Regulatory Law in Ireland

We dedicate this book to our families

Regulatory Law in Ireland

Niamh Connery BCL, LLM, Solicitor

David Hodnett BA, MSc, Solicitor

Published by
Tottel Publishing Ltd
Maxwelton House
41–43 Boltro Road
Haywards Heath
West Sussex
RH16 1BJ

Tottel Publishing Ltd
Fitzwilliam Business Centre
26 Upper Pembroke Street
Dublin 2

ISBN 978 1 84766 254 5
© Tottel Publishing Ltd 2009

British Library Cataloguing-in-Publication Data
A catalogue record for this book is available from the British Library

Typeset by Marie Armah-Kwantreng, Dublin, Ireland
Printed in the UK by
CPI William Clowes Beccles NR34 7TL

FOREWORD

To most of the population, including many lawyers, the contents of this book may seem arcane, technical and remote from everyday concerns including those of the legal practices of all but a few specialists. And yet its subject is one of the most in influential forces that have been at work in Irish life over the last half-century – the inexorable expansion of administrative intervention in the routines of much of daily life.

The book is, at least in this jurisdiction, the first attempt to describe and explain the legal framework which governs the roles of the myriad agencies established to police a vast range of commercial activities, services and infrastructures with which most of us have to deal on a regular basis.

We appear now to be watched over by protective authorities of many kinds; regulators, ombudsmen and commissioners who licence and control, amongst many others, our entertainment, our telephones, our banks and even our taxis. Most of the time we are indifferent to their existence. For older people these developments at least mean that one no longer needs political influence to get a telephone line; for all of us, it is suddenly heartening that there appear to be plenty of taxis around both day and night. On the other hand, there is the vague understanding that the existence of all these regulators is in some way responsible for the frantic and annoying warnings in every advertisement that 'terms and conditions apply' and that the advertiser is regulated by someone or other.

Then there are the occasional protests from those affected by these regimes: the bus company which feels let down by the system when apparently driven out of the market by a dominant incumbent; or the taxi drivers who complain that deregulation has led to far too much competition. These are the inevitable indices of the tension inherent in the market model which has been pursued both here and in the other Community Member States since 1973. This recognises that, at least in developed economies, most commercial services are provided more efficiently by a private enterprise in a competitive market than by state monopolies.

The privatisation of the old state monopolies and the deregulation of public services previously provided through state-sponsored entities, required the establishment of mechanisms which would both set standards to ensure that public interest objectives continued to be achieved – that letters continue to be delivered and transport to run in rural areas for example – and that the market could become and remain competitive and not dominated by the former incumbents to the exclusion of new entrants. The difficulty in getting the balance correct in different markets can perhaps be gauged by comparing the progress made to date in the markets for taxi services, phones and electricity generation.

These and the other markets in which deregulation has been introduced have, of course, greatly different characteristics so that the regulatory regimes put in place to police their operation require different supervisory structures with different powers of intervention. The barriers to entry to the taxi trade are radically different compared with those facing an entrepreneur who wants to start a bank or an electricity generating station.

It is the legislative and administrative framework that provides the legal basis for this economic organisation which the two authors describe and analyse in this work.

Starting from the somewhat meagre constitutional provisions defining the role of the State in promoting and controlling economic and commercial activities, they examine the Irish regulatory system both from the economic perspective of its policy objectives and from the viewpoint of its administrative structures and the legal constraints under which it operates in representative sectors.

Regulatory supervision operates, of course, primarily on a sector-specific basis with individual regimes being put in place separately for distinct industries or services – energy, communications, broadcasting and so forth. But regimes are also in place which operate across the economy generally either for the purpose of ensuring that all competition remains undistorted as in the case of the Competition Authority, or in order to pursue a particular public interest objective, as in the case of Data Protection for example.

The authors describe how a number of the most important regimes have evolved or been created and take the reader through the often complicated legislative provisions from which the individual regimes derive their objectives and their powers. The accessibility of these regimes is frequently clouded by the fact that several of the regulatory agencies are the creatures of both domestic legislation and European Community directives. The full primary and secondary legislative framework for the regulation of financial services thus runs to a list three pages long.

The authors also describe and explain some of the important common features of the controls that exist over the functioning of the offices of the regulators, the mechanisms for appeal against their decisions and the availability of judicial control over the exercise of their powers.

As has frequently been observed in all common law countries, judicial review has been one of the areas of judicial activity which has seen the greatest expansion and development since 1945 and a good deal, if not most, of this burgeoning case-load can be attributed to the demand for judicial intervention to control the lawful exercise of the powers delegated by central government to 'independent' regulatory authorities.

In the final chapter of the book, the authors provide an overview of the approach of the courts to this task, one which has come as a relatively new experience to a judiciary for which, historically, the invocation of the prerogative orders to intervene in economic decisions would have been a novel proposition.

The book greatly benefits from the special expertise and experience of its two authors in this field both in their current positions as legal advisors respectively in the Commission for Aviation Regulation and the Commission for Communications Regulation and in their earlier careers as practitioners in competition and regulatory law.

For its depth of analysis of the economic and policy objectives of the Irish regulatory system and for its breadth of exposition of the legal framework and individual structures of the principal regimes, this work is an important contribution to Irish administrative law texts and will be an indispensable tool for lawyers, administrators and economists working in the field.

John D Cooke
The High Court
Dublin
30 January 2009

ACKNOWLEDGMENTS

We would like to thank the following people for their kind help with this book:

The Honourable Mr Justice John Cooke for his kind foreword.

Ms Niamh Hyland BL for her comments on the aviation chapter.

Mr Philip Andrews, Solicitor, for his comments on the broadcasting chapter.

Ms Helen Martin BL for her comments on the communications chapter.

Ms Isolde Goggin for her comments on the competition chapter.

Ms Diane Balding, Solicitor, for her comments on the energy chapter.

Mr John Fish, Solicitor, and Ms Lindsay Stevens, Solicitor, for their comments on the banking and financial regulation chapter.

Dr Dermot Nolan for his comments on the regulation of economics chapter.

Mr Ronan Munro BL for his comments the enforcement chapter.

Ms Noreen Mackey BL for her comments on the chapter on appeals.

Mr Anthony Collins SC for his comments on the judicial review chapter.

All views expressed and any errors are of course the authors' own. Any views expressed are not attributable either to the Commission for Communications Regulation or to the Commission for Aviation Regulation. We have attempted to state the law as we found it as at 31 December 2008.

We would like to thank our editor Amy Hayes for her continued patience and perseverance, Marie Armah-Kwantreng for typesetting the book and also Sandra Mulvey.

Contents

Contents

Contents

TABLE OF CASES

TABLE OF STATUTES

TABLE OF STATUTORY INSTRUMENTS

BUNREACHT NA hÉIREANN

TABLE OF EUROPEAN LEGISLATION

Acts and Treaties

EC Treaty

Conventions

Chapter 1

INTRODUCTION

1.001 Regulatory law is constantly changing and is highly political in nature. Throughout the sectors covered, readers will notice that principal acts that are less than a decade old have been substantially revised or amended many times. As economics is a means to an end, so too is regulation. It must be responsive to change and recognise new objectives and can only then be useful.

BACKGROUND

1.002 State intervention in economic organisation is the reason for regulatory law in Ireland. Using a structured legal approach, the State has consciously changed how business is done and is to be done in regulated sectors. In one sense, the government of enterprise is the enterprise of government. The firm has a central role in industrial organisation and indeed regulation. The judiciary has an independent role to intercede as required between the State and these undertakings to clarify the law, particularly in the broader context of Irish jurisprudence. Therefore, regulatory law is of interest not only to lawyers but also to government policy-makers, economists, regulated firms and their business advisers, together with academics and those other commentators who report on the interaction of these groups on a daily basis – the media. The purpose of this book is to set out the manner in which the State has intervened in a number of sectors that are regulated by independent Regulators whose powers have been devolved from Ministers, or assigned to them as agents of the State in the broader context of the internal market of the European Union. These sectors are aviation, broadcasting, communications, energy and financial services. In addition, competition is discussed because it affects all sectors. Direct intervention is coupled with integration in the broader Irish legal context and the book also discusses issues that arise for Regulators in the context of enforcement, appeals and judicial review. The motivation for regulation is, in part, economics and, accordingly, the book briefly introduces some economic reasons for regulation and discusses some of the motivations underlying regulatory bodies. The book also references the principal recent decisions of Regulators, in which are outlined the policies and methodologies used by them.

1.003 Much of the material in this book concerns the economic regulation of former State monopolies.[1] The Europe-led liberalisation of sectors such as communications, energy and financial services created licensing or authorisation systems so that other players could enter the markets and compete with the previous State monopolist(s). It also led to the establishment of independent Regulators which are separate from the incumbent and also from the relevant government department. In order to ensure that

---

1   It has been said that State monopolies are like children, that you never like them until you have one of your own and when you do, yours is different from all the rest and special – Mary Harney TD – Europe Competition Day – Dublin Castle, 29 April 2004.

the State monopolist would 'play nicely' with the new entrants, sector-specific regulatory rules were developed in each of the sectors. The application of those rules is overseen and enforced by the Regulators with the assistance of the courts, as required. In addition, the rules of competition law apply to ensure *inter alia* that there is no abuse of dominance. Decisions of the Regulators are subject to judicial oversight either by way of appeal or judicial review.

1.004 The warning has been given before that economic policy is only a means to an end. As Meenan has stated, the ultimate justification for economic policy is not the creation of wealth for its own sake; the purpose of creating wealth is to improve the conditions in which people live.[2] The purpose of economic policy is for Kettle's 'great human conspiracy',[3] otherwise known as the State, to succeed. To the extent that the State has adopted economic policy in the sectors mentioned above and established Regulators to implement that policy, the success of the economic policy must be measured by its contribution to the increased welfare of the State, both from a material and social perspective.

1.005 The goals of Irish politics and economics are echoed in the basic law of the State – *Bunreacht na hÉireann*. The Constitution also speaks of the desire to provide for the citizens of the State and the organisation of their underlying economy. It is conscious also of the role of regulation. It would seem fitting, therefore, at this point to briefly consider the constitutional aspect of regulatory law before going on to introduce in a more detailed manner the sector-specific approach of this book.

THE CONSTITUTIONAL POSITION OF ECONOMIC REGULATION

1.006 Bunreacht na hÉireann was adopted by the Irish people in 1937 and expressly provides a constitutional basis for economic regulation. This is set out in Arts 43 and 45 of Bunreacht na hÉireann. Article 43 deals with private property. It states:

> The State acknowledges that man, in virtue of his rational being, has the natural right, antecedent to positive law, to the private ownership of external goods.

> The State accordingly guarantees to pass no law attempting to abolish the right of private ownership or the general right to transfer, bequeath, and inherit property.

> The State recognises, however, that the exercise of the rights mentioned in the foregoing provisions of this Article ought, in civil society, to be regulated by the principles of social justice.

> The State, accordingly, may as the occasion requires delimit by law the exercise of the said rights with a view to reconciling their exercise with the exigencies of the common good.

---

2   Meenan, *The Irish Economy Since 1922* (Liverpool University Press, 1970), p xx of the Introduction.

3   Kettle defined the State as a great human conspiracy for good, in the days before the present Irish State existed – Kettle, *The Day's Burden* (Maunsel, 1910), p 22.

Arguably, Art 43 codifies the earlier US Supreme Court judgments on the use of regulation to prevent monopolistic exploitation of consumers, namely *Munn*[4] and *Nebbia*.[5]

1.007 Article 45 goes on to set out the directive principles of social policy. It specifically warns that the principles of social policy set out in Art 45 are intended for the general guidance of the Oireachtas. The application of those principles in the making of laws is specifically stated to be in the care of the Oireachtas, and should not be cognisable by any court under any provision of the Constitution. In this way, they cannot be relied upon as the legal basis for a challenge to an act, measure or instrument done, made or taken by the government. However, they can be looked to for guidance, especially when considering the application of other articles of the Constitution.

Article 45.2 provides that the State shall direct its policy towards securing:

(ii) That the ownership and control of the material resources of the community may be so distributed amongst private individuals and the various classes as best to subserve the common good.

(iii) That, especially, the operation of free competition shall not be allowed so to develop as to result in the concentration of the ownership or control of essential commodities in a few individuals to the common detriment.

Article 45.3 states that:

1° The State shall favour and, where necessary supplement private initiative in industry and commerce.

2° The State shall endeavour to secure that private enterprise shall be so conducted as to ensure reasonable efficiency in the production and distribution of goods and as to protect the public against unjust exploitation.

1.008 In the context of economic regulation, the notion of 'reasonable efficiency in the production and distribution of goods'[6] merits further consideration. It seems that the

---

4 The important principle promulgated by the US Supreme Court judgment in *Munn v Illinois* 94 US 113 (1877) was that: 'property does become clothed with public interest when used in a manner to make it of public consequence, and affect the community at large. When, therefore, one devotes his property to a use in which the public has an interest, he in effect, grants to the public an interest in that use, and must submit to be controlled by the public for the common good.'

5 In 1934 in *Nebia v New York* (1934) 291 US 502, 531–532, 536–537 the US Supreme Court rejected the notion that there was anything constitutionally sacrosanct about private price-determination and declared that if any industry could, for good and sufficient reasons, be subjected to public regulation, there was no constitutional bar to its being subjected to price regulation in particular: 'So far as the requirement for due process is concerned, and in the absence of other constitutional restriction, a State is free to adopt whatever economic policy may reasonably be deemed to promote public welfare and to enforce that policy by legislation adapted to its purpose.'

6 In particular, the use of the word 'reasonable' merits consideration. The main sense of the English language definition of the adjective reasonable is: '1. fair and sensible. 2. *archaic* able to reason logically. 3. as much as is appropriate or fair; moderate.' Subsenses are given as: (i) fairly good (ii) relatively inexpensive' – Pearsall (ed), *The Concise Oxford Dictionary* (10th edn, revised, Oxford University Press, 2001), p 1193.

word 'reasonable' used in the Constitution means that Art 45 equates to the following: 'ensure reasonable [fair, sensible, fairly good, relatively inexpensive] efficiency in the production and distribution of goods'. The economic concept of efficiency does not equate with making reasonable endeavours ('fairly good'); it equates to the optimal outcome of all endeavours at a given time. Economists' conceptions of efficiency tend to eschew commenting on fairness and distribution. It is assumed by economists that overall allocation comprises many smaller allocative choices made by rational economic actors – otherwise known as Adam Smith's 'invisible hand'.[7] Therefore, *efficiency* does not necessarily relate to 'fair' or 'sensible' in the context of the meaning of the word 'reasonable' as used in Art 45. Whether economic choices are all driven by rational thinking or otherwise cannot be measured. Perhaps the framers of the Constitution realised that 'reasonable' in the circumstances may not be measured and consequently the provisions are directive only.

Furthermore, Art 45.4.1° provides that, 'The State pledges itself to safeguard with especial care the economic interests of the weaker sections of the community'. An economist might recognise these sentiments as presaging consumer protection and social welfare legislation. In the course of considering the constitutional context of economic regulation, the unenumerated rights of the citizen may also be recalled. The doctrine of unenumerated rights springs from the wording of Art 40.3, which states:

> The State guarantees in its laws to respect, and as far as practicable, by its laws to defend and vindicate the personal rights of the citizen.
>
> The State shall, in particular, by its laws protect as best it may from unjust attack and, in the case of injustice done, vindicate the life, person, good name, and property rights of every citizen.

1.009 Ultimately, as Casey discusses,[8] it falls upon the courts to determine which unenumerated rights the Constitution implicitly guarantees. In discharging this function, the courts have drawn upon a wide variety of sources. They have, in some instances, invoked other provisions of the Constitution, such as the directive principles of social policy in Art 45. The right to earn a living was first recognised by Kenny J in *Murtagh Properties v Cleary*.[9] In the course of his judgment, Kenny J referred to *Ryan v Attorney General*[10] as having established that the Constitution protected rights that were not specifically enumerated therein. The right to earn a livelihood derived from Art 45.2, which states that:

> The State shall, in particular, direct its policy towards securing:—
>
> That the citizens (all of whom, men and women equally, have the right to an adequate means of livelihood) may through their occupations find the means of making reasonable provision for their domestic needs.

---

7   Adam Smith wrote of the invisible hand in The *Wealth of Nations* IV 2.9 (1776). This principle illustrates how the self-interest of individuals moves together to promote economic progress. In a free market, each individual maximising revenue, assists the market to maximise the total revenue of society as a whole, given that total revenue is the sum of the individual parts.

8   Casey, *Constitutional Law* (2nd edn, Sweet & Maxwell, 1992).

9   *Murtagh Properties v Cleary* [1972] IR 330.

10 *Ryan v Attorney General* [1965] IR 294.

It was argued before the court that it could not have regard to Art 45, which is expressed to be for the guidance of the Oireachtas only and which states that the application of its social policy principles in the making of laws 'shall not be cognisable by any court under any of the provisions of this Constitution.' However, Kenny J said that this did not mean that the courts could not have regard to the terms of the Article. They had no jurisdiction to consider the application of its principles in the making of laws, but this did not mean they could not take it into consideration in deciding whether a claimed constitutional right existed.

The principle of the right to earn a livelihood has resonance in sectors that are concerned with regulating freedom of entry, for example licensed sectors (although it must be recalled that undertakings are not considered to fall within the scope of Art 40.3).

1.010 The question of a statutory monopoly and its impact on the right to earn a livelihood were canvassed in *Attorney General and Minister for Posts and Telegraphs v Paperlink Ltd.*[11] In 1981 the defendant company had begun to operate a courier service in and around Dublin. This involved, as Costello J found, delivering letters in breach of the statutory monopoly conferred on the Minister by the Post Office Act 1908, s 34(2), and the plaintiffs were seeking to restrain this. The defendants pleaded that s 34(2) was unconstitutional as it was an invalid restriction on their freedom to earn a livelihood. The State monopoly thereby established, it was contended, was an unjust attack on their right to earn a livelihood, in violation of Art 40.3.2° – the defendants sought to draw support from the provisions of Art 45.3.1°: 'The State shall favour and, where necessary, supplement private initiative in industry and commerce.' The defendants argued that the onus was on the State to justify any interference with private initiative in matters of commerce.

1.011 Costello J rejected the defendants' arguments. He agreed that the State had a duty by its laws, derived from Art 40.3, to protect as best it might from unjust attack the personal right to earn a livelihood. He also accepted that the courts could consider Art 45 for the limited purposes of ascertaining what personal rights were included under Art 40.3.1°, and what legitimate limitations in the interests of the common good the State might impose on such rights. However, in his view, Art 45.3.1° must not be pushed too far. It demonstrated a view that the social order should not be based on a system in which all the means of production were owned by the State, and a preference for one in which industry and commerce were mainly carried on by private citizens rather than State agencies. However, it did not follow that the Oireachtas could not legislate to establish State trading corporations or public utilities, nor was it legitimate to infer that the State was called upon in legal proceedings to justify a State monopoly.

1.012 The defendants went on to argue that the monopoly was inefficiently administered, and that it was possible to organise one less restrictive of their rights. Consequently, they argued, the 'attack' on those rights was 'unjust'. In Costello J's view, while it would not be in the public interest that a statutory monopoly was inefficiently administered, this – if it were the fact – could not make the relevant Act

---

11   *Attorney General and Minister for Posts and Telegraphs v Paperlink Ltd* [1984] ILRM 373.

unconstitutional. He held that inefficiency in administration would not of itself mean that anyone's constitutional rights were being infringed. In addition, evidence as to alternative ways of organising the postal service could not be admitted. This would involve the court in an unconstitutional departure from its role as laid down in the Constitution. Costello J continued:[12]

> This court is not the forum in which to decide whether a postal service organised on lines advocated by the defendants' experts is one which meets the requirements of the common good. These are matters for the Oireachtas to determine. I must, of course, defend the citizen's rights from unjust attack, and hold if necessary that an existing law has placed an excessive limit on the citizen's right to earn a livelihood. But to carry out the inquiry which the defendants ask me to perform and, thereafter, make a determination on an alternative to the existing postal service, would amount to an unwarranted and unconstitutional interference with the powers of government exclusively conferred on the executive and the Oireachtas, a point strikingly illustrated by the fact that as this case was at hearing the Dáil itself was considering a Bill to establish a different method of organising the postal system to that contained in the 1908 Act. Just as the courts must not permit the legislature to interfere with the judicial function, so too they must be astute to see that they do not themselves depart from their constitutionally defined role.

1.013 In *Hand v Dublin Corporation*[13] the plaintiffs were street traders in Dublin who, by the terms of their Casual Trading Act 1980, required licences to operate (market entry regulation). In this case, the plaintiffs had contravened the Act's provisions. Their applications for licences were refused. The plaintiffs claimed that this was an unjustified attack on their constitutional right to a livelihood, because the disqualification it imposed was out of proportion to the nature of the offences committed by them. The Supreme Court rejected the claim. Griffin J, delivering the judgment of the court, pointed out the right to earn a livelihood was not unqualified; thus it could be subjected to legitimate legal constraints. In enacting legislation, the Oireachtas had to strike a balance between the legitimate rights and interests of those affected by it. These included members of the public using the streets, those lawfully engaged in casual trading and those carrying on business in premises in the neighbourhood of the casual trading area. The refusal of a licence was not unjust or unreasonable, and consequently did not violate the rights protected by Art 40.3.2° of the Constitution.

THE RULE OF LAW

1.014 Given that the rule of law is central to the system of competition and regulation discussed in this book, it is useful to briefly recall what 'the rule of law' actually means. At the heart of the rule of law there are four interrelated notions.[14]

---

12 *Attorney General and Minister for Posts and Telegraphs v Paperlink Ltd* [1984] ILRM 373, 388–389.

13 *Hand v Dublin Corporation* [1991] 1 IR 409.

14   Morgan and Hogan, *Administrative Law in Ireland* (3rd edn, Round Hall Sweet & Maxwell, 1998) at p 8.

1.015 The first is the principle of legality, which means that executive or administrative acts that affect legal rights, interests or legitimate expectations must have legal justification. Where such justification does not exist, the aggrieved party may have recourse to the courts to have this decision invalidated. An illustration of this principle is supplied by *DPP v Fagan*.[15] Denham J in her dissenting judgment made the following observation on the rule of law principles:

> A cornerstone of the rule of law is that persons in authority must be able to justify their actions, if called upon to do so, by reference to a specific rule in statute or common law. Thus it is appropriate to look for a positive law authorising the action in question.

The rule of law is implemented in practice in a number of ways. The principle of *ultra vires* requires that administrative authorities such as Regulators show they possess legal authority to act by reference to legislation. Furthermore, the courts will review the exercise of a Regulator's discretionary power according to settled principles of reasonableness and compliance with constitutional justice.

1.016 The second principle is that everyone, including the government and its servants, is subject to the law. This principle was affirmed in cases such as *Macauley v Minister for Posts and Telegraphs*[16] (where a statutory provision requiring the prior permission of the Attorney General before an action could be taken against a Minister of State was found to be unconstitutional); *Byrne v Ireland*[17] (holding that the former Crown immunity from suit had not survived the enactment of the Constitution); and *Howard v Commissioners of Public Works*[18] (holding that the common law rule whereby the State was presumed not to be bound by the application of statute had not survived the enactment of the Constitution).

1.017 The third aspect of the rule of law is that the legality of executive or administrative acts is to be determined by judges who are independent of the government. The principle of judicial independence is enshrined in Art 34.1 of the Constitution.[19] Legislative attempts to prevent – or even altogether to curb – the review

---

15 *DPP v Fagan* [1994] 2 IR 265 at 288.

16 *Macauley v Minister for Posts and Telegraphs* [1966] IR 345.

17 *Byrne v Ireland* [1972] IR 241.

18 *Howard v Commissioners of Public Works* [1994] 1 IR 101. A further aspect of this principle is that the government may not exercise a dispensing power, ie waive or suspend the operation of statute law. In *Hoey v Minister for Justice* [1994] 3 IR 329 (a case concerning a local authority's statutory obligation to repair the courthouse in Drogheda) the Minister sought to defend a mandamus application by saying that he had written to the local authority to inform it that he did not require it to provide courthouse accommodation in Drogheda since this was satisfied by the provision of suitable premises in Dundalk. Lynch J rejected this argument, saying (at 343): 'It is not open to the Executive by arrangements made with the local authority to alter the law by lifting obligations which statute has imposed on a local authority.'

19 See, generally, *Buckley v Attorney General* [1950] IR 67; *In Re Haughey* [1971] IR 217; and *State (McEldowney) v Kelleher* [1983] IR 289.

of administrative action have been viewed with disfavour by the judiciary.[20] As part of the separation of powers, the ability of the judiciary to substitute its decision for a decision of a Regulator which is based on technical or economic assessments may be constrained to some extent.

1.018 The final aspect of the rule of law is that the law must be public and precise; the law should be ascertainable and its operation predictable. This principle underlies the presumption against retrospectivity[21] and the related principle of legal certainty, which are discussed further below. The reason for this rule is that it provides for citizens and firms to arrange their behaviour to conform with the law.

TOWARDS A COMMON POSITION ON REGULATION

1.019 Certain regulatory issues apply to many of the sectors examined in this book and indeed to many of the regulated sectors that are outside the scope of this book.

European Community Law Basis

1.020 Most of the sector-specific regulation is based on European Community (EC)[22] law. Since the Treaty of Rome came into existence in 1957, there has been ever-increasing harmonisation of European economic policy through the creation and increased integration of the Internal Market. The liberalisation of sectors is driven by DG Internal Market, a directorate general in the European Commission[23] which seeks to ensure that harmonious, barrier-free conditions exist throughout the European Union (EU). The Internal Market provides for the free movement of goods, services, citizens and capital throughout the EU. The uniform application of EC law throughout the EU is important for the freedom of establishment of enterprises and the free

---

20   In *State (Pine Valley Developments Ltd) v Dublin County Council* [1984] IR 407 at 426 Henchy J commented that the courts 'should be reluctant to surrender their inherent right to enter on a question of the validity of what are prima facie justiciable matters'. See also the comments of O'Higgins CJ in *Condon v Minister for Labour* [1981] IR 62 at 69: 'A strong, healthy and concerned public opinion may, in the words of Edmund Burke, "snuff the approach of tyranny in every tainted breeze", but effective resistance to unwarranted encroachment on constitutional guarantees and rights, depends, in the ultimate analysis on the courts. If access to the courts is denied or prevented or obstructed, then such encroachment, being unchallenged, may become habitual, and, therefore, unacceptable.'

21   *Hamilton v Hamilton* [1982] IR 466; *O'H v O'H* [1990] 2 IR 558.

22   EU law comprises three pillars, the first of which is that EC law is binding, has supremacy and has direct effect, ie it may be relied upon by citizens in private actions – *Van Gend en Loos* Case C–26/62 [1963] ECR 1. The two remaining pillars are common foreign and security policy and justice and home affairs, which are more similar to international law or intergovernmental law.

23   In general, the European Commission produces the policy and legislative proposals on which the Council and European Parliament may adopt legislation (the co-decision procedure is the norm for regulatory legislative acts). The European Commission also polices compliance with EC law amongst Member States.

movement of services. Competition policy also drives sector liberalisation and DG Competition, another directorate general of the European Commission, also plays a role in respect of the application of the competition rules, in particular art 81 (restrictive agreements), art 82 (abuse of dominance), art 86 (special and exclusive rights and services of general economic interest), and art 87 (state aid).

1.021 Regulatory law in Ireland can be considered in many circumstances to be applied EC law. While a substantive portion of the various regulatory frameworks is contained in EC regulations, which are directly applicable without the need for further implementation, most of the relevant provisions are contained in EC directives, which have to be transposed in Ireland, either by way of primary or secondary legislation. New directives are constantly being adopted at the EC level. This leads to provisions, in particular in secondary legislation, being 'lost in translation' as provisions may be inaccurately transposed into Irish law or copied into Irish law with no guidance provided as to how concepts that are often civil law based are to be applied in a common law jurisdiction such as Ireland. This leads to a lack of legal certainty for Regulators, regulated entities and the courts.

1.022 Regulators are emanations of the State.[24] Due to the EC law concept of vertical direct effect,[25] Regulators would be expected to ensure that the underlying directive provisions are being applied correctly by them, even where the secondary legislation wrongly transposes the directive provisions.[26] Certain regulated entities which are also considered to be emanations of the State[27] would also have to do so. Even in respect of entities that could not be considered to be emanations of the State, due to the *Von Colson*[28] principle, courts are obliged to interpret national implementing provisions in light of the underlying provisions of the directive on which they are based, provided that a *contra legum* interpretation is not the result. It is not always an easy task to interpret provisions of secondary legislation in line with the provisions of the directive on which they are based without at times engaging in Herculean leaps of logic. In addition, there is a lack of consolidation of secondary legislation and a lack of transparency in respect of the location of the applicable legislation (usually secondary legislation) relating to a particular sector which further obscures matters, particularly in light of the maxim *ignorantia juris non excusat* – ignorance of the law is no excuse.

1.023 The standard of review and scope of review procedures to be applied in the case of an appeal are often unclear and frequently involves previously untried matters or a novel area of law. However, just when the parties involved – that is the Regulator, the courts and the regulated entities – get to grips with the law, the legislation is amended

---

24 *Becker v Finanzamt Munster-Innenstadt* Case C–8/81 [1982] ECR 53; *Brinkmann Tabakfabriken GmbH v Skatteministeriet* [1998] ECR I–5255.

25 *Van Duyn v Home Office* Case C–41/74 [1974] ECR 1337.

26 To ensure against an action of State liability under *Brasserie du Pêcheur SA v Federal Republic of Germany; R v Secretary of State for Transport, ex parte Factortame Ltd* [1996] ECR I–1029 or *Coppinger v Waterford County Council* [1998] 4 IR 220.

27 *Foster v British Gas Plc* Case C–188/89 [1990] ECR I–3313.

28 *Von Colson v Land Nordrhein-Westphalen* Case C–14/83 [1984] ECR 1891.

or revised. The swathe of consultation documents, common positions, recommendations, notices, guidelines, directives and regulations being produced at an EC level (and in the case of directives requiring implementation into Irish law) is extensive. Domestically, the number of consultations, responses to consultations, expert reports, decisions and secondary legislation also contributes to the Kafkaesque nature of sector-specific regulation. The codification and consolidation of sector-specific law should be considered, in particular in respect of the various statutory instruments.

1.024 The European Commission retains a supervisory role in respect of the national regulatory authorities (NRAs). In the communications sector, the European Commission can veto certain decisions of the Regulator.[29] Under competition law and the Modernisation Regulation,[30] the national competition authorities (in Ireland the Competition Authority, the courts and the Commission for Communications Regulation in certain instances) must notify the opening of an investigation where EC competition rules also apply, and must notify proposed decisions where EC competition rules apply, via the European Competition Network (ECN) to the European Commission. Within networks similar to the ECN, the NRAs must co-operate with each other and the Commission to ensure the uniform application of EC law, for example through the European Regulators Group for Communications Networks and Services (ERG), the European Energy Regulators Group (ERGEG) and the Committee of European Securities Regulators (CESR). Despite the principle of subsidiarity,[31] and the decentralisation of competition law, the European Commission does appear, if anything, to be seeking to increase its own supervisory role.

The Role of the Incumbent and Services of General Economic Interest

1.025 The role of the incumbent, from one perspective, is to resist regulation and entrench its market position and, at worst, hinder or, at best, certainly not assist, market entrance by potential competitors. Due to the legacy of State ownership, the incumbent is often heavily unionised and unable to adapt to market conditions or to change as quickly as its competitors. From another perspective, it may often not be possible to bring about the seismic organisational changes in as short a space of time as may be required to turn a former State monopoly into the ideal of the 'efficient operator'. The incumbent may be subject to a geographically uniform tariff obligation and some form of universal service or public service obligation so it may not cherry-pick more lucrative customers or geographic areas, as its competitors may. The public service

---

29 Relating to market analysis.

30 Regulation 1/2003.

31 Article 5 of the EC Treaty provides: 'In areas which do not fall within its exclusive competence, the Community shall take action, in accordance with the principle of subsidiarity, only if and in so far as the objectives of the proposed action cannot be sufficiently achieved by the Member States and can therefore, by reason of the scale or effects of the proposed action, be better achieved by the Community.'

obligation has a social service and geographic cohesion element to it. This may not be inherently profit-making nor a service which a rational, profit-maximising, efficient operator would necessarily provide. Nonetheless, it is a social or public service which incumbents are expected to carry out, despite no longer being nationalised.

1.026 In return for carrying out a public service obligation, should the incumbent be compensated and, if so, on what basis? If compensation is required, the query arises as to whether this should be funded by industry by way of a levy charged on all the players in the industry, or whether consumers should contribute directly to the public service fund, or alternatively whether the fund should be State funded. If it is State funded, the issue arises as to whether it puts a burden on public funds and whether that might constitute a State aid. It then has to be considered whether the provisions of art 86(2) of the EC Treaty[32] can exempt the funding of a universal service fund from the State aid provisions. If not, is it necessary to run a public procurement tender pursuant to the Altmark criteria[33] before the public service obligation contract could be awarded in order to ensure that the State aid rules do not apply? Consideration may also need to be given to whether there is only one possible provider[34] in this regard.

1.027 Many of the sectors covered by this book concern services of general economic interest (also known as public service obligations or universal service obligations). Such services include energy, telecommunications, broadcasting and postal services, and may also include transport, water supply and waste management (the latter sectors are not covered by this book). Article 16 of the EC Treaty confirms the place of services of general economic interest among the shared values of the EU and their role in promoting social and territorial cohesion. The European

---

32 See para **2.028**.

33 *Altmark Trans GmbH v Nahverkehrsgesellschaft Altmark GmbH* Case C–280/00 Judgement of 24 July 2003 [2003] ECR I 7747, which sets out the following four criteria for when a public service fund is not a State aid: (i) the recipient undertaking must have a public service obligation (PSO) to discharge, and this obligation must be clearly defined; (ii) the parameters for calculating the compensation must be established beforehand in an objective and transparent manner to avoid it conferring an economic advantage which may favour the recipient undertaking over competing undertakings; (iii) the compensation cannot exceed what is necessary to cover all or part of the costs incurred in the discharge of the PSO, taking into account the relevant receipts and a reasonable profit for discharging those obligations; and (iv) where the undertaking which is to discharge the PSO is not chosen pursuant to a public procurement procedure which would allow for the selection of the tenderer capable of providing those services at the least cost to the Community, the level of compensation needed must be determined on the basis of an analysis of the costs which a typical undertaking, well run and adequately provided with means of transport so as to be able to meet the necessary public service requirements, would have incurred in discharging those obligations, taking into account the relevant receipts and a reasonable profit for discharging the obligations.

34 Arrowsmith, *The Law of Public and Utilities Procurement* (2nd edn, Sweet & Maxwell, 2005) 6.205.

Commission has issued various communications on services of general economic interest.[35] Article 86(2) of the EC Treaty provides that:

> Undertakings entrusted with the operation of services of general economic interest or having the character of a revenue-producing monopoly shall be subject to the rules contained in this Treaty, in particular to the rules on competition, in so far as the application of such rules does not obstruct the performance, in law or in fact, of the particular tasks assigned to them.

In this way, the internal market and competition rules only apply inasmuch as the application of those rules does not affect carrying out the service of general economic interest. This is essentially a derogation from the Treaty rules provided certain conditions are satisfied such as the proportionality of the compensation provided to the undertakings entrusted with the operation of services of general economic interest.[36] Member States need to be proportionate in that any restrictions of competition or limitations on the fundamental freedoms[37] do not exceed what is necessary to guarantee effective fulfilment of the service of general economic interest.

Protection of Competition

1.028 The objective for many Regulators is to open up the relevant market to competition. It is often alleged that the role of the Regulator in sector-specific regulation becomes that of protecting competitors rather than competition or consumer welfare, which would be the case under pure competition law. The protection of what may transpire to be unviable competitors is often criticised as the Regulator tries to add weight to the new entrants' positions and tilt the balance in negotiating power away from the incumbent. Such protection can come in the form of non-discrimination obligations on the incumbent, which is the regulatory law translation of the biblical direction 'thou shalt love thy neighbour as thyself'.[38] The discussion of functional or structural separation and access obligations may also arise where the incumbent is vertically integrated. The Regulator's role as between the players on the market loosely

---

35 Services of General Interest in Europe, OJ C 281 26 September 1996; Services of General Interest in Europe, 2001/C 17/04; 2005/842/EC Commission Decision of 28 November 2005 on the application of art 86(2) to State Aid in the form of public service compensation; 2004 White Paper COM (2004) 374 of 12 May 2004; Resolution of the European Parliament (A6-0275/2006 of 26 September 2006) Services of General Economic Interest Opinion prepared by the State Aid Group, 29 June 2006; Commission Staff Working Document, 20 November 2007 SEC (2007) 1516 on frequently asked questions on the application of art 86(2) to State Aid; and, most recently, the Communication from The Commission on Services of General Interest, including social services of general interest: a new European Commitment, 20 November 2007 COM (2007)725 final.

36 *Corbeau* Case C–320/91 [1993] ECR I 2533; *Almelo* Case C–393/92 [1994] ECR I 1477; *Altmark Trans GmbH and Regierungsprasidium Magdeburg v Nahverkehrsgesellschaft Altmark GmbH* [2003] ECR I 7747.

37 Free movement of goods, services, persons and capital.

38 Particularly when thou art vertically integrated!

translates to that of a referee ensuring fair play is upheld in the market and resolving disputes that arise between players. The question of what happens if these new entrants fail may be particularly pertinent in the current economic climate. Is the incumbent expected to be a provider of last resort in addition to carrying out the public service obligation? The rationale for economic regulation of infrastructure or networks is also to be questioned. Just how much network competition and how many competing networks are viable in a country the size of Ireland with relatively low population density and a high rural population?

Role and Independence of the Regulator

1.029 The task of the Regulators is to implement State economic policy. Much of the economic policy codified in the laws discussed in this book has arisen due to Ireland's participation in broader economic areas such as the European Union. Consequently, many of these legal instruments have their genesis in the State's central economic policy of participation in the Internal Market of the European Union. Diverse ministerial powers are divested to the various national regulatory authorities. There is therefore somewhat of a domestic policy gap. Notwithstanding that policy at a high level originates in the European Commission and that there are policy divisions within the various relevant departments, the statutory role of the Regulators to feed into this policy with its grass-roots experience of regulation in Ireland is somewhat limited. Although the Competition Authority has an advisory function, the other Regulators do not. However, their input is provided formally through the various European Regulators' groups and to the various departments, but only when requested. Nonetheless, this local policy deficit can create the risk of Ireland being reactive rather than proactive[39] in respect of its economic regulation.

1.030 Regulators are often required by EC law to be independent. Just how independent are the Regulators from the relevant department, and the relevant Minister, should also be borne in mind, particularly where the Minister may issue the Regulator with policy directions. It is also questionable just how independent the Minister is in situations where he or she is the controlling shareholder in the incumbent. The concept of regulatory capture also exists, where there is a concern that the incumbent can, over time, exert undue influence over the Regulator.[40] This is particularly of concern since prior to the liberalisation and the privatisation of many of these sectors, the role of the Regulator, Minister and incumbent was carried out by one and the same entity. In the financial services sector, with the recent changes[41] to the

---

39 An obvious recent exception is where Ireland led the way with its reaction to the financial crisis in its Credit Institutions (Financial Support) Act 2008.

40 Also known as gamekeeper turned poacher, which can be summarised as follows: 'Regulation is not about the public interest at all, but is a process, by which interest groups seek to promote their private interest ... Over time, regulatory agencies come to be dominated by the industries regulated.' Posner, 'Theories of Economic Regulation', 5 *The Bell Journal of Economics and Management Science* 335 (1974).

41 Credit Institutions (Financial Support) Act 2008; Credit Institutions (Financial Support) Scheme 2008 (SI 411/2008).

merger control rules whereby the Minister for Finance may appoint directors to the board of directors of credit institutions to protect the public interest, the degree of independence of these regulated entities from the Minister may also be queried.

Tools Available to the Regulators

1.031 The Regulators often play an important role in licensing or authorisation. The power to refuse a licence or withdraw a license or authorisation is a powerful tool in a Regulator's toolbox. The Regulators may approve or refuse certain proposed price increases by the regulated entity. In some instances, price control measures are imposed *ex ante*, such as obligations of cost orientation or price caps. There can be disagreements between Regulators and the regulated entity over the rate of return in respect of the regulated assets. There can also be disagreements over the cost of the assets that form the relevant asset base for pricing models.

1.032 The Regulators often have the role of designating the public service provider to carry out the public service obligation and of deciding on the public service fund, if any, to be established in this regard.

1.033 In relation to network sectors, the Regulators can often seek to impose access obligations on the incumbent, where access to the vertically integrated incumbent's network is necessary for new entrants. Incumbents may often be subject to non-discrimination obligations to ensure that they treat new entrants in the same manner as they treat their own downstream arms and also to ensure equivalent treatment in equivalent circumstances as between other entities. The players in regulated sectors may also be subjected to various transparency obligations by Regulators.

1.034 Civil financial sanctions cannot be imposed by all Regulators for the principal constitutional reason[42] that justice has to be done in the courts. Where the financial penalties are very high, these are often considered akin to imposing a penalty, which can only be done under criminal law.[43] EC law, of course, takes precedence even

---

42   Article 34.1: 'Justice shall be administered in courts established by law by judges appointed in the manner provided by this Constitution, and, save in such special and limited cases as may be prescribed by law, shall be administered in public.'

Article 37.1: 'Nothing in this Constitution shall operate to invalidate the exercise of limited functions and powers of a judicial nature, in matters other than criminal matters, by any person or body of persons duly authorised by law to exercise such functions and powers, notwithstanding that such person or such body of persons is not a judge or a court appointed or established as such under this Constitution.'

43   *Melling v O Mathghamhna* [1962] IR 1 which held that where a penalty is too high it is viewed as punitive and indicative of a criminal matter. Also Art 38 provides:

1. No person shall be tried on any criminal charge save in due course of law.

2. Minor offences may be tried by courts of summary jurisdiction.

5. Save in the case of the trial of offences under section 2, section 3 or section 4 of this Article no person shall be tried on any criminal charge without a jury.

over the provisions of the Constitution.[44] If a provision in a Directive were to state that 'National Regulatory Authorities shall' impose civil financial sanctions, then this would override any constitutional issues. However, where the provisions of a Directive state 'Member States shall' or 'Member States may' impose financial sanctions, the choice is left to the Member State as to how this particular provision of the directive is to be implemented. The practice in Ireland is to create a range of regulatory either-way[45] offences, rather than to impose civil financial sanctions. The Financial Regulator may, however, impose civil financial sanctions up to €5m, in the case of a corporate body, and up to €500,000, in the case of an individual. Under the Broadcasting Bill 2008, the Broadcasting Authority of Ireland's Compliance Committee may apply to the High Court for the imposition of a financial sanction in respect of a breach by a broadcaster of the provisions of the Bill. The civil sanction which may be imposed by the court is up to €250,000. The Commission for Communications Regulation may apply to the court and seek a civil financial penalty for breaches of certain regulatory obligations. The Competition Authority, the Commission for Aviation Regulation and the Commission for Communications Regulation may apply to court using criminal powers in order to have significant financial penalties imposed.

1.035 Without civil financial sanctions and the ability to impose those, a Regulator's role is limited and the 'manners' it can put on an incumbent in order to keep it honest are also restricted. If a regulatory breach is treated as an either-way offence, an attempt to secure a conviction to the requisite standard of beyond reasonable doubt in relation to what can often be viewed as a technical offence in order to impose significant financial penalties, may be difficult before Irish courts. Regarding many of these breaches, while it may be appropriate to impose a civil sanction, it may not be appropriate to consider a breach an indictable criminal offence simply in order to impose financial sanctions.

1.036 The structural separation of vertically integrated incumbents is a tool increasingly being considered by Regulators. This may involve the splitting out the downstream business from the upstream business of an incumbent and requiring, for example, the downstream business to be transferred to a new company say 'NewCo'. NewCo could then be hived off by way of a sale, if appropriate. This helps to ensure that the upstream business will deal with the downstream business on an arms' length basis, it also assists in reducing incentives to discriminate in favour of the downstream business. Structural separation is being considered in particular in the energy sector.

1.037 The Regulators also have substantive information-gathering powers and may investigate or carry out authorised officer inspections or visits ('dawn raids') where they are concerned that there may be a breach of obligations.

---

44 Article 29.4.10°: 'No provision of this Constitution invalidates laws enacted, acts done or measures adopted by the State which are necessitated by the obligations of membership of the European Union or of the Communities, or prevents laws enacted, acts done or measures adopted by the European Union or by the Communities or by institutions thereof, or by bodies competent under the Treaties establishing the Communities, from having the force of law in the State.'

45 An either-way offence is an offence that may be tried summarily or on indictment.

Appeals and Review

1.038 It is, of course, imperative that the decisions of Regulators be subject to judicial scrutiny and oversight. However, delays waiting for appeals to be heard can cause market failure because delays may allow an incumbent to operate without being subject to regulation. Suspension of the effect of a Regulator's decision works to the advantage of an incumbent. This particular form of 'regulatory gaming' needs to be guarded against. Smaller operators or players often do not have the requisite deep pockets to take on an incumbent in private enforcement actions but rely on the intervention of the Regulator, whether by way of dispute resolution or through regulation and enforcement of regulation, to keep the incumbent honest. If a Regulator's work is frustrated by tactical appeals, there may be difficulty in regulating effectively. While of course a company's property rights have to be respected and investment and innovation encouraged, suspension of Regulators' decisions should only be granted under an injunctive type balance-of-convenience test. A suspension of a decision of the European Commission by the Court of First Instance[46] is only granted where three grounds are satisfied:

    (i)   that there is a *prima facie* case;

    (ii)   that the matter is urgent; and

   (iii)   that there is a risk of serious and irreparable harm.

1.039 The interim measure of suspension must outweigh other interests in the proceedings. There is a high evidential burden before the Court of First Instance of proving actual harm that will be suffered, not just potential harm which might be suffered. Damages should not be awarded against a regulatory body where it is carrying out its statutory duty in good faith where suspension is not granted. A further query arises as to whether a Regulator could be obliged to give undertakings as to damages[47] where the regulatory body is seeking statutory injunctive relief from the court again as part of carrying out its statutory functions, rather than where it is seeking injunctive relief under equity. It is also often not clear how the right of appeal is to be exercised in conjunction with an entity's right to seek judicial review. This can be particularly problematic when there is a specialist *ad hoc* appeal panel to be established in order to exercise the right of appeal; an entity may need immediate relief and may in that instance also need to seek recourse to the court system by way of judicial review in order to obtain injunctive relief. The sometimes poorly-drafted statutory instruments can at times leave little guidance to all involved as to the procedures to be followed in this instance.[48] Where appeals are made to specialist appeal panels, it is often less than obvious what the relevant standard of review and scope of review are to be. In addition, the specialist appeal panels may often establish their own procedures in the absence of statutory guidelines and are frequently not

---

46   *Endesa SA v Commission* T–417/05 R, Order of the President of the CFI, 1 February 2006.

47   In England or Australia Regulators are generally not so obliged.

48   The provisions or rather lack thereof relating the process and scope of aviation regulation appeals left what was described by Kelly J as a 'witches brew of questions' in *Aer Rianta v Commissioner for Aviation Regulation* [2001] No 707 JR (13 November 2001, unreported), HC.

bound to follow previous procedures.[49] In a case where the Regulator is funded by the regulated entities, an unfair concept can also emerge in that, regardless of the outcome, the regulated entity or the incumbent is paying for the litigation either directly or indirectly (through a levy) where it seeks to rely on its right of appeal.

Increased Consumer Choice

1.040 The principle of competition as set out in art 3(g) of the EC Treaty aims to achieve the optimal supply of goods and services to consumers through the prevention of harmful restrictions on trade, thereby ensuring consumer welfare, provided that the protection of services of general interest do not require more specific regulation. The objectives of competition policy can be divided into economic policy and socio-political objectives. The purpose of competition policy is to allow consumers to benefit from efficiency advantages which, it is assumed, will be passed on. There are counter arguments that consumers are better off with larger businesses which can benefit from economies of scale and also that competition deters successful entrepreneurship and encourages free-riders. There is also a concern that the privatisation of certain entities may in fact have resulted in asset stripping and higher prices for consumers rather than investment or innovation. As State control over network infrastructure is relinquished and private enterprises are charged with carrying out services of general economic interest, the State retains an obligation to guarantee the provision to consumers of these essential services. The questions remain: is economic regulation working? Are there sectors where there may be limited scope for competition?

1.041 Regulation has certainly produced increased consumer choice. For example, in communications there are fixed-line, mobile, fixed-wireless, cable and satellite operators, whereas previously there was just the State monopoly. In postal services, there are now many logistics companies offering a choice of parcel and courier services. There is a choice of airlines and airports with low-cost carriers increasing consumer choice. There is an increased choice of television and radio channels. In the financial services sector, there is a choice of banks and financial service providers. It would appear that liberalisation, or the opening up of sectors to competition, has yielded more consumer choice; however, it is not clear that in all instances it has yielded lower prices and maximised consumer welfare. Many of the Regulators are charged with express consumer protection roles and adopt, accordingly, various consumer protection measures. In that context, the aim of regulation is consumer protection and sustainable consumer choice, to complement, the general consumer protection remit of the National Consumer Agency[50] under the Consumer Protection Act 2007.

---

49 As in the case of the appeal panel established under s 40 of the Aviation Regulation Act 2001.

50 It was announced in October 2008 that this agency is to be merged with the Competition Authority – http://www.budget.gov.ie, Budget 2009: Annex D Rationalisation of State Agencies.

Common Principles

1.042 There are common principles that underpin the various regulatory deliberations and decisions. These principles include proportionality and legitimate expectation and are considered together with some of the other more common principles in this section.

Proportionality

1.043 Proportionality was established as a general principle of EC law by the courts,[51] and one which could be used to challenge the legality of State action that falls within the realm of the application of EC law. Proportionality involves, in effect, balancing means and ends.[52]

The test for proportionality in Ireland is set out in *Heaney v Ireland*[53] where Costello J considered that to be proportionate, a decision must:[54]

   (i)   be rationally connected to its objective and not be arbitrary, unfair or based on irrational considerations;

  (ii)   impair rights as little as possible; and

 (iii)   be such that its effect on rights is proportional to the objective to be achieved.

Legal certainty and legitimate expectation

1.044 Good order allows people plan with a sense of security and invest with confidence, which is vital for a healthy economy. Legal certainty relates to the principle of non-retroactivity and the protection of legitimate expectation in particular.[55] Legal certainty requires that undertakings should be able to act and in particular plan, secure in the knowledge of the legal environment in which they are active and with full knowledge of the legal consequences of their actions. Retroactivity occurs where a law is introduced and applied to events which have already taken place. Where policy changes cause a loss to an undertaking, the doctrine of legitimate expectation may apply.

1.045 In *Glencar Exploration PLC v Mayo County Council* Fennelly J observed that:

> In order to succeed in a claim based on failure of a public authority to respect legitimate expectations, it seems to me to be necessary to establish three matters. Because of the essentially provisional nature of these remarks, I would emphasise that these propositions cannot be regarded as definitive. Firstly, the public authority must have made a statement or adopted a position amounting to a promise or representation, express or implied, as to how it will act in respect of

---

51   *Hauer v Land Rheinland-Pfalz* 44/79 [1979] ECR 3727.

52   See Craig and de Burca, *EU Law Text, Cases and Materials* (2nd edn, Oxford University Press, 1998), pp 349*ff.*

53   *Heaney v Ireland* [1994] 3 IR 593.

54   Para 607.

55   See Craig and de Burca, *EU Law Text, Cases and Materials* (2nd edn, Oxford, 1998), pp 357*ff.*

an identifiable area of its activity. I will call this the representation. Secondly, the representation must be addressed or conveyed either directly or indirectly to an identifiable person or group of persons, affected actually or potentially, in such a way that it forms part of a transaction definitively entered into or a relationship between that person and group and the public authority or that the person or group has acted on the faith of the representation. Thirdly, it must be such as to create an expectation reasonably entertained by the person or group that the public authority will abide by the representation to the extent that it would be unjust to permit the public authority to resile from it. Refinements or extensions of these propositions are obviously possible. Equally they are qualified by considerations of the public interest including the principle that freedom to exercise properly a statutory power is to be respected. However, the propositions I have endeavoured to formulate seem to me to be preconditions for the right to invoke the doctrine.[56]

1.046 In the case of *Power v Minister for Social and Family Affairs*,[57] MacMenamin J granted a declaration of legitimate expectation on the basis that legitimate expectation arose in circumstances where: (i) a public authority issued a statement or adopted a position amounting to a specific promise or representation, express or implied, as to how it would act in respect of an identifiable area of its activity; (ii) the representation was conveyed to an identifiable group of persons; and (iii) the representation formed part of a transaction definitively entered into by those identifiable persons on foot of those representations.

1.047 The doctrine of legitimate expectation applies to the exercise of public functions by a public body.[58] In *Carna Foods Ltd v Eagle Star Insurance Co (Ireland) Ltd*, McCracken J, in addressing a submission that it was 'an unjust and an unfair contractual term to allow the defendant to refuse cover without giving reasons',[59] observed that 'where a decision is taken to exercise a function in the public realm, the person affected is entitled to know the reasons for the decision. This is because statutory powers must be determined and exercised reasonably.'[60]

Non-discrimination and transparency

1.048 The principle of non-discrimination under EC law is binding on Member States within the scope of the application of EC law. It is generally used to ensure that there is no discrimination on grounds of nationality further to art 12 of the EC Treaty.[61]

---

56   *Glencar Exploration PLC v Mayo County Council* [2002] 1 IR 84, 162–163, applied in *Power v Minister for Social and Family Affairs* [2007] 1 IR 543, 553 *per* MacMenamin J.

57   *Power v Minister for Social and Family Affairs* [2007] 1 IR 543.

58   See the definition of the scope of the doctrine of legitimate expectations in *Abrahamson v Law Society of Ireland* [1996] 1 IR 403, 423 *per* McCracken J, applied in *Power v Minister for Social and Family Affairs* [2007] 1 IR 543, 554 *per* MacMenamin J.

59   *Carna Foods Ltd v Eagle Star Insurance Co (Ireland) Ltd* [1995] 2 ILRM 474, 477.

60   *Carna Foods Ltd v Eagle Star Insurance Co (Ireland) Ltd* [1995] 2 ILRM 474, 477.

61   See Craig and de Burca, *EU Law Text, Cases and Materials* (2nd edn, Oxford, 1998) pp 364*ff*.

The principle of openness of the legislative process is an essential requirement, as is the right of public access to information. Article 255 of the EC Treaty provides that any natural or legal person shall have a right of access to European institutions' documents, subject to certain restrictions on the grounds of public or private interest. This principle of transparency[62] relates to the duty to give reasons. In Ireland, the Freedom of Information Act (see para **2.052**) gives a statutory basis to the principle of transparency.

Fit and proper

1.049 Many licensing regimes require that applicants, amongst other things, demonstrate that they are fit and proper persons to hold a licence to trade. This is not defined as a concept. It is left to the discretion of the Regulator to apply the concept. In relation to its application as a notion, the principles that emerge are that being a 'fit' person relates to honesty, ability and knowledge. Ability and knowledge are applicable directly to the job and may be easily identified as lacking. Considering someone as honest or not may be more problematic. Can one presume a person to be honest until it is shown otherwise by their past conduct? If past conduct is known, then how should it be taken into account? The relevance of past conduct to the present activity is important. Similarly, the time that has elapsed since the past conduct is important. One must also be guided by considering against what ill the public is being protected by regulation in that field of activity.

1.050 The concept of a person's fitness to conduct a type of regulated business is not heavily litigated in Ireland, but there are some notable exceptions. This is probably for two reasons: firstly, because some of the most obvious licensed businesses, such as public houses and auctioneers, are licensed by the District Courts and any issues are argued on the spot, resolved locally and do not make it into the law reports. Secondly, many of the issues are resolved by licensing authorities by the exercise of good judgement and common sense, allied to the fact that many licensing regimes are codified in terms of what are grounds for grant, refusal or revocation and there is little room for manoeuvre. There are exceptions. In Ireland there have been some cases involving solicitors – see, for example, *In Re Burke*.[63] Further afield in Australia, the accountants acting as tax agents are to the fore.[64] On the basis of such cases, it appears that if either a new applicant or licence renewal applicant was a person who in the

---

62   See Craig and de Burca, *EU Law Text, Cases and Materials* (2nd edn, Oxford, 1998), pp 368*ff.*

63   *In Re Burke* [2001] IESC 4. See also *Balkan Tours v The Minister for Transport* [1988] ILRM 101.

64   See, for example, *Hughes & Vale Valley Pty Ltd v New South Wales (No 2)* (1955) 93 CLR at 156; *Cowlinshaw v Tax Agent's Board of Queensland* [2000] FCA 827 (20 June 2000); See *also In Re Su and the Tax Agent's Board of South Australia* 13 ATR 192 at 195 and *Tax Agent's Board of Queensland v Haddad* (1994) 48 FCR 223 at 226. *In Ingle v O' Brien* (1975) 109 ILTR at p 7 Pringle J held that simply because the applicant taxi driver was convicted in the District Court of carriage offences did not entitle the licensing authorities, by that mere fact, to revoke the applicant's licence.

recent past was convicted of either irregular trading offences, tax offences or fraud, or possibly other crimes of dishonesty or breach of trust, then one may make argue that they are neither fit nor proper persons to hold a licence. Is the recent past within the last five years? There is no statutory guidance on this question.

Data Protection

1.051 The roles of the various Regulators discussed in this book are also complemented by the role of the Data Protection Commissioner. The relevant legislation is the Data Protection Act 1988, as amended by the Data Protection (Amendment) Act 2003. The Data Protection Acts set out the general principle that individuals should be in a position to control how data relating to them is used. 'Data controllers' – people or organisations holding information about individuals – must comply with certain standards in handling personal data and respect the individual's right to privacy. Data protection law allows individuals to access and correct data. The Data Protection Commissioner is responsible for upholding the rights of individuals as set out in the Data Protection Acts, and enforcing the obligations *vis-à-vis* data controllers. The Data Protection Commissioner is appointed by the government and is independent in the exercise of his or her functions. Individuals who consider that their rights are being infringed can complain to the Data Protection Commissioner who will investigate the matter and seek to resolve it. The Data Protection Commissioner also has *vires* in the enforcement of electronic communications data protection and privacy regulations.[65] These regulations make the sending, for example, of unsolicited direct marketing messages by electronic means, an offence.

Freedom of Information

1.052 The Freedom of Information Act 1997, as amended by the Freedom of Information (Amendment) Act 2003, provides that all public bodies must publish certain information. The Act is administered by the Information Commissioner who is independent of the government in the performance of her functions. The main functions of the Information Commissioner include:

(i)   reviewing (on application) decisions of public bodies in relation to freedom of information (FOI) requests and, where necessary, making binding decisions on the matter; and

(ii) reviewing the operation of the Freedom of Information Acts to ensure that public bodies comply with the provisions of the legislation.

FOI requests are frequently used to obtain access to information relating to Regulators' decisions as an alternative and in advance of discovery. In that regard, there are a number of provisions in the Act that provide grounds upon which a refusal to release information may be based.[66]

---

65   Under SI 535/2003 as amended by SI 526/2008 – the Commission for Communications Regulation also has a role provided for under these Regulations.

66   See, for example, ss 20, 22, 23, 26 and 27 of the Freedom of Information Act.

Proceeds of Crime

1.053 Ironically, in an era of instant communication and publication, lack of accurate and reliable information is still a key factor that puts customers at risk of victimisation by criminals. Increasingly, the public demands State-led retribution for being either directly victimised by illegal traders or indirectly victimised due to the wider impact of the criminal behaviour of enterprises holding themselves out as legitimate economic enterprises. The fraud of customers through a scheme, organised by a banker or a bank robber, may result in the State responding with a trial by jury, loss of liberty, loss of licence and disqualification as a director, but what becomes of the customer's money? This is the question asked by the customer. Economic crime leads to proceeds of crime. As an alternative or in addition to prosecuting before the court with a view to applying fines, regulatory authorities should consider liaising with the Criminal Assets Bureau (CAB) regarding the proceeds of economic crime. Almost the entirety of the economic activity described in this book is a crime in the breach. Many of the principal offences are legislated in such a way as may be prosecuted as indictable offences being serious crimes. Accordingly, proceeds of those breaches are proceeds of crime as defined in the Proceeds of Crime Act 1996. Whether crime is organised in the backroom or the boardroom, it still merits State prosecution. Crime organised in the boardroom is more invidious than other crime in that some or many of the perpetrators (eg the workers) may be unwitting accomplices to the guiding minds of the criminal enterprise and may be ultimately victims themselves. In those circumstances, the State must not hesitate in using all means at its disposal to combat such crime.

BETTER REGULATION: GETTING THERE?

1.054 The Department of the Taoiseach published a white paper called 'Regulating Better', which set out six principles of better regulation in January 2004.[67] The six principles were transparency, necessity, consistency, accountability, proportionality and effectiveness. The white paper fleshed out each of these principles. In respect of *transparency*, the principle was to consult before regulating, provide greater clarity about public service obligations and ensure that regulation was straightforward, clear and accessible. In respect of *necessity*, it was intended to ensure that there would be sufficient evidence in place before regulating, to reduce red tape and to keep the various institutions and frameworks under review. In respect of *consistency*, the aim was to ensure greater consistency across regulatory bodies and that the rules be consistent. In respect of *accountability*, it was intended to strengthen the accountability in the regulatory process and to improve the appeals procedure. Regarding *proportionality*, light touch regulation was advocated to ensure that the burden of complying, and the penalty for not complying, were fair. Regulators were to engage in a regulatory impact assessment when regulating. With respect to *effectiveness*, it was intended to ensure that new regulation was targeted more effectively and adequately enforced and complied with. Since the white paper, the appeals process in respect of

---

67   Available on the website of the Better Regulation unit of the Department of the Taoiseach (http://www.betterregulation.ie).

electronic communications has been improved. There is also wider consultation and regulatory impact assessments are being increasingly undertaken. In respect of the sectors examined in this book, there has been consolidation of the regulatory agencies. The Broadcasting Commission of Ireland, the Broadcasting Complaints Commission and the RTÉ Authority are now being merged to form the Broadcasting Authority of Ireland. In October 2008, the budget announced the merger of the Competition Authority with the National Consumer Agency.[68] It is interesting to note that part of the action plan for better regulation did propose that the office of the Attorney General would work with the Government departments to promote guidelines on drafting statutory instruments and that departments would be encouraged to simplify and codify by consolidating statutory instruments that have been amended more than three times. Consideration was also given at that time to the more effective scrutiny of statutory instruments by the Houses of the Oireachtas as part of the transparency goal. Since the European Communities Act 2007, statutory instruments that implement EC law and provide for indictable offences (fines of up to €500,000 and imprisonment of up to three years on indictment) must be laid before each House of the Oireachtas for a period of 21 days. Further, as part of the proportionality element of the action plan for better regulation, the Government was to examine the issue of empowering courts and Regulators to apply effective and economically meaningful penalties for non-compliance with regulation. The Government was also to consider the extent to which the criminal justice system can appropriately deal with complex regulatory issues in an efficient manner.[69] It remains to be seen if these overtures in relation to better regulation will be further developed amidst the cacophony of competing demands on the Government.

1.055 It is against the above backdrop that this book was written. This book is a reference book. The sector-specific chapters seek to guide the reader through the maze of primary and secondary legislation as well as relevant case law. Part of the regulatory burden is the time spent identifying applicable law and digesting relevant cases. Hopefully, readers will find the book to be a useful asset in the exposition and presentation of the relevant legal basis. The chapters attempt to examine regulatory issues from a practical perspective, briefly considering, as appropriate, the historical background and how the law in each particular sector is developing. In addition, the chapters address the functions of the various Regulators, including their investigative powers. There are separate chapters on the economics of regulation, the criminal enforcement of regulatory offences, appeals and judicial review. Overall, this book is a guide to the various regulatory regimes in Ireland and how these regimes apply in practice. This book attempts to state the law as we have found it. Because of the scope of the topics covered and the dynamic nature of regulatory law, we have made little or no attempt to comment upon how it should be.

---

68   http://www.budget.gov.ie, Budget 2009: Annex D Rationalisation of State Agencies.

69   Page 46 of the White Paper on Regulating Better.

Chapter 2

ECONOMIC REGULATION

INTRODUCTION

2.001 This chapter seeks to briefly introduce some of the principal economic reasons for regulation and the strategies and methods used to regulate economics. Given that this book deals mainly with the legal structures of regulation, it is appropriate to give some broader context to the legal approaches and underlying policy choices described elsewhere in this book. This chapter then goes on to discuss some aspects of regulatory agencies.

2.002 Regulation has been defined as 'a State imposed limitation on the discretion that may be exercised by individuals or organisations, which is supported by the threat of sanction.'[1] Put another way, the essence of regulation is the explicit replacement of competition with governmental orders as the principal institutional device for assuring good performance.[2] Two prime requirements of competition as the governing market institution – freedom of entry and independence of action – are deliberately replaced. Instead, the State determines price, quality and conditions of trade, often through the agency of Regulators. It is the manner in which this has been done in Ireland that is the subject matter of this book. This chapter seeks to set out, in brief, some of the principal reasons, strategies, methods and agency types that are deployed by the State in economic regulation. It is beyond the scope of this book to discuss comprehensively the underlying economics of regulation. However, certain economic ideas encountered are briefly considered in this chapter.

2.003 As has long been noted, the key feature of the State is the power to coerce. Regulation is the use of that power for the purpose of restricting the decisions of economic agents. Economic regulation typically refers to State-imposed restrictions on individuals' and firms' decisions over price, quantity and entry and exit. When an industry is regulated, industry performance, in terms of allocative and productive efficiency, is determined both by market forces and administrative processes. However, clearly the State cannot regulate every decision, as it would be physically impossible to carry out the resulting requisite monitoring. Consequently, market forces can be expected to play a role, regardless of the degree of government intervention.[3] The question arises: when or why should the State intervene to regulate markets?

---

1   Stone, *Regulation and its Alternatives*, (Congressional Quarterly Press, 1982), p 10.

2   Kahn, *The Economics of Regulation* (MIT Press, 1998).

3   Even in the centrally planned economy of the former Soviet Union, market forces were at work. Although production and prices were set by the state, the (effective) market-clearing price was set in the market, ie by people and firms. If a product was scarce and desirable, eg food, people would queue for it. The effective price to those people was the price set by the state plus the value of time spent queuing. (contd .../)

Competition versus Regulation

2.004 The objectives of competition policy can be divided into economic policy and socio-political objectives. By protecting consumers from the exploitation of market power and by the achievement of optimal consumer welfare, the aim of competition policy is to allow consumers to benefit from efficiency advantages which it assumes will be passed on. There are counter-arguments that consumers are better off with larger businesses that can benefit from economies of scale and that competition deters successful entrepreneurship and encourages free riders.[4] For example, it may not be appropriate to 'punish' an undertaking for being successful and becoming a monopolist.[5] '[A] single producer may be the survivor out of a group of active companies, merely by virtue of his superior skill, foresight and industry .... The successful competitor, having been urged to compete, must not be turned upon when he wins.'[6] However, competition alone cannot always work as an alternative to regulation.

2.005 Economic liberalism,[7] regards competition[8] as the superior method of economic organisation, not only because it is in most circumstances the most efficient method known, but, even more so, because it is the only method known by which the activities of individuals can be adjusted to each other without coercive or arbitrary intervention of government. Consequently, one of the main arguments in favour of competition is that it dispenses with the need for 'conscious social control' and that it gives undertakings a chance to decide whether the prospects of a particular occupation are sufficient to compensate for the disadvantages and risks connected with it.[9] The benefits of competition are lower prices, innovative products, wider choice and greater efficiency than could be obtained under a monopoly. Social welfare is considered to be maximised under conditions of perfect competition.[10] In such a market where there are

---

3　(contd) To achieve supply and demand equilibrium, people would queue until the effective price (cash plus time) cleared the market. Also, for example, before 1993, by virtue of airline regulation in the European Community, prices were regulated but not the quality of service. Firms responded by shifting competition from the price dimension to the quality dimension.

4　For example, the argument that Microsoft is being punished for its success and forced to open up its systems to those companies that were less successful.

5　Whish, *Competition Law* (8th edn, LexisNexis UK, 2008), p 15.

6　Judge Learned Hand in *US v Aluminum Co of America* 148 F2d 416 (2nd Cir 1945).

7　Hayek, *The Road to Serfdom* (University of Chicago Press, 1944 (reprinted in 1994)). In his introduction to the 1994 edition, Friedman states, 'I use the term liberal, as Hayek does in the book, and also in his preface to the 1956 paperback edition, in the original nineteenth–century sense of limited government and free markets, not in the corrupted sense it has acquired in the United States, in which it also means almost the opposite.'

8　The liberal concept of competition had its origin in Adam Smith's *An Inquiry into the Nature and Causes of the Wealth of Nations* (1776).

9　Hayek, *The Road to Serfdom* (University of Chicago Press, 1944 (reprinted in 1994)), p 41.

10　Perfect competition occurs where there are a large numbers of buyers and sellers all producing homogeneous products, consumers have perfect information, there are no barriers to entry or exit, costs are kept to a minimum, and prices never rise above marginal cost of production.

many suppliers, there are allocative,[11] productive[12] and dynamic[13] efficiencies. This model is the polar opposite of a monopoly. In the case of a monopoly, it is considered that a monopolist is responsible for all output. A monopolist can increase prices by reducing volume of production. The monopolist can earn monopoly profits if he refrains from expanding production, thus output will be lower than under perfect competition. Since the monopolist may charge higher prices than under conditions of perfect competition, wealth is transferred from the consumer to the monopolist. There are allocative,[14] productive[15] and dynamic[16] inefficiencies. Given that both of these theories are somewhat divorced from real market practice, a theory of workable competition,[17] which considered *inter alia* oligopolitic markets (only a few suppliers), was developed in order to produce a more practical economic policy.

Limitations to competition

2.006 In general, the competition rules can deal with market conditions on an ex-post basis satisfactorily. However, in relation to certain sectors that were previously State monopolies, this may not be the case. As State control over network infrastructure is relinquished and private enterprises are charged with carrying out services of general economic interest, the State retains an obligation to guarantee the provision to consumers of these essential services. In all such instances, there must be some substitute for competition by regulation.[18]

2.007 Where it is impracticable to make the enjoyment of certain services dependent on the payment of a price, competition will not produce the services,[19] and the price

---

11 This means that resources are allocated between goods and services in such a way that the net gain to the consumer when buying the product is at its optimum. Production will be expanded to the point where marginal revenue equals marginal cost.

12 Under perfect competition, goods will be produced at the lowest cost possible, because if a producer were to charge above cost other competitors would move into the market.

13 Under perfect competition, producers innovate constantly.

14 This is because society's resources are not distributed in the most efficient way.

15 The monopolist is not constrained by competitive forces to reduce costs, outdated processes may be used and the monopolist becomes X-inefficient: Liebenstein, 'Allocative Efficiency v X-Efficiency' (1966) 56 *Am Ec Rev* 392–415.

16 The monopolist may not be under pressure to innovate. However, other economists consider that it is only where monopoly profits are available, that expensive research in order to innovate can be carried out.

17 Clark, 'Toward a Concept of Workable Competition' (1940) *AER* 30, 241; Sosnick, 'A Critique of Concepts of Workable Competition' (1958) 72 *Quarterly Journal of Economics* 380.

18 Here meaning the regulation of production. In other words, if consumers do not pay for the pollution through price directly, society must decide how it will pay. Society equals consumers plus producers.

19 For example, a fireworks display. These cost a lot of money to be put on as a show. However, the show can be watched for free for miles around by those in good vantage points of that part of the sky above. There is no capability to charge for entry to see the show to the exclusion of others. Hence, private enterprises have no incentive to produce the show.

system becomes similarly ineffective when the damage caused to others by certain uses of property cannot be effectively charged to the owner of that property.[20] In all these instances there is divergence between the items that enter into private calculation and those that affect social welfare; and, whenever this divergence becomes important, some method other than competition may have to be found to supply the services in question. For example, neither the provision of signposts on the roads, nor, in most circumstances, that of the roads themselves, can be paid for by every individual user; equally, certain harmful effects of deforestation, of some methods of farming, or of the smoke and noise of factories cannot be confined to the owner of the property in question or to those who are willing to submit to the damage for an agreed compensation.[21]

2.008 Spulber[22] argues that a market failure test may be proposed as a guide to determining the desirability of government intervention. The test has essentially three steps. It must first be established that market failure has occurred. 'Market failure' is defined as a departure of the market equilibrium allocation from the set of Pareto optimal allocation[23] such that no consumers can be made better off without making another consumer worse off. The optimal allocation may in fact be a 'second-best-optimum', subject to institutional, technological and informational constraints. These constraints mean a trade-off in the allocation due to competing objectives such that it becomes what is termed 'second best' optimum. The second step of the test is to determine whether government regulation can alleviate the misallocation of resources or correct the cause of the market failure, particularly when faced with similar institutional, technological or informational constraints. Finally, it must be shown that the potential benefits of regulatory remedies justify market intervention with any attendant administrative costs and induced allocative inefficiencies.

2.009 Natural monopoly is often given as an example of justified State regulatory intervention. In the case of a natural monopoly, the cost of production is lowest where output is produced by one firm. It generally refers to a property of productive technology often in conjunction with market demand, such that a single firm is able to serve the market at less cost than two or more firms.[24] Natural monopoly is due to economies of scale or economies of multiple output production; increasing returns to scale[25] must occur up to output levels that are significant relative to market demand evaluated at prices that cover the firm's costs. Natural monopoly is generally attributed to utility industries (electricity, electronic communications, post, natural gas, water) and transportation (railroads, canals). In these industries, multiple-entry of firms

---

20   Such as certain types of pollution.

21   Economists call the results of the negativities escaping from the confines so mentioned *externalities*.

22   Spulber, *Regulation and Markets* (MIT Press, 1989), p 3.

23   Economically efficient. Named after Vilfredo Pareto.

24   Spulber, *Regulation and Markets* (MIT Press, 1989), p 3.

25   Increasing returns to scale occur if output more than doubles following the doubling of all inputs.

would result in costly duplication of transmission networks and other facilities (eg lines, pipelines and tracks.) The possibility of competitive entry is the principal limitation on monopoly power in a market economy.[26]

Due to the nature of natural monopolies, they are often associated with government regulation of prices, service and entry. However, identification of increasing returns to scale does little more than describe productive technology.[27] Spulber argues that this is not sufficient to establish market failure and therefore cannot serve as a basis for regulatory policy. It must be established that economies of scale somehow prevent competition from achieving an efficient allocation of resources and that regulation can provide a remedy.

Contestable markets

2.010 The contestable markets theory is often considered in respect of the deregulation of utility industries. When studying competition in markets where firms have increasing returns to scale, economists use the contestable markets theory.[28]

---

26 It has been said that how badly a monopoly can perform in the long run (relative to the performance that could be achieved under competition) depends on the height of the barriers to entry into the market. See Bain, *Barriers to New Competition* (Harvard University Press, 1956). The US Supreme Court has defined monopoly power under the Sherman Act as the power 'to raise prices or to exclude competition when it is desired to do so', *American Tobacco Co et al v US* 328 US 781. But these two conditions are not alternatives, as the court implied; the first is in the long run dependent on the second.

27 Economies of scale can be defined as factors that cause the average cost of producing a commodity to fall as output of the commodity rises. *Penguin Dictionary of Economics* (7th edn, Penguin Books, 2003) p 114. For example, a firm or industry that would less than double its costs if it doubled output would enjoy economies of scale. Economies of scale generally result from technological factors that ensure the optimal size of production of the firm is large: (a) with high fixed cost in plant and machinery, the larger its production, the lower the cost per unit of the fixed inputs, eg one may generate electricity without a generating station, but once you build a generating station, it is inefficient to only produce small amounts of electricity with it, hence electricity companies tend to be large; (b) large firms can also arrange for the specialisation of labour and machines; and (c) only large firms can afford the high costs of research and development. There are also non-technological non-firm economies of scale: the development of an industry may lead to clusters of skilled labour in a geographical area, specialist suppliers of components and other services. Economies of scope, by contrast, are factors that make it cheaper to produce a range of related products than to produce each of the individual products on their own. Economies of scope can provide a basis for corporate diversification. For example, cutlery and crockery are now manufactured and produced as sets of complementary but distinct products.

28 See Panzar and Willig, 'Free Entry and the Sustainability of Natural Monopoly' (1977) *Bell Journal of Economics*, 8, Spring, pp 1–22; Baumol, Bailey, Willig, 'Weak Invisible Hand Theorems on the sustainability of Prices in a Multiproduct Natural Monopoly' (1977) *American Economic Review*, 67, June, pp 350–365; Baumol, Panzar. and Willig, *Contestable Markets and the Theory of Industry Structure* (Harcourt Brace Jovanovich, 1988).

The basic definition of contestable market theory requires the following:

(a)   the firms all have the same technology, which is used efficiently, and products are homogenous;

(b)   there are no barriers to market entry or exit; and

(c)   perfect information on prices is available to all consumers and firms, and firms have complete demand information.

The model of perfect competition assumes that in addition to free entry, identical technology and perfect information, there are a large number of price-taking firms. The notion of a perfectly contestable market allows a relaxation of the restriction on the number of firms (market structure) and on the behaviour of firms (firm conduct). In particular, market equilibrium in a contestable market may consist of one or a few firms with potential competition provided by the threat of entry. Firms compete by adjusting both prices and output supplied. The forces of price competition and the potential for entry serve to eliminate monopoly rents even with a small number of firms. The contestable market model is used to study competition in the presence of significant scale economies.

2.011 As Spulber notes, it is evident that the notion of a perfectly contestable market is an 'ideal case', much as the perfectly competitive market represents an abstract ideal. In studying contestable markets, the observer may isolate the effects of increasing returns to scale on market equilibrium and outputs. The extent to which market failure may be attributed to scale economies can then be examined. If contestable markets function well under scale economies, then scale economies cannot serve to rationalise regulation. Merely asserting that technology exhibits natural monopoly will not demonstrate the need for regulatory intervention. On the other hand, if market failure can be shown to result from a combination of scale economies and the departure of markets from the ideal of 'contestability,' regulatory policy must then respond to a broader range of underlying circumstances.

Regulation and Market Failure

2.012 Regulations may be classified and their effectiveness evaluated on the basis of the market failure they attempt to remedy.[29] Regulation of entry and quality of service in utility industries attempts to address imperfections in the competition associated with 'barriers to entry.' Environmental regulations directed at air and water pollution or natural resource depletion are aimed at 'externalities', where transactions create costs for third parties. Finally, regulation of product quality, workplace safety or contract terms is directed at 'internalities', that is costs or benefits of market transactions that are not reflected in terms of exchange.

REASONS FOR REGULATION

2.013 The section below attempts to set out some of the technical justifications for regulation, that is to say justification for government to act in the public interest. Many reasons relate to 'market failure', where unregulated markets will fail to produce a

---

29   Spulber, *Regulation and Markets* (MIT Press, 1989), p 8.

desirable result in the context of the public interest. There may, in fact, be an absence of a market – eg households cannot buy clean air or peace and quiet in their localities.[30] Baldwin and Cave[31] have identified twelve types of rationale behind State intervention.

Monopolies and Natural Monopolies

2.014 'Monopoly' describes a situation where there is one seller in the market. This may occur if a product is unique, ie there is no close substitute and there are substantial barriers restricting entry by other firms into the market and exit is difficult. Where a monopoly occurs, the market 'fails' because competition is deficient. Against the public interest, a monopolist may be seen to reduce output, but raise prices to compensate for revenue lost by lower production. Thus the monopolist takes advantage of its position by making less and selling for higher prices. Consumers lose out (they pay more for less) and there is a transfer of income from the consumers to the producer.

2.015 A potential response to monopolies is the use of competition law to provide for a potentially competitive environment. However, this is unhelpful if the monopoly is a natural monopoly, ie the economies of scale in the market are such that one firm alone can supply the market at lowest cost. It is thus least costly to society to have one firm producing. As Baldwin and Cave note, determining whether a natural monopoly exists requires a comparison of demand for the product with the extent of the economies of scale available in production. If a natural monopoly exists, it may be seen to also produce less for more, as noted above. Competition law would provide for other entrants in the market, but the replication by those firms of the means of production and supply would, by definition, impose inefficient costs on society; thus regulation of prices, quality and output, as well as access, may be called for.

2.016 Not all aspects of a supply process may be naturally monopolistic. As Ogus points out,[32] the economies of scale phenomenon may affect only one part of a given process – for instance, the transmission of, say, electricity rather than its generation.[33] Therefore, the task of Government and Regulator is to identify those parts of a process that are naturally monopolistic so that these can be regulated.

Windfall Profits

2.017 Some argue that there is a case for regulation where windfall profit may occur for a firm by chance, as opposed to design.[34] Many firms incur exceptional profits due

---

30   Baldwin and Cave, *Understanding Regulation: Theory, Strategy and Practice* (OUP, 1999), p 9.
31   Baldwin and Cave, *Understanding Regulation: Theory, Strategy and Practice* (OUP, 1999), ch 2.
32   Ogus, *Regulation: Legal Form and Economic Theory* (OUP, 1994), p 31.
33   Yarrow, 'Regulation and Competition in the Electricity Supply Industry', in Kay, Mayer and Thompson, *Privatisation and Regulation* (OUP, 1996).
34   Such arguments appear unpersuasive when using the example of a firm with boats in a suddenly flooded desert area.

to the sale of an asset (for example a new invention); however, for government to try and capture any such profits as windfall profits might chill initiative and innovation.

Externalities

2.018 The reason for regulating externalities (also called spill-overs) is that the price of a product does not reflect the true cost to society of producing that good, and excessive consumption accordingly results. Pollution, a by-product in many manufacturing processes, is not factored into price. Society bears the extra cost of pollution (the externality), such as the cost of poor quality air, excess noise, polluted water and so on. The resultant process is inefficient as too many resources are attracted to polluting activities and too few resources to pollution avoidance or the adoption of pollution-free production methods. The rationale for regulation is to eliminate this inefficiency, thus protecting society or third parties suffering from externalities, by compelling the internalisation by the manufacturer of spill-over effects on the *polluter pays* principle.

Information Inadequacies

2.019 Competitive markets can only function if consumers are sufficiently well informed to evaluate competing products.[35] If consumers are not well informed for various reasons, then regulation, by making information more extensively accessible, accurate and affordable, may protect consumers against information inadequacies and the consequences thereof, and may encourage the operation of healthy, competitive markets.[36]

Continuity and Availability of Service

2.020 Socially desired levels of continuity or availability of service may not always be provided by the market. For example, some markets are seasonal. It may be wasteful to open, close and re-open the service provider, and socially undesirable to discontinue service provision in between. Other markets have customers concentrated in urban cluster as well as remote rural customers. The temptation is for the producer to serve only the easily reached urban customers at the expense of others, as the cost of serving the rural customers at the same price may reduce overall profits. In both cases, regulation may be justified in order to produce socially desirable results, even though the cross-subsidisation effects of maintaining a service during a seasonal trough or

---

35   See Hayek, 'The Use of Knowledge in Society' (1945) 35 *American Economic Review* 519; Breyer, *Regulation and its Reform* (Harvard UP, 1982), pp 26–28; Ogus, *Regulation: Legal Form and Economic Theory* (OUP, 1994), pp 38–41.

36   As Breyer notes, until the US government required disclosure, accurate information was unavailable to most buyers there concerning the durability of light bulbs, nicotine contents of cigarettes, fuel economy for cars or care requirements for textiles.

extending a service to remote locations may be criticised as inefficient and unfair. Such instances pose difficult economic policy questions regarding State intervention.[37]

Anti-Competitive Behaviour and Predatory Pricing

2.021 Markets may be deficient not merely because competition is lacking; they may produce undesirable effects because firms behave in an anti-competitive manner. One manifestation of such behaviour is predatory pricing. This occurs when a firm prices below costs, in the hope of driving competitors from the market, achieving a degree of domination and then using its dominant position to recover the costs of predation and increase profits at the expense of consumers. This assumes that entry into the market takes time for that period to arise. In such a circumstance, the objective for Regulators is to sustain competition and protect consumers from the ill effects of market domination by making predatory behaviour or other forms of anti-competitive behaviour illegal.

Public Goods and Moral Hazard

2.022 Some commodities, such as security and defence services, may bring generally socially desirable shared benefits. However, it may, be very costly for those paying for such services to prevent non-payers ('free riders') from enjoying the benefits of those services. Consequently, the market may fail to such commodities and regulation may be required – often to overcome the free rider problem by imposing taxes.

Similarly, when there is an instance of moral hazard – where someone other than the consumer pays for the service – such as medical bills paid by the State or an insurance company, the regulatory constraints may be required if excessive consumption of services is to be avoided.

Unequal Bargaining Power

2.023 One precondition for the efficient allocation of resources in a market is equal bargaining power. If bargaining power is unequal, regulation may be justified to protect certain interests, such as the health and safety of workers who individually may not be able to negotiate that outcome. Related to unequal bargaining power is an information deficit on one side of the bargain. Regulation may seek to redress this issue by imposing transparency obligations.

---

37 It has been long recognised in legal circles that the unvarnished application of the common law can lead to outcomes that are socially regarded as unjust. Equity demands another solution. Thus, the law of equity arose and is turned to in circumstances that merit its application. In the examples mentioned above, the unvarnished application of economic thinking requires a political solution for a just social outcome. By analogy, therefore, should regulation only arise as a political response when the economic solution proposed is socially unacceptable, ie it does not equate with the public interest? A difficulty with such a question is obvious: what is the public interest? Who measures it and how is it defined? It is outside the scope of this book to discuss the issue further. However, if one makes a case for regulation on this basis, once the public interest is satisfied or changes, then surely the case of re-regulation or deregulation must follow.

Scarcity and Rationing

2.024 In certain times of crises, regulation may take the place of market price and allocate goods according to some other set of priorities.

Distributional Justice and Social Policy

2.025 Allocative efficiency attempts to maximise welfare but is not concerned with the distribution of that welfare amongst individuals or groups in society. The State, by contrast, may be keenly interested in that issue for reasons of social cohesion, order or paternalism. For example, victims may be compensated, discrimination prohibited or passengers required to wear seatbelts for their own safety.

Rationalisation and Co-ordination

2.026 Centralised regulation holds the advantage over individual private law arrangements where information can be more efficiently communicated through public channels, and economies of scale can be achieved by having one public agency responsible for upholding standards. As Baldwin and Cave note,[38] this rationale for regulation is based more on the desire to enable effective action to take place than on the need to prohibit undesirable behaviour.

Planning

2.027 Markets may ensure that the individual's current consumer preferences are met, but they are less able to meet the demands of future generations or to satisfy altruistic concerns, such as the future state of the environment. Centralised planning and taxation for payment may be used to address these issues and also to overcome free-rider problems.

It is important to note that often a number of these reasons to regulate may co-exist in a given sector.

STRATEGIES OF REGULATION

2.028 The State controls activities in various ways that reflect the special capacity government has to influence industrial, economic or social policy. These have been described as follows:[39]

To command – where the legal authority and the command of law is used to pursue policy objectives;

To deploy wealth – where contracts, grants, loans, subsidies or other incentives are used to influence conduct;

---

38 Baldwin and Cave, *Understanding Regulation: Theory, Strategy and Practice* (OUP, 1999), p 15.

39 See Hood, *The Tools of Government* (London, 1983); Daintith, 'The Techniques of Government' in Jowell and Oliver (eds), *The Changing Constitution* (3rd edn, OUP, 1994). See also Baldwin and Cave, *Understanding Regulation: Theory, Strategy and Practice* (OUP, 1999), ch 4.

To harness markets – where governments channel competitive forces to particular ends (for example, by using auctions to achieve benefits for consumers);

To inform – where information is deployed strategically (so as to empower consumers and competing undertakings who may themselves be customers of vertically integrated monopolists);

To act directly – where the State takes physical action (possibly to contain a hazard or a nuisance); and

To confer protected rights – where rights and liability rules are structured and allocated so as to create desired incentives and constraints (for example when rights to clean water are created in order to deter polluters).

2.029 Various strategies are associated with the use of the above capacities or resources of the State.

(i) Command and control regulation is the exercise of influence by imposing standards backed by criminal sanctions. Certain forms of conduct may be prohibited, positive actions demanded or conditions for entry in a sector set out in law. Often the rules will be set by the State and then implemented and enforced by other agencies. Associated with command and control regulation is licensing to screen entry into an activity, control of quality, service production, allocation of resources, products or commodities and price charged to customers.[40]

(ii) Self-regulation and enforced self-regulation is a substitute for control and command regulation. It often involves a trade association monitoring and enforcing a set of rules against its own members. If subject to State oversight, it can be classified as enforced self-regulation.

(iii) Regulating by means of *incentive-based regimes* offers an escape from highly restrictive, rule-bound, control and command regimes.[41] In such a regime the regulated firm, can be induced to behave in accordance with the public interest by the State or a Regulator imposing negative or positive taxes or deploying grants and subsidies from the public purse. Thus, not only can taxes be used to penalise polluters, but rewards can be given for reductions in pollution, or financial assistance can be given to those who build pollution-reducing mechanisms into their production or operational processes. An example of this is the taxation of motor cars according to CO_2 emissions.

---

40 Difficulties with this form of regulation include the possibility for regulatory capture and 'legalism' – complex, inflexible rules leading to litigation, delay and possibly further regulation. Enforcement is also difficult for many of the same reasons.

41 See Ogus, *Regulation: Legal Form and Economic Theory* (OUP, 1994), ch 11; Daintith, 'The Techniques of Government' in Jowell and Oliver (eds), *The Changing Constitution* (3rd edn, OUP, 1994); Breyer and Stewart, 'The Discontents of Legalism: Interest Group Relations in Administrative Regulation' (1985) *Wisconsin LR* 685. On the limitations of incentive-based regimes, see Braithwaite, 'The Limits of Economics in Controlling Harmful Conduct' (1982) 16 *Law and Society Review* 481.

(iv) Market harnessing controls may also be used to as a form of regulation. Examples of this type of strategy include competition law, franchising, regulation by contract and tradable permits.

Competition law may be used instead of, or in conjunction with, regulation in order to channel market forces; for example, in order to promote levels of competition that provide desirable services to consumers and the public.[42]

Franchising is a system of control that can be employed in naturally monopolistic sectors to replace competition in the market with competition for the market. The idea is predicated on the assumption that applicants for franchises make competitive bids for an exclusive (or at least protected) right to serve the market, based on assumptions of efficiency in service provision – to the benefit of consumers.[43]

2.030 *Regulation by contract* is when State departments or agencies use the State's wealth and spending power to achieve desired objectives by specifying these in contracts.

2.031 The use of *tradable permits* is an attempt to harness markets by requiring use of such permits by those engaged in an activity that has been deemed to require control. In a typical regime, the State or Regulator issues a given number of permits and each of these allows a specified course of behaviour. Following the initial allocation, permits may be traded and this allows, say, a generating company to switch to cleaner fuels and sell its excess allowances to other firms. It has been suggested by Baldwin and Cave that the initial distribution of permits may be carried out by auction or according to public interest criteria.[44] The incentives within such a system are provided by the market in permits.

2.032 *(v) Disclosure rules* generally involve prohibitions on false or misleading information (such as advertising) or the mandatory disclosure of information; for example, obliging suppliers to provide information to consumers on price, composition, quantity or quality, such as in the food and drink industry. Passengers and holiday-makers also benefit from disclosure rules regarding details of air travel and package holidays.

2.033 *(vi)* A Government may decide to regulate by *direct action*. It may provide the infrastructure to a desired standard and then franchise its use for the provision of the service. For example, the State might own the bus transport network but put out to

---

42   For a review of the New Zealand experience of this approach, see: New Zealand Commerce Commission, *Telecommunications Industry Inquiry Report* (Wellington, June 1992); Blanchard, 'Telecommunications Regulation in New Zealand; How effective is "light handed regulation"'? (1994) 18 *Telecommunications Policy* 154–164.

43   For example, a 'beauty contest' for a licence may be a competition for the right to have an exclusive licence for a market, or one of only very few licences.

44   Baldwin and Cave, *Understanding Regulation: Theory, Strategy and Practice* (OUP, 1999), p 47.

tender or franchise the provision of bus services.[45] A difficulty with direct action is that private firms tend not to invest in the State-funded aspect of the market. Thus innovation in that element may be lost.

2.034 *(vii)* The State may also impose a system of *rights and liabilities* in relation to an activity. For example, a prospective polluter may be deterred by the knowledge that those affected locally have the right to sue for damages in the event and he bears the liability to make good that damage. This is a weak form of regulation if those rights attach to individuals as the time and expense of litigation may be prohibitive. Alternatively, the State could give itself the right to sue for damages against such a company, on behalf of a local community, either as a Minister or local authority. Such damage as is quantified could then be awarded to the Exchequer or local authority for ultimate redistribution to the community. Such a system would provide the polluter with a well-resourced, committed adversary. Compensation in the form of damages would flow back to the community. A court might direct that damages remitted to the State be used to remedy in the best way possible the particular damage incurred. There is a legal difficulty in Ireland in so far as administrative fines may not in general be imposed against offenders – such fines must be imposed by the courts in due course of law. In addition, the State suffers no personal, quantifiable damage in many cases and thus cannot show damage. The system described above looks at this difficulty from a different angle – a change in the civil liability law would provide for the State, acting on behalf of identifiable persons, to absorb their damage and sue for recompense. Insurance companies act in a similar way in circumstances when a customer is compensated by them; they may step in to his shoes by subrogation, absorb his rights and sue for the money back from the liable culprit. Here the State might pursue the perpetrator of the harm through the courts for damages in a similar manner, but expressed as a statutory right. Such a system crosses over into the next regulatory strategy discussed below.

2.035 *(viii) Public compensation and social insurance schemes* are another form of attempting to exercise control in certain circumstances. For example, some economic incentive schemes are insurance schemes whereby the State pays out to, say, employees for the sins of their employers, who pay premiums to the State based on their past performance. Workplace health and safety schemes are an example.[46] Say the State compensated persons who suffered damage from workplace accidents in return for those persons assigning any claim against the employer to the State; then the State would require firms participating in such markets to pay it premiums to cover the provision of commensurate levels of insurance for defined risks in order to compensate those persons who have suffered damage.

---

45   See Glaister, Kennedy and Travers, *London Bus Tendering* (Greater London Group, London School of Economics, 1995), and Glaister, *Deregulation and Privatisation: British Experience* (World Bank, 1998).

46   See Bailey (ed), *Economic Incentives to Improve the Working Environment* (European Foundation for the Improvement of Living and Working Conditions, 1994).

METHODS OF REGULATION

2.036 As Viscussi *et al* note, although economic regulation can encompass restrictions on a wide array of firm decisions, the three key decision variables controlled by regulation are price, quantity[47] and the number of firms.[48] Also frequently controlled is third-party access to the incumbent's natural monopoly network. Less frequently controlled variables include product quality and investment.[49] Set out below is an outline on each of these approaches. However, it is beyond the scope of this chapter to discuss any in the comprehensive fashion their detail or relative merit.

Control of Price

2.037 Price regulation may either set a particular price that firms must charge or may restrict firms to setting prices within some range. If the concern of the Government is with a regulated monopolist setting prices too high, regulation may specify a maximum price that can be charged – for example, airport or air traffic control charges. If the regulated firm has some unregulated competitors, the Regulator may also be concerned with the regulated firm engaging in predatory pricing. In that situation, regulation is likely to include a minimum as well as a maximum price.[50]

Sometimes, regulation may put an entire price structure in place. For example, in the electronic communications market and the energy markets, where one has a variety of different tariffs, the specification of a price structure, as opposed to just a single price, increases the complexity of implementing economic regulation.

2.038 One purpose of regulation is to protect buyers from monopolistic exploitation – but buyers can be exploited just as effectively by giving them poor or unsafe service as by charging excessive prices. It has been argued by Kahn[51] that the nature of our

---

47 It is essentially impossible to simultaneously control price and quantity in a market situation. Whether a private monopoly or a regulated firm, you either set the price and observe how much is sold or set the quantity and observe what the price becomes.

48 For an excellent discussion on some effects of price and entry regulation, see Viscussi, Vernon and Harrington, *Economics of Regulation and Antitrust* (3rd edn, MIT Press, 2000), pp 504–513. They discuss the emergence of: (i) non-price competition – quality improvements, warranties, advertising; (ii) productive inefficiency – higher wages, continued operation of inefficient firms; (iii) cross-subsidisation – universal service obligations; (iv) reduced capital formation due to service of unprofitable markets; and (v) effects on innovation.

49 In his 1957 study, Nobel Laureate Robert Solow concluded that 90 per cent of the doubling of per capita non-farm output in the US over the period 1909–1949 was due to technical advance – 'Technical Change and Aggregate Production Function,' (August 1957) *Review of Economic Studies* 39: 312–20. Viscussi *et al* argue that, given the importance of technological innovation in economy, it is essential to consider the ramifications of regulation on the pace of technological progress.

50 Placing a minimum on prices that may be charged by a regulated firm may counter or limit that firm from charging at lower levels to prevent entry as opposed to forcing exit.

51 Kahn, *The Economics of Regulation* (MIT Press, 1998), p 21/I.

dependence on public utility services is typically such that customers may be more interested in the reliability, continuity and safety of the service, rather than the price they have to pay.[52] That said, price regulation is a central feature of public utility regulation. It is through the regulation of price that the levels and permissible kinds of costs are controlled: by allowing or disallowing payments for various inputs, by supervising methods of financing and controlling financial structures.

2.039 Price regulation is also a means by which a Regulator may achieve the ultimate objective of limiting industry profit. A Regulator often sets price so that the regulated firm earns a reasonable rate of return. This is not always the case in Ireland[53] but has been utilised in the past in the US in the regulation of public utilities and has been used in other regulated industries such as the airline industry in the US (prior to its deregulation). It is also a familiar principle in the EU in allowing the provider of a public service obligation to recover a reasonable rate of return for carrying out a service of general economic interest.[54] As firm profit is determined by a variety of factors (with price being just one of them), a Regulator may have a difficult time in achieving its goal of a reasonable rate of return. Regulatory lag in changing price in response to new cost and demand conditions can result in a regulated firm earning either too high or too low a rate of return. During the inflationary period of the 1970s,

---

52   Kahn, *The Economics of Regulation* (MIT Press, 1998), p 21/I. Kahn suggests another purpose is to prevent 'destructive' competition – but he argues it would seem that sellers can compete just as destructively by offering better or more service for the same price as by offering the same service at lower prices. It would seem that his argument here is that regulation can be used to counter the excesses of creative destruction by slowing down the rate of technological innovation by removing the impetus for innovation by some form of regulation. Allan Greenspan explains the notion of creative destruction briefly in *The Age of Turbulence – Adventures in a New World* (Penguin Allen Lane, 2007) at p 48. 'Working with heavy industry gave me a profound appreciation of the central dynamic of capitalism. 'Creative destruction' is an idea that was articulated by the Harvard economist Joseph Schumpeter in 1942. Like many powerful ideas, his is simple: a market economy will incessantly revitalise itself from within by scrapping old and failing businesses and then reallocating resources to newer, more productive ones.'

53   The Electronic Communications Access Regulations 2003 (SI 305/2003) provide that the Regulator shall take into account any relevant investment made by the operator and allow the operator a reasonable rate of return on adequate capital employed, taking into account the risks involved. It also provides that the Regulator may take account of prices available in comparable competitive markets.

54   *Altmark Trans GmbH and Regierungsprasidium Magdeburg v Nahverkerhrsgesellschaft Altmark GmbH* [2003] ECR I 7747 refers to reasonable profit. As does Commission Decision of 28 November 2005 on the application of art 86(2) of the EC Treaty to State Aid in the form of public service compensation grants to certain undertakings entrusted with the operation of services of general economic interest. Reasonable profit in this context means a rate of return on own capital that takes account of the risk, or absence of risk, incurred by an undertaking by virtue of the intervention by the Member State, particularly where there are special or exclusive rights. This rate shall not normally exceed the average rate for the sector concerned in recent years. In determining reasonable profit, the member states may introduce incentive criteria relating to the quality of service provided and gains in productive efficiency (para 5.4 of the Decision).

rising inputs prices resulted in public utilities often earning a below normal rate of return because the regulatory agency was slow to adjust price. Alternatively, a regulated firm that experiences an innovation in its production technology will reap above normal profits until the Regulator realises the cost function has shifted down and responds by lowering price. This approach to price regulation is known as rate-of-return regulation.

2.040 As Baldwin and Cave note,[55] rate-of-return regulation has one obvious flaw and one more subtle one. The more obvious flaw is that the company in question has no incentive to operate efficiently, as it knows that it will be able to recover increasing cost with a substantial increase in price. Assuming price reviews take place with sufficient frequency, the firm pays no penalty for inefficiency. The less obvious flaw is the incentive for the firm to over invest in capital equipment. Suppose that the Regulator calculates the allowable rate of return on assets at 15 per cent per year, whereas the firm's cost of capital – the return required to keep investors replacing and expanding assets in the firm – is only 10 per cent per year. In these conditions, the Regulator's estimate allows the firm's investors an excess rate of return of 5 per cent per year on whatever investment they put into the business. Thus they have an incentive to artificially inflate the asset base by adopting very capital-intensive techniques and by unnecessary extravagance in designing plants (sometime known as gold plating). The more they invest, the greater the excess returns. This phenomenon, known as the Averch-Johnson effect,[56] will skew inefficiency in the direction of excessive use of capital, and as Baldwin and Cave note,[57] it may be difficult for a Regulator to identify such extravagance by inspecting investment plans, especially if comparable firms are subject to the same incentives. This consequence is, however, secondary to the lack of incentive to control costs of production that is encountered under rate-of-return regulation.

2.041 Due to these effects, rate-of-return regulation has been described as a 'low powered' incentive mechanism – as the firm benefits little from any efficiency gain. This is because cost savings made will almost immediately be taken from the firm and given to consumers in the form of lower prices. of the question then arise as to what would amount to a 'high powered' incentive mechanism. Clearly, a distinguishing feature is that the firm retains, at least temporarily, a substantial proportion of the benefits of any greater efficiency. This may be achieved by decoupling the revenues that a firm can generate from the costs that it incurs.

2.042 This type of alternative approach to rate-of-return regulation is 'incentive regulation'. This approach to regulation is influenced by the fact that in competitive markets, firms seek to gain advantage over one another by realising efficiencies.

---

55 Baldwin and Cave, *Understanding Regulation: Theory, Strategy and Practice* (OUP, 1999), pp 224–226; see also Spulber, *Regulation and Markets* (MIT Press, 1989) at pp 287–290.

56 Averch and Johnson, 'Behaviour of the Firm under Regulatory Constraint' (1962) 92 *American Economic Review* 1052–69.

57 Baldwin and Cave, *Understanding Regulation: Theory, Strategy and Practice* (OUP, 1999) p 225.

Competition forces companies to employ the most efficient production methods. They gain the benefits of greater efficiency as profits and, ultimately, their customers may gain through lower prices as other firms react, catch up technologically and lower prices to recover market share. In this way, competition will eventually result in the benefits of efficiency being shared with customers through lower prices.

2.043 In a regulated market, a Regulator may attempt to create similar incentives for a firm to seek productive efficiencies and later force it to share the benefits of greater efficiencies with its customers through lower prices. As with rate-of-return regulation, it does this by capping the firm's prices, which are set such that the firm can recover efficiently incurred costs while keeping any additional profits earned from further efficiencies realised beyond those underlying the 'price cap.' A price cap is usually for a fixed period. The benefit of additional efficiencies realised within that period is later shared with the firm's customers when the Regulator sets the next price cap by basing the new price cap on the more efficient cost base achieved by the regulated entity. This regime is also known as price capping by RPI – X regulation (in Ireland CPI – X).[58] It was first applied on a large scale in the UK in British Telecom in 1984.[59]

2.044 A simple but very high powered incentive mechanism would operate by setting a price path for the firm's products prices indefinitely into the future – requiring them, for instance, to fall by 2 per cent per year in real terms. In such circumstances, a firm not subject to competition would be able to 'keep' in perpetuity the benefits of any costs savings that it achieved. However, as Baldwin and Cave observe,[60] this is not, practical, as setting prices in advance for an indefinite period is likely, within a decade or less, either to drive the firm into bankruptcy, if they are set too low, or to allow profits to grow to a politically unacceptable level, if they are set too high. The key to CPI – X regulation is to reset the price cap at defined intervals that are neither too long to create financial difficulties for the firm, nor too short to realise efficiencies that may later be passed on to customers.

2.045 In incentive regulation, price caps are not supposed to be immediately revised up or down according to the firm's performance relative to the forecast performance. Within the defined period, the regulated entity should be confident that any profit earned through additional efficiency can be retained by the firm until the end of the defined period. Such certainty is central to the cost-reducing incentives inherent in price caps based on incentive regulation.

---

58 Where CPI stands for the change in the consumer price index for the preceding year within the regulatory period. 'X' is an efficiency factor set by the Regulator. 'X' may be a positive or negative number. Where x = 0 then prices may increase in line with CPI. Where x = CPI then prices are static.

59 See Littlechild, *Regulation of British Telecommunication's Profitability*, (Department of Industry, 1983).

60 Baldwin and Cave, *Understanding Regulation: Theory, Strategy and Practice* (OUP, 1999), p 226.

2.046 The operation of a price cap can be explained by way of a simple example.[61] Supposing the Regulator believes the firms costs will be €1,000 per annum for each year of a regulatory period, and that it forecasts 100 passengers per annum. It would, therefore, set a per passenger cap of €10 per passenger, allowing the firm to recover its costs. Suppose that during the period the firm discovers how to operate at a cost of €900 while still serving 100 customers. In this scenario it would earn a profit of €100. It keeps this until the next price cap, at which time the Regulator would lower the price cap to €9 per passenger to reflect the lower costs. Therefore, both the airport and the passengers benefit from the price cap through profit incentives and lower charges. It is important to recognise that if the Regulator revised the cap down to €9 as soon as the saving was made, the incentive to undertake the efficiency would be undermined. Therefore, price cap periods that are too short undermine the incentive properties of price cap regulation, while periods that are too long share a smaller proportion of potential savings with consumers.

Calculating a price cap

2.047 Price caps are derived from a series of inputs sometimes known as 'regulatory building blocks' calculated at the time of making a price cap. These building blocks are:

   (i)   an estimate of efficient future operating expenditures;

   (ii)   plus a return on capital;

   (iii) plus a depreciation allowance;

   (iv) less an estimate of future commercial revenues.

The sum of these building blocks is divided by the unit to be regulated; for example, a forecast of passengers using an airport to give the maximum per passenger airport charge.

Forward-looking long-run incremental cost (LRIC) is also sometimes used as a pricing mechanism for regulating utilities.

Control of Quantity

2.048 A common form of quantity regulation that is often imposed is to 'meet all demand at the regulated price'.[62] This requirement is used in regulating energy, electronic communications and postal utilities. The reason for this is to provide for a universal service to consumers that does not discriminate as to the location of those consumers. Finally, regulation may place restrictions upon the prices that firms set while leaving their quantity decision unregulated; for example, airport passenger

---

61   See further,Commission for Aviation Regulation, *Maximum Levels of Airport Charges at Dublin Airport Issues Paper*, Commission Paper 6/2008,24 October 2008 available at http://www.car.ie for a discussion on the operation of a price cap.

62   See further, Viscussi, Vernon and Harrington, *Economics of Regulation and Antitrust* (3rd edn, MIT Press, 2000), p 299.

charges. Restrictions on the quantity of product or service that is sold may be used either with or without price regulation.

Control of Entry and Exit

2.049 In Ireland, the two main variables that Regulators have controlled are price and the number of firms, the latter through restrictions on entry and exit.[63] These forms of control are important because they are key determinants of both allocative and productive efficiency. Entry may be regulated on several levels. Entry by new firms may be controlled by licensing or the grant of a monopoly right. In addition to controlling entry by new firms, a Regulator may also control entry or exit by existing firms. An example of both co-existing is the allocation of landing slots at a co-ordinated airport.[64] Ownership and control rules based on nationality similarly restrict entry.[65]

Control of Other Variables

Quality of service

2.050 The other main variable that is often regulated is the quality of the product or service that is produced.[66] For example, a Regulator may specify minimum standards for reliability of a service such as energy in order to avoid blackouts. In addition, product quality may also be controlled for safety reasons. In the past, in Ireland, there was minimal regulation of quality; one reason was the cost of implementing it. In more recent times, the Commission for Communications Regulation has taken an active role in relation to quality of service standards in postal delivery[67] and in relation to quality of service standards provided in fixed line electronic communications. In addition, the Commission for Energy Regulation has an express statutory role in relation to safety standards in energy. Generally, economic regulation has not placed severe restrictions on the quality of products or services that firms offer, with the notable exception of product safety.

---

63 Viscussi, Vernon and Harrington, *Economics of Regulation and Antitrust* (3rd edn, MIT Press, 2000) p 299.

64 Slot co-ordination is a complex form of regulation, found at the busiest international airports, including Dublin, designed to allocate scarce resources ('slots') amongst existing air carriers using the airport and new entrants. In addition, all firms need to be licensed before they can even enter the market.

65 For example, air carriers are not entitled to an Irish Air Carrier Operating License unless they can demonstrate that majority ownership and ongoing effective control at all times reside with EEA Member States or their nationals – art 4 of Council Regulation 1008/2008 on the licensing of air carriers.

66 Viscussi, Vernon and Harrington, *Economics of Regulation and Antitrust* (3rd edn, MIT Press, 2000), p 300.

67 The target for delivery of domestic mail is D + 1 where D = Day.

2.051 Generally, primary responsibility for quality remains with the supplying company instead of with the regulatory agency. As Kahn observes,[68] the reasons for this are fairly clear. Service standards are often much more difficult to specify by the promulgation of rules. The only role the Regulator can usually play is a negative one – formulating minimum standards and using periodic inspections to see that they are met; investigating customer complaints and issuing orders when service has been poor, when management or subordinates have been inefficient or unfair; or insisting that the companies take on or retain un-remunerative business.

2.052 There is another reason[69] why Regulators have at times in certain sectors left the quality of service, far more than price, to the companies themselves – the latter will have a strong interest in providing good, ample and expanding service, so long as they can recoup their costs in the prices they charge. In this respect, more so than as regards price, the interest of the monopolist on the one hand and the consumer on the other are more nearly coincident than in conflict.[70] Why so? Kahn offers the following reasons:[71]

1. Maintaining and improving the quality and quantity of service typically is costly. Any regulated monopolist who is prevented by regulation from fully exploiting the inelasticity of his demand[72] but assured (albeit with a regulatory lag) of his ability to incorporate these additional costs in his cost-of-service and hence of recouping them in his price, will presumably be less hesitant than a non-regulated monopolist to incur them.

2. Improvement and extension of service will often involve an expansion of the company's invested capital – that is, its regulated asset base[73] – on which it is entitled to a return. The regulated monopolist, therefore, will have some temptation to err in the direction of expanding and improving his services and thus increasing his regulated base beyond the point of economic optimality, instead of the reverse.

3. A public utility company is peculiarly exposed to public criticism if its service is inadequate. This exposure is increased by the possibility of customers complaining to the Regulator.[74]

---

68   Kahn, *The Economics of Regulation* (MIT Press, 1998), p 22/I.

69   Kahn, *The Economics of Regulation* (MIT Press, 1998), p 24/I.

70   Indeed, the greater danger might be that the companies place excessive, instead of inadequate, emphasis on providing high quality service, at the expense of economy – 'gold plating'.

71   Kahn, *The Economics of Regulation* (MIT Press, 1998), p 24/I.

72   Assuming the monopolist is at that time facing inelastic demand.

73   Also known as the rate base.

74   This is true in Ireland where many of the regulated entities are the best-known companies in the country and major employers with a nationwide presence.

Investment

2.053 Another variable that is sometimes regulated is firm investment. In contrast to other variables, regulation of investment means government intervention into the production process; that is, a firm's choice of technology and inputs. An example of how this is indirectly achieved is by regulating price by reference to projected allowed capital expenditure.[75]

Access

2.054 The electricity, gas, post and electronic communications networks all have certain natural monopolistic characteristics in relation to elements of those markets, since duplication or multiplication of this network infrastructure may at times be connected with economically unjustifiable costs.[76] The opening of networks by legal means is necessary since supplying the consumer may only be possible through the natural monopoly and therefore access to these networks needs to be opened up to all service providers. It is, however, the case that the behaviour of such a natural monopolist may be constrained by competing infrastructures, for example, mobile telephony services may compete with fixed line, and courier services with postal services.

Public or consumer interest/social requirements

2.055 The customer interest in relation to utilities has a number of facets: price, quality, access and fears about loss of service. In brief, consumers desire that there be ready and dependable access to an acceptable standard of utility services at a reasonable cost. Sector-specific regulation has a function too in relation to overcoming any tendency by incumbents to try to keep competitors out of the market, restrict their own activities to profitable aspects only, or reduce quality of service.[77]

2.056 The provision of utilities services to certain groups of consumers (such as those in remote locations with low population density or disadvantaged groups) does not always generate a pure economic return to the service provider. However, in the interests of economic, social and regional cohesion, it is important that there be no discrimination in the availability of services to particular groups, that access be provided on reasonable terms and that due account be taken of government's objectives for the groups. In Ireland, examples of public service obligations are found in the broadcasting, electronic communications, energy and postal sectors. The legislation establishing the Commission for Energy Regulation imposes a duty on the Commission to 'take account of the needs of rural customers, the disadvantaged and the elderly.'[78] Such customer concerns are not unique to Ireland. Provisions addressing

---

75 Examples in Ireland are the setting of prices in both electricity and airports.
76 Hirsch, Montag and Sacker, *Competition Law: European Community Practice and Procedure* (Sweet & Maxwell, 2008), p 22.
77 *Governance and Accountability* in *the Regulatory Process: Policy Proposals,* Department of Public Enterprise, March 2000, page 30.
78 Electricity Regulation Act 1999, s 9(5)(c).

such concerns are a feature of EC legislation. In the European Union special recognition is given to services of general economic interest[79] and services of general interest.[80] The importance of such provisions has been endorsed by the inclusion in the Amsterdam Treaty of a new article to address this issue.[81]

2.057 In addition in the regulatory process, there can be other matters, for example the protection of the environment or research and development, that fall outside the scope of normal competitive markets.

APPROACHES TO REGULATORY BODIES IN IRELAND

2.058 The separation of regulatory functions from the other duties of government and their transfer to independent statutory bodies involves a delegation of power from the centre.[82] Arising from changes in national policy and EU competition policy and the influence of the process of liberalisation of economic services at EU level, the trend in Ireland has been towards the statutory transfer of responsibility for regulatory functions from the Minister to independent bodies[83] that are charged with the

---

79   Such as public service obligations in energy, postal, electronic communications, and broadcasting.

80   Such as health and social services.

81   Treaty of Amsterdam, art 16.

82   Mary O'Rourke TD, Minister for Public Enterprise, *Governance and Accountability in the Regulatory Process: Policy Proposals,* Department of Public Enterprise, March 2003, available on http://www.transport.ie.

83   A powerful attack on these independent bodies was launched by former Minister Rory Quinn, speaking during the debate in Dáil Éireann on the Aviation Regulation Bill 2001: 'These are the independent Regulators where the Government hives off not the responsibility to provide a service nor a watchdog function, but the central core function of Government itself, the regulation of an industry or sector. A characteristic of these Regulators – a worrying one as some people would suggest – is that they seem to be answerable to no one. Independence cannot go any further than that. There is a reason for doing that in some of the cases I have mentioned. The need to create these Regulators arose with the shift away from public monopoly in public services like telecommunications. Originally the Government was the Regulator and provider of the service. Later, after Telecom Éireann was hived off, it owned the service provider. When the monopoly was broken up and other players were invited in, it was clear that the Government could not be a player and a referee at the same time. When the telecommunications Regulator was being set up I said I thought we had got it the wrong way around. The Government was giving up its referee role in order to continue being a player. This was some years ago. I said then that it should have given up being a player to continue being a referee. I said that because it seemed that a telecommunications referee should be more than an impartial arbiter or non-biased referee between competing parties. There was also a national development agency which the referee should be insisting on as a basic rule of the game. The referee should have an interest in what game is being played and how it is being played. He or she should be indifferent to the detail of who won but they should ensure there is fair play. The only reason for having a Regulator is that the Government should not be referee and player. (contd .../)

regulation of certain domestic markets, mainly utilities.[84] Later chapters deal in greater detail with such independent Regulators: the Broadcasting Commission of Ireland and its proposed successor the Broadcasting Authority of Ireland, the Competition Authority, The Commission for Aviation Regulation, the Central Bank and Financial Services Authority, the Commission for Energy Regulation and the Commission for Communications Regulation. Set out below are some of the policy considerations in establishing and structuring regulatory bodies.

Regulatory Objectives and Development

2.059 In many cases, the policy impetus for the establishment of a Regulator has been the desire to see a move from monopoly supply to more competitive markets. This entails access by new players to the network of the incumbent. Consequently, intervention is required to facilitate such things as market entry, fair market conditions, customer protection and a basic level of services at efficient prices. This requires a range of interventions, which differs from the range of tasks undertaken in regulating traditional monopoly markets. Such markets in their transition phases are dynamic, require various forms of ex-ante intervention and demand a dedicated and expert focus.[85] A separate political impetus towards regulation emerges out of economic growth and the increasing number and sophistication of interaction which increases the workload of the rule-making body – the legislature.[86] Posner (1974)[87] provides an interesting commentary as follows:

> legislative bodies are a type of firm in which the costs of productions are extremely high and moreover, rise very sharply with increases in output. The reason is that legislative 'production' is a process of negotiation among a large group, the legislators, and the analysis of transaction costs in other contexts suggest that bargaining among a number of individuals is a costly process (and explains why legislatures require only a majority and not a unanimous vote in the conduct of their business). Because costs of bargaining rise rapidly with the number of bargainers, a legislature cannot respond efficiently to a growth in workload by increasing the number of its members. Hence, as the business of a legislature rises, it can be

---

83 (contd) If the Government is not to be a player, then in the national interest it should continue to be referee rather than handing the power over to someone else. The Bill should not proceed past Second Stage.'

84 'In using the word "independent", I mean that regulation of the sector is undertaken by a body that is unconnected with any of the operators in the sector. It is inappropriate that the Minister, as shareholder of Bord Gáis Éireann, should, at the same time, regulate the competitive gas market on a day to day basis' – Minister of State at the Department of Public Enterprise, Mr Jacob: Gas (Interim) (Regulation) Bill 2001: Second Stage. Seanad Éireann – Vol 168 – 3 October 2001.

85 *Governance and Accountability in the Regulatory Process: Policy Proposals*, p 6, Department of Public Enterprise, March 2000, available at www.betterregulation.ie.

86 Mulreany and Weir, 'Regulation and Governance', 55 (2007) *Administration Journal*, Institute of Public Administration of Ireland, No 1, p 184.

87 Posner, 'Theories of Economic Regulation', (1974) 5 *Bell Journal of Economics and Management Science*, 155.

expected to delegate more and more of its work to agencies, and to exercise progressively less control over those agencies.

The Minister's Policy Role

2.060 The focus of Ministers is now on the area of policy development – covering all stages from the strategic analysis for development of the sectors, to the follow-through of legislation to enable policy implementation. Regulators operate within the policy parameters of the regulatory framework laid down by the Minister. The provision of such a regulatory framework, in turn, requires that the Regulators have the necessary powers and resources and that there are clear-cut and transparent accountability systems.[88]

Level of Regulation

2.061 A key policy decision for the State is to determine the level at which regulation should occur. Regulation can be targeted at one of three levels:

(i)   *Industry level regulation:* in this scenario, a separate regulatory body is established for each industry. The Broadcasting Authority of Ireland and the Central Bank and Financial Services Authority of Ireland fall into this category as their remit is to oversee the operation of the broadcasting and financial services industries, respectively.

(ii) *Sectoral level regulation:* the remit of a sectoral Regulator spans several industries operating in the same, or in converging, sectors. The Commission for Communications Regulation is a sectoral Regulator, whose remit extends across the telecommunications, postal and broadcasting industries where technological advances are blurring some former distinctions so that competition is emerging between these industries. The Commission for Energy Regulation's remit covers gas and electricity. The remit of the Commission for Aviation Regulation covers air carriers, airports, and the travel trade.

(iii) *Overall utility regulation:* a general utility Regulator would have responsibility for overseeing the operation of all markets in the utilities, including electricity, gas, airports, telecommunications, post and others.[89]

Composition of Regulatory Authorities

2.062 The top-level structure of a regulatory authority can comprise an individual Regulator, a multi-member regulatory board, or some combination of these models.[90]

---

88   *Governance and Accountability in the Regulatory Process: Policy Proposals*, p 7, Department of Public Enterprise, March 2000.

89   This is used in various EU member states, such as Germany where there is a network Regulator with jurisdiction over various network industries such as post, energy and telecommunications.

90   *Governance and Accountability in the Regulatory Process: Policy Proposals*, pp 11–13, Department of Public Enterprise, March 2000.

Individual Regulator

2.063 One important advantage of a single-person regulatory authority is a level of consistency that may be expected between the various decisions of the individual. A further benefit is that he or she will have the potential to execute their functions quicker than a multi-member board that requires discussion and agreement between the various members. The possibility of the delays that might be generated by a conflict between board members in relation to a particular decision is avoided.

2.064 On the other hand, an individual Regulator may result in a regulatory process identified with a personality. In addition, one person could not be expected to have a comprehensive range of expertise relevant to the sectors being regulated. It has been suggested that individual Regulators could be more susceptible to regulatory capture.[91] Cave has noted,[92] that there is comparatively little evidence in Northern Europe of regulatory capture compared with the US and that there is more evidence of legislator capture whereby well mobilised and high profile producer interests influence legislation.[93]

Regulatory board

2.065 It has been suggested that a regulatory board would be likely to offer a more comprehensive and wide-ranging perspective on regulatory issues than would occur where the regulatory authority is headed by an individual.[94] In addition, a regulatory board could be seen as being more diverse and less vulnerable to claims of regulatory capture. Consequently, the decisions of such a board might be perceived to be more robust. However, group structures may involve a more protracted regulatory decision-making process. Many of the decisions to be made by a Regulator are very significant, both for those involved in the regulated industries, and for the economy as a whole. It has been suggested, therefore, that it would be more appropriate that these decisions be made by a board of several members rather than by a single individual.

Variations to the basic models

2.066 The individual member and the multi-member board models as discussed above are the two basic structural options. Several variations on these models also arise, which attempt to combine the efficiency of the individual model with the range and continuity of experience offered by the board structure.

Advisory panel: Such a model provides a Regulator with access to expert advice from diverse perspectives, while decisions, including the decision to accept or reject the expert advice, would remain in the hands of the individual Regulator.

---

91 'Regulatory capture' occurs where a Regulator comes to equate regulation in the interest of the regulated with regulation in the public interest.

92 Cave, Speech at the Institute of Public Administration, Dublin, November 2006.

93 See also, Baldwin and Cave, *Understanding Regulation: Theory, Strategy and Practice* (OUP, 1999).

94 Governance and Accountability in the Regulatory Process: Policy Proposals, pp 11–13, Department of Public Enterprise, March 2000 at p 11.

Full-time and part-time Regulators: Another possibility suggested is that of a board structure with both part-time, non-executive and full-time, executive board members.

Single-member or multi-member commission: A further option that has been adopted in relation to certain Regulators in Ireland[95] is where the legislation provides for a commission comprising between one and three persons. This means that regulation can be carried out either by an individual Regulator (a one-person commission) or a regulatory board (a three-person commission). The inherent flexibility of this approach allows the decision on the appropriateness of the individual/board structures to be reconsidered from time to time in the light of changing circumstances.

ENFORCEMENT OF THE REGULATORY FRAMEWORK

2.067 In the regulation of the sectors discussed in this book, there is overlap between each of the sectoral Regulators and the Competition Authority.[96] The Competition Authority implements and enforces the comprehensive body of competition law, which applies to all sectors. In the case of sectoral Regulators, they have powers to enforce their decisions and to ensure compliance with licence conditions, particularly with regard to operators with significant market power. This necessarily involves them in competition issues, while also having responsibility for taking a pro-active approach to ensuring that their decisions take into account their potential impact on competition.[97]

The credibility of a regulatory body is dependent on it having powers to enforce the regulatory framework. Enforcement powers can be considered under three broad headings: investigative, remedial and punitive.

Investigative Powers[98]

2.068 Information is central to the work of a Regulator. As there is a heavy dependence on the regulated entities as the source of a large portion of this information, it is important that a Regulator has statutory powers to acquire relevant information. In many cases, Regulators have the power to request (compel) that information be given over to them. To this end, the Regulator can appoint authorised officers, who, in general, have the power to: (i) enter the premises of a regulated firm, (ii) require the production of any records concerning regulatory matters, (iii) inspect or take extracts from such documents, (iv) require the regulated firm or persons to give such

---

95 This structure is used in the legislation establishing the Commission for Communications Regulation, the Commission for Energy Regulation and the Commission for Aviation Regulation.

96 *Governance and Accountability in the Regulatory Process: Policy Proposals*, Department of Public Enterprise, p 26, March 2003.

97 The Commission for Communications Regulation has an express jurisdiction to deal with competition law matters within electronic communications.

98 *Governance and Accountability in the Regulatory Process: Policy Proposals*, Department of Public Enterprise, p 34, March 2003.

information as the authorised officer may reasonably require, and (v) inspect equipment. Generally, obstruction of an authorised officer is a statutory offence.

Remedial Measures

2.069 Remedial measures are a half-way house to prosecution for breach of the regulatory regime. An example is the power to require a regulated entity to discontinue malpractice (such as anti-competitive stance, breach of a licence condition etc). For example, the Commission for Aviation Regulation can direct an airline to comply with the provisions of the denied boarding regulations.[99]

Punitive Powers

2.070 Punitive measures[100] are designed to punish contravention of the legislation. Generally, such action should strike a balance between being effective as a deterrent and being commensurate with the violation for which it can be imposed. A significant punitive act is revocation or restriction of a licence or other form of authorisation permitting the regulated entity to operate in the regulated industry.[101] Clearly, there may be different degrees of transgression, ranging from tardiness in responding to requests of a Regulator, to more blatant breaches of the regulatory rules. It is important, therefore, that Regulators have a range of responses available to them to enforce compliance.

2.071 Equally, one can argue that another approach to enforcing compliance with what is in fact, criminal law, although disguised as economic regulation, is for Regulators to have no enforcement powers at all. This would then leave the enforcement of these criminal laws in the realm of An Garda Síochána and the Office of the Director of Public Prosecutions. Both organisations are better suited to enforcing criminal law than Regulators for a variety of reasons: (i) it is what they are trained to do, (ii) they have expertise in implementing criminal law statutes, (iii) they have the manpower and networks to do so, and (iv) they will be culturally different in outlook, for example, suspects of crime may not find themselves visited but rather arrested and detained for questioning concerning the alleged commission by them of serious crime. If the crimes recited in economic regulation statutes are designed to create a culture change, then arguably the agents of change should be experienced traditional law enforcement agencies.[102]

---

99 Aviation Regulation Act 2001, s 45A, as inserted by Aviation Act 2006, s 5.

100 Governance and Accountability in the Regulatory Process: Policy Proposals, Department of Public Enterprise, pp 36–37, March 2003.

101 Equally, it is possible that revocation of a licence is for other reasons involving the company, which are not punitive but may be automatic or consequential to events, such as insolvency or change of ownership.

102 For example, in the USA, the Federal Bureau of Investigation (FBI) and US Marshalls do the work done in Ireland by authorised officers of the various Regulators.

2.072 In addition, by way of civil law enforcement, the Financial Regulator may impose financial sanctions. The Commission for Communications Regulation may apply to the court to have a financial penalty imposed by way of civil enforcement. Both these powers are the result of provisions contained in underlying EC Directives. The European Commission itself may also impose financial sanctions by way of civil law enforcement.

CONCLUSION

2.073 It has been said that, '[t]he evils of natural monopoly are exaggerated, the effectiveness of regulation in controlling them is highly questionable, and regulation costs a great deal.'[103] In this regard, there is a marked policy within the EU of ex-ante regulation being transitory in nature, to be rolled back as and when markets prove to be effectively competitive so that ex-post competition rules can replace regulation. Nonetheless, the utility markets are characterised by the de-monopolisation or liberalisation of previous State-owned monopolies, together with the privatisation or partial privatisation of those undertakings. Releasing legacy State-owned monopolies into a free market economy, where there may be no effective competition, at least for the early years, requires regulation to ensure that prices are not excessive and to ensure that tactics are not adopted to preclude new entrants. This form of regulation may naturally sunset over time, to be replaced by the rules of competition when markets become sufficiently competitive and barriers to entry are lowered. The second limb of utility regulation, namely ensuring the provision of the service of general economic interest, is not likely to dissipate over time. The danger would be that, with the withdrawal of the State involvement, these services would not be provided. Providers of a public service obligation may need to be able to make sufficient profits so as to be able to perform this socio-political function. The challenge of regulation is to ensure the competitive orientation of recently privatised undertakings that continue to fulfil public duties in the form of public service obligations. This guarantee of efficient as well as reliable and secure networks is expressed by regulation. In this way, regulation touches on both private (in terms of competitive and non-discriminatory access to third parties) and public law (in terms of security of supply, and public service obligations). It may be that the task of regulating is not as transitory as may have been initially considered, as the process of transformation from State-protected monopolies to the free enterprise competition law system may involve the longer term State task of ensuring efficient infrastructure satisfies services of general economic interest. For this reason, regulatory law might not be a specialised type of competition law, with a limited shelf life. It may be that regulation and competition are complementary, rather than substitutes, since abuse-preventing prophylactic regulation may complement abuse-suppressing ex-post competition rules, in relation to many of the sectors discussed in this book.

---

103 Posner, *Natural Monopoly and its Regulation* (Washington DC, Cato Institution, 1999) at
    p 106.

Chapter 3

AVIATION REGULATION

APPROACH OF THIS CHAPTER

3.001 This chapter examines the regulation of aviation in Ireland. The Department of Transport is the government department responsible for leading developments in this area. The relevant Regulator is the Commission for Aviation Regulation (the Commission).

GENERAL AND INTRODUCTION

3.002 The Commission was established by the Minister for Public Enterprise by reference to a theme. The Minister[1] sought to assign to the Regulator all the relevant aspects, from an economic perspective, of the chain of events in which air carriers are involved, stretching from the licensing stage through to the allocation of departure and arrival slots and up to the regulation of groundhandling and the determination of airport charges.

3.003 The Minister for Finance is the only shareholder in the 'State airports' – Dublin, Cork and Shannon – owned by Dublin Airport Authority (DAA).[2] Initially, the Minister for Transport and then (briefly) Public Enterprise[3] had executive responsibility on behalf of the Government for those airport's development, operation and management including approving airport charges. A primary motivation for setting up an independent Regulator with responsibility for regulating airport charges was the potential for conflict between the Government's shareholder role as owner of the airport and the regulatory role in relation to approval of airport charges. The objective of the legislation in respect of the Irish airports is to ensure that regulation of charges is carried out in a manner that will facilitate the development of cost-effective and efficient services that will meet the needs of users. Also added to the Regulator's brief was the determination of a cap for certain air traffic control charges, specifically those imposed by the Irish Aviation Authority for services rendered to aircraft at the approach and take-off stages. It was, in the Minister's view, a logical progression to include the regulation of these charges, together with airport charges, in the

---

1   Minister for Public Enterprise, Mary O'Rourke: Seanad Éireann – Vol 163 – 17 May 2000, Aviation Regulation Bill 2000, Second Stage.

2   Aer Rianta was renamed Dublin Airport Authority by the State Airports Act 2004. 'State Airport' is defined in the same Act as an airport in the State that is managed and controlled by Dublin Airport Authority or, from the relevant appointed day, a company – ie Dublin, Cork or Shannon Airport Authority.

3   In this chapter, references to 'the Minister' relate to the Minister for Transport.

Regulator's remit. En-route charges[4] are also part of the normal cost base of the airlines, however, the principles upon which these charges are based are determined by the relevant international aviation bodies and are imposed for the use of Irish airspace as opposed to the use of Irish airports. Consequently, these charges are not regulated domestically.

3.004 The broad framework for the amendments to the 2001 legislation on airport charges emerged following extensive interaction with Aer Rianta – now renamed Dublin Airport Authority – and its advisers.[5] Those amendments appear at Pt 3 of the State Airports Act 2004 (the 2004 Act), which makes changes to the Aviation Regulation Act 2001 (the 2001 Act) as considered necessary to effect the restructuring of Aer Rianta[6] and to complement the reforms described elsewhere in that Act. In brief, the restructuring foreseen is that Cork and Shannon Airports will be spun out of the Dublin Airport Authority group to separate State-owned Airport Authority plcs. Both Cork and Shannon are explicitly excluded from airport charges regulation by the 2004 Act. The Minister for Transport stated that post-restructuring it will no longer be appropriate to price regulate Cork and Shannon airports because they will not have market dominance in the same way that Dublin Airport has and will continue to have.

THE RELEVANT LEGISLATIVE FRAMEWORK

3.005 The legislative framework for aviation and travel trade includes the following Acts:

(a)   Air Navigation and Transport Act 1965;

(b)   Transport (Tour Operators and Travel Agents) Act 1982;

(c)   Package Holidays and Travel Trade Act 1995;

(d)   Air Navigation and Transport (Amendment) Act 1998;

(e)   Aviation Regulation Act 2001;

(f)   The State Airports Act 2004; and

(g)   The Aviation Act 2006.

The framework also includes the following statutory instruments:

(i)   Tour Operators and Travel Agents (Bonding) Regulations 1983 (SI 102/1983);

(ii)   Tour Operators (Licensing) Regulations 1993 (SI 182/1993);

---

4   En route charges are levied by the IAA in respect of air traffic control services used by air carriers flying over Ireland and through Irish controlled airspace.

5   Seamus Brennan, Minister for Transport, Dáil Éireann – Vol 588 – 24 June 2004, State Airports Bill 2004, Second Stage.

6   To date, this restructuring of Aer Rianta into separate airport authorities, with the management of the airports vested in each one, has not occurred. Cork and Shannon Airport Authority have yet to have ownership and statutory responsibility for the airports vested in them.

(iii) European Communities (Access to the Groundhandling Market at Community Airports) Regulations 1998 (SI 505/1998);

(iv) Aviation Regulation Act 2001 (Levy No 8) Regulations 2007 (SI 840/2007);

(v) European Communities (Common Rules for the Operation of Air Services in the Community) Regulations (SI 426/2008); and

(vi) European Communities (Rights of Disabled Persons and Persons with Reduced Mobility when travelling by Air) Regulations 2008 (SI 299/2008).

The following EC regulations are also part of the framework:

(I) Regulation EEC/95/93 on common rules for the allocation of slots at Community airports;

(II) Regulation EC/261/2004 establishing common rules on compensation and assistance to passengers in the event of denied boarding and of cancellation or long delay of flights;

(III) Regulation EC/1107/2006 concerning the rights of disabled persons and persons with reduced mobility when travelling by air; and

(IV) Regulation EC/1008/2008 on common rules for the operation of air services in the community.

THE COMMISSION FOR AVIATION REGULATION

3.006 The Commission for Aviation Regulation was established on 27 February 2001 as a body corporate with perpetual succession, a common seal, power to sue and be sued in its corporate name, and to acquire, hold and dispose of land or an interest in land and any other property.[7] It is deemed to have such powers as are necessary for, or incidental to, the performance of its functions under the 2001 Act.[8]

The 2001 Act states that, in carrying out its functions in relation to economic regulation, the Commission shall ensure that all determinations, conditions attaching thereto, amendments thereof and requests shall be objectively justified and shall be non-discriminatory, proportionate and transparent.[9]

Appointment and Term of Office of Members

3.007 Section 11 of the 2001 Act deals with the selection, appointment and term of office of the Commission in detail. In summary, the Commission shall consist of at least one, but not more than three, members, each of whom shall be appointed by the Minister on such terms and conditions of appointment, including remuneration, as the Minister may fix, with the consent of the Minister for Finance, to hold office in a full-time capacity for a period of not less than three, and not more than five, years. Each member of the Commission shall be known as a Commissioner for Aviation

---

7   Aviation Regulation Act 2001, s 5(2).

8   Aviation Regulation Act 2001, s 5(3).

9   Aviation Regulation Act 2001, s 5(4).

Regulation. The legislation also provides under s 13 that the Commission may appoint a member of staff as Deputy Commissioner.

Independence

3.008 Section 6 of the 2001 Act provides that the Commission shall be independent in the exercise of its functions.

Seal

3.009 The 2001 Act provides that the Commission shall have a seal[10] and that when it is affixed to certain documents, it shall be authenticated by the signature of:

(a)   a Commissioner; or

(b)   a member of the staff of the Commission, authorised by the Commission to act in that behalf.

Judicial notice shall be taken of the seal of the Commission and every document purporting to be an instrument made by, and to be sealed with, the seal of the Commission (purporting to be authenticated in accordance with s 30) shall be received in evidence and deemed to be such instrument without proof unless the contrary is shown. Certain public documents are thus sealed by the Commission, such as licenses, warrants of appointment of authorised officers and the levy statutory instrument.

Borrowings, Levies and Fees

3.010 For the purpose of meeting expenses properly incurred by the Commission in the discharge of its functions under the 2001 Act, the Commission shall make regulations imposing a levy to meet, but not to exceed, the estimated operating costs and expenses of the Commission, to be paid each year beginning with such year as specified in the regulations on such classes of undertakings as may be specified by the Commission by way of statutory instrument.[11] Every Statutory Instrument made by the Commission under s 23 shall be laid before each House of the Oireachtas as soon as may be after it is made and, if a resolution annulling the regulation is passed by either such House within the next 21 days on which that House has sat after the regulation is laid before it, the regulation shall be annulled accordingly, without prejudice to the validity of anything previously done thereunder. Thus, the Commission levy is a statutory instrument in the name of, and for the benefit of, the Commission.

3.011 Pursuant to the Aviation Regulation Act 2001 (Levy No 8) Regulations 2007,[12] the categories of undertakings subject to the levy for the year 2008 are: certain airport authorities, air terminal service providers (air traffic control), licensed air carriers,

---

10   Aviation Regulation Act 2001, s 30.

11   Aviation Regulation Act 2001, s 23.

12   SI 840/2007.

ground handlers, tour operators and travel agents. They are levied in respect of the Commission's functions with regard to the regulation of airport and aviation terminal services charges, slot allocation, air passenger consumer protection work and airline, tour operator, travel agent and ground handler licensing and approval.

Functions and Transfer of Functions

3.012 The 2001 Act and subsequent amendments to that Act set out the functions of the Commission, many of which are the former functions of the Ministers for Transport and Public Enterprise. References to 'the Minister' contained in any Act or instrument relating to any functions so transferred, are to be construed as references to the Commission.[13]

The functions of the Commission are as follows:

(i) The regulation of airport charges;[14]

(ii) The regulation of aviation terminal services charges;[15]

(iii) To be the competent authority within the State for the licensing of air carriers under Council Regulation EC/1008/2008, which is the successor to Council Regulation 2407/92 mentioned in the 2001 Act.[16] Previously it had this power pursuant to the Air Navigation and Transport Act 1965 (Section 8) Regulations 1993;[17]

(iv) To be the competent authority within the State for the purposes of the European Communities (Access to the Groundhandling Market at Community Airports) Regulations 1998.[18] Accordingly, it has a role in approving undertakings that wish to provide groundhandling services[19] at the State airports and the approval of access fees for the use of airport installations;

(v) To be the competent authority in the State for the purposes of Council Regulation EEC/95/93 on slot allocation other than the functions of the co-

---

13 Aviation Regulation Act 2001, s 9.

14 Aviation Regulation Act 2001, s 7.

15 Aviation Regulation Act 2001, s 7.

16 The European Communities (Common Rules for the Operation of Air Services in the Community) Regulations (SI 426/2008) re-designated the Commission as the air carrier licensing authority in the State for the purposes of Regulation (EC) No 1008/2008.

17 SI 323/1993. These regulations were later revoked by SI 426/2008. The Commission remains the licensing authority for air carriers.

18 SI 505/1998. Aviation Regulation Act 2001, s 9(2)(c).

19 Examples of groundhandling services are handling baggage, checking-in passengers, fuelling planes and catering for planes. The regulations distinguish between carriers who do this for themselves (self-handlers) and companies who provide the services for other companies (third-party handlers).

ordinator.[20] The Commission also has the function of appointing a co-ordinator under art 4 of Council Regulation EEC/95/93;[21]

(vi) To be the licensing authority for travel agents and tour operators within the State pursuant to the Transport (Tour Operators and Travel Agents) Act 1982, as amended by the Package Holidays and Travel Trade Act 1995.[22] In that role it also administers the consumer protection bonds that those entities must put in place to get a licence;

(vii) To be the national enforcement body for the purposes of Regulation EC/1107/2006 of the European Parliament and of the Council of 5 July 2006 concerning the rights of disabled persons and persons with reduced mobility when travelling by air;[23]

(viii) To be the national enforcement body for the purposes of Regulation EC/ 261/2004 of the European Parliament and of the Council of 11 February 2004 establishing common rules on compensation and assistance to passengers in the event of denied boarding and of cancellation or long delay of flights.[24]

Ministerial Direction

3.013 Section 10 of the 2001 Act provides that the Minister may give such general policy directions (including directions in respect of the contribution of airports to the regions in which they are located) to the Commission as he or she considers appropriate to be followed by the Commission in the exercise of its functions when making an airport charges or aviation terminal services charges determination and that the Commission shall comply with any such directions. The Minister has used this power three times to date in respect of both the 2001 and 2005 airport charges determinations and the 2006/7 interim review of the 2005 determination.[25]

---

20 Aviation Regulation Act 2001, s 8(1).

21 Aviation Regulation Act 2001, s 8(2).

22 Aviation Regulation Act 2001, s 9(2)(a) and (b).

23 EC (Rights of Disabled Persons and Persons with Reduced Mobility when Travelling by Air) Regulations 2008 (SI 299/2008), reg 3.

24 Aviation Regulation Act 2001, s 8(4), as inserted by Aviation Act 2006, s 5(1)(b).

25 These policy directions are published and available on the Commission's website (http://www.aviationreg.ie) as annexes to the respective determinations. In addition, the scope of that power was briefly considered by Mr Justice O'Sullivan in the case of *Aer Rianta cpt v Commissioner for Aviation Regulation* [2003] IEHC 168 when he stated: 'it is also clear that the ministerial direction itself is cast in the language of generality. The obligation cast upon the [Commission] is to make every reasonable effort: it is not an obligation to achieve a particular result or to aim for a policy objective in a particular way. Indeed given the wide language of s 10 itself, which refers to making a general policy direction, a specific direction might well be open to question.'

THE REGULATED ACTIVITY AND THE REGULATED ENTITIES

Airport Charges

3.014 It is a function of the Commission, in making a determination in respect of maximum airport charges at Dublin Airport, to adhere to three objectives.[26] Those modified objectives of the Commission are to:

   (i)   facilitate the efficient and economic development and operation of Dublin Airport which meet the requirements of current and prospective users of the airport;

   (ii) protect the reasonable interests of current and prospective users of Dublin Airport; and

   (iii) enable the Dublin Airport Authority to operate and develop Dublin Airport in a sustainable and financially viable manner.

The Minister's stated intention was that these primary objectives would oblige the Commission to balance economic efficiency and the reasonable interests of users, and to ensure the airport's financial sustainability in a way that would promote its long-term development, having regard to its contribution to the economy.[27]

3.015 Section 32 of the 2001 Act[28] provides the procedure by which a determination on airport charges and any review of such charges shall be made.[29] Statute decreed that the first determination on airport charges be made within six months of the establishment day of the Commission, by 26 of August 2001. The airports affected by the regulatory determination were Cork, Dublin and Shannon Airports, the 'State airports' owned

---

26   Aviation Regulation Act 2001, s 33, as substituted by State Airports Act 2004, s 22(4).

27   The State Airports Bill 2004 was subjected to a fierce attack in the Dáil. Calling for the House to reject the amendments to the 2001 Act, Deputy Róisín Shorthall (Labour) stated: 'The Bill provides for a fundamental change in the airport regulatory regime, so fundamental as to effectively dismantle it. Instead of only allowing for the inclusion of recognised assets and only acting in the consumer interest in calculating the price cap, s 21(4) proposes that the Commission for Aviation Regulation shall in future have due regard to the restructuring, including the modified functions of the Dublin Airport Authority and, critically, costs or liabilities for which the Dublin Airport Authority is responsible, as well as policy statements published by or on behalf of the Government. The Bill proposes a requirement that the Regulator include liabilities, in this case politically-created liabilities, in calculating the price cap. This is nonsense. It is also proposed that the Commission take account of general Government policy for the economic and social development of the State. Economic regulation of Dublin Airport is to be perverted.'

28   As amended by State Airports Act 2004, s 22.

29   See: Commission for Aviation Regulation, *Maximum Levels of Airport Charges at Dublin Airport*, Commission Paper CP3/2005, Determination on Maximum Levels of Airport Charges, 29 September 2005; Commission for Aviation Regulation, *Maximum Levels of Airport Charges at Dublin Airport, Decision of the Commission further to a Referral by the 2006 Aviation Appeal Panel*, Commission Paper CP5/2006, 22 June 2006; Commission for Aviation Regulation, *Maximum Levels of Airport Charges at Dublin Airport, Final Decision on Interim Review of 2005 Determination*, Commission Paper 6/2007, 30 July 2007.

and managed by Aer Rianta cpt.[30] The regulatory period of the determination was to run for five years until August 2006. This never occurred due to important changes introduced by the State Airports Act 2004. The 2004 Act provided for the establishment of Cork, Dublin and Shannon Airports Authorities, which, to date, has not occurred.[31] The 2004 Act also directed a new airport charges determination to be made prior to October 2005 to supersede the earlier first determination. It also provided that this determination, and those subsequent to it, would only apply to airport charges levied at Dublin Airport by DAA.[32] It provided for some changes in the procedure to be adopted in making an airport charges determination.

3.016 The 2001 Act, as amended, now provides that a determination on airport charges shall be in force for a period of not less than four years. The Commission is given quite a lot of scope in how it sets charges. A determination may:

  (a)   provide:

       (i)   for an overall limit on the level of airport charges,

       (ii)   for limits to apply to particular categories of such charges, or

       (iii) for a combination of any such limits; and

  (b)   operate to restrict increases in any such charges, or to require reductions in them, whether by reference to any formula or otherwise, or provide for different limits to apply in relation to different periods of time falling within the period to which the determination relates.[33]

At present the Commission sets an airport charge that is expressed as an annual maximum yield per departing passenger from Dublin Airport for the duration of the determination.[34] It is important to note that this is not an overall revenue cap. It is a yield cap per passenger for a period of years. In this way, the revenue collected depends on the number of passengers travelling. This reflects the fact that the airport's passenger forecast is taken into account when setting the price cap. Simply put, if DAA forecasts 100 million passengers in a four-year period and 120 million travel, DAA is entitled to collect the revenue generated by the extra twenty million passengers.

---

30 'cuideachta phoiblí theoranta' or 'cpt' is the Irish language phrase meaning public limited company or 'plc' – Companies (Amendment) Act 1983, s 4.

31 On dates yet to be confirmed, Cork and Shannon Airport Authorities may have the relevant airport assets, liabilities, contracts, rights, obligations etc vested in them and assume full responsibility for the management, development and operation of Cork and Shannon airports. In the interim, the board of the Dublin Airport Authority has transferred significant day-to-day operational responsibility, under delegated authority, to the boards of the Cork and Shannon Airport Authorities.

32 Aviation Regulation Act 2001, s 32, as amended by State Airports Act 2004, s 22.

33 Aviation Regulation Act 2001, s 32(6).

34 The Commission's compliance statement, in respect of Dublin airport, calculated the 2008 airport charges price cap of €7.38 per passenger, which is based on the consumer price index, the relevant 'X' factor, the Commission's actual and budgeted costs, relevant interest rates and a correction term based on the under-recovery of airport charges during 2006.

Equally, if only 80 million travel, they have to bear the loss. The DAA thus has an incentive to attempt to forecast passenger numbers at Dublin accurately and plan the development of the airport accordingly.

3.017 Prior to making a determination, the Commission shall:

(a)   give notice to any person concerned stating that it proposes to make a determination;

(b)   publish such notice in a daily newspaper published and circulating in the State; and

(c)   specify the period (being not less than one month from the publication of the notice) within which representations with respect to the proposed determination may be made by interested parties or the public.[35]

It has been the practice of the Commission to give the required formal notice of the making of a determination[36] by publishing a draft determination. This means that interested parties have significant information with which to engage in during the consultation period. The Commission must then consider any representations that are made and may either accept or reject them. On making a determination,[37] the Commission makes a report on the determination, giving an account of its reasons for making that determination, together with its reasons for accepting or rejecting any representations made. A report on the making of the determination shall be sent by the Commission to the Minister and to DAA. In addition, the Commission must give the general public notice that it has made a determination and make the report available. The Commission does so by notices in the national press and also by publishing the determination, the report and the technical annexes that generally accompany the report on its website.

3.018 The Commission requires information from DAA about its costs, development plans, commercial revenue and forecasted passenger numbers in order to have sufficient information to make a determination. Accordingly, the Commission may make a statutory request to an airport authority in writing to provide information (including accounts, estimates, returns, projections or any other records) which it is in possession of or which can be obtained by the airport authority.[38] If DAA were to refuse, the Commission could seek a court order to enforce its statutory information request.[39]

---

35   Aviation Regulation Act 2001, s 32(7)

36   Aviation Regulation Act 2001, s 32(7).

37   In this regard, the obligation on the Commission in s 5(4) of the 2001 Act should be noted, namely that '[i]n carrying out its functions, the Commission shall ensure that all determinations, conditions attaching thereto, amendments thereof and requests shall be objectively justified and shall be non-discriminatory, proportionate and transparent.'

38   Aviation Regulation Act 2001, s 32(13).

39   Aviation Regulation Act 2001, s 39.

3.019 The 2001 Act provides that a determination may be reviewed within the regulatory period by the Commission either:

(i)   at its own initiative; or

(ii)   at the request of DAA or a user concerned in respect of the determination;[40]

if it considers that there are substantial grounds for so doing.

Once it has reviewed the determination, it may, if it sees fit, amend the determination. Any such amendment would be in force for the remainder of the period of the determination. The process of the review is the same as that for making a determination (as described above) – a public consultation followed by publication of the result with a report on the reasons.

3.020 In making a determination, the objectives of the Commission are as outlined at para **3.014** above. In addition, in making a determination, the Commission shall have due regard to:

(i)   the restructuring including the modified functions of DAA;

(ii)   the level of investment in airport facilities at Dublin Airport, in line with safety requirements and commercial operations in order to meet the needs of current and prospective users of Dublin Airport;

(iii) the level of operational income of DAA from Dublin Airport, and the level of income of DAA from any arrangements entered into by it for the purposes of the restructuring under the State Airports Act 2004;

(iv)   costs or liabilities for which DAA is responsible;

(v)   the level and quality of services offered at Dublin Airport by DAA and the reasonable interests of the current and prospective users of these services;

(vi)   policy statements, published by or on behalf of the government or a Minister of the government and notified to the Commission by the Minister in relation to the economic and social development of the State;

(vii) the cost competitiveness of airport services at Dublin Airport;

(viii) imposing the minimum restrictions on DAA consistent with the functions of the Commission; and

(ix)   such national and international obligations as are relevant to the functions of the Commission and DAA.

The objectives and factors set out above are those introduced as the new s 33 of the 2001 Act, as inserted by s 22 of the State Airports Act 2004. Upon their introduction, although many of the concepts were familiar, the Commission consulted with the industry as to the implication for airport charges regulation. Set out below is the summary of the Commission's view expressed after that consultation:[41]

> Having regard to the provisions contained in the 2004 Act and in light of the nature
> and purpose of economic regulation, the Commission is of the view that the new

---

40   Aviation Regulation Act 2001, s 32(14)(a).

41   *The Commission for Aviation Regulation's conclusions on the impact of the amendments to the Aviation Regulation Act 2001, on the regulation of maximum levels of airport charges in Ireland,* Commission Paper CP9/2004, 21 December 2004, p 8 (http://www.aviationreg.ie).

statutory objectives permit the continuation by the Commission of the regulation of airport charges imposed at Dublin Airport by DAA by reference to the economic concepts of productive, dynamic and allocative efficiency.[42] As set out below, these concepts continue to promote the statutory objectives of the Commission, as amended. By directly stating the Commission's objective as being to facilitate the efficient and economic development and operation of Dublin Airport, the amendment has strengthened the emphasis on economic efficiency as a principle of airport charges regulation.

Dublin airport authority

3.021 A seminal shift in the management of Dublin Airport occurred with the enactment of the Air Navigation and Transport (Amendment) Act 1998. By virtue of s 16 of this Act, a reconstituted Aer Rianta cpt was given the duty to manage and develop Dublin Airport, which was vested in it by s 14 of that Act. Thus, for the first time in the history of the State, the Executive was no longer directly legally responsible for the management and development of Dublin Airport.[43]. Airport charges levied by (what is now) DAA at Dublin Airport are the main subject of economic regulation by the Commission. The positions of the DAA and the Commission relative to each other are encapsulated by an important amendment to s 39 of the Act of 1998, which substitutes 'subject to section 32 of the Aviation Regulation Act, 2001' for 'with the approval of the Minister.'[44] What this means is that the imposition of airport charges at Dublin Airport by DAA is subject to the determination of maximum levels of airport charges to be levied at Dublin Airport as determined by the Commission pursuant to the 2001 Act. Thus, the Commission now regulates or 'controls' the setting of airport charges at Dublin Airport.[45]

Where a person fails to comply with a determination on airport charges or aviation terminal services charges or a statutory information request made by the Commission

---

42   The Commission noted in CP9/2004 that the Competition Authority in its response to CP7/2004 agreed with this approach.

43   The Minister for Finance remains the only shareholder as per Air Navigation and Transport (Amendment) Act 1998, Pt II.

44   Aviation Regulation Act 2001, s 34.

45   In *Aer Rianta cpt v Commissioner for Aviation Regulation* [2003] IEHC 168 Aer Rianta sought to judicially review the Commission's first airport charges determination. In the course of finding for the Commission, Mr Justice O'Sullivan considered the meaning of 'regulate': 'As has been made clear the principal function of the [Commission] is to regulate airport charges including those of [Aer Rianta]. The word "regulate" is not defined and therefore should carry its ordinary meaning. According to the *Concise Oxford Dictionary* the word means "control by rule" or "subject to restriction". There seems to be nothing in the 2001 Act to suggest that the word carries a special meaning and in particular it is not defined. Accordingly, the principal function of the [Commission] is to control airport charges by rule or subject them to restriction.' Ryanair later also unsuccessfully brought judicial review proceedings against the second airport charges determination: see the judgments in *Ryanair Ltd v Commission for Aviation Regulation* [2008] IEHC 98, Clarke J and *Ryanair Ltd v Commission for Aviation Regulation* [2008] IEHC 148, Clarke J.

in the context of making such a determination, the Commission may apply to the High Court for an order requiring the person to comply with the determination or request.[46]

Aviation Terminal Services Charges

3.022 By virtue of s 35 of the 2001 Act, the Commission determines maximum levels of aviation terminal services charges that may be imposed by the Irish Aviation Authority at airports in Ireland.[47] These are air traffic control charges relating to the approach, landing and take-off of airplanes at airports. The procedure by which such determinations are made is similar to the process for an airport charges determination. There have been some amendments to s 35 by s 23 of the State Airports Act 2004. Under the amended provisions, a determination shall be in force for a period of not less than four years.

3.023 As with airport charges, a determination may:

  (a)   provide:

      (i)   for an overall limit on the level of aviation terminal services charges,

      (ii)   for limits to apply to particular categories of such charges, or

      (iii)   for a combination of any such limits;

  (b)   operate to restrict increases in any such charges, or to require reductions in them, whether by reference to any formula or otherwise; or

  (c)   provide for different limits to apply in relation to different periods of time falling within the period to which the determination relates.

3.024 Prior to making a determination, the Commission shall:

  (a)   give notice to any person concerned stating that it proposes to make a determination;

  (b)   publish such notice in a daily newspaper published and circulating in the State; and

  (c)   specify the period (being not less than two months[48] from the publication of the notice) within which representations with respect to the proposed determination may be made by interested parties or the public.

As with airport charges, it has been the practice of the Commission to give formal notice of the making of a determination by publishing a draft determination. All the other provisions regarding the making of a determination, information requests of the Irish Aviation Authority (IAA), reporting and review are identical to those in place regarding airport charges.

---

46   Aviation Regulation Act 2001, s 39.

47   See Commission for Aviation Regulation, *Determination and Report on the Maximum Level of Aviation Terminal Service Charges that may be imposed by the Irish Aviation Authority*, 23 March 2007 (http://www.aviationreg.ie).

48   Note that respondents to notification of an airport charges determination have two months.

3.025 By virtue of s 36 of the 2001 Act, when making a determination on aviation terminal service charges, the Commission shall aim to facilitate the development and operation of safe, cost-effective terminal services which meets international standards and shall have due regard to:

(a) the relevant charging principles of the International Civil Aviation Organisation and of Eurocontrol;

(b) the level of investment in aviation terminal services by the IAA, in line with safety requirements and commercial operations, in order to meet current and prospective needs of the airline industry;

(c) the efficient and effective use of all resources by the Authority;

(d) the level of the Authority's income from aviation terminal services and other revenue earned by the Authority generally;

(e) operating and other costs incurred by the Authority in providing aviation terminal services;

(f) the level and quality of aviation terminal services, and the reasonable interests of the users of these services; and

(g) the cost competitiveness of aviation terminal services with respect to international practice.

The manner in which the Commission has sought to do so in 2002 and again in 2007 broadly speaking, has been similar to that adopted in relation to the setting of airport charges. The Commission made the level of the 2007 price cap conditional on the IAA building new Air Traffic Control (ATC) towers at Cork and Dublin Airports. This is the first time such 'trigger' conditions have been used in a price cap in Ireland. The idea is that having 'triggers' built into the price cap protects users from having to pay higher charges until such time as the IAA is ready to start providing users with the benefits associated with these investments. The price cap for 2008 was estimated to be €2.28 per tonne of maximum take-off weight (MTOW). During consultation for the 2007 Determination, the IAA anticipated that the Cork ATC tower will be completed in 2009.

These determinations are publicly available.[49]

Irish Aviation Authority

3.026 The IAA is a commercial State-sponsored company that was established on 1 January 1994 to provide air navigation services in Irish-controlled airspace and to regulate safety standards within the Irish civil aviation industry.

Aviation terminal service charges as imposed by the IAA at Irish airports are one of the main subjects of regulation by the Commission. The positions of the IAA and Commission relative to each other are encapsulated by an important amendment to s 43(1)(a) of the Irish Aviation Authority Act 1993, which involves the insertion of 'and section 35 of the Aviation Regulation Act, 2001' after 'subject to subsection

---

49   http://www.aviationreg.ie.

(3).'[50] What this means is that the levying of aviation terminal service charges by IAA at certain Irish airports is subject to the determination on maximum levels of aviation terminal services charges as determined by the Commission pursuant to the Aviation Regulation Act 2001.

Licensing of Air Carriers

3.027 The 2001 Act also transferred the air carrier licensing function of the Minister to the Commission. The rules and regulations underpinning that function were repealed and replaced in 2008. The Commission for Aviation Regulation remains responsible for licensing Irish airlines.[51]

Air carrier licensing

3.028 An Air Carrier Operating Licence (ACOL) permits the holder to engage in the carriage by air of passengers, mail and/or cargo for remuneration and/or hire. By virtue of the EC regulations, no undertaking established in the Community shall be permitted within the territory of the Community to carry by air passengers, mail and/or cargo for remuneration and/or hire unless the undertaking has been granted the appropriate operating licence.

The Commission will not grant an operating licence to an undertaking unless it is satisfied that the undertaking complies with Council Regulation EC/1008/2008 of the European Parliament and of the Council of 24 September 2008 on common rules for the operation of air services in the Community and is in possession of an air operator's certificate.[52]

3.029 Previously, the Minister for Transport had the power under s 8 of the Air Navigation and Transport Act 1965 to grant or refuse to any person an authorisation entitling that person to operate an air service to, from, within or over the territory of the State. He also had the power to make regulations for the purpose of the section. The reason such an authorisation was necessary is because s 6 of the Act prohibits the operation of an air service to, from, within or over the territory of the State unless, *inter alia*, an authorisation under s 8 is in place.[53] In the Act an 'air service' is defined as a flight or flights by one or more aircraft carrying passengers, cargo or mail for reward. The European regulations provide for Community air carriers authorised by the appropriate national competent authority (now the Commission for Aviation

---

50   Aviation Regulation Act 2001, s 37.

51   It is designated by the European Communities (Common Rules for the Operation of Air Services in the Community) Regulations 2008 (SI 426/2008).

52   31.10.2008 OJ L 293/3. Commercial air carriers in Ireland need two authorisations – the Air Operator Certificate (AOC), which is granted by the IAA and relates to safety and technical matters, and the ACOL, which relates to commercial and legal requirements and is granted by the Commission. The Commission will not grant an ACOL unless a carrier can show it has the relevant AOC.

53   This section was commenced on 1 June 1996 by the Air Navigation and Transport Act, 1965 (Commencement of Sections 6 and 19) Order 1966, SI 94/966.

Regulation) to operate air services to, from within or over their territories. This is an evolution from the provisions of the 1965 Act set out above. However, important sections of that Act remain in force.

3.030 Section 12 of the 1965 Act deems the owner, hirer or commander of any aircraft who has breached a provision of the 1965 Act to be guilty of a criminal offence. Further to this provision, in Ireland, it is a criminal offence to operate an air carrier without a licence. The penalties for this offence were amended by s 10 of the Air Transport Act 1986. Persons are liable on summary conviction for breach of s 8 to a term of imprisonment of not more than six months and/or a fine of IR£1000 (€1,270), or upon conviction on indictment to a term of imprisonment not exceeding six months and/or a fine of IR£100,000 (€127,000).

New criteria

3.031 In order to be eligible for an operating license, the applicant must satisfy all the conditions for granting an operating licence set out in art 4 of Council Regulation EC/1008/2008.

> An undertaking shall be granted an operating licence by the competent licensing authority of a Member State provided that:
>
> (a) its principal place of business is located in that Member State;
>
> (b) it holds a valid AOC[54] issued by a national authority of the same Member State whose competent licensing authority is responsible for granting, refusing, revoking or suspending the operating licence of the Community air carrier;
>
> (c) it has one or more aircraft at its disposal through ownership or a dry lease agreement;
>
> (d) its main occupation is to operate air services in isolation or combined with any other commercial operation of aircraft or the repair and maintenance of aircraft;
>
> (e) its company structure allows the competent licensing authority to implement the provisions of this Chapter;[55]
>
> (f) Member States and/or nationals of Member States own more than 50 per cent of the undertaking and effectively control[56] it, whether directly or indirectly through one or more intermediate undertakings, except as provided for in an agreement with a third country to which the Community is a party;[57]

---

54 Air operator certificate.

55 Chapter II of the Regulation.

56 The regulation defines 'effective control' as meaning a relationship constituted by rights, contracts or any other means which, either separately or jointly and having regard to the considerations of fact or law involved, confer the possibility of directly or indirectly exercising a decisive influence on an undertaking, in particular by:

(a) the right to use all or part of the assets of an undertaking;

(b) rights or contracts which confer a decisive influence on the composition, voting or decisions of the bodies of an undertaking or otherwise confer a decisive influence on the running of the business of the undertaking.

57 These countries are the Member States of the EC, European Free Trade Association and Switzerland.

(g) it meets the financial conditions specified in Article 5 [of Council Regulation EC/1008/2008];

(h) it complies with the insurance requirements specified in Article 11 and in Regulation (EC) No 785/2004; and

(i) it complies with the provisions on good repute as specified in Article 7 [of Council Regulation EC/1008/2008].

Air Carrier Operating Licences are divided into two categories related to capacity and maximum take-off weight: Category A licences[58] and Category B licences.[59]

By virtue of art 8 of Council Regulation EC/1008/2008, an operating licence shall be valid as long as the Community air carrier complies with the requirements of that regulation. This is dependent on the air carrier being able upon request to demonstrate to the competent licensing authority that it meets all the requirements of the Regulation.[60]

Groundhandling

3.032 Section 9(2)(c) of the 2001 Act transferred the functions contained in the European Communities (access to the groundhandling market at Community airports) Regulations 1998 (the Groundhandling Regulations)[61] to the Commission. Accordingly, it is the competent authority in Ireland for the purposes of Council Directive 96/67/EC on access to the groundhandling market at Community airports. The Directive was intended as a first step towards the gradual opening up of access to the groundhandling market and helping reduce the operating costs of air carriers, improving quality of service and facilitating effective competition in that market. Groundhandling broadly comprises all those services required by an aircraft between landing and take-off (eg marshalling aircraft, loading or unloading, refuelling, baggage handling, passenger handling, aircraft maintenance etc). An airline may choose to provide services for itself ('self-handling') or contract with another company ('third-party handling'), be it an airline or a dedicated groundhandling company. Prior approval must be obtained from the Commission before engaging in groundhandling operations. Applicants must complete an application form and also meet a number of requirements before an approval to operate as a ground handler can be issued. Groundhandling approvals are issued for a period of five years and approval is subject

---

58 Category A licence holders are permitted to carry passengers, cargo and/or mail on aircraft with 20 seats or more.

59 Category B license holders are permitted to carry passengers, cargo and/or mail on aircraft with fewer than 20 seats and/or less than 10 tonnes MTOW (maximum take-off weight).

60 Of the 18 licensed Irish airlines, eight hold Category A licences which permit them to carry passengers, cargo and/or mail on aircraft with 20 seats or more. This group includes household names such as Aer Arann, Aer Lingus, CityJet and Ryanair. The remaining ten operators hold Category B licences, permitting them to carry passengers, cargo and/or mail on aircraft with fewer than 20 seats and/or less than 10 tonnes MTOW. This group includes CHC (Ireland) Ltd, which performs search and rescue operations around Ireland on behalf of the Department of Transport.

61 SI 505/1998.

to the holder satisfying certain conditions at all times. After the five-year timeframe, groundhandling approvals can be renewed following the successful completion of the licensing renewal process.

Approvals and compliance

3.033 Regulation 12(1) of the Groundhandling Regulations states that, prior to engaging in groundhandling activities at an airport to which the regulations apply,[62] each supplier of groundhandling services and each self-handler shall apply in writing to the Commission for Aviation Regulation for approval in that behalf. Suppliers may be either:

(a) 'self-handlers', ie suppliers who provide the groundhandling service independently and who conclude 'no contract of any description with a third party for the provision of such services; or

(b) 'third-party handlers', ie suppliers who provide the service pursuant to or with the assistance of a contract with another party.[63]

In compliance with the Groundhandling Regulations, financial information is submitted by approved ground handlers to the Commission on an annual basis. In addition, for groundhandling companies providing services to third parties, the Groundhandling Regulations require the submission of separate accounts to the Commission. Updated insurance details are also submitted by approved ground handlers on an annual basis in order to ensure compliance with the minimum levels of insurance cover required for ground handlers operating at Irish airports where the Groundhandling Regulations apply.

Access fees to airport installations

3.034 Under reg 14(3) of the Groundhandling Regulations, an airport authority is entitled to impose a fee for access to airport installations[64] granted to providers of groundhandling services at the State airports. Where a decision is taken by the airport authority to impose a fee in respect of access to airport installations, the airport

---

62 In Ireland this means Cork, Dublin and Shannon based on the cargo and passenger thresholds set out in the Directive. Pursuant to reg 7(1) of SI 505/1998, the groundhandling rules apply at Irish airports open to commercial traffic whose annual traffic is not less than two million passenger movements or 50,000 tonnes of freight. At present those thresholds are met by Dublin, Cork and Shannon Airports.

63 As of 31 December 2007 there were 15 companies approved as self-handlers, with a further 41 approved as third-party handlers.

64 As Quirke J noted in *Ryanair Ltd v Commission for Aviation Regulation*, a check-in desk is an 'installation' within the meaning of the Directive and of the Regulations. A rent charged for the exclusive right to occupy a particular desk is an 'access to installations fee' within the meaning of the Directive and of the Regulations – see *Flughafen Hannover– Langenhagen GmbH v Deutsche Lufthansa AG* Case C–363/01; *Flughafen Hannover– Langenhagen GmbH* [2003] ECR I–11893. (contd .../)

authority is required to submit to the Commission in advance[65] a request for approval of the proposed fee in accordance with the criteria set out in the Groundhandling Regulations.[66] When making a decision on access fees, the Commission must ensure that those fees comply with the provisions of reg 14(3) of the Groundhandling Regulations and in particular that they are 'relevant, objective, transparent and non-discriminatory.'[67]

Slot Allocation and Appointment of Schedules Co-ordinator

3.035 Section 8(1) of the 2001 Act provides that the Commission shall be the competent authority for the purposes of Council Regulation EEC/95/93,[68] other than the functions of co-ordinator. Section 8(2) provides that the Commission shall have the function of appointing a co-ordinator under art 4 of Council Regulation EEC/95/93.

---

64 (contd) In *Commission v Italy* Case C–460/02 [2004] ECR I – 11547 the Court of Justice confirmed its decision in *Flughafen Hanover* and that the objective of the Directive was 'to ensure the opening up of the groundhandling market which … must help … to reduce the operating costs of airlines' in order to achieve its stated aim, which includes 'the creation of appropriate conditions for intra-community competition in the sector.'

65 The issue of lack of prior approval for imposing a check-in desk fee was at the centre of the case in *Ryanair Ltd v Aer Rianta Cpt* [2003] 2 IR 143, [2003] IESC 19, when the Supreme Court, *per* Keane CJ, made an art 234 reference on the correct interpretation of the Directive. That reference was overtaken by events as the *Flughafen Hanover* case was decided. The effect of the lack of approval was that the charge was invalid and a refund in order.

66 *Ryanair Ltd v Commission for Aviation Regulation* [2006] IEHC 291, Mr Justice Quirke. In early 2005, an application for judicial review was made by Ryanair in respect of the Commission's Decision in CP8/2004 approving such fees. CP8/2004 published (on 6 October 2004) the Commission's decision approving an earlier request from the former Aer Rianta (now the DAA) for the approval of an annual and hourly fee structure in respect of check-in desk rental at the three State airports. In addition, the decision granted approval for a fee in respect of use of the CUTE (Common User Terminal Equipment) facility at Shannon airport by way of a fee per embarking passenger. The decision also provided that the DAA be permitted to increase the check-in desk fee (in respect of Shannon and Cork airports) in line with inflation as of 1 July each year. The Commission's decision granted approval to the DAA in respect of the above-mentioned fees from the date of the decision. The challenge by Ryanair related to the treatment by the Commission of the DAA's costs in respect of the CUTE facility at Dublin Airport. Ryanair's claim was dismissed.

67 In *Ryanair Ltd v Commission for Aviation Regulation* [2008] IEHC 278, Ryanair sought to impugn the decision made by the Commission on 10 March 2008 permitting DAA to charge certain fees in respect of check-in desks at Dublin Airport. That challenge instituted by way of special summons was dismissed by Kelly J as it was held that judicial review was the appropriate form of proceedings for Ryanair's complaint.

68 Council Regulation (EEC) No 95/93 of 18 January 1993 on common rules for the allocation of slots at Community airports (OJ L 14, 22.1.1993), as amended by Regulation (EC) No 793/2004 of the European Parliament and of the Council of 21 April 2004.

Slot allocation

3.036 A 'slot' is permission to use the full range of airport infrastructure necessary to operate an air service at an airport at a specific time of day. The Commission is responsible for the designation, if necessary, of Irish airports as schedules facilitated or co-ordinated and subsequent appointment of a schedules facilitator or co-ordinator as a result of such a designation. A 'schedules facilitated' airport is one where the various requirements of airlines operating at the airport can be met through a broad measure of consensus as to the allocation of slots. A 'co-ordinated' airport is, in effect, one where slots are allocated on a prescriptive basis and the relevant airport authority can impose sanctions where airlines do not meet the requirements of the airport authority allocating the slots. The Slot Co-ordinator is the independent person who assigns slots at an airport to airlines. At present the Slot Co-ordinator is Airport Coordination Limited.[69] The scheduling status at Dublin Airport is controversial.[70]

In February 2007, in accordance with the provisions of art 3 of Council Regulation EEC/95/93, as amended by Regulation EC/793/2004, the Commission designated Dublin Airport as co-ordinated with effect from the start of the Winter 2007 scheduling season.[71] What this means, amongst other things, is that airlines, in order to land and take off at Dublin Airport need to have a predetermined slot assigned to them to do so.

Slot trading

3.037 Article 8(4) of Council Regulation EEC/95/93, as amended, specifies that slots may be 'freely exchanged' between air carriers by mutual agreement or as a result of a takeover. Any slot exchanges of this type must be transparent and be agreed by the co-ordinator. The general view within the European Community is that 'freely exchanged' means a voluntary swap, not a simple sale (ie a transfer for a cash consideration). At

---

69 Airport Coordination Limited (ACL) is an independent UK based company. It is responsible for schedules facilitation and slot allocation at 21 airports in Ireland, the UK and the EU including Dublin and Heathrow. ACL is owned by a group of nine airlines including British Airways, Virgin Atlantic Airways and Easy Jet.

70 *Ryanair Ltd v Commission for Aviation Regulation* [2006] IEHC 252, Mr Justice O'Higgins gave judgment on 3 July 2006. In that case Ryanair sought a declaration that the decision by the respondent made on 26 April 2005 to alter the designation of Dublin Airport from 'schedule facilitated' to 'coordinated' for the purposes of Regulation (EC) No 95/1993, as amended by Regulation (EC) No 793/2004 on common rules for the allocations of slots at Community airports was *ultra vires* its powers under the said Regulation and under the Aviation Regulation Act 2001. Ryanair was granted *certiorari* quashing the decision. That High Court judgment is on appeal.

71 Commission for Aviation Regulation Decision on the scheduling status of Dublin Airport from the start of Winter 2007 in accordance with the provisions of Council Regulation (EEC) No 95/93, as amended by Regulation (EC) 793/2004 on Common Rules for the Allocation of Slots at Community Airports, Commission Paper CP3/2007, 13 February 2007 (http://www.aviationreg.ie).

present, there is an ongoing EC-wide debate as to amending this regulation to allow for a simple sale transfer.[72]

3.038 Article 14(5) of Council Regulation EEC/95/93, which was inserted by Regulation EC/793/2004, obliges Member states to ensure that effective, proportionate and dissuasive sanctions or equivalent measures are available to deal with repeated and intentional operation of air services at times significantly different from allocated slots, or the use of slots in a significantly different way from that indicated at the time of allocation, where this causes prejudice to airport or air traffic operations.

Tour Operators and Travel Agents Trade

3.039 Sections 9(2)(a) and 9(2)(b) of the 2001 Act transferred the functions of the Minister contained in the Transport (Tour Operators and Travel Agents) Act 1982 (the 1982 Act) and the Package Holidays and Travel Trade Act 1995 to the Commission for Aviation Regulation on its establishment day.[73]

3.040 The Transport (Tour Operators and Travel Agents) Act 1982, as amended by the Package Holidays and Travel Trade Act 1995 and regulations made in accordance with those Acts, are the primary pieces of legislation regarding the regulation of the travel trade in Ireland. Section 4 of the 1982 Act sets out a blanket ban on persons carrying on the business of a tour operator or holding themselves out as such unless they have a licence issued under the Act. Section 5 of the 1982 Act sets out a blanket ban on persons carrying on the business of a travel agent or holding themselves out as such unless they have a licence issued under the Act.[74]

3.041 A key concept in the licensing scheme is the organisation or retail of an 'overseas travel contract'. This is defined in s 2(1) of the 1982 Act as a contract for the carriage of a party to the contract (with or without any other person) by air, sea or land transport commencing in the State to a place outside the State or Northern Ireland, whether the provision of the carriage is the sole subject matter of the contract or is associated with the provision thereunder of any accommodation, facility or service.

'Tour operator' is defined in the 1982 Act, as amended,[75] as a person other than a carrier who arranges for the purpose of selling or offering for sale to any person accommodation for travel by air, sea or land transport commencing in the State to destinations outside the State or Northern Ireland or who holds himself out by

---

72   See also *R v Airport Coordination Ltd, ex parte States of Guernsey Transport Board* [1999] EWHC Admin 264 in which Mr Justice Kay found that notwithstanding the high probability that BA had given Air UK, the only provider of flights to Guernsey from Heathrow, a money payment as well as slots in return for its more useful slots at Heathrow, these slots were 'freely exchanged' within the meaning of art 8(4).

73   Aviation Regulation Act 2001, s 9(2).

74   As of 31 December 2007 a total of 364 firms had travel trade licences – 290 Travel Agents and 74 Tour Operators. This is down from 371 in 2006 and 399 in 2005.

75   By s 27 of the Package Holidays Act 1995.

advertising or otherwise as one who may make available such accommodation, either solely or in association with other accommodation, facilities or other services.

A 'travel agent' means a person other than a carrier who as agent sells or offers to sell to, or purchases or offers to purchase on behalf of, any person, accommodation on air, sea or land transport commencing in the State to destinations outside the State or Northern Ireland or who holds himself out by advertising or otherwise as one who may make available such accommodation, either solely or in association with other accommodation, facilities or services.

Thus, tour operators and travel agents only need a licence to organise and retail travel commencing in Ireland to destinations outside the State. The organisation and retail of travel within the State does not require a licence.

3.042 Applications for a Tour Operator licence are made pursuant to the Tour Operators (Licensing) Regulations 1993 (SI 182/1993) in the form and containing the information required as set out in the First Schedule to those regulations.

Applications for a Travel Agents licence are made under the Travel Agents (Licensing) Regulations 1993 (SI 183/1993) in the form and containing the information required as set out in the First Schedule to those regulations.

Tour operators' and travel agents' bonds

3.043 Under s 13 the 1982 Act, tour operators and travel agents are required, in order to get a license, to be bonded in respect of the sale and offering for sale, of overseas travel originating within the State to destinations outside the State or Northern Ireland. In the event of failure of a tour operator or travel agent to meet its financial or contractual obligations, the Commission is responsible for administering the bond. This work consists of assessing the eligibility of individual claims from customers of the failed tour operator or travel agent, making the appropriate refunds and, where necessary, making arrangements for the repatriation of customers.

The bond may be either cash or guarantee and in the form set out in the Tour Operators and Travel Agents (Bonding) Regulations 1983 (SI 102/1983).

Appeals

3.044 Section 9 of the 1982 Act provides a right of appeal against decisions of the Minister (now the Commission) to either refuse or revoke a licence. It states that:

'(1) Whenever the Minister proposes to revoke, other than pursuant to section 10 of this Act [insolvency/bankruptcy], or to vary the terms and conditions of, a licence granted under this Act, he shall notify the holder of the licence of his proposal and of the reasons for such proposal and shall, if any representations are made in writing by such holder within seven days, consider the representations.

(2) Whenever the Minister refuses to grant a licence or decides, having considered any representations that may have been made by the holder of a licence, to revoke the licence or to vary any term or condition of the licence, he shall notify the applicant for, or as the case may be, the holder of, the licence of the refusal or decision and such applicant or such holder may within seven days appeal to the High Court against such refusal or such decision.

The 1982 Act goes onto provide that:

(3) On the hearing of an appeal under this section in relation to a refusal to grant a licence under this Act or in relation to a decision of the Minister to revoke, or vary the terms and conditions of, a licence granted under this Act, the High Court may either confirm the refusal or decision or may allow the appeal and, where an appeal is allowed, the Minister shall grant the licence or shall not revoke, or vary the terms and conditions of the licence as the case may be.

(4) A decision of the High Court on an appeal under this section shall be final save that, by leave of that Court, an appeal from the decision shall he to the Supreme Court on a specified question of law.

(5) An appeal shall not lie in any case where the Minister refuses to grant a licence to an applicant who does not comply with the provisions of section 13 [the Bond] of this Act or in any case where the Minister revokes a licence pursuant to section 10 [insolvency] of this Act.

(6) Where, after the commencement of *Part III* of this Act, a person appeals against a decision of the Minister to revoke or vary any term or condition of a licence or appeals against a refusal of the Minister to grant a licence, such person shall not, pending the determination of the appeal, carry on business as a tour operator or travel agent unless he complies with the provisions of section 13 of this Act.

These provisions were considered in the recent case of *Manorcastle Limited v Commission for Aviation Limited*,[76] an ultimately unsuccessful appeal against the decision of the Commission not to grant a licence to a tour operator who had sought the renewal of its licence.

Offences

3.045 It is an offence contrary to s 20 of the 1982 Act to carry on business as either a tour operator or travel agent without a licence or to hold oneself out as such. The offence is indictable but may be tried summarily with the consent of the DPP, the accused and the District Court Judge, if he considers it a minor offence.

Pursuant to s 21 of the 1982 Act, where the offence is committed by a body corporate, the directors of the company may also be charged with consenting or conniving with the commission of the offence. The penalties for the offences were amended by s 32 of the Package Holidays and Travel Trade Act 1995. Offences contrary to s 20 attract penalties in the District Court of either a term of imprisonment not exceeding 12 months or a fine not exceeding IR£1,500 or both. Upon conviction after trial on indictment, the accused is liable to a fine of up to IR£100,000 and/or to a term of imprisonment not exceeding five years. Summary proceedings may be brought by the Commission in its own name, pursuant to s 21 of the 1982 Act.

---

76 *Manorcastle Ltd v Commission for Aviation Regulation* [2008] IEHC 386 *ex tempore* judgment of Charleton J.

Persons with Reduced Mobility

3.046 On the 25 July 2008, the Commission was designated as National Enforcement Body (NEB) for the purposes of Regulation EC/1107/2006 of the European Parliament and of the Council of 5 July 2006 concerning the rights of disabled persons and persons with reduced mobility when travelling by air.[77]

Regulation EC/1107/2006[78] came into effect in full on 26 July 2008. Articles 3 and 4, which deal with the prevention of refusal of carriage, have been in force since 26 July 2007. This regulation establishes rules for the protection of and provision of assistance to disabled persons and persons with reduced mobility travelling by air, both to protect them against discrimination and to ensure that they receive assistance. It is an attempt to harmonise the assistance provided to persons of reduced mobility in airports and on board aircraft.

The provisions of the regulation apply to persons with reduced mobility departing from, arriving to or transiting through an airport in the EU on a commercial air service. The rights set down in respect of prevention of refusal of carriage (except in limited circumstances) and the right to assistance by air carriers also apply to passengers departing from an airport outside of the EU to an EU Member State, if the carrier is an EU licensed airline.

3.047 Disabled persons or persons with reduced mobility are defined in art 2, which states:

> a disabled person or person with reduced mobility means any person whose mobility when using transport is reduced due to any physical disability (sensory or locomotor, permanent or temporary), intellectual disability or impairment, or any other cause of disability, or age, and whose situation needs appropriate attention and the adaption to his or her particular needs of the service made available to all passengers.

3.048 Airport managing bodies and airlines are obliged to provide the assistance foreseen by the regulation. Details of the assistance to be provided are set out in Annex I of the Regulation for airport managing bodies and Annex II for airlines. In this regard, art 8 of the regulation provides that the managing body of an airport may, on a non-discriminatory basis, levy a specific charge on airport users for the purpose of funding this assistance, which it may either provide directly or sub-contract. This specific charge shall be reasonable, cost-related, transparent and established by the managing body of the airport in co-operation with airport users, through the Airport Users Committee, where one exists, or any other appropriate entity. It shall be shared among airport users in proportion to the total number of all passengers carried to and from that airport.

3.049 As NEB, the Commission deals with complaints regarding the assistance provided to persons with reduced mobility at airports in Ireland, as well as complaints

---

77   European Communities (Rights of Disabled Persons and Persons with Reduced Mobility when Travelling by Air) Regulations 2008 (SI 299/2008), reg 3.

78   26.7.2006 Official Journal of the European Union L 204/1.

relating to the care and assistance received whilst on board an airline which is licensed in Ireland.

Pursuant to the European Communities (Rights of Disabled Persons and Persons with Reduced Mobility when Travelling by Air) Regulations 2008, the Commission may issue general directions under reg 4 to air carriers, their agents, tour operators or the managing bodies of airports in relation to compliance with the regulation. Such undertakings are obliged to comply with these directions.

In addition, the Commission, either on its own initiative or following a complaint to it by a disabled person or person with reduced mobility, being of the opinion that an air carrier or its agent or a tour operator or managing body of an airport is failing to comply with or is infringing the regulation, may issue a direction under reg 6 to the carrier, agent, operator or body to comply with the article concerned of the regulation, or cease the infringement and to comply with any requirements of the direction. Non-compliance with such a specific direction is an offence.

Where such a direction has been given to a person who:

(a)   has not made representations to the Commission within the period of 14 days of the issue of the direction, after such period; or

(b)   has made such representations and the Commission has replied confirming the direction with or without variation, and the person after the reply is given, fails, without reasonable excuse, to comply with the direction, the person commits an offence and is liable:

(i)   on summary conviction, to a fine not exceeding €5,000, or

(ii)   on conviction on indictment, to a fine not exceeding €150,000.

Denied Boarding Regulations

3.050 Regulation EC/261/2004 of the European Parliament and of the Council of 11 February 2004 establishing common rules on compensation and assistance to passengers in the event of denied boarding and of cancellation or long delay of flights[79] came into effect on 17 February 2005.[80] The aim of this regulation was to establish

---

79   The validity of the regulation was challenged by the airlines in *The Queen on the application of International Air Transport Association, European Low Fares Airline Association v Department for Transport* Case C–344/04 [2006] ECR I 403, a reference for a preliminary ruling under art 234 EC from the High Court of Justice of England and Wales, Queen's Bench Division (Administrative Court).The challenge was rejected by the European Court of Justice, stating: 'Examination of the questions referred to the Court has revealed no factor of such a kind as to affect the validity of arts 5, 6 and 7 of Regulation (EC) No 261/2004 of the European Parliament and of the Council of 11 February 2004 establishing common rules on compensation and assistance to passengers in the event of denied boarding and of cancellation or long delay of flights, and repealing Regulation (EEC) No 295/91.'

80   17.2.2004 L 46/1 Official Journal of the European Union.

common rules on compensation and assistance to passengers in the following situations:

(i) denied boarding;

(ii) cancellation;

(iii) delay; and

(iv) downgrading.

The Commission for Aviation Regulation was designated as the NEB for Ireland on 31 May 2005.[81]

3.051 The rights afforded by the Denied Boarding Regulation apply to the following:

(i) all passengers departing from EU/EEA[82] airports; and

(ii) all passengers departing from outside the EU/EEA but arriving at an EU/EEA airport on an EU/EEA licensed carrier (unless they have already received compensation or assistance in that third country).

Pursuant to art 3 of the Denied Boarding Regulation, passengers must be able to demonstrate that they:

(a) have a confirmed reservation on the flight concerned and, except in the case of cancellation referred to in art 5, present themselves for check-in:

(i) as stipulated and at the time indicated in advance and in writing (including by electronic means) by the air carrier, the tour operator or an authorised travel agent, or, if no time is indicated,

(ii) not later than 45 minutes before the published departure time; or

(b) have been transferred by an air carrier or tour operator from the flight for which they held a reservation to another flight, irrespective of the reason.

3.052 The Denied Boarding Regulation does not apply to passengers travelling free of charge or at a reduced fare not available to the public, nor does it apply to passengers who have not checked in on time. It is important to note that tickets purchased under 'Frequent Flyer Programmes' are not regarded as reduced fare tickets for the purpose of the Regulation. Other issues, such as lost or damaged baggage, personal injury and refunds of taxes and charges are not governed by the Regulation.

In brief, the Denied Boarding Regulation applies in circumstances where a qualifying passenger has been denied boarding, has suffered a cancellation, a long delay or downgrading in particular circumstances set out at length and in great complexity. The responsible operating airline is then liable to provide care,

---

81 The European Communities (Compensation and Assistance to Air Passengers) (Denied Boarding, Cancellation or Long Delay of Flights) Regulations 2005 (SI 274/2005), later revoked by Aviation Act 2006, s 5(2). Section 5(1)(b) of that later Act designated the Commission afresh by amending Aviation Regulation Act 2001, s 8(4).

82 European Union/European Economic Area – this is the EU together with Iceland, Norway and Lichtenstein. Switzerland has a separate agreement with the EU.

reimbursement, rerouting or compensation according the particular circumstances, unless it has a good excuse, which it is obliged to show.

In addition, the operating air carrier is obliged to inform passengers of their rights. In this regard, it must ensure that at check-in, a clearly legible notice containing the following text is displayed in a manner clearly visible to passengers: 'If you are denied boarding or if your flight is cancelled or delayed for at least two hours, ask at the check-in counter or boarding gate for the text stating your rights, particularly with regard to compensation and assistance'. This is a mandatory provision of the regulation and is set out at art 14.

3.053 Enforcement of the regulation is divided between the various Member States. The Commission for Aviation Regulation, the Irish NEB, processes complaints that arise from flights departing from Irish airports or those arriving at Irish airports from non-EU countries on EU-licensed carriers.

Pursuant to s 45(A) of the Aviation Regulation Act 2001,[83] the Commission is now empowered to issue a direction to the carrier to comply with the EC regulation or to cease the infringement and to comply with any instructions contained in the direction. Where a direction has been issued to an air carrier and it fails to comply with the direction, the carrier commits an offence and is liable:

(i)   on summary conviction, to a fine not exceeding €5,000; or

(ii)   on conviction on indictment, to a fine not exceeding €150,000.

ENFORCEMENT

Authorised Officers

3.054 Pursuant to s 42 of the 2001 Act, the Commission may appoint persons to be authorised officers for the purposes of the Act. This is a broad power and is not restricted to members of staff of the Commission. Thus, theoretically, although it has never been done, members of An Garda Síochána may be appointed as authorised officers of the Commission.

Authorised officers must, on their appointment, be furnished by the Commission with a certificate of their appointment and when exercising a power conferred by the Act shall, if requested by any person thereby affected, produce such certificate to that person for inspection. These certificates are generally under seal. As with other offices, for security reasons, copies are produced or given to the persons who enquire. The categories of person identified as potentially being the subject of visits from authorised officers are as follows:

(a)   an airport authority;

(b)   a supplier of aviation terminal services;

(c)   any person responsible for the carriage of passengers, mail or freight by air to or from an airport;

---

83   As inserted by Aviation Act 2006, s 5.

(d) a supplier of groundhandling services;

(e) a tour operator or a travel agent; and

(f) an organiser.[84]

One should note that, in so far as some of these persons may be obliged to hold a licence to act lawfully, it is their activity that defines them, not the holding of a licence. Thus, authorised officers may act against a person illegally trading.

3.055 According to s 42, for the purposes of the exercise by the Commission of its functions under the 2001 Act, including all the functions transferred to it, authorised officers may—

(a) enter at any reasonable time any premises or place owned or occupied by a person to whom this section applies and search and inspect the premises and any books, documents or records found therein,

(b) require any such person to produce to him or her any books, documents or records relating to the provision of airport or aviation services which are in the person's power or control, and in the case of information in a non-legible form to reproduce it in a legible form, and to give to the officer such information as he or she may reasonably require in relation to any entries in such books, documents or records,

(c) secure for later inspection any premises or part thereof in which books, documents or records relating to the provision of airport or aviation services are kept or there are reasonable grounds for believing that such books, documents or records are kept,

(d) inspect and take extracts from or make copies of any such books, documents or records (including in the case of information in a non-legible form a copy of or extract from such information in a permanent legible form),

(e) remove and retain such books, documents or records for such period as may be reasonable for further examination,

(f) require the person to maintain such books, documents or records for such period of time, as may be reasonable, as the authorised officer directs,

(g) require the person to give to the officer any information which he or she may reasonably require with regard to the provision of airport or aviation services,

(h) require any person on the premises or place having charge of, or otherwise concerned with the operation of, the data equipment or any associated apparatus or material, to afford the officer all reasonable assistance in relation thereto.

3.056 Where an authorised officer in exercise of his or her powers under s 42 is prevented from entering any premises or place, an application may be made under s 43 for a warrant to authorise such entry. This provision means that such entry must not be by force. An interesting point arises: if officers enter but are asked to leave, the subject of the visit may be subject to an obstruction prosecution at a later date. This is because, according to s 42(7), a person to whom this section applies who:

(a) obstructs, impedes or assaults an authorised officer in the exercise of a power under this section,

---

84 An 'organiser' has a meaning given to it by the Package Holidays and Travel Trade Act 1995. Usually, an 'organiser' is in fact either a tour operator or travel agent.

(b) fails or refuses to comply with a requirement under this section,

(c) alters, suppresses or destroys any books, documents or records which the person concerned has been required to produce, or may reasonably expect to be required to produce,

(d) gives to the Commission or to an authorised officer information which is false or misleading, in a material respect, or

(e) falsely represents himself or herself to be an authorised officer,

shall be guilty of an offence and shall be liable on summary conviction to a fine not exceeding IR£1,500.

3.057 Therefore, if authorised officers peacefully enter a premises, identify themselves and make lawful demands before being asked to leave, that request to leave is implicitly a rejection of that lawful demand. Accordingly, it may be argued that once authorised officers enter premises open for business, asking them to leave may be construed as an act of obstruction.

Authorised officers are not entitled to demand and/or force entry to premises as a right unless they get a search warrant.

The rules are different for entry by authorised officers at a person's private dwelling. An authorised officer shall not, other than with the consent of the occupier, enter a private dwelling, unless he or she has obtained a warrant under s 43 authorising such entry. Thus, a person in a private dwelling may ask authorised officers not possessing a search warrant to leave without putting him or herself in jeopardy.

Searches

3.058 Section 43 of the 2001 Act provides that if a judge of the District Court is satisfied on the sworn information of an authorised officer that there are reasonable grounds for suspecting that information required by an authorised officer for the purpose of this Act is held at any premises or place, the judge may issue a warrant authorising the authorised officer, accompanied if the officer considers it necessary by other authorised officers or members of An Garda Síochána, at any time or times, within one month from the date of issue of the warrant, on production, if so required, of the warrant, to enter, if need be by reasonable force, the premises or place, and exercise all or any of the powers conferred on an authorised officer under s 42.

3.059 An application for a search warrant is made by way of Sworn Information,[85] a document that is akin to an affidavit and sets out the reasonable grounds of suspicion held by an authorised officer. This information is sworn before a District Judge for the District Court area within which the premises or dwelling is situated. This is an important jurisdictional point. An information sworn and warrant granted in the wrong District Court area may well be held to be illegal at a later stage, thus jeopardising evidence garnered from that search. The procedure is that the District Court Clerk will hand the judge the written information and the deponent will then give sworn oral

---

85 A 'Sworn Information' is a document which is akin to an affidavit setting out the reasonable grounds of suspicion held by an authorised officer. Formally, the contents are conveyed by way of oral evidence under oath to a District Court Judge.

evidence to the judge as to the reasonable suspicion held. Often, in the interests of secrecy, this application is heard in chambers. If the judge is satisfied to grant the warrant, he or she will sign the information sworn, hand it back to the deponent and then issue the search warrant, which will be prepared beforehand and brought to the application. A search warrant issued in this way is in the nature of an order of the District Court. It is important to note that in an investigation context, sight by the subject of a search of the Sworn Information only occurs at the pre-trial stage, once charges are pressed. If this does not occur, then it is not disclosed. By contrast, the subject of a search is entitled to be shown the search warrant authorising entry and, in fact, it is the practice of the Commission to simply hand over a copy on the day.

3.060 Many search warrants recite the bulk of the search warrant section of the appropriate Act to ensure the inclusion of the exercising of all powers therein. As adverted to above, the Commission is entitled to name officers on the warrant, including members of An Garda Síochána. It is important to note that a search warrant of this type is against a place, not a person, and for this reason the use of the correct address is important. This is especially so where entry may be by force.[86] Obstruction of a search pursuant to warrant is an offence.

APPEALS

3.061 Following a Commission determination on either airport charges or aviation terminal services charges, the Minister for Transport may, if requested, establish an appeal panel to consider appeals as provided for under s 40 of the 2001 Act.[87] The Minister has done so three times in relation to airport charges.[88]

Those entitled to request the setting up of an appeal panel are restricted to DAA, in respect of a determination under s 32(2), the IAA, in respect of a determination under s 35(2), and 'users' in respect of a determination under ss 32(2) or 35(2). Such a request to the Minister to establish an appeal panel must be made in writing.

3.062 Generally, the Minister is obliged to set up an appeal panel unless he is of the opinion that the request is vexatious, frivolous or without substance, in which case he may refuse to establish an appeal panel to consider the appeal. A refusal by the Minister to establish the appeal panel shall be in writing and state the reasons for the refusal. It may also occur that a Minister may refuse to set up an appeal panel if the subject matter of the complaint is not in fact a determination on either airport or air terminal services charges.

---

86 The case of the *People (Attorney General) v O'Brien* [1965] IR 142 centres on an error as to the address of the premises recited on the face of the search warrant. The legality of the search was consequently called into question.

87 Aviation Regulation Act 2001, section 40, as amended by of State Airports Act, section 24.

88 See http://www.aviationreg.ie for the Commission's responses to the two referrals it has received to date from aviation appeal panels: CP2/2002 – *Commission decision on matter referred by the Appeal Panel in relation to the 2001 Determination on airport charges*; CP5/ 2006 – *Maximum Levels of Airport charges at Dublin Airport: Decision of the Commission further to a referral by the 2006 Aviation Appeal Panel*.

3.063 Once set up, an appeal panel shall consist of at least three, but not more than five, persons appointed by the Minister, one of whom shall be designated by the Minister to be the chairperson of the appeal panel. The appeal panel is entitled to determine its own procedure. This fact has led to the situation whereby in each of the appeal panels set up thus far in relation to airport charges, different procedures have been followed.

The appeal is limited in nature. An appeal panel is obliged to consider the determination and, not later than three months from the date of its establishment, may confirm the determination or, if it considers that in relation to the provisions of ss 33 or 36[89] there are sufficient grounds for doing so, refer the decision in relation to the determination back to the Commission for review. Once it has done this, the appeal panel must notify the appellant of this step. It then stands dissolved.

Thereafter, the Commission, where it has received a referral from an appeal panel, shall, within two month of receipt of the referral, either affirm or vary its original determination and notify the appellant of the reasons for its decision. In addition, a notice of such a decision shall be given by publishing the notice in a daily newspaper published and circulating in the State and by such means as the Commission may determine.[90]

3.064 It is clear from the foregoing that this is not an independent appeal of a determination. Rather it is a mechanism whereby the Commission may be formally requested to revisit elements of its decision for grounds shown. To date, it has mainly been used as an error correction mechanism and an attempt to further argue points of view in relation to the treatment of planned and actual expenditure at airports when setting airport charges. The lack of set procedures is a significant drawback and was criticised in the High Court, which described the section providing for appeals as a 'witches brew of uncertainty.'[91]

See **Ch 10** on appeals for further details.

JUDICIAL REVIEW OF DETERMINATION OF COMMISSION

3.065 Section 38 of the 2001 Act restricts a person wishing to question the validity of a determination, a review of a determination or a request for information to assist

---

89 Sections 33 and 36 set out the mandatory statutory factors that the Commission must take into account when making determinations on airport charges and aviation terminal services charges respectively.

90 Copies of the Commission's decisions on referral from an appeal panel in relation to both the first (2001) and second (2005) airport charges determinations are available on the Commission's website (http://www.aviationreg.ie).

91 Comment by Mr Justice Kelly in *Aer Rianta v Commission for Aviation Regulation* (14 November 2001, unreported), HC. The Commision for Aviation was on notice of the application by Aer Rianta, such application having been made pursuant to s 38 of the Aviation Act 2001. The Commission sought to have the judicial review proceedings adjourned pending the outcome ofthe then current appeal procedure. Mr Justice Kelly declined that application and later granted Aer Rianta leave to bring judicial review proceedings on 10 December 2001.

making a determination to doing so by way of an application for leave to apply for judicial review. The section goes on to set out particular judicial review rules for airport charges and aviation terminal services charges determinations.

Such an application for leave to apply for judicial review shall:

(a) be made within the period of two months commencing on the date on which notice of the determination under this Part was first published, unless the High Court considers that there is good and sufficient reason for extending the period within which the application shall be made, and

(b) be made by motion on notice (grounded in the manner specified in the Order in respect of an ex parte motion for leave) to the Commission and the person concerned,

and such leave shall not be granted unless the High Court is satisfied that there are substantial grounds for contending that the determination is invalid or ought to be quashed.

Under the section, the High Court is entitled at its discretion, before hearing an application for leave, to direct that notice of the application be also served on such other persons as the court may specify. The application shall not affect the validity of the determination and its operation unless, upon an application to the High Court, that court suspends the determination until the application is determined or withdrawn.

3.066 Pursuant to s 38(5), the determination of the High Court of an application for leave to apply for judicial review as aforesaid or of an application for such judicial review shall be final and no appeal shall lie from the decision of the High Court[92] to the Supreme Court in either case, save with the leave of the High Court, which leave shall only be granted where the High Court or the Supreme Court certifies that the decision involves a point of law of exceptional public importance and that it is desirable in the public interest that an appeal should be taken to the Supreme Court. Such leave to appeal to the Supreme Court was granted to Aer Rianta in 2003,[93] however, that appeal did not proceed further.

3.067 Where an application is made for judicial review in respect of part only of a determination, the High Court may, if it so thinks fit, declare to be invalid or quash the part or any provision thereof without declaring to be invalid or quashing the remainder of the determination or part, as the case may be, and if the court does so, it may make any consequential amendments to the remainder of the order or part, as the case may be.

---

92 Bar a finding of the High Court in so far as it involves the question as to the validity of any law having regard to the provisions of the Constitution.

93 *Aer Rianta v Commission for Aviation Regulation* (14 November 2001, unreported), HC Judgment of Mr Justice O'Sullivan on 4 June 2003 certifying one ground of appeal.

Chapter 4

FINANCIAL SERVICES REGULATION

APPROACH OF THIS CHAPTER

4.001 This chapter examines the regulation of financial services from a practical perspective. It is useful in the regulation of financial services to understand its historical foundations and also to understand how this area is currently developing. The Department of Finance is responsible for leading developments in this area. The relevant Regulators are the Central Bank and the Irish Financial Services Regulatory Authority.

FINANCIAL SERVICES

General

4.002 'Financial capital' is a term for liquid instruments, whether or not those liquid instruments are recognised tender. To act as a store of value, financial capital must have the capacity to be reliably saved, stored and retrieved, and it must be predictably useful when it is so retrieved. 'Liquidity' describes how easily an item can be traded for another item, or into common currency. Money is the most liquid form of financial capital because it is universally recognised and accepted as common currency. In economics, money is a broad term that refers to any instrument that can be used in the resolution of debt and includes commodity money,[1] representative money,[2] credit money,[3] fiat money[4] and electronic money.[5]

---

1   The value comes from the commodity out of which it is made, eg gold, silver, barley – the Shekel derived its name from to an ancient unit of weight and currency in Mesopotamia circa 3000 BC and referred to a specific mass of barley.

2   Representative money is money that consists of physical tokens, such as certificates or coins, which can be reliably exchanged for a fixed quantity of a commodity such as gold or silver. It stands in direct and fixed relation to the commodity which backs it, while not itself being composed of that commodity.

3   Credit money is any claim against a physical or legal person that can be used to purchase goods and services. Credit money supply moves in line with the business cycle. When lenders are optimistic, they increase their lending activity, which creates new money. This may trigger inflation and bull markets. When creditors are pessimistic (when debt level is perceived as too high or there are high levels of defaults), creditors reduce their lending activity and money becomes tight or illiquid. Bear markets, characterised by bankruptcies and market recessions, may follow.

4   Fiat money is any money whose value is determined by legal means. Fiat money is symbolic of a commodity or a government promise. Incidentally, the first banknotes were used in China in the seventh century, and the first banknotes used in Europe were issued by Stockholm's Bank in 1661.

5   This may be in the form of value stored digitally on a technical device such as a chip card or, indeed, a computer memory.

History

4.003 The history of financial services in the State originated with the Coinage Act 1926, which authorised the Minister for Finance to issue token coins of silver, nickel and bronze. A Banking Commission in 1926 was appointed under the chairmanship of a previous Director of the US Federal Reserve Board.[6] Most of the essential points of the Banking Commission's recommendations contained in its First Interim Report were included in the Currency Act 1927. The Irish pound[7] or punt was introduced as a Free State pound in 1927 and remained in existence until the changeover to the euro in 2002. The Central Bank of Ireland (Banc Ceannais na hÉireann) was founded in 1943 and its powers were extended with the Central Bank Act 1971, which saw the transition of the bank from a currency board to a fully functional central bank. Provision for the decimalisation of the Irish punt was made under the Decimal Currency Acts 1969 and 1970, and the system formally commenced on 15 February 1971.

4.004 The 1970s[8] also saw the introduction of the European Currency Unit (ECU), which comprised a basket of the Community's currencies, which would be used as the denominator for fixing exchange rates. In 1978, at the European Council meeting in Brussels, it was agreed to set up the European Monetary System (EMS) as a system of 'fixed but adjustable' exchange rates. Ireland joined the EMS in March 1979. When in 1979 sterling gained support from rising oil prices and appreciated strongly against all EMS currencies, as an EMS member, the punt could not follow and the link between the Irish pound and sterling was broken as Ireland had to devalue against the sterling. The early 1990s saw a currency crisis within the EMS.[9] The Irish authorities

---

6   Prof Henry Parker-Willis.

7   For most of its existence, the Irish pound had a fixed link to sterling. In the 1970s, this link failed to deliver price stability due to high inflation in the UK which lead to Ireland joining the European Monetary System (EMS). This was prompted by the breakdown of the Bretton Woods System which existed from 1944–1971 whereby gold was the base currency underpinning the system (gold standard) which functioned as the worldwide monetary system of fixed exchange rates.

8   Borrowing to fund spending and global economic issues in the wake of the first oil crisis were considered to have caused high unemployment and mass emigration in Ireland in the 1970s. Tax rates increased significantly and the currency had to be devalued several times.

9   When sterling left the Exchange Rate Mechanism (ERM) in 1992, pressure on the Irish pound developed. Initially, this was based on fears of a unilateral devaluation of the Irish pound to reverse its sharp appreciation against sterling. There were expectations of a general realignment, but the Irish pound held firm. In January 1993 the defence of the Irish pound was abandoned (Kelly, *The Irish Pound: From Origins to EMU* (Central Bank of Ireland, 2003)). One of the most notable features of the currency crisis were the unprecedented levels to which Irish interest rates were increased in defence of the currency – similar to the Thai Baht during the Asian Financial Crisis of July 1997. While defence of the Irish pound had been costly, interest rates soon dropped back to normal levels (Kelly, *The Irish Pound: From Origins to EMU* (Central Bank of Ireland, 2003)).

reluctantly decided on a downward realignment against the other currencies on 30 January 1993. The cash changeover to the euro began on 1 January 2002, when euro notes and coins became legal tender.

4.005 In 2003, the Central Bank was renamed the Central Bank and Financial Services Authority of Ireland to reflect its new role in financial services and the economy. The bank now operates in two constituent parts, the existing Central Bank and the Financial Regulator. The European Central Bank (ECB)[10] is the ultimate central bank for Ireland and is responsible for monetary policy for the member countries of the eurozone.

Recent Times

4.006 Issues such as nationalisation,[11] bank bailouts, shotgun mergers,[12] bank runs and bankruptcy[13] had not been seen for some time[14] until the 'credit crunch' that is ongoing at the time of writing. It will inevitably produce a new set of regulatory reforms and involve co-ordinated global intervention to deal with a crisis which started in the sub-prime mortgage market in the US and led to contracted liquidity in the global credit markets and banking system.

4.007 Through a system allowing for credit default swaps (CDS), the crisis travelled from the mortgage lenders with whom the risk of payment default originated, who were the first to be affected as borrowers became unable to make payments, to major banks and financial institutions around the world. With securitisation,[15]

---

10 Established by the European Union (EU) in 1998 with headquarters in Frankfurt, Germany.

11 There is a history of nationalisation of financial services entities in Ireland. In March 1985, the Irish government had to take over the Insurance Corporation of Ireland, a subsidiary of Allied Irish Banks (AIB), and assist the bank after the insurer started incurring substantial losses. In order to prevent the bankruptcy of AIB, the State purchased ICI for £1 and assumed its debts.

12 In September 2008 a sale of Merrill Lynch to Bank of America was agreed and Lloyds TSB bid for HBOS with little or no regard to merger control rules, which seemed to have been abandoned in the crisis. Morgan Stanley agreed to sell 20 per cent of its business to Mitsubishi UFJ, Japan's biggest bank, and ceased being an investment bank. Bear Stearns was sold in a fire sale to JP Morgan Chase in May 2008. Commerzbank bought Dresdner Bank and Wachovia was sold in a fire sale to Citibank.

13 Lehman Brothers filed for Chapter 11 bankruptcy protection.

14 The Great Depression which commenced in the United States in 1930s subsequent to the Stock Market Crash of Black Tuesday, October 1929; Denmark, Norway, Sweden and Finland nationalised large segments of their banking systems in the late 1980s; the Asian Financial Crisis of 1997; the Russian (Ruble) crisis of 1998.

15 Securitisation is a structured finance process which involves the pooling and repackaging of cash-flow-producing financial assets into securities that are then sold to investors.

87

many mortgage lenders had passed the rights to the mortgage payments and related credit/default risk to third-party investors via mortgage-backed securities and collateralised debt obligations. The area of financial regulation is complex and it now appears that not only were certain structured investment vehicles not understood by Regulators throughout the globe, but some of the previous giants of Wall Street may not have fully appreciated the complexity of the financial engineering involved. The collapse of the investment banks in the US closed down the wholesale banking market in September 2008.

4.008 The turmoil in the banking sector had already seen a run on a UK bank – Northern Rock – in 2007, which prompted the UK Treasury to pledge that it would guarantee all moneys invested in this bank and in February 2008, that bank was taken into State ownership.[16] Investment banks seeking to deleverage or reduce their debt had assets on their books that were historically low in value and given there was no credit available, there were no interested buyers with available funds. As a result, deleveraging was made extremely difficult. The liquidity concerns drove central banks around the world to take collective action to provide funds to member banks[17] and introduce a co-ordinated interest rate cut.[18] Agreement on a US bailout package of €700bn was finally reached by US Congress in October 2008.[19] Concerns were raised about what was perceived as 'Main Street' bailing out Wall Street.[20] The crisis resulted

---

16   Bradford & Bingley became the second bank nationalised in the UK after Northern Rock. Iceland's banks, including Glitnir, were also nationalised. The Federal National Mortgage Association (Fannie Mae) and the Federal Home Loan Mortgage Corporation (Freddie Mac), both mortgage-backing entities in the United States, were placed into conservatorship with the US government in September 2008 and the US government took a 79.9 per cent equity stake in insurance giant AIG and provided emergency loans significantly above the LIBOR (London Interbank Offered Rate). German banks Sachsen and IKB were also rescued with government money. Fortis, the Dutch/Belgian bank was in part 'nationalised' by Belgium, Luxembourg and Holland, also in September.

17   19 September 2008.

18   8 October 2008.

19   This represented the biggest expansion of government's role in the financial system since the Great Depression of the 1930s. The assets were indirectly to be acquired by the US taxpayer who would have assumed a huge quantity of Wall Street's bad debts, which led to the phrase 'socialism for the risk and free market economy for the poor.' It was followed by similar financial rescue packages around the world, including Germany, UK, France, Netherlands, Russia, South Korea, Singapore. In Ireland the rescue package was in the form of the Credit Institutions (Financial Support) Act 2008.

20   The last two surviving independent investment banks on Wall Street were Goldman Sachs and Morgan Stanley. The US had separated investment and commercial banks since 1933 to protect investors following abuses that led to the 1929 Wall Street Crash. In 2008 this move was reversed and Goldman Sacs and Morgan Stanley are to operate as commercial banks and come directly under the Federal Reserve's regulatory oversight. They will now be subject to capital requirements and able to acquire deposit holders rather than act as independent broker dealers.

in a dramatic fall in stock exchanges the world over.[21] Despite the short selling[22] bans[23] in place, bank shares continued to fall.

4.009 State aid issues and merger control issues were quickly swept aside despite initial objections from Competition Commissioner Nellie Kroes. The Federal Reserve approved the change in status in September 2008 of Goldman Sachs and Morgan Stanley and the five-day anti-trust waiting period was waived by the Federal Reserve and the banks became bank holding companies. This provoked concerns that anti-trust control appeared to be treated as an optional extra which could be waived in times of urgency. Under the UK Enterprise Act 2002, the Secretary of State may override a decision of the Office of Fair Trading to refer a merger to the Competition Commission on the grounds of public interest. In addition, the Secretary of State has powers to override the Competition Commission's decision to block a merger on the grounds of public interest (having taken into account competition concerns). Although the EC Merger Regulation[24] has an exemption for failing firms in terms of merger control, a similar provision was not provided for in the Irish Competition Act 2002, nor was there a provision allowing for State intervention on the grounds of public interest. In October 2008, the government adopted the Credit Institutions (Financial Support) Act 2008, which amended the Competition Act 2002. Section 7 provides that in the case of a merger involving credit institutions, the Minister for Finance may approve a merger, notwithstanding that the merger would substantially lessen competition, where he considers it necessary to maintain the stability of the Irish financial system and that there would be a serious threat to that stability if the merger did not proceed.

4.010 EU banks must provide deposit guarantees of €20,000 under the EU Deposit Guarantee Schemes Directive. In October 2008, in the form of the Credit Institutions (Financial Support) Act 2008, together with the Credit Institutions (Financial Support) Scheme 2008, Ireland provided guarantees under the deposit guarantee scheme of unlimited amount. It also guaranteed liabilities including the wholesale debts of banks but excluding intra-group borrowing and any debt owed to the ECB by those who

---

21 The stock market in Ireland reportedly fell even more on 29 September 2008 than it did on 19 October 1987 or Black Monday: Reddan, 'Banks hit as credit market turmoil spreads' (2008) *Irish Times*, 30 September. The Russian stock market closed its stocks to trading on 19 September 2008 to try and prevent a free fall of shares.

22 Short selling occurs where an investor believes that the price of an asset, such as shares, is going to fall and agrees to sell that asset in the relevant market at a certain price without having actually purchased the asset. Instead of actually buying shares, investors borrow the asset they wish to short sell normally from a broker and agree to sell these shares at a particular price. As the share price falls, they purchase the shares at the new lower market price and benefit from the difference between the lower purchase price and the agreed higher sale price.

23 In September 2008, the Securities and Exchange Commission in the US restricted short selling of shares in hundreds of companies exposed to the credit crunch crisis. Similar measures were taken around the globe. In Ireland bans apply to shares in AIB, Bank of Ireland, Anglo Irish Bank and Irish Life & Permanent.

24 EC Merger Regulation Council Regulation (EC) No 139/2004 of 20 January 2004.

partake in the scheme, provided they sign up to a guarantee acceptance deed which involves quarterly charges. The Minister may also appoint non-executive directors to the board of any institution availing of this scheme to protect the public interest.[25]

4.011 Deregulation and light-touch regulation would appear not to have worked for certain aspects of the banking sector, rather they led to a lack of transparency and a lack of prudence in relation to risk taking.

ECONOMIC POLICY AND THE POLITICAL DIMENSION

4.012 In order to regulate the markets and the supply of money, a central bank and a financial Regulator is required.

Monetary policy is the process by which a government, central bank or monetary authority manages the money supply to achieve specific goals. A failed monetary policy may have significant detrimental effects on an economy. These may include hyperinflation, stagflation, recession, unemployment, shortages of imported goods, inability to export goods, and even total monetary collapse and the adoption of a much less efficient barter economy. Governments and central banks have taken both interventionist and free-market approaches to monetary policy.

4.013 Transparency is required in order to have effective regulation of a sector and it was the lack of transparency[26] that appears to have fuelled the financial crisis taking place at the time of writing. Investment banks had largely escaped regulatory oversight. More capital, lower leverage and more disclosure seem now inevitable. Better regulation of financial institutions is being promised by the US, the UK and the EU. The EU Internal Market Commissioner Charlie McCreevy is considering a range of reform proposals and it is likely that the current crisis will prompt a range of new Directives and regulations in the financial services sector. It is likely that new EU proposals will lead to greater transparency, with hedge funds and private equity funds being monitored more closely, as well as increased capital requirements and increased guarantees for deposits.

4.014 Questions have been asked about the role of financial Regulators. Directives such as the Capital Requirements Directives do not seem to have been able to adequately address the recent wholesale banking crisis. It is unclear whether it was the lack of transparency as to what was taking place within firms that led to the lack of oversight by the various regulatory agencies across the globe that caused the crisis, or whether this merely exasperated it. The fact that taxpayers across the globe will now have to bear the brunt of the capital markets crisis will have ramifications for economies across the globe for the coming years. Free market economics were disposed of swiftly during the height of the crisis with the Federal Reserve and various central banks expected to rescue the big players and the markets to ensure financial

---

25   The European Commission issued a decision not to raise objections under State aid rules on 13 October 2008.

26   The economist Joseph Stigliz suggested that there needed to be a move to the 'psychology of supervision away from the presumption that institutions know what they are doing'.

stability for the global economy. Previous concerns about merger control laws, golden shares and State aid rules seem to have been suspended. When the shock waves of the credit quake will end is, at the time of writing, uncertain; however, it is likely that it will bring about sweeping reforms in the regulation of the financial sector and tightened regulation of the wholesale banking market with increased regulatory oversight and transparency obligations.

THE RELEVANT LEGISLATIVE FRAMEWORK

4.015 The legislative framework under which the Financial Regulator and the Central Bank work is complicated and is largely based on various complex EU Directives.

Structure of the European Regulatory Framework for Financial Service

4.016

- (i) The Markets in Financial Instruments Directives[27] – implemented in Ireland by the Market in Financial Instruments and Miscellaneous Provision Act 2007 and the Markets in Financial Instruments Regulations (SI 60/2007, SI 663/2007 and SI 773/2007);

- (ii) Prospectus Directive (Directive 2003/71/EC) – implemented by 2005 Regulations (Prospectus Regulations 1 July 2005 (SI 324/2005));

- (iii) Market Abuse Directive (Directive 2003/6/EC) – implemented by 2005 Regulations (Market Abuse Regulations 6 July 2005 (SI 342/2005));

- (iv) Transparency Directive (Directive 2004/109/EC) – implemented by 2007 Regulations (Transparency Regulations 13 June 2007 (SI 277/2007));

- (v) Capital Requirements Directives (Directives 2006/48/EC and 2006/49/EC) – implemented into Irish law via the European Communities (Capital Adequacy of Investment Firms) Regulations 2006 (SI 660/2006) and European Communities (Capital Adequacy of Credit Institutions) Regulations 2006 (SI 661/2006);

- (vi) Large Exposures Directive 92/121/EEC – implemented by the Central Bank;

- (vii) Directive 2000/46/EC on the taking up, pursuit of and prudential supervision of the business of electronic money – implemented by SI 221/2002;

- (viii) Financial Conglomerate's Directive 2002/87/EC of the European Parliament and of the Council of 16 December 2002 on the supplementary supervision of credit institutions, insurance undertakings and investment firms in a financial conglomerate – implemented by the European Communities (Financial Conglomerates) Regulations 2004 (SI 727/2004);

---

27 Directive 2007/44/EC of the European Parliament and of the Council of 5 September 2007, Council Directive 92/49/EEC and Directives 2002/83/EC, 2004/39/EC, 2005/68/EC and 2006/48/EC as regards procedural rules and evaluation criteria for the prudential assessment of acquisitions and increase of holdings in the financial sector.

   (ix) Money Laundering Directive, Council Directive 91/308/EEC of 10 June 1991 on prevention of the use of the financial system for the purpose of money laundering; Second Anti Money Laundering Directive 2001/97/EC and Third EU Anti Money Laundering Directive 2005/60/EC – implemented by the Criminal Justice Act 1994, as amended, and the Criminal Justice (Terrorist Offences) Act 2005;

   (x) Takeover Bids Directive 2004/25/EC – implemented by the European Communities (Takeover Bids (Directive 2004/25/EC)) Regulations 2006 (SI 255/2006);

   (xi) Prudential supervision of pension funds Directive 2003/41/EC – implemented by SI 592/2005, SI 593/2005 and SI 594/2005;

   (xii) Directives 92/96/EEC, 92/49/EEC (the 'Life and Non-Life Framework Directives') and Directive 98/78/EC (the Insurance Groups Directive) – implemented by the European Communities (Life Assurance) Framework Regulations 1994 which implemented the First, Second and Third EU Life Assurance Directives (the 'Life Directives') in Ireland; the European Communities (Supplementary Supervision of Insurance Undertakings in an Insurance Group) Regulations 1999 should also be taken into account when calculating regulatory capital requirements by an applicant for authorisation that forms part of an insurance or reinsurance group;

   (xiii) Reinsurance Directive 2005/68/EC – implemented by European Communities (Reinsurance) Regulations 2006 and 2007 (SI 380/2006 and SI 306/2007);

   (xiv) Insurance Mediation Directive 2002/92/EC – implemented by SI 12/2005;

   (xv) Distance Marketing of Financial Services Directive 2002/65/EC – implemented by SI 853/2004 European Communities (Distance Marketing of Consumer Financial Services) Regulations 2004;

   (xvi) Reorganisation and Winding up of Banks Directive 2001/24/EC – implemented by European Communities (Reorganisation and Winding-up of Credit Institutions) Regulations 2004 (SI 198/2004);

   (xvii) Financial Collateral Arrangements Directive 2002/47/EC implemented by SI 1/2004 European Communities (Financial Collateral Arrangements) Regulations 2004;

   (xviii) Undertakings for Collective Investment in Transferable Securities Directives to allow collective investment schemes to operate freely throughout the EU on the basis of a single authorisation from one Member State (UCITS Directives 2001/107/EC and 2001/108/EC) – implemented by way of European Communities (Undertakings for Collective Investment in Transferable Securities) Regulations (SI 211/2003), which was then amended by SI 212/2003 and SI 497/2003 in order to give effect to the Product Directive and the Management Directive, respectively, and it was later amended by the European Communities (Undertakings for Collective Investment in Transferable Securities) (Amendment) Regulations 2006 (SI 287/2006);

   (xix) Winding Up of Insurance Undertakings Directive 2001/17/EC – implemented by SI 168/2003;

(xx) Investment Services Directive (93/22/EEC) – implemented by way of SI 267/ 1996.

Structure of the National Regulatory Framework for Financial Services

4.017

   (i) Insurance Acts 1909 to 2000;

   (ii) Central Bank Act 1942;

   (iii) Central Bank Act 1971 (as amended);

   (iv) Central Bank Act 1989;

   (v) Trustee Savings Bank Act 1989;

   (vi) Stock Exchange Act 1991;

   (vii) ACC Bank Act 1992;

   (viii) ICC Bank Act 1992;

   (ix) Investment Intermediaries Act 1995;

   (x) Consumer Credit Act 1995;

   (xi) Stock Exchange Act 1995;

   (xii) Central Bank Act 1997;

   (xiii) Investor Compensation Act 1998;

   (xiv) Asset Covered Securities Act 2001;

   (xv) Dormant Accounts Act 2001;

   (xvi) Pensions (Amendment) Act 2002;

   (xvii) Unclaimed Life Assurance Policies Act 2003;

   (xviii) Central Bank and Financial Services Authority of Ireland Act 2003;

   (xix) Central Bank and Financial Services Authority of Ireland Act 2004;

   (xx) Investment Funds, Companies and Miscellaneous Provisions Acts 2005 and 2006;

   (xxi) Markets in Financial Instruments and Miscellaneous Provisions Act 2007;

   (xxii) Credit Institutions (Financial Support) Act 2008 and Credit Institutions (Financial Support) Scheme 2008 (SI 411/2008).

THE ESTABLISHED ENTITIES – CENTRAL BANK AND FINANCIAL SERVICES AUTHORITY OF IRELAND

4.018 The Central Bank of Ireland, which came into being in 1943, was restructured and renamed on 1 May 2003. The Bank, formerly called 'Banc Ceannais na hÉireann' in Irish and the 'Central Bank of Ireland' in English, continues, but with the corporate name of 'Banc Ceannais agus Údaras Seirbhísí Airgeadais na hÉireann' in Irish and the 'Central Bank and Financial Services Authority of Ireland' in English.[28] This body carries out all of the activities formerly carried out by the Central Bank of Ireland and additional regulatory and consumer protection functions for the financial services sector. It was the Central Bank and Financial Services Authority of Ireland Act 2003 (the 2003 Act) which led to the establishment of the new Financial Services Regulator. There are two Regulators involved in the regulation of the financial services sector in Ireland, the Central Bank and Irish Financial Services Regulatory Authority (the Financial Regulator). The Financial Regulator reports to both the Minister for Finance and the Board of the Central Bank.

4.019 The Financial Regulator is responsible for the regulation of all financial services firms in Ireland. It also has a role in the protection of the consumers of those firms. Its main aims are to help consumers to make informed decisions on their financial affairs in a safe and fair market, and to foster sound, growing and solvent financial institutions which give consumers confidence that their deposits and investments are secure. There are 13,000 firms and entities that come under Financial Regulator's direct supervision.[29] The Financial Regulator is a distinct component of the Central Bank and Financial Services Authority of Ireland. All Irish financial institutions including those previously regulated by the Central Bank: Department of Enterprise, Trade and Employment (DETE); Office of the Director of Consumer Affairs (ODCA) and Registrar of Friendly Societies, come within its ambit. The Financial Regulator contributes to the work of the Central Bank in discharging its responsibility in relation to the maintenance of overall financial stability of the State.

4.020 The Central Bank and Financial Services Authority of Ireland Act 2004 (2004 Act) created a statutory financial services ombudsman for consumers. Consultative consumer and industry panels have also been appointed where matters of policy and practice can be discussed. In addition, this legislation created new enforcement powers for the Financial Regulator, including fining and public censure powers.

Central Bank

4.021 The Central Bank is responsible for monetary policy functions, financial stability, economic analysis, currency and payment systems, investment of foreign and domestic assets and the provision of central services. In relation to monetary policy, the Central Bank became part of the Economic and Monetary Union (EMU) in Europe in 1999. The national central banks of the euro area together with the European Central Bank (ECB) form the 'Eurosystem'. The primary objective of the Eurosystem is to maintain price stability in the euro area. Price stability has been identified by the ECB

---

28   Section 5 of the Principal Act, the Central Bank Act 1942, is substituted by s 4 of the Central Bank and Financial Services Authority of Ireland Act 2003. The Bank is required to have a seal which is to be judicially noticed.

29   From the speech of Patrick Neary of IFSRA on 17 September 2008 to the Institute of Directors.

as the most effective means by which Eurosystem monetary policy can support economic growth in the national economies of the member states.

Functions of the board

4.022 The Board of the Central Bank has a number of legislated functions.[30] It performs the functions of the Bank under ss 6B to 6K[31] of the Central Bank Act 1942 as inserted. These sections generally concern the organisation, staff and administration of the Central Bank and the Financial Regulator. However, s 6G states that the Bank shall continue to keep and operate the fund called the general fund. The Board is directed by the legislation that it shall pay into the general fund all money received by the Bank and shall pay from that fund all amounts that the Bank is required to pay. Surplus income is to be paid as into the Exchequer in such manner as the Minister directs.[32] The Board, on behalf of the Bank, may at any time pending such determination pay into the Exchequer such sums on account of surplus income as may be agreed on by the Minister and the Bank. The Board is empowered to do whatever is necessary for, or in connection with, or reasonably incidental to, the performance of its functions.[33]

Composition of the board

4.023 The Board of Directors of the Bank comprises the following persons:[34]

    (i)   the Governor;

   (ii)   the Director General of the Bank;

  (iii)   the Secretary General of the Department of Finance;

  (iv)   the Chairperson of the Regulatory Authority;

   (v)   the Chief Executive of that Authority; and

  (vi)   seven other directors appointed by the Minister.

Of the other directors, four are to be members of the Regulatory Authority.[35] The Governor is the Chairperson of the Board.

---

30 Section 18D of the Central Bank Act 1942 as inserted by s 13 of the 2003 Act.

31 Sections 6B to 6K of the Central Bank Act 1942 as inserted by s 7 of the 2003 Act.

32 Pursuant to s 6J of the Central Bank Act 1942 as inserted by s 7 of the 2003 Act, profits, income and chargeable gains of the Bank are exempt from corporation tax, income tax and capital gains tax despite any contrary provisions of any enactment providing for corporation tax, income tax or capital gains tax.

33 Section 18D(2) of the Central Bank Act 1942 as inserted by s 13 of the 2003 Act.

34 Section 18B(1) of the Central Bank Act 1942 as inserted by s 13 of the 2003 Act.

35 All told there are six directors who are from the Regulatory Authority. The quorum of the board is seven. Of that at least four must be central bank directors solely as opposed to also being members of the regulatory authority.

Governor of the Central Bank

4.024 The President of Ireland, on the advice of the government, appoints the Governor of the Central Bank[36] who holds office for seven years.[37] Upon appointment, that person is disqualified from being a director of a credit institution, financial institution or insurance undertaking and must relinquish any such directorships within ten days of appointment. It is clear that the Governor once appointed is expected to devote himself exclusively to that job with the diligence and integrity required. Thus the Governor personifies the Central Bank and is invested with significant responsibilities and powers.

4.025 The Governor is responsible for:[38]

    (i)   the holding and managing by the Bank of the foreign reserves of the State;

    (ii)   promoting the efficient and effective operation of payment and settlement systems;[39] and

    (iii) performing such other functions as are imposed by law.

The Governor has sole responsibility for the performance of the functions imposed and the exercise of powers conferred on the Bank by or under the Rome Treaty or the ESCB Statute.[40] Subject to the requirements of the Rome Treaty and the ESCB Statute, he is obliged to inform the Board of the performance of these functions and exercise of these powers. Similar to the Bank, the Governor has power to do whatever is necessary for, or in connection with, or reasonably incidental to, carrying out the Governor's responsibilities.

---

36   Section 19 of the Central Bank Act 1942 as substituted by s 14 of the 2003 Act.

37   By contrast, an ordinary appointed Director holds office as such for a period of five years pursuant to s 24 of the Central Bank Act 1942 as substituted by s 20 of the 2003 Act.

38   Section 19A of the Central Bank Act 1942 as inserted by s 15 of the 2003 Act.

39   This aspect of the Central Bank's job is akin to utility regulation in so far as the payment and settlement system is as ubiquitous now in the transactions of daily personal and public business as to be a utility service.

40   This is the protocol on the Statute of the European System of Central Banks and of the European Central Bank, which established the European System of Central Banks and the European Central Bank as provided for in art 8 of the Treaty Establishing the European Community. The Statute established both the ECB and the European System of Central Banks (ESCB) as from 1 June 1998. See Protocol annexed to the Treaty establishing the European Community (OJ C 191, 29.7.1992, p 68), as amended by the Treaty of Amsterdam (OJ C 340, 10.11.1997, p 1), the Treaty of Nice (OJ C 80, 10.3.2001, p 1), Council Decision 2003/223/EC (OJ L 83, 1.4.2003, p 66) and the Act concerning the conditions of Accession of the Czech Republic, the Republic of Estonia, the Republic of Cyprus, the Republic of Latvia, the Republic of Lithuania, the Republic of Hungary, the Republic of Malta, the Republic of Poland, the Republic of Slovenia and the Slovak Republic and the adjustments to the Treaties on which the European Union is founded (OJ L 236, 23.9.2003, p 33) – unofficial consolidated version.

The Financial Regulator

4.026 The Irish Financial Services Regulatory Authority is a separate but constituent part of the Bank. It is also referred to by its acronym 'IFSRA' as well as the 'Financial Regulatory' and 'Regulatory Authority', for ease of reference it will be referred to as the Financial Regulator in the remainder of this chapter. It discharges many functions of the Central Bank and is subject to control by the board of the Central Bank. For example, where the Board of the Central Bank is considering budgetary, funding or staffing issues relating to the Financial Regulator, there is no quorum unless there are enough members of the Board present to ensure that:

(i)   if there is an even number of members present, at least half of them are not members of the Financial Regulator;[41]

(ii) if there is an uneven number of members present, the majority of them are not members of the Financial Regulator.

4.027 The Financial Regulator comprises a Chairman together with nine members. The divisions include a prudential division dealing with financial institutions and funds authorisation, banking supervision, insurance supervision, investment services providers supervision and markets supervision; a consumer division dealing with consumer protection codes and consumer information; a registrar of credit unions division; and a legal and enforcement division.

4.028 Chapter 1 of the 2003 Act establishes the Financial Regulator. Section 33B sets out the powers and constitution of the Financial Regulator. It provides that the Financial Regulator is a constituent part of the Central Bank. Section 33D provides that either the Governor or the Board of the Central Bank may issue to the Financial Regulator guidelines as to the policies and principles that that Authority is required to implement in performing functions, or exercising powers, of the Central Bank. The Financial Regulator is required to comply with guidelines issued to it. The Guidelines issued by the Governor or the Board under this section shall be in writing and the Governor or the Board shall cause them to be published in Iris Oifigiúil (Official Journal) as soon as practicable after they are issued. Section 33E provides that the Financial Regulator shall comprise no fewer than eight and no more than ten members, of whom one is the Chief Executive, one is the Consumer Director and no fewer than six and no more than eight are persons appointed by the Minister for Finance after consulting the Minister for Enterprise, Trade and Employment.

4.029 A person appointed as Chief Executive holds office for a period not exceeding five years. The other members of the Financial Regulator may appoint a person to hold the office of Chief Executive for a further period, not exceeding five years, to take effect at the end of the first period. The Chief Executive has the power to do whatever

---

41   The Bank board must meet with a majority of Central Bank directors who are not members of the Regulatory Authority.

is necessary for, or in connection with, or reasonably incidental to, carrying out the Chief Executive's responsibilities. In carrying out or exercising the Chief Executive's responsibilities or powers, the Chief Executive is to ensure that the resources of the Financial Regulator allocated for carrying out those responsibilities or exercising those powers are used effectively, efficiently and economically.

4.030 Section 33I provides that the Minister for Finance is to appoint one of the members, other than the Chief Executive or the Consumer Director, to be Chairperson of the Financial Regulator. A member appointed as Chairperson holds office for up to five years. Section 33Q provides that the other members of the Financial Regulator shall appoint a person as the Consumer Director of that Authority. A person appointed as Consumer Director holds office for a period of up to five years, which may be renewed for up to another five years. Section 33X provides that the Financial Regulator is to appoint a person as the Registrar of Credit Unions. A person appointed as Registrar holds office for a period not exceeding five years.

4.031 Currently, the Financial Regulator has a staffing complement of 380 people, according to the 2008 Report on Projected Income and Expenditure published on its website. The funding levy raised €22.3m from industry in 2007, according to its Annual Report. The Financial Regulator aims to maintain the levy at approximately 50 per cent of its budget with the balance of the total annual costs being provided by the Central Bank in accordance with s 33(L) of the Central Bank Act 1942 (as inserted by s 26 of the 2003 Act). In 2007, the Central Bank, with the approval of the Minister for Finance, bore the full cost of certain securities market supervision activities carried out within the Financial Regulator.

The Financial Services Ombudsman

4.032 The Financial Services Ombudsman was established under the Central Bank and Financial Services Authority of Ireland Act 2004[42] (the 2004 Act). The Financial Services Ombudsman is a statutory officer who deals independently with unresolved complaints from consumers about their individual dealings with all financial service providers. It is a free service to the complainant.

Central Bank Functions and Objectives

4.033 The Bank has a number of legislated functions that included the functions and powers conferred on the Bank by or under the Rome Treaty or the ESCB Statute.[43] In discharging its functions and exercising its powers as part of the European System of

---

42   Section 16 and schedules 6 and 7.

43   Section 6 of the Central Bank Act 1942 as substituted by s 6 of the 2003 Act.

Central Banks, the primary objective of the Bank is to maintain price stability.[44] In particular, the Bank has the following functions:[45]

(a) to carry out the efficient and effective co-ordination of:

    (i) the activities of the constituent parts of the Bank, and

    (ii) activities undertaken by any of those parts with persons who provide services to, or receive services from, the Bank, and

    (iii) the exchange of information among those parts and between any of those parts and any of those persons;

(b) to promote the development within the State of the financial services industry (but in such a way as not to affect the objective of the Bank in contributing to the stability of the State's financial system);[46]

(c) where appropriate, to represent and co-ordinate the representation of the Bank on international financial bodies and at international meetings relating to financial or economic matters;

(d) to establish and maintain, either directly or indirectly, contact with the monetary authorities established in other countries and in territories;

(e) whenever it thinks fit, to provide to governments of, and financial institutions and other bodies established in, other countries and in territories advice or other assistance on matters within its expertise and, when appropriate, to co-ordinate application of the resources of its constituent parts for that purpose;

(f) to provide banking services to its constituent parts;

(g) to provide for the collection and study of data that deal with monetary and credit problems and to publish information about that data;

(h) to provide advice and assistance to the Central Statistics Office about the collection, compilation, analysis and interpretation of statistics relating to the balance of payments, national accounts and other financial statistics and, where appropriate, to collect data for that purpose;

(i) to perform such other functions as are imposed on it by or under this and any other Act or law.

4.034 The Bank has power to do whatever is necessary for, or in connection with, or reasonably incidental to, the performance of its functions. In particular, the powers of the Bank are deemed to include powers of a kind that, in accordance with normal banking practice, may be exercised by a bank. The Bank is required to perform its functions and exercise its powers in a manner consistent with the Rome Treaty and the ESCB Statute. Interestingly, the Bank can perform its functions and exercise its powers

---

44   Section 6A(6) of the Central Bank Act 1942 as inserted by s 7 of the 2003 Act: 'Without prejudice to the objective of maintaining price stability, the Bank is required to support the general economic policies of the European Union with a view to contributing to the achievement of the objectives of that Union as laid down in art 2 of the Rome Treaty' [common market, economic and monetary union etc.].

45   Section 5A(1) of the Central Bank Act 1942 as substituted by s 5 of the 2003 Act.

46   The Governor has a personal role in achieving this function.

both within the State and elsewhere. The powers of the Bank include the power to do all or any of the following:[47]

    (a) subject to paragraph (b), acquire, hold, dispose of or otherwise deal in all kinds of property (including real property, securities, coins, gold or silver bullion and other precious metals, and any kinds of currency or currency units);

    (b) acquire, hold or dispose of shares in a bank or other institution formed wholly or mainly by banks that are the principal currency authority in their respective countries, but only with the approval of the Minister;

    (c) enter into, carry out, assign or accept the assignment of, vary or rescind, any contract, agreement or other obligation;

    (d) provide loans and other kinds of financial accommodation to credit institutions and other persons on the security of such assets and on such terms and conditions as the Board considers appropriate;

    (e) give guarantees and make payments under them;

    (f) receive funds on deposit;

    (g) open accounts in other countries or act as agent, depository, or correspondent of any credit institution carrying on business in or outside the State;

    (h) re-discount exchequer notes or bills, local authority bills, bills of exchange and promissory notes on such terms and conditions as the Board considers appropriate;

    (i) keep registers of securities generally;

    (j) operate or participate in a depository of securities or other instruments;

    (k) keep the accounts for the clearing and settlement of securities or payment instruments;

    (l) become a member of, or a party to, the establishment or operation of one or more payment systems;

    (m) operate or participate in a system that provides a settlement service for transactions in securities or other instruments for its members;

    (n) enter into agreements with depositories of securities or of other instruments, and carry out transactions under the terms of those agreements so far as necessary for the settlement of transactions between members of those depositories and the members of any depository operated by the Bank;

    (o) transfer assets, income or liabilities to the European Central Bank where required under the ESCB Statute.

4.035 As a member of the Eurosystem, the Central Bank's main responsibilities include:[48]

    (i) *Contributing to the maintenance of price stability (low inflation) and a stable financial system.*

    The Central Bank seeks to achieve this through co-operation with the ECB and other national central banks in producing economic forecasts for use in determining monetary policy and by implementing Eurosystem monetary policy and exchange rate policy decisions efficiently. It works in close co-operation with the Financial Regulator to ensure that financial stability is maintained in Ireland.

---

47   Section 5B of the Central Bank Act 1942 as substituted.

48   Information taken from http://www.centralbank.ie, accessed on 10 December 2008.

(ii) *Ensuring safe and reliable payment and settlement systems, to enable firms and individuals to make payments to each other.*

Euro zone monetary policy operations are implemented through the inter-central-bank system known as TARGET. It includes the national real-time gross settlement systems of the EU countries and the ECB. Nearly every EU credit institution is linked to TARGET and although the system was primarily developed to meet the needs of the single monetary policy, it can also be used for transmitting both interbank and customer payments. One may say that this pan-European banking payment and settlement system echoes the energy, aviation and telecommunications sectors in that it is an essential network facility, access to which is required by regulated entities to carry on business. Access is limited to licence holders.

(iii) *Producing and distributing euro banknotes and coins and ensuring the security and integrity of the euro currency.*

The ECB has the sole right to issue euro banknotes and approves the volume of euro coins to be issued in euro area countries. As the Irish member of the 'Eurosystem', the Central Bank issues euro banknotes and coins in Ireland and is responsible for ensuring the quality and authenticity of euro banknotes.

(iv) *Managing foreign exchange assets, on behalf of the European Central Bank.*

Upon the creation of the European Monetary Union, the euro area national central banks transferred a part of their foreign reserves to the ECB. In the case of Ireland this amounted to €451m. These reserves continue to be managed by the Central Bank on behalf of the ECB, in accordance with the investment policy of the ECB.

4.036 In carrying out the above functions, the Bank has the following objectives:[49]

(a) contributing to the stability of the financial system;

(b) promoting the efficient and effective operation of payment and settlement systems; and

(c) discharging such other functions and powers as are conferred or imposed on it by the Rome Treaty, the ESCB Statute or any enactment.[50]

Financial Regulator Functions and Objectives

4.037 The Financial Regulator has the following statutory functions:[51]

(a) to perform the functions the Bank has under or in respect of the enactments and statutory instruments specified in Schedule 2;

---

49   Section 6A(2) as inserted.

50   By virtue of s 6A(3) the Minister may, from time to time, request the Governor, the Board or the Financial Regulator to consult with the Minister, in relation to their respective functions, as regards the performance by the Bank of any function of the Bank, or request the Governor to report on the pursuit of the primary objective of the Bank.

51   Section 33C of the Central Bank Act 1942 as inserted.

(b) in respect of functions of the Bank under sections 18 and 23 of the Central Bank Act 1971[52] —

    (i) in so far as relates to the performance of functions imposed on the Financial Regulator by this section, to perform those functions of the Bank, and

    (ii) in any other case and by agreement with the Governor, to contribute to the performance of those functions of the Bank;

(c) whenever requested to do so, to provide the Governor and the Board with advice, information and assistance with respect to the performance of their respective functions under the Central Bank Acts;

(d) to perform such other functions as are expressly imposed on it by this or under any other Act or law.

In performing its functions and exercising its powers, the Financial Regulator is required to promote the best interests of users of financial services in a way that is consistent with the orderly and proper functioning of financial markets, and the orderly and prudent supervision of providers of those services.

The Financial Regulator must also take such action as it considers appropriate to increase awareness among members of the public of available financial services and the cost to consumers, and risks and benefits associated with the provision of those services.

4.038 As with the Central Bank, the Financial Regulator has power to do whatever is necessary for, or in connection with, or reasonably incidental to, the performance of its functions. It is required to perform these functions and exercise its powers in a way that is consistent with the Rome Treaty and the ESCB Statute. In addition, in performing its functions and exercising its powers, the Financial Regulator has a duty to act in a way that is consistent with the performance by the Governor and the Board of their respective functions in relation to the Bank. Accordingly, the Financial Regulator has to report to the Governor on its activities.[53]

4.039 Importantly, if any matter relating to the financial stability of the State's financial system arises in connection with the performance or exercise by the Financial Regulator of its functions or powers, the Financial Regulator shall consult the Governor on that matter.[54] Where the Financial Regulator considers it prudent in the circumstances, it may send a report to the Minister on any matter to which this subsection relates. The Financial Regulator may otherwise act on that matter only with the agreement of the Governor. Such matters include (but are not limited to) the issue, revocation and suspension of a licence or other authority.

---

52 Section 18 concerns furnishing of information to the Bank; s 19 involves publication of business statements by holders of licences; s 20 requires displaying of financial statements by holders of licences; s 21 provides for directions by Bank to holders of licences; s 22 provides for directions by Bank in relation to advertisements of holders of licences; and s 23 provides for the regulation of ratios between assets and liabilities of holders of licences.

53 Section 33C(8) as inserted.

54 This provision, s 33C(9) of the Central Bank Act 1942 as inserted, provides a formal link between IFSRA and Central Bank, particularly in relation to licensing.

4.040 The Financial Regulator can also perform its functions and exercise its powers both within the State and elsewhere. In performing its functions and exercising its powers, the objectives of the Financial Regulator are set out in s 33P of the Central Bank Act 1942. These are as follows:

(1) The Financial Regulator shall, at least 3 months before the beginning of each financial year—

(a) prepare for the year a strategic plan that complies with this section, and

(b) submit the plan to the Minister.

(2) A strategic plan must specify—

(a) the objectives of the Financial Regulator's activities for the financial year concerned, and

(b) the nature and scope of the activities to be undertaken, and

(c) the strategies and policies for achieving those objectives, and

(d) targets and criteria for assessing the performance of the Authority, and

(e) the uses for which it is proposed to apply the Authority's resources.

(3) If the Minister has in writing notified the Financial Regulator of any requirements with respect to the form in which its strategic plan is to be prepared, the plan must comply with those requirements.

(4) As soon as practicable after receiving the Financial Regulator's strategic plan, the Minister shall arrange for the plan to be laid before both Houses of the Oireachtas.

(5) As soon as practicable after becoming aware that subsection (4) has been complied with, the Financial Regulator shall publish its strategic plan and take all reasonably practical steps to implement it.

Financial Services Ombudsman

4.041 Section 57BK of the Central Bank and Financial Services Authority of Ireland Act 2004 sets out the functions of the Financial Services Ombudsman, which are as follows:

(1) The principal function of the Financial Services Ombudsman is to deal with complaints made under this Part by mediation and, where necessary, by investigation and adjudication

(2) Subject to this Part, the Financial Services Ombudsman has such powers as are necessary to enable that Ombudsman to perform the principal function referred to in subsection (1).

(3) The Financial Services Ombudsman may authorise any Deputy Financial Services Ombudsman or any other Bureau staff member, by name, office or appointment, to perform any of the functions, or exercise any of the powers, imposed or conferred on the Financial Services Ombudsman by this or any other Act.

(4) The Financial Services Ombudsman is entitled to perform the functions imposed, and exercise the powers conferred, by this Act free from interference by any other person and, when dealing with a particular complaint, is required to act in an informal manner and according to equity, good conscience and the substantial merits of the complaint without regard to technicality or legal form.

LEVIES AND FEES

4.042 The government gave the power to the Chief Executive of the Financial Regulator, pursuant to s 33J of the 2003 Act, to raise a levy directly from the firms it regulates. Section 33J(1) provides that the purpose of this section is 'to enable the Regulatory Authority to have sufficient funds to enable it to perform its functions and exercise its powers.' Subsection (2) provides that the 'Chief Executive, with the agreement of the other members of the Regulatory Authority, may make regulations prescribing levies to be paid by persons who are subject to regulation under the designated enactments and designated statutory instruments.'

4.043 The total levy payable is used to fund approximately 50 per cent of the cost of the Financial Regulator's budget. The other 50 per cent is paid by the Central Bank of Ireland. The regulations detailing the levy amounts payable for 2007 were made on 19 June 2007.[55] The 2007 levy calculations were based on an allocation of the Financial Regulator's 2007 budget, the methodology of which was subjected to an independent review by Deloitte. Overall, according to the Financial Regulator's website, there was a high level of compliance with the Regulations in 2007, with the majority of regulated financial service providers paying the levy on a timely basis. Total expenditure for the year ended 31 December 2007, which comprised direct and indirect costs, amounted to €49.3m. This compares with a budgeted figure for the year of €51.6 million.

4.044 The Central Bank Act 1942 (Sections 33J and 33K) Regulations 2008 became law in July 2008.[56] All financial service providers are liable to pay an annual levy. The levy must be paid no later than 28 days from the date on the levy notice. If a financial services provider fails to pay the levy by the required date, the Financial Regulator may take steps to recover the amount of the levy. Recovery action may include court proceedings. The Financial Regulator is expected to receive €55.7m for 2008 in terms of funding from industry levies, as per its Statement of Estimated Income and Expenditure projected for the year end 31 December 2008 published on its website.[57]

All regulated entities that held an authorisation as at 31 December 2007 are required to pay their contribution of the 2008 levy. All Collective Investment Schemes that were authorised as at 31 March 2008 are required to pay the 2008 levy.

4.045 The Financial Regulator sends almost all financial service providers a levy notice after the regulations are made. However, if a regulated entity does not receive a levy notice, it is still legally obliged to pay the levy calculated in accordance with the appropriate industry category in the regulations. Annual fees which were payable by insurance companies, credit unions, mortgage intermediaries and moneylenders have been abolished and replaced with the levy requirement.

4.046 The method of calculation of the levy varies depending on the industry classification of a financial services provider. There are 12 categories (A–L) contained

---

55 Central Bank Act 1942 (Sections 33J and 33K) Regulations 2007 SI 294/2007.

56 SI 297/2008.

57 http://www.ifsra.gov.ie, accessed on 10 December 2008.

in the Sch to the Regulations. A financial service provider may fall into more than one industry category. In such cases, the financial services provider must pay the levy for each category. For example, a credit union (Category F) may also hold a multi-agency intermediary authorisation (Category C) and is therefore obliged to pay the levy for both categories. The levy that a financial services provider must pay for each category will depend on the basis of calculation for that industry category. The basis of calculation for intermediaries (Category C) is based upon self-declared annual income. The levy for life insurance undertakings (Category B) is based upon the amount of gross global premium income reported in the undertaking's annual return (prudential levy) together with the total of gross premium income written on Irish risk business (consumer levy).

4.047 A financial service provider may appeal the levy amount to the Chief Executive but must do so within the timeframe and in the manner set out in the Regulations. A financial services provider may only dispute the amount of assessment; it cannot dispute an amount correctly calculated from the Sch to the Regulations. In order to appeal, a financial services provider must dispute the calculation of the levy because of either an incorrect figure, or because of the use of an incorrect category or categories. It must include with the grounds for appeal any supporting documentation and pay the undisputed balance of the levy. After an appeal is considered and the financial services provider is notified of the decision, the financial services provider must pay the balance of the levy owing (if any) within ten days.

4.048 Section 33K provides for fees and sets out that the 'Chief Executive may, with the agreement of the other members of the Financial Regulator, make regs prescribing fees for the purpose of any enactment that provides for the payment of a fee by reference to this section.' The Prospectus Regulations provide that fees shall be payable pursuant to s 33K of the Central Bank Act 1942 in respect of the performance by the Financial Regulator of its functions under the Prospectus Regulations. The Financial Regulator has published regulations drawn up in accordance with s 33K of the Central Bank Act 1942 setting out details of the fees payable by persons seeking approval of documents under the Prospectus Regulations and providing for the collection and recovery of these fees.

THE REGULATED ACTIVITY AND THE REGULATED ENTITIES

4.049 The Financial Regulator regulates all entities active in the financial services sector. The matters within the Financial Regulator's remit include the following activities (discussed in paras **4.050–4.153** below).

Banking and Credit Institution Supervision

4.050 Achieving an integrated market for banks and financial conglomerates is a core component of the European free movement of services and freedom of establishment policy in the area of financial services.

The European Commission's policies in the field of regulation of banks and financial conglomerates are contained in the financial services action plan. These policies are based on the principles of mutual recognition and the 'single passport', a system which allows financial services operators legally established in one Member State to establish themselves or provide their services in the other Member States without further authorisation requirements.

4.051 Regulated and safe financial institutions are required for mutual recognition and the single passport. Since they are necessary for financial stability in the EU, they required the establishment of a common framework ensuring prudential oversight and consumer protection across the European internal market.

A package of legislation had to be implemented by the various member states in this regard. As of 14 September 2008, Ireland had implemented all the Directives which formed part of this package except for the Third Money Laundering Directive. The Financial Services Action Plan, launched in 1999, was largely completed by 2004.

4.052 Given the increasingly global aspects of financial services, there are a number of international fora – outside the EU – that also shape regulation in this field, notably the G-10 Basel Committee on Banking Supervision, the Banking Supervision Committee of the European Central Bank and the Joint Forum on Financial Conglomerates.

4.053 The Basel Accords refer to the banking supervision Accords (recommendations on banking laws and regulations) of Basel I and Basel II issued by the Basel Committee on Banking Supervision. The Basel Committee maintains its secretariat at the Bank of International Settlements in Basel, Switzerland. The Basel Committee consists of representatives from central banks and regulatory authorities of the Group of Ten (G-10) countries, plus others (specifically Luxembourg and Spain). The committee does not have the authority to enforce recommendations, although most member countries (and others) tend to implement the Committee's policies. This means that recommendations are enforced through national (or EU-wide) laws and regulations, rather than as a result of the committee's recommendations – thus some time may pass between recommendations and implementation as law at the national level.

4.054 Basel I is the round of deliberations by central bankers from around the world and, in 1988, the Basel Committee published a set of minimal capital requirements for banks. This is also known as the 1988 Basel Accord, and was enforced by law in the G-10 countries in 1992, with Japanese banks permitted an extended transition period.

4.055 Basel II is the second of the Basel Accords. The purpose of Basel II, which was initially published in June 2004, is to create an international standard that banking Regulators can use when creating regulations about how much capital banks need to put aside to guard against the types of financial and operational risks they face. Basel II sought to have an international standard to help protect the international financial system from the types of problems that might arise should a major bank or a series of banks collapse. It sought to set up rigorous risk and capital management requirements designed to ensure that a bank holds capital reserves appropriate to the risk the bank exposes itself to through its lending and investment practices. Generally speaking, these rules mean that the greater risk to which the bank is exposed, the greater the amount of capital the bank needs to hold to safeguard its solvency and overall economic stability.

Register

4.056 The Financial Regulator keeps a register of all the firms that it regulates, which is approximately 13,000 firms.

The Financial Regulator keeps the following registers:

(i) Register of Life and Non Life Insurance Companies;

(ii) Register of Authorised Reinsurance Undertakings and Special Purpose Reinsurance Vehicles (RI SPRV);

(iii) Register of Credit Unions;

(iv) Register of Investment Firms (MiFID);

(v) Register of Investment Product Intermediaries (Section 31 Register);

(vi) Register of Investment Business Firms authorised under s 10 of the Investment Intermediaries Act (Section 10 Register);

(vii) Register of Mortgage Intermediaries;

(viii) Register of Moneylenders; and

(ix) It also keeps a register of designated credit institutions.

Under the Asset Covered Securities Act 2001, the Financial Regulator is required to issue a number of regulations and regulatory notices. The purpose of the Act is to establish a legal framework for the issue of credit-enhanced, asset-backed bonds by Irish credit institutions. The main features of the Asset Covered Securities Act is that only authorised Irish credit institutions can apply to the Financial Regulator for designation. An authorised Irish credit institution may then request to be registered by the Financial Regulator as a designated credit institution (DCI) under the Act. Upon registration, a DCI may engage in the activities permitted under the Act, ie issue asset backed securities. Only credit institutions designated by the Financial Regulator can issue securities under the Act. The Financial Regulator is responsible for the supervision of DCIs. A DCI must ensure that at least 90 per cent of its business is in the provision of mortgage or public sector credit. The securities issued are secured on a pool of assets. Unlike conventional securitisations, the pool of assets remains on the balance sheet of the issuing DCI, although the assets are ring-fenced. The Act sets out certain criteria regarding composition of the cover assets pool.

4.057 The Act also sets out certain criteria regarding management of the cover assets pool in terms of duration, interest-rate matching and currency. DCIs are required to appoint a cover asset monitor (CAM) and this appointment must be approved by the Financial Regulator. The CAM is an independent party whose main duty is the protection of the bondholders' interest by monitoring the asset pools in order to ensure compliance with the provisions of the Act, eg a DCI cannot enter or remove an asset from the pool without the prior approval of the CAM.

Authorisation and prudential supervision

4.058 Banking supervision relates to the prudential supervision of banks and building societies (together referred to as 'credit institutions'). The objectives of such supervision are to:

   (i)   foster a stable banking system; and

   (ii)   provide a degree of protection to depositors with individual credit institutions.

Banking supervision encompasses the authorisation of banks and building societies, their prudential supervision and the development of supervisory guidance and requirements for their operation. Prudential supervision involves monitoring the business of banks and building societies and how they are controlled, and checking compliance with statutory and non-statutory requirements. The Financial Regulator is responsible for the authorisation and prudential supervision of all credit institutions in the State, as well as the Irish branches of banks located outside the European Economic Area (EEA).

4.059 Section 7 of the Central Bank Act 1971, as amended, (the 'Act') provides that:

> Subject to the provisions of this Act, a person, other than a Bank, shall not, in or outside the State, carry on banking business or hold himself out or represent himself as a banker or as carrying on banking business or on behalf of any other person accept deposits or other repayable funds from the public, unless he is the holder of a licence.

Article 6 of Directive 2006/48/EC of the European Parliament and of the Council of 14 June 2006 relating to the taking up and pursuit of the business of credit institutions requires that 'Member States shall require credit institutions to obtain authorisation before commencing their activities'. The Financial Regulator is the competent authority in Ireland for the issuing of such authorisations or licences. Its fundamental approach to supervision (including authorisation or licensing) is that it is principles led. Responsibility for the proper management and control of a credit institution, and the integrity of its systems, rests with the board of directors and its senior management. Ethical behaviour and transparency in business dealings are key values expected of boards and senior management. Applicants should contact the Financial Regulator (Financial Institutions and Funds Authorisation Department) in order to arrange a preliminary meeting. The Financial Regulator sets out the Licensing and Supervision Requirements and Standards for Credit Institutions ('the Requirements') on its website – www.ifsra.ie.

4.060 The authorisation function is a key element in meeting the objectives of banking supervision. Criteria for the authorisation of banks and building societies are set out in legislation, as augmented by conditions and standards set out in the Requirements. In considering applications for authorisation,[58] the Financial Regulator considers ownership, management competence, corporate structure and controls, business plans and financial backing.

---

58   Section 7 of the Central Bank Act 1971 and art 6 of Directive 2006/48/EC.

It is illegal to take deposits in Ireland without being authorised to do so by the Financial Regulator or by another EEA competent authority.

4.061 In accordance with EU legislation, EEA credit institutions are entitled to establish in Ireland on a branch basis or to provide services on a cross-border basis (ie without having a physical presence in Ireland). 'Passporting' of services in this way is subject to a notification procedure through the home country Regulator to the Financial Regulator. The home country Regulator is largely responsible for the prudential supervision of these institutions.

4.062 Ongoing prudential supervision involves monitoring the business of banks and building societies and how it is planned, managed and controlled, and checking compliance with statutory and non-statutory requirements. This process is interactive in nature and entails frequent dialogue with the banks and building societies, as well as the submission of extensive financial data by the supervised entities. As such, the process involves both qualitative and quantitative activities, including:

(i)   analysis of regularly collected financial data;

(ii)   regular meetings with management;

(iii)   review of internal audit, risk management and compliance reports;

(iv)   on-site visits;

(v)   meetings with other supervisors; and

(vi)   meetings with external auditors.

4.063 In the case of Irish branches of EEA banks and building societies, responsibility for the supervision of liquidity is shared between the Financial Regulator and the home country Regulator. The Financial Regulator is also responsible for ensuring that EEA branches are in compliance with Irish anti-money laundering procedures. Statistics are collected from the Irish branches of EEA credit institutions on a monthly basis and the Financial Regulator holds review meetings with branch management.

Capital Requirements Directives

4.064 The Capital Requirements Directives were in preparation for almost the entire timeframe of the Financial Services Action Plan, from 1999 to 2004, and are intended to better align financial institutions' capital with the risks that they face. Their drafting tied in closely with the work of the Basel Committee on a capital adequacy framework, commonly known as Basel II. The Basel II requirements apply on a global level so it was necessary to ensure that EU legislation, while being fully compatible with the Basel II requirements, would also reflect the specific features of the European context. The Capital Requirements Directives were adopted in June 2006.

These Directives cover credit institutions listed under the Central Bank Act 1971, investment firms authorised under the Investment Intermediaries Act 1995 and stockbrokers authorised under the Stock Exchange Act 1991. The Capital Requirements Directives are transposed into Irish law via the European Communities (Capital Adequacy of Investment Firms) Regulations 2006 (SI 660/2006) and European Communities (Capital Adequacy of Credit Institutions) Regulations 2006

(SI 661/2006). The Statutory Instruments together with a notice published by the Financial Regulator form the framework for the Capital Requirements Directives (CRDs) in Ireland.

Supervisory disclosure is utilised to ensure transparency. Its aim is to make information related to prudential supervision available in a timely manner to all interested parties, including credit institutions, investment firms, other market participants, other supervisors and consumers. The framework for supervisory disclosure aims to provide information without seeking to interpret or validate disclosures. The role of disclosure is specifically set forth in the CRDs which comprise Directive 2006/48/EC relating to the taking up and pursuit of the business of credit institutions and Directive 2006/49/EC on the capital adequacy of investment firms and credit institutions. In accordance with art 144 of Directive 2006/48/EC, the Financial Regulator displays and provides access to information regarding the laws, regulations, administrative rules and general guidance adopted by Ireland in the field of prudential regulation and supervision. The Financial Regulator also displays aggregate statistical data on key aspects of the implementation of the prudential framework in Ireland. The supervisory practice to be disclosed includes the way in which Ireland exercises the options and national discretions available in EU banking legislation and the general criteria and methodologies used by the Financial Regulator in the Supervisory Review and Evaluation Process (SREP).

It is also possible to access the Supervisory Disclosure pages of each national authority through the Committee of European Banking Supervisors (CEBS) Member States' Supervisory Disclosures. The Financial Regulator's approach to the implementation of the CRDs in Ireland is guided by a set of implementation principles which are available on its website.

Deposit protection

4.065 The European Communities (Deposit Guarantee Schemes) Regulations 1995 implemented the European Union Council Directive on Deposit Guarantee Schemes (Directive 1994/19/EC) and were amended by the Central Bank Act 1997, the European Communities (Deposit Guarantee Schemes) Regulations 1999, the European Communities (Deposit Guarantee Schemes) Regulations 2002 and the European Communities (Deposit Guarantee Schemes) Regulations 2003. The maximum amount payable to any depositor until September 2008 was 90 per cent of the aggregate deposits held by that depositor, subject to a maximum compensation payment of €20,000. The Scheme was initially extended in September 2008 to protect 100 per cent of deposits up to €100,000. The guaranteed level was also then extended to credit union savers.

The Irish deposit protection scheme is funded by credit institutions, which are authorised by the Central Bank. The system is also administered by the Central Bank. Deposits with credit institutions authorised in another EEA country and operating in Ireland on a branch basis are covered under that country's system. In this way, levels of protection vary from Member State to Member State.

4.066 The level of contribution required from each credit institution is 0.2 per cent of deposits held at all branches of the credit institution in the EEA, including deposits on current accounts and share accounts with a building society, but excluding interbank deposits and deposits represented by negotiable certificates of deposit. Each contribution is maintained in a Deposit Protection Account at the Central Bank. Deposits eligible for cover under the deposit protection scheme are deposits denominated in any currency held at EEA branches of credit institutions authorised in Ireland. Certain deposits are not eligible for cover, such as: interbank deposits; deposits by the governments or municipal, local, regional or provincial authorities of any State; deposits by a person who had responsibility for or who profited from the failure of the credit institution; deposits by the directors, secretary, chief executive or their close families; deposits by financial institutions; deposits by pension funds and deposits by large companies.

4.067 Under the Regulations, the compensation payment process is initiated by:

(i)   the Central Bank determining that a credit institution is unable to repay deposits due to its financial condition; or

(ii) a court making a ruling, for reasons directly related to a credit institution's financial circumstances, that suspends depositors' ability to make claims against that institution.

The Central Bank (or liquidator, where one has been appointed) is expected to pay compensation to depositors within three months of a determination that deposits are unavailable, or of a ruling by the court (subject to the terms and conditions set out in the regulations).

All balances held in the depositor's name (including balances held in a joint account), together with any interest due, will be aggregated for the purpose of calculating the funds owed to the depositor by the institution. Joint account balances will be apportioned equally between each account holder for this purpose and aggregated with any other balances held by that account holder.

In normal circumstances, debts owed to the institution by the depositor will be deducted from the aggregate deposit balance in calculating the compensation payment to be made to the depositor.

4.068 From October 2008, under the Credit Institutions (Financial Support) Act 2008 (the 2008 Act) together with the Credit Institutions (Financial Support) Scheme 2008, guarantees under the deposit guarantee scheme are now of an unlimited amount. The Scheme guarantees those institutions eligible on the basis that they are 'systemically important credit institutions', which the Minister may specify by order under s 6 of the 2008 Act. Under the Scheme, the Minister stands as guarantor of the covered liabilities which include all retail and corporate deposits, interbank deposits, senior unsecured debt, asset-covered securities and dated subordinated debt. It excludes intragroup borrowing and any debt owed to the ECB. To partake in the scheme involves signing up to a guarantee acceptance deed, which involves quarterly charges. The covered institution will also, at the direction of the Minister, appoint at least one, but no more than two, non-executive directors to its board from a panel approved by the Minister during the period of guarantee. It applies from 30 September 2008 to 29 September 2010.[59]

Securities Market Regulation – 'Lamfalussy Directives'

4.069 The Lamfalussy Directives – adopted on the basis of the so-called 'Lamfalussy approach' – fall into two categories: 'level 1 Directives', which set out framework principles, and 'level 2 Directives', which set out the implementing measures that allow these principles to be put into practice. They are based on the final report from the Committee of Wise Men on the Regulation of European Securities Markets, which was chaired by Alexandre Lamfalussy in 2001. The Lamfalussy Committee called for a four-level approach to European regulation to allow the EU to respond to developments in financial markets. Level 1 consists of legislative acts, namely Directives or regulations. In adopting each directive or regulation, the Council and the Parliament will agree, on the basis of a Commission proposal, on the nature and extent of detailed technical implementing measures to be decided at Level 2. At Level 2, the European Securities Committee, the future regulatory committee, will assist the Commission in adopting the relevant implementing measures. Such measures will be used to ensure that technical provisions can be kept up to date with market developments. Level 3 measures will have the objective of improving the common and uniform implementation of Level 1 and 2 acts in the member states. The Committee of European Securities Regulators will have particular responsibility for this. At Level 4, the Commission will strengthen the enforcement of Community law.

4.070 There are four 'level 1 Directives':

    (i)   Directive on Markets in Financial Instruments;

    (ii)   Market Abuse Directive;

    (iii) Prospectus Directive; and

    (iv) Transparency Directive.

4.071 All four pieces of legislation form an essential part of the Commission's Financial Services Action Plan:

    (i)   The Directive on Markets in Financial Instruments, creates an effective 'single passport', which allows investment firms to operate across the EU whilst ensuring a high level of protection for investors;

    (ii)   The Market Abuse Directive aims to prevent insider dealing and market manipulation. This is essential, if investor confidence is to be maintained;

    (iii) The Prospectus Directive, provides issuers (including small and medium sized enterprises (SMEs)) with a single passport which allows them to raise

---

59   The European Commission issued a decision not to raise objections on the grounds of State aid rules on 13 October 2008 as a result of the scheme being revised to make it non-discriminatory and limited in duration to two years.

investment capital on a pan-European basis. This allows them to in effect 'shop around' seeking out the cheapest capital available;

(iv) The Transparency Directive is also important for investor confidence. It sets out uniform rules for the disclosure of accurate, comprehensive and timely information by issuers throughout the EU.[60]

The Irish Financial Services Regulatory Authority (Financial Regulator) has been appointed the competent authority for the purpose of these Directives. The Markets Supervision Department is responsible, within the Financial Regulator, for carrying out the competent authority obligations provided for in these regulations.

CESR

4.072 CESR is an independent Committee of European Securities Regulators. The role of CESR includes improving co-ordination among security Regulators and working to ensure more consistent and timely day-to-day implementation of community legislation in member states. The Financial Regulator is a member of CESR.

Market in Financial Instruments Directive

4.073 The Markets in Financial Instruments Directive (MiFID) and its implementing measures together establish a comprehensive legislative framework at European level relating to the establishment and conduct of investment firms, multilateral trading facilities and regulated markets. On 1 November 2007, MiFID entered into force. The aim of this Directive is to create a robust, common regulatory framework for Europe's securities markets. MiFID seeks to increase competition among exchanges, multilateral trading facilities (MTFs) and investment firms, giving them a 'single passport' to operate throughout the EU on the basis of authorisation in their home Member State. This is to ensure high levels of investor protection.

The 'passport' enables authorised investment firms, banks and exchanges to provide their services freely across borders by harmonising national rules for investment services and the operation of exchanges. It benefits investors, issuers and market participants by promoting efficient and competitive markets by allowing banks and other investment institutions to compete fairly with stock exchanges as trading venues in their own right.

4.074 MiFID is the successor of the old Investment Services Directive passport. The body vested with the monitoring of firms covered by MiFID is CESR. It is transposed into Irish law by way of SI 773/2007, SI 663/2007, SI 60/2007 and the Market in Financial Instruments and Miscellaneous Provision Act 2007.

---

60 European Commission DG Internal Market – securities – transposition of Lamfalussy Directives 9 January 2008 - www.ec.europa.eu/internal_market/securities/transp_sition/index_en.htm.

Prospectus (Directive 2003/71/EC) Regulations 2005

4.075 The Prospectus (Directive 2003/71/EC) Regulations 2005 (SI 324/2005) (the Prospectus Regulations) transposed Directive 2003/71/EC of the European Parliament and of the Council of 4 November 2003 on the prospectus to be published when securities are offered to the public or admitted to trading and amending Directive 2001/34/EC. The aim of this Directive is to ensure investor protection and market efficiency, in accordance with high regulatory standards. The Prospectus Regulations made by the Minister for Enterprise, Trade and Employment came into operation on 1 July 2005. The Financial Regulator has been appointed the competent authority for the purpose of the Prospectus Regulations.

Prospectus Regulations

4.076 In summary, the Prospectus Regulations require, *inter alia*, persons who make an offer of securities to the public or seek admission of securities to trading on an EEA regulated market, such as that operated by the Irish Stock Exchange, to publish a prospectus which is subject to prior approval by the Financial Regulator. The Prospectus Regulations specify certain exemptions from this provision. A person who has had a prospectus approved by the competent authority of their home Member State may, subject to notification procedures, offer securities to the public or seek admission of securities to trading on a regulated market in the other Member States of the EEA, without having the prospectus approved by the competent authorities of the host Member State. Ireland is, subject to certain exemptions, the home Member State for Irish registered companies or persons from a non-EEA Member State who opt for Ireland as their home Member State. The Prospectus Regulations also impose annual reporting obligations on issuers.

4.077 The Financial Regulator has delegated certain tasks relating to the scrutiny of prospectuses to the Irish Stock Exchange. However, approval of a prospectus rests with the Financial Regulator. In this regard, applicants:

   (i)   seeking admission of securities to trading on an EEA regulated market, including the Irish Stock Exchange; or

   (ii) making an offer of securities to the public within the EEA, though not seeking admission to trading on an EEA regulated market;

should submit the draft prospectus to the Irish Stock Exchange in accordance with the Prospectus Rules. The Prospectus Regulations also provide for a system for the investigation of potential prescribed contraventions of the Prospectus Regulations, in addition to enforcement action, including administrative sanctions that can be imposed by the Financial Regulator. Prospectuses approved by the Financial Regulator are available on the Approved Prospectuses page of its website. All currently valid prospectuses approved by the competent authority of another EEA Member State and passported into Ireland are available on the Passport Notifications section of the Financial Regulator's website.

Prospectus rules

4.078 The Financial Regulator has published amended Prospectus Rules (the Prospectus Rules) under s 51 of the Investment Funds, Companies and Miscellaneous Provisions Act 2005. The Prospectus Rules, published in March 2006, have been amended to address issues raised by the respondents to a consultation and also to reflect changes arising from the Financial Regulator's experience as competent authority since March 2006. These Prospectus Rules came into force on 15 September 2008.

Passport notifications

4.079 The Financial Regulator receives passport notifications when valid prospectuses approved by the competent authority of another EEA Member State are passported into Ireland for the purposes of an offer of securities to the public or the admission of securities to trading on a regulated market in the State in accordance with the provisions of the Prospectus Directive 2003/71/EC and implementing regulations from 2005.

Market Abuse (Directive 2003/6/EC) Regulations 2005

4.080 The Market Abuse Regulations (SI 342/2005) transposed Directive 2003/6/EC of the European Parliament and of the Council of 28 January 2003 on insider dealing and market manipulation (market abuse) and its implementing Directives, 2003/124/EC and 2003/125/EC both of 22 December 2003, and 2004/72/EC of 29 April 2004. The objective of the Market Abuse Directive, its Implementing Directives and Implementing Regulation (EC) No 2273/2003 of 22 December 2003, is to ensure the integrity of Community financial markets and to enhance investor confidence in those markets. The Market Abuse Regulations made by the Minister for Enterprise, Trade and Employment, came into operation on 6 July 2005. The Financial Regulator is the competent authority for the purposes of the Market Abuse Regulations.

4.081 The Market Abuse Regulations provide for the prohibition of insider dealing and market manipulation in respect of financial instruments admitted to trading on an EEA regulated market, such as the main market of the Irish Stock Exchange. The prohibition also applies in respect of a financial instrument for which a request for admission to trading on a regulated market has been sought, irrespective of whether the transaction actually takes place on that regulated market.

The Market Abuse Regulations also include specific obligations on:

- persons professionally arranging transactions to notify suspicious transactions to the Financial Regulator;
- issuers of financial instruments to publicly disclose inside information without delay;
- issuers of financial instruments to draw up lists of persons with access to insider information;
- those involved in the management of issuers of financial instruments to comply with notification rules regarding managers' transactions; and

- persons, including the media and journalists, involved in the preparation and dissemination of recommendations regarding, *inter alia*, the presentation and the disclosure of significant financial interests and conflicts of interests.[61]

4.082 The Financial Regulator has issued Market Abuse Rules under s 34 of the Investment Funds, Companies and Miscellaneous Provisions Act 2005. The Market Abuse Rules of March 2006 set out procedural and administrative requirements and guidance in respect of the Market Abuse Regulations. Persons obliged to make disclosures or notifications to the Financial Regulator under the Market Abuse Regulations must do so in accordance with the Market Abuse Rules. The Financial Regulator may publish further rules and/or guidance in respect of the Market Abuse Regulations.[62]

4.083 As part of this role, CESR has produced two sets of guidance to the Market on the operation of the Market Abuse Directive: (1) Market Abuse CESR Guidance issued on 11 May 2005 and (2) Market Abuse CESR Guidance issued on 12 July 2007. As a member of CESR, in considering whether the Market Abuse Regulation has been complied with, the Financial Regulator will take into account any relevant guidance as set out in these CESR documents.

4.084 A person who enters into transactions or issues orders to trade which appear to constitute market manipulation may be able to establish that the reasons for entering into such transactions or orders to trade were legitimate and in conformity with accepted market practice in the regulated market concerned. Accepted Market Practices (AMPs) are practices that are reasonably expected in one or more financial markets and are accepted by the Financial Regulator in accordance with certain criteria as specified in Sch 1 of the Market Abuse Regulations. In accordance with such criteria, the Financial Regulator shall consult, as appropriate, relevant bodies such as issuers, financial service providers, consumers, other authorities and market operators before issuing a decision as to whether to accept an AMP. To date, there are no AMPs accepted by the Financial Regulator in relation to the main market of the Irish Stock Exchange.[63]

4.085 Part 3 of the Market Abuse Regulations applies to persons, including the media and journalists, involved in the preparation and dissemination of recommendations. In particular, Pt 3 provides *inter alia* that specific public disclosures must be made in respect of such recommendations. Part 3 also provides for a possible exemption from a number of the public disclosure requirements for journalists where they are subject to a regulatory regime (which may be a self-regulation regime) which the Financial Regulator is satisfied is equivalent appropriate regulation and which achieves similar effects to the requirements of Pt 3. To date, the Financial Regulator has not accepted

---

61   http://www.financialregulator.ie.
62   http://www.financialregulator.ie.
63   http://www.financialregulator.ie.

any regulatory regime as constituting equivalent appropriate regulation.[64] There have been several settlement agreements under the Market Abuse Regulations.[65]

Short selling

4.086 With effect from 19 September 2008, the Market Abuse Rules (from March 2006) were amended by the insertion of Rule 10.1 to prohibit short selling of banking stock. The Rules provide that a person, other than a market maker,[66] may not enter into any transaction, transactions or arrangements which have the effect of generating a net economic benefit which would arise from a fall in the price of the shares of either the Governor and Company of the Bank of Ireland, Allied Irish Banks Plc, Irish Life and Permanent Plc or Anglo Irish Bank Corporation Plc. Rule 10.2 provides that on 23 September 2008, and each business day thereafter, by 3.30pm each person who has on that day an economic interest involving 0.25 per cent or more of the issued share capital to which Rule 10.1 would have applied if entered into after the issuance of that Rule, shall make a disclosure setting out the name of the person who has the position, the company in which the position is held and the amount of that position. The prohibition in Rule 10.1 applies to any new short positions, including increases in existing short positions. Where a person has an existing short position on 18 September 2008, the rule does not prevent that short position being continued, nor does it prevent trading to reduce or close out the short position. Where a net short position arises, but does not arise because the person entered into transactions after 18 September to create that short position, Rule 10.1 does not apply, but Rule 10.2 may apply depending solely on whether 0.25 per cent of the shares of the company are involved or not. These rules apply to spread betting and contracts for difference and to all other ways in which an economic interest, whether direct or indirect, can be created.

The Transparency Directive

4.087 The Transparency Regulations (SI 277/2007) implementing the Transparency Directive (2004/109/EC) seek to enhance the information made available about issuers whose securities are admitted to trading on a regulated market situated or operating within a Member State. The European Commission has adopted measures supplementing the EC legal framework established by the Directive on transparency obligations of listed companies. The Transparency Directive and its implementing measures improve the quality of information available to investors on companies' performances and financial positions as well as on changes in major shareholdings.

---

64 http://www.financialregulator.ie.

65 http://www.financialregulator.ie.

66 'Market maker' in relation to an investment instrument means a person who (otherwise than in his capacity as manager of a collective investment scheme) holds himself out as able and willing to enter into transactions of sale and purchase in that investment instrument at prices determined generally and continuously rather than in respect of each transaction.

The European Commission's implementing measures supplement the Transparency Directive with regard to:

   (i)   issuers' disclosure of financial information in half-yearly reports;

   (ii)   investors' disclosure of major holdings;

   (iii) minimum standards for the pan-European dissemination of regulated information to the public; and

   (iv) minimum requirements for accepting equivalence of third-country regulations in respect of some elements of the Directive.

These implementing measures do not go beyond the requirements already contained in the Transparency Directive.

Insurance

4.088 The Financial Regulator is the designated EU Insurance Supervisory Authority of Ireland. The Insurance Supervision Department responsibilities include life, non-life and re-insurance services encompassing:

   (i)   fostering sound and solvent financial institutions;

   (ii)   the prudential supervision of insurance and re-insurance companies ('undertakings') with head offices in Ireland and of the Irish branches of companies with head offices outside of the EEA in accordance with EU Directives and the Insurance Acts and Regulations;

   (iii) issues related to the functioning of the insurance market;

   (iv) insurance legislation and policy development; and

   (v)   related EU and international issues.

4.089 The relevant statutory instrument in relation to life assurance is the European Communities (Life Assurance) Framework Regulations 1994 (SI 360/1994), which was amended by the European Communities (Life Assurance) Framework (Amendment) Regulations 2007 (SI 352/2007). This implements the First, Second and Third EU Life Assurance Directives (the 'Life Directives')[67] in Ireland. Directive 2002/12/EC on solvency margin requirements for life assurance undertakings also applies to this sector, as does the Unclaimed Life Assurance Policies Act 2003 (discussed further below at paras **4.152–153**).

4.090 The Non-Life Framework Directive 92/49/EEC is implemented by the European Communities (Non-Life Insurance) Framework Regulations 1994 (SI 359/1994), which was amended by the European Communities (Non-Life Insurance) Framework (Amendment) Regulations 2007 (SI 354/2007). Directive 2002/13/EC amending Directive 73/239/EEC also applies and concerns the solvency margin requirements for non-life insurance undertakings.

---

67   Directive 92/96/EEC.

4.091 Directive 98/78/EC of the European Parliament and of the Council of 27 October 1998 on the supplementary supervision of insurance undertakings in an insurance group – the Insurance Groups Directive – is implemented to adjust the margin of solvency to avoid double counting of capital by insurance groups and is amended by the Solvency I Directives (2002/13/EC and 2002/83/EC).

4.092 The European Communities (Supplementary Supervision of Insurance Undertakings in an Insurance Group) Regulations 1999 (SI 399/1999) are also taken into account when calculating regulatory capital requirements by an applicant for authorisation that forms part of an insurance or reinsurance group.

Also relevant to this sector are the provisions of the Financial Conglomerate Regulations[68] implementing Directive 2002/87/EC.

4.093 The European Communities (International Financial Reporting Standards and Miscellaneous Amendments) Regulations 2005 (SI 116/2005) are also relevant to this sector. These regulations implement into Irish law the European provisions dealing with accounting under international financial reporting standards. These regulations give full effect to Regulation (EC) No 1606/2002, Directive 78/660/EEC, Directive 83/349/EEC, Directive 86/635/EEC, Directive 91/674/EEC and Directive 2003/51/EC, which all deal with financial reporting standards.

4.094 The Reinsurance Directive 2005/68/EC is implemented by the European Communities (Reinsurance) Regulations 2006 and 2007 (SI 380/2006 and SI 306/2007). The first of these regulations, which transposed the Reinsurance Directive (Directive 2005/68/EC), was signed into Irish law on 15 July 2006. This was amended by the European Communities (Insurance and Reinsurance Groups Supplementary Supervision) Regulations 2007.[69]

Investment Services

4.095 The Financial Regulator is responsible for supervising a range of non-bank firms providing investment services in a range of investment instruments. The firms range from large securities houses owned by major multinational financial institutions to smaller operations. The activities involved include broking activities, securities trading, discretionary portfolio management and investment advice, while the instruments involved include equities and bonds, up to, and including, complex derivative products. The legislative framework governing the authorisation and ongoing supervision of investment firms and exchanges is set out in the Investment Intermediaries Act 1995 and the Stock Exchange Act 1995 and, in the case of futures exchanges, the Central Bank Act 1989. Within the Financial Regulator, the Securities and Exchanges Supervision department is responsible for the ongoing prudential supervision of investment firms and exchanges. The Securities and Exchanges Supervision department currently supervises approximately 140 investment firms, the Irish Stock Exchange and two futures and options exchanges – FINEX

---

68   European Communities (Financial Conglomerates) Regulations 2004 (SI 727/2004).

69   SI 366/2007 European Communities (Insurance and Reinsurance Groups Supplementary Supervision) Regulations 2007.

Europe[70] and NYMEX[71] Europe. The Financial Regulator keeps a register of firms authorised under the Investment Intermediaries Act 1995, a register of appointed investment product intermediaries maintained under s 31 of the Investment Intermediaries Act and a list of stockbrokers authorised under the Stock Exchange Act 1995.[72] The MiFID discussed above in paras **4.073–4.074** is the most significant piece of financial services legislation agreed in recent times and applies to both investment firms and credit institutions when providing investment services.

Funds

4.096 The IFSC & Funds Supervision department in the Financial Regulator is responsible for the authorisation and subsequent supervision of collective investment schemes. Collective investment schemes are also commonly known as funds.

The Financial Regulator's role in supervising collective investment schemes covers not only the scheme itself but also firms based in Ireland which provide services to such schemes. These service providers, which consist of administration, trustee and management companies, are authorised by the Financial Regulator under the Investment Intermediaries Act 1995 or approved under collective investment scheme legislation, as appropriate. Service providers are supervised in a broadly similar process to that described for the investment services industry. In addition, each scheme must provide Net Asset Value (NAV) returns to the Financial Regulator on a monthly basis, as well as annual audited accounts and half-yearly unaudited accounts for each scheme. Collective investment schemes are established for the purpose of investing the pooled funds of investors (held as units or shares in the scheme) in assets in accordance with investment objectives published in a prospectus.[73]

4.097 There are two main categories of funds authorised by the Financial Regulator: UCITS (Undertakings for Collective Investment in Transferable Securities) and Non-UCITS. UCITS have their basis in EC legislation and once authorised in one Member State, they may be marketed throughout the EU without further authorisation. This is described as an EU passport. UCITS are largely retail in nature. Non-UCITS are those funds authorised by the Financial Regulator which do not have a similar EU passport. Non-UCITS can be marketed to both retail and institutional investors.

4.098 The legislative basis for the Financial Regulator's supervisory function in relation to collective investment schemes is set out in several government Acts and Regulations dating from 1989. The Undertakings for Collective Investment in Transferable Securities Directives (2001/107/EC and 2001/108/EC) allow collective

---

70   FINEX is the currency futures and options division of the New York Board of Trade, which has a trading floor in Dublin.

71   The New York Mercantile Exchange.

72   http://www.financialregulator.ie.

73   http://www.financialregulator.ie.

investment schemes to operate freely throughout the EU on the basis of a single authorisation from one Member State. See **para 4.016** above for further information.

4.099 The regulation of a scheme consists of a detailed assessment of the promoter and other parties related to the scheme. It also involves the imposition and enforcement of detailed supervisory requirements which are set out in notices devised by the Financial Regulator and which cover, *inter alia*, investment and borrowing restrictions and disclosure of information to investors.

The Financial Regulator's authorisation process, which is based on the legislation and notices published by the Regulator, has evolved from 1989. The Financial Regulator has undertaken to issue first comments on fund application within three weeks of filing a complete application and, where documentation is in order and the fund not complex, to authorise a fund within eight weeks.

Insurance and Investment Intermediaries and Mortgage Intermediaries

4.100 Investment and insurance intermediaries fall to be regulated by the Financial Regulator under the Investment Intermediaries Act 1995, as amended. The status of these intermediaries falls into two categories: Authorised Advisors (AA) or Multi-Agency Intermediaries (MAI) which includes Restricted Activity Investment Product Intermediaries (RAIPI). The Financial Regulator maintains a register of investment product intermediaries (in accordance with s 31(4) of the Investment Intermediaries Act 1995), who are authorised to provide investment and insurance services. This register provides the status of each intermediary and a list of product producers from whom it holds an appointment. A product producer is usually a bank, building society or insurance company but may also be an AA or an MAI, which may sell its own products either directly or through intermediaries.[74]

Persons providing insurance or reinsurance mediation activities are also required to be registered as insurance or reinsurance intermediaries under the European Communities (Insurance Mediation) Regulations 2005. The application form for registration is on the Financial Regulator's website.

4.101 The Financial Regulator has supervisory responsibility for three professional bodies that have been approved to regulate their own members in respect of the provision of investment business services by these members. The provision of such services is on the basis that these services are incidental to the main professional services provided by the member.

The following institutes fall into this category:

(i)   Institute of Chartered Accountants in Ireland (ICAI);

(ii) Association of Chartered Certified Accountants (ACCA); and

(iii) Institute of Certified Public Accountants (CPA).

4.102 Investment and insurance intermediaries are required to comply with the relevant statutory provisions and also with the requirements as set out in the Consumer

---

74   http://www.financialregulator.ie.

Protection Code and the Handbook of Prudential Requirements. The Financial Regulator also carries out on-site inspections of investment and insurance intermediaries to ensure that they are complying with their obligations.

4.103 Mortgage intermediaries are regulated under the Consumer Credit Act 1995 (the 1995 Act). A mortgage intermediary is defined as 'any person, other than a mortgage lender or credit institution, who in return for a commission, payment or consideration of any kind in relation to a credit transaction, arranges or offers to arrange the provision of a housing loan by a mortgage lender.'[75]

Under s 116 of the 1995 Act a person shall not engage in the business of being a mortgage intermediary unless he is the holder of an authorisation granted for that purpose by the Financial Regulator and holds a letter of appointment in writing from each undertaking for which he is an intermediary. An application must be accompanied by the following:

(i)   tax clearance certificate;

(ii)   letters of appointment; and

(iii) certificate of incorporation or business name (where appropriate).

An authorisation is valid for 12 months from the date specified on the authorisation.

4.104 The Financial Regulator may refuse an authorisation on a number of grounds, but mainly for failure to supply the appropriate documentation or if the candidate holds certain licences (moneylending, gaming, publican or pawn-broking) or in the opinion of the Financial Regulator they are not fit and proper to hold an authorisation. The Financial Regulator may suspend or revoke an authorisation if the intermediary has been convicted of a criminal offence since becoming the holder of an authorisation. There are procedures laid down in the 1995 Act that have to be followed by the Financial Regulator in these circumstances. If the Financial Regulator refuses or revokes an authorisation, the intermediary has the right to appeal to the Circuit Court – the decision of the court is final.

Intermediaries are regulated by site visits, monitoring of advertisements, complaints from consumers or their competitors and through an agreement that is in place between the Financial Regulator and the finance houses that commission is not paid to any intermediary that is not properly authorised.

Credit Unions

4.105 Credit Unions are mutual non-profit-making organisations whose principal activities are the accepting of shares and deposits from members and the making of loans to members at reasonable rates of interest.[76] Credit unions have a special co-operative flavour to their organisation and character. This reflects the history of the movement and is clear from the legislation with which they must comply in order to enjoy the status of credit union. Simply put, one cannot join any credit union in the

---

75   Section 2.
76   http://www.ifsra.ie.

same manner as seeking to open a bank account with the bank of your choice. Members of an individual credit union must be linked to each other by some type of 'common bond'.

4.106 The Registrar of Credit Unions is responsible for the registration, regulation and supervision of credit unions and the maintenance of a public record file on each credit union. A Registrar of Credit Unions in discharging his duties recognises that the credit union movement is not motivated by profit and is volunteer-based. Nonetheless, regulation is good for the movement and the solvency and safety of members' funds is of critical importance. The Registrar concentrates on issues of transparency, good value and fair play for the many members of credit unions. The Registrar has the authority to inspect any credit union. These inspections are generally carried out under s 90 of the Credit Union Act 1997 (the 1997 Act). Investigations may also be carried out under s 92 of the 1997 Act.

A society may be registered as a credit union if the Registrar is satisfied that each of the following conditions is fulfilled:[77]

(i) the society is formed for specified objects and limited purposes set out by statute (set out below);[78]

(ii) admission to membership of the society is restricted to persons each of whom has, in relation to all the other members, at least one of the common bonds specified in s 6(3) of the Credit Union Act 1997;

(iii) it has at least 15 members who are of full age;

(iv) its rules comply with s 13 of the 1997 Act;

(v) the place which under those rules is, or is to be, the society's registered office is in the State;

(vi) if registered, it will participate in a savings protection scheme approved under s 46(1) of the 1997 Act; and

(vii) it has in force (or will have in force if registered) such a policy of insurance as is required by s 47 of the 1997 Act.

4.107 According to s 6(2) of the 1997 Act, the objects and purposes for which a credit union may be formed are:

(a) the promotion of thrift among its members by the accumulation of their savings;

(b) the creation of sources of credit for the mutual benefit of its members at a fair and reasonable rate of interest;

(c) the use and control of members' savings for their mutual benefit;

(d) the training and education of its members in the wise use of money;

---

77 Section 6 of the Credit Union Act 1997. The Registrar issues a Certificate of the Acknowledgement of Registry, when the application is satisfactory. Other relevant instruments are the Credit Union Act 1997 (Commencement) Order 1997 and the Credit Union Act 1997 (Fees) Regulations 1998. Under s 5(3) of the Credit Union Act 1997, societies which were registered as credit unions under the Industrial and Provident Societies Acts 1893 to 1978 were deemed to be registered as credit unions under the Credit Union Act 1997.

78 Section 6(1)(a) and (2) of the Credit Union Act 1997.

    (e) the education of its members in their economic, social and cultural well-being as members of the community;

    (f) the improvement of the well-being and spirit of the members' community; and

    (g) subject to section 48, the provision to its members of such additional services as are for their mutual benefit.

Section 6(3) of the 1997 Act states that the common bond that one must be able to demonstrate as existing between the members is any one of the following:

    (a) following a particular occupation;

    (b) residing or being employed in a particular locality;

    (c) being employed by a particular employer or having retired from employment with a particular employer;

    (d) being a member of a *bona fide* organisation or being otherwise associated with other members of the society for a purpose other than that of forming a society to be registered as a credit union;

    (e) any other common bond approved by the Registrar.

As noted above membership of credit unions also involves availing of a savings protection scheme (SPS). The SPS was the subject of a recent Supreme Court judgment on the Irish League of Credit Unions. Please see para **7.072** of the chapter on Competition in this regard. Credit unions are now also part of the Deposit Protection Scheme detailed at paras **4.065*ff*** above.

Registrar of Credit Unions

4.108 The Registrar of Credit Unions is appointed by the Financial Regulator.[79] The appointment is for a period not exceeding five years, which does not take effect until the Minister approves it. The Registrar is responsible:[80]

    (a) as the delegate of the Financial Regulator, for managing the performance and exercise of the functions and powers of the Bank under the 1997 Act; and

    (b) if management of the performance and exercise of the functions and powers of the Bank under any other Act or law are delegated to the Registrar, for managing the performance and exercise of those functions and powers.

The Registrar has power to do whatever is necessary for or in connection with, or reasonably incidental to, carrying out the Registrar's responsibilities. In carrying out the responsibilities and exercising the powers imposed or conferred on him, the Registrar is, through the Chief Executive, subject to the control of the Financial Regulator and is required to comply with directions duly given by the Financial Regulator with respect to the carrying out of those responsibilities or the exercise of those powers.

---

79 Section 33X of the Central Bank Act 1942 as inserted by s 26 of the 2003 Act.
80 Section 33AA as inserted.

4.109 In issuing directions to the Registrar, the Financial Regulator is obliged to have regard to the particular nature of credit unions, in particular, by reference to:[81]

(i) the conditions for the registration of a credit union as set out in s 6 of the Credit Union Act 1997 and to the objects and common bonds referred to in that section, and

(ii) the voluntary ethos of credit unions.

The Registrar is required to report annually, and from time to time as requested, to the Chief Executive of the Financial Regulator as to the discharge and exercise by him of his duties and powers.[82] In addition, the Registrar must, at the end of each financial year, provide the Bank with sufficient information about the financial affairs of the Registrar as will enable the Bank to make its own annual report.

Credit Union Act 1997

4.110 The primary responsibility of the Registrar is to administer the system of regulation and supervision of credit unions provided for by the Credit Union Act 1997 with a view to the maintenance of the financial stability and well-being of credit unions generally.[83] In exercising this power, the Registrar may consult the Advisory Committee[84] and such other bodies as appear to him to be expert or knowledgeable in matters relating to credit unions.

4.111 A credit union is obliged at all times to keep a proportion of its total assets in liquid form, being such a proportion and having such a composition as to enable the credit union to meet its liabilities as they arise. Consequently, a credit union must have regard to the range and scale of its business and the composition of its assets and liabilities. The Registrar is entitled from time to time by notice in writing to require a credit union to maintain, between its assets and its liabilities:

(i) a ratio specified in the requirement;

(ii) a ratio which does not exceed a ratio so specified; or

(iii) a ratio which is not less than a ratio so specified;

and a ratio may be so specified as a percentage of the assets or liabilities concerned.

A requirement of the Registrar as regards such liquid assets may be expressed to apply in one or more of the following ways: in relation to all credit unions or to credit unions of a category or categories specified in the requirement.

---

81 Section 33AA(4)(c).

82 Sections 33AC and 33AD.

83 Section 84 of the 1997 Act.

84 Credit Union Act 1997, s 180 provides for the continuation of the Credit Union Advisory Committee, which was first established by Credit Union Act 1966, s 27. The role of the seven person Advisory Committee is advise the Minister or the Registrar in relation to *(a)* the improvement of the management of credit unions; *(b)* the protection of the interests of members and creditors of credit unions; and *(c)* other matters relating to credit unions upon which the Minister, the Registrar or such other persons as may be specified by the Minister may from time to time seek the advice of the Committee.

4.112 In Ireland the liquidity limits are goals that have been agreed by the Irish League of Credit Unions in negotiation with the Registrar. Financial Performance ratios (known as PEARLS[85]) have been adapted to suit the Irish context – different PEARLS are used. A Prudential Return is now made to the Registrar by credit unions, pursuant to s 91 of the 1997 Act reporting on the implementation of these ratios.[86]

The liquid investment to uncommitted savings is regarded as the key ratio. The goal for this ratio is 20 per cent and it measures liquid funds versus uncommitted savings available to meet withdrawers' demand.

Moneylenders

4.113 A moneylender is defined as 'a person who carries on the business of moneylending or who advertises or announces himself or holds himself out in any way as carrying on that business,'[87] where moneylending means credit supplied by a moneylender to a consumer on foot of a moneylending agreement.

4.114 Moneylenders are regulated under the 1995 Act. Under s 93(1) of the 1995 Act a person shall not engage in the business of being a moneylender unless he is the holder of a license granted for that purpose by the Financial Regulator authorising that person to engage in the business of moneylending in any District Court district. A moneylending agreement is a credit agreement into which a moneylender enters or offers to enter with a consumer in which one or more of the following apply:

(a) the agreement was concluded away from the business premises of the moneylender or the business premises of the supplier of goods or services under the agreement;

(b) any negotiations for, or in relation to the credit were conducted at a place other than the business premises of the moneylender or the business premises of the supplier of goods or services under the agreement;

(c) repayments under the agreement will, or may, be paid by the consumer to the moneylender or his representative at any place other than the business premises of the moneylender or the business premises of the supplier of goods or services under the agreement; or

(d) where the total cost of credit to the consumer under the agreement is in excess of an APR of 23 per cent, or such other rate as may be prescribed.

A moneylender must ensure that any moneylending agreement to which he is a party shall contain in a prominent position the words 'Moneylending agreement'.

4.115 Prior to submitting an application for a moneylender's license, the applicant must publish notice of his intention to apply for a license in any national or local newspaper published in the State and circulating in the District Court district that the

---

85   This is an acronym connoting – **P**rotection, **E**ffective Financial Structure, **A**sset Quality, **R**ates of Return and Costs, **L**iquidity and **S**igns of Growth.

86   Irish League of Credit Unions Annual Report 2007, http://www.ilcu.ie, pp 79–90.

87   Section 2 of the Consumer Credit Act 1995.

applicant intends to engage, or engages, in the business of moneylending. The application for a moneylending license should then be made in writing to the Financial Regulator and should contain that information detailed in s 93(3) of the 1995 Act.

4.116 The Financial Regulator may refuse a license on a number of grounds under s 93(10) of the 1995 Act. These grounds include, but are not limited to, failure to supply the appropriate documentation, or the possession of certain licences (bookmaking, gaming, publican or pawn-broking) or the opinion of the Financial Regulator that the applicant is not fit and proper to hold an authorisation or the cost of credit to be charged is excessive or any of the terms or conditions attaching thereto are unfair.

4.117 Once granted, an authorisation is valid for 12 months from the date specified. However, the Financial Regulator may suspend or revoke an authorisation if the moneylender has been convicted of a criminal offence since becoming the holder of a license. Procedures laid down in the 1995 Act have to be followed by the Financial Regulator in these circumstances. If the Financial Regulator refuses or revokes an authorisation, the intermediary has the right to appeal to the Circuit Court.

4.118 Moneylenders are regulated by site visits, monitoring their advertisements, investigation of complaints from consumers or from their competitors and by the publishing of Codes of Practice setting out conduct regarding moneylending agreements.

Money Transmitters and Bureaux de Change

4.119 'Money transmission service' means a service that involves transmitting money by any means. 'Bureaux de change business' means a business that provides members of the public with a service that involves buying or selling foreign currency.

4.120 In accordance with the provisions of Pt V of the 1997 Act, the Financial Regulator is responsible for the authorisation and supervision of bureaux de change. The Central Bank and Financial Services Authority of Ireland Act 2004 widened the scope of bureaux de change provisions contained to include money transmission business in order to give effect to Financial Action Task Force (FATF) Special Recommendation VI on Alternative Remittance. Authorisation is in the context of ensuring the effective implementation of the money laundering and prevention of financing terrorism provisions of the Criminal Justice Act 1994 (as amended). The supervisory regime was introduced to comply with the recommendations of the FATF – the OECD-sponsored body on money laundering, which requires member countries to authorise and supervise bureaux de change and money transmitters for anti-money laundering purposes and the prevention of financing of terrorism.

4.121 In assessing applications for authorisation, the Financial Regulator focuses on the ownership of bureaux de change and money transmitters and the adequacy of procedures to counter money laundering. In particular, the Financial Regulator seeks to ensure that the shareholders, partners, directors and senior management are fit and proper persons and that the internal controls and procedures which the applicant has in place satisfy the provisions of the Criminal Justice Act 1994 (as amended) and the relevant provisions of the Money Laundering Guidance Notes for Credit Institutions and Guidance on the Offence of Financing Terrorism and the Financial Sanctions Regime of Terrorism, which were issued by the Money Laundering Steering Committee.

Home Reversion Firms and Retail Credit Firms

4.122 In November 2007, Pt V of the Central Bank Act 1997 was amended by the Markets in Financial Instruments and Miscellaneous Provisions Act 2007. With effect from 1 February 2008, the Financial Regulator is the body responsible for the authorisation and supervision of retail credit firms and home reversion firms.

4.123 Part V of the 1997 Act provides for a regulatory regime for retail credit firms and home reversion firms in Ireland. Chapter 1 of Pt V of the 1997 Act defines 'retail credit firm', 'home reversion firm', 'credit' and 'home reversion agreement', while Chapter 3 deals with, *inter alia*, the authorisation of retail credit firms and home reversion firms. Chapters 1 and 2 of Pt V of the 1997 Act must be examined to determine whether or not authorisation under the legislation is required.

4.124 The Financial Regulator's fundamental approach to supervision (including authorisation) is that it is principles-led. Responsibility for the proper management and control of a retail credit firm or a home reversion firm, and the integrity of its systems, rests with the board of directors and its senior management or any other persons responsible for the operation of such firms. Ethical behaviour and transparency in business dealings are key values expected by the Financial Regulator. Section 31A of the 1997 Act sets out the requirements which must be satisfied in order for an authorisation to be granted.

It is an offence, after 30 April 2008, to operate as a retail credit firm or home reversion firm without having applied to the Financial Regulator for authorisation.

Consumer

4.125 The Financial Regulator has a key responsibility for giving confidence to consumers that their deposits and investments are safe and that their claims can be met, particularly during the credit crunch which is taking place at the time of writing. In turn, this contributes to a stable financial system and to the reputation and good standing of the Irish financial sector. The financial services industry is increasingly global and this poses challenges to both the industry and its Regulator.

4.126 The Financial Regulator is responsible for the development of codes of conduct and other requirements applicable to regulated entities authorised by or registered with the Financial Regulator. In March 2004, the Financial Regulator commenced a review of existing codes in order to unify and develop the conduct of business requirements of these codes under one Consumer Protection Code (the Code). This review was carried out with the aid of two public consultations. The Code was published on 25 July 2006. The Code contains provisions that cover all aspects of a regulated entity's relationship with a consumer, from advertising and marketing, to knowing the consumer and offering suitable products, to ensuring that consumers are treated fairly. The provisions of the Code are effective from 1 August 2006. The Code's principal aims are to:

(i)   ensure a consumer-focused standard of protection for buyers of financial products and services;

(ii)   ensure that there is the same level of protection for consumers regardless of the type of regulated entity they choose to deal with; and

(iii) facilitate competition by contributing to a level playing field.[88]

4.127 The Financial Regulator also engaged in public consultations on another consumer protection matter – minimum competency requirements. The minimum competency requirements (the Requirements), which were published on 25 July 2006, introduced a competency framework that is designed to establish minimum standards for regulated entities. Firms are required to ensure that individuals who provide advice on or sell retail financial products or who undertake certain specified activities on their behalf acquire the competencies set out in the Requirements. In addition, individuals are required to undertake a programme of Continuing Professional Development on an ongoing basis. The Requirements came into force on 1 January 2007.

Fit and Proper Standards for Directors and Managers of Financial Services Entities

4.128 Directors and Managers of financial services entities are responsible for the proper running of these entities. To ensure the proper discharge of this responsibility, it is important that Directors and Managers ('approved persons') have the skills and personal qualities, such as honesty, integrity, diligence, independent-mindedness and fairness to ensure that the entity is run ethically, in compliance with relevant legislation and in a manner that treats its customers fairly.

4.129 EC and Irish law require that the Directors and Managers of financial services entities regulated by the Financial Regulator meet standards of competence and probity. These standards are usually referred to in shorthand as 'fit and proper' standards. 'Fitness' requires that a person appointed as a Director or Manager has the necessary qualifications, skills and experience to perform the duties of that position. 'Probity' requires that a person is honest, fair and ethical. Before proposing a new Director or Manager, the appointing entity should satisfy itself that the proposed appointee meets the fit and proper standards. The entity then passes its proposal to the Financial Regulator, attesting that it is satisfied that the person is fit and proper. This is the 'fit and proper test' and involves the completion of an Individual Questionnaire (IQ) by the applicant.

4.130 The Financial Regulator has operated fit and proper[89] tests in the various financial service sectors subject to its oversight, in conformity with the relevant

---

88   http://www.financialregulator.ie/frame_main.asp?pg=/industry/in_car_intr.asp&nv=/ industry/in_nav.asp

89   Fit and proper standards are further discussed in **Ch 3** on Aviation Regulation.

legislation. A common framework applies a common process across all industry sectors. The common framework has been developed in light of a consultative process that involved two public consultations.

Anti-Money Laundering

4.131 Financial institutions designated under the Criminal Justice Act 1994 (the 1994 Act) are obliged to take the necessary measures to effectively counteract money laundering[90] in accordance with the provisions of the 1994 Act and the relevant sectoral Guidance Notes which have been issued with the approval of the Money Laundering Steering Committee. The Steering Committee is chaired by the Department of Finance and includes representatives from relevant Government Departments, the Financial Regulator, the Garda Síochána and the major representative bodies in the financial sector. The 1994 Act and the Guidance Notes set out measures to counteract money laundering and terrorist financing in line with the forty recommendations and the nine special recommendations (on terrorist financing) of the FATF and the EU Directives on prevention of the use of the financial system for the purpose of money laundering and terrorist financing.

4.132 There are separate anti-money laundering guidance notes published on the Financial Regulator's website for each of the following sectors:

  (i)   credit institutions;

  (ii) financial institutions (excluding credit institutions);

  (iii) stockbrokers; and

  (iv) insurance and retail investment products (for use by life assurance companies and intermediaries).

4.133 The Financial Regulator, as part of its supervision process, assesses the adequacy of procedures adopted by the institutions, which it supervises to counter money laundering and the degree of compliance with such procedures. The Financial Regulator uses the Money Laundering Guidance Notes as criteria against which it assesses the adequacy of institutions' internal controls, policies and procedures to counter money laundering. The Financial Regulator from time to time conducts inspections of institutions to assess their compliance with the guidance notes. The Central Bank/Financial Regulator is obliged by the Criminal Justice Act 1994 to report to the Garda Síochána and Revenue Commissioners where it suspects that an offence under ss 31 or 32 of the Act has been, or is being, committed by an institution under its supervision (s 57(2) of the Act). It is an offence punishable by imprisonment of up to

---

90 Money laundering is an offence. The 1994 Act makes provision for international co-operation in respect of certain criminal law enforcement procedures and for the forfeiture of property used in crime and provides for related matters, such as imposing an obligation on designated bodies (banks and a wide range of financial institutions), to take measures to combat money laundering in line with the provisions of the Money Laundering Directive. Money Laundering was first made an offence on 14 November 1994.

five years or a fine, or both, for the failure of the Central Bank/Financial Regulator to comply with this requirement (s 57(5)).

4.134 Member states are required to bring into force the laws, regulations and administrative provisions necessary to comply with the Third EU Anti-Money Laundering Directive 2005/60/EC (and Directive 2006/70/EC)[91] on the prevention of the use of the financial system for the purpose of money laundering and terrorist financing by 15 December 2007. On 12 February 2008, the Minister for Justice, Equality and Law Reform received government approval for the drafting of a Criminal Justice (Money Laundering) Bill, which will give effect to the Third EU Money Laundering Directive.

4.135 The type of revised provisions that will impact on the obligation of the financial sector arise from a move away from the narrow focus of customer identification to a broader focus on 'customer due diligence', which includes obtaining information on the purpose and nature of the intended business relationship and ongoing monitoring of the business relationship. There are also requirements to adapt a risk-based approach, which will give rise to simplified customer due diligence measures in certain cases and enhanced due diligence in other cases.

4.136 The Criminal Justice (Money Laundering) Bill 2008 will transpose the Third Directive into Irish law. It contains references to the risk-based approach, enhanced and simplified customer due diligence, beneficial ownership – defined broadly as owning 25 per cent of a company or more – and politically exposed persons.

According to a European Union press release of 5 June 2008,[92] the EC is pursuing infringement actions against 15 member states for failing to adopt and implement the Third EU Anti-Money Laundering Directive into national law by the deadline of 15 December 2007. The Commission has commenced infringement proceedings against these countries, which include Ireland, pursuant to art 226 of the EC Treaty (previously art 169).

The Second Anti-Money Laundering Directive was implemented *inter alia* by the Criminal Justice Act 1994 (Section 32) (Amendment) Regulations 2003 (SI 242/2003). The Criminal Justice Act 1994 was passed by both houses of the Oireachtas and signed by the President on 30 June 1994. The Act makes provisions for the recovery of the proceeds of drug trafficking and other offences, including that of financing terrorism since 2005.

4.137 In late 1996, Ireland ratified and fully implemented the 1988 Vienna Convention and the 1959 and 1990 Council of Europe Conventions, thus allowing it to provide a full range of mutual legal assistance to a large number of countries. In 1996, it also enacted the Criminal Assets Bureau Act 1996 and the Proceeds of Crime Act 1996.

---

91 Directive (2006/70/EC) laying down implementing measures for Directive 2005/60/EC of the European Parliament and of the Council as regards the definition of 'politically exposed persons' and the technical criteria for simplified customer due diligence procedures and for exemption on grounds of a financial activity conducted on an occasional or very limited basis.

92 Ref: IP/08/860.

The first Act created the Criminal Assets Bureau, an independent statutory body comprising staff from a number of government agencies, and provided them with certain compulsory powers. The second Act provides for a process of civil forfeiture whereby property which is the proceeds of crime can be frozen[93] and ultimately confiscated, without any need for criminal proceedings against any person. A number of technical changes were made to the Act by the Proceeds of Crime (Amendment) Act 2005. These remove any doubts as to when a person may be said to be in possession or control of property for the purposes of the Act. The enactment of the Disclosure of Certain Information for Taxation and Other Purposes Act 1996 provides for the effective exchange of information between the Garda Síochána and the Revenue Commissioners and enables the Revenue Commissioners to provide information to the Gardaí where there are reasonable grounds for suspecting that the information relates to a person who has derived profits from an unlawful activity.

4.138 In relation to the financial sector, amendments were enacted in 1996 to complete the requirements for institutions subject to the Criminal Justice Act 1994, while the establishment in 1994 of a Money Laundering Steering Committee led to guidance notes being issued for credit institutions, financial institutions, credit unions, stockbrokers and life assurance companies and intermediaries. Consideration is being given to extending the money laundering provisions of the 1994 Act to company formation agents. Section 58 of the Criminal Act 1994 (as amended) creates the offence of tipping off.

Prohibition on Disclosure and Supervisory Disclosures

4.139 A feature of financial services regulation is the existence of detailed rules on disclosure of information. A number of persons involved in the regulation of the financial sector are subject to a detailed prohibition on disclosure of confidential information that has come to their attention due to the nature of their position.[94] According to the Central Bank Act 1942, the prohibition applies to the following persons:

    (i)   the Governor and every former Governor;

   (ii)   every Director and every former Director;

  (iii)   every member, member's deputy appointed under para 4 of Sch 3, former member and former member's deputy who had been so appointed, of the Financial Regulator;

  (iv)   the Chief Executive and every former Chief Executive of the Financial Regulator;

   (v)   the Consumer Director and every former Consumer Director of the Financial Regulator;

  (vi)   the Registrar of Credit Unions and every former Registrar of Credit Unions;

 (vii)   every other officer or employee and every other former officer or employee of the Bank;

---

93   This is further discussed in **Ch 9** on criminal law enforcement.

94   Part IIIA, s 33AK of the Central Bank Act 1942, as inserted by s 26 of the 2003 Act.

(viii) every person who is or was formerly employed as a consultant, auditor or in any other capacity by the Bank or any constituent part of the Bank.[95]

4.140 The above-mentioned persons are barred from disclosing confidential information concerning[96]:

(i) the business of any person or body[97] whether corporate or incorporate that has come to the person's knowledge through the person's office or employment with the Central Bank, or

(ii) any matter arising in connection with the performance of the functions of the Central Bank or the exercise of its powers,

if such disclosure is prohibited by the Rome Treaty, the ESCB Statute or the Supervisory Directives.

4.141 There is a duty of disclosure on directors of supervised entities,[98] if so requested by the Central Bank, to inform it on the extent of any disclosure duly made by or on behalf of them or the entity to any authority, whether within the State or otherwise. Where such a request is made, the directors or those charged with the direction of a supervised entity must give to the Central Bank all the information so requested that is in their possession or under their control, within:

(i) 30 days of receipt of the request; or

(ii) such longer period as the Central Bank may allow when making the request or subsequently.

In responding to a request for information, under s 33AK, the directors or those charged with the direction of the supervised entity concerned must exercise due diligence and shall not, by any act or omission, give or cause to be given to the Central Bank false or misleading information.

4.142 The Central Bank is under a duty to disclose ('report'), as appropriate, to:

(i) the Garda Síochána;

(ii) the Revenue Commissioners;

---

95   For example, the Financial Regulator. The section quoted is the Central Bank Act 1942, s 33AK.

96   Section 33AK(1)(b), as inserted by s 26 of the 2003 Act.

97   The legislation distinguishes between credit institutions and financial institutions – s 18A of the Central Bank Act 1942 as inserted by s 13 of the 2003 Act. 'Credit institution' means an undertaking whose business is to receive deposits or other repayable funds from the public and to grant credit on its own account but does not include the European Central Bank; 'financial institution' means an undertaking, other than a credit institution, that provides one or more of the kinds of financial services that are set out in the Schedule to the European Communities (Licensing and Supervision of Credit Institutions) Regulations 1992 (SI 395/1992). In addition, 'insurance undertaking' has the meaning given by the Insurance Act 1989.

98   'Supervised entity' means any person or body in relation to which the Bank exercises functions under the designated enactments or the designated statutory instruments.

   (iii) the Director of Corporate Enforcement;

   (iv) the Competition Authority;

   (v) any other body, whether within the State or otherwise, charged with the detection or investigation of a criminal offence; or

   (vi) any other body charged with the detection or investigation of a contravention of:

       (a) the Companies Acts 1963 to 2001, or

       (b) the Competition Act 2002, or in so far as any commencement Order under that Act does not relate to the repeal of provisions of the Competition Acts 1991 and 1996, which would otherwise be subsisting those Acts, any information relevant to that body that leads the Bank to suspect that:

          (i) a criminal offence may have been committed by a supervised entity, or

          (ii) a supervised entity may have contravened a provision of the Companies or Competition Acts.[99]

This duty to report does not apply if the Central Bank is satisfied that the supervised entity has already reported the information concerned to the relevant body.

4.143 Information contained in such a report by the Central Bank may only be used by the body to which it is addressed for the purposes of:

   (i) the detection or investigation of a contravention of a provision of the Companies Act and/or Competition Act; or

   (ii) any investigation which may lead to a prosecution for a criminal offence and any prosecution for the alleged offence.[100]

4.144 In relation to a supervised entity, where the Central Bank identifies information:

   (i) which it believes is or is likely to be material to an authority concerned with the enforcement of any law, and

   (ii) which it believes it is unable to disclose to that authority, and

   (iii) in respect of which it is not satisfied that the information has been disclosed to that authority by the directors, or those charged with the direction, of the supervised entity, then, the Central Bank shall issue to the directors or others duly charged with the direction of the supervised entity a document, to be known as a Disclosure Issue Notice, and the notice shall:

       (I) specify the name of the authority concerned, and

       (II) identify the information that the Central Bank has identified as causing it to issue the Disclosure Issue Notice.[101]

4.145 The Central Bank must advise the authority concerned when a Disclosure Issue Notice is issued.

Where a Disclosure Issue Notice is issued in respect of a company to which s 158 of the Companies Act 1963 applies (which relates to the directors' report), the directors' report shall comply with sub-s (6B) of that section.

---

99 Central Bank Act 1942, s 33AK(3).

100 Central Bank Act 1942, s 33AK(3)(c).

101 Central Bank Act 1942, s 33AK(4)(a).

4.146 Subject to the above-mentioned general bar on disclosure, the Central Bank may disclose confidential information:[102]

(i)   required for the purposes of criminal proceedings;

(ii)   to any institution of the European Community because of the State's membership of the Community, or to the European Central Bank for the purpose of complying with the Rome Treaty or the ESCB Statute;

(iii) to an approved stock exchange, within the meaning of the Stock Exchange Act 1995 where the Central Bank considers it necessary to do so, either for the proper and orderly regulation of stock exchanges and their member firms or for the protection of investors, or for both;

(iv)   to a financial futures and options exchange, within the meaning of s 97 of the Central Bank Act 1989, whose rules have been approved by the Central Bank under Ch VIII of the Central Bank Act 1989, where the Central Bank considers it necessary to do so for the proper and orderly regulation of futures and options exchanges and their members;

(v)   to an inspector appointed under the Companies Acts 1963 to 2001, or s 57 of the Stock Exchange Act 1995;

(vi)   to an officer of statistics (as defined by s 20 of the Statistics Act 1993) in connection with the collection, compilation, analysis or interpretation of data relating to balance of payments, national accounts or any other financial statistics prepared for those purposes;

(vii) for the purpose of complying with ss 57(2) or 57A(3) of the Criminal Justice Act 1994 on Money Laundering;

(viii) to the Director of Corporate Enforcement for the purpose of any investigation under Pt II (as amended) of the Companies Act 1990, or to an officer of the Director of Corporate Enforcement for the purposes of the Director's functions and in accordance with the terms of the Supervisory Directives, where applicable;

(ix)   if the Central Bank is satisfied that the disclosure is necessary to protect consumers of relevant financial services or to safeguard the interests of the Central Bank, or

(x)   if the disclosure arises in relation to:

   (a)   the operations of the Central Bank in any financial market,

   (b)   the issue by the Central Bank or the European Central Bank of legal tender, or

   (c)   the pursuit by the Central Bank of the objectives set out in s 6A of the Central Bank Act 1942.

Any person or entity to whom confidential information is provided under this provision must comply with the provisions on professional secrecy in the Supervisory

---

102 This is not a complete list – see s 33AK of the Central Bank Act 1942, as inserted by s 26 of the 2003 Act.

Directives[103] in holding and dealing with information provided to them by the Central Bank.

4.147 A person who contravenes the provisions on disclosure commits an offence and is liable:

> (i)   on conviction on indictment to a fine not exceeding €30,000 or to imprisonment for a term not exceeding five years, or both; or
>
> (ii) on summary conviction to a fine not exceeding €3,000 or to imprisonment for a term not exceeding 12 months, or both.[104]

Electronic Money

4.148 An electronic money institution (EMI) is an undertaking, other than a credit institution, that issues means of payment in the form of e-money and is duly authorised to do so.

The European Communities (Electronic Money) Regulations 2002 (SI 221/2002) implement Directive 2000/46/EC on the taking up, pursuit of and prudential supervision of the business of electronic money institutions. The Financial Regulator is the competent authority responsible for the authorisation and supervision of EMIs.

4.149 Under the regulation, e-money is defined as monetary value as represented by a claim on the issuer, which is:

> (i)   stored on an electronic device;
>
> (ii)   issued on receipt of funds of an amount not less in value than the monetary value issued; and
>
> (iii) accepted as means of payment by undertakings other than the issuer.

4.150 The supervisory regime provided for in the regulation for EMIs is similar to those which apply to other regulated entities – eg fitness and probity of relevant parties; sound internal control systems, sound administrative and accounting principles; adequate capital levels, liquidity, etc. There are certain features and requirements that are unique to E-money and EMIs. These include:

> (i)   EMIs must not undertake or carry on business other than issuing e-money and the provision of financial and non financial services closely related to issuing e-money;
>
> (ii)   each EMI must have initial capital of at least €1m; on an ongoing basis it must maintain capital equal to 2 per cent of e-money issued or €1m, whichever is the higher;

---

103 'Supervisory Directives' means: (a) Directive 2000/12/EC of the European Parliament and of the Council of 20 March 2000; (b) Council Directive 93/22/EEC of 10 May 1993; (c) Council Directive 85/611/EEC of 20 December 1985; (d) Council Directive 92/49/EEC of 18 June 1992; and (e) Council Directive 92/96/EEC of 10 November 1992.

104 Central Bank Act 1942, s 33AK(8)(c).

(iii) the maximum storage capacity of each issued electronic device should not exceed €5,000;

(iv) small issuers of e-money may benefit from a waiver of certain requirements under certain conditions;

(v) the bearer of e-money has the right at all times to demand repayment from the EMI of any balance outstanding on the device; and

(vi) an EMI can only invest its assets in cash or near cash items (ie assets carrying a zero weighting in the context of banks' capital adequacy requirements).

Dormant Accounts

4.151 The purpose of the Dormant Accounts Act 2001 is to facilitate rejoining account holders with their dormant funds held in banks, building societies and An Post. A dormant account is an account that has shown no activity for 15 years. Unclaimed money is transferred to a fund managed by the National Treasury Management Agency (NTMA) and paid out by the Dormant Accounts Fund Disbursement Board. The rights of original account holders (or their successors) are not affected by the transfer to the fund and they can always reclaim the funds (including interest). Funds can be claimed by contacting the institution where the account was held – the bank, building society or An Post – and completing the relevant claim form. Institutions are obliged to publish a notice in two national newspapers in October each year about the transfer of funds under the 2001 Act. The Dormant Accounts Fund Disbursements Board will distribute the funds to programmes designed to assist the personal, educational and social development of persons who are economically, educationally or socially disadvantaged or persons with a disability and to projects that are designed to assist primary school students with learning disabilities.

Unclaimed Life Assurance Policies

4.152 The purpose of the Unclaimed Life Assurance Policies Act 2003 is to reunite policyholders with funds held in unclaimed life assurance policies. As in the case of dormant accounts, funds from unclaimed policies will be transferred to a fund administered by the NTMA and disbursed by the Dormant Accounts Fund Disbursement Board. Policies held by overseas residents are not covered by the 2003 Act. The original policy holder (or their successors) can always reclaim their funds at any time by contacting the life assurance company where the original policy was held and completing the relevant claim form.

4.153 Personal pension policies (those not included in an employer's pension scheme) are also covered by the legislation and will be classed as 'unclaimed' where more than five years have passed – without communication from the policyholder – from the latest retirement date in the policy. A notice will be published in two or more national newspapers in October of each year relating to the transfer of funds under the Act. The Dormant Accounts Fund Disbursements Board will distribute the funds to programmes designed to assist the personal, educational and social development of persons who are economically, educationally or socially disadvantaged or persons with a disability and to projects that are designed to assist primary school students with learning disabilities.

ENFORCEMENT

4.154 Enforcement by the Financial Regulator can be both civil and criminal. This section will examine both the civil and criminal aspects of the enforcement of the Financial Regulator's powers. In general, enforcement can happen by way of a complaint being made or by way of the Regulator investigating a matter on its own initiative.

Civil Enforcement

Complaints to the Financial Services Ombudsman

4.155 Section 57BY of the Central Bank and Financial Services Authority of Ireland Act 2004 (the 2004 Act) provides that the Financial Services Ombudsman shall investigate a complaint if he is satisfied that the complaint is within his jurisdiction.

The Ombudsman has recently revised its procedures for the dealing with complaints in light of the recent case of *Davy v Financial Services Ombudsman*.[105] The High Court ruled that the Financial Services Ombudsman had failed to follow fair procedures in the way in which he upheld a complaint by Enfield Credit Union against stockbrokers J & E Davy. As a result of the judicial review, the court quashed the decision of the Financial Services Ombudsman by an order of *certiorari* and directed the Ombudsman to conduct a new investigation into the complaint against Davy, according to 12 detailed procedures outlined by the court. These procedures includes conducting an oral hearing, a full exchange of complaint documentation and guaranteeing the right of reply. Charleton J stressed that when determining complaints, both complainants and respondents must be treated equally. The court noted that under s 57CI(3) of the Central Bank Act 1942 as inserted by s 16 of the Central Bank and Financial Services Authority of Ireland Act 2004, the Financial Services Ombudsman is obliged to give reasons for any findings. Such findings can be concise.[106] In making adjudication under the Central Bank Act, given there is a right of appeal to the High Court in the event there is dissatisfaction with the decision of the Ombudsman, the Ombudsman is required to stipulate what part of the Act and what legal basis constitutes his findings.

Authorised officers

4.156 A notable feature of financial services regulation is the possibility for overseeing the relevant institutions through inspection by authorised officers appointed by either

---

105 *J & E Davy trading as Davy v Financial Services Ombudsman & Ors* [2008] IEHC 256, Charleton J.

106 In *International Fishing Vessels Ltd v Minister for Marine* [1989] IR 149, the applicant was refused a fisheries licence by being furnished with a letter that simply turned down his application. On judicial review, the High Court held that he was entitled to reasons.

the Governor of the Central Bank, the Chief Executive of the Financial Regulator or the Registrar of Credit Unions under a variety of statutes.

A number of provisions in various banking Acts provide for regulation of the industry by appointing persons to inspect and investigate the business of financial institutions. Authorised officers may be appointed by the Governor of the Central Bank or the Chief Executive of the Financial Regulator, to conduct investigations in the business of various types of financial institution under a number of pieces of legislation,[107] principally:

(i) s 17 of the Central Bank Act 1971;

(ii) s 41 of the Building Societies Act 1989;

(iii) s 24A of the Trustee Savings Bank, 1989;

(iv) s 36 of the Stock Exchange Act 1995;

(v) s 64 of the Investment Intermediaries Act 1995; and

(vi) reg 6 of the European Communities (UCITS) Regulations 1989.[108]

A separate analogous power resides with the Registrar of Credit Unions pursuant to s 90 of the Credit Unions Act 1997.

4.157 An authorised officers under these Acts may be either a member of staff of the Central Bank or Financial Regulator or another suitably qualified person. Authorised officers are subject to broadly similar provisions under each of the above-mentioned pieces of legislation. Broadly stated, these provisions are as follows:

(1) A responsible authority[109] may authorise in writing a qualified person[110] to investigate the business, or any aspect of that business, and to report on the outcome of the investigation.

(2) An authorised person may, at any reasonable time on production of evidence of the person's authorisation, enter the business premises for the purpose of carrying out such an investigation.

(3) An authorised person who has entered premises may do all or any of the following:

(a) inspect the premises;

(b) request any person on the premises who apparently has control of, or access to, documents or material relating to the business of the body concerned to produce the documents or material to the authorised person for inspection;

(c) inspect documents and material so produced, or found in the course of inspecting the premises, and, in the case of documents, take copies of them or of any parts of them;

---

107 All relevant sections of legislation are as amended by s 31 of the Central Bank and Financial Services Authority of Ireland 2003.

108 SI 78/1989.

109 Meaning the Governor of the Central Bank, the Chief Executive of the Financial Regulator or the Registrar of Credit Unions, as appropriate.

110 Officer or employee of the Central Bank or the Financial Regulator, or some other person who in the opinion of the relevant responsible authority has the qualifications and experience necessary to exercise the powers conferred.

(d)   if a person who is requested to produce a particular document or material relating to that business is unable to produce it, request the person to state, to the best of that person's knowledge and belief, where the document or material is located;

(e)   request any person (including a person who is not on the premises at the relevant time) who appears to the authorised person to have or to have access to information relating to the documents or material, or to the business of body, to provide that information or to answer questions with respect to the documents or material or that business.

(4)   A person to whom a request for such abovementioned information is made shall:

(a)   comply with the request so far as it is possible to do so; and

(b)   give such other assistance and information to the authorised person with respect to the business of body concerned as is reasonable in the circumstances.

(5)   The requirement to comply with a request for information also extends to:

(a)   a liquidator of the body concerned;

(b)   any person who is or has been an officer, employee or agent of body; or

(c)   other persons who in the opinion of the authorised officer are in possession of relevant information.

(6)   If any person from whom production of a document or material is required claims a lien on the document or material, its production does not affect the lien.

Nothing in these sections requires a legal practitioner to produce a document or material containing a privileged communication made by or to the practitioner as such or to provide information contained in such a communication.

Civil financial sanctions

Administrative sanction procedure

4.158 Currently, the Financial Regulator is unique in Ireland in that he may impose administrative sanctions under civil law, unlike other Regulators where constitutional grounds are often cited as a reason why Regulators may not impose administrative or civil financial sanctions. The Financial Regulator has entered into various settlement agreements and imposed monetary penalties in respect of its powers in this regard.[111] No challenges have been made in respect of the exercise of its powers in this area. If

---

111 On 24 October 2008, the Financial Regulator published a settlement agreement with Quinn Insurance Limited and Mr Sean Quinn. The company was required to pay a monetary penalty of €3,250,000 to the Financial Regulator. Settlement agreements which also produced significant fines involved Fexco Stockbroking Ltd in March 2008 with a fine in the sum of €80,000, and €50,000 was levied on the Irish Nationwide Building Society in October 2008. Mr Sean Quinn (senior) was also personally required to pay a monetary penalty of €200,000. The previous highest personal monetary penalty as part of a settlement agreement was no more than €20,000 in August 2008. See paras **4.168–4.170** below for further details on settlement agreements.

challenged to the court, it will be interesting to see how this unique power is considered in light of the Constitution. Ireland is obliged under EC law to impose civil financial sanctions in relation to market abuse. Article 14 of the Market Abuse Directive, which prohibits insider dealing and market manipulation, provides:

Without prejudice to the right of Member States to impose criminal sanctions, Member States shall ensure, in conformity with their national law, that the appropriate administrative measures can be taken or administrative sanctions be imposed against the persons responsible where the provisions adopted in the implementation of this Directive have not been complied with. Member States shall ensure that these measures are effective, proportionate and dissuasive.

The word 'shall' is pivotal in this Article, since in this way, the provision of administrative sanctions would be necessitated by Ireland's membership of the EU and in that regard would fall within the exception of Art 29.4.10° of the Constitution.[112] This provision states that no provision[113] of the Constitution invalidates laws enacted or measures adopted which are necessitated by the obligations of membership of the EU or of the Communities, or prevent laws enacted or measures adopted by the Institutions of the EU or Communities from having the force of law in the State.

4.159 Article 38.1 of the Constitution provides that: 'No person shall be tried on any criminal charge save in due course of law.'[114] It may be recalled that Art 34.1 provides that 'Justice shall be administered in courts established by law by judges appointed in the manner provided by this Constitution and save in such special and limited cases as may be prescribed by law shall be administered in public.' It has been consistently held under Irish law that the imposition of a significant financial penalty may amount to the matter being considered penal or criminal in effect.[115] However, where EC law requires administrative sanctions, that is, where the administrative sanction requirement is underpinned by articles in an EC Directive (or an EC regulation) using the construct 'shall' as opposed to 'may', then the EC provision in this way 'trumps'[116] the constitutional bias against civil administrative sanctions by virtue of the effect of Art 29.4.10°. Where there is no such EC law requirement, where, for example, the

112 *Meagher v Minister for Agriculture* [1994] 1 IR 329; *Maher v Minister for Agriculture* [2001] 2 IR 139.

113 It has been noted that the reference to 'provision' excludes *inter alia* the preamble of Bunreacht na hÉireann and constitutional law outside the scope of Bunreacht na hÉireann such as natural law: Phelan, *Revolt or Revolution: The Constitutional Boundaries of the European Community* (Thomson Round Hall, 1997), p 350.

114 It shall be noted that the use of the word 'person' in this context would not appear to exclude a legal person such as a company. See also *National Irish Bank Ltd (under investigation), Re* [1999] 1 ILRM 321.

115 *Melling v O Mathghamhna* [1962] IR 1; *Conroy v the Attorney General* [1965] IR 411; *In Re Haughey* [1971] IR 217, *Kostan v Ireland* [1978] ILRM 12; *O'Sullivan v Hartnett* [1983] ILRM 79; *Montemuino v Minister for Communications Marine and Natural Resources, Ireland and the AG* [2008] IEHC 157.

116 For reference to the new legal order created by EC law: *Van Gend en Loos* 26/62 [1963] ECR 1; *Costa v Enel* 6/64 [1964] ECR 585. See also Cahill, Connery, Kennedy & Power, *European Law* (4th edn, Oxford University Press, 2008), Ch 4.

construct 'may' as opposed to 'shall' is used, Art 29.4.10° may not be used to justify the imposition of a civil administrative sanction in this regard.

4.160 The Financial Regulator published guidelines as to how administrative sanction procedures will be followed on its website under a document called 'Outline of the Administrative Sanctions Procedure'.[117] The 2004 Act amended the Central Bank Act 1942 and provided the Financial Regulator with the power to administer sanctions in respect of prescribed contraventions by regulated financial service providers and persons concerned in the management of regulated financial service providers.[118] The relevant legislative provisions are contained in Pt IIIC of the Central Bank Act 1942, as amended. Formal guidance was issued pursuant to s 33BD of the Central Bank Act 1942, as amended. There is also a publication on the Financial Services Regulator's website detailing the structures and procedures of the Financial Regulator's Administrative Sanctions Procedure.

4.161 If the Financial Regulator is concerned that a prescribed contravention may be or may have been committed, an examination into the issue may be commenced to establish whether there are reasonable grounds for a suspicion that a regulated financial service provider and/or a person concerned in the management of a regulated financial service is committing or has committed a prescribed contravention.

The Financial Regulator will obtain information about the suspected prescribed contravention. Once the examination has been concluded, a decision will then be taken about whether to establish an inquiry. A decision will not be taken to establish an inquiry before the regulated financial service provider concerned and/or the person(s) concerned in its management has had a reasonable opportunity to respond.

An inquiry may be held where there are reasonable grounds to suspect that there is or has been a prescribed contravention. The inquiry shall decide if the prescribed contravention has occurred and determine the appropriate sanctions.

4.162 As an alternative, the Administrative Sanctions Procedure provides that, at any time before the conclusion of an inquiry, the matter may be resolved by entering into a settlement agreement. This is a written agreement which binds both the Financial Regulator and the regulated financial service provider and/or person(s) concerned in the management of the regulated financial service provider.

4.163 Decisions of an inquiry may be appealed to the Financial Services Appeals Tribunal and to the High Court. A prescribed contravention is defined in s 33AN of the Central Bank Act 1942, as amended, as a contravention of:

(a) a provision of a designated enactment or designated statutory instrument;

(b) a code made, or a direction given, under such a provision;

---

117 http://www.financialregulator.ie/data/in_asp/outline%200f/
%20Administrative%20Sanctions%20Procedure%20_%20October&202005.pdf.

118 The following section is based on the guidelines issued by Liam O'Reilly, Chief Executive for, and on behalf of, the Irish Financial Services Regulatory Authority on 7 October 2005, in exercise of its powers including its powers under s 33BD of the Central Bank Act 1942 as inserted by the 2004 Act.

(c) any condition or requirement imposed under a provision of a designated enactment, designated statutory instrument, code or direction, or

(d) any obligation imposed on any person by Pt IIIC of the Central Bank Act 1942 or imposed by the Financial Regulator pursuant to a power exercised under Pt IIIC of the Central Bank Act 1942.

4.164 The list of designated enactments and designated statutory instruments is located in Sch 2 of the Central Bank Act 1942 (as amended by s 31 of the 2003 Act). Section 20 of the 2004 Act further amends Sch 2 of the Central Bank Act 1942. Section 87(2) of the Investment Funds, Companies and Miscellaneous Provisions Act 2005 further amends the list of designated enactments in Sch 2 of Central Bank Act 1942. Section 87(1) of the Investment Funds, Companies and Miscellaneous Provisions Act 2005 amends s 33AN of the Central Bank Act 1942 by narrowing the scope of designated enactments and designated statutory instruments – for the purposes of Pt IIIC of the Central Bank Act 1942. Schedule 2 of the Central Bank Act 1942 is not an exhaustive list as there are many instances where the Financial Regulator issues codes, imposes conditions, directions or requirements, pursuant to legislation, directions or codes. Some of these obligations are imposed on a bilateral basis. These obligations will be known to the Financial Regulator and the financial service provider involved.

4.165 Section 33AN of the Central Bank Act 1942 provides that 'contravene' includes fail to comply, and also includes:

(i) attempting to contravene;

(ii) aiding, abetting, counselling or procuring a person to commit a contravention, inducing, or attempting to induce, a person (whether by threats or promises or otherwise) to commit a contravention;

(iii) being (directly or indirectly) knowingly concerned in, or a party to, a contravention;

(iv) conspiring with others to commit a contravention.

In respect of prescribed contraventions, the Financial Regulator may deal with the issue in a number of ways. Depending on the seriousness of the prescribed contravention, the Financial Regulator may decide to take no further action, resolve the matter by taking supervisory action, agree a settlement, refer the case to inquiry for determination and sanction, initiate a summary criminal prosecution and/or refer the case to another authority or enforcement body.

4.166 The decision to take enforcement action will be determined on a case-by-case basis, taking into account the full circumstances of each case. The following overriding objectives will be considered:

(i) the enforcement action should promote compliance by the regulated financial service provider or persons concerned in its management;

(ii) the enforcement action should promote compliance within the industry or sector;

(iii) the enforcement action should be proportionate, and be likely to support the economic, efficient and effective pursuit of the strategic objectives of the Financial Regulator.

According to the procedures, in some cases no further action will be taken. No further action may also be appropriate if the matter giving rise for concern is minor in nature and where immediate remedial action has been taken and full co-operation has been provided.

Supervisory warnings

4.167 In some cases, it is set out in the procedures that where it appears that a prescribed contravention has occurred, the Financial Regulator may decide that the case may most appropriately be dealt with by taking supervisory action. This will be particularly appropriate if the prescribed contravention has limited regulatory significance or can be fully dealt with without applying sanctions. The Financial Regulator may issue a supervisory warning where there are reasonable grounds to suspect a breach of statutory or regulatory requirements has occurred. Supervisory warnings may be issued where full co-operation is received and the problem was rectified immediately and other considerations supporting enforcement do not apply. If it proves necessary to issue a supervisory warning, that shall form part of the compliance record of the regulated financial service provider or person concerned in its management. In relation to further prescribed contraventions, such a warning may influence the Financial Regulator's decision about whether to commence enforcement action, to agree a settlement or to hold an inquiry. Supervisory warnings may also be considered cumulatively. Where a supervisory warning is taken into account by the Financial Regulator in determining whether enforcement action should take place, the age of the warning shall be taken into account. Supervisory warnings will not be taken into account in deciding whether a breach has occurred or the level of sanctions to apply. It is important to note that unlike settlement agreements, supervisory warnings may not be taken into account in determining appropriate sanctions pursuant to the Administrative Sanctions Procedure if any further prescribed contraventions occur.

Settlement agreements

4.168 Section 33AV of the Central Bank Act 1942 (as amended) provides that if the Financial Regulator suspects on reasonable grounds that:

(i) a regulated financial service provider is committing or has committed a prescribed contravention; or

(ii) a person concerned in the management of the financial service provider is participating or has participated in such contravention,

the Financial Regulator may enter into a settlement agreement to resolve the suspected contravention.

Settlement is voluntary. A settlement may be agreed at any time up to the conclusion of the inquiry. The settlement agreement must be in writing and is binding on the Financial Regulator and the regulated financial service provider or person concerned in its management. The terms of the settlement agreement may contain the name of the regulated financial service provider or person concerned in its management, the sanctions imposed, together with any other terms, and require the agreement to be published. The Financial Regulator has a preference for publicising settlement agreements (the amount of detail may, of course, vary) but accepts that there may be occasions when this preference is not in the public interest. The terms of each settlement agreement shall be decided on a case-by-case basis.

4.169 A firm or individual who is subject to the Administrative Sanctions Procedure may discuss the possibility of a settlement agreement with the staff of the Financial Regulator on an informal basis. Settlement discussions will be conducted on a 'without prejudice' basis. In this way, the contents of the settlement discussions will not be made known to an inquiry if no settlement agreement is reached and the case is subsequently referred to inquiry. Settlement discussions may be revealed to the inquiry at the stage when sanctions are being considered.

4.170 The Financial Regulator expects the firm in question to act promptly and to take the necessary remedial action to deal with its concerns before any settlement agreement can be contemplated. Settlement agreements shall be concluded only where the basis for settlement is consistent with the general approach to regulation that the Financial Regulator adopts, and is fair having regard to all the facts known, and that to conclude a settlement agreement will contribute to the efficient, effective and economic use of resources. It is important to note that a settlement agreement shall form part of the firm's compliance record. In relation to further prescribed contraventions, a settlement agreement may influence the Financial Regulator's decision about whether to commence enforcement action, to agree a settlement or to hold an inquiry and in determining appropriate sanctions. Unlike supervisory warnings, settlement agreements may be taken into account in determining appropriate sanctions pursuant to the Administrative Sanctions Procedure if any further prescribed contraventions occur. Where a settlement agreement is taken into account by the Financial Regulator, the age of the agreement shall be taken into account. Details of various settlement agreements entered into by the Financial Regulator are published on its website.[119]

Examination

4.171 If the Financial Regulator has a concern that a prescribed contravention may be or may have been committed, an examination into the issue may be commenced to establish whether there are reasonable grounds for a suspicion that a regulated financial service provider and/or a person concerned in the management of a regulated financial service provider is committing or has committed a prescribed contravention. Examinations will usually be conducted by the supervisory function of the Financial Regulator. Additionally, the Financial Regulator may engage external experts to assist in the examination. The Financial Regulator will obtain information about the prescribed contravention. This will usually involve the Financial Regulator writing to the regulated financial service provider and/or persons concerned in its management,

---

119 See para **4.158** above in this regard.

setting out the concern(s) and requiring information, comments and explanations. The Financial Regulator may require the regulated financial service provider and/or persons concerned in its management to engage external experts to assist in the examination. The Financial Regulator may require further information and may conduct interviews and take statements. In the course of the examination, the Financial Regulator may also need to contact third parties who may have information about the suspected prescribed contravention. These actions may be undertaken by external experts engaged by the Financial Regulator. The purpose of the examination shall be to gather sufficient information about a suspected prescribed contravention so that a decision may be taken about whether or not an inquiry should be held. Once the examination has been concluded, a report appending all relevant information will be prepared for consideration by the person(s) in the supervisory function who are designated to decide whether to establish an inquiry. Before the decision about establishing an inquiry is taken, a copy of the report appending all relevant information will be sent to the regulated financial service provider and/or person(s) concerned in its management. The report will identify precisely the prescribed contravention that is being alleged.

4.172 The regulated financial service provider or person concerned in its management shall be given a reasonable opportunity to make written representations and submit any additional information about the prescribed contravention and whether an inquiry should be held. These representations, together with the report appending all relevant information, will be placed before the person(s) designated to take the decision about holding an inquiry and shall be considered as part of the decision on whether to hold an inquiry.

Treatment of confidential information

4.173 The Financial Regulator's examination will remain confidential. There are certain circumstances where the Financial Regulator is *required* by law to make disclosure and there are certain circumstances where the Financial Regulator is *permitted* by law to make disclosures.

Inquiry

4.174 If it is determined that there are reasonable grounds to suspect that a prescribed contravention is being or has been committed, the case may be referred to an inquiry held pursuant to the Administrative Sanctions Procedure and, if appropriate, sanctions may be imposed. The purpose of the inquiry is to determine whether a prescribed contravention is being or has been committed and to determine the appropriate sanctions to apply. Section 33AP of the Central Bank Act 1942 provides that a written inquiry notice will be sent in advance of an inquiry being held. The notice will:

    (i)   set out the suspected contraventions;

   (ii)   specify the grounds upon which the suspicions are based;

  (iii)   specify the date, time and place of the inquiry;

(iv)   invite the financial service provider or person concerned in its management to attend the inquiry and/or to make written submissions;

(v)   set out the procedure that is envisaged.

In addition to the inquiry notice, the following information will be furnished:

(i)   details of the information relevant to the issue (statements, documents and any other relevant material); and

(ii)   a report prepared by or for the Financial Regulator setting out the relevant prescribed contravention(s) and the facts and matters relied on in support of the case.

4.175 The regulated financial service provider or person concerned in its management shall be asked to:

(i)   confirm if the alleged prescribed contravention(s) is/are admitted or denied;

(ii)   identify agreed facts;

(iii)   submit representations on the alleged prescribed contraventions; and

(iv)   submit any representations on the procedure.

4.176 In every case, the Regulated Financial Service Provider or person concerned in its management is entitled to make written representations to the inquiry. Section 33AP(3) of the Central Bank Act 1942 provides that these representations must be submitted in advance of the inquiry.

4.177 The Financial Regulator may decide not to adopt the approach of a full oral hearing in respect of every inquiry. Section 33AY(1) of the Central Bank Act 1942 provides for the inquiry to be conducted with as little formality and technicality, and with as much expedition, as a proper consideration of the matters will allow. Section 33AP(5) of the Central Bank Act 1942 provides that the inquiry may be held in the absence of the regulated financial service provider or person concerned in its management so long as an opportunity to attend the inquiry or make written submissions has been provided. The options will be:

(a)   a consideration of the case on the basis of the written representations and documents alone;

(b)   a consideration of the case on the basis of both written and oral information and, if relevant, depositions;

(c)   the factors that will be taken into account in determining the procedure to be adopted are:

(i)   the complexity of the case,

(ii)   the benefit that oral examination would add to the written representations, and

(iii)   the unique facts of the case.

4.178 The inquiry will consider representations on the appropriate procedure to adopt prior to finalising its approach. Once the inquiry has determined the approach to be adopted, it then may give further directions about submission of information, documents or attendance at the inquiry.

If the case is admitted, the inquiry shall write and request:

(a) consent to dispense with an inquiry; and

(b) offer sanctions so that the need to hold a sanctions inquiry is avoided.

If no response is received or consent is not given, then an inquiry shall be held to determine sanctions pursuant to s 33AR(1) and (2) of the Central Bank Act 1942.

If the case is denied or no reply is received, then an inquiry shall be held to determine whether the allegation is proven and what appropriate sanctions, if any, should be imposed.

4.179 Section 33AZ of the Central Bank Act 1942 provides for inquiries to be held in public, save where the parties agree to hold the inquiry in private or where information may arise of a confidential nature or relating to an offence against a law of the State or unfairly prejudicing a person's reputation. A decision not to hold the inquiry in public may be varied or revoked at any time. The decision to hold the inquiry in public or private (either in whole or in part) will be taken on a case-by-case basis. The inquiry will seek the views of the parties on holding the inquiry in private or public and will come to its conclusions having had regard to the nature of the subject matter before the inquiry, the representations made and the public interest.

4.180 The purpose of an inquiry shall be to determine on the balance of probabilities if there has been a prescribed contravention. It will also determine what sanctions to apply. The burden of proof rests with the Financial Regulator. Pursuant to s 33BD of the Central Bank Act 1942, binding guidelines about the procedure have been published and are available for downloading from the Financial Regulator's website or a copy can be obtained by writing to the address at the back of this document.

Section 33AY(2) of the Central Bank Act 1942 provides that the inquiry is not bound by the rules of evidence and may consider any relevant information brought to its attention. The inquiry will adhere to the requirements of natural and constitutional justice.

4.181 An inquiry will be conducted by one or more persons, being officers of the Financial Regulator or employees of the Central Bank who shall not also be directly responsible for authorisation, ongoing supervision of the regulated financial service provider or person concerned in its management, or examination of the prescribed contravention. This team may be assisted by other officers of the Financial Regulator or members of staff of the Central Bank or agents of the Financial Regulator who shall not, however, decide the matters before the inquiry. The Chief Executive shall approve the team for each inquiry and shall nominate the presiding person. All decisions of the inquiry shall be determined by a majority of the votes of the members of the inquiry team present, with each member having one vote. Additionally, the presiding person shall have the power to take decisions relating to procedural matters, in advance of and between inquiry meetings.

4.182 If it is determined that there has been a prescribed contravention, written notification of the findings of fact and the grounds upon which they are based, together with the sanctions imposed, if any, will be provided.

Sanctions

4.183 The following sanctions may be imposed:

(a)   caution or reprimand;

(b)   direction to refund or withhold all or part of an amount of money charged or paid, or to be charged or paid, for the provision of a financial service;

(c)   monetary penalty (not exceeding €5,000,000 in the case of a corporate and unincorporated body, not exceeding €500,000 in the case of a person);

(d)   direction disqualifying a person from being concerned in the management of a regulated financial service provider;

(e)   direction to cease the contravention if it is found the contravention is continuing; or

(f)   direction to pay all or part of the costs of the investigation and inquiry.

4.184 In determining sanctions, all the circumstances of the case will be taken into account. Additionally, regard will be had to the following factors:

1.   *Nature and seriousness*

(a)   Whether the contravention was deliberate, dishonest or reckless;

(b)   duration and frequency of the contravention; the amount of any benefit gained or loss avoided due to the contravention;

(c)   whether the contravention reveals serious or systemic weaknesses of the management systems or internal controls relating to all or part of the business;

(d)   the extent to which the contravention departs from the required standard;

(e)   the impact of the contravention on the orderliness of the financial markets, including whether public confidence in those markets has been damaged;

(f)   the loss or risk of loss caused to consumers or other market users;

(g)   the nature and extent of any financial crime facilitated, occasioned or otherwise attributable to the contravention;

(h)   whether there are a number of smaller issues, which individually may not justify administrative sanction, but which do so when taken collectively; and

(i)   any potential or pending criminal proceedings in respect of the contravention which will be prejudiced or barred if a monetary penalty is imposed pursuant to the Administrative Sanctions Procedure.

2.   *The conduct of the regulated financial service provider or person concerned in its management after the contravention*

(a)   How quickly, effectively and completely the financial service provider or person concerned in its management brought the contravention to the attention of the Financial Regulator or any other relevant Financial Regulator;

(b)   the degree of co-operation with the Financial Regulator or other agency provided during the examination of the contravention;

(c)   any remedial steps taken since the contravention was identified, including: identifying whether consumers have suffered loss and compensating them; taking disciplinary action against staff involved (where appropriate); addressing any systemic failures; and taking action designed to ensure that similar problems do not arise in the future;

(d)   the likelihood that the same type of contravention will re-occur if no administrative sanction is imposed; and

(e)   whether the contravention was admitted or denied.

3.   *The previous record of the regulated financial service provider or person concerned in its management*

(a)   Whether the Financial Regulator has taken any previous action resulting in a settlement, sanctions or there are relevant previous criminal convictions;

(b)   whether the regulated financial service provider or person concerned in its management has previously been requested to take remedial action; and

(c)   general compliance history.

4.   *General considerations*

(a)   Prevalence of the contravention;

(b)   action taken by the Financial Regulator in previous similar cases; and

(c)   any other relevant consideration.

Section 33AS(3)(a) and (b) of the Central Bank Act 1942 provides that if the conduct engaged in by the regulated financial service provider or person concerned in its management constitutes two or more prescribed contraventions, only one monetary penalty may be imposed in respect of the same conduct. Section 33AS(1) and (2) of the Central Bank Act 1942 provides that the amount of the monetary penalty should not be in such an amount as would be likely to cause the regulated financial service provider to cease business or in the case of a person to be adjudged bankrupt.

Publicity

4.185 Section 33BC of the Central Bank Act 1942 provides that in the event of an adverse decision following an inquiry, or where sanctions are agreed, details shall be published, save where the information is confidential, pertains to a criminal offence or would unfairly prejudice a person's reputation. Subject to these special and particular safeguards set out in legislation, findings of an occurrence of a prescribed contravention concerning a named regulated financial service provider or person concerned in its management and the sanctions to apply will be published in all cases.

4.186 The Financial Regulator has also published various publicity notices on its website in respect of investigations under the Market Abuse Regulations. It has entered into various settlement agreements in relation to those investigations. The Market Abuse Regulations, *inter alia*, provide for the investigation of possible contraventions of the regulatory requirements provided in the Market Abuse Regulations and Rules. The Market Abuse Regulations provide for enforcement action, including the option of administrative sanctions that can be imposed by the Financial Regulator. The Financial Regulator may conduct an examination into possible 'prescribed contraventions' (as defined in reg 34 of the Market Abuse Regulations) of the Market Abuse Regulations and Rules. The Market Abuse Regulations provide that once the examination has concluded and the Financial Regulator has reason to suspect that a prescribed contravention is being or has been committed, a decision will then be taken about whether to appoint one or more assessors. The assessor(s) shall decide if the prescribed contravention has occurred and determine the appropriate sanctions. The Financial Regulator has appointed a panel of assessors.

4.187 The legislation provides that, at any time up to the conclusion of an assessment, the Financial Regulator may enter into a binding settlement agreement with an entity or individual to resolve the matter. Where an entity or individual enters into such an agreement at an early point in the process, the terms of the settlement will reflect the savings in time, resources and money which would result.

On its website the Financial Regulator states that it will not hesitate to use sanctions where appropriate; however, its goal is to resolve issues to the benefit of the market and consumer speedily and efficiently.

Consequences of a finding of non-compliance

4.188 The Financial Regulator has the power to caution or reprimand. It can also direct to refund or withhold all or part of an amount of money charged or paid, or to be charged or paid, for the provision of a financial service. It can impose a monetary penalty of up to €5m in the case of a corporate and unincorporated body, and up to €500,000 in the case of a person. It can issue a direction disqualifying a person from being concerned in the management of a regulated financial service provider. Furthermore, it can issue directions to cease the contravention if it is found the contravention is continuing. It can issue directions to pay all or part of the costs of the investigation and inquiry.

Criminal Enforcement

Penalties and punishments

4.189 The Financial Regulator also has criminal powers of enforcement. The criminal offences created in respect of financial services are divided into two types: indictable offences and summary offences. Indictable offences, which are the more serious cases, are heard by a judge and jury in the Circuit Criminal Court or the Central Criminal Court. They carry the most serious penalties if the court convicts the accused and are subject to appeal to the Court of Criminal Appeal. Summary offences, which are the less serious offences, are heard by a judge without a jury in the District Court, and on appeal in the Circuit Court. The Financial Regulator will be given discretion for prosecuting various summary offences. When determining whether or not to prosecute, the Financial Regulator follows the DPP's Guidelines For Prosecutors, which are published on the DPP's website.[120]

Breaches of criminal law committed by a regulated financial service provider or person concerned in its management for which the Financial Regulator may initiate a summary prosecution, may also be prescribed contraventions.

4.190 The Financial Regulator may impose a sanction via the Administrative Sanctions Procedure, in addition to bringing a criminal prosecution itself or a prosecution being brought by another body or agency. However, certain restrictions apply in circumstances where both a criminal prosecution and administrative sanctions are possible. No criminal prosecution may be brought if the Administrative Sanctions Procedure leads to the imposition of a monetary penalty. If a criminal prosecution has been brought in respect of an offence that also involves a prescribed contravention, and the financial service provider or person concerned in its management is found either guilty or not guilty, then no monetary penalty may be imposed pursuant to the Administrative Sanctions Procedure.[121]

4.191 In light of the limited penalties available pursuant to summary criminal prosecutions, as a matter of general policy, the Financial Regulator has decided to pursue prescribed contraventions pursuant to the Administrative Sanctions Procedure instead of bringing a summary prosecution. Only in exceptional circumstances will the Financial Regulator pursue a prescribed contravention via the criminal courts.

4.192 Where appropriate, the Financial Regulator may refer the suspected prescribed contravention to the Garda Síochána and/or the DPP for consideration of prosecution. The suspected prescribed contravention may also be referred to other enforcement agencies or bodies for consideration of prosecution. If such a referral is made, the Financial Regulator will consider what action is appropriate in the circumstances and apply a public interest test in deciding whether to forbear in relation to any matter being pursued by another agency or body. The restrictions that apply in circumstances where both a criminal prosecution and administrative sanctions are possible, as described in paras **4.158***ff*, will be relevant to this consideration.

4.193 Section 33AT(2)(a) and (b) of the Central Bank Act 1942 provides that no monetary penalty may be imposed if the regulated financial service provider or person concerned in its management has been found guilty or not guilty of committing a criminal offence and that offence involves a prescribed contravention. Section 33AT(1) of the Central Bank Act 1942 provides that if a monetary penalty is imposed by or

---

120 http://www.dppireland.ie.

121 A version of *Ne bis in Idem* or double jeopardy may be thus avoided, although in this instance, rather than a second prosecution in relation to the same facts, a second 'administrative sanction procedure' in relation to the same facts is prohibited.

agreed with the inquiry and the relevant prescribed contravention is also a criminal offence, then no prosecution may be brought in respect of that offence.

APPEALS AND JUDICIAL REVIEW

4.194 Decisions of the Financial Regulator are also, of course, open to judicial review and may also be appealed to the Irish Financial Services Appeals Tribunal. Appeals in respect of financial services are addressed in **Ch 10** on appeals. Judicial Review is dealt with in detail in **Ch 11**.

Chapter 5

BROADCASTING

APPROACH OF THIS CHAPTER

5.001 This chapter examines broadcasting regulatory issues from a practical perspective. As with the other sectors, it is useful in the regulation of broadcasting to understand its historical foundations and how this area is developing. The regulation of the broadcasting sector is characterised currently by the presence of several Regulators, namely, the RTÉ Authority, the Broadcasting Commission of Ireland (BCI) and the Broadcasting Complaints Commission (BCC). Once the Broadcasting Bill 2008 is enacted,[1] it is intended that all of these Regulators will be merged into one new Regulator, namely, the Broadcasting Authority of Ireland (BAI). The Commission for Communications Regulation (ComReg) also plays a role in respect of the broadcasting sector. The Department of Communications, Energy and Natural Resources is the responsible Department for leading policy developments in this area.

HISTORY OF BROADCASTING

5.002 Broadcasting had diverse origins across the globe. Very early radio transmissions only carried the dots and dashes of wireless telegraphy. At first, the concept of broadcasting was new and unusual – with telegraphs, communication had been one-to-one, rather than one-to-many. One of the first signals of significant power that carried voice and music was accomplished in 1906.[2] In Ireland, the first broadcast was made in 1916 in Dublin in Morse code to the effect that an Irish Republic had been declared. Until that point, telegraphy had been point-to-point narrowcast. In the UK, the first experimental broadcasts, from Marconi's factory in Chelmsford, began in 1920. Two years later, a consortium of radio manufacturers formed the British Broadcasting Company, which later became the British Broadcasting Corporation (BBC). The John Logie Baird system was one of the first systems of picture transmission –transmitting pictures between London and Glasgow using telephone lines in 1927. A year later, radio waves were used to transmit pictures between London and New York.[3] While Ireland had been one of the first movers in Europe in respect of radio, it was relatively slow to commence television broadcasting. The first voice broadcast took place in 1925 in Dublin by 2RN and radio service began on 1 January 1926 with 2RN. The first high-power station was established in Athlone in 1932. 2RN (which operated in Dublin), 6CK (which operated in Cork), together with the station

---

1   This was originally scheduled for December 2008 but the timing was since pushed back.

2   By Reginald Fessenden when he made a Christmas Eve broadcast to ships at sea from Massachusetts.

3   His company, Baird Television Development Company, made the first programme for the BBC (broadcast on 30 September 1929).

established in Athlone became known as 'Radio Athlone' or 'Raidio Áth Luain'. It was receivable almost nationwide. Radio Athlone became known as 'Radio Éireann' in 1938, which became one of the founding organisations of the European Broadcasting Union in 1950.

5.003 The Department of Finance at the time had quite a limited budget and could not approve expenditure for anything considered to be a 'luxury' such as television. In the late 1950s, a Television Committee was formed. The broadcasting service in Ireland was at that time operated as a section of the Department of Posts and Telegraphs. In 1960 under the Broadcasting Authority Act 1960, Radio Éireann was converted from an arm of the Department of Posts and Telegraphs into a semi-State body and given responsibility for television. Eamonn Andrews was appointed as the chairman. Teilifís Éireann began broadcasting on New Year's Eve 1961. The opening address by President de Valera described the benefits and disadvantages of the new medium; he went on to say that like 'atomic energy, it can be used for incalculable good, but it can also do irreparable harm'. The name of the semi-State body was changed to Radio Teilifís Éireann under the Broadcasting Authority (Amendment) Act 1966, and both the radio and television services became known as RTÉ in that year. The first official colour transmissions were made in 1969. All of RTÉ's studios at Donnybrook, Dublin were equipped for colour broadcasts by 1976. In 1978, RTÉ 2, a second television channel was launched which was renamed Network 2 in 1987. A new Irish-language TV service, Teilifís na Gaeilge (now TG4), began broadcasting in 1996. TG4 became independent on 1 April 2007 and a board of Teilifís na Gaeilge was appointed in March 2007.

5.004 The launch of TV3 took some time to complete. In 1989, Ireland's newly-formed independent Regulator, the Independent Radio and Television Commission (IRTC), was charged with inviting applications from prospective broadcasters for the exclusive right to negotiate a television programme service contract with the IRTC. The successful applicant, announced in April 1989, was a consortium, TV3. TV3 was unable to secure the necessary financing and the IRTC withdrew the offer in 1991. This was followed by legal and regulatory battles, culminating in 1993 in the invitation to the original consortium to begin new negotiations for a broadcasting contract. In February 1997, a new consortium reached an agreement with CanWest Global Communications Corp., a Canada-based international broadcaster, regarding the development and operation of TV3. In October 1997, the newly formed partnership signed a broadcasting contract with the IRTC, and TV3 was launched in September 1998 as Ireland's first free-to-air commercial channel not dependent on State funding or TV license fees.[4] The BCI (the successor to the IRTC) most recently issued a contract in March 2006 to Channel 6 pursuant to the Broadcasting Act 2001.

---

4   According to the European Commission decision on TV3's State aid complaint detailed in paras **5.160***ff*, in terms of audience shares, RTÉ One and Two had, during the period from 2001 to 2006, a constant share of around 40 per cent (all day) and 44–45 per cent (peak time), TG4 had 2–3 per cent (all day as well as peak time) and TV3 had 12–14 per cent (all day and peak time). Non-Irish channels such as the BBC had a market share of around 13 per cent.

5.005 In respect of national broadcasting on radio, Radio 1 has existed since 1938, RTÉ 2fm commenced broadcasting as RTÉ Radio 2 in 1979. RTÉ Lyric FM came on air in 1999, replacing FM3 Classical Music. RTÉ Raidió na Gaeltachta, an exclusively Irish language service, first began broadcasting in 1972. Digital Audio Broadcasting (DAB) test broadcasts of RTÉ's four stations began on 1 January 2006 along the east coast of Ireland, also carrying the private Today FM and World Radio Network English for Europe, to which RTÉ is a contributing broadcaster. Newstalk 106–108 fm went national in 2006.

5.006 From the outset, RTÉ faced competition from British TV channels such as the BBC, ITV, S4C and UTV broadcasting from Northern Ireland and Wales, whose signals spilled over into the Republic. In the 1990s, more competition came from satellite television, especially from BSkyB, which is based in the UK.

5.007 Under s 31 of the Broadcasting Authority Act 1960, the Minister for Posts and Telegraphs of the day could direct RTÉ 'not to broadcast any matter, or any matter of any particular class'. In 1971, the first such direction was issued, directing RTÉ not to broadcast 'any matter that could be calculated to promote the aims or activities of any organisation which engages in, promotes, encourages or advocates the attaining of any particular objectives by violent means'. In 1977, a new direction in the form of the Broadcasting Authority Act 1960 (Section 31) Order 1977 was issued where RTÉ was explicitly banned from broadcasting statements by spokespersons of Sinn Féin,[5] the Provisional IRA or any terrorist organisation banned in Northern Ireland by the Parliament of the United Kingdom. These directions were generally reissued on an annual basis until the final one of 1993.

5.008 In 2004, RTÉ and the Minister for Communications, Marine and Natural Resources agreed that, in the future, RTÉ would operate under a public service broadcasting charter. Further to a European Commission investigation as a result of a TV3 State aid complaint, it is intended that the Broadcasting Bill 2008 will abolish the current RTÉ legal structure, change the station into a company incorporated under the Companies' Acts, and separate out its regulatory role. RTÉ and TG4 will become separate companies limited by guarantee, with the Minister as the sole member of both companies. Under the draft legislation, RTÉ will now be legally obliged to agree a public service broadcasting charter every five years and publish a statement of commitments every year. It will be under the jurisdiction of the proposed BAI.

5.009 A pilot Digital Terrestrial Television (DTT) programme is being undertaken with a view to the analogue system, which is currently in place nationwide, being replaced with a digital system. The 'analogue switch off' date is expected to occur in 2012. On 21 July 2008, Boxer DTT Ltd, a consortium made up of Communicorp, Boxer TV Access in Sweden and BT Ireland was awarded a contract by the BCI to operate the national commercial pay DTT service. RTÉ will operate the free-to-air Multiplex (MUX) and will carry TV3, together with RTÉ1, RTÉ2 and TG4.

---

5   See paras **5.153** and **5.154**.

5.010 Indeed, broadcasting did open up a new world to Ireland with topics which were previously taboo being ventilated openly and it has been credited with bringing about major changes in the social fabric and national identity.

INTRODUCTION

5.011 The RTÉ Authority is responsible for the supervision of RTÉ. RTÉ operates three national TV services, RTÉ One, RTÉ Two and TG4, together with four national radio stations, RTÉ1, 2FM, Radio na Gaeltachata and Lyric FM. TG4 (previously Teilifís na Gaeilge) maintains a national television broadcasting service primarily in the Irish language. TG4 has been an independent statutory body since April 2007, having previously operated as part of the RTÉ family. RTÉ is the main public service broadcaster in Ireland. RTÉ's operations are divided into six main business divisions: RTÉ Television, RTÉ Radio, RTÉ News and Current Affairs, RTÉ Performing Groups, RTÉ Publishing and RTÉ NL (Networks). RTÉ's core activity is the broadcast of public service, free-to-air television (RTÉ One and RTÉ Two) and radio. Its television broadcasting can be received by over 99 per cent of the population in Ireland. RTÉ's commercial activities consist primarily of the sale of advertising and sponsorship and of the provision of transmission network service to broadcasters (through RTÉ NL), including the renting out of surplus tower or mast space. In addition, RTÉ generates commercial revenue from the release of television programmes on DVD/VHS and radio programmes on audio CD, the sales of television programmes, the sale of television facilities (including studio facilities and fixed contribution links to programme makers and broadcasters) and the sale of radio archive material and clips. Furthermore, RTÉ Publishing earns commercial revenue from the sale of the *RTÉ Guide* (a television and radio listing magazine).

5.012 The BCI is responsible for the licensing and regulation of the independent television and radio sector, which includes TV3, Today FM and Newstalk. BCI is also responsible for licensing certain new digital television services and for the development of codes of programming and advertising standards for television and radio. Non-EU applicants for broadcasting contracts are required by the BCI to have their place of residence or registered office within the EU.

The BCC deals with complaints made in relation to programme material and advertising on television and radio.

The BAI will be established under the Broadcasting Bill 2008 and will take over the functions of the RTÉ Authority, the BCI and the BCC.

ECONOMIC POLICY AND THE POLITICAL DIMENSION

5.013 Overlaps in the areas of telecommunications, information technology and media make these difficult areas to regulate prospectively. There is no bright line between these sectors. Regulators have the challenge of trying to legislate in a technology-neutral manner so as not to preclude any technology from developing and not to stifle innovation. The roll out of TV over mobile phones and TV over Internet, as well as Video on Demand (VoD) and Video over Broadband (VoB) are blurring the boundaries between media and communications. Mobile phones with mp3 players and radios further blur these already grey boundaries. An example of this is where consideration had to be given as to whether each mobile handset needed a wireless telegraphy license similar to the requirement to have a TV license as a result. In 2003, an order amending the Wireless Telegraphy Act 1926 exempted mobile telephones from the requirement to have a television license.[6]

5.014 Ireland's laws on the regulation of the broadcasting sector are based on primary legislation and on various EC Directives. Primary legislation includes the various broadcasting statutes as well as the Wireless Telegraphy Act 1926. EC Directives such as the Television without Frontiers Directive[7] (TVWF) may be transposed into Irish law by way of statute, such as the Broadcasting (Major Events Television Coverage) Act 1999 and the Broadcasting (Major Events Television Coverage) (Amendment) Act 2003. There is also the new Audiovisual Media Services Directive,[8] which has yet to be transposed into Irish law; however, the Broadcasting Bill 2008 will implement this particular Directive. Other Directives are transposed by way of secondary legislation, that is statutory instruments.

5.015 According to the Department of Communications, Energy and Natural Resources briefing to Minister Eamon Ryan of July 2007,[9] the government's policy in communications and broadcasting is to provide a supportive legislative and regulatory environment and to develop a leading edge R&D reputation in the information communications and digital technologies. The Broadcasting Policy Division of the Department is responsible for the development of the legislative and regulatory framework for the broadcasting sector and the funding of public service broadcasters and the development of the sector generally. The Department currently has corporate governance responsibility for RTÉ, TG4, the BCI and the BCC. RTÉ is the national public service broadcaster and is a statutorily independent body.

5.016 The Broadcasting Policy Division is responsible for arranging for the collection of the TV license fee by An Post and for making payments to RTÉ. The Division also manages exchequer funding of TG4, the BCI, the BCC and the Broadcasting Fund. The Division advises on whether the RTÉ license fee should be increased and recently concluded a five-year review of the TV license as a means of financing public service broadcasting, which resulted in an increase in the cost of a TV licence by €2. The current cost of a TV licence is €160. Licenses are discussed further at paras **5.098ff** below.

The policy as stated on the Department's website under the Broadcasting Policy Division is to develop a legislative framework to facilitate the provision of quality broadcasting services in Ireland. It is also to optimise the opportunities presented by

---

6   Wireless Telegraphy Act 1926 (Section 3) (Exemption of Mobile Telephones) (Amendment) Order 2003.
7   Directive 89/552/EEC, as amended by Directive 97/36/EC.
8   Directive 2007/65/EC.
9   Introductory brief from the Department of Communications, Energy and Natural Resources to Minister Eamon Ryan, July 2007; published on the website of the department of Communications, Energy and Natural Resources (http://www.dcenr.gov.ie).

the emerging technologies for new Irish-based broadcasting services. The Division furthermore seeks to ensure that the approach taken to issues arising from the convergence of telecommunications and broadcasting will optimise the contribution of broadcasters, programme-makers, infrastructure operators and other interested stakeholders to the development of the information society of Ireland.

5.017 Separately, there are State aid issues arising out of a complaint by TV3 to the European Commission in relation to the funding of RTÉ and TG4. The draft Broadcasting Bill 2008 is considered by the European Commission to resolve this issue. See paras **5.260***ff* for a further discussion of this particular State aid issue.

THE REGULATORS

5.018 As set out above, there are several Regulators involved in the regulation of the broadcasting sector in Ireland: the RTÉ Authority, the BCI, the BCC and ComReg. Once the Broadcasting Bill 2008 is adopted, the new Regulator will be the BAI who will act together with ComReg in this sector. In this way there will be a single content Regulator, namely the BAI. Each Regulator will be now discussed in turn below.

RTÉ Authority

5.019 Radio Teilifís Éireann (RTÉ) was established as a non-profit-making organisation and statutory corporation under the Broadcasting Authority Act 1960 (the 1960 Act). This Act established the RTÉ Authority as the Regulator and operator (and therein may lie the problem) of television broadcasting services and the then existing publicly-owned radio services. RTÉ, the public service broadcaster, is regulated and operated by the RTÉ Authority established under the Broadcasting Authority Act 1960. The regulation of RTÉ will change once the Broadcasting Bill 2008 is enacted.

RTÉ's functions are laid down in the Broadcasting Authority Act 1960, as amended, and in the Broadcasting Act 2001. Its duties and powers are set out in s 16(1) of the 1960 Act, which provides that 'the Authority' (RTÉ) shall establish and maintain a national television broadcasting service and shall have all such ancillary powers as are necessary for that purpose. Section 16(2) lists a number of specific powers granted. According to s 17 of the 1960 Act, RTÉ shall in its programming reflect the interests and concerns of the whole community, as well as the varied elements which make up the culture of the people of Ireland, and have special regard for the elements which distinguish that culture and, in particular, for the Irish language. It shall uphold the democratic values and have regard to the need for the formation of public awareness and understanding of the values and traditions of countries other than Ireland.

5.020 Section 28(1) provides that the national television and sound broadcasting service maintained by RTÉ is a public service that shall continue to be a free-to-air service and be made available, in so far as it is reasonably practicable, to the whole community on the island of Ireland. Pursuant to s 28(2), its programme schedules are to provide a comprehensive range of programmes in Irish and English that reflect the cultural diversity of Ireland, including programmes that entertain, inform and educate; cover sport events, religious and cultural activities; and cater for the expectations of the community generally, as well as members of the community with special or minority interests. Programmes shall also cover news and current affairs in Irish and English, including proceedings in the Houses of the Oireachtas and the European Parliament.

5.021 RTÉ's remit was further specified in the public service broadcasting charter, which was published by the Department of Communications, Marine and Natural Resources for the first time in June 2004. The charter is a statement of principles that clarifies what is expected of RTÉ, including RTÉ's accountability. At present, the charter does not have a statutory basis. RTÉ issued a set of guiding principles 'Implementing the Public Service Broadcasting Charter', in which RTÉ sets out the commitment to meet the expectations outlined in the charter and presents RTÉ's vision, mission, values, goals and strategic corporate plan. Since 2003, RTÉ has published annual statements of commitments, including more specific commitments on how to deliver on its public service obligations. These statements are to facilitate measurement and independent verification at the end of each year. As part of its annual reporting, RTÉ has committed to demonstrating how each specific commitment has been met. As the public service broadcaster, it both produces programmes and broadcasts on television, radio and the Internet.

5.022 RTÉ is a statutory body run by an Authority appointed by the government. General management of the organisation is in the hands of the Executive Board headed by the Director-General. State-sponsored bodies may be organised as statutory corporations with a board appointed by the sponsor Minister. RTÉ and TG4 are such corporations. RTÉ's board is known as the RTÉ Authority and is appointed by the Minister for Communications, Energy and Natural Resources (the Minister). The members of the RTÉ Authority are appointed by the Cabinet upon the recommendation of the. The RTÉ Authority is currently both the legal owner of RTÉ and its Regulator. RTÉ's headquarters are in Montrose in Dublin. The RTÉ Authority appoints the Director-General of RTÉ who, in effect, fulfils the dual role of Chief Executive and Editor-in-Chief.

5.023 RTÉ receives income from two main sources: the television licence fee and commercial revenue, including the sale of advertising and sponsorship. Within the State, it is necessary to pay a fee of €160 per annum in order to legally possess any piece of equipment capable of receiving television signals (not necessarily those of RTÉ). This money is collected by An Post on behalf of the Minister. In respect of revenue from sales and advertising, there are quotas in place to limit the amount of revenue RTÉ may procure through advertising, in view of the corporation's licence fee income. The licence fee does not fund RTÉ 2fm, RTÉ Aertel, *RTÉ Guide* or the website rte.ie. According to RTÉ's 2007 annual report (published on its website), it received €195.7m in licence fee revenue and €245.5m in commercial revenue in 2007.

RTÉ owns 100 per cent of a number of subsidiaries, such as RTÉ Commercial Enterprises Limited (publications and other commercial activities), RTÉ Music Limited (music publishing) and RTÉ NL (management of transmission network assets).

5.024 TG4 offers a third public service channel and its focus is on Irish language programmes. TG4 is now also established as an independent statutory body. The RTÉ Irish language channel, TG4, was operated as a subsidiary of RTÉ (Serbhisí Teilifís na Gaeilge Teoranta) prior to its separation from RTÉ. The Broadcasting Act 2001 provides the legislative basis for establishing TG4 as an independent entity. The government published the Teilifís Na Gaeilge (Establishment Day) Order 2007,[10] which established TG4 as an independent statutory body from 1 April 2007. The functions laid down in the Broadcasting Authority Act 1960 also applied to TG4. The Broadcasting Act 2001 sets out these functions separately with a particular focus on TG4's programmes in the Irish language. TG4's new legislative basis will be set out in the Broadcasting Bill 2008.

Under the Broadcasting Bill 2008, RTÉ and Teilifís na Gaeilge will become companies limited by guarantee.

5.025 Within RTÉ, the RTÉ Authority has the task of ensuring that RTÉ meets all of its obligations. The RTÉ Authority is required to forward to the Minister information and annual reports concerning financial performance, as well as information regarding the performance of RTÉ's functions. The Minister submits these documents to each House of the Oireachtas. Compliance with RTÉ's commitments is subject to control in the context of the annual reviews on a possible licence fee adjustment. The Broadcasting Authority Acts 1960–2001 set out the functions and objectives of the Authority. The Authority is relatively well funded as a result of license fees. It does not currently maintain a strong degree of independence from the government. The RTÉ Authority will be dissolved by the Broadcasting Bill 2008 and replaced by the BAI.

BCI

5.026 The Regulator for independent media is the Broadcasting Commission of Ireland (BCI).[11] The BCI is an independent statutory organisation, which was established in September 2001. It has regulatory and control functions with regard to commercial television and radio services in Ireland. The BCI at the time of writing has a staff of approximately 40. The ten members of the BCI, including the Chairperson, were appointed on 2 December 2003 by the then Minister for Communications, Marine and Natural Resources.

5.027 The BCI's key functions include the licensing of independent broadcasting services, the development of codes and rules in relation to programming and advertising standards, and the monitoring of all licensed services to ensure that licence holders comply with their statutory obligations and terms of their contracts. There is, however, no specific competence for supervising how RTÉ delivers on its duties. BCI regulates the content of independent broadcasters. The Radio and Television Act 1988 provided for the establishment of the Independent Radio and Television Commission, which was renamed the BCI under the Broadcasting Act 2001. The Broadcasting Act 2001 provides for the issue by the BCI of contracts in respect of various television

---

10   SI 98/2007.
11   See http://www.dci.ie.

programme services, eg digital, satellite and cable-MMD content contracts. The BCI most recently issued a contract in March 2006 to Channel 6, pursuant to the Broadcasting Act 2001. The BCI is also responsible for licensing regional, local, community, community of interest and institutional radio services. The framework for the ownership and control policy of the BCI is set out in the Radio and Television Act 1988 and the Broadcasting Act 2001. The Radio and Television Act 1988 requires the BCI in awarding a sound broadcasting contract (or when consenting to a change of control) to have regard, *inter alia*, to the desirability of allowing any person or group of persons to have control of or substantial interests in an 'undue number' of sound broadcasting services or an 'undue amount' of communications media in a specified area.

5.028 The BCI will be dissolved under the Broadcasting Bill 2008 and its functions will be subsumed into the BAI. Some of the key areas within the BCI's remit at the time of writing are as follows.

Cross-ownership

5.029 The BCI has issued an ownership and control policy statement in which it sets out its policy on cross-ownership. The policy objectives include:

(a) promoting plurality of ownership in the communications media, with particular reference to radio and television services;

(b) promoting diversity in viewpoint, outlet and source;

(c) ensuring that broadcasting contracts are held by persons who have available to them the necessary character, expertise, experience and financial resources; and

(d) ensuring that the ethos of a broadcasting service is such that it will best serve the needs of the audience it is licensed to service.

The BCI interprets an undue amount of communications media as 'more than a reasonable share of the range of communications media available to audiences in the franchise area'. The BCI's interpretation of an undue number of sound broadcasting services is that more than 25 per cent of total services licensed under the Act would be unacceptable. Less than 15 per cent would be acceptable. The range in between requires careful consideration.

In addition, the media merger rules of the Competition Act 2002 require the Minister for Enterprise, Trade and Employment to have regard to the spread of ownership and control of media businesses in the State in deciding whether to permit a media merger. Please see para **7.091** of the Competition chapter, **Ch 7**, for more information in this regard.

5.030 On 23 May 2007, the BCI made a number of announcements regarding ownership and control of national, regional and local radio stations.[12] The BCI considered three ownership and control issues regarding: the proposed sale of Emap

---

12 See http://www.bci.ie/news_information/press138.html.

radio services; the proposed sale of WLR FM, the Waterford City and County service; and the proposed sale of Beat FM, the regional youth radio service for the south-east. Emap had indicated to the BCI that it proposed to sell its three Irish radio services – Today FM, FM104 and Highland Radio. In this context, it requested that the BCI waive the two-year moratorium condition in the BCI's Ownership and Control Policy (2005), in respect of the Today FM service. Today FM was awarded a renewal of its ten-year contract in February 2006. The BCI agreed to waive the two-year moratorium requirement, as requested, having had regard to a number of issues, such as:

(a)   That there was no other applicant for the licence;

(b)   Emap's track record to date in the control and operation of its Irish radio interests, including Today FM;

(c)   the Irish radio services held by Emap continued to be managed from Ireland and under Irish management since their acquisition; and

(d)   the uncertainty which delay could create for staff of Today FM and, potentially, the other stations involved in the sale.

According to BCI, the two-year moratorium on the sale of a commercial radio licence contains within it an overriding flexibility which enables the BCI to consider particular and unique circumstances. The BCI also agreed to the sale of the majority shareholding in WLR FM and Beat FM to Thomas Crosbie Holdings (TCH) Ltd. TCH will take control of 75 per cent of both services, with Des Whelan, Chief Executive of WLR FM and a Director of Beat FM, holding the remaining 25 per cent. Final approval was made subject to a number of conditions.

In the Communicorp/ Emap case,[13] the BCI refused to approve the acquisition of FM104 by Communicorp by reference to the BCI ownership and control policy. This was the first case where BCI took such a far reaching position. The BCI decided the matter on the basis of the undue control of media in a particular area test, suggesting that BCI considered that access to newspaper and TV in a geographic area was not sufficient to assuage media plurality concerns associated with the relevant Dublin radio stations coming under common control. In its review of the Communicorp/SRH deal, the BCI ultimately prevented Communicorp from acquiring another Dublin based radio station FM104 on the grounds that the BCI 'was not satisfied that Communicorp would not hold an undue amount of communications media in Dublin City and County franchise area following completion of the transaction. Accordingly, the BCI did not grant approval to the proposed acquisition.'[14]

5.031 Pursuant to the Competition Act 2002, the BCI had entered into a co-operation agreement with the Competition Authority in order to facilitate co-operation, avoid duplication and ensure consistency between the parties in so far as their activities consist of, or relate to, the determination of a competition issue. The agreements

---

13   Please see Competition Authority Decision M/07/040 Determination of Merger Notification Communicorp/SRH dated 7 December 2007 –www.tca.ie.

14   BCI Decision of 9 October 2007 –as referred to in the Competition Authority Decision M/ 07/040 Determination of Merger Notification Communicorp/SRH dated 7 December 2007 –www.tca.ie.

provide for the exchange of information between the parties, forbearance to act when one party is already considering a particular issue and consultation between the parties prior to determination of a competition issue of interest to both parties. The co-operation agreement between the BCI and the Competition Authority governs situations where both parties have an interest in a particular issue.

Sound contracts

5.032 Under the Radio and Television Act 1988, the BCI is empowered to grant sound broadcasting contracts. In determining the most suitable applicant for the award of a sound broadcasting contract, the BCI is obliged to have regard to the:

(a) character of the applicant;

(b) adequacy of the expertise, experience and financial resources of the applicant;

(c) quality, range and type of programmes proposed to be provided, including programmes in the Irish language;

(d) extent to which the applicant will create new opportunities for Irish talent in music, drama and entertainment;

(e) desirability of having a diversity of services catering for a wide range of tastes; and

(f) desirability of allowing any person or group to have control or substantial interests in an undue amount of the communications media.[15]

For the purpose of awarding sound broadcasting contracts, Ireland is divided into various regions and, therefore, the applicable requirements vary depending on the region in question. The BCI sets out the relevant and applicable criteria in a guide to submissions, and negotiates with a successful applicant on average for a period of six to nine months. There is no timescale provided for in legislation and a final contract is signed close to the date for commencement of broadcasting. Fees payable in respect of sound broadcasting licences vary depending on the region. The BCI had encountered early difficulties in relation to radio stations, particularly in light of the failure the first commercial nationwide radio station. This has led to an emphasis on commercial viability, in the BCI licensing approach.

TV contracts

5.033 Under the Radio and Television Act 1988, the BCI was given the authority to award a television programme service contract. The criteria set out above in relation to sound broadcasting contracts is applied in relation to this award. In addition, the BCI is charged with ensuring that the television programme service:

(a) is responsive to the interests and concerns of the whole community, is mindful of the need for understanding and peace within the whole of Ireland, reflects the varied elements which make up the culture of the people of the whole island of Ireland and has special regard for the elements which distinguish that culture and in particular the Irish language;

---

15   Radio and TV Act 1988, s 6(2).

(b) upholds the democratic values enshrined in the written Irish Constitution, especially those relating to the freedom of expression;

(c) has regard to the need for the formation of public awareness and understanding of the values and traditions of countries other than the State, including in particular those of such countries which are Member States of the EU; and

(d) includes a reasonable proportion of news and current affairs programmes.[16]

A reasonable proportion of such television programme services must be produced in the State or in another Member State of the EU and be devoted to original programme material produced by persons other than the contractor, its subsidiary, its parent or existing broadcasting organisations.

TV3 and Channel 6 have been awarded such contracts.

5.034 The Broadcasting Act 2001 provides for the award of digital content contracts,[17] satellite content contracts,[18] local content contracts,[19] community content contracts[20] and cable-MMDs[21] content contracts by the BCI. There is no timescale provided for in the Broadcasting Act 2001 in respect of the award of such contracts. The Broadcasting Act 2001 further provides that the holder of a cable or MMDs transmission licence must comply with certain specified conditions in order to transmit a broadcasting service. The BCI has somewhat different powers vis-à-vis contracts under the 2001 Act and vis-à-vis contracts under the 1988 Act. There has been a 2006 review of the BCI's licensing function mandated by the Minister yet this dichotomy appears to have been replicated to some extent in the Broadcasting Bill 2008.

Advertising

5.035 Advertising is regulated by a number of different legislative and voluntary instruments of both a national and European nature, depending on the subject matter of the advertisement and the medium of advertisement used. Under the Broadcasting Act 2001, the BCI is mandated to prepare a code specifying standards to be complied with and rules and practices to be observed in respect of advertising, tele-shopping, sponsorship and other forms of commercial promotion used in any broadcasting service.[22] Broadcasters in Ireland are required to comply with the advertising codes both under statute and as a condition of their broadcasting contracts (licences) with the BCI.

5.036 The BCI has formulated codes in relation to children's advertising and access rules, and is currently consulting on a General Advertising Code under the 2001 Act. General advertising rules can currently be found in the existing Codes of Standards,

---

16   Broadcasting Authority Act 1960, s 17.

17   Broadcasting Authority Act 1960, s 12.

18   Broadcasting Authority Act 1960, s 36.

19   Broadcasting Authority Act 1960, s 38.

20   Broadcasting Authority Act 1960, s 39.

21   Broadcasting Authority Act 1960, s 41.

22   Broadcasting Authority Act 1960, s 31.

Practice and Prohibitions in Advertising, Sponsorship, and Other Forms of Commercial Promotion in Broadcasting Services, which was prepared by the Minister for Arts, Culture and the Gaeltacht under the Radio and Television Act 1988. A further code of conduct applies to advertising with the State broadcaster, RTÉ. A voluntary self-regulatory code is also in operation and is administered by the Advertising Standards Authority of Ireland.

5.037 In addition to broadcasting legislation, there are numerous other relevant national and European rules relating to advertising of specific types of products and services. Examples of such products and services include tobacco, pharmaceutical products, health foods, airfares, package holidays, solicitors' services and financial services. There are also national rules relating to the type of advertising practices permitted, examples of which include consumer information requirements, misleading advertising rules, unsolicited commercial communications, and rules on merchandise marks, gaming and lotteries. The National Consumer Agency (NCA) established in May 2007 is the relevant authority to deal with many consumer issues. The NCA derives its authority from the Consumer Protection Act 2007.

Must-carry obligation

5.038 'Must-carry obligations' are provisions which specify a basic package of programmes that must be carried by operators' broadcasting distribution networks. Section 34 of the Broadcasting Act 2001 provides for must-carry obligations. These obligations relate to holders of licences granted by ComReg, authorising the transmission, or re-transmission, by means of satellite (s 36), a cable or MMD system (s 37) of programme material. The obligations relate to community content or free-to-air services and national sound broadcasting services, respectively. No provision is made for a financing mechanism. Section 34 provides that the television programme service contractor may provide such other broadcasting services (whether free-to-air or not) as it considers appropriate, including broadcasting services of a community, local or regional character.

BCC

5.039 The Broadcasting Complaints Commission's functions are set out in the Broadcasting Act 2001.[23] The Broadcasting Complaints Commission (BCC) is an independent statutory body. The BCC members were nominated by Government in 2005 and will hold office for a period of five years or until such time as a new body is established under the Broadcasting Bill 2008, whichever is the lesser. Any breach of the BCI's advertising codes may be investigated by the BCC. It considers complaints about broadcast material, both programmes and advertisements, in relation to:

   (i)   impartiality in news and current affairs;

  (ii)   taste and decency including a code of programme standards;

 (iii)   law and order;

---

23   Broadcasting Authority Act 1960, s 22 *et seq.*

   (iv)   privacy of an individual;

   (v)   slander;

   (vi)   published matter in relation to RTÉ and ministerial prohibitions;

   (vii)   general advertising codes; and

   (viii)   the children's advertising code.[24]

5.040 Section 24 of the Broadcasting Act 2001 sets out the functions of the BCC. It provides that the BCC may investigate and decide upon complaints. A complaint must be in writing and be made to the BCC not more than 30 days after:

   (i)   if it relates to one broadcast, the date of the broadcast; or

   (ii)   if it relates to two or more unrelated broadcasts, the date of the earlier or earliest, as the case may be, of those broadcasts; and

   (iii)   if it relates to two or more related broadcasts of which at least two are made on different dates, the later or latest of those dates.

When the BCC proposes to investigate a complaint, it shall afford to the broadcaster to whom the complaint relates an opportunity to comment on the complaint. As soon as the BCC decides on a complaint, it sends to the person who made the complaint, the broadcaster concerned and (if the complaint is in respect of a broadcast made on a broadcasting service which is not a free-to-air service provided by the RTÉ Authority or Teilifís na Gaeilge) the BCI, a statement in writing of its decision.

5.041 Unless it considers it inappropriate to do so, the BCC will, as soon as may be after the making of the decision, publish particulars of its decision on a complaint in such manner as it considers suitable and, where it considers that the publication should be by the broadcaster concerned, or should include publication by the broadcaster concerned, the particulars shall be published by the broadcaster concerned in such manner as is agreed between the BCC and the broadcaster concerned. The BCC shall not have any power to award to any party costs or expenses.

    The BCC will be dissolved under the Broadcasting Bill 2008 and its functions will be subsumed into the BAI.

ComReg

5.042 ComReg's role in respect of the broadcasting sector covers the issuing of associated licences under Ireland's Wireless Telegraphy Acts 1926–1988 in respect of wireless equipment and the assignment of required radio spectrum. Broadcasting over radio and TV requires capacity on spectrum, which is a finite resource. Regulation of spectrum involves the allocation of spectrum bandwidth to various uses, including mobile telephony, radio and television. Spectrum management is important to ensure that interference is prevented. Wireless telegraphy licences may be required under the Wireless Telegraphy Acts 1926–1988. Section 3 provides that no person may keep an apparatus for wireless telegraphy other than pursuant to a licence granted under this

---

24   http://www.bci.ie/faqs/faq_about_bcc_htm.

Act. Section 5 empowers ComReg to grant licences in this regard. Fees for wireless telegraphy licences vary. For wireless services, such as mobile and fixed wireless, a licence must be obtained under the Wireless Telegraphy Acts in connection with the use of wireless telegraphy apparatus. ComReg may limit the number of wireless telegraphy licences issued under s 5 of the Wireless Telegraphy Act 1926, as amended, to the extent required to ensure the efficient use of radio frequencies.

5.043 ComReg also has regulatory powers where Electronic Communications Networks (ECNs) are used to broadcast services. Authorisation is required under the European Communities (Electronic Communications Networks and Services) (Authorisation) Regulations 2003 (the Authorisation Regulations),[25] which are part of the Electronic Communications Regulatory Framework. Pursuant to the Framework Regulations,[26] ComReg conducted a review of the market for wholesale broadcasting transmission services and designated RTÉ NL as having significant market power (SMP) in the wholesale market for radio broadcasting transmission services on national analogue terrestrial networks, and the wholesale market for television broadcasting transmission services on national analogue terrestrial networks. ComReg imposed obligations of transparency, non-discrimination and accounting separation on RTÉ NL in this regard.[27]

5.044 An annual levy may be payable in respect of 'broadcast transmission networks'. This levy is payable under s 30 of the Communications Regulation Act 2002, together with the Authorisation Regulations. Annual levies are payable in respect of broadcasting transmission networks pursuant to the Levy Order SI 346/2003.[28] The levy is subscriber-based for pay TV and is per transmitter for the operation of free-to-air TV. The amount of the annual levy payable depends upon the nature of the transmission network and will be based upon an annual charge of €0.50 per subscriber connected to the network or a charge of €100 per transmitter as follows:

(i) a terrestrial transmission network licensed under the Broadcasting Act 1960 or the Radio and Television Act 1988, as amended, is subject to an annual charge of €100 per transmitter;

(ii) a provider of ultra high frequency (UHF) deflector networks is subject to an annual charge of €0.50 per subscriber connected;

(iii) a provider of electronic communications networks for cable or multipoint microwave distribution system (MMDS) is subject to an annual payment of €0.50 per subscriber connected to the network;

(iv) a digital terrestrial television network carrying free-to-air services is subject to an annual charge of €100 per transmitter carrying free-to-air services; and

25 SI 306/2003.
26 SI 307/2003.
27 ComReg Decision D16/04, Wholesale Broadcasting Transmission Services Markets, 22 December 2004.
28 As amended by SI 392/2003.

(v)   a digital terrestrial television network carrying pay-television services is subject to an annual charge of €0.50 per subscriber connected.[29]

A levy exemption applies where the amount payable by an operator is less than €1,000 per levy year.

See **Ch 6** on ComReg for further details on ComReg's jurisdiction in this area.

It is proposed under the Broadcasting Bill 2008 that ComReg will have duties in respect of DTT.

BAI

5.045 The proposed Broadcasting Bill 2008 will see the establishment of a new broadcasting and audio-visual content Regulator, the Broadcasting Authority of Ireland (BAI), in respect of both public and private broadcasters, which will take over the responsibilities of the BCI and the RTÉ Authority.

The Broadcasting Authority of Ireland will encapsulate the existing regulatory functions of the BCI, the BCC and the RTÉ Authority. The BAI will be operationally independent and will be funded primarily by a sectoral levy applicable to all broadcasters in the country. The Broadcasting Bill 2008 aims to ensure that the new BAI has an adequate range of proportionate enforcement mechanisms available to it. The Broadcasting Bill does not provide that the current BCI board members will continue on the BAI Board, rather the term of any member of the BCI terminates on the establishment of the BAI,[30] conversely, any member of the RTE board continues as a member of the BAI further to s 178(3) of the Bill. The BCI staff will however be transferred to the new agency, further to s 15(6) of the Broadcasting Bill. In addition, the Bill provides for the appointment of the BCI chief executive as the interim chief executive of the BAI.[31] Paragraphs **5.061***ff* of this chapter consider the BAI in more detail.

THE RELEVANT LEGISLATIVE FRAMEWORK

Structure of the European Regulatory Framework for Television without Frontiers Directive

5.046 The Television without Frontiers Directive (TVWF) regulates the reception and retransmission of TV broadcasts from one Member State to another. The directive deals with the regulation of broadcasters, quotas for the inclusion of recent European works, advertising, protection of minors and coverage of events of major importance to society. The directive is the basis on which Ireland prepares a list of sporting events that Ireland determines should remain available on free-to-air television services. The first TVWF Directive dated from 1989 and was amended in 1997. It provides that Member States shall ensure that broadcasters reserve for European works a majority

---

29   SI 392/2003.
30   Section 173(3) of the Broadcasting Bill.
31   Sections 14(7) and 14(12) of the Broadcasting Bill.

proportion of their transmission time, excluding the time appointed to news, sports events, games, advertising and teletext services. Member States shall ensure that broadcasters reserve at least ten per cent of their transmission time, excluding the time appointed to news, sports events, games, advertising and teletext services or alternatively at the discretion of the Member State at least ten per cent of their programming budget for European works created by producers who are independent of broadcasters. Advertising, sponsorship and teleshopping rules are also included as are rules on the amount and timing of advertising together with rules controlling the nature of the advertising such as a ban on tobacco advertising and controls on alcohol advertising. The directive also covers the designation of certain events of major importance to society that should be available on free television. Finally, it deals with the protection of minors and the rights of reply. The European Commission started its review of the TVWF and published its proposals in December 2005 and a general approach was put in place for 2006, yielding a common position text put to Council in 2007. This directive is known as the Audio Visual Media Services Directive.[32]

Directive on Audiovisual Media Services

5.047 Directive 2007/65/EC amends the Television without Frontiers Directive and renames it 'Audiovisual Media Services Directive' (AMS Directive). The amending directive was adopted on 11 December and entered into force on 19 December 2007. Member States have two years to transpose the new provisions into national law, so that the modernised legal framework for audio-visual media services will be fully applicable by the end of 2009. The implementation of the directive brings about a review of Ireland's approach to TV regulation, codes and rules, and the development of the broadcasting sector as well as jurisdiction issues.

5.048 The AMS Directive provides that each broadcaster is only subject to the national regulations of one Member State. It means that even where a UK broadcaster carries advertising that is only available to Irish viewers, that it is the UK codes and rules that apply to such advertising. With the growth in the number of channels available in a digital era, it is increasingly likely that new channels will be developed by a broadcaster in one Member State and targeted at an audience in another Member State. The programme codes and standards of the targeted Member State would, however, not apply. Ireland raised the jurisdiction issue during its Presidency of the EU. This has resulted in a co-operation clause whereby Ireland can now complain to the Regulator in another country if one of its licensed broadcasters is targeting Irish citizens in breach of Irish codes; for example, if advertising relates to a product which is banned from being advertised in Ireland. The Regulator complained to in the other jurisdiction would have to request the broadcaster to desist. This, however, would not be binding on the broadcaster.

5.049 Currently, while British Sky Broadcasting (BSkyB) provides satellite television in Ireland, the UK's Independent Television Commission licences and regulates BSkyB's programme channels and regulates the advertising carried on those channels.

---

32 Directive 2007/65/EC.

When a broadcasting service does not originate in Ireland, any content regulation is the responsibility of the country of origin. The new directive makes further changes to the current framework. The scope of the directive has been broadened to include both linear services – for example, scheduled broadcasting via traditional TV, the Internet or mobile phones which pushes content to viewers – and non-linear services, such as on-demand film or news which the viewer pulls from a network. The directive imposes a lighter basic tier of regulation on non-linear services.

5.050 As well as setting rules for advertising, promotion of European content, consumer protection and accessibility, other new obligations under the directive relate to media literacy and short news reports. The new directive identifies the importance of media pluralism and media literacy in a world with increasing access to content, the increased commercialisation of that content and the range of technological platforms involved. The original TVWF Directive needed to be amended to address the fact that advances in technology and the manner in which the audio-visual sector has developed have resulted in a regulatory environment where similar audio-visual services are not subject to similar regulation. The level of regulation also differs from Member State to Member State, which frustrates the goal of a common market. Certain content services that are similar in nature to traditional TV services are available on non-traditional networks and are not subject to broadcasting regulation. The new AMS Directive addresses the technological and market developments of recent years to ensure a competitive playing field between service-providers exists. It establishes common minimum rules for all audio-visual media services irrespective of the transmission platform. The Broadcasting Bill 2008 makes proposals regarding media literacy and proposes a study of issues around media literacy and media pluralism in Ireland. It is intended that the Broadcasting Bill 2008 will implement the AMS Directive in Ireland.

Structure of the National Regulatory Framework for Broadcasting

The Wireless Telegraphy Acts 1926–1988

5.051 These Acts deals with licenses of wireless telegraphy apparatus to be used over spectrum.

Broadcasting Authority Acts 1960–2001

5.052 These Acts established the RTÉ Authority.

Radio and Television Act 1988

5.053 The Radio and Television Act 1988 provided for the establishment of commercially owned radio broadcasters, both locally and nationally. The Radio and Television Act 1988 also provided for the establishment of the Independent Radio and Television Commission, the forerunner of the BCI.

Broadcasting Act 2001

5.054 This Act established the BCI.

Broadcasting (Funding) Act 2003

5.055 This Act allows for the funding of new and additional programmes on Irish radio and TV from 5 per cent of the net proceeds of the TV license fee. The BCI has drawn up a scheme called the Sound and Vision Scheme and has allocated over €30m to finance the making of new TV and radio programmes. The scheme is directed at new and additional high-quality programming on Irish culture, heritage and history, including programmes in the Irish language. The fund also supports adult literacy programmes and the archiving of broadcast material. The fund is open to independent producers and all broadcasters licensed in Ireland.

Broadcasting (Major Events Television Coverage) Act 1999, as amended in 2003

5.056 This Act implements the TVWF Directive in Ireland, which allows Member States to designate certain sporting and cultural events of sufficient importance to be designated for free television services. The legislation also provides for an arbitration system whereby qualifying terrestrial TV broadcasters cannot secure a deal with the holders of sports rights. In such instances, the broadcasters can apply to the High Court for an order directing that an event organizer provide access to a listed event subject to the payment of reasonable market rates and such terms as determined by the High Court. The TVWF Directive is also implemented by way of the European Communities (Television Broadcasting) Regulations 1999, which provide that a television broadcaster, where practicable and by appropriate means, must progressively reserve for European works a majority proportion of its transmission time (excluding the time appointed to news, sporting events, games, advertising and teletext services), having regard to its various public responsibilities. At a minimum, the proportion of transmission time cannot be lower than the average proportion of transmission time devoted to European works, if any, in 1988. The regulations further provide that a broadcaster, where practicable and by appropriate means, shall progressively reserve at least ten per cent of its transmission time (excluding the time applied to news, sports events, games, advertising and teletext services) for European works created by producers who are independent of broadcasters, or reserve ten per cent of its programming budget for European works which are created by producers who are independent of broadcasters, having regard to its various public responsibilities. An adequate proportion of works must comprise recent works, ie works which are transmitted within five years of their production. The TVWF Directive has been modernised and replaced with the AMS Directive, which was adopted in 2007.

Broadcasting (Amendment) Act 2007

5.057 This Act allows for the development of Digital Terrestrial Television (DTT) in Ireland. It seeks to establish a new model for licensing DTT in Ireland and to allow for progress to be made towards analogue switch-off. The Act provides for DTT and also for the potential use of surplus spectrum freed up by the switch from analogue to digital for 'other services'. The Act also seeks to amend the remit of RTÉ to allow it to utilise public funding in the provision of a broadcasting services to Irish emigrant communities abroad.

Television Licences Regulations 2007[33]

5.058 These regulations are made further to ss 5 and 6(1) of the Wireless Telegraphy Act 1926 and the Broadcasting (Transfer of Departmental Administration and Ministerial Functions) Order 2002 (SI 299/2002) (as adapted by the Communications, Marine and Natural Resources (Alteration of Name of Department and Title of Minister) Order 2007 (SI 706/2007)), with the consent of the Minister for Finance. A 'television licence' is a licence granted by the Minister under s 5 of the Wireless Telegraphy Act 1926 to a person to keep and have possession of a television set (within the meaning of the Wireless Telegraphy Act 1972) in a specified place in the State or in a specified vehicle, ship or aircraft. Licences are issued through the Irish Post Office, An Post.

5.059 Pursuant to the Wireless Telegraphy Act 1926, every person or undertaking that has a television, or equipment capable of receiving a television signal, must pay a television license. The licence fee is collected through An Post, which subsequently transfers the moneys to the Department of Communications, Energy and Natural Resources. Each year, the Minister allocates almost the totality of revenues from the license fee (net of collection costs) to RTÉ. In 2002, the Irish government decided to base the annual adjustment of the licence fee on the consumer price index, with an adjustment for the extent to which RTÉ's programme output commitments were achieved. Any such possible increase in the licence fee level is preceded by an annual review, the exact terms of which are set by the Minister. The review is carried out by an independent expert who also makes recommendations to the Minister. The Minster may then decide to increase the licence fee level. The last such increase was decided by the Minister in 2007. Based on the Television Licences Regulation 2007, the level of the licence fee was increased as of 1 January 2008 to €160. The amount paid to RTÉ shall only be used for the programme schedules set out in s 28(2) of the Broadcasting Authority Act 1960, for complying with its duties under s 17 of the Broadcasting Authority Act 1960, in exercising its powers under s 16 of the same Act (with the exception, however, of the powers related to subscription or pay-per-view services as well as programme schedules transmitted by electronic means), but also for providing, pursuant to its powers, any service (other than a broadcasting service) for the benefit of the public.

The Broadcasting Bill 2008

5.060 This Bill is designed to modernise the legislative framework for broadcasting in Ireland. It will establish a single content Regulator for all commercial, community and public service broadcasters in Ireland, to be known as the BAI. It will provide a right-of-reply mechanism to persons whose reputation and good name have been damaged by an assertion of incorrect facts in a TV or radio programme. The right of replay is

---

33   SI 851/2007.

intended to provide a proportionate, low cost and expeditious remedy to such persons. The growth in new and innovative technologies in the broadcast of television services means that the Bill re-examines the definition of a TV set to take into account mobile TV. The Bill proposes to extend the existing public service remit of RTÉ and TG4 to incorporate the broadcasting of public service programming to Irish communities in the UK, the use of new web-based technologies, and the assistance of relevant public bodies in the dissemination of information in the event of an emergency. The Bill also proposes mechanisms to review the level of public funding that is made available to RTÉ and TG4 to deliver on their public service mandates.

THE NEW ESTABLISHED ENTITY – THE BROADCASTING AUTHORITY OF IRELAND

5.061 Draft heads of the Broadcasting Bill 2008 were published in July 2006 by the Department of Communications and were consulted on by way of an e-consultation process. The Joint Oireachtas Committee returned its report in April 2007. The Office of the Parliamentary Counsel drafted the Broadcasting Bill 2008. The Bill establishes the BAI, which will carry on the function of the existing BCI, but will have increased supervisory functions with regard to public service broadcasters. It allows for a levy to be paid by the broadcasting sector for the funding of the BAI. The Bill develops new procedures around license enforcement, right of reply, legal definitions regarding TV licenses, codes and rules, and contract award. It overhauls the existing framework relating to public service broadcasters and the allocation of public funding and consolidates the key broadcasting legislation since 1960. The Bill is aimed to address many of the issues raised by the European Commission in its investigation into the allegation of State aid discussed in paras **5.160***ff*. Issues arising out of the review of the licensing framework have also fed into the Bill. In addition, the Bill is intended to address aspects of the transposition of the new AMS Directive.

5.062 Under the Bill, the BAI will have nine members, five of whom shall be appointed by the Government on the nomination of the Minister, and four of whom shall be appointed by the Government on the nomination of the Minister having regard to the advice of the Joint Oireachtas Committee with responsibility for broadcasting matters. There will be two statutory Committees under the umbrella of the BAI: the Contract Awards Committee, which will have eight members, and the Compliance Committee, which will also have eight members. Interestingly, s 8 of the Bill provides that not less than four of the members of the BAI shall be men and not less than four of them shall be women. Section 9 also, interestingly, provides for a key skill set requirements list and states that a person shall not be appointed unless he or she has had experience of, or shown capacity in, one or more of the listed areas. The listed areas relate to broadcasting, media, trade unions, business or commercial affairs, the Irish language and Gaeltacht, disability, arts music and culture, science or environment, legal or regulatory, and social education or community affairs. Section 15 provides that the BAI may appoint staff and provides that the existing staff of the BCI would transfer to the BAI. Section 18 allows the BAI to appoint consultants and advisors. Section 23 requires the BAI to draw up a code of conduct with regard to conflicts of interest and ethical behaviour.

BAI FUNCTIONS

5.063 The functions of the BAI are set out in s 26 of the Broadcasting Bill 2008. The Contract Awards Committee functions are set out in s 27 of the Broadcasting Bill. The Compliance Committee functions are set out in s 28 of the Broadcasting Bill. The Broadcasting Bill 2008 transfers the functions of the BCI and BCC to BAI. The principal functions of the BAI are to:

   (i)   prepare a strategy for the provision of broadcasting services in the State, in addition to those provided by RTÉ, TG4 and the Irish Film Channel;

  (ii)   prepare a strategy statement;

 (iii)   direct the Contract Awards Committee to make arrangements to invite considerations and make recommendations to the BAI and the BAI shall follow such recommendations or proposals;

 (iv)   prepare or make broadcasting codes and rules;

  (v)   prepare and implement schemes for the granting of funds;

 (vi)   make a levy order;

 (vii)   prepare a scheme under s 49(3), which provides that the BAI shall prepare within six months of its establishment, following a period of public consultation, a scheme for the exercise of the right of reply;

(viii)   consult with the Minister as to the sectoral impact of a proposal under certain sections;

 (ix)   prepare guidance to RTÉ and TG4 as to the fulfilment of their public service obligation;

  (x)   undertake a review under s 124, which provides that the BAI shall, on an annual and five-year basis, conduct reviews and make recommendations to the Minister as to the requisite level of public funding to fulfil public service obligations;

 (xi)   make a recommendation under s 123, which provides that the Minister, with the approval of the Minster for Finance, may pay to RTÉ out of moneys provided by the Oireachtas an amount equal to the total receipts in that year in respect of television licence fees less certain deductions, such as expenses incurred by the Minster in relation to the collection of those fees. The amount paid to RTÉ shall be used solely for the purposes of pursuing its public service objects and paying amounts levied on RTÉ. The Minister, with the consent of the Minister for Finance, may from time to time, pay to TG4 money for the purposes of defraying the expenses incurred by TG4 in pursuing its public service objects, and paying amounts levied on TG4;

 (xii)   make a result under s 115, which provides that the Minister may at the request of the BAI and after consultation with RTÉ require RTÉ to co-operate with a holder of a sound broadcasting contract in respect of infrastructure sharing; and

(xiii)   liaise and consult with ComReg in the preparation of the allocation plan for the frequency range dedicated to sound and TV broadcasting.

5.064 The BAI also has ancillary functions, which are to:

(i) collect and disseminate information on the broadcasting sector in the State;

(ii) monitor developments in broadcasting internationally;

(iii) initiate, organise and promote research relating to broadcasting;

(iv) collect and disseminate information in relation to the skills requirement of the broadcasting sector;

(v) co-operate with other bodies to promote training in areas of skill shortages;

(vi) co-operate with other bodies outside the State that exercise a similar function; and

(vii) promote media literacy including co-operation with broadcasters and educationalists.

5.065 The function of the Contract Award Committee is to make recommendations to the BAI regarding broadcasting services in addition to those provided by RTÉ and TG4.

The principal functions of the Compliance Committee are to:

(i) monitor and enforce compliance by contractors with the terms and conditions of any contract entered into by the BAI on the recommendation of the Contract Award Committee;

(ii) monitor and enforce compliance by broadcasters with their obligations under the Act;

(iii) monitor and enforce compliance by RTÉ and TG4 with their public service obligations under the Act;

(iv) monitor and enforce compliance by broadcasters with any broadcasting code or rule; and

(v) investigate complaints and requests for dispute resolution.

BAI OBJECTIVES

5.066 The objectives of the BAI and the Committees are set out in s 25 of the Broadcasting Bill 2008. These are to ensure:

(i) that the number and categories of broadcasting services made available in the State best serve the needs of the people, bearing in mind languages, traditions, and religious, ethical and cultural diversity;

(ii) that the democratic values enshrined in the Constitution, especially those relating to freedom of expression, are upheld; and

(iii) the provision of open and pluralistic broadcasting services.

In addition, the Committees shall:

(i) stimulate the provision of high-quality, diverse and innovative programming by commercial, community and public service broadcasters and independent products;

(ii) facilitate public service broadcasters in the fulfilment of their public service objects;

(iii) promote diversity in control of the more influential commercial and community broadcasting services;

(iv) provide a regulatory environment that will facilitate the development of a broadcasting sector in Ireland that is responsible to audience needs and in particular is accessible to people with disabilities; and

(v) facilitate the development of Irish language programming and broadcasting services.

5.067 The BAI and the Committees in performing their functions shall seek to ensure that measures taken:

(i) are proportionate having regard to the objectives;

(ii) are applied across the range of broadcasting services taking account of the degree of influence that the different types of broadcasting services are able to exert in shaping audience views in the State;

(iii) are mindful of the object, functions and duties set for public service broadcasters;

(iv) will produce regulatory arrangements that are stable and predictable; and

(v) will readily accommodate and encourage technological development and its application by the broadcasting sector.

BAI INDEPENDENCE

5.068 Section 24 of the Broadcasting Bill 2008 provides for the independence of the BAI. Section 38, however, provides that it must submit reports to the Minister. In addition, s 26 provides that the Minister may confer on the BAI by order such other additional functions in relation to broadcasting services as he or she may consider necessary. Such an order should be laid before each House of the Oireachtas for 21 days. These sections may serve to limit the independence conferred under s 24. In addition, it is likely that RTÉ will still retain a stronghold over its public service remit in that it will prepare the public service broadcasting charter outlining the activities that it will undertake over a five-year period in order to fulfil its public service object under s 101. This limits the power of the BAI in this regard, given that it is RTÉ that prepares its public service charter rather than the BAI. The BAI may, of course, provide guidance to RTÉ and TG4 as to the fulfilment of their public service obligations; however, this is somewhat more diluted than having direct control over what constitutes fulfilment of the public service obligation (PSO). The BAI shall, of course, monitor and enforce compliance by RTÉ and TG4 with their PSOs under the Act; however, again given that the remit to define these PSOs are left with RTÉ and TG4, respectively, under s 101 of the Act, this could be a relatively weak power. It will remain to be seen how the Compliance Committee apply these sections in practice.

BAI BORROWINGS, LEVIES AND FEES

5.069 Section 35 of the Broadcasting Bill 2008 sets out that the BAI may, for the purpose of the performance of its functions, borrow money, but shall only do so with the consent of the Minister for Communications, Energy and Natural Resources and the Minister for Finance. Section 33 deals with levies and fees. It provides that, for the purpose of meeting expenses properly incurred by the BAI, the Contract Awards Committee and the Compliance Committee in the performance of their functions, the BAI shall make an order imposing a levy on public service broadcasters and broadcasting contractors. Whenever a levy order is made, public service broadcasters and each broadcasting contractor shall pay to the BAI such amount as shall be appropriate having regard to the terms of the levy order.

5.070 A levy order shall provide for the collection, payment and administration of a levy, including all or any of the following:

    (i)   the method of calculation of the levy;

    (ii) the times at which payment will be made and the form of payment;

    (iii) the keeping, inspection and provision of records relating to the levy; and

    (iv) any exemptions, deferrals or refunds of the levy.

Any surplus of levy income over the expenses incurred by the BAI in the discharge of its functions relevant to that levy in a particular financial year shall either be retained by the BAI to be offset against levy obligations for the subsequent year, or be refunded proportionately to the providers of broadcasting services on whom the levy is imposed. The BAI may recover as a simple contract debt in any court of competent jurisdiction a levy from any person by whom it is payable. A levy order shall be laid before each House of the Oireachtas by the BAI as soon as may be after it is made. Either House of the Oireachtas may, by resolution passed within 21 sitting days after the day on which a levy order was laid before it pass a resolution annulling the order.

5.071 Section 34 allows for Exchequer funding. The BAI will be obliged to prepare accounts and an annual report under ss 37 and 38 respectively of the Broadcasting Bill. It will be seen from this whether it will be an Authority with independent financial means and the ability to be able to regulate fearlessly, rather than merely a paper tiger.

THE REGULATED ACTIVITY AND THE REGULATED ENTITIES

5.072 The RTÉ Authority currently regulates RTÉ and TG4. BCI currently regulates commercial entities such as Today FM and TV3 in relation to content. BCC currently regulates all entities in respect of complaints within its remit. The BAI will regulate all entities. Section 32 of the Broadcasting Bill 2008 requires the BAI and the Committees to review the regulatory burden they impose on broadcasters.

The matters within the BAI's remit are discussed in the following paragraphs.

Broadcasters' Duties, Codes and Rules

5.073 The rules concerning broadcasters' duties, codes and rules, including rules and codes relating to advertising, are set out in Pt 3 of the Broadcasting Bill 2008. Section 39 imposes certain duties on broadcasters and s 40 requires broadcasters to record and hold every broadcast made by them for review by the Compliance Committee. Section 41 imposes certain requirements in respect of advertising. Section 42 requires the BAI to prepare codes governing standards and practices to be observed by broadcasters and provides for the continuance of certain BCI codes. Section 43 provides for rules in respect of access to broadcasting services by people with disabilities, and in respect of the maximum duration and frequency of advertisements. The section also provides for the continuance of rules by the BCI. Section 44 provides for public consultation in relation to rules or codes. Section 45 provides that any broadcasting code or rule may be annulled by either House of the Oireachtas.

Broadcasting Contracts and Content Provision Contracts

5.074 Part 6 of the Broadcasting Bill 2008 deals with Broadcasting Contracts and Content Provision Contracts. Section 59 provides that the BAI may not award a broadcasting contract without an associated Wireless Telegraphy Act (WTA) license issued by ComReg. Section 60 provides that ComReg may vary the terms and conditions of a WTA license issued for the purpose of a broadcasting contract. Section 61 provides that the Minister may suspend WTA licences during a national emergency. The BAI may also, at the request of the Minister, require a commercial or community radio or TV broadcaster to allocate broadcast time for government announcements in the event of an emergency. Section 63 provides that the BAI may, on the recommendation of the Contract Awards Committee, award sound broadcasting contracts. Section 65 provides for the process by which the Contracts Awards Committee seeks applications for the award of broadcasting contracts. Section 66 outlines the criteria against which such applications are considered. Section 70 provides for the award of analogue TV broadcasting contracts and provides for the continuance of the existing contract held by TV3. Section 71 provides that the BAI may award content provision contracts to broadcasters to make their services available on broadcasting platforms such as cable, IPTV,[34] satellite, DTT and mobile TV systems. The holder of a contract under this section is subject to the broadcasting duties, codes and rules outlined in the section above. Section 75 provides that the BAI may, after consultation with ComReg, prepare rules in respect of electronic programme guides regarding the schedule of programme material. Section 76 sets out the rules in relation to the must-carry obligations of certain services on MMD systems and s 77 sets out the rules for must-carry obligations of TV services provided by RTÉ, TG4 and the TV programme service contractor of national radio services provided by RTÉ and broadcasting contractors on certain types of broadcasting transmission networks. In addition, s 77 sets out a must-carry obligation of TV services provided by RTÉ and TG4.

---

34 Internet Protocol Television.

5.075 Section 77 deals with the following matters in relation to must-carry obligations. Where the BAI is of the view, after carrying out a review and after consultation with ComReg, that a type or class of network system, rather than an individual network system, is not used by a significant number of end-users as their principal means of receiving transmissions of programme material, it may propose to the Minister the full or partial removal of the obligations set out in this section on that type or class of network system. The Minister may make an order to that effect. A network provider shall ensure the re-transmission, by or through his network, of each free-to- air service provided by RTÉ, TG4 and the free-to-air service provided under s 70 by the television service programme contractor where RTÉ, TG4 or the contractor requests the network provider to re-transmit.

A network provider shall re-transmit each national sound broadcasting service provided by RTÉ and each sound broadcasting contractor which RTÉ or the contractor concerned requests the holder to re-transmit. The network provider shall not impose a charge in relation to the making available to a person of any service referred to in s 77, if he imposes a charge in relation to the making available of any *other* service to that person.

5.076 The BAI may require a network provider to transmit as a broadcasting service, by means of its network, programme material supplied under one or more specified community content provision contract, the holders of which are members of the local community that is served by the network and who request the network provider to transmit the programme material. A network provider shall not impose a charge in this regard, if he imposes a charge on that person in relation to any other service to that person.

5.077 The BAI shall report to the Minister on an annual basis in relation to the operation of this section. An order under this section shall be laid before each House of the Oireachtas by the Minister as soon as may be after it is made. Either House of the Oireachtas may, by resolution passed within 21 sitting days after the day on which an order was laid before it, pass a resolution annulling the order. The annulment of an order takes effect immediately on the passing of the resolution but does not affect anything that was done under the order before the passing of the resolution.

Public Service Broadcasting

5.078 In response to criticisms levelled at the lack of independence of the RTÉ Authority, the Broadcasting Bill 2008 deals with public service broadcasting. Section 79 provides for the continuation of RTÉ and TG4 as corporate bodies. Section 81 provides for the appointment by government of the members of the boards of RTÉ and TG4, and s 82 outlines the experience board members require. Section 86 provides for the suspension or exclusion from memberships of the board in certain specified circumstances. Section 95 requires RTÉ and TG4 to draw up codes of conduct in respect of controls on interest and ethical behaviour to apply to the board members, staff and advisers. Section 98 provides that RTÉ and TG4 are to be independent in the pursuit of their statutory objectives. Section 101 requires that they would prepare public service broadcasting charters outlining the activities that RTÉ and TG4 propose to undertake over a five-year period in order to fulfil their public service objects (five-year plans). This may limit the extent to which the BAI controls the public service broadcasting obligation given that it is RTÉ and TG4 that determines its scope in the first instance. In most utility regulation, it is the Regulator that determines the scope of the PSO rather than the regulated entity. Section 105 provides that RTÉ and TG4 are to act prudently to ensure that their revenue matches their expenditure. Section 106 details provisions regarding advertising and sponsorship. Section 108 concerns the exploitation of commercial opportunities and provides that such exploitation shall be at arm's length basis and should be used to subsidise public service broadcasting objects.

5.079 Section 114 outlines the objects and associated powers of RTÉ. The objectives of RTÉ are to:

(a) establish, maintain and operate a national television and sound broadcasting service which shall have the character of a public service, be a free-to-air service and be made available, in so far as it is reasonably practicable, to the whole community on the island of Ireland;

(b) establish and maintain a website and teletext services in connection with the services of RTÉ;

(c) establish and maintain orchestras, choirs and other cultural performing groups in connection with the services of RTÉ;

(d) assist and co-operate with the relevant public bodies in preparation for, and execution of, the dissemination of relevant information to the public in the event of a major emergency;

(e) establish and maintain archives and libraries containing materials relevant to the objects of RTÉ;

(f) establish, maintain and operate a television broadcasting service and a sound broadcasting service which shall have the character of a public service, which services shall be made available, in so far as RTÉ considers reasonably practicable, to Irish communities outside the island of Ireland;

(g) subject to the consent of the Minister, the Minister having consulted with the BAI, establish, maintain and operate, in so far as it is reasonably practicable, community, local, or regional broadcasting services, which shall have the character of a public service, and be available free-to-air;

(h) subject to the consent of the Minister, the Minister having consulted with the BAI, establish and maintain non-broadcast, non-linear audio-visual media services, in so far as it is reasonably practicable, which shall have the character of a public broadcasting service (such consent not being required in respect of services which are ancillary to a broadcasting service provided);

(i) establish, maintain, and operate one or more national multiplexes; and

(j) so far as it is reasonably practicable, exploit such commercial opportunities as may arise in pursuit of the objects.

5.080 In pursuit of the objects, RTÉ shall:

(a) be responsive to the interests and concerns of the whole community, be mindful of the need for understanding and peace within the whole island of

Ireland, ensure that the programmes reflect the varied elements which make up the culture of the people of the whole island of Ireland, and have special regard for the elements which distinguish that culture and in particular for the Irish language;

(b) uphold the democratic values enshrined in the Constitution, especially those relating to freedom of expression; and

(c) have regard to the need for the formation of public awareness and understanding of the values and traditions of countries other than the State, including in particular those of other Member States in the EU.

5.081 RTÉ shall ensure that the programme schedules of the broadcasting services:

(a) provide a comprehensive range of programmes in the Irish and English languages that reflect the cultural diversity of the whole island of Ireland and include programmes that entertain, inform and educate, provide coverage of sporting, religious and cultural activities and cater for the expectations of the community generally as well as members of the community with special or minority interests and which, in every case, respect human dignity;

(b) provide programmes of news and current affairs in the Irish and English languages, including programmes that provide coverage of proceedings in the Houses of the Oireachtas and the European Parliament; and

(c) facilitate or assist contemporary cultural expression and encourage or promote innovation and experimentation in broadcasting.

5.082 The principal express powers of RTÉ in pursuance of the objects outlined above shall be to:

(a) establish, maintain and operate broadcasting stations and to acquire, install and operate apparatus for wireless telegraphy;

(b) subject to any regulations under the Wireless Telegraphy Act 1926, provide for the distribution by means of wired broadcast relay stations of programmes broadcast by RTÉ and such other programmes as RTÉ may decide;

(c) originate programmes and procure programmes from any source;

(d) make contracts, agreements and arrangements incidental or conducive to the objects of RTÉ;

(e) acquire and make use of copyrights, patents, licences, privileges and concessions;

(f) collect news and information and subscribe to news services and such other services as may be conducive to the objects of RTÉ;

(g) subscribe to such international associations, and to such educational, musical and dramatic bodies and such other bodies promoting entertainment or culture, as may be conducive to the objects of RTÉ;

(h) organise, provide and subsidise concerts, entertainments, education and other activities in connection with a broadcasting service or for any purpose

183

incidental to it and, in relation to any such concert or entertainment, provide or procure accommodation and, if desired, make charges for admission;

(i) prepare, publish and distribute, with or without charge, such magazines, books, papers and other printed matter as may seem to RTÉ to be conducive or incidental to its objects;

(j) arrange with other broadcasting companies or authorities for the distribution, receipt, exchange and relay of programmes (whether live or recorded);

(k) compile, publish and distribute, with or without charge, recorded aural and visual material;

(l) provide programmes of news and current affairs in the Irish and English languages, including programmes that provide coverage of proceedings in the Houses of the Oireachtas and the European Parliament;

(m) facilitate or assist contemporary cultural expression and encourage or promote innovation and experimentation in broadcasting;

(n) invest in, originate or procure films;

(o) establish and maintain websites;

(p) establish and maintain an electronic communications network subject to any enactment or rule of law;

(q) establish and maintain an electronic communications service meaning a service which consists wholly or mainly in the conveyance of signals on electronic communications networks, subject to the provisions of any enactment or rule of law;

(r) make available the broadcasting services of RTÉ in so far as reasonably practicable by any and all means of transmission, relaying or distribution, whether by way of broadcast (which includes terrestrial sound and television broadcasting networks, cable networks or satellite networks), or by any form of electronic means (which includes fixed terrestrial networks, mobile terrestrial networks, including the Internet and other electronic communications networks) and whether now known or hereinafter invented on a linear or non-linear basis; and

(s) invest any of its funds in any manner in which a trustee is empowered by law to invest trust funds.

RTÉ shall have all such powers as are necessary or incidental to the attainment of the objects and which are not inconsistent with the Broadcasting Bill 2008.

Programming

5.083 The television broadcasting service and the sound broadcasting service established and maintained shall have the character of a public service. RTÉ shall endeavour to ensure that the programme schedules of the television broadcasting service and the sound broadcasting service established and maintained are, in so far as it is reasonably practicable, representative of the programme schedules of the national television broadcasting services referred to in the Broadcasting Bill 2008.

Infrastructure sharing

5.084 Section 115 provides that, at the request of the BAI and after consultation with RTÉ, the Minister may direct RTÉ to require it to co-operate with the holder of a broadcasting contract in respect of access to and use of RTÉ's transmission infrastructure. The co-operation covers the use of any mast, tower, site or other installation or facility needed in connection with the provision of transmission facilities for sound broadcasting services under the sound broadcasting contract. A sound broadcaster shall make to RTÉ such periodical or other payments in respect of any such facilities as the Minister after consultation with RTÉ and the BAI directs. No provisions are made as to the conditions of this access such as, in particular, price, appropriate price models to be applied or non-discrimination obligations.

Licensing

5.085 Section 121 provides that ComReg shall issue a WTA licence to RTÉ and TG4 in respect of the provision of broadcasting services by them.

Funding

5.086 Section 123 provides that the Minister may, with the approval of the Minster for Finance, pay to RTÉ out of moneys provided by the Oireachtas an amount equal to the total receipts in that year in respect of television licence fees, less certain deductions such as expenses incurred by the Minster in relation to the collection of those fees and amounts paid to BAI in respect of the Broadcasting Fund. This section also provides that the Minister may, subject to the consent of the Minister for Finance, make Exchequer funding available to RTÉ and TG4 for public services purposes. The amount paid to RTÉ shall be used solely for the purposes of pursuing its public service objects and paying amounts levied on RTÉ. The Minister, with the consent of the Minister for Finance, may from time to time, pay to RTÉ such an amount as he or she determines to be reasonable for the purposes of defraying the expenses incurred by RTÉ in the pursuance of its PSOs. The Minister, with the consent of the Minister for Finance, may from time to time, pay to TG4 such an amount as he or she determines to be reasonable for the purposes of defraying the expenses incurred by TG4 in pursuing its PSOs, and paying amounts levied on TG4.

5.087 Section 124 provides that on an annual and five-year basis, the BAI will conduct reviews and make recommendations to the Minster as to the requisite level of public funding to fulfil public service objects. Section 124 provides that the BAI shall, in each year, carry out a review of the extent to which a corporation has during the previous financial year fulfilled the commitments stated in an annual statement of commitments for that financial year and the adequacy or otherwise of public funding to enable the corporation to meet its PSOs. The BAI shall on the basis of the review recommend in a report to the Minister an annual television licence fee modification and the amount of any payment to be made to TG4. The BAI shall within a period of not more than three years after the passing of this Act, and every five years thereafter, or as directed by the Minister, carry out a review of the adequacy or otherwise, of public funding to enable a corporation to meet its PSOs. The BAI shall on the basis of the review make in a report to the Minister a recommendation as to the requisite level of public funding required to permit the corporation to fulfil its public service objects further to s 123. The government's response to the recommendation of the BAI is to be laid before each House of the Oireachtas.

Digital Broadcasting and Analogue Switch Off

5.088 In 1999, Ireland first considered introducing DTT. Legislation was enacted in 2001[35] to allow for this; however, the response to a public tender competition to award the licenses was not successful and the process ended in 2003. The Broadcasting (Amendment) Act 2007 amended the 2001 DTT legislation to put forward a new framework for the roll out of national DTT. The Broadcasting (Amendment) Act 2007 was commenced in April 2007.

5.089 In line with other EU countries, Ireland is moving from the current analogue terrestrial system to a digital one. Digital TV offers better quality new services and more channels. It can provide universal free-to-air digital TV. Once DTT is rolled out and in place, Ireland will be obliged to switch off the analogue channels. This will involve a substantial campaign to raise public awareness in this regard to ensure that everyone will be switched over to the new system before the old system is switched off. The spectrum will be divided into a system of multiplexes,[36] which is a much more efficient use of spectrum rather than spectrum channels. For example, currently four spectrum channels are taken up by RTÉ One, RTÉ Two, TV3 and TG4. Once these channels are available on DTT, each spectrum channel will accommodate a multiplex which can allow for up to 8 channels. This frees up spectrum for other uses.

5.090 It is interesting to note that spectrum below 1GHz rarely becomes available in that the existing spectrum framework dates to 1961.[37] This spectrum will now become available when analogue TV is switched over to digital TV. Surplus spectrum that will be freed up from the analogue to digital switchover could be re-allocated, although the processes through which this spectrum could be re-allocated have not been finalised. This surplus spectrum is known as the digital dividend. According to the European Commission, the:

> [D]igital dividend is a unique opportunity to meet the fast growing demand for wireless communications services. It opens up sufficient spectrum for broadcasters to

---

35 Broadcasting Act 2001.

36 Multiplexing (known as 'muxing') is a term used to refer to a process where multiple signals or digital data streams are combined into one signal over a shared medium. In the case of DTT, it is a group of digital TV channels that are combined together for broadcast. A device that performs the multiplexing is called a multiplexer (MUX). According to the 2007 Act, 'multiplex' means an electronic system which combines programme material and related and other data in a digital form and the transmission of that material and data so combined by means of wireless telegraphy directly or indirectly for reception by the general public.

37 Presentation by Philip Rutnam of OfCom at the ComReg Digital Dividend Conference on 1 October 2008, available on ComReg's website (http://www.comreg.ie).

significantly develop and expand their services while at the same time ensuring that other important social and economic uses, such as broadband applications to overcome the "digital divide", have access to this valuable resource. The digital dividend therefore potentially creates a "win/win" situation for all interests.[38]

5.091 In Ireland, given the proximity to the UK (in particular Northern Ireland and Wales), overspill issues are currently well managed. With the advent of DTT, these overspill issues need to be managed particularly in terms of the expectation that currently UK TV channels are *de facto* available on free-to-air services in Ireland and *vice versa*. In addition, any new use of the digital dividend needs to be co-ordinated in respect of overspill. The EU has indicated that it expects all Member States to have reached analogue switch-off by 2012. To date, Ireland has not formally committed to a precise date although, as part of the National Development Plan, it is anticipated that the 2012 date is a target that Ireland will seek to meet. The Department of Communications, Energy and Natural Resources has stated that it is aiming to meet the EU date of 2012.[39] Analogue switch off is happening in the US on 17 February 2009 so no doubt Ireland and Europe can learn from any teething difficulties experienced by the US.

5.092 74 per cent of Irish households already avail of pay TV.[40] Other delivery methods (mobile handsets, personal computers) are also being used. It is questionable how much of a take up of DTT there will be in Ireland given it would only be of interest to the last 26 per cent of the population. Consideration also has to be given to the desirability of High Definition TV, which takes up more spectrum than standard TV. Nonetheless, it is thought that 20 to 30 channels could become available over DTT. Once national roll-out is well underway, a date for analogue switch-off can be decided upon. In 2006, the Department of Communications, Marine and Natural Resources commenced a pilot programme to start a roll-out of the service in Ireland, which has been running successfully with 12 TV channels, High Definition Channels and radio channels. This DTT pilot programme has been run by RTÉ NL since 2006 and is due to finish in 2008 – supposedly in preparation for digital switch-off. The Broadcasting Bill 2008 allows consideration by the Minister of a date for analogue switch-off. The

---

38 European Commission (13.11.2007), *Reaping the full benefits of the digital dividend in Europe: A common approach to the use of the spectrum released by the digital switchover*, COM(2007) 700 final.

39 Speech made by Minister Eamon Ryan at the ComReg Digital Dividend Conference on 1 October 2008.

40 Europe Economics Report to ComReg on Digital Dividend, dated 1 October 2008. Interestingly, according to the European Commission in its decision on TV3's State aid complaint (see paras **5.160***ff* of this chapter), in 2005 around 21.5 per cent of Irish television households were 'Irish terrestrial households', ie they received only the four Irish channels: RTÉ One, RTÉ Two, TG4 and TV3. Approximately 15.7 per cent of Irish television households were 'Multi terrestrial households', ie they received the four Irish channels and at least one of the UK channels. In total there are, however, around ten Irish television channels operating on the island, in addition to the about six to ten foreign channels (mainly British) which are targeting Ireland.

Bill provides that the Minister for Communications may, following consideration of a report from the BCI or the RTÉ Authority, issue a policy direction in this regard.

Digital Audio Broadcasting (DAB) is currently on trial in Greater Dublin, the Northeast, Cork and Limerick.[41] A DVB-H[42] trial was undertaken between RTÉ and O$_2$ in 2007, whereby RTÉ One and RTÉ Two linear broadcasts were available via DVB-H.

5.093 The Broadcasting (Amendment) Act 2007 reserves six multiplexes for TV broadcasting: two are reserved for RTÉ, and four are allocated to BCI for use by commercial TV. It sets out the new framework for the development of DTT in Ireland. Under this Act, RTÉ, TG4, ComReg and BCI all have new statutory obligations. RTÉ has a duty to roll-out a DTT multiplex at a national level for free-to-air digital TV, which must carry at least RTÉ One, RTÉ Two, TV3 and TG4. The BCI has been allocated three multiplexes, which it had to put out to licensing. The contracts were advertised by BCI on 7 March 2008. The BCI considered the applications received from three consortia. On 21 July 2008, the BCI announced its decision with regard to the award of the three national DTT multiplex contracts – it awarded the contracts in principle to Boxer DTT Ltd. The award of the contracts is subject to clarifications and the successful outcome of contract negotiations, which will take place in the coming months. RTÉ, pursuant to the Broadcasting Amendment Act 2007, is obliged to operate the free-to-air MUX.[43]

5.094 Section 5 of the Broadcasting Amendment Act 2007 sets out that it shall be a duty of ComReg, at the request of the RTÉ Authority, to issue to the RTÉ Authority under s 16(3)(a) of the 1960 Act, a licence in respect of the establishment, maintenance and operation of a single television multiplex, which multiplex shall, in so far as it is reasonably practicable, be capable of being transmitted by digital terrestrial means to the whole community in the State. The same section provides that it shall also be the duty of ComReg, at the request of the BCI, to issue to the BCI under the Wireless Telegraphy Acts 1926 to 1988, licences in respect of the establishment, maintenance and operation of four television multiplexes, which multiplexes shall, in so far as it is reasonably practicable, be capable of being transmitted by digital terrestrial means to the whole community in the State, in accordance with contracts to be entered into by the BCI. During any emergency declared under s 10 of the Wireless Telegraphy Act 1926, the Minister may suspend any licence issued under this section and, while any such suspension continues, the Minister may operate any service which was provided under the suspended licence or require such service to be operated as he directs. Section 6 provides that it shall be a duty of ComReg, at the request of the RTÉ Authority, to issue under s 16(3)(a) of the 1960 Act a licence in respect of the establishment, maintenance and operation of a single sound broadcasting multiplex, which multiplex shall, in so far as it is reasonably practicable, be capable of being transmitted by digital terrestrial means to the whole community in the State. Likewise it shall be a duty of ComReg, at the request of the BCI, to issue to the BCI under the

---

41 Presentation by Cathal Goan, Director-General, RTÉ, 1 October 2008 at ComReg conference on Digital Dividend, available on (http://www.comreg.ie).

42 Digital Video Broadcast Handheld.

43 Multiplex.

Wireless Telegraphy Acts 1926 to 1988 licences in respect of the establishment, maintenance and operation of one sound broadcasting multiplex, which multiplex shall, in so far as it is reasonably practicable, be capable of being transmitted by digital terrestrial means to the whole community in the State, in accordance with contracts to be entered into by the BCI. These licenses may also be suspended in the event of an emergency declared under s 10 of the Wireless Telegraphy Act 1926.

5.095 Section 130 of the Broadcasting Bill 2008 provides for the establishment and operation of multiplexes by RTÉ and outlines associated conditions which ensure that RTÉ and TG4 channels are carried on the first RTÉ multiplex. It also provides for the carriage on the RTÉ multiplex, if required by the Minster, of other TV services of a public service nature, and of the TV programme service contractor, if requested by the BAI. Channels carried by RTÉ on the first RTÉ multiplex may make payments to RTÉ in respect of this provision and may request an increase in capacity for the carriage of their service. TV3 will therefore have to pay RTÉ for carrying TV3 on the first multiplex. No provision is made for the basis on which this cost of carriage should be charged. Section 131 provides that the BAI shall make arrangements for the establishment and operation of multiplexes in addition to those provided by RTÉ. Section 132 sets out that ComReg shall make available licences for DTT services for both RTÉ and the other multiplex service providers. Section 133 provides that ComReg should make available licenses to RTÉ and other providers in respect of digital sound broadcasting. Section 135 provides that ComReg may make regulations with the Minister's consent prescribing fees to be paid by the holders of licences in respect of multiplex contracts awarded by the BAI. Section 136 provides that the BAI shall direct the Contract Awards Committee to invite applications for the award of contracts to establish and operate multiplexes. Section 137 sets out the award criteria for these contracts. Section 139 provides for consideration by the Minister of a date for analogue switch-off, having consulted with the relevant stakeholders. The Minister may issue policy direction to ComReg under s 13 of the Communications Regulation Act 2002 to begin the process of analogue switch-off, and this may require ComReg to revoke existing licences to facilitate analogue switch-off. It also provides for RTÉ and the BAI to provide information to the public with regard to analogue switch off.

5.096 ComReg has published a consultation entitled 'Licensing Digital Terrestrial Television',[44] which consulted on proposed licence conditions for the DTT multiplex licences to be issued to RTÉ and the BCI under the Wireless and Telegraphy Act 1926 and the Broadcasting (Amendment) Act 2007. ComReg published a 'License for Digital Terrestrial Television'[45] and 'Technical conditions for Digital Terrestrial Television'.[46] ComReg's position on the DTT multiplex licence conditions is set out in its response to consultation document and includes the following conditions:[47]

   (a)   the licence duration shall be 12 years;

---

44   ComReg Document No 07/65 dated 31 August 2007.

45   ComReg Document No 07/90a dated 9 November 2007.

46   ComReg Document No 07/90b dated 9 November 2007.

47   ComReg Document No 07/90 dated 9 November 2007.

(b)   there shall be annual licence fees with phased implementation in the start-up phase of DTT, including a 50 per cent discount in the early years of the DTT licences, with the following structure:

    (i)   initial annual licence fees of €57,000 in the period from the award of the DTT licences up to 1 July 2012,

    (ii)   thereafter, an annual licence fee of €114,000 indexed to inflation, using CPI, for the remainder of the licence period,

    (iii)   the first indexation will take place with effect from 1 July 2013 based on the increase, if any, in CPI in the period 1 July 2012 to 30 June 2013;

(c)   there are roll-out obligations in each of the licences issued to the BCI, such that these licences reflect the roll-out agreed by the BCI with its multiplex contractor to whom the rights and obligations of the multiplex licence will be passed on;

(d)   there are sanctions for non-compliance with licence conditions, including:

    (i)   licence revocation, suspension, term reduction, reduction of geographical coverage area and re-allocation of spectrum thus recovered; and

(e)   ComReg also sets out the technical conditions related to the operation of the transmission networks that will be used to carry the DTT multiplexes.

These terms and conditions are set out in Wireless Telegraphy (Digital Terrestrial Television License) Regulations 2008.[48]

5.097 In respect of digital sound broadcasting, ComReg published a consultation on 16 September 2008.[49] The purpose of this document is to consult on the proposed licence conditions for digital terrestrial sound broadcasting multiplex licences ('Digital Sound Broadcasting Multiplex licences') to be issued to RTÉ and the BCI. This consultation arises following a request from RTÉ for a Digital Sound Broadcasting Multiplex licence, pursuant to s 6(1) of the Broadcasting (Amendment) Act 2007 (the 2007 Act), for digital radio broadcasting using Band III spectrum (174 to 230MHz). Digital Sound Broadcasting Multiplex licences will be issued by ComReg to RTÉ and the BCI, as required by the 2007 Act, under the Broadcasting Authority Act 1960 and the Wireless Telegraphy Acts 1926 to 1988. ComReg expects that the first multiplex licence to enable digital radio broadcasting in Ireland will be issued following completion of this consultation process. This consultation identifies the requirements imposed by relevant legislation and proposes licence conditions which seek to ensure the efficient use of the radio spectrum going forward and which maximise the benefits to consumers and broadcasters of digital radio in Ireland. The process involves consulting on a range of technical and non-technical licence conditions considered relevant by ComReg within this context. ComReg's preliminary views on the proposed

---

48   SI 198/2008.

49   ComReg Document No 08/79.

Digital Sound Broadcasting Multiplex licence conditions are set out in its consultation document and it is proposed that the following licence conditions would be included:

(a) the licence would be of ten years' duration;

(b) there would be sanctions for non-compliance with the licence conditions, which may include licence termination, suspension, term reduction, reduction of geographical coverage area, licence revocation and re-allocation of spectrum recovered;

(c) there would be technical conditions attached to multiplex licences; and

(d) it is proposed that there would be an initial annual licence fees of €20,000 per multiplex, indexed to inflation on an annual basis using the CPI and subject to a fees review on the fifth anniversary of the commencement date of the licence.

TV Licences

5.098 Another important issue currently is whether TV-enabled mobile phones need TV licences. Mobile-TV can be a more limited version of traditional TV, where the TV programmes are transmitted to individual subscribing customers over a mobile network, rather than broadcast in the sense of conventional television. A mobile phone, capable of receiving live broadcast television, is a wireless telegraphy apparatus not dissimilar in this sense to a television set, and whether it would require a television licence had to be considered. 3G mobile phones may be exempt from the television licensing requirements of s 3 of the Act of 1926 by reason of s 4 of the Wireless Telegraphy Act 1926 (Section 3) (Exemption of Mobile Telephones) (Amendment) Order 2003 (the 2003 Order).[50] It provides:

> The following class of apparatus for wireless telegraphy, namely, mobile telephones, is hereby declared to be a class of apparatus for wireless telegraphy to which Section 3 of the Wireless Telegraphy Act, 1926, does not apply.'

5.099 There are currently no specific regulations that apply to broadcasting to mobile devices given that this is an emerging technology. In December 2006, ComReg published a 'Briefing Note on Mobile Television'.[51] ComReg stated that the definition of mobile TV in the Briefing Note covered both advanced forms of traditional broadcast TV to mobile users as well as video download type services targeted at mobile users. ComReg also noted that much of the policy and regulation relating to broadcasting in Ireland revolves around content, advertising and related user protection, which are beyond the scope of ComReg's remit. In its briefing note, ComReg indicated that it may need to consider important issues raised in the area of

---

50 SI 158/2003.

51 ComReg Document No 06/62.

content that will affect the converged mobile TV landscape. ComReg stated that regulatory intervention by ComReg (though not necessarily by other bodies) is likely to be lightest where the mobile TV industry is structured in the form of separate competing arrangements. ComReg also indicated that broadcasting to mobile devices would raise issues in respect of spectrum-related regulation, which would be necessary in terms of frequency management for both the mobile and broadcasting sectors.

5.100 Part 9 of the Broadcasting Bill 2008 deals with TV licences. It provides that the Minister may by order specify that individual rooms within a premises are to be regarded as separate premises for the purpose of television set licensing. Section 142 establishes that possession of a television set requires a licence and that the Minster may exempt certain classes of television set from the licensing requirement. The Minster may grant a TV license to possess a TV set at a premises. Section 145 provides that An Post, or a person designated by the Minster, may act as the Minster's agent as regards the grant of TV licenses and the collection of license fees. This section also provides for the role of the Department of Social and Family Affairs as regards the issue of lifetime TV licences. Section 148 provides that it is an offence not to hold a TV license in respect of the possession of a TV set and sets out the maximum fines applicable on summary conviction. Section 149 provides for the operation of a fixed penalty payment mechanism in respect of a failure to hold a TV licence. It is capped at one-third of the value of the licence fee. Section 151 amends the definition of a television set contained in the Wireless Telegraphy Act. 'Television set' means any electronic apparatus capable of receiving and exhibiting television broadcasts broadcast for general reception (whether or not its use for that purpose is dependent on the use of anything else in conjunction with it), and any software or assembly comprising such apparatus and other apparatus. This could, therefore, include mobile phones unless mobile TV is provided to subscribers that pay for that mobile operator's service and this, therefore, constitutes broadcasts to a closed user group rather than broadcasts for general reception.

5.101 In respect of general TV licences, when approving a significant increase in the level of the license fee in 2002, the government decided that the license fee should be subject to an annual adjustment based on a formula of $CPI - X$, with the value of X to be decided following a review of RTÉ's performance. The intention is that the new BAI will conduct the review. In the interim, the Department of Communications, Energy and Natural Resources engages independent consultants to carry out this review. The license fee was increased in 2006 and in 2008 as a result of this review. Within the State, it is necessary to pay a fee of €160 per annum in order to legally possess any piece of equipment capable of receiving television signals (not necessarily just those of RTÉ).

5.102 The State pays for 'TV Licence Inspectors' who have the power to obtain and execute search warrants of private houses. Failure to possess a valid television licence can result in a fine and a criminal record. An Post acts as the Minister's agent in collecting TV license fees on foot of the Postal and Telecommunications Services Act 1983. In the past, the Department of Communications, Energy and Natural Resources worked closely with An Post and RTÉ to introduce a range of new measures to improve the efficiency of license-fee collection to reduce the level of evasion. In 2004, the office of the Comptroller & Auditor General published a report dealing with the efficiency of license fee collections and the Department is implementing these recommendations. The Department has now got a service level agreement in place with An Post. The Broadcasting Bill 2008 contains amendments that would allow for the collection contract to be put out to tender and consideration to be received for carrying out this collection service. Almost a third of license fees come from free licenses and are paid directly by the Department of Social and Family Affairs. These are for families whose incomes are below a certain level.

Broadcasting Fund

5.103 In December 2002, it was decided that 5 per cent of the net proceeds of the TV license fee would be made available to support a scheme to fund new and additional programmes on Irish radio and TV. Legislation to provide for the establishment of the fund was enacted in December 2003, namely the Broadcasting (Funding) Act 2003. The BCI has drawn up a scheme called the Sound and Vision Scheme and has allocated over €30m to finance the making of new TV and radio programmes. The BCI recently announces a fourth round of funding for TV. The scheme is directed at new and additional high quality programming on Irish culture, heritage and history, including programmes in the Irish language. The fund also supports adult literacy programmes and the archiving of broadcast material. The fund is open to independent producers and all broadcasters licensed in Ireland.

5.104 Part 10 of the Broadcasting Bill deals with the broadcasting fund. Section 153 provides for the preparation of a grant scheme by the BAI, the terms of which are to be agreed with the Minister. Section 154 sets out the objectives of the broadcasting funding scheme. Section 155 provides for payments by the Minister equivalent to 5 per cent of the net revenue received from the sale of television set licence fees for the purposes of a broadcasting funding scheme.

Major Events Television Coverage

5.105 The government publishes a list in the Official Journal of the EU of events of major national importance that should be available free to air. By doing so, it seeks to ensure that events of major national importance will not end up only on pay per view and out of the reach of those who wish to view them. The aim is to prevent a two-tier television system, which could deprive the public of involvement in events that are part of its national identity. Access to such events should not be restricted only to those who can afford to pay the rates demanded by subscription or pay-per-view television services. The concept is that the public should not be excluded from seeing major events on television because of pay TV subscription rates. Among the list of events are: the Summer Olympics; the All-Ireland Senior Inter-County Football and Hurling Finals; Ireland's home and away qualifying games, Ireland's games and the opening games, the semi-finals and the final in the European Football Championship and the

FIFA World Cup Tournaments; Ireland's games in the Rugby World Cup Finals Tournament and the Irish Grand National, the Irish Derby, together with the Nations Cup at the Dublin Horse Show. This is provided for by the Television without Frontiers Directive and is carried on by the Audiovisual Media Services Directive.

5.106 Part 11 of the Broadcasting Bill 2008 seeks to deal with major events television coverage. Section 161 provides that the Minister may by order determine and designate events of major importance to society to be available free to air. Section 162 provides for a consultation process where it is intended to designate an event of major importance. Section 163 sets out the duties of the broadcaster, whether they are qualified or not, in respect of acquiring rights with respect to designated events. Section 164 sets out the duties of a broadcaster in respect of events designated as being of major importance by a Member State of the EU. Section 165 provides for civil remedies where it is alleged that a broadcaster has not complied with these obligations. Section 166 provides that the High Court may on application by a broadcaster make an order determining reasonable market rates for an event. Section 167 covers the circumstance where an event organizer has not, within 56 days of the event taking place, entered into a contract with a qualifying broadcaster for broadcasting rights to a designated event. The qualifying broadcaster may apply to the High Court for an order directing that access to the event be provided, subject to the payment of reasonable market rates and such other terms as may be determined by the court. The court may direct, upon terms the court considers just and proper, an event organizer to give a qualifying broadcaster access to a designated event before the High Court has fixed all the terms for the acquisition of the broadcasting rights including the fixing of reasonable market rates. This section also provides that, where an existing contract is in place between an event organizer and a non-qualifying broadcaster, the High Court shall on receipt of an application from a qualifying broadcaster decide to whom and in what proportion moneys in respect of reasonable market rates should be paid. Section 167 also provides that the High Court may adjust, as it considers appropriate, the terms of an existing contract between an event organizer and a non-qualifying broadcaster. These provisions could be viewed as wide-reaching powers in respect of costly sports broadcasting rights.

5.107 Section 168 provides for arbitration arrangements in respect of instances where an event organizer who is willing to sell broadcasting rights to a designated event has not been able to agree a price with a qualifying broadcaster for access to the event. Section 169 provides for the criteria which the High Court or arbitrator must have regard to when determining reasonable market rates or terms. These include:

   (a) previous fees (if any) for the event or similar events;

   (b) time of day for live coverage of the event;

   (c) the period for which rights are offered;

   (d) the revenue potential associated with the live or deferred coverage of the event;

(e) the purposes of art 3j of the Audiovisual Media Services Directive[52] and the rights conferred on Member States of the European Communities to regulate the exercise of broadcasting rights; and

(f) such other matters as may appear to be relevant.

5.108 Section 170 provides that the Minister may in the public interest require an event organizer to provide the Minister with a copy of any agreement entered into by an event organizer with any broadcaster in respect of a designated event. Section 171 provides for the power to issue directions and notifications and s 172 sets a three-year review timetable for the Minister to determine which events are major events.

ENFORCEMENT

5.109 Enforcement of the Broadcasting Bill 2008 will be both civil and criminal. This section will examine both the civil and criminal aspects of the enforcement of the BAI's powers in the area of broadcasting. In general, enforcement can happen by way of a complaint being made to a Regulator or by way of the BAI investigating a matter on its own initiative. There is also a process for dispute resolution where a dispute arises.

Civil Enforcement

Complaints and requests for dispute resolutions

5.110 Section 47 of the Broadcasting Bill requires broadcasters to consider complaints and to establish a mechanism for dealing with complaints. Section 48 allows the Compliance Committee to investigate complaints. Section 49 of the Broadcasting Bill provides for a right-of-reply mechanism for persons whose honour and reputation have been impugned by an assertion of incorrect facts in a broadcast.

5.111 Section 47 provides that a broadcaster shall give due and adequate consideration to a complaint on one or more of the grounds specified in s 48(1), made in writing by a person in respect of the broadcasting service provided by the broadcaster which, in the opinion of the broadcaster, has been made in good faith and is not of a frivolous or vexatious nature. A complaint shall be made to the broadcaster not more than 30 days after:

(a) in case the complaint relates to one broadcast, the date of the broadcast;

---

52 Council Directive 89/552/EEC of 3 October 1989 on the co-ordination of certain provisions laid down by law, regulation or administrative action in Member States concerning the pursuit of television broadcasting activities as amended by Directive 97/36/EC of the European Parliament and of the Council of 30 June 1997 and by Directive 2007/65/EC of the European Parliament and of the Council of 18 December 2007. Article 3j of the Audiovisual Media Services directive requires that 'The Member States shall take appropriate measures to ensure that audio-visual media services under their jurisdiction are gradually and where feasible made accessible to people with a visual or hearing disability.'

(b)   in the case of two or more unrelated broadcasts, the date of the earlier or earliest, as the case may be, of those broadcasts; or

(c)   in case the complaint relates to two or more related broadcasts of which at least two are made on different dates, the later or latest of those dates.

5.112 A broadcaster shall prepare and implement a code of practice for the handling of complaints. The code of practice shall make provision for the following matters:

(a)   an initial point of contact for complainants;

(b)   a time period within which the broadcaster shall respond to complaints; and

(c)   the procedures to be followed by the broadcaster in the resolution of complaints.

A broadcaster shall publish on a website maintained by the broadcaster, and generally make available, a copy of a code of practice prepared. The Compliance Committee may prepare and publish guidance for broadcasters for the purposes of ensuring compliance with preparing a code of practice. A broadcaster shall provide a copy of its code of practice to the Compliance Committee who shall cause such information to be published on a website maintained by the BAI. A broadcaster shall keep a record of complaints made and of any reply made thereto for a period of two years from the date of receipt of the complaint. A broadcaster shall, if directed by the Compliance Committee, make available for inspection by the Compliance Committee all records kept by the broadcaster in this regard.

5.113 Section 48 provides that the Compliance Committee may investigate complaints. The Compliance Committee can investigate and decide upon the following types of complaints:

(a)   a complaint that in broadcasting news given by it and specified in the complaint, a broadcaster did not comply with one or more of the requirements of s 39(1)(a) and (b);[53]

(b)   a complaint that in broadcasting a programme a broadcaster either did not comply with one or more of the requirements in s 39(1)(a) and (b) or was in breach of the prohibition contained in s 39(1)(d);[54]

---

53   Section 39(1) provides that every broadcaster shall ensure that: '(a) all news broadcast by the broadcaster is reported and presented in an objective and impartial manner and without any expression of the broadcaster's own views, and (b) the broadcast treatment of current affairs, including matters which are either of public controversy or the subject of current public debate, is fair to all interests concerned and that the broadcast matter is presented in an objective and impartial manner and without any expression of his or her own views, except that should it prove impracticable in relation to a single broadcast to apply this paragraph, two or more related broadcasts may be considered as a whole, if the broadcasts are transmitted within a reasonable period of each other.'

54   Section 39(1)(d) provides that: 'anything which may reasonably be regarded as offending against good taste or decency, or as being likely to promote, or incite to, crime or as tending to undermine the authority of the State, is not broadcast by the broadcaster.'

(c)   a complaint that there was an encroachment by a broadcaster contrary to s 39(1)(e);[55]

(d)   a complaint that a broadcaster failed to comply with a provision of a broadcasting code providing for the matters referred to in s 42(2)(a) to (d) and s 42(2)(f), (g) and (h).[56]

A complaint shall be in writing and be made to the Compliance Committee not more than 30 days after:

(a)   in case the complaint relates to one broadcast the date of the broadcast;

(b)   in the case of two or more unrelated broadcasts, the date of the earlier or earliest, as the case may be, of those broadcasts; and

(c)   in case the complaint relates to two or more related broadcasts of which at least two are made on different dates, the later or latest of those dates.

5.114 The Compliance Committee may, at its discretion, refer the complaint in the first instance to the broadcaster, for consideration in accordance with a code of practice. Where the Compliance Committee proposes to investigate a complaint, the Committee shall afford to the broadcaster to whom the complaint relates seven days (or such further period not exceeding 21 days as the Committee allows) to comment on the complaint. Where a complaint is made to the Compliance Committee and a person employed by the broadcaster in the making of any programme the subject of the complaint requests that the Compliance Committee afford to him or her an opportunity

---

55   Section 39(1)(e) provides that: 'in programmes broadcast by the broadcaster, and in the means employed to make such programmes, the privacy of any individual is not unreasonably encroached upon.'

56   Broadcasting codes shall provide: '(a) that all news broadcast by a broadcaster is reported and presented in an objective and impartial manner and without any expression of the broadcaster's own views, (b) that the broadcast treatment of current affairs, including matters which are either of public controversy or the subject of current public debate, is fair to all interests concerned and that the broadcast matter is presented in an objective and impartial manner and without any expression of the broadcaster's own views, (c) that anything being likely to promote, or incite to, crime, or as tending to undermine the authority of the State, is not broadcast by a broadcaster, (d) that in programmes broadcast by a broadcaster, and in the means employed to make such programmes, the privacy of any individual is not unreasonably encroached upon, (f) that matters involving taste and decency of programme material, in particular, in respect of the portrayal of violence and sexual conduct, shall be presented by a broadcaster: (i) with due sensitivity to the convictions or feelings of the audience, and (ii) with due regard to the impact of such programming on the physical, mental or moral development of children, (g) that advertising, teleshopping material, sponsorship and other forms of commercial promotion employed in any broadcasting service, in particular advertising and other such activities which relate to matters likely to be of direct or indirect interest to children, protects the interests of children having particular regard to the general public health interests of children, (h) that advertising, teleshopping material, sponsorship and other forms of commercial promotion employed in any broadcasting service, other than advertising and other activities as aforesaid falling within paragraph (g), protect the interests of the audience.'

to comment on the complaint, the Compliance Committee shall, having considered the reasons, afford to the person seven days (or such further period not exceeding 21 days as the Committee allows) to comment on the complaint. In addition, if the making of any programme the subject of the complaint was commissioned by the broadcaster concerned, and the person commissioned to make that programme requests the Compliance Committee to afford to him or her an opportunity to comment on the complaint, the Compliance Committee shall, having considered the reasons so specified, afford to the person seven days (or such further period not exceeding 21 days as the Committee allows) to comment on the complaint. In each case, it is only where the Committee is satisfied that there is an appropriate interest involved, such as:

(i)   an interest of the person being an interest which the Compliance Committee considers relevant to the person's employment by the broadcaster concerned; or

(ii)   the prospects of the person obtaining further commissions in respect of programmes from the broadcaster concerned, may, because of the complaint, be adversely affected.

5.115 When the Compliance Committee proposes to consider a complaint that a broadcaster failed to comply with the provision of a broadcasting code providing for the matters referred to in s 42(2)(g) or (h), the Compliance Committee shall afford the relevant advertiser seven days (or such further period not exceeding 21 days as the Committee allows) to comment on the relevant advertisement.

As soon as may be after it decides on a complaint made under this section, the Compliance Committee shall send to the person who made the complaint, and the broadcaster concerned, a statement in writing of its decision, including the reasons for its decision.

In case the Compliance Committee decides on a complaint that a broadcaster failed to comply with the provision of a broadcasting code providing for the matters referred to in s 42(2)(g) or (h), the Compliance Committee shall send to the person with whom the broadcaster agreed to broadcast the relevant advertisement (if he or she is not the person who made the complaint) a statement in writing of its decision.

5.116 The consideration by the Compliance Committee of a complaint made to them under s 48 may be carried out by the Compliance Committee in private further to s 48(9). Unless they consider it inappropriate to do so, the Compliance Committee shall, as soon as may be after the making of the decision, publish particulars of their decision on a complaint in such a manner as they consider suitable and, where they consider that the publication should be by the broadcaster, or should include publication by the broadcaster, the particulars shall be published by the broadcaster in such manner as shall be agreed between the Compliance Committee and the broadcaster concerned. The broadcaster shall, unless the Compliance Committee consider it inappropriate for the broadcaster to do so, broadcast the Compliance Committee's decision on every complaint considered by the Compliance Committee in which the Compliance Committee found in favour, in whole or in part, of the person who made the complaint, within 21 days of such decision and at a time and in a manner corresponding to that in which the broadcast to which the complaint relates took place.

As regards proceedings under this section, the Compliance Committee does not have any power to award to any party costs or expenses.

5.117 The Compliance Committee does not have to investigate a complaint which, in the opinion of the Compliance Committee, is not made in good faith or is frivolous or vexatious, nor, unless the Compliance Committee considers that there are special reasons for investigating the complaint (which reasons shall be stated by the Compliance Committee when giving their decision), does it have to investigate a complaint which is withdrawn.

5.118 Where a matter has been the subject of multiple complaints made under s 48 or multiple complaints in respect of a broadcast transmitted from another jurisdiction targeted at audiences in the State, the Compliance Committee may review the matter concerned and as it considers appropriate, report the findings to the Minister and to the relevant public body in such form and manner as the Committee thinks fit.

5.119 The Compliance Committee shall endeavour to decide upon a complaint as soon as practicable after such a complaint is received. The Compliance Committee may, where it deems it appropriate, hold an oral hearing in respect of proceedings under this section. The Compliance Committee may also deem a complaint made to a broadcaster rather than the Compliance Committee within the time periods specified in s 47 as having been made within the time periods specified in s 47.

5.120 Section 49 deals with right of reply. It provides that any person whose honour or reputation has been impugned by an assertion of incorrect facts or information in a broadcast shall have a right of reply. 'Right of reply' means the broadcast by a broadcaster of a statement prepared in accordance with a scheme according to the section. A 'scheme' is provided for under s 49 where it provides that the BAI shall prepare, within six months of the establishment day, following a period of public consultation, a scheme for the exercise of the right of reply. A scheme shall set out the procedures to be followed in the exercise of the right of reply. In preparing a scheme, the BAI shall ensure that:

(a) a right of reply shall be broadcast:

  (i) within a reasonable time period subsequent to the request for a right of reply being made, and

  (ii) at a time and in a manner appropriate to the broadcast to which the request refers; and

(b) a right of reply shall:

  (i) state to what extent the information contained in the broadcast is incorrect or misleading, and

  (ii) be limited to factual assertions necessary to rectify an incomplete or otherwise distorting assertion.

The scheme shall be published by the BAI on its website. The scheme shall be laid before each House of the Oireachtas by the Minister as soon as may be after it is made. Either House of the Oireachtas may, by resolution passed within 21 sitting days after the day on which a scheme was laid before it, annul the scheme. The annulment of a scheme takes effect immediately on the passing of the resolution concerned but does not affect anything that was done under the scheme before the passing of the resolution. The BAI shall review and report to the Minister on the operation, effectiveness and impact of a scheme not later than three years from the date on which it comes into operation and every five years thereafter or at such time as may be requested by the Minister. A copy of this report shall be laid by the Minister before each House of the Oireachtas as soon as may be after it has been made to him or her.

5.121 A person who wishes to exercise a right of reply in accordance with a scheme shall make a request in writing addressed to the broadcaster concerned stating that the request is made under s 49 and containing sufficient particulars to enable the identification of the part of the broadcast which asserted incorrect facts impugning the honour or reputation of the requester, and if the requester requires the right of reply to be given in a particular form or manner, specifying what this is (provided it is in accordance with the terms of any scheme). A request for a right of reply shall be made not later than ten days after the making of the broadcast referred to in the request, unless otherwise agreed between the requester and the broadcaster concerned. The broadcaster shall, as soon as may be, but not later than ten days after the receipt of a request decide whether to grant or refuse the request, and cause notice in writing of the decision to be given to the requester. Where notice of a decision is not given to the requester, a decision refusing to grant the request shall be deemed to have been made upon the expiration of the notice period. A broadcaster shall give due and adequate consideration to any request which in the opinion of the broadcaster has been made in good faith and is not of a frivolous or vexatious nature, by a member of the public in respect of the broadcasting service provided by the broadcaster and shall keep due and proper records for a period of two years of all such requests and of any reply made to them or of any action taken on foot of them. A broadcaster shall, if directed by the Compliance Committee, make available for inspection by the Compliance Committee all records kept by him or her in this regard. No charge shall be made for the processing of a request by a broadcaster. In a defamation action, the granting of a request for a right of reply under this section by a defendant in respect of a statement to which the action relates does not constitute an express or implied admission of liability by that defendant, and is not relevant to the determination of liability in the action. In a defamation action, the defendant may give evidence in mitigation of damage, that he or she granted or offered to grant a right of reply under this section to the plaintiff in respect of the statement to which the action relates, either before the bringing of the action, or as soon as practicable thereafter, in circumstances where the action was commenced before there was an opportunity to grant or offer to grant a right of reply. In a defamation action, a defendant who intends to give evidence shall, at the time of the filing or delivery of the defence to the action, notify the plaintiff in writing of his or her intention to give such evidence. Evidence of the granting of a right of reply under this section by a broadcaster in respect of a statement to which the action relates is not admissible in any civil proceedings as evidence of liability of the defendant.

5.122 The Compliance Committee, on application in writing, by a requester, may within 21 days after the receipt of such an application, review such a decision to refuse by a broadcaster and affirm the decision, or annul the decision and require the broadcaster concerned to broadcast the Compliance Committee's decision including any correction of inaccurate facts or information within seven days of the decision being communicated to the broadcaster. The correction shall take place at a time and in a manner corresponding to that in which the broadcast to which the request relates took place. An application for review shall be made to the Compliance Committee within ten days of receipt of a decision to refuse. Where the Compliance Committee proposes to investigate an application for review, the Compliance Committee shall afford to the broadcaster to whom the application relates an opportunity to comment on the application. As soon as it decides on an application made for review, the Compliance Committee shall send to the person who made the application, and the broadcaster concerned, a statement in writing of the decision, including the reasons for their decision. The Compliance Committee may reject any request for a right of reply where it is of the opinion that:

(a) the request is of a frivolous or vexatious nature or was not made in good faith;

(b) the request is manifestly unnecessary owing to the minor significance of the error in the broadcast complained of;

(c) a proposed right of reply cites untrue information or assertions;

(d) a proposed right of reply is a personal opinion;

(e) a proposed right of reply is an assessment or warning against the future conduct of a person;

(f) satisfaction of the proposed right of reply would involve a punishable act;

(g) satisfaction of the proposed right of reply would transgress standards of public decency;

(h) satisfaction of the proposed right of reply would render the broadcaster liable to civil law proceedings;

(i) satisfaction of the proposed right of reply would breach a broadcaster's statutory obligation;

(j) satisfaction of the proposed right of reply would breach the terms of a broadcaster's contract with the BAI under Pt 6 of the Broadcasting Bill;

(k) the person who was injured by the contested information has no legally justifiable actual interest in the publication of a right of reply;

(l) the original broadcast also contained a statement from the person affected and such contents are equivalent to a reply;

(m) the original broadcast also contained a statement from the person affected and the text of the original statement had prior agreement of the person who feels he or she has been injured;

(n) an equivalent editorial correction has been made and the person affected informed;

(o) the content of the proposed right of reply would violate the rights of a third party;

(p) the matter concerned relates to reports on public sessions of the Houses of the Oireachtas or the courts;

    (q)   the matter concerned relates to a party political broadcast;

    (r)   the matter concerned relates to a broadcast under s 3 of the Referendum Act 1998;[57]

    (s)   the broadcast of a right of reply is not in the public interest; or

    (t)   the application was not made within the period specified.

5.123 Where the Compliance Committee finds that the broadcaster has failed to comply with a decision, the Compliance Committee shall notify the broadcaster of those findings and give the broadcaster an opportunity to make representations in relation to the notification or remedy any non-compliance, not later ten days after issue of the notification, or such period as is agreed by the Compliance Committee with the broadcaster concerned.

Where, at the end of this period, the Compliance Committee is of the opinion that the broadcaster concerned has not complied with such notification, the Compliance Committee may recommend to the BAI that the BAI apply to the High Court for such order as may be appropriate in order to ensure compliance with the notification. Where the application is made to the High Court, it shall be heard by a judge sitting alone. The court may, as it thinks fit, on the hearing of the application make an order:

    (a)   compelling compliance with the notification;

    (b)   varying the direction; or

    (c)   refusing the application.

Dispute resolution

5.124 There are several provisions in the Broadcasting Bill 2008 that refer to the referral and resolution of disputes.

Section 76 sets out a dispute resolution process where a dispute arises in relation to s 70 of the Broadcasting Bill. If a dispute arises between the holder of an MMD licence and RTÉ/TG4 or between the holder of an MMD licence and a contractor relating to the placement by the licence holder of a broadcasting service on the free-to-air service system provided by RTÉ/TG4 or a contractor, the dispute shall be referred to the BAI for its determination, and the determination of the BAI in the matter shall be final.

5.125 Section 77, which deals with must-carry obligations, also provides for the resolution of disputes.

---

57   Pursuant to s 3(1), the Referendum Commission shall have the function 'to publish and distribute such statements in such manner and by such means including the use of television, radio and other electronic media as the Commission considers most likely to bring them to the attention of the electorate and to ensure as far as practicable that the means employed enable those with a sight or hearing disability to read or hear the statements concerned ... [and] to foster and promote and, where appropriate, to facilitate debate or discussion in a manner that is fair to all interests concerned in relation to the proposal aforesaid.'

If a dispute arises between a network provider and RTÉ, TG4 or a television programme service contractor in relation to the placement by the network provider on the free-to-air service system provided by RTÉ/TG4 or a contractor, the dispute shall be referred to the BAI for its determination, and the determination of the BAI in the matter shall be final further to s 77(3) and s 77(4) of the Broadcasting Bill.

5.126 Both RTÉ and TG4 have to ensure that dispute procedures are in place to resolve disputes arising under s 111 (Access to Archive material) and s 112 (the Code of Fair Trading Practice). These provide that RTÉ and TG4 shall ensure that provision is made for resolving disputes arising in respect of the operation of a scheme (by independent arbitration or otherwise) in a manner that appears to the Minister to be appropriate.

5.127 Section 159, which deals with major TV events, also has dispute resolution provisions. A broadcaster who provides near universal coverage of a designated event is deemed to be a qualifying broadcaster. Two or more broadcasters who enter into a contract or arrangement to jointly provide near universal coverage of a designated event shall be deemed to be a single broadcaster with respect to that event. A broadcaster may request the Minister to resolve any dispute as to the extent of a free television service being provided by a broadcaster in the State for the purpose of this section and the definition of 'near universal coverage' is also contained in s 159.

Investigations by Compliance Committee

5.128 The Broadcasting Bill 2008 gives powers to the Compliance Committee in respect of information gathering and investigations. However, these powers are not as extensive as other organisations would have. The relevant provisions are set out in s 50. Section 50 allows the Compliance Committee of the BAI to conduct an investigation into the affairs of a broadcasting contractor or in respect of compliance with terms of a contract or a Wireless Telegraphy Act (WTA) licence. The BAI may suspend or terminate a broadcasting contract on the recommendation of the Compliance Committee under s 51. This is a significant sanction and would likely be subject to the principle of proportionality and, of course, is subject to a right of appeal to the High Court. An investigation may also be instigated if the Compliance Committee has reasonable grounds for concerns about breaches by a broadcaster of certain requirements. Section 53 provides that the Compliance Committee may appoint investigating officers to investigate and report on apparent breaches by a broadcaster of certain requirements. Section 54 sets out the procedures to be followed by the investigating officer in any investigation of an apparent breach.

5.129 Section 50 provides that the Compliance Committee may conduct an investigation if it has reasonable grounds for believing:

(a) a contractor is not providing a service in accordance with the terms of the contractor's contract;

(b) the manner in which a service is being operated is causing interference or is being operated without a licence under the WTA; or

(c) any apparatus for wireless telegraphy is injuriously affected.

It may conduct an investigation into the operational, programming, financial, technical or other affairs of a holder of a contract under Pts 6[58] or 8[59] of the Broadcasting Bill 2008. The contractor shall co-operate in any such investigation.

5.130 The Compliance Committee may, for the purposes of an investigation, require the contractor concerned to:

(a) produce to the investigator such information or records in the contractor's possession or control relevant to the investigation;

(b) allow the investigator to enter the premises of the contractor to conduct such inspections and make such examinations of broadcasting equipment found there; and

(c) where appropriate, attend before the investigator for the purposes of the investigation.

5.131 Where an investigator, having conducted an investigation, forms a view that a contractor is not providing the service referred to or is causing interference, then he or she shall notify the finding to the contractor and afford that contractor an opportunity to make submissions in accordance with any rules made at a hearing before the Compliance Committee in respect of the matter under investigation.

The contractor concerned is to supply the Compliance Committee with such information and records that the Compliance Committee considers necessary for the purposes of a hearing. After consideration of submissions made by the contractor concerned, the Compliance Committee may make a finding of non-compliance or may make such other finding as it considers appropriate in the circumstances.

5.132 The Compliance Committee is obliged to set out rules providing for the conduct of a hearing which will indicate the period in which submissions are to be made. The rules may include the provision for an oral or other form of hearing, as appropriate. All expenses reasonably incurred in relation to an investigation under s 50 conducted by an investigator shall be borne by the contractor concerned where the Compliance Committee confirms any findings of the investigator.

5.133 Section 53 provides that the Compliance Committee shall appoint a member of the staff of the BAI (or such other person as the Committee considers to be suitably qualified) to be an investigating officer where it is of the opinion that there are circumstances suggesting that it is appropriate to investigate and report on any apparent breach by a broadcaster of a requirement of ss 39(1);[60] 40(1), (2) or (3);[61]

---

58   Part 6 deals with commercial broadcasting, ie not public service obligation broadcasting.

59   Part 8 deals with digital broadcasting.

60   Section 39(1) imposes certain duties on broadcasters.

61   Section 40 requires broadcasters to record and hold for a specified period any broadcasts made by them for the purpose of the performance of the functions of the Compliance Committee.

41(2), (3) or (4);[62] 106(3) or (4)[63] or a broadcasting code or rule. The terms of appointment of an investigating officer under s 53 shall relate to the particular breach being investigated and may define the scope of the investigation, as regards the matters or the period to which the investigation is to extend, and may limit the investigation to matters connected with particular circumstances.

5.134 Where the Compliance Committee appoints an investigating officer to investigate and report on an apparent breach by a broadcaster, the investigating officer shall:

(a) notify the broadcaster of the matter under investigation;

(b) supply the broadcaster with copies of any documents relevant to the investigation; and

(c) afford to the broadcaster an opportunity to respond, within seven days of the date of the notification (or such further period not exceeding 21 days as the Committee allows), to the matter under investigation.

It is the duty of the broadcaster concerned to co-operate in any such investigation and to provide the investigating officer with such information as he or she considers necessary for the purposes of the investigation.

5.135 Where the Compliance Committee appoints an investigating officer to investigate and report on a breach and either a person employed by the broadcaster concerned, or a person commissioned to make a programme, requests, for reasons specified by the person, that the Compliance Committee afford to him or her an opportunity to comment within seven days (or such further period not exceeding 21 days as the Committee allows) on the matter under investigation, then the Compliance Committee shall, having considered the reasons so specified, require the investigating officer to afford to the person such an opportunity, if they are satisfied that:

(a) an interest of the person, which the Compliance Committee considers relevant to the person's employment by the broadcaster concerned, is involved;

(b) the prospects of the person obtaining further commissions in respect of programmes from the broadcaster concerned, may, because of the matter under investigation, be adversely affected; or

(c) it is in the interests of fairness to do so, having regard to any potential consequences for the good name of the person.

Where the Compliance Committee proposes to investigate non-compliance by a broadcaster with a broadcasting code that provides for any of the matters referred to in s 42(2)(g) or (h),[64] the investigating officer shall afford to the person employing such matter in a broadcasting service an opportunity to comment within seven days of notification (or such further period not exceeding 21 days as the Committee allows) in relation to the matter under investigation. An investigating officer may require the

---

62 Section 41 sets out requirements in relation to the broadcast of advertisements.

63 These subsections pertain to RTÉ and TG4 as regards advertising and sponsorship.

64 These subsections relate to advertising targeted at children and adults, respectively.

broadcaster concerned to provide to the investigating officer such information or records in the broadcaster's possession or control relevant to the investigation, and if appropriate, attend before the investigating officer for the purposes of the investigation.

Consequences of a finding of non-compliance – termination and suspension & financial sanctions

Termination & suspension

5.136 Section 51 provides that the BAI may terminate any contract entered into by the BAI under Pt 6 or Pt 8 of the Act or suspend any contract for such period as the Compliance Committee considers reasonable and specifies in its recommendation to the BAI:

(a) if any false or misleading information of a material nature was given to the Contract Awards Committee by or on behalf of the holder of the contract before it was entered into; or

(b) if the holder of the contract has, upon a finding by the Compliance Committee subsequent to the investigation, failed on one or more occasions to comply with a term or condition of the contract and the nature of that failure is of such seriousness as warrants the termination or suspension by the BAI of the contract.

The BAI also has the power to suspend or terminate the contract where the Compliance Committee recommends that the contract be suspended or terminated.

Where the Compliance Committee proposes to consider making a recommendation, the Committee shall by notification afford the holder of the contract concerned an opportunity to make submissions, in accordance with any rules made under s 50 at a hearing before the Committee in respect of the matter.

A contract terminated or suspended shall:

(a) in case it is terminated, cease to have effect; and

(b) in case it is suspended, cease to have effect for the period for which it is suspended.

5.137 Section 54 of the Broadcasting Bill details a compliance procedure entailing notification to the broadcaster and provides undertakings with an opportunity to remedy any perceived non-compliance. Section 54 provides that where an investigating officer forms the view that there has been a breach in respect of any matter which he or she is investigating or that the broadcaster has failed to co-operate with the investigation, the officer shall report this to the Compliance Committee. The report of an investigating officer in relation to an investigation to the Compliance Committee shall include:

(i) the investigating officer's findings in relation to the matter;

(ii) any response or comment received from the broadcaster;

(iii) details of any failure by the broadcaster concerned to comply with the investigation; and

(iv)   the recommendation of the investigating officer.

5.138 Where an investigating officer forms a view that there has been a breach by the broadcaster concerned or that the broadcaster has not co-operated with the investigation, the broadcaster shall be afforded the opportunity of making a submission to the Compliance Committee within ten days of being notified of the investigating officer's views and recommendation.

Where the Compliance Committee, having considered the report and any submissions finds that there has been a breach by the broadcaster, or the broadcaster has failed to co-operate in an investigation, the Committee may recommend to the Authority (and the Authority shall comply with the recommendation) that the Authority shall either:

(i)   apply to the court for a determination that there has been a breach or a failure to co-operate with an investigation by the broadcaster concerned; or

(ii)   notify the broadcaster concerned.

5.139 A notification shall set out reasons for the notification. It shall state that the BAI intends to apply to the court for a determination that there has been a breach or a failure to co-operate with an investigation, unless the broadcaster concerned requests, in writing within 14 days of the date of the notification, that the BAI deal with the matter. The BAI may indicate in the notification the amount of financial sanction (not exceeding €250,000) that it intends to recommend to the court if the matter is dealt with by the court under s 55.

5.140 Where a broadcaster makes a request to do so, the BAI shall afford the broadcaster an opportunity to make submissions at a hearing before the BAI. Where a broadcaster takes the opportunity to make submissions at a hearing, the members of the BAI conducting the hearing shall not include any person who was a member of the Compliance Committee that appointed the investigating officer under s 53 to investigate the alleged breach and made a recommendation under s 53. The BAI shall make rules providing for the conduct of a hearing. The rules may include the provision for an oral or other form of hearing, as appropriate, and for the taking of evidence whether orally or otherwise, as appropriate, and the applicable rules of evidence. The BAI may not award costs or expenses to any party in relation to a hearing.

Civil financial sanctions

5.141 Section 54 provides that the Compliance Committee may apply to the High Court for the imposition of a financial sanction in respect of a breach by a broadcaster of the Broadcasting Bill. Under s 55, the undertaking is required to make a payment to remedy any non-compliance. Section 55 provides that the High Court may make a determination in respect of a breach and may impose a civil financial sanction of up to €250,000. Please see **Ch 4** on Financial Services Regulation, paras **4.158***ff* for a discussion of the constitutionality of civil sanctions under the provisions of the Central Bank and Financial Services Authority of Ireland Act 2004. The constitutionality of the provision in the Broadcasting Bill providing for civil financial sanctions in the order of €250,000 may fall to be tested by the courts.

5.142 Section 56 sets out the matters to be considered in determining the amount of financial sanction. It provides that in doing so, the BAI or the court shall take into account the circumstances of the breach or the failure to co-operate with an investigation in question, as the case may be, and shall, where appropriate, have regard to:

   (a)   the need to ensure that any financial sanction imposed:

       (i)   is appropriate and proportionate to the breach or the failure to comply with an investigation, and

      (ii)   will act as a sufficient incentive to ensure future compliance in respect of the requirement breached;

   (b)   the seriousness of the breach;

   (c)   the turnover of the broadcaster in the financial year ending in the year previous to the breach and the ability of the broadcaster to pay the amount;

   (d)   the extent of any failure to co-operate with the investigation;

   (e)   any excuse or explanation offered by the broadcaster for the breach or failure to co-operate with the investigation;

   (f)   any gain (financial or otherwise) made by the broadcaster or by any person in which the broadcaster has a financial interest as a consequence of the breach;

   (g)   the appropriateness of the time when the programme concerned was broadcast;

   (h)   the degree of harm caused or increased cost incurred by audiences, consumers or other sectoral or market participants as a consequence of the breach;

   (i)   audience expectations as to the nature of a programme's content;

   (j)   the duration of the breach;

   (k)   repeated breaches by the broadcaster;

   (l)   continuation by the broadcaster of:

       (i)   the breach, or

      (ii)   the broadcasting of the matter to which an investigation relates after being notified of the investigation;

  (m)   the extent to which:

       (i)   the management of the broadcaster knew, or ought to have known, that the breach was occurring or would occur, and

      (ii)   any breach was caused by a third party, or any relevant circumstances beyond the control of the broadcaster,

   (n)   the absence, ineffectiveness or repeated failure of internal mechanisms or procedures of the broadcaster intended to prevent the breach by the broadcaster;

   (o)   the extent to which the broadcaster has taken steps in advance to identify and mitigate external factors that might result in a breach;

(p)   the extent and timeliness of any steps taken to end the breach in question, and any steps taken for remedying the consequences of the breach;

(q)   submissions by the broadcaster on the appropriate amount of a financial sanction;

(r)   whether a financial sanction in respect of similar conduct has already been imposed on the broadcaster by the BAI or another person; and

(s)   any precedents set by the court or BAI in respect of previous breaches or failures to comply with an investigation.

Criminal Enforcement

Penalties and punishments

5.143 The BAI also has criminal powers of enforcement. The criminal offences created in respect of broadcasting are divided into two types: indictable offences and summary offences. Indictable offences, the more serious cases, are heard by a judge and jury in the Circuit Criminal Court or the Central Criminal Court and carry the most serious penalties if the court convicts the accused. They are subject to appeal to the Court of Criminal Appeal. Summary offences are heard by a judge without a jury in the District Court and on appeal in the Circuit Court. The BAI will be given a discretion for prosecuting various summary offences. When determining whether or not to prosecute, the BAI will likely follow the DPP's *Guidelines For Prosecutors*, which is available on the DPP's website.

5.144 Section 78 of the Broadcasting Bill 2008 deals with offences under broadcasting contracts and content provision contracts for commercial and community broadcasters, that is the offences for the purposes of Pt 6 of the Broadcasting Bill. It provides that a person who contravenes s 71(1)[65] or s 74(2)[66] commits an offence liable, on summary conviction, to a fine not exceeding €5,000 or, on conviction on indictment, to a fine not exceeding €100,000.

5.145 There are also criminal offences in respect of TV licences. Section 145 provides that an 'issuing agent' (An Post or another person designated by the Minister) may, on payment of the appropriate licence fee, issue on behalf of the Minister a television licence. The Minister may by order designate a person other than An Post to be an issuing agent for the purposes of this section. An issuing agent may:

(a)   collect fees in respect of television licences; and

(b)   identify persons who have television sets not authorised by a licence.

Summary proceedings may be brought and prosecuted by an issuing agent for an offence under s 147(3) or s 148. Section 147 provides that a special notice may be

---

65   Section 71(1) provides that a person shall not supply a compilation of programme material otherwise than under and in accordance with a content provision contract.

66   Section 74(2) provides that a person shall not prepare or make available for use an electronic programme guide otherwise than under and in accordance with an electronic programme guide contract.

issued to a person requiring the person to complete and return a form of declaration, including a statement as to whether or not the person has in their possession a television set and has or has not a current television licence. If a person fails within 28 days to complete and return the declaration, it is presumed that they have a television set without a licence. The section provides that a person commits an offence if they make any false or misleading statements in respect of the completion of a special notice or declaration under this section.

Section 148 provides that it is an offence not to hold a television licence in respect of the possession of a television set and sets out the maximum fine applicable on summary conviction of such an offence, which is €5,000.

5.146 Sections 149 provides for the operation of a fixed penalty payment mechanism in respect of a failure to hold a television licence. A fixed penalty payment notice may only be applied after the issue of two reminder notifications and a minimum period of 56 days. The extent of a fixed penalty payment notice is capped at one-third of the value of the television licence fee. Section 149(6) provides that, in a prosecution for an offence under s 148, the onus of proving that a payment pursuant to a notice under s 149 has been made lies with the defendant.

5.147 Section 150 provides for the prosecution of offences for failure to hold a television licence. It also sets out certain presumptions. It provides that summary proceedings for an offence under Pt 9 of the Broadcasting Bill may be brought by the Minister or the issuing agent (ie An Post) concerned. In a prosecution for an offence under s 148 in which it is shown that a television set was in a particular premises or specified place on a particular day, it shall be presumed, until the contrary is shown by the defendant, that on that day the television set was in the possession of the person who was then the occupier of the premises or specified place. In a prosecution for an offence under s 148 in which it appears that a person kept or had in his possession a television set at the time to which the prosecution relates, it shall be presumed, until the contrary is shown by the defendant, that he did not at such time hold a television licence. In a prosecution for an offence under s 148 in which it is shown that a notice under s 147 has been sent by registered post, it shall be presumed, until the contrary is shown by the defendant, that the person to whom the notice was sent has not complied with the requirements of that section. In s 150 'occupier' in relation to premises, means a person who as owner, tenant or otherwise is in occupation. Where an offence has been committed by a body corporate and is proved to have been committed with the consent or connivance of, or to be attributable to any neglect on the part of, a director, manager, secretary or other similar officer of the body corporate, or any person who was purporting to act in any such capacity, he or she, as well as the body corporate, commits that offence and is liable to be proceeded against accordingly.

5.148 Section 179 provides for the updating of fines in respect of certain broadcasting and wireless telegraphy related offences. These are offences under the Wireless Telegraphy Act 1926–1988, the Broadcasting Offences Act 1968 and the Broadcasting Act 1990.

APPEALS

5.149 Please see **Ch 10** for details on the provisions relating to appeal of decisions of the BAI.

THE RULES RELATING TO JUDICIAL REVIEW

5.150 Decisions of the BAI are also, of course, open to judicial review. Judicial review is a process whereby the supervisory jurisdiction of the High Court is invoked in relation to the procedures adopted in reaching decisions taken by bodies such as BAI in the exercise of powers conferred by public law. Injunctive relief could also be obtained. Please see **Ch 11** for general information on judicial review of regulatory bodies.

RELEVANT CASES

5.151 The following cases relate to the regulation of the broadcasting sector.

5.152 *State (Lynch) v Cooney*:[67] This case was a judicial review of an order by the Minister for Posts and Telegraphs made under s 31 of the Broadcasting Authority Act 1960. Mr Lynch was a member of Sinn Féin and RTÉ had agreed to carry Sinn Féin party political broadcasts on television and radio. However, the Minister intervened and directed RTÉ to refrain from broadcasting a matter that would invite support for Sinn Féin by means of the Broadcasting Authority Act (section 31) (No 2) Order 1982. The Supreme Court in this case considered that the Minister's power under s 31 had to be based on an opinion that was '*bona fide* held and factually sustainable and not unreasonable'. It held that the Minister had compelling grounds for believing that Sinn Féin was seeking to broadcast views aimed at undermining the authority of the State and that the Minister was justified in forming an opinion in relation to the matter prior to making an order under the section.

5.153 *Laurence O'Toole v RTÉ (No 2)*:[68] This case also involved the consideration of s 31. RTÉ refused to broadcast an interview with the chairman and spokesperson of a strike committee when there was a strike taking place at the Gateaux Factory in Finglas, Dublin. The man in question, Mr O'Toole, as it happened was also a member of Sinn Féin. The issue arose as to whether broadcasting an interview was prohibited by a s 31 Order solely on the basis that Mr O'Toole was a member of Sinn Féin. It was argued by the applicant that RTÉ could have pre-recorded the interview to ensure that it complied with the s 31 Order. The High Court found in favour of the applicant and the Supreme Court dismissed the appeal by RTÉ, upholding the High Court's finding. Finlay CJ held that the purpose of the s 31 Order was to prohibit the broadcasting of material that could likely undermine the authority of the State. However, the matters discussed by Mr O'Toole's broadcast did not come within the category of matters prohibited by the order, given at the interview was in the context of his role as a

---

67 *State (Lynch) v Cooney* [1982] IR 337.
68 *Laurence O'Toole v RTÉ (No 2)* [1993] ILRM 458.

spokesperson of a strike committee. To impose such a ban on Mr O'Toole would have gone outside the scope of the order.

5.154 R*adio Limerick One Limited v Independent Radio and Television Commission:*[69] In this case the IRTC, the forerunner of the BCI, terminated Radio Limerick One's licence on grounds of serious breaches. The most serious breaches included the 'blacking out' of part of a news bulletin, the use of outside broadcasts as a form of illicit advertising, the failure to provide tapes to the IRTC of programmes broadcast and the alleged refusal to co-operate with a request from the IRTC to inspect the station's operations. Radio Limerick One brought a judicial review action before the High Court seeking to have the IRTC's decision to terminate quashed. Both the High Court and, on appeal, the Supreme Court dimissed the action. They found that the IRTC had not acted disproportionately in terminating the licence given the serious breaches involved. The Supreme Court did find that the permanent withdrawal of a licence could in some cases be unreasonable where such a sanction was not proportionate to the gravity of the breach involved.

5.155 *Colgan v IRTC:*[70] This case concerned a challenge by a member of an organisation called Youth Defence to a decision of the IRTC (the forerunner of the BCI) prohibiting the broadcast of an advertisement that the organisation had prepared. The IRTC considered that the objective of Youth Defence was to bring about a change in policy by seeking a referendum regarding abortion in the State. In the IRTC's view, this was a broadcast of an advertisement that was directed towards a religious or political end and was prohibited further to s 10 of the Radio and Television Act 1988. The court considered that the advertisement had a political aim and the IRTC was correct in prohibiting the advertisement.

5.156 *TV3 Television Co Ltd v Independent Radio and Television Commission:*[71] This case involved a judicial review by the TV3 consortium of the IRTC's decision to withdraw the conditional grant of the contract from TV3 following extensive negotiations. The IRTC decided to make an award subject to contract in April 1989, but withdrew this offer in October 1991. The IRTC's decision was based on the difficulty which the consortium experienced with receiving investment. The High Court found that the decision of the IRTC to grant the award, subject to contract, amounted to a determination and also the decision to withdraw this was the IRTC exercising a statutory function to which the principles of constitutional justice applied. The court noticed that TV3 had not been given notice of the proposed decision of the IRTC, nor did the IRTC specify that the difficulties with the investment issues were grounds for withdrawing the offer, nor did it give TV3 an opportunity to be heard. The High Court granted an order of *certiorari* quashing the decision of the IRTC. The Supreme Court upheld the decision of the High Court on appeal. The Supreme Court agreed that the decision was subject to the requirements of natural and constitutional

---

69   *Radio Limerick One Limited v Independent Radio and Television Commission* [1997] 2 IR 291.

70   *Colgan v IRTC* [1999] 1 ILRM 22; [2000] 2 IR 490.

71   *TV3 Television Co Ltd v Independent Radio and Television Commission* [1994] 2 IR 439.

justice. Accordingly, the court found that there should have been a warning given to TV3 that the offer would be withdrawn if certain terms were not complied with.

5.157 *Spin Communications Ltd Trading as Storm FM v IRTC:*[72] The applicant sought to judicially review the IRTC decision to award a sound broadcasting contract to Maypril Ltd trading as Spin FM, alleging bias on the part of an IRTC member who had participated in the decision. This was on the basis that the member had written to the applicants expressing concern about the image of a nightclub run by one of the applicants, which had allegedly been associated with drugs. The Supreme Court noted that one of the requirements in s 6 of the Radio and Television Act 1988 was that the IRTC should have regard to the character of applicants, which is especially relevant where the IRTC is awarding a licence for a radio service that will target young people. The court found that the drug issue was a relevant factor in the IRTC's decision and that there was no evidence of bias on the part of the IRTC member in that the member had not prejudged the application. The Supreme Court upheld the High Court's decision finding there had been no bias.

5.158 *Magill TV Guide/ITP, BBC and RTÉ:* [73] This case resulted in the European Court finding that RTÉ, BBC and ITV had each abused their respective dominant positions in the market for listing television programming by prohibiting the reproduction of TV listings. Magill had sought to publish TV listings for all stations thereby competing with the respective guides from each station – in RTÉ's case, the *RTÉ Guide*. This case involved a refusal to supply case under art 86 (now 82) of the EC Treaty and is considered to be one of the best examples of the doctrine of essential facilities at work before the European Commission and European Court, although it is important to note that neither the court nor the Commission used the expression 'essential facility' or explicitly stated that the case amounted to a refusal to grant access to an essential facility.

5.159 *Phantom FM (Dublin Rock Radio) Case:*[74] In this judicial review case, the Supreme Court (Denham J, McCracken J, and Kearns J) was divided on whether greater account should have been taken of the pirate radio history of the members of the Dublin Rock Radio consortium trading under the name Phantom FM. The applicant in this case, Zed FM, sought an order determining that the decision of the BCI granting a sound broadcasting contract to Phantom FM should be quashed. There are ten criteria under s 6 of the Radio and Television Act 1988 which the BCI has to take into account in granting a sound broadcasting contract. The contentious criteria were contained in s 6(2)(a) of the 1988 Act which refers to 'The character of the applicant, or, if the applicant is a body corporate, the character of the body and its directors, manger, secretary, or other similar officer and its members, and the persons entitled to the beneficial ownership of its shares' and also contained in s 6(2)(b) of the 1988 Act

---

72 *Spin Communications Ltd Trading as Storm FM v IRTC* [2001] 4 IR 411; [2002] 1 ILRM 98.
73 *Magill TV Guide/ITP, BBC and RTÉ* [1989] OJ L78/43.
74 *Scrollside Ltd, Trading as 'Zed FM' v Broadcasting Commission of Ireland* [2006] IESC 24.

which refers to 'The adequacy of the expertise and experience and of the financial resources that will be available to each applicant and the extent to which the applicant accords with good economic principles'. In the High Court, O'Sullivan J had previously found in favour of the BCI. The Supreme Court ultimately found in favour of the BCI and upheld the High Court judgement. However, Kearns J in the Supreme Court was of the minority view that the appeal should be allowed in that the BCI's decision was not in line with the BCI's own stated policy. Denham J, supported by McCracken J, was of the view that the grounds of appeal should be dismissed and the order of the High Court should be affirmed. Denham J in her judgement referred to the fact that 'To succeed on such an application the applicant has to achieve a high bar, meet a significant burden of proof, to show that the decision of the specialist decision maker, in this case the respondent, should be declared void by the courts. The courts approach with caution the review of a specialist body. Such a body has particular expertise to apply to decision making in their arena. That specialist knowledge is not held by the courts. The process of review by way of judicial review is not a full appeal, but rather a review of the process and fair procedures. In this case it is in essence a review of the inclusion in a decision by the respondent of the factor that members of Dublin Rock had gained experience and expertise in pirate radio.'

5.160 *State Aid Investigation into RTÉ:*[75] In 1999, the Department for Communications received notification from the European Commission that it had received a complaint from TV3 alleging infringements of the State aid rules contained in arts 87–89 of the EC Treaty relating to the payment of license fee revenue and direct grants to RTÉ, TG4 and to the price of accessing the national broadcasting transmission network. In 2001, the European Commission published guidelines as to how it would proceed with its investigation. In February 2004, the European Commission formally wrote to Ireland re-starting the investigation into the appropriateness of the funding for RTÉ and TG4.[76] Ireland responded in 2004. In 2005, the European Commission sent Ireland an art 17 letter[77] setting out its preliminary views in relation to the compatibility of the funding arrangements for RTÉ with the requirements of the EC Treaty. The European Commission considered that the payments of license fee revenues constituted State aid within the meaning of art 87(1) of the EC Treaty. Considering that the legal basis for the license fee was adopted prior to Ireland's accession to the EEC in 1973, and remained applicable without significant subsequent alterations, the European Commission also considered that the licence fee funding could be regarded as existing aid. As regards the compatibility of the licence fee funding regime, the European Commission had concerns regarding the definition of the public service remit, entrustment and control of the public service obligations, the proportionality of the aid and whether commercial activities were benefiting from the aid. The European

---

75   *State Aid investigation into RTÉ* Case E 4/2005. Relevant documents are published on the State Aid Register on the European Commission, Competition DG's website, http://ec.europa.eu/competition/index_en.html.

76   State Aid No E 4/2005 State financing of RTÉ and TG4 – Ireland.

77   Article 17 of Council Regulation No 659/1999 laying down detailed rules for the application of art 93 EC [now art 88 EC], OJ L 83, 27.03.1999, p 1 (the Procedural Regulation).

Commission indicated ways in which compliance with State aid rules could be achieved. The European Commission considered that there were no satisfactory ex-post controls to verify whether State funding exceeded the net public service costs (over-compensation), whether commercial activities had unduly benefited from licence fee revenues (cross-subsidisation) or whether RTÉ's commercial activities were in line with market principles (market-conform behaviour). Having assessed the information and arguments subsequently submitted by Ireland, the European Commission, in accordance with art 18 of the Procedural Regulation,[78] concluded that the existing aid scheme was not compatible with the Common Market.

5.161 Ireland responded in 2005 and 2006. Following discussions as to how to address preliminary concerns identified in the art 17 letter, negotiations took place that led to the resolution of these issues in January 2008. The Irish government submitted a letter of commitment on 30 January 2008 that certain steps would be formally undertaken in the context of the Broadcasting Bill 2008. These commitments are to a large extent reflected in the draft Bill. The steps include amending the current financing regime so that the European Commission's concerns regarding the incompatibility of the current financing regime were dispelled and the investigation closed.

5.162 The European Commission considered that the commitments given by the Irish authorities were adequate to provide for a sufficiently precise and clear public service definition. In the European Commission's opinion, the enunciation of objects and duties clarifies the exact scope of the public service tasks and thus the activities which may benefit from State funds. The European Commission was satisfied with the commitments and explanations provided by the Irish authorities as to how activities such as the publication of books or audio-visual material would be treated (in the context of the Broadcasting Charter, as well as the annual statements of commitments), following consultation with the BAI, as purely commercial activity or, where a public service need is shown, as a public service so that the scope of publicly funded activities would be known in advance and could be checked afterwards.

5.163 The legal requirements for RTÉ and TG4 to adopt a Charter as well as annual statements of commitments, help to clarify the scope and limits of the public service remits. RTÉ is supposed to consult with the BAI (and the Minister) on the statements of commitment and their impact on the market and the BAI will also be responsible for checking compliance with the annual statements of commitments in its annual reviews. The European Commission considered that the evaluation procedure that was to be introduced would be an adequate means to determine to what extent new services serve the democratic, social and cultural needs of society and, in this way, to establish the public service character of the services in question. Ministerial consent is to be required before RTÉ can engage in certain new activities. The European Commission was satisfied that the granting of Ministerial consent would be preceded by a public value and market impact assessment.

---

78 Council Regulation No 659/1999 laying down detailed rules for the application of art 93 EC [now art 88 EC], OJ L 83, 27.03.1999, p 1 (the Procedural Regulation).

5.164 The European Commission welcomed the establishment of the independent BAI to ensure effective supervision and compliance of the public service broadcasters' fulfilment of the public service obligations, and considered that they satisfied the requirement for adequate control. The European Commission noted the *ex-post* control that the BAI exercised over RTÉ and TG4, in that the BAI must undertake reviews of the extent to which RTÉ and TG4 have met their commitments under their annual statement of commitments. The European Commission also noted the *ex-ante* advisory functions of the BAI, in that it advises the Minister on RTÉ and TG4's strategic plans, the public service charter and the annual commitments. It noted that part of the BAI's duties comprise the ex-ante assessment of the public value and sector impact of certain alterations and extensions to the public service remit as referred to above. The European Commission was of the view that the clearer public service remit would allow the BAI to have more effective control, including control of the extent to which public service broadcasters stay within the limits of their mission.

5.165 The commitments given by the Irish authorities to ensure RTÉ respects the requirements of the Transparency Directive mean that RTÉ will keep separate accounts distinguishing between public service activities, which are based on clearly established, consistently applied and objectively justifiable principles within the meaning of art 4(1) of the Transparency Directive.

5.166 The European Commission noted that the Broadcasting Bill 2008 foresees that the BAI, after having consulted the Minister, will prepare and publish guidance to RTÉ as regards the cost accounting principles and methods to follow in its annual reporting. The European Commission considered that the commitments given by the Irish authorities would ensure that the compensation granted to public service broadcasters would not exceed what is necessary for the fulfilment of the public service tasks (ie would be limited to the net public service costs). This will be ensured through the commitment given by Ireland that the public funds can only be granted in relation to public service tasks, while commercial revenues are deducted. In addition, the European Commission was satisfied that the regular reviews carried out by the BAI would ensure that there is a proper control of possible overcompensation. The European Commission expressed itself to be satisfied that the control of over-compensation, including the possibility for public service broadcasters to transfer a certain surplus to the following financial year would be carried out by the BAI in line with European Commission practice.

5.167 The European Commission considered that the commitments given by the Irish authorities contained the necessary safeguards to ensure that public service broadcasters carry out their commercial activities (whether intra-group or with unrelated companies) on market terms and that the financial needs of public service broadcasters are not unnecessarily increased through any such non-market-conforming behaviour since the net public service costs will be determined after having deducted commercial revenues generated in full compliance with market principles. The European Commission noted in particular that the arm's length principle applies also to investments of public service broadcasters and that commercial activities shall be operated in an efficient manner so as to maximise revenues. The revenue maximisation should be sufficient to ensure that RTÉ does not undercut prices, for instance on the advertisement market. The European Commission was satisfied that compliance with market principles was subject to control by the BAI. In this respect, the European Commission noted that the BAI must prepare and submit to the Minister a report on compliance.

With the submission of the commitments, Ireland agreed to implement the appropriate measures. The European Commission noted the commitments provided by Ireland and recorded acceptance in accordance with art 19 of the Procedural Regulation and closed the procedure. The European Commission has asked Ireland to notify the European Commission of the entry into force of the Broadcasting Bill 2008 and to submit the final law to the European Commission before December 2008.

Ireland had committed to implementing the announced amendments by December 2008. The European Commission announced its intention to close its investigation on 27 February 2008, since it is considered that the draft Broadcasting Bill 2008 would resolve the issues.[79] The Broadcasting Bill 2008 was not yet enacted at the time of writing.

---

79 The non-confidential notice of the decision was published on 17 May 2008 in the OJ with the letter dated 27 February 2008 from the European Commission to Ireland.

Chapter 6

COMMUNICATIONS REGULATION

APPROACH OF THIS CHAPTER

6.001 This chapter examines issues from both practical and academic perspectives. It is useful in the regulation of communications, which includes electronic communications (that is telecommunications) and post, to understand its foundations since these can give a good indication as to how regulatory law in this area may develop in the future. The regulation of communications involves an interdisciplinary approach that embraces law, economics and politics.

HISTORY OF ELECTRONIC COMMUNICATIONS REGULATION

Global and European

6.002 In 1865, the first International Telegraph Convention was signed in Paris and the International Telegraph Union was established. Subsequently, the first Telegraph Regulations were put in place.[1] It could be said that this was the first true communications regulatory law framework package. The International Telegraph Union in 1885 drew up international legislation governing telephony and the first provisions for international telephone service were put in place.[2] In 1896, a preliminary radio conference was convened to study the question of international regulations for radiotelegraphy communications. The first International Radiotelegraphy Conference was held in 1906 in Berlin and the first International Radiotelegraph Convention was signed that same year. The annex to this Convention contained the regulations governing wireless telegraphy, also known as the Radio Regulations.[3] In 1963, the first steps were taken to allocate frequencies in Geneva.[4]

---

1   The principles of telegraphic communication were pioneered in Ireland in the 1790s by Richard Lovell Edgeworth. In 1837 the electric telegraph was invented by Wheatstone and Fothergill Cooke. On 24 May 1844, Samuel Morse sent his first public message over a telegraph, which led to the development of telecommunications. By the mid 1850s, telegraphy was available as a service to the general public. Telegraph lines, however, did not cross national borders. Each country used a different system and messages had to be transcribed, translated and handed over at frontiers, then re-transmitted over the telegraph network of the neighbouring country. Due to the difficulties this created, many countries established arrangements that facilitated the interconnection of their national networks.

2   In 1876 Alexander Graham Bell patented his invention of the telephone and in 1895–96 the first signals were transmitted by a radio-relay system, which led to the development of wireless telegraphy and the use of this technique for maritime communications. In 1902 the first radio transmissions of the human voice took place.

3   1906 also heralded the first trials of broadcasting (voice and music) using radiotelephony.

4   In 1963, and the world's first telecommunication satellite, Syncom-1, was put in orbit.

Subsequent conferences put in place regulations governing the use, by satellites, of the radio-frequency spectrum and associated orbital slots.

6.003 In 1982, Groupe Speciale Mobile (GSM) was formed by the Confederation of European Posts and Telecommunications (CEPT) to design a pan-European mobile technology. In 1986 the EU heads of State reserved 900MHz spectrum band for GSM.[5] In the 1980s many countries moved from State-owned telecommunications infrastructure to a policy geared towards privatisation of communications networks and services.[67] In 2000, the general packet radio service (GPRS) (2.5G) was launched and in 2001, the first 3G network went live.

6.004 In 1990, the European Commission developed a framework for the liberalisation of the telecommunications sector. This transformed a sector typically characterised by State monopolies into one comprising commercial and innovative companies, for the most part. In addition, in order to ensure that remote areas or less financially attractive parts of the country were protected, the EC concept of universal service or a basic telephony and narrowband service was developed. At a European level, the electronic communications market was fully opened up to competition, ie 'liberalised', in 1998. Currently *ex ante* regulation is only applied to markets that are still insufficiently competitive due to, for example, infrastructure bottlenecks. In respect of those markets where there is sufficient competition, the ordinary rules of competition apply *ex post*. In 1999, the European Commission undertook a review of the telecommunications sector[8] and considered that a regime was needed to manage the transition to competitive markets, which envisaged a light-handed regulatory approach while ensuring that the dominant players did not abuse their positions. As markets became more competitive, regulation would be rolled back and limited to areas where objectives could not be achieved by competition rules alone. The policy objectives were:

(i) to promote an open and competitive European market for communications;

(ii) to benefit the European citizen by ensuring affordable access to a universal service specified at a European level; and

(iii) to consolidate the internal market in an environment of increasing convergence.

---

5 In 1991, the first GSM call was made in Finland. In 1992, the first international roaming agreement was signed between Telecom Finland and Vodafone (UK) and the first short message service (SMS) was sent.

6 Carney, *Regulatory Law* (Cavendish Publishing, 2004).

7 In 1992, allocations were made to serve the needs of a new kind of space service using non-geostationary satellites, known as Global Mobile Personal Communications by Satellite (GMPCS). In 1993 the first hand portable terminals were launched and in 1997 the first tri-band handsets were launched. In 1999 the first wireless application protocol (WAP) trials began. In 2000–01 the dotcom bubble collapsed and investment in many innovative consumer services was suspended.

8 Towards a new framework for electronic communications infrastructure and associated services, COM [1999] 539.

6.005 At the Lisbon Summit in 2000, the European Commission created the i2010 initiative, which stressed the importance of the role of Information and Communication Technologies (ICTs) for Europe's competitiveness. The aim was that by the year 2010 the EU would be a knowledge- or an information-based economy, moving away from Europe's traditional reliance on manufacturing.

6.006 In 2002, a revised regulatory regime or European regulatory framework for the communications sector was adopted, which consisted of a package of directives.[9] The eventual goal of the regulatory package is deregulation and the application of competition law *ex post* rather than a reliance on sector-specific regulation, also known as *ex ante* regulation.[10] The test of dominance, known in the regulatory framework package as significant market power (SMP), is generally the trigger for sector-specific regulation. There has already been a movement to deregulation in respect of the retail markets, and in the most recent European Commission list of recommended markets,[11] there are now only seven markets identified by the European Commission as suitable for *ex ante* review, reduced from 18 in the previous recommendation.[12]

6.007 Now high-speed wireless devices capable of handling voice, data and connection to online services, such as the Internet, are the norm and broadband is being rolled out across the country. Next Generation Networks involving fibre to the home or to the street-side cabinet are being considered. In addition, Voice over Internet Protocol (VoIP) is also becoming widespread and is threatening traditional voice call revenues and further blurring the boundaries within ICT. Convergence between fixed line and mobile services is also taking place both in terms of voice and data with the increased use of mobile broadband.

6.008 The current developments in the electronic communications market are Next Generation Networks (NGNs), structural and functional separation, VoIP and convergence. NGNs will radically improve the infrastructure used to deliver electronic

---

9   There were five principles underpinning the regulatory framework, which were distilled from the 1999 Review: 1. Regulation should be based on clearly defined policy objectives; 2. Regulation should be the minimum necessary to meet those policy objectives; 3. Regulation should further enhance legal certainty in a dynamic market; 4. Regulation should be aimed at being technologically neutral; 5. Rules should be enforced as close as practical to the activities being regulated – Farr and Oakley, *EU Communications Law* (2nd edn, Sweet & Maxwell, 2006).

10 This is because competition law (Competition Act 2002, ss 4 and 5 or EC Treaty, arts 81 and 82) is applied *ex post*, or after the fact once the harm has happened on the market, whereas sector-specific regulation is applied *ex ante*, before the harm takes place to try and ensure that rules are in place to prevent the harm from occurring.

11 Revised European Commission recommendation on relevant product and service markets within the electronic communications sector susceptible to *ex ante* regulation in accordance with Directive 2002/21/EC of the European Parliament and of the Council on a common regulatory framework for electronic communications networks and services dated 17 December 2007 OJ L 344/65.

12 Recommendation on relevant product and services within the electronic communications sector susceptible to *ex ante* regulation, OJ 2003 L114/45.

communications services. NGNs, for the most part, propose to replace the copper wires used in electronic communications with fibre optic cable, which can deliver much higher speeds and efficiencies. Fibre to the kerb (FTTK), fibre to the node (FTTN) and fibre to the home (FTTH) are all being considered. In order to encourage investment in this area, operators need regulatory certainty as to whether this new fibre optic cable will be regulated, and if so, to what extent and whether there will be any 'regulatory holidays' given, in particular in respect of access or price control obligations in order to facilitate the roll out of NGN. To date, the strong signal from the European Commission is that there will be no regulatory holidays since legislation is technology neutral.[13]

6.009 Structural separation is being considered, which would involve separating the network arm of an operator from its retail or services end. Structural separation may assist with eliminating some of the regulatory issues that arise in respect of incumbents as it would help to solve issues surrounding discrimination and lack of transparency. In addition, there would automatically be accounting separation in a structurally separated entity. Functional separation is also being considered.[14]

6.010 Increased use of VoIP will challenge both mobile and fixed operators' revenues, tariffs and business models. VoIP usage is becoming increasingly common, with a VoIP operator offering free on-net calls, ie between its customers regardless of location, and very competitive rates for off-net calls, ie to customers of another network. These calls travel over the Internet with voice being converted into data packets.

6.011 Convergence in the area of telecommunications, information technology and media makes it a complex area to regulate prospectively. The traditional divisions between telecommunications and IT have become so increasingly blurred that current regulatory speak refers to electronic communications, rather than telecommunications. This is particularly so with VoIP and Voice over Broadband (VoB). In addition, given the increased usage of mobile phones, the roll out of 3G and the increased use of wireless broadband, the boundary between the already indistinct waters of fixed and mobile has been further muddied. With the roll out of TV over mobile phones and TV over Internet, as well as Video on Demand (VOD), there is indeed no bright line between media and communications. Mobile phones with mp3 players and radios further cloud these opaque distinctions. Regulators have the challenge of trying to legislate in a technology-neutral manner so as not to preclude any technology from developing and not to stifle innovation.

Nowadays, electronic communications have an important impact on growth, jobs and social inclusion in the EU. The 13th implementation report, published on 13

---

13   Draft Recommendation and Explanatory Memorandum on the regulated access to Next Generation Access Networks (NGA), available at http://ec.europa.eu/information_society/policy/ecomm/doc/library/public_consult/nga/dr_recomm_nga.pdf.

14   Organisational or functional separation has already been adopted in the UK by BT. BT gave undertakings to separate its business in September 2005 and now has separate network wholesale and retail divisions.

March 2008, states that the electronic communications sector was worth €293bn in 2007.[15] It is expected that the directives, proposed on the back of the current review of the existing framework, will be adopted by 2009 and implemented in the various Member States by 2010.

Telecoms regulation has led to market liberalisation and competition, with significant progress leading to a reduction of regulation in areas where competition is functioning. In the fixed sector, however, incumbent operators still have considerable reach and the market shares of alternative providers remain relatively low. Across the EU, 86.5 per cent[16] of consumers are still offered access to the fixed network over the incumbent's infrastructure.

Ireland

6.012 In 1983, the Postal and Telecommunications Services Act was adopted and Bord Telecom Éireann remained a State-controlled monopoly, with the Minister for Posts and Telegraphs as its shareholder.[17] Bord Telecom Éireann had special and exclusive rights. From the early 1990s, the Irish government's policy in the electronic communications sector has been to open up the electronic communications networks and services to promote competition and to ensure efficient services and technologically advanced networks are in place to improve Ireland's competitiveness.[18]

---

15   Communication from the European Commission to the European Parliament, the Council, the European Economic and Social Committee and the Committee of the Regions progress report on the Single European Electronic Communications Market 2007 (13th report), dated 13 March 2008.

16   Communication from the European Commission to the European Parliament, the Council, the European Economic and Social Committee and the Committee of the Regions progress report on the Single European Electronic Communications Market 2007 (13th report), dated 13 March 2008.

17   The Minister for Finance held one share in Bord Telecom Éireann under s 19 of the 1983 Act.

18   In 1992, Ireland implemented the Open Network Provision Directive (90/387/EEC), which provided for the liberalisation of telecommunications services other than voice telephony. In 1994, Ireland implemented the leased lines Directive (92/44/EEC), which obliged Telecom Éireann to provide leased lines to other operators, such as BT. In 1995, Directive 95/51/EC abolished restrictions on the use of cable TV networks for the provision of already liberalised telecommunications services. In 1996, ESAT was awarded the second 2G licence. In 1996, Directive 96/2/EC allowed direct interconnection of mobile networks with other mobile and fixed networks. Also in 1996, Directive 96/19/EC required full competition with the exception of voice telephony and public telecommunications networks, such exception only to remain in place until 1998. In 1998, Meteor was announced as the successful applicant for a third 2G licence. In 1998, full liberalisation took place in Ireland. In 1999, Telecom Éireann was listed and regulations transposing Directive 98/61/EC on number portability and carrier pre-selection came into effect. In 2000, the European Commission adopted a regulation on unbundled local loop. For a full history of liberalisation of telecommunications in Ireland, see: http://www.dcenr.gov.ie/ Communications/Reports+and+Publications/History+of+Liberalisation/ History+of+Liberalisation.htm (accessed on 7 January 2009).

The Telecommunications (Miscellaneous Provisions) Act 1996 allowed for private investment in Telecom Éireann and KPN/Telia took an equity stake in the company. This Act also allowed for the establishment of the Office of the Director of Telecommunications Regulation (ODTR). At the time, however, this was criticised as not going far enough since, '[d]ifficulties arose from the fact that the Minister was also a shareholder [in Telecom Eireann and] … [t]he Minster remain[ed] responsible for critical areas of national telecommunications policy.'[19]

6.013 In 1997, the Department of Transport Energy and Communications set out in its statement of strategy for the regulation of telecommunications as follows:

> The Department currently carries out three functions in the sectors for which it is responsible – regulation, discharging the State's shareholding function as well as policy development. It is clearly unsatisfactory to continue to carry out these three functions in one Department when the possibility exists of companies from the private sector entering those markets which up to now have been characterised for the most part by State owned monopolies. Ownership interests should not dictate or be perceived to dictate how a sector is regulated and to that extent it is essential that the regulatory function be separated clearly and transparently from the shareholder function … it is fundamental that the development of policy and legislation remain with the Minister.[20]

In 1998, the telecommunications market was fully liberalised in Ireland, which meant that other companies could compete to provide services in all telecommunications services. A substantial, if phased, paradigm shift had taken place in Ireland as the telecommunications sector went from being under State control, protected from competition and heavily unionised, to having open competition with commercial international companies active in the market.

6.014 The primary legislation that established the current national regulatory authority in Ireland was the Communications Regulation Act 2002, as amended by the Communications Regulation (Amendment) Act 2007. The 2002 Act changed the name of the ODTR to the Commission for Communications Regulation (ComReg) and increased the Regulator's enforcement powers. The 2007 Act increased penalties for breaches of certain obligations and granted additional information-gathering powers to the Minister for Communications and to ComReg. It gave ComReg concurrent competition powers in the sphere of electronic communications together with the Competition Authority and the courts. It established an emergency call-handling service and transferred responsibility for the oversight and management of the Irish '.ie' domain registry to ComReg.

6.015 The relatively low level of broadband penetration in Ireland remains a political bone of contention. In March 2006, it was announced that the European Commission had authorised, in line with State aid rules, a new programme to boost broadband availability in Ireland by creating open-access metropolitan area networks (MANs),

---

19   Baker and McKenzie, *Telecommunications Laws in Europe* (4th edn, Butterworths, 1998).

20   Statement of Strategy, Department of Transport, Energy and Communications, 1997.

which are fibre networks, in over 120 Irish towns at a cost of €170m. The government recently launched the National Development Plan (NDP) 2007–2013 in which it indicated that it will allocate €435m to the Communications and Broadband Programme over this period. The government intends to build on the success of the NDP 2000–2006 by completing the construction of the MANs. A new scheme to deliver broadband to areas of the country that would not be reached by the MANs programme is also being developed for implementation over the 2007–2013 period, and is known as the National Broadband Scheme (NBS). The NBS is to ensure that a minimum level of broadband services will be available across the State and will provide broadband services to certain areas in Ireland in which broadband services are not available at present. Hutchinson 3G Ireland Ltd was announced as the preferred bidder in November 2008 and the detail of the scheme was announced by the Minister for Communications in January 2009.

ComReg stated in its Quarterly Key Data Report that there are over one million active broadband subscriptions in Ireland at present.[21] Over all, electronic communications network and service revenues were estimated to be €4.46bn at the end of June 2008 in Ireland. Ireland's Internet penetration rate is above the European average. Ireland's household broadband penetration rate was 57 per cent as at March 2008.[22]

6.016 Wholesale bottlenecks such as local loop unbundling (LLU) remain contentious. Price is also important in opening up markets and is subject to regulatory intervention. NGN and the question of how to regulate Next Generation Access (NGA) in a manner that facilitates access and promotes competition balanced against the protection of commercial interests, such as securing innovation and investment, is being considered by the European Commission,[23] ComReg[24] and the Department of Communications.[25]

Although Ireland has committed to the WTO Basic Telecommunications Agreement without exceptions, Ireland's laws in this area are primarily based on EC-led directives,[26] which are transposed into Irish law by way of statutory instruments. The underlying policies in Ireland accordingly come from the European Commission's regulatory package.

---

21 S3.3 ComReg document 08/75, 'Irish Communications Report – Key Data Report – Q2 2008.'

22 S3.3 ComReg document 08/75, 'Irish Communications Report – Key Data Report – Q2 2008.'

23 Draft Recommendation and Explanatory Memorandum on the regulated access to Next Generation access Networks (NGA), available at: http://ec.europa.eu/information_society/ policy/ecomm/doc/library/public_consult/nga/dr_recomm_nga.pdf.

24 ComReg Document No 07/40, July 2007.

25 Government consultation on Next Generation Broadband, dated 3 July 2008.

26 Framework Directive 2000/21/EC; Access Directive 2002/19/EC; Authorisation Directive 2002/20/EC and Universal Service Directive 2002/22/EC, together with the Data Protection and Privacy Directive 2002/58/EC and 2002/77/EC Directive on competition in the markets for electronic communications networks and services.

HISTORY OF POSTAL REGULATION

Global and European

6.017 Before the introduction of uniform penny postage[27] in the UK, postage usually had to be paid for by the recipient.[28] Prepaid postage was introduced in other countries during the 1840s and had a huge impact upon communications, similar to the more recent communications "revolution" caused by the Internet and mobile telephony. On 9 October 1874,[29] the Treaty of Berne established the General Postal Union, the forerunner of the Universal Postal Union (UPU). It succeeded in unifying a confusing maze of international postal services and regulations providing for the reciprocal exchange of letters. This removed barriers previously in place that had impeded the free flow of mail and growth of an international mail system. The UPU is the primary forum for postal cooperation and ensures a universal network of services. It is a specialised agency of the United Nations with 191 members, and it sets the rules for international mail exchanges and makes recommendations to improve the quality of service for customers.

6.018 The 1992 Green Paper on the Development of the Single Market for Postal Services[30] (the 'Green Paper') was the European Commission's first legislative initiative towards developing a common postal policy and a single market for the provision of postal services. The European Commission justified the necessity for action at European level on the basis that:

    (i)   the concept of the universal service had evolved independently in each Member State (particularly with regard to its scope and level of service);

---

27   The first known postal item, found in Egypt, dates from 255 BC. Even before then, postal services existed in the form of messengers serving kings or emperors. Over time, religious orders and universities added their own message delivery systems to exchange news and information. Relay stations were set up along the messengers' routes to speed up delivery over long distances. Private individuals also began to use the messengers to communicate with one another. During the seventeenth and eighteenth centuries, the exchange of mail between countries was largely governed by bilateral postal agreements. By the nineteenth century, the web of bilateral agreements had become so complex that it began to impede the rapidly developing trade and commercial sectors. The need for order and simplification in the international postal services led to national postal reforms. The most significant reform occurred in Britain in 1840, whereby a system was introduced for postage on letters to be prepaid. Uniform rates were also introduced for all domestic letters of a particular weight, regardless of the distance travelled. Rowland Hill was responsible for introducing the world's first prepaid postage stamp – known as the Penny Black stamp – which first went on sale in May 1840.

28   The Penny Black represented the beginning of the communications era and made it affordable for people to communicate. Before the reforms, people used to have to pay a certain amount depending on how many sheets of paper they used and how far the letter travelled. After the reforms, it only cost one penny to send a letter, which greatly reduced the cost of postage. This was to be paid for by the person who sent the letter. This is often referred to as the first example of the 'calling party pays' principle.

29   A day now celebrated around the world as World Post Day.

30   COM (91) 476 Final.

(ii)   service performance for cross-border mail services varied significantly resulting in a lack of certainty with regard to deliveries;

(iii)   the divergences in service levels contributed to market distortions in other sectors;[31] and

(iv)   the divergences frustrated the realisation of a cohesive Community, given the role played by postal services in terms of both communication and the delivery of goods.

6.019 In December 1997, the Council adopted the Postal Directive[32] (the First Postal Directive) and the Notice on the application of the competition rules to the postal sector and on assessment of certain State measures relating to postal services (the Postal Notice).[33] In May 2002, the Council adopted the Second Postal Directive,[34] which amended the Postal Directive. In particular, it required opening of the market to competition by further limiting the scope of postal services that could be reserved to the universal service provider (USP).[35]

The First Postal Directive identifies common rules in respect of six specific areas. These are as follows:

(i)   the provision of a universal postal service within the Community;

(ii)   the scope of the services that may be reserved to USPs and the conditions governing the provision of non-reserved services;

(iii)   tariff principles and transparency of accounts for universal service provision;

(iv)   the setting of quality standards for universal service provision and the creation of a system to ensure compliance with these standards;

(v)   the harmonisation of technical standards; and

(vi)   the creation of independent national regulatory authorities.

---

31   The Green Paper (p 3) noted that one unnamed Member State with a poor standard of postal service had a mail order sector one-fifth the size of other Member States with economies of a similar size.

32   Directive 97/67/EC on common rules for the development of the internal market of Community postal services and the improvement of quality of service. This followed substantial policy development contained in the June 1993 communication from the European Commission to the Council and the European Parliament on guidelines for the development of Community postal services (COM (93) 247 Final). The Council responded by way of a resolution on the development of Community postal services (OJ 1994 C48/2). In July 1995, the European Commission adopted a proposal for a directive on postal services and a draft notice providing guidance on the application of competition rules in the postal sector.

33   98/C 39/02.

34   Directive 2002/39/EC, amending Directive 97/67/EC with regard to the further opening to competition of Community postal services.

35   Hereafter, references to 'the Postal Directive' will be to Directive 97/67/EC, as amended by Directive 2002/39/EC, unless otherwise stated.

The Postal Directives provide for a step-by-step opening of the European market for postal services, in which each step represents a controlled reduction of the reservable area (see para **6.024**) while, on the other hand, continuing the universal service.[36] The Third Postal Directive[37] represents a final step in the liberalisation of the postal sector and foresees full market opening by 31 December 2010.

6.020 Postal services play a pivotal role in the economy and society of the EU.[38] Although technological innovations such as email compete with the primacy of letter mail as a vehicle for communication and trade, the publishing, insurance, banking and advertising sectors are all still heavily reliant on postal infrastructure. Ecommerce and mail order companies are dependent on reliable and cost-efficient parcel delivery.[39] The provision of a universal postal service is essential to the geographic and social cohesion of the EU.

Ireland

6.021 The policy in Ireland in respect of postal services is driven primarily by Europe and entails the liberalisation of the postal sector. The Third Postal Directive was adopted on 27 February 2008. The final date for the implementation of the new directive is 31 December 2010, with the possibility for some Member States[40] to postpone full market opening by two more years (31 December 2012). The Minister for Communications, Energy and Natural Resources (the Minister), Eamon Ryan TD, launched a public consultation process[41] about the issues to be addressed in transposing the directive into Irish law. The implementing legislation will be drafted following this consultation.

6.022 The challenge in regulating the postal sector is striking the balance between the benefits of competition and innovation, and ensuring the continued existence of the universal service under economically viable conditions. It is this duality between the economic policy driver 'market opening' – considered essential to bring economic efficiency to the postal sector, and the political policy driver 'the universal service', which is necessary for geographic and social cohesion that distinguishes the regulation of the postal sector.

---

36   See consideration 14 of Directive 2002/39/EC.

37   Directive 2008/6/EC of the European Parliament and of the Council of 20 February 2008 amending Directive 97/67/EC with regard to the full accomplishment of the internal market of Community postal services.

38   In 2004, postal services in the EU generated approximately €90bn in turnover, or 1 percent of the EU's GDP, and directly employed 1.71 million people.

39   Speech of Commissioner Charlie McCreevy (Deutsche Post World Net Event 2005, Brussels, 23 November 2005).

40   Czech Republic, Greece, Cyprus, Latvia, Lithuania, Luxembourg, Hungary, Malta, Poland, Romania and Slovakia, with the inclusion of a temporary reciprocity clause applying to those member states that make use of this transitional period.

41   The closing date for responses was July 2008.

6.023 At the time of writing, the incumbent has a statutory monopoly in respect of the reserved area. This is an area based on weight and price thresholds, which is exclusively the remit of the public postal operator, in Ireland, An Post, pending full market opening. Currently, the weight threshold is 50 grams and the price threshold is 2.5 times the standard price for basic priority mail items. The ability of a Member State to reserve any part of the postal services market to the incumbent universal service operator is limited to what is necessary to ensure the maintenance of universal service.

6.024 There are three policy areas in the regulation of postal services:

(i) the scope of the area of postal services reserved to the incumbent postal operator;

(ii) the universal service obligations imposed on the incumbent postal services provider; and

(iii) the question of any price controls on the services provided by the incumbent universal service provider.

This is quite apart from the application of general competition law to an incumbent operator occupying a dominant position.

6.025 Each of these policy areas is, of course, interrelated in that the ability of an incumbent to fulfil its universal service obligation depends to some extent on the competition that it faces from other operators. Its ability to meet competition and fulfil its universal service obligation is affected by the pricing flexibility in respect of its services. Due to the labour-intensive nature of postal services, full network competition may in practice be unattainable outside of urban areas. The specific characteristic of a postal network also raises the question of whether network access is essential for the development of competition in the postal services market in that access seekers may argue that the postal network is a natural monopoly which may not be replicated.[42] This, in turn, focuses on the key question of price and the terms on which an incumbent could be required to grant such access, which would impact on the ability to generate revenue and, in turn, cover the costs of the universal service to complete the circle.

In terms of the market, it would appear that mail volumes in Ireland are increasing slightly year on year.[43]

THE LEGISLATIVE FRAMEWORK

6.026 As discussed above, the Communications Regulation Act 2002 and the Communications Regulation (Amendment) Act 2007 govern the establishment and

---

42 This argument was, however, rejected *in Corbeau (Criminal Proceedings against Paul Corbeau* Case C–320/91 ECR (1993) I–2533) which considered that the public postal network did not constitute an essential facility.

43 ComReg Postal Business and Residential Services Surveys 2007, Milward Brown IMS, both dated 31 January 2008.

functioning of ComReg. The purpose of this section is to get an understanding of the legislative framework in which ComReg operates. This section is divided into the relevant legislative framework for electronic communications and the relevant legislative framework for postal services.

Electronic Communications

Structure of the european regulatory framework for electronic communications

6.027 The European regulatory framework consists of the following key legislative texts:

  (i)   Directive 2002/21, the Framework Directive, and four specific directives, namely:

      (a)   Directive 2002/20, the Authorisation Directive,

      (b)   Directive 2002/19, the Access Directive,

      (c)   Directive 2002/22, the Universal Service directive, and

      (d)   Directive 2002/58, the Privacy Directive;

  (ii)   European Commission Recommendation on relevant product and services markets, most recently revised in 2007;[44]

  (iii)   European Commission guidelines on market analysis and assessment of significant market power;[45]

  (iv)   Directive 2002/77 on competition in the markets for Electronic Communications services; and

  (v)   Regulation No 717/2007 on mobile roaming services in a single market.

Structure of the national regulatory framework for electronic communications

6.028 Relevant Acts of the Oireachtas include:

  (i)   Postal and Telecommunications Services Act 1983;

  (ii)   Wireless Telegraphy Acts 1926–1988;

  (iii)   Telecommunications (Miscellaneous Provisions) Act 1996;

  (iv)   Communications Regulation Act 2002, as amended by the Communications Regulation (Amendment) Act 2007;

---

44   Revised Commission recommendation on relevant product and service markets within the electronic communications sector susceptible to *ex ante* regulation in accordance with Directive 2002/21/EC of the European Parliament and of the Council on a common regulatory framework for electronic communications networks and services, dated 17 December 2007 (OJ L 344/65).

45   Commission Guidelines on market analysis and the assessment of significant market power under the Community regulatory framework for electronic communications networks and services ([2002] OJ C 165/6).

(v)   Competition Act 2002, as amended by the Communications Regulation (Amendment) Act 2007;

(vi)   Data Protection Acts 1988 and 2003;

(vii)   Electronic Commerce Act 2000, as amended;

(viii)   Consumer Protection Act 2007; and

(ix)   Freedom of Information Acts 1997–2003.

Key statutory instruments include:

(i)   European Communities (Electronic Communications Networks and Services) (Framework) Regulations 2003 (SI 307/2003, amended by SI 271/2007);

(ii)   European Communities (Electronic Communications Networks and Services) (Access) Regulations 2003 (SI 305/2003, amended by SI 373/2007);

(iii)   European Communities (Electronic Communications Networks and Services) (Authorisation) Regulations 2003 (SI 306/2003, amended by SI 372/2007);

(iv)   European Communities (Electronic Communications Networks and Services) (Universal Service and Users Rights) Regulations 2003 (SI 308/2003, amended by SI 374/2007);

(v)   European Communities (Electronic Communications Networks and Services) Data Protection and Privacy Regulations 2003 (SI 535/2003 amended by SI 526/2008);

(vi)   European Communities (Implementation of the Rules on Competition laid down in Articles 81 and 82 of the EC Treaty) Regulations 2004 (SI 195/2004), as amended by SI 525/2007);

(vii)   European Communities (Satellite Telecommunications Service) Regulations 1997 (SI 372/1997);

(viii)   Broadcasting Amendment Act (Digital Terrestrial Television Licence Fees) Regulations, 2007 (SI 796/2007).

(ix)   Communications Regulation Act 2002 (Section 30) Levy 25 Order 2003 (SI 346/2003);

(x)   Communications (Mobile Telephone Roaming) Regulations 2007 (SI 792/2007);

(xi)   Telecommunications Tariff Regulation (Revocation) Order, 2007 (SI 665 of 2007);

(xii)   Various Regulations adopted under the Wireless Telegraphy Act 1926.

Post

Structure of the european regulatory framework for post

6.029 The European regulatory framework consists of the following key legislative texts:

(i)   Directive 97/67/EC (the First Postal Directive);

(ii)   Directive 2002/39/EC (the Second Postal Directive); and

(iii)   Directive 2008/6/EC (the Third Postal Directive).

Structure of the national regulatory framework for post

6.030 Relevant Acts of the Oireachtas include:

(i)   Post Office Act 1908;

(ii)   Post Office (Evasion of Postage) Act 1937;

(iii) Postal and Telecommunications Services Act 1983, as amended; and

(iv)   Communications Regulation Act 2002, as amended.

Important statutory instruments include:

(i)   Inland Post Warrant 1939 (SI 202/1939), as amended;

(ii)   Foreign Post Warrant 1949 (SI 267/1949), as amended;

(iii) Foreign Parcel Post Warrant 1953 (SI 418/1953), as amended;

(iv)   European Communities (Postal Services) Regulations 2002 (SI 616/2002);

(v)   Communications Regulation Act 2002 (section 30) Postal Levy Order 2005 (SI 319/2005); and

(vi)   European Communities (Postal Services) (Amendment) Regulations 2008 (SI 135/2008).

THE REGULATOR

6.031 The Regulator for communications in Ireland is the Commission for Communications Regulations (ComReg), which was established by the Communications Regulation Act 2002 (the 2002 Act). ComReg is responsible for the regulation of the electronic communications sector and the postal sector in Ireland. Through its management of radio spectrum, ComReg also plays a role in the broadcasting sector.

The 2002 Act dissolved ComReg's predecessor, the ODTR, and transferred the functions of the ODTR to ComReg. The 2002 Act sets out the functions and objectives of ComReg. ComReg is a funded by a combination of levies and spectrum license fees. ComReg's annual report and accounts are published on its website, http://www.comreg.ie. For the year ending June 2006, according to its annual report, ComReg's net income was €32m, its expenditure was €18.6m and it remitted approximately €13m to the exchequer.[46] It is based in Abbey Street in Dublin and currently employs approximately 120 people.[47] ComReg may engage such consultants

---

46   ComReg is obliged by s 32 of the 2002 Act to prepare accounts and an annual report.

47   Section 20 provides that ComReg may, with the consent of the Minister for Communications and the Minister for Finance, determine the number, grading, remuneration and other conditions of service of staff.

or advisers as it considers necessary to assist it in the discharge of its functions.[48] ComReg is divided into three main divisions: market framework, retail and wholesale.

6.032 Section 14 of the 2002 Act sets out that there shall be at least one member and not more than three members of ComReg. Each member is known as a 'Commissioner'. Section 15 provides that each member shall be appointed by the Minister on such terms and conditions, including remuneration, as the Minister may fix with the consent of the Minister for Finance. Section 15 further provides that a person may not be appointed as a Commissioner unless the civil service and Local Appointments Commissioners, after holding a competition, select him or her for appointment as a Commissioner. This provision underpins the independence of the Commissioners. A Commissioner is appointed on a full-time basis for a period of at least three years and not more than five years. A Commissioner shall not serve more than two terms of office as a Commissioner. There are currently three Commissioners, one of whom is the Chairperson.[49] The chairperson has a casting vote in the event of a tied vote. Section 21 provides for the delegation of powers and enables the exercise of ComReg's functions to be carried out by or through any member of staff or authorised officer, as ComReg shall deem proper.

6.033 Section 6 of the 2002 Act establishes ComReg as a body corporate with perpetual succession, a seal and power to sue and be sued. Section 7 provides that the seal shall be authenticated by the signature of a Commissioner or a member of staff duly authorised in that regard.

6.034 ComReg is independent in the exercise of its functions. Section 11 provides for the independence of ComReg, which is essential in the exercise of its role as Regulator. In the past, the regulatory arm was simply another limb of the government, for example, the Minister for Post and Telecommunications carried out many of the functions now assigned to ComReg.

6.035 In terms of policy-making and policy development procedure, the government has powers to issue directions to ComReg, some of which are subject to public consultation prior to their issue. The Department of Communications, Energy and Natural Resources (DCENR) is the relevant government department. Ministerial directions were addressed to ComReg in 2003 and 2004[50] after public consultation on

---

48 Section 22.

49 Section 16 provides that, where there is more than one Commissioner, the Minister shall point one of them to be the chairperson. Section 17 provides that, where there is only one Commissioner, the Commission is to designate a member of its staff as a deputy member of the Commission who shall assume and carry out with the authority of the Commission all of ComReg's functions in the absence of the Commissioner. Section 18 provides for the resignation of a Commission or who must tender his or her resignation to the Minister. A Commissioner may also be removed from office by the Minister if the Commissioner has become incapable of effectively performing his or her duties or for stated misbehaviour.

50 Policy Directions issued in February 2003 and March 2004 to ComReg pursuant to Communications Regulation Act 2002, s 13.

proposed policy directions. These directions outline the policy objectives that ComReg must consider when it is applying its powers under the European regulatory framework and under the Communications Regulation Act 2002. Section 13(1) of the 2002 Act provides that the Minister may give policy directions to ComReg.[51] Such policy directions must be followed by ComReg in exercising its functions.

This section has to be balanced with the independence of the Regulator, which is discussed in more detail above (paras **6.036–6.038**). It is important that any directions given by the Minister should not fetter the Regulator. A policy direction does not grant a new function to the Regulator but rather serves to guide the Regulator in the exercise of its existing functions.

6.036 In the regulation of the electronic communications sector, ComReg is responsible for ensuring compliance by undertakings in that sector with their statutory obligations, managing the radio frequency spectrum and national numbering resources, and ensuring compliance in relation to the placing on the market and putting into service of radio equipment. ComReg is also responsible for specific aspects of data protection and privacy rules as they relate to electronic communications. The Communications Regulation (Amendment) Act 2007 also transfers responsibility to ComReg for the oversight and management of the '.ie' domain registry. The framework within which ComReg regulates the electronic communications industry is driven by the European Commission and the European Regulators' Group (ERG). The Communications Regulation (Amendment) Act 2007 gives ComReg competition powers, which enable it to pursue issues arising in respect of electronic communications under competition law. ComReg is a member of the European Competition Network (ECN). ComReg is therefore both a national regulatory authority (NRA) and a national competition authority (NCA) in respect of electronic communications.

6.037 ComReg's role in respect of the broadcasting sector covers the issuing of associated licences under Ireland's Wireless Telegraphy Acts in respect of wireless equipment and the assignment of required radio spectrum. Please see **Ch 5** for further details on the regulation of the broadcasting sector.

6.038 ComReg is the national regulatory authority for the postal sector in Ireland. ComReg administers the general authorisation process in relation to postal operators. It also ensures compliance with the various statutory obligations imposed on the universal service provider (An Post) and on the other postal operators.

---

51   Section 13(1) provides 'In the interests of the proper and effective regulation of the electronic communications and postal markets, the management of the radio frequency spectrum in the State and the formulation of policy applicable to such proper and effective regulation and management, the Minister may give such policy directions to the Commission as he or she considers appropriate to be followed by the Commission in the exercise of its functions. The Commission shall comply with any such direction.'

FUNCTIONS AND OBJECTIVES

Functions

6.039 Section 10 of the 2002 Act sets out the functions of ComReg and provides as follows:

> 10.—(1) The functions of the Commission are—
>
> (a) to ensure compliance by undertakings with obligations in relation to the supply of and access to electronic communications services, electronic communications networks and associated facilities and the transmission of such services on such networks,
>
> (b) to manage the radio frequency spectrum and the national numbering resource, in accordance with a direction under section 13,
>
> (c) to ensure compliance by providers of postal services with obligations in relation to the provision of postal services,
>
> (ca) to monitor the quality and efficiency of the emergency call answering service established under Part 6,[52]
>
> (d) to carry out investigations into matters relating to the supply of, and access to, electronic communications services, electronic communications networks and associated facilities and the transmission of such services on such networks,[53]
>
> (da) for the purpose of contributing to an open and competitive market and also for statistical purposes, to collect, compile, extract, disseminate and publish information from undertakings relating to the provision of electronic communications services, electronic communications networks and associated facilities and the transmission of such services on those networks, and[54]
>
> (e) to ensure compliance, as appropriate, by persons in relation to the placing on the market of communications equipment and the placing on the market and putting into service of radio equipment.
>
> (2) The Commission may carry out an investigation referred to in subsection (1) either on its own initiative or as a result of a complaint made by an end user or an undertaking.[55]
>
> (3) The Commission shall have all such powers as are necessary for or incidental to the performance of its functions under this or any other Act. …[56]

6.040 ComReg has functions under the Competition Act 2002, as amended by Pt 4 of the Communications Regulation (Amendment) Act 2007, and these are set out *inter alia* in Pt 4A of the Competition Act. Section 47A of the Competition Act 2002 provides:

> The Commission has, in addition to its other functions under this Act or any other enactment, the function of investigating, either on its own initiative or in response to a

---

52 As inserted by Communications Regulation (Amendment) Act 2007, s 5 – 22/2007.
53 As inserted by Communications Regulation (Amendment) Act 2007, s 5 – 22/2007.
54 As inserted by Communications Regulation (Amendment) Act 2007, s 5 – 22/2007.
55 As amended by Communications Regulation (Amendment) Act 2007, s 5 – 22/2007.
56 As amended by Communications Regulation (Amendment) Act 2007, s 5 – 22/2007.

complaint made to it by any person, the existence of an agreement, decision or practice of a kind specified in section 4, or the occurrence of an abuse of the kind specified in section 5, involving the provision of an electronic communications service or electronic communications network, or associated facilities.

In addition, ComReg has various functions under the statutory instruments that implement the European regulatory framework in respect of electronic communications and post.

Objectives

6.041 The objectives of ComReg are set out in s 12 of the Communications Regulation Act 2002. These include promoting competition, contributing to the development of the internal market and promoting the interests of users within the EU.[57] In the area of electronic communications, ComReg's objectives reflect the objectives set for national regulatory authorities in the Framework Directive.[58] ComReg also has as one of its objectives the efficient management and use of the radio frequency (RF) spectrum and numbers.[59] In respect of the postal sector, ComReg's objective is to promote the development of the postal sector and, in particular, the availability of a universal postal service within, to and from the State at an affordable price for the benefit of all users.[60]

6.042 Regarding the promotion of competition, ComReg is to take all reasonable measures aimed at achieving those objectives including:

(i) ensuring that users, including disabled users, derive maximum benefit in terms of choice, price and quality,

(ii) ensuring that there is no distortion or restriction of competition in the electronic communications sector,

(iii) encouraging efficient investment in infrastructure and promoting innovation, and

(iv) encouraging efficient use and ensuring the effective management of radio frequencies and numbering resources.[61]

In carrying out its functions, ComReg shall seek to ensure that measures taken by it are proportionate.[62] ComReg also has as one of its objectives ensuring that the exercise of its functions aimed at achieving the objectives does not result in discrimination in favour of or against particular types of technology for the transmission of electronic communications services.[63]

---

57   Communications Regulation Act 2002, s 12(1)(a).

58   Directive 2002/21/EC of the European Parliament and of the Council of 7 March 2002 on a common regulatory framework for electronic communication networks and services.

59   Communications Regulation Act 2002, s 12(1)(b).

60   Communications Regulation Act 2002, s 12(1)(c).

61   Communications Regulation Act 2002, s 12(2)(a).

62   Communications Regulation Act 2002, s 12(3).

63   Communications Regulation Act 2002, s 12(6).

BORROWINGS, LEVIES AND FEES

6.043 Section 29 of the 2002 Act provides that ComReg may for the purpose of the performance of its functions borrow money, but shall only do so with the consent of the Minister for Communications and the Minister for Finance. Section 30 provides for levies and fees. Any surplus of levy income over the expenses incurred by ComReg in the discharge of its functions relevant to this levy in the levy period will either be retained to be offset against levy obligations for the subsequent year, or refunded proportionately to the applicable undertakings on whom the levy is imposed.

Licence fees are also payable in respect of licences issued in accordance with the Wireless Telegraphy Acts. The amount of these fees varies. Some spectrum licence fees – for example 3G licences – are substantial. To date, ComReg has made a surplus each year and that surplus is remitted to the Minister for Finance.

An annual levy is also payable in respect of broadcast transmission networks. This is set out in **Ch 5** on broadcasting.

Electronic Communications

6.044 Annual levies are payable in accordance with s 30 of the Communications Regulation Act 2002 by operators of an Electronic Communications Network (ECN) and providers of an Electronic Communications Service (ECS), excluding broadcasting transmission networks. The amount of the annual levy for an ECN or an ECS is set out in a levy order.[64] The amount payable is 0.2 per cent of relevant turnover in the relevant financial year of the authorised service provider, unless relevant turnover is less than €500,000, in which case no levy is payable. The 'relevant turnover' is the gross Irish revenue excluding VAT in respect of the provision of an ECN and/or ECS.

Post

6.045 For the purpose of postal operators, s 30 also applies and sets out that, for the purpose of meeting expenses properly incurred by the Commission in the discharge of its functions in relation to postal services, the Commission may make an order imposing a levy on providers of postal services. The Postal Levy Order is contained in SI 319/2005. It applies to undertakings with a relevant turnover in excess of €1,500,000 in a relevant financial year. The amount of the levy imposed on the universal service provider, ie An Post, in respect of each levy period (essentially one year) is the aggregate of:

(a) 0.25 per cent of the relevant turnover, for the relevant financial year, of the universal service provider arising from the provision of the universal service; and

(b) €15,000, where the relevant turnover, for the relevant financial year, of the universal service provider arising from the provision of postal services falling outside the scope of the universal service is equal to or greater than €20m, or,

---

64 SI 346/2003.

€1000, where the relevant turnover, for the relevant financial year, of the universal service provider arising from the provision of postal services falling outside the scope of the universal service is less than €20m.

The amount of the levy imposed on other authorised postal operators is either:

(a)   €1,000, where the relevant turnover of the applicable undertaking is less than €20m; or

(b)   €15,000, where the relevant turnover of the applicable undertaking is greater than or equal to €20m.

THE REGULATED ACTIVITY AND THE REGULATED ENTITIES – ELECTRONIC COMMUNICATIONS

6.046 Following the structure of the earlier parts of this chapter, this section will first address ComReg's role in relation to the electronic communications sector and then subsequently the postal sector. ComReg has concurrent competition law powers together with the Competition Authority in respect of electronic communications.

6.047 There is a technology-neutral approach to the regulation of electronic communications in Ireland, which is in line with the EU regulatory framework. The Framework Directive, which was transposed in Ireland by the Framework Regulations (see para **6.029** above), provides that the convergence of the telecoms, media and information technology sectors means all transmission networks and services should be covered by a single regulatory framework. The statutory instruments implementing the EU regulatory framework cover all ECNs and ECSs, irrespective of their means of transmission and regardless of the type of information conveyed.

An ECN is a transmission system and involves, where applicable, switching or routing equipment and other resources that permit the conveyance of signals by wire, by radio, by optical or by other electromagnetic means, including satellite networks, fixed (circuit- and packet-switched, including the Internet) and mobile terrestrial networks, electricity cable systems, to the extent that they are used for the purpose of transmitting signals, networks used for radio and television broadcasting, and cable television networks, irrespective of the type of information conveyed.

An ECS is a service normally provided for remuneration which consists wholly or mainly of the conveyance of signals on electronic communications networks, including telecoms services and transmission services in networks used for broadcasting, but excluding: (a) a service providing, or exercising editorial control over, content transmitted using electronic communications networks and services; and (b) an information society service as defined in art 1 of Directive 98/34/EC, which does not consist wholly or mainly of the conveyance of signals on electronic communications networks.

General Authorisation

6.048 In terms of ownership, the Irish government no longer holds shares in any electronic communications operator, although it does own the Metropolitan Area

Networks (MANs). All entities providing an ECS or operating an ECN need to obtain a general authorisation from ComReg. Authorisations have replaced the previous licensing system, although licences are still in place in respect of wireless telegraphy (see **para 6.034** below). Unlike a license, once a party has notified ComReg and completed the general authorisation form, it is deemed authorised. The regime set out in the Authorisation Regulations, which implement the Authorisation Directive (see **para 6.028** above), confers a general right to provide an ECN and/or ECS, provided certain conditions are complied with. These conditions are set down in the general authorisation[65] Under reg 4 of the Authorisation Regulations, persons wishing to provide an ECN and/or ECS to third parties must notify ComReg in advance. The notification must contain certain minimum information and, on receipt of a complete notification, ComReg will add the notifying to party to its register of authorised undertakings.[66] There is no waiting period and the general authorisation is not limited in duration. Regulation 15(1) of the Authorisation Regulations provides that ComReg may amend the rights, conditions and procedures concerning the general authorisation, wireless telegraphy licences and rights of use, provided that any such amendments are objectively justified and proportionate. Before making any amendment under reg 15(1), ComReg must publicly consult on its intended proposal for a period, other than in exceptional circumstances, of not less than 28 days.[67] A general authorisation is not transferable. An authorisation is personal to an authorised person. An authorised person may not sub-authorise or grant or otherwise transfer any right, interest or entitlement in a general authorisation. Unlike certain jurisdictions outside of the EU, there are no foreign ownership restrictions on providing these services. Additional obligations apply in respect of an authorised operator designated as having significant market power (SMP), and to a universal service provider.

Licences

6.049 In addition to complying with the conditions of the general authorisation, mobile phone operators and providers of fixed wireless services need to obtain a licence in connection with the use of wireless telegraphy apparatus under the Wireless Telegraphy Acts 1926 to 1988 ('the Wireless Telegraphy Acts').[68] A licence must also be obtained under the Wireless Telegraphy Acts in respect of the installation, maintenance and use of fixed satellite earth stations. Various statutory instruments

---

65 Available to view at
    http://www.comreg.ie/publications/general_authorisation.597.103212.p.html
    ComReg Document No. 03/81R1 dated 5 November 2008.

66 Which can be viewed at http://www.comreg.ie.

67 As ComReg did in the case of amending the general authorisation to include consumer protection conditions to deal with operator exit ComReg Document No 03/81R1 dated 5 November 2008.

68 It is expected that a new Radiocommunications Act, which will replace the Wireless Telegraphy Acts 1926–1988 will be introduced over the next few years.

have been passed exempting satellite earth stations[69] from the requirements of the Wireless Telegraphy Acts. Satellite earth station equipment should comply with the provisions of the European Communities (Satellite Earth Station Equipment) Regulations 1998.

6.050 With the exception of the award of the first mobile telephony licence, the award of all mobile telephony licences has been by way of a competitive comparative bidding procedure. *Orange Communications Ltd v Director of Telecommunications Regulation*[70] involved a challenge to the award of a spectrum licence to Meteor (see paras **6.212–6.213** at the end of this chapter on relevant case law).

6.051 Specific wireless telegraphy regulations have been adopted in respect of wireless apparatus to be used in the provision of 2G and 3G mobile services.[71] A code of practice has also been agreed between ComReg and the authorised 3G mobile service providers in Ireland in respect of the sharing of radio sites. Three 3G mobile telecoms licences were originally awarded to operators in Ireland. Hutchison 3G Ireland Ltd was awarded an 'A' licence, and Vodafone and O_2 were awarded 'B' licences. The 'A' Licence differs from the 'B' Licences in respect of coverage requirements, access conditions and the amount of spectrum access fees payable, which are less than the 'B' Licences. Coverage requirements were more onerous under the 'A' Licence, which also carries a Mobile Virtual Network Operator (MVNO) obligation. Smart Telecom (Smart) had successfully bid for the fourth 3G licence; however, the licence was not ultimately awarded by ComReg to Smart due to failure on the part of Smart to meet the terms of the tender process. Smart unsuccessfully challenged ComReg's decision in the

---

69   Wireless Telegraphy Act 1926 (Section 3) (Exemption of Satellite Earth Stations for Satellite Personal Communications Services (S-PCS)) Order 1998 (SI 214 of 1998); Wireless Telegraphy Act 1926 (Section 3) (Exemption of Mobile Satellite Earth Stations for Satellite Personal Communication Systems operating in bands below 1 GHz (S-PCS<1, 25 GHz)) Order 2000 (SI 173/2000); Wireless Telegraphy (Fixed Satellite Earth Stations) Regulations 2000 (SI 261/2000); Wireless Telegraphy Act 1926 (Section 3) (Exemption 20 of Certain Fixed Satellite Receiving Earth Stations) Order 2000 (SI 273/2000); Wireless Telegraphy Act 1926 (Section 3) (Exemption of Certain Classes of Fixed Satellite Earth Stations) Order 2003 (SI 505/2003); Wireless Telegraphy (Fixed Satellite Earth Stations and Teleport Facility) Regulations (SI 295/2007).

70   *Orange Communications Ltd v Director of Telecommunications Regulation* [2000] 4 IR 136.

71   Wireless Telegraphy Act 1926 (Section 3) (Exemption of Mobile Telephones) Order 1997 (SI 409 of 1997); Wireless Telegraphy (GSM and TACS Mobile Telephony Licence) Regulations 1997 (SI 468 of 1997); Wireless Telegraphy (GSM and TACS Mobile Telephony Licence) Regulations 1999 (SI 442 of 1999); Wireless Telegraphy (Third Generation and GSM Mobile Telephony Licence) Regulations 2002 (SI 345 of 45 2002); Wireless Telegraphy Act 1926 (Section 3) (Exemption of Mobile Telephones) (Amendment) Order (SI 158/2003); Wireless Telegraphy (Third Generation and GSM Mobile Telephony Licence) (Amendment) Regulations, 2003 (SI 340/2003); Wireless Telegraphy Act 1926 (section 3) (Exemption of Apparatus for Mobile Communication Services on Aircraft) Order 2008 (SI 178/2008).

High Court.[72] The fourth 3G licence was then offered to and accepted by Meteor on behalf of Eircom in March 2007.

Fixed Wireless Point to Multipoint Access (FWPMA) licences were awarded by means of a licence competition.[73] Fixed Wireless Access Local Area (FWALA) licences[74] have also been awarded by ComReg to wireless broadband service providers in Ireland.

6.052 Currently, spectrum trading is not permitted under Irish legislation. Spectrum trading allows a licensee to transfer the right to use all or part of the licensed spectrum, usually in return for some financial consideration. Trading can take several forms, which include transfer of licences, reconfiguration, partial trading of spectrum, spectrum leasing and change of spectrum use. There is at present no specific regulatory framework for the assignment of unused spectrum. ComReg published a spectrum management document that outlined its strategy statement for the period 2005–2007 (Document No 05/72). ComReg stated that it was considering opportunities to permit one or more forms of spectrum trading in relation to specific services, to test its appropriateness and operation in the Irish market as part of its broader work on spectrum liberalisation and refarming.[75] Currently, the 900 and 1800 MHz bands are used for 2G technology. In ComReg's 2008–2010 spectrum strategy statement dated 1 July 2008 (Document No 08/50), in respect of spectrum trading, ComReg considered the potential benefits of spectrum trading for specific licence categories and concluded that secondary markets could potentially play a role in ensuring the efficient assignment and use of the spectrum in some areas. However, ComReg considers that the use of spectrum trading (and other innovations in the development of rights of use) needs to be underpinned by a revision of existing primary legislation. ComReg considered the liberalisation of the GSM spectrum bands to facilitate the growth of the public mobile services and innovation through the use of 3G and other technologies in these bands. It furthermore considered the digital dividend which will be yielded as a result of Digital Terrestrial Television (please see **Ch 5** on broadcasting for more detail in this regard). It also considered the release of substantial additional spectrum below 4 GHz, to meet market demand and to support

---

72 *Smart Mobile Ltd v Commission for Communication Regulation* [2006] IEHC 338, Kelly J. See **Ch 11** on judicial review for further details on this case.

73 The relevant Statutory Instruments adopted in relation to Fixed Wireless Point to Multipoint include Wireless Telegraphy (Fixed Wireless Point-to-Multipoint Access Licence) Regulations 1999 (SI 287 of 1999); Wireless Telegraphy (Fixed Wireless Access Local Area Licence) Regulations 2003 (SI 79/2003); Wireless Telegraphy (Fixed Wireless Point to Multi Point Access License) Regulations 2003 (SI 338/2003); Wireless Telegraphy (National Point-to-Point and Point-to-Multipoint Block Licences) Regulations 2006 (SI 296/2006); Wireless Telegraphy (National Point-to-Point and Point-to-Multipoint Block Licences) Regulations, 2007 (SI 762/2007).

74 Under the Wireless Telegraphy (Fixed Wireless Access Local Area Licence) Regulations 2003 (SI 79/2003).

75 Reassigning electromagnetic spectrum for services with higher value. The frequency bands are reassigned to communications services that may yield greater economic or social benefit.

the expected requirement for additional spectrum to facilitate broadband and multimedia mobile services.

6.053 Wireless Access Policy for Electronic Communications (WAPECS)[76] is a framework for the provision of electronic communications services within a set of frequency bands to be identified and agreed between European Union Member States in which a range of ECNs and ECSs may be offered on a technology- and service-neutral basis, provided that certain technical requirements are met, ie interference is avoided, the effective and efficient use of the spectrum is ensured and authorisation conditions do not distort competition. The term 'WAPECS' has been used to signal a move away from too narrowly specified allocations and applications, for which specific spectrum is designated. Under this definition of WAPECS, it is envisaged that technologies will be stimulated to deliver all electronic communications services within their capabilities, making use of any frequency band and networks.

6.054 In respect of a wireless telegraphy licence, ComReg must make a decision on the granting of a licence as soon as possible after the receipt of a complete application. In the case of radio frequencies that have been allocated for specific purposes within the national frequency plan, ComReg must make a decision within six weeks of receipt of a complete application. Where ComReg decides to use a competitive or comparative selection procedure for the purposes of granting a licence, it may extend this six-week period for as long as is necessary to ensure that such procedures are fair, reasonable, open and transparent to all interested parties, but for no longer than eight months. These time limits are without prejudice to any applicable international agreements relating to the use of radio frequencies, or orbital positions or satellite co-ordination.

6.055 Wireless telegraphy licences are annual in nature and must be renewed annually. The current 2G mobile licences were granted for a term of 15 years and are renewed on an annual basis. The current 3G mobile licences were granted for a term of 20 years and are also renewed on an annual basis. The holder of a wireless telegraphy licence may not, without the consent of ComReg (which shall not be unreasonably withheld), assign a licence.

6.056 A foreshore licence is also required from the Department of Communications, Energy and Natural Resources, in respect of the landing of a submarine cable in Ireland.

Significant Market Power

6.057 ComReg has designated various operators as having significant market power (SMP) in a range of markets as part of the European regulatory framework. One of the aims of the framework is to decrease sector-specific regulation as competition becomes more effective in the electronic communications sector. Only in markets that

---

76 In March 2008, the European Commission's Communications Committee (CoCom) expressed a positive opinion on the Draft Commission Recommendation (RSCOM08–16) on the 'nontechnical conditions attached to rights of use for radio frequencies under the regulatory framework for electronic communications in the context of the (WAPECS)'.

are still not competitive should *ex ante* or sector-specific regulation be imposed. On all other markets where there is sufficient competition, the ordinary competition rules should apply *ex post*.[77] In this way, for those markets where there is not yet effective competition, ComReg can take action before any anti-competitive behaviour has taken place, ie before there is any abuse of a dominant position or before there is any agreement which could restrict competition. Since the Regulator takes action before the fact, this is known as *ex ante* regulation. The competition rules which prohibit anti-competitive arrangements or abuses of dominance operate conversely *ex post*, or after the fact, in that a Regulator investigates the anti-competitive behaviour that has already taken place. The need to impose regulatory obligations in some markets is due to the fact that competition law remedies may not be sufficient to deal with market failure and to ensure effective and sustainable competition in markets that are characterised by high and non-transitory barriers to entry.

6.058 The Framework Regulations, which implement the Framework Directive, require that market reviews are carried out before SMP regulation is imposed so that obligations are only imposed where the market is not effectively competitive. A market is not effectively competitive if there are one or more players with SMP on that market. SMP essentially equates to the competition law concept of dominance.[78] The test for dominance comes from the *United Brands* case[79] and is whether an undertaking has a position of economic strength that allows it to act independently of its competitors, customers and, ultimately, consumers. The SMP test is set out in art 14(2) of the Framework Directive and implemented in Ireland by way of reg 25 of the Framework Regulations. There are several steps involved requiring lengthy and detailed analysis before an operator can be designated with SMP.

Market definition

6.059 ComReg must take a list of recommended markets that the European Commission has produced and define product and geographic markets in accordance with the principles of competition law and having regard to national circumstances. The European Commission issued a list of defined markets for the purposes of market reviews, which is set out in the Recommendation on relevant product and services market.[80] The first recommendation was published in 2003 and contained 18 markets. In line with the general erosion of sector-specific regulation, a revised

---

77 EC Treaty, arts 81 and 82 and Competition Act 2002, ss 4 and 5. See the competition chapter, **Ch 7**, for more information.

78 A position of economic strength can be enjoyed individually (single dominance) or jointly with others (joint or collective dominance).

79 *United Brands* Case C–27/76, [1978] ECR 207, [1978] 1 CMLR 429.

80 Revised Commission recommendation on relevant product and service markets within the electronic communications sector susceptible to ex ante regulation in accordance with Directive 2002/21/EC of the European Parliament and of the Council on a common regulatory framework for electronic communications networks and services dated 17 December 2007 OJ L 344/65.

Recommendation was published in 2007 and contains merely seven markets. The seven markets fall into one of two categories as follows:

Retail level

1. Access to the public telephone network at a fixed location for residential and non-residential customers.

Wholesale level

2. Call origination on the public telephone network provided at a fixed location. Call origination is taken to include call conveyance, delineated in such a way as to be consistent, in a national context, with the delineated boundaries for the market for call transit and for call termination on the public telephone network provided at a fixed location.

3. Call termination on individual public telephone networks provided at a fixed location. Call termination is taken to include call conveyance, delineated in such a way as to be consistent, in a national context, with the delineated boundaries for the market for call origination and the market for call transit on the public telephone network provided at a fixed location.

4. Wholesale (physical) network infrastructure access (including shared or fully unbundled access) at a fixed location.

5. Wholesale broadband access. This market comprises non-physical or virtual network access including 'bit-stream' access at a fixed location. This market is situated downstream from the physical access covered by market four listed above.

6. Wholesale terminating segments of leased lines, irrespective of the technology used to provide leased or dedicated capacity.

7. Voice call termination on individual mobile networks.

6.060 ComReg must take the recommended market from the Recommendation and consider the market definition in accordance with the principles of competition law. It must consider the national circumstances and the relevant geographic markets. The European Commission has issued guidelines to assist national regulatory authorities carrying out assessments of SMP in relevant markets.[81] ComReg must take the utmost account of the Recommendation and the guidelines when defining relevant markets.[82] ComReg has to determine the geographic scope of the relevant markets, which may be national or sub-national or local.[83] These markets are always assessed on a forward-looking basis since ComReg has to take into account likely future developments on that market. If the European Commission identifies a market as transnational, the NRAs must jointly conduct the relevant market analysis in a concerted fashion. The

---

81 Commission Guidelines on Market Analysis and the assessment of significant market power under the Community regulatory framework for electronic communications networks and services ([2002] OJ C 165/6).

82 Framework Regulations, reg 26.

83 They may of course also be regional or EU-wide or global.

European Commission decided that the mobile roaming market was transnational and so it issued a regulation in this regard.[84] Similar to all other NRAs in the EU, ComReg may identify markets which differ from those set out in the Recommendation, provided that the Commission does not disagree. ComReg also has to consult with the other NRAs in this regard. This procedure is set out in arts 6 and 7 of the Framework Directive, and so these are known as art 7 markets. When identifying markets other than the recommended relevant markets, NRAs should ensure that the following three-pronged test is cumulatively met:

(a)   the presence of high and non-transitory barriers to entry – these may be of a structural, legal or regulatory nature;

(b)   a market structure which does not tend towards effective competition within the relevant time horizon – the application of this criterion involves examining the state of competition behind the barriers to entry; and

(c)   the insufficiency of competition law alone to adequately address the market failure(s) concerned.

The markets specified in the Recommendation may differ from markets that may be defined under competition law. Certain other other regulated markets are identified in arts 18 and 19 of the Universal Service Directive. In relation to those markets which have been 'dropped' from the European Commission's revised Recommendation, the SMP findings and remedies remain in place until these markets are analysed in light of the revised Recommendation. ComReg is obliged to analyse these markets as soon as practical after the adoption of the Recommendation pursuant to art 15 of the Framework Directive as implemented by reg 26 of the Framework Regulations.

Market analysis

6.061 ComReg may impose obligations on SMP operators in the defined markets, since these markets are not considered to be effectively competitive. It is not merely a matter of taking the listed markets, defining them in light of local market conditions and divvying out SMP designations. In accordance with reg 27 of the Framework Regulations, which implements art 15(3) of the Framework Directive, ComReg has to prospectively analyse the product and services markets set out in the Recommendation. This task is known as conducting a market analysis. Regulation 27 of the Framework Regulations, which implements art 16 of the Framework Directive, provides that when carrying out a market analysis, ComReg must take the utmost account of the Commission Guidelines on market analysis and assessment of SMP. ComReg has to decide if the market is effectively competitive. A market which is effectively competitive is a market where there are no undertakings with SMP and a market which is not effectively competitive is one where there are one or more undertakings with SMP.

---

84   Regulation No 717/2007 on Mobile Roaming Services in a Single Market.

6.062 Paragraph 78 of the Guidelines includes a list of factors to be taken into account when assessing market power. These factors include:

    (i)   overall size of the undertaking;

   (ii)   technological advantages or superiority;

  (iii)   absence of or low countervailing buying power;

  (iv)   easy or privileged access to capital markets and financial resources;

   (v)   product and services diversification;

  (vi)   economies of scale;

 (vii)   economies of scope;

(viii)   vertical integration;

  (ix)   a highly developed distribution and sales network;

   (x)   absence of potential competition;

  (xi)   barriers to expansion; and

 (xii)   control of infrastructure not easily duplicated.

SMP

6.063 The existence of SMP might result from a combination of the above criteria, which, taken separately, may not necessarily be conclusive.

Where an undertaking is designated as having SMP further to reg 27(4) on a particular market for the purposes of *ex ante* regulation, this does not automatically mean that the entity has a position of dominance for the purposes of s 5 of the Competition Act or art 82 of the EC Treaty. It is solely for the purposes of art 14 of the Framework Directive, as implemented by reg 25 of the Framework Regulations.

Remedies

6.064 Where there is an SMP player, a remedy has to be imposed[85] pursuant to art 8 of the Access Directive and reg 9 of the Access Regulations. Regulation 9(6) of the Access Regulations requires that any obligations imposed must:

    (a) be based on the nature of the problem identified,

    (b) be proportionate and justified in the light of the objectives laid down in section 12 of the Act of 2002, and

    (c) only be imposed following consultation in accordance with Regulations 19[86] and 20[87] of the Framework Regulations.

These remedies are contained in the Access Directive, as implemented by the Access Regulations, where it relates to a wholesale market, and the Universal Service

---

85   Regulation 27(4) of the Framework Regulations.

86   Public consultation.

87   Pre-notification to the European Commission further to Framework Directive, art 7(3).

Directive, as implemented by the Universal Service Regulations, where it relates to a retail market or carrier pre-selection. Where a market is effectively competitive, ie no entity has SMP, then no obligations should be imposed and any existing obligations should be removed.[88]

6.065 Where an undertaking is designated as having SMP on a wholesale market, the obligations which may be imposed are set out in arts 9 to 13 of the Access Directive or regs 10 to 14 of the Access Regulations. The tools in the Regulator's tool box include imposing obligations of transparency, non-discrimination, access (to include interconnection), accounting separation, cost accounting and price control. Some of these naturally go hand in hand, such as transparency and non-discrimination.

In the case of retail markets, regulatory controls may be included if this is appropriate in accordance with arts 17 to 19 of the Universal Service Directive, as transposed by regs 14, 15 and 16 of the Universal Service Regulations.

6.066 Designation of an entity as having SMP and the imposition of remedies is done by way of public consultation further to art 6 of the Framework Directive, as transposed by reg 19 of the Framework Regulations, and each consultation is published on ComReg's website (http://www.comreg.ie). Adequate right of reply is given to the SMP entity. The right of appeal is enshrined in art 4 of the Framework Directive, as transposed by regs 3 and 4 of the Framework Regulations, and is dealt with in more detail in **Ch 10** on appeals. ComReg consults with the European Commission pursuant to art 7(3) of the Framework Directive, as transposed by reg 20 of the Framework Regulations, and the Competition Authority pursuant to reg 27 of the Framework Regulations, before designating SMP and imposing remedies.

SMP findings to date

6.067 ComReg originally designated Eircom as having SMP in the market for retail leased lines up to 2MB, in the terminating segments of leased lines and the trunk segment of leased lines markets, in Decision No D7/05 Market Analysis: Retail Leased Lines and Wholesale Terminating and Trunk Segments of Leased Lines (National), dated 30 March 2005. ComReg conducted a second round review of these markets and found Eircom only to have SMP on the market for wholesale terminating segment of leased lines in Decision D06.08 dated 22 December 2008. This decision is currently under appeal at the time of writing.

ComReg designated Eircom as having SMP in respect of the market for wholesale unbundled access (including shared access) to metallic loops and sub-loops (LLU) pursuant to ComReg Decision No D8/04 Market Analysis: Wholesale Unbundled Access (including shared access) to Metallic Loops and Sub-loops, dated 15 June 2004. ComReg has commenced a fresh review of this market in light of the revised Recommendation and it is being proposed that Eircom has SMP on the market for wholesale physical network infrastructure access at a fixed location. A final decision in this regard will likely be adopted in the first half of 2009.

---

88   There is an exception in respect of concerns about end-to-end connectivity set out in reg 6 of the Access Regulations.

ComReg has designated Eircom as having SMP in respect of the market for wholesale broadband access (WBA) pursuant to Decision No 03/05, dated 24 March 2005, Market Analysis: Wholesale Broadband Access, as amended by Decision No D01/06, dated 13 January 2006, which concerned Retail Minus Wholesale Price Control for the WBA Market.

6.068 Eircom was found to have SMP on the market for Access to the Public Telephone Network provided at a Fixed Location on 24 August 2007 (fixed retail narrow band access) and ComReg imposed a full suite of remedies, including transparency, access, cost accounting etc. The remedies basically support the wholesale line rental (WLR) and carrier pre-selection (CPS) products, which Eircom is required to offer to its competitors and new entrants with ancillary obligations to make sure those products operate efficiently and for the benefit of users. ComReg also decided to apply a price cap in respect of this market, and the final decision on that was implemented in October 2007. The price cap sets a CPI[89] – 0 target for a three-year period with an identical sub-cap on line rental.

6.069 In respect of wholesale call origination and transit, ComReg found Eircom had SMP in the markets on 5 October 2007 and imposed a suite of remedies designed to ensure that alternative operators could readily access the wholesale inputs needed for them to compete effectively in the retail calls market.

The fixed wholesale call termination market review was completed on 21 December 2007. In relation to termination, ComReg found that Eircom, plus five smaller operators, had SMP in their individual networks. ComReg proposed a range of remedies mindful of proportionality and thus imposed somewhat less burdensome remedies on some of the smaller operators.

6.070 Vodafone, O_2, Meteor and Hutchison 3G Ireland (3) were designated as having SMP in the market for wholesale voice call termination on individual mobile networks in ComReg Decision No D9/04 of July 2004, 'Market Analysis: Wholesale Voice Call Termination on Individual Mobile Networks'. In Ireland, the originating calling party, ie the party making the call, is responsible for charges to terminate a call on mobile networks. ComReg has imposed access obligations, non-discrimination obligations, price control and transparency obligations on Vodafone, O_2 and Meteor. ComReg has, in addition, imposed accounting separation and cost accounting obligations on Vodafone and O_2.

6.071 Ireland's fourth mobile operator, 3, successfully challenged ComReg's first decision to designate it as having SMP in the relevant market, as a result of which this aspect of ComReg's original decision was annulled by an electronic communications appeal panel. ComReg since completed a new market analysis in respect of Wholesale Voice Call Termination on 3's Mobile Network and found 3 to have SMP on this market (ComReg Decision No 05/08, dated 1 December 2008). ComReg imposed obligations of transparency, non-discrimination and price control. This decision is currently under appeal at the time of writing.

---

89   Consumer price index.

6.072 RTÉ was designated as having SMP on the national market for wholesale broadcasting transmission services in Decision No D16/04 of December 2004, Wholesale Broadcasting Transmission Services Markets – SMP Obligations.

6.073 In August 2006, ComReg published its Response to Consultation on its 'Market Analysis on Wholesale International Roaming' (ComReg Document No 06/35). In this Response, ComReg concluded that no undertaking had a position of single or joint dominance. In June 2007, the European Parliament and Council published Regulation EC/717/2007 on roaming on public mobile telephone networks within the Community (the Roaming Regulation). This regulation caps the wholesale charges that mobile phone operators charge each other for carrying calls from foreign networks. It was proposed that operators will be allowed to add to their wholesale cost a retail mark-up of up to 30 per cent. This retail mark-up would apply to calls made and received while roaming. It came into effect at the end of Summer 2007. The Roaming Regulation also introduced a number of obligations designed to ensure greater price transparency for consumers availing of international roaming services.[90]

Additional markets

6.074 ComReg had designated additional markets to those recommended by the European Commission. The additional markets include retail and wholesale payphone access and calls.

Regulation 6 of the Access Regulations also allows ComReg to impose the obligations referred to in regs 10 to 14 of the Access Regulations on undertakings in the absence of SMP to the extent that it is necessary to ensure end-to-end connectivity. Regulation 6 therefore allows for an obligation to interconnect networks, however, only where it is necessary to ensure end-to-end connectivity. This power has not been invoked to date.

Removal of SMP

6.075 In relation to the fixed retail calls markets, these markets were notified to the European Commission in 2005, but were re-reviewed subsequently in light of the Commission's draft recommendation (at the time of the review). ComReg decided to examine the three criteria[91] for these markets. Using the Commission's 'modified Greenfield' approach, ComReg found that, in the presence of wholesale regulation, the first criterion was not met. ComReg considered that a price cap on calls was no longer necessary, and that issues arising could be dealt with using *ex post* competition powers.

---

90 Communications (Mobile Telephone Roaming) Regulations 2007 (SI 792/2007) was adopted to ensure full effect of the provisions of the Roaming Regulation and deals with dispute resolution, the creation of offences as well as providing for an enforcement procedure under which a civil financial penalty of €500,000 may be ordered by the High Court to be paid.

91 (a) The presence of high and non-transitory barriers to entry; (b) a market structure which does not tend towards effective competition; and (c) competition law alone is insufficient to adequately address the market failure(s) concerned.

ComReg made a final decision on these markets on 28 December 2007 and concluded that they were not suitable for *ex ante* regulation.

Universal Service Obligation

6.076 The Universal Service Directive[92] and implementing regulations seek to establish a minimum set of high-quality services to all end-users at an affordable price[93] through obligations on the universal service provider (USP) and providers of publicly available electronic communications networks and services (PATS). For example, there is an obligation on all PATS providers in accordance with reg 18 of the Universal Service Regulations, to ensure that end-user contracts contain certain minimum content.

6.077 In order to ensure the effective provision of the universal service, a USP has to be designated to carry out the service. Pursuant to the Universal Service Regulations and ComReg's Decision in Document No 06/32, 'The Future Provision of Telephony Services under Universal Service Obligations', dated 25 July 2006, Eircom is designated as the USP and is designated as the USP until June 2009. As the USP, Eircom is obliged to provide access at a fixed location. It must satisfy any reasonable request to provide connections to the public telephone network and access to publicly available telephone services. Any connection provided by Eircom must be capable of local, national and international telephone calls, facsimile communications and narrowband Internet access, ie data communications at data rates that are sufficient to permit functional Internet access (currently 28.8kbps). The USP is required to consider all requests for connections as reasonable if the expenditure involved in meeting the request is less than €7,000 and the cost to the applicant shall not exceed the standard connection charge. Requests for connections which involve expenditure in excess of €7,000 are to be considered reasonable if the applicant agrees to pay the standard connection charge plus incremental costs above €7,000. The USP is required to provide end-users with a directory of subscribers, free of charge and updated at least once a year, based upon information supplied to it in accordance with the National Directory Database (NDD). The NDD is a database of subscriber numbers and is operated by Eircom. Eircom must keep a record in the NDD of all subscribers of publicly available telephone services in the State, including fixed and mobile numbers, and allow access to this information to other undertakings in accordance with terms and conditions approved by ComReg. As USP, Eircom must also ensure that public pay telephones are provided to meet the reasonable needs of end-users in terms of geographic coverage, number of telephones, accessibility of such telephones to users with disabilities and the quality of services.

6.078 The USP must also take specific measures aimed at users with disabilities. Eircom must provide inductive couplers, which allow users with a hearing aid set to

---

92 Directive 2002/22/EC of the European Parliament and of the Council of 7 March 2002 on universal service and users' rights relating to electronic communications networks and services.

93 Carney, *Regulatory Law* (Cavendish Publishing, 2004), chapter on Telecommunications.

connect to their telephone in order to allow them to hear incoming speech clearly; amplifier phones, which allow the user to increase the volume of incoming speech; and teleflash visual alert, which shows a flashing light or makes a loud noise when the telephone rings. In respect of users who are hearing or speech impaired, a text relay service must be provided with facilities for the receipt and translation of voice messages into text and the conveyance of that text to the text phone of customers of any operator, and vice versa. For users with limited dexterity or mobility, the USP must provide push button telephone sets with speed and automatic redial buttons allowing pre-programmed telephone numbers (typically the most-called numbers) or last-called telephone numbers to be dialled without having to re-enter the telephone number, or hands-free/loudspeaker phones, which mean that the handset does not need to be used at all. In respect of users with restricted vision, the USP must provide restricted vision telephones that can help people with restricted vision to find other numbers more easily and Braille-billing free of charge.

6.079 The Universal Service regulations require that the USP adheres to the principle of maintaining affordability for universal services. Currently, affordability is maintained by way of a number of different measures, which include the price cap regime, the Department for Social and Family Affairs (DSFA) free telephone rental allowance under the household benefit scheme, and the vulnerable user scheme.

6.080 Eircom is required to publish information on its quality of service performance in providing universal services. Eircom submitted an application to ComReg for universal service funding. In response to Eircom's request, ComReg has issued a Consultation (ComReg Document No 07/07, dated 2 February 2007). Articles 12 and 13 of the Universal Service Directive allow for the costing and funding of the universal service, respectively. These articles are transposed into Irish law by regs 11 and 12 of the Universal Service Regulations.

Numbering

6.081 All undertakings and users of telephone numbers from Ireland's National Numbering Scheme must comply with the Irish Numbering Conventions (the Conventions). The Conventions set down rules relating to the allocation and permitted use of numbers allocated from the National Numbering Scheme. ComReg does not charge any fees for number allocations, at present.

In the case of a number that has been allocated for a specific purpose within the National Numbering Scheme, ComReg must make a decision within three weeks of receipt of a complete application. Where ComReg decides, after public consultation, that rights of use for numbers of exceptional economic value are to be granted through competitive or comparative selection procedures, ComReg may extend the period of three weeks by a further three weeks.

VoIP

6.082 There is no special regulatory treatment for Internet services. Regulation is technology-neutral. Internet service providers (ISPs) are providers of ECNs and/or

ECSs, depending on whether they operate their own transmission system, and will therefore require authorisation and be entitled to offer their services subject to compliance with the general conditions of authorisation. The degree of authorisation depends on whether the Voice over Internet Protocol (VoIP) service simply involves downloading software and remains at all times on-net – VoIP in. Where services go off-net – VoIP out – onto electronic communications networks, then these require authorisation.

6.083 ComReg has published relevant guides on VoIP regulation in Ireland.[94] Geographic numbers were made available to VoIP service providers on certain conditions, together with a new range of non-geographic numbers – the '076' range. VoIP services can be ECSs or publicly available telephone service (PATS). Whether ECS or PATS, it is necessary to obtain an authorisation under the Authorisation Regulations in Ireland. There are different obligations and rights depending on whether a VoIP company is designated as providing ECS or PATS. PATS means a service available to the public for originating and receiving national and international calls and access to emergency services. PATS are provided through a number, or numbers, in a national or international telephone numbering plan, and may include the following services: the provision of operator assistance, directory enquiry services, directories, provision of public pay phones, and provision of special facilities for customers with disabilities or with special social needs.

6.084 For example, VoIP PATS providers are obliged to offer lifeline services such as access to emergency numbers, whereas ECS providers are only obliged to undertake best endeavours to ensure that delivery of emergency calls is achieved, although users must be advised of any limitations. Those who offer VoIP as PATS are obliged to offer their customers a listing in the NDD and also to facilitate directory enquiry and operator assistance services with a best endeavours obligation applying to ECS.

Interception

6.085 The interception of telecoms messages is dealt with in the Interception of Postal Packets and Telecommunications Messages (Regulation) Act 1993. Authorised operators are required to comply with directions given by the Minister for Justice to intercept telecoms messages for the purpose of criminal investigation or in the interests of the security of the Irish State.

Data Retention Obligations

6.086 The Criminal Justice (Terrorist Offences) Act 2005 provides that the Irish Garda Commissioner may request mobile phone or fixed-line service providers to retain traffic data or location data or both for a period of three years for the purpose of prevention, detection, investigation or prosecution of crime (including but not limited

---

94   The most recent of which was published in August 2006, 'Result of the VoIP Framework Review' (ComReg Document No 06/45).

to terrorist offences), or in order to safeguard the security of the Irish State. The 2005 Act does not make any provision for operators and service providers to be compensated for retaining traffic or location data. Digital Rights Ireland Ltd (DRI) is currently contesting the constitutionality of the provisions of the Criminal Justice (Terrorist Offences) Act 2005 in the Irish High Court, as well as contesting the European Directive 2006/24/EC of 15 March 2006 on the retention of data generated or processed in connection with the provision of publicly available electronic communications services.[95] The Irish Human Rights Commission is appearing as *amicus curiae* in the challenge to data retention laws.[96] Separately, Ireland is pursuing a case in the European Court of Justice (ECJ) against the Council of the European Union and the European Parliament, whereby it is seeking the annulment of Directive 2006/24/EC, on the grounds that it was not adopted on an appropriate legal basis (Case C–301/06).[97] The Advocate General of the ECJ delivered his opinion on 14 October 2008, stating that the European Directive on data retention is founded on an appropriate legal basis, and invited the court to dismiss the action.

Unsolicited Communications

6.087 In 2003, Ireland implemented Directive 2002/58/EC through the introduction of the European Communities (Electronic Communications Networks and Services) (Data Protection and Privacy) Regulations 2003 (SI 535/2003). Under the regulations, individuals cannot be subjected to unsolicited direct marketing calls, emails or SMS messages unless they have given their prior consent. Where a subscriber is a customer, electronic mail, the definition of which includes SMS text messaging, can be used for direct marketing purposes if an easy-to-use, free-of-charge opportunity is given to object to the use of electronic contact details when such detail is originally collected and on the occasion of each message. This customer exception only applies to the direct marketing by a business of its own similar products and services to its customers. Individuals can sign up to a central 'opt-out' register, to indicate that they do not wish to receive unsolicited telephone calls. Failure to comply with these regulations is an offence and is subject to a fine. The Data Protection Commissioner is the relevant body in respect of these matters, together with ComReg.

.ie Domain Name

6.088 The Communications Regulation (Amendment) Act 2007 brought about changes to the Electronic Commerce Act 2000 that relate to the transfer of the management of the .ie domain name from the Minister to ComReg.

---

95 *Digital Rights Ireland Ltd v Minister for Communications, Marine and Natural Resources* (2006, unreported), HC

96 Leave granted by McKechnie J on 1 July 2008.

97 The public hearing was held on 1 July 2008.

Regulator of Premium Rate Telecommunications Services

6.089 New legislation is proposed to bring the role of the Regulator of Premium Rate Telecommunications Services (RegTel) within the ambit of ComReg. RegTel is the current independent Regulator of the content and promotion of premium rate telecommunications services. RegTel operates through a code of practice that is observed by companies or individuals offering premium rate services in Ireland. RegTel is a not-for-profit limited company and is financed by a charge on call revenue. The Minister proposed in 2008 to fold RegTel into ComReg.

The Regulated Activity and the Regulated Entities – Postal Services

6.090 ComReg also has responsibility for regulating the postal sector. An Post is the incumbent and was established as a public company under the Postal and Telecommunications Services Act 1983 (the 1983 Act). The Minister for Communications, Energy and Natural Resources (the Minister) is its ultimate shareholder.[98] Section 12 of the 1983 Act sets out the principal objects of An Post, which include the provision of a national postal service within the State and between the State and places outside the State, meeting the needs of the State for comprehensive and efficient postal services and, so far as An Post considers reasonably practicable, satisfaction of all such reasonable demands for such services throughout the State. Section 13 of the 1983 Act sets out the general duties of An Post, which are to conduct its affairs so as to ensure that charges for services are kept at the minimum rate consistent with meeting approved financial targets, that the revenues of the company are not less than is sufficient to meet all charges properly chargeable to revenue account, to generate a reasonable proportion of capital needs and to remunerate capital and repay borrowings. Section 13(2) provides that ss 12 and 13 do not impose on An Post any form of duty or liability enforceable by proceedings before a court.

6.091 Section 64 of the 1983 Act limits An Post's liability in respect of carrying out its functions. Section 83 of the 1983 Act provides An Post's powers in respect of items in its network. An Post may refuse, return or dispose of postal packets that do not comply with schemes under s 70 of the 1983 Act or other provisions of the 1983 Act, or that consist of objectionable matter. This section also provides that An Post may open postal packets that are undeliverable. Section 84 of the 1983 Act provides that it is an offence for anyone to open a postal packet or disclose the existence or contents of a postal packet or tamper with a postal packet without the agreement of the addressee. The exception is if the person is acting further to s 83 or some other lawful authority.

6.092 There are no foreign ownership restrictions applicable to authorisation to provide postal services. The following section discusses the regulated sector that is both the reserved and the non-reserved area. It will also discuss the scope of the universal service obligation (USO) and other issues that have an impact on liberalisation, such as VAT on basic postal services, terminal dues, complaints and

---

98   Although the Minister for Finance holds one share in An Post, s 19 of the 1983 Act.

redress procedures, and quality of service. ComReg's strategy[99] in relation to postal services in light of the Third Postal Directive is set out in ComReg's document called The Postal Strategy Statement (2008–2010) and is to 'act as an advocate for the consumer and all those interested in providing customer focused and efficient postal services.'

General authorisation

6.093 All providers of postal services must obtain an authorisation. The procedures put in place for the authorisation of non-reserved services both inside and outside the scope of the USO should be transparent, non-discriminatory, proportionate and based on objective criteria further to art 9 of the Postal Directive. The reasons for refusing an authorisation must be communicated to the applicant and an appeal procedure must be available in the case of refusal.

6.094 Article 9(4) of the Postal Directive provides for the creation of compensation funds (to which authorised service providers contribute) in circumstances in which Member States determine that the provision of the USO is an unfair financial burden for the USP. In practice, this provision has remained largely unavailed of in light of Member States' preference for the reservation of services to public postal operators as a mechanism for funding the USO. However, such compensation funds may find a new relevance in light of the Third Postal Directive.

6.095 For non-reserved services that are outside the scope of the USO, Member States may introduce general authorisations. For non-reserved services that fall inside the scope of the USO, Member States may provide for authorisation procedures including the granting of individual licences to the extent necessary to ensure compliance with essential requirements and to safeguard the universal service.[100] The granting of authorisations for the provision of non-reserved services that fall inside the scope of the USO may:

(i)   where appropriate, be made subject to USOs;

(ii) if necessary, impose requirements concerning the quality and availability of the relevant services; and

(iii) be made subject to an obligation not to infringe the exclusive or special rights granted to the USP.

An Post is the universal service provider in Ireland.

---

99 Section 31 of the 2002 Act states that ComReg must 'draw up and adopt a strategy statement reflecting its statutory functions' every two years.

100 Postal Directive, arts 9 and 2(14) set out how a general authorisation does not require the undertaking concerned to obtain an explicit decision by the NRA before exercising the rights stemming from the authorisation. A general authorisation may be provided for by way of legislation or a 'class licence' and may require registration or declaration procedures. An individual licence is granted on foot of a decision by the NRA and may grant an undertaking specific rights or subject the undertaking's operations to specific obligations supplementing the general authorisation where applicable.

6.096 Regulation 7 provides that a postal service provider (other than a USP) with an annual turnover of more than €500,000, exclusive of VAT, shall apply to the Regulator for an authorisation (postal service authorisation) to provide a postal service. Where the Regulator is satisfied that an applicant can provide a postal service, the Regulator shall grant the applicant a postal service authorisation where the applicant gives the Regulator a written declaration that the postal services provided by the applicant do not infringe the reserved area. As part of obtaining an authorisation, entities have to give an undertaking that they will not breach An Post's reserved area.

Regulatory concerns in respect of the postal sector

Universal service

6.097 Article 3 of the Postal Directive, as transposed by reg 4 of the Postal Regulations,[101] requires that obligations should be imposed on the provider of the universal service and that the reserved area (statutory monopoly for the incumbent) should be reduced. The universal service shall include, as a minimum, the following:

(i)   the clearance, sorting, transport and distribution of postal items of up to 2kg;

(ii) the clearance, sorting, transport and distribution of postal packages of up to 10kg (with an option to increase this to 20kg);

(iii) the delivery of postal packages received from other Member States weighing up to 20kg; and

(iv) services for registered items and insured items.

The USP is required to apply a uniform tariff in Ireland. Regulation 4 of the Postal Regulations fleshes out An Post's obligation as the USP[102] and includes a requirement for delivery and collection at least five days a week to every home and premises.

6.098 The Postal Directive and the implementing statutory instrument contain various provisions concerning pricing and accounting for the universal service[103] and, specifically, in respect of the reserved services. As regards the universal service, prices should be affordable such that all users have access to the services, and should be cost-orientated, transparent and non-discriminatory.[104] The application of a uniform tariff does not preclude the USP from concluding individual agreements on prices with customers (ie in practice a lower price, for example for bulk mail under transparent and non-discriminatory conditions).[105] The USP is required to keep separate accounts for the following: each of the services in the reserved area, non-reserved services that are part of the universal service, and services outside the universal service. Internal

---

101 SI 616/2002.

102 Regulation 4(2)(a) designates An Post as the USP.

103 Postal Directive, arts 12–15; Postal Regulations, regs 9–11.

104 Postal Regulations, reg 9.

105 Postal Regulations, reg 9(1)(d) and (3).

accounting systems must operate on the basis of consistently applied and objectively justifiable cost accounting principles.[106]

6.099 Accordingly, the main regulatory obligations on incumbent USPs can typically be divided into the following categories:

(i)   obligations to provide a universal service in line with the definition of the scope of the universal service;[107]

(ii)   quality of service requirements;[108]

(iii)   financial requirements, including transparency of tariffs[109] and separation of accounts;[110]

(iv)   pricing controls;[111]

(v)   obligation of non-discrimination in respect of tariffs;[112] and

(vi)   obligations to ensure a uniform tariff for the universal service.[113]

The need to safeguard the universal service is a pre-condition for granting any reserved area to the incumbent USP.

6.100 Under the Postal Directive, Member States are required to ensure that postal users enjoy the right to a universal service ensuring the permanent provision of a postal service of specified quality at all points in their territory at affordable prices. In practice, this requirement amounts to an obligation on Member States to ensure that (save for circumstances or geographic conditions that are deemed to be exceptional by the NRA) every working day, and not less than five days a week, there is one clearance (ie collection) of postal items from letter boxes (or other comparable facilities) and one delivery of postal items to the home or premises of every natural or legal person. The universal service must include (as a minimum) the clearance, sorting, transport and distribution of postal items of up to 2 kilograms in weight and of packages of up to 10 kilograms in weight. NRAs may increase the weight limit of universal service coverage for packages up to 20 kilograms.[114] Member States must ensure (notwithstanding the

---

106 Article 14(3) contains detailed provisions on cost allocation, whereby costs that can be directly assigned must be so assigned and common costs should be allocated on the basis of the origin of the costs, or, if this is not possible, on the basis of any indirect linkage to another cost category, failing which they must be allocated on the basis of a general allocator computed by using the ratio of all expenses directly or indirectly assigned or allocated, to each of the reserved and non-reserved services. Regulation 11 of the Postal Regulations implements this provision into Irish law.

107 Postal Regulations, reg 4.

108 Postal Regulations, regs 12 and 13.

109 Postal Regulations, reg 9.

110 Postal Regulations, reg 11. ComReg has issued An Post with an Accounting Direction Document No: 06/63, dated 8 December 2006 pursuant to Postal Regulations, reg 11(2).

111 Postal Regulations, reg 9 but also Postal Regulations, reg 8(4).

112 Postal Regulations, reg 9.

113 Postal Regulations, reg 9.

114 Postal Directive, art 3(5) – In Ireland the USO is up to 20kg further to Postal Regulations, reg 4.

weight limit applicable in that Member State for the universal service coverage for packages) that the delivery of packages received from other Member States of up to 20 kilograms in weight is covered by the universal service.

6.101 The First and Second Postal Directives did not expressly address the manner in which the USP was to be selected. In practice, this issue has proven to be uncontroversial since Member States' postal sectors are generally characterised by the presence of an incumbent public postal operator (PPO) that has traditionally borne the USO. In Ireland, An Post is the designated USP pursuant to reg 4(2)(a) of the Postal Regulations. ComReg published a working definition of the Universal Postal Service on 15 November 2005 in ComReg Document No 05/85.

Quality of service

6.102 Under reg 12 of the Postal Regulations, quality of service standards are to be set and published by ComReg for the universal service. Regulation 13(1) provides that ComReg must set out quality standards for domestic mail, which are to be notified to the European Commission and which are to be compatible with the standards for intra-Community cross-border services contained in the Sch to the Postal Regulations. On 1 June 2004, ComReg set An Post a D+1[115] quality of service target of 94 per cent for the delivery of single piece priority mail. This means that ComReg has required An Post to achieve this next-day delivery target in respect of single piece priority mail or ordinary day-to-day correspondence posted by consumers and some businesses. ComReg set the 94 per cent target for An Post following a public consultation.[116] ComReg received new powers from the Minister in 2008 to issue directions to An Post regarding quality of service.[117] Regulation 13 of the Postal Regulations has now been amended to insert a new reg 13(5), which provides that for the purpose of ensuring that the USP takes corrective action in respect of quality of service, the Regulator may give a direction to a USP to take such action.

The reserved area

6.103 A rationale behind the reservation of services to the USP has been to ensure that the USP is capable of discharging its USO under financially balanced conditions.[118] In the absence of a reserved area, it would be possible for competing postal providers (not bound by a USO) to provide those elements of the reserved services that are profitable (eg the clearance, sorting and delivery of letter post within large cities) without bearing the costs of those elements of the reserved services that are loss-making (eg the provision of similar services in outlying and rural areas), a practice known as 'cream-skimming' or 'cherry picking'.[119] Such a scenario could potentially undermine the viability of the continued provision of the USO and could also permit inefficient entry

---

115 D = day, D + 1 = next day delivery.

116 Regulation 4(1)(i) allows ComReg to issue directions to An Post in respect of the quality of the postal service to be provided after consultation with interested parties.

117 European Communities (Postal Services) (Amendment) Regulations 2008 (SI 135/2008).

118 Recital 16 to the Postal Directive.

119 See *Criminal Proceedings against Paul Corbeau* Case C–320/91, par 18.

into the market if postal operators that are less efficient than the USP were able to exploit any price differential resulting from a constraint on the USP's pricing.[120]

6.104 Accordingly, to the extent necessary to ensure the maintenance of the universal service, Member States may reserve to the USP the clearance, sorting, transport and delivery of items of domestic correspondence and incoming cross-border correspondence of up to 50 grams in weight and costing less than two-and-a-half times the basic tariff. All outgoing cross-border mail has been open to competition since 1 January 2003. This legal monopoly was deemed necessary in order for An Post to be able to meet its USO. The reserved area relates to 'items of correspondence' (which includes any communications in written form on any kind of physical medium to be conveyed and delivered at the address indicated by the sender on the item itself or on its wrapping, with the exception of books, catalogues newspapers and periodicals). This means that competing postal providers in Ireland are currently not permitted to provide these services. An Post's legal monopoly was challenged in *Attorney General and Minister for Post and Telegraphs v Paperlink Ltd*,[121] which was a challenge brought by a courier company on the grounds that the statutory monopoly then conferred by s 34(2) of the Post Office Act 1908 was unconstitutional. The challenge was unsuccessful.[122]

6.105 The Third Postal Directive dictates the minimum pace of liberalisation in the Member States from 2009. This Directive has to be implemented in Ireland by 31 December 2010. Full liberalisation of the postal sector is now to be achieved by 2011. This means that as of 2011, An Post will no longer have any statutory monopoly.

6.106 Although not provided for in the Directive, it would appear that the exclusive or reserved area rights granted by a Member State to a USP cannot extend beyond the scope of the universal service itself. This would seem to be the case in light of the ruling of the ECJ in the landmark *Corbeau* case.[123] It was held that exclusive rights in favour of a USP are not justified under art 86 of the EC Treaty as regards specific services which are dissociable from the universal service itself (the service of general interest), where these meet special needs of economic operators and call for certain additional services not offered by the traditional postal service, and can be performed without compromising the economic equilibrium of the service of general economic interest.[124]

---

120 'The USO in a liberalised postal sector: what are the options?', Oxera Agenda, March 2007, http://www.oxera.com.

121 *AG and Minister for Post and Telegraphs v Paperlink Ltd* [1984] ILRM 373.

122 *Regulatory Law* (Law Society and Cavendish Publishing, 2004), Postal Regulation chapter by David Dodd.

123 *Criminal Proceedings against Paul Corbeau* Case C–320/91 ECR (1993) I–2533.

124 Flynn and Rizza note that the ECJ did not identify the precise nature of the Régie des Postes' abusive conduct, nor, indeed, did it state whether any abuse had actually occurred: Flynn and Rizza, 'Postal Services and EC Competition Law: A review and analysis of EC Case-Law', 24(4) *World Competition* 475. (contd .../)

6.107 The *Corbeau* test was restated by the ECJ in May 2001 in the judgment of *TNT Traco SpA v Poste Italiane SpA*.[125] The ECJ held that the imposition by a USP of postal dues (based on universal service postage prices) on the provision by independent operators of express postal services, could only be justified with reference to art 86(2) of the EC Treaty if the maintenance of such rights was necessary for the USP to be able to perform its public service tasks or to perform them under economically acceptable and financially stable conditions. Further, the ECJ concluded that compatibility with arts 82 and 86 of the EC Treaty meant that the proceeds from the postal dues could not exceed the amount of the losses incurred in the operation of the universal service by the USP, that the USP must also be required to pay the same dues when itself providing an express mail service not forming part of the universal service, and that none of the costs of that service could be subsidised from the universal service.[126]

The European Commission's willingness to use its enforcement powers under art 86(3) of the EC Treaty rather than issue proceedings under art 226 of the EC Treaty is evidenced in its approach *inter alia* in the *SNELPD* case.[127]

---

124 (contd) Hancher has suggested that the ECJ's approach was based on a vigilance towards Member States attempting to expand the monopoly held by PPOs over basic services to cover emerging markets for new 'value-added' postal services, eg express courier services: Case note by Leigh Hancher CML Rev, 1994, p 105.

125 *TNT Traco SpA v Poste Italiane SpA* Case C–340/99, ECR (2001) I–4109.

126 Indeed, the case law in the area has focused on instances where national rules have attempted to extend the scope of the PPO's monopoly to cover value-added services. This point is illustrated by two Commission decisions taken prior to the ECJ's judgment in *Corbeau*: Commission Decision 90/16/EEC concerning the provision in the Netherlands of express courier services and Commission Decision 90/456/EEC concerning the provision in Spain of international express courier services. In both instances, the Commission found that national rules that prevented PPOs from providing international express courier services in competition to the incumbent PPOs were in breach of art 86(1) EC read in conjunction with art 82 EC. It did so on the basis that in neither instance did the courier services in question form part of the basic postal service, nor was the reservation of such services to the PPO necessary to protect the financial equilibrium of the PPO or its ability to finance the basic postal service. In the *Italian Hybrid Mail* decision 2001/176/EC: Commission Decision of 21 December 2000 concerning proceedings pursuant to art 86 of the EC Treaty in relation to the provision of certain new postal services with a guaranteed day- or time-certain delivery in Italy (2001) OJ L 63/59) an Italian rule prevented PPOs from providing hybrid mail services (a new form of postal service characterised *inter alia* by guaranteeing delivery either on a pre-arranged day or at a pre-arranged time) despite the fact that Poste Italiane did not itself provide such services. The Commission stated that the reservation to an incumbent in one market of the right to provide services on a neighbouring market contravened art 86(1) EC in conjunction with art 82 EC .

127 The *SNELPD* case was decided upon in the Commission Decision 2002/344/EC of 23 October 2001, (2002) O.J. L 120/19 and concerned the lack of exhaustive and independent scrutiny of the charges and technical conditions applied by La Poste to mail preparation firms for access to its reserved services. This resulted in the establishment of an independent Regulator in France for postal services.(contd .../)

6.108 In the Postal Notice,[128] the European Commission had indicated that the subsidisation of non-reserved services from income generated through reserved services was likely to amount to a breach of art 82 EC in circumstances where it was not necessary in order to sustain the USO.[129] In *Deutsche Post I*[130] the European Commission found that Deutsche Post had used profits generated from its monopoly over letter post (ie the reserved area) to finance fidelity rebates and predatory pricing in the market for business parcel services, which was open to competition (ie outside the reserved area) in breach of art 82 of the EC Treaty.[131] Accordingly, if a public postal operator (PPO) which produces profits in the reserved area[132] provides any services in the non-reserved area and fails to recover the incremental costs of each of these services, then it is presumed to have funded the loss generated by that service with the profits generated from the reserved services and such cross-subsidisation could amount to predatory pricing and a breach of art 82 EC.[133] In order to alleviate the European Commission's concerns with regard to the financial relations between Deutsche Post's activities in the reserved and non-reserved areas, Deutsche Post undertook to transfer its business parcel services to a separate company (NewCo). NewCo would be free to source its necessary inputs (eg sorting, transport and delivery services) either from Deutsche Post, third parties or itself.[134] This was the first

---

127 (contd) See Baratta, Buigues, Fehrenbach, Johansson and Lüder, *The Application of EC Competition Rules in the Postal Sector*, Paper presented at the Second Conference on 'Competition and Universal Service in the Postal Sector', Toulouse 10EI, 6–7 December 2001.

128 Notice on the application of the competition rules to the postal sector and on assessment of certain State measures relating to postal services, 98/C 39/02 (Postal Notice).

129 Paragraph 3.3 of the application of the competition rules to the Postal Notice.

130 *Deutsche Post AG* Case COMP/35.151, Commission Decision of 20 March 2001.

131 In determining that such cross-subsidisation amounted to a breach of Deutsche Post's dominant position, the European Commission defined the following standard for the analysis of cost allocation between reserved and non-reserved services: 'cross-subsidization occurs where the earnings from a given service do not suffice to cover the incremental costs of providing that service and where there is another service or bundle of services the earnings from which exceed the stand-alone costs.' At para 6.

132 Conversely, UPS Europe was unsuccessful in its complaint that Deutsche Post used funds from the reserved area to fund acquisitions and that this was abuse. Having had its complaint rejected by the European Commission, UPS Europe appealed to the Court of First Instance (CFI) in *UPS Europe v Commission* Case T-175/99 [2002] ECR II-1915. The CFI concluded that the use of funds generated in the reserved area to fund the acquisition of joint control of an undertaking active in a neighbouring market open to competition does not amount to a breach of art 82 unless it can be shown that the funds in question were derived from abusive practices on the part of the dominant undertaking in the reserved area.

133 A further example of a PPO exploiting revenues generated in the reserved area in order to extend its dominance into the non-reserved area arose in Commission Decision of 2002/180 5 December 2001 relating to a proceeding under art 82 of the EC Treaty – *De Post/La Poste* Case COMP/37.859, OJ L 61 of 2 March 2002. The European Commission concluded that De Post/La Poste's behaviour had breached art 82 EC and fined it €2.5m.

134 Deutsche Post was fined €24m as result of the illegal rebates it had provided to customers.

European Commission decision adopted under art 82 EC that led to a structural remedy.[135]

Remail

6.109 Whereas incoming cross-border letter mail may be reserved to USPs, the collection and forwarding of outgoing cross-border letter mail has been opened to competition. This liberalisation has facilitated the development of remail. Remail involves the rerouting of mail between countries so as to take advantage of varying postal tariffs and levels of terminal dues.[136] There are different types of remail.[137] Remail can be physical or non-physical. In the case of non-physical remail, the content of the letters is transmitted by electronic data transfer from Country A to Country B, where the information is printed out for delivery in Country A, B or C. Article 43 of the Universal Postal Union (UPU) Convention provides that:

> A member country shall not be bound to forward or deliver to the addressee letter-post items which senders resident in its territory post or cause to be posted in a foreign country with the object of profiting by the lower charges in force there. The same shall apply to such items posted in large quantities, whether or not such postings are made with a view to benefiting from lower charges.

6.110 The current prevalent view on ABA remail is that it amounts to a circumvention of the statutory postal monopoly, ie the reserved area of the PPOs. Interception of remail may be lawful and so would not constitute an abuse within the meaning of art 82 of the EC Treaty, if remail[138] prevents the PPO of the country of destination from recovering its costs in delivering the mail in so far as terminal dues are not based on real costs. However, the PPO may only recover the difference between the terminal

---

135 See Baratta, Buigues, Fehrenbach, Johansson and Lüder, *The Application of EC Competition Rules in the Postal Sector*, Paper presented at the Second Conference on 'Competition and Universal Service in the Postal Sector', Toulouse 10EI, 6–7 December 2001, p 12.

136 Terminal dues are the compensation for the costs of the delivery of cross-border mail between countries.

137 If mail originating in Country A (and destined for addressees in Country A) is transported to Country B and posted back to addressees in Country A, this is referred to as ABA remail. ABB remail refers to mail which originates in Country A, but is posted in Country B for delivery in Country B. A third scenario involves mail originating in Country A (and destined for addressees in Country C), which is transported to Country B before being posted to addressees in Country C. This is referred to as ABC remail.

138 Remail was also examined in *Deutsche Post II* Case COMP/36.915, 26 July 2001. The European Commission in that case determined that the mail in question did not in fact originate in Germany and was, accordingly, not remail. In this case, the European Commission concluded that Deutsche Post had abused its dominant position by discriminating, by refusal to supply, by excessive pricing, by limiting markets and restricting development of mail services.

dues actually received and the domestic tariff that should have been received from the sender. To seek to recover the full domestic tariff would be viewed as abusive.[139]

6.111 The ECJ has also had the opportunity to consider ABA remail[140] in a case concerning non-physical remail. In this case, Deutsche Post intercepted letters sent in accordance with art 43(3) of the UPU Convention, and demanded postage at the domestic rate in respect of each of the letters sent, which it delivered in Germany. The ECJ recognised that the postal services of a Member State cannot simultaneously bear the costs entailed in the performance of the service of general economic interest of forwarding and delivering international mail items and the loss of income resulting from the loss of bulk mail to other postal systems. In such a case, the ECJ found that it must be regarded as justified, for the purposes of the performance, in economically balanced conditions, of the task of general interest entrusted to Deutsche Post to treat cross-border mail as internal mail and, consequently, to charge internal postage.[141]

Pricing controls

6.112 The Postal Directive imposes a basic requirement that tariffs for each of the services comprising the universal service must be transparent, non-discriminatory, affordable, ensuring that all users have access to the services, and geared to costs under art 12 of the Postal Directive, as transposed into Irish law by reg 9 of the Postal Regulations. Regulation 8(4) of the Postal Regulations provides that ComReg's concurrence is required in respect of the increase of charges by An Post under a scheme in the reserved area. This SI amends a piece of primary legislation, namely s 70(2) of the 1983 Act. Outside the reserved area, ComReg's prior concurrence is not stipulated to be so required. ComReg has *ex post* control outside the reserved area to ensure that pricing complies with the general tariff obligations such as that prices are transparent, geared to costs and non-discriminatory further to reg 9(3) of the Postal Regulations.

---

139 In the European Commission's 2003 exemption in respect of remuneration in the form of terminal dues for cross-border mail, commonly referred to as REIMS, the European Commission took a favourable view in regard to PPOs' attempts to resist incoming remail as the obligation to offer third-party access does not apply to ABA remail.

140 *Deutsche Post AG v Gesellschaft fur Zahlungssysteme GmbH GZS* Case C–147/97 and *Citicorp Kartenservice GmbH* Case C–148/97, 10 February 2000.

141 It was held that in the absence of an agreement fixing terminal dues in relation to the actual costs of processing and delivering incoming trans-border mail, it was not contrary to art 86 EC, read in conjunction with arts 82 EC and 49 EC, for a body such as Deutsche Post to exercise the right provided for by art 43(3) of the UPU Convention to charge internal postage on items of mail posted in large quantities with the postal services of a Member State other than the Member State to which that body belongs.It would be contrary to art 86(1) EC, read in conjunction with art 82EC, in so far as the result is that such a body may demand the entire internal postage applicable in the Member State to which it belongs without deducting the terminal dues paid. In Ireland, the Post Office (Evasion of Postage) Act 1937 may be relevant in this regard.

6.113 Member States may require uniform tariffs to be applied throughout their national territory. The provision of uniform tariffs is clearly at odds with the principle that prices must be geared to costs. There is inherently a degree of cross-subsidisation where uniform tariffs are applied to the provision of a given service. USPs applying uniform tariffs will not recover the costs of delivering to outlying and peripheral areas. At the same time, tariffs applied in urban areas may well significantly exceed costs.[142] Some commentators have suggested that the provision of uniform tariffs should be read as an exception to the requirement that tariffs be geared to costs.[143] The application of a uniform tariff does not prevent the USP from concluding individual agreements on prices with customers, provided that such agreements do not breach the principles of transparency and non-discrimination. To this end, tariffs must take account of avoided costs as a result, for example, from work sharing arrangements as compared with the standard service.[144]

6.114 As noted above, the cross-subsidisation of universal services outside of the reserved area out of revenues generated by the reserved services is prohibited, except to the extent to which it is shown to be necessary to maintain the viability of those universal services. The purpose of this requirement is to prevent the USP from using revenue generated from its reserved services to restrict competition in those elements of the universal service which are not reserved and are, therefore, open to competition.[145] The Postal Directive lays down minimum standards for the separation of accounts of USPs. Member States must require USPs to keep separate accounts within their internal accounting systems at least for each of the services within the reserved area and for the non-reserved services as a whole.[146] ComReg issued An Post with an Accounting Direction on 8 December 2006 pursuant to reg 11(2) of the Postal Regulations.[147]

6.115 In respect of pricing, An Post has a VAT exemption in respect of the provision of public postal services pursuant to art 13 of the Sixth VAT Directive.[148] Although

---

142 Paragraph 3.2 of the Postal Notice specifically provides that, 'Cross-subsidisation does not distort competition when the costs of reserved activities are subsidised by the revenue generated by other reserved services since there is no competition possible as to these services. This form of subsidisation may sometimes be necessary to enable ... operators ... to provide a service universally, and on the same conditions to everybody. For instance unprofitable mail delivery in rural areas is subsidised through revenues generated by activities open to competition.'

143 Bishop, Caffarra, Kuhn and Whish, 'Liberalising Postal Services: On the Limits of Competition Policy Intervention'(1998) *Kings College London Occasional Papers*, Series 1; Paragraph 3.2.2 of the European Commission's Explanatory Memorandum to its Proposal for a Third Postal Directive.

144 Postal Directive, art 12, fifth indent; Postal Regulations, reg 9(3).

145 Postal Directive, art 12, sixth indent.

146 Postal Directive, art 14; Postal Regulations, reg 11.

147 Document No 06/63.

148 Directive 77/388/EEC. (contd .../)

attempts have been made to amend this directive in this regard, unanimity is required at Council level in respect of fiscal policy, which can be difficult to obtain.

Terminal dues

6.116 The Postal Directive sets out basic principles to be adhered to by USPs in any arrangements entered into providing compensation for the costs of the delivery of cross-border mail between Member States. Such compensation is paid in the form of 'terminal dues'. USPs are to be encouraged by Member States to ensure that agreements which they enter into with other USPs regarding terminal dues for intra-Community cross-border mail respect the following principles:

 (i)   terminal dues shall be fixed in relation to the costs of processing and delivering incoming cross-border mail;

 (ii) levels of remuneration shall be related to the quality of service achieved; and

 (iii) terminal dues shall be transparent and non-discriminatory.[149]

6.117 The current system for the payment of terminal dues between USPs is provided for in the Agreement for the Remuneration of Mandatory Deliveries of Cross-Border Mails (the REIMS Agreement). Originally PPOs did not directly compensate each other for the costs of delivery of international mail since it was assumed that the flows of mail between countries balanced themselves out over time.[150] However, with the evolution in the flow of cross-border mail, significant imbalances began to develop. In 1969, the Universal Postal Union (UPU), an international organisation of which nearly every country in the world is a member, developed a system of terminal dues which set a fixed rate per kilogram of cross-border mail. This system was considered by many to be unsatisfactory since it was unreflective of the real costs of handling cross-border mail.[151]

6.118 Accordingly, a number of European countries entered into discussions in the context of the European Conference of Postal and Telecommunications Administrations (CEPT), a sub-group within the UPU, in order to develop a more satisfactory system of terminal dues for the exchange of cross-border mail in Europe. In 1987, CEPT members concluded an agreement (the CEPT Agreement) providing for a system whereby terminal dues would be calculated on the basis of two elements: a rate per item and a rate per kilogram (also known as items per kilo or IPKs). In 1993,

---

148 (contd) The European Commission has opened infringements against Germany, the UK and Sweden pursuant to art 226 of the EC Treaty in this regard and issued in July 2007 reasoned opinions to the three countries – file numbers 2006/2046 (Sweden), 2006/2047 (UK) and 2006/2048 (Germany).

149 Postal Directive, art 13; Postal Regulations, reg 10.

150 For further background to the issue of terminal dues generally, see Reeves, 'Terminal Problems in the Postal Sector?' [2000] *ECLR* 283. For a discussion of terminal dues in the broader international context, see Campbell, 'Evolution of Terminal Dues and Remail Provisions in European and International Postal Law' (2002) *Journal of Network Industries* 3:1.

151 It is generally cheaper to deliver one item of mail weighing 1 kilogram than 50 letters weighing 20 grams each.

on foot of a complaint lodged to the European Commission, the Commission issued a statement of objections to the effect that the CEPT Agreement was in breach of art 81 (then 85) EC since it fixed a uniform rate for the delivery of cross-border mail. The European Commission did not ultimately prohibit the CEPT Agreement, however, since the CEPT Agreement was replaced in 1995 by the REIMS Agreement.[152]

6.119 Under the REIMS Agreement, terminal dues were to be linked to the domestic tariffs of the signatory countries and were to reach 80 per cent of domestic tariffs provided that certain quality of service targets were met (it was amended by the Commission to reduce this percentage). REIMS I expired in September 1997. A successor agreement (the REIMS II Agreement) was concluded and was notified to the European Commission in October 1999. The European Commission found that the REIMS II Agreement infringed art 81 EC since it fixed the terminal dues which the participant PPOs paid each other on the market for inbound cross-border mail.[153] The European Commission noted that the alternative to the regime envisaged under the REIMS II Agreement was a network of bilateral agreements between PPOs, the content of which would not necessarily be identical.[154] The European Commission concluded that the REIMS II Agreement satisfied the criteria set out in art 81(3) of the EC Treaty. The exemption was to expire on 31 December 2001.

6.120 In 2001, the participant PPOs re-notified the REIMS II Agreement to the European Commission subject to some slight amendments; rather than 80 per cent, terminal dues were to reach 78.5 per cent in 2005 and 2006.[155] The European Commission concluded that the re-notified REIMS II Agreement satisfied art 81(3) EC subject to the following conditions. Firstly, the European Commission was not satisfied that an increase in terminal dues to 80 per cent of domestic tariffs was in line with the cost information provided by the participant PPOs. Secondly, the participant parties had to provide access to third-party postal service providers on the same terms and conditions as applied between the participant PPOs. The exemption expired on 31 December 2006. The REIMS II Agreement remains in place. However, as a result of the European Commission's Modernisation Regulation – Regulation 1/2003, re-notification of the REIMS II Agreement is no longer possible (please see chapter 7 on Competition for further details on Regulation 1/2003). At the time of writing, negotiations have begun on a successor REIMS agreement.[156]

---

152 IECC unsuccessfully challenged the European Commission's failure to prohibit the CEPT Agreement before the CFI and ECJ; *IECC v Commission* Case C-449/98 P.

153 *REIMS II* Notification Case COMP/C/38.170.

154 However, in practice since each PPO is likely to be found to be dominant in its own national market for the delivery of inbound cross-border mail, there could only be a limited extent to which a receiving PPO could vary the terms and conditions upon which it delivered inbound cross-border mail without leaving itself exposed to accusations of abusing its dominant position through unjustifiable discrimination.

155 Commission Decision of 23 October 2003, *REIMS II Notification Case* COMP/C/38.170.

156 At the time of writing neither the Royal Mail in the UK or TNT in Holland are members of REIMS.

The provision of downstream access to postal networks

6.121 The First and Second Postal Directives do not provide for any regulatory obligations concerning access to incumbent postal networks. Some Member States consider access to the postal network a fundamental element of liberalisation, while others regard access to postal networks as unnecessary for the entry of new postal operators to the market. A postal network is not a physical infrastructure network like telecommunications or energy networks. Within a densely populated urban area giving rise to considerable volumes of inner city mail, it is arguably not unduly difficult to replicate a localised collection, sorting and delivery network, although clearly modern sorting equipment is expensive. However, the establishment of long-distance conveyance and sorting networks capable of reaching remote areas involves much greater investments in infrastructure. Thus, the wider the overall area and the more remote the individual delivery destinations, the greater the possibility that the postal network has the characteristics of a natural monopoly.[157]

6.122 Article 12 of the Postal Directive provides that where a USP grants access to its network by providing a service consisting of less than the complete range of features offered for the clearance, transport, sorting and delivery of postal items, for example to businesses, bulk mailers or consolidators, the USP shall (in addition to applying the principles of transparency and non-discrimination) set tariffs that take account of the avoided costs, as compared with providing the full clearance, transport, sorting and delivery service. Further, the tariffs and conditions must apply equally both as between different third parties and as between third parties and USPs supplying equivalent services. Any such tariffs must also be available to private customers who post under similar conditions, ie those who carry out an equivalent degree of mail preparation for an equivalent volume of mail items.

6.123 The European Commission took a very significant decision in the application of art 86(1) combined with art 82 of the EC Treaty concerning *La Poste of France* 'on the lack of exhaustive and independent scrutiny of the scales of charges and technical conditions applied by La Poste to mail preparation firms for access to its reserved services'.[158] The Commission decided[159] that the French government had allowed a situation to persist in which the public undertaking La Poste was faced with a risk of conflict of interest as the monopoly provider of basic postal services, in relation to determining the terms of access to its reserved services and especially its postal network, because of its activities as a competitor on the upstream market for mail preparation services. In such circumstances, it was the responsibility of the State to ensure an effective monitoring system so as to re-establish effective competition on the upstream market by ensuring that the drawing up of technical specifications and the monitoring of their application would be carried out by a body that was independent of La Poste. The Commission concluded that the conflict of interest on the part of La

---

157 It is interesting to note, however, that in *Corbeau* the notion that the public postal network was an essential facility was rejected.

158 Decision of 23 October 2001, OJ (2002) L120/19 Commission Decision 2002/344/EC.

159 Following the reasoning of the ECJ in Case C–18/88, GB-Inno-BM (1991) ECR I–5941.

Poste constituted an abuse without the need to show commitment of an actual abuse in order for there to be an infringement of art 86(1) EC. It was a material factor that lack of satisfactory independent monitoring and regulation of La Poste in relation to the imposition of terms of access for mail preparation firms to its downstream network would involve discrimination between the conditions applied to La Poste's own subsidiaries and the two competing independent mail preparation firms, both as regards the specific terms and conditions applied and the strictness with which they were enforced.

6.124 This European Commission decision was followed by a similar decision under art 86 EC against a provision of the German Postal Act, in October 2004.[160] The European Commission concluded that certain provisions which prevent commercial mail preparation firms from earning discounts for handing over pre-sorted letter post at Deutsche Post's sorting offices induced Deutsche Post to discriminate against such mail preparation firms. The discrimination resulted from the fact that individual large users (senders) were allowed to feed self-prepared mail directly into sorting offices and receive volume-related discounts, whilst postal consolidators or intermediaries were prevented from obtaining comparable discounts for mail preparation.[161] Although Germany and Deutsche Post appealed this to the European Court of First Instance (CFI) claiming that the European Commission's decision was not consistent with art 82 of the EC Treaty and the Postal Directive[162] on 7 May 2008, the appellants withdrew their challenge of the Commission Decision and the cases were struck from the register of the CFI.

The Third Postal Directive

6.125 As noted above, the Third Postal Directive[163] envisages the accomplishment of the postal internal market (ie full liberalisation and the removal of the reserved area) by 2011.[164] Implementing legislation will need to be adopted to transpose the Third Postal Directive into Irish law. ComReg responded to the Department of Communications, Energy and Natural Resources' consultation on the Third Postal Directive and the liberalisation of the postal sector on 27 June 2008 in ComReg Document No: 08/47.

The key provisions of the Third Postal Directive are set out in the following paragraphs.

(a) Full liberalisation and the removal of the reserved area

6.126 Several Member States have already liberalised their postal markets beyond what is required under the Postal Directive. Most notably, the UK fully opened its

---

160 *BdKEP/Deutsche Post* COMP 38.745.

161 European Commission press release IP/04/1254, 20 October 2004: http://europa.eu.int/comm/competition/antitrust/cases/decisions/38745/en.pdf.

162 *Germany v Commission* Case T–490/04, and *Deutsche Post AG v Commission*, Case T–493/04, OJ (2005) See 31/29.

163 Directive 2008/6/EC of 20 February 2008, amending Directive 97/67/EC, with regard to the full accomplishment of the internal market of Community postal services.

164 Some Member States such as Greece have a derogation until 31 December 2012.

postal market on 1 January 2006, joining Sweden and Finland, which had previously taken this step. Article 7 of the Postal Directive is now amended so as to prohibit Member States from granting or maintaining in force exclusive or special rights for the establishment and provision of postal services.

(b) Scope of uso and financing the uso

6.127 While the European Commission has reaffirmed its commitment to universal service, vigorous debate is ongoing regarding its future financing. This debate involves a fundamental rethinking of the manner in which the dual imperatives of market opening and universal service are balanced. The universal service will continue to guarantee, in principle, one clearance and one delivery to the home or premises of every natural or legal person every working day, even in remote or sparsely populated areas.[165]

6.128 The European Commission recognises that by prohibiting Member States from reserving services to the USP, it may in effect remove the traditional mechanism by which the USO has been financed. The Third Postal Directive goes further still in so far in as it envisages a movement away from a situation in which Member States designate the incumbent PPO as the USP. To this end, the Third Postal Directive would require that Member States ensure the provision of universal services by procuring such services in accordance with the applicable public procurement rules.[166] Article 4 of the Postal Directive will be amended in this regard.

6.129 What is not expressly clear from the Third Postal Directive is whether Member States may simply re-designate the existing USP (which in most instances will be the incumbent PPO) or whether they will have to go to the market in all instances. ComReg in its response to the Department's consultation suggests that designation of a single USP may not be appropriate in a liberalised market. The alternatives to designation are 'market provision' and 'public procurement'. ComReg considers that these two methods can be used in combination, with public procurement being used to fill in any gaps in market provision.

6.130 With regard to financing the universal service, where necessary, the Third Postal Directive envisages two mechanisms:

(i)   direct compensation from public funds; and

(ii) sharing the net cost of the universal service between providers of services and/ or users.

---

165 With the caveat, as exists currently, 'save in circumstances or geographical conditions deemed exceptional.'

166 Such tendering competitions are likely to be in the form of 'reverse auctions' whereby operators bid on the basis of the subsidy they would require to provide the service in question. See 'The USO in a liberalised postal sector: what are the options?' Oxera Agenda, March 2007, fn 9, www.http://oxera.com.

This latter mechanism may involve the use of compensation funds. Such compensation funds are currently provided for in art 9 of the Postal Directive. Article 9 is amended to prohibit Member States from imposing certain conditions as part of the authorisation process, including limiting the number of licensees and the imposition of concurrent requirements to both bear a USO and contribute to its funding.[167]

6.131 The former mechanism, ie direct compensation from public funds, need not necessarily raise State aid issues where the Altmark Principles[168] are complied with or if art 86(2) may be validly invoked. The four *Altmark* principles are as follows:

> First, the recipient undertaking must actually have public service obligations to discharge, and the obligations must be clearly defined. In the main proceedings, the national court will therefore have to examine whether the public service obligations which were imposed on Altmark Trans are clear from the national legislation and/or the licences at issue in the main proceedings.

> Second, the parameters on the basis of which the compensation is calculated must be established in advance in an objective and transparent manner, to avoid it conferring an economic advantage which may favour the recipient undertaking over competing undertakings. Payment by a Member State of compensation for the loss incurred by an undertaking without the parameters of such compensation having been established beforehand, where it turns out after the event that the operation of certain services in connection with the discharge of public service obligations was not economically viable, therefore constitutes a financial measure which falls within the concept of State aid within the meaning of art 92(1) of the Treaty.

> Third, the compensation cannot exceed what is necessary to cover all or part of the costs incurred in the discharge of public service obligations, taking into account the relevant receipts and a reasonable profit for discharging those obligations. Compliance with such a condition is essential to ensure that the recipient undertaking is not given any advantage which distorts or threatens to distort competition by strengthening that undertaking's competitive position.

> Fourth, where the undertaking which is to discharge public service obligations, in a specific case, is not chosen pursuant to a public procurement procedure which would allow for the selection of the tenderer capable of providing those services at the least cost to the community, the level of compensation needed must be determined on the

---

167 Proposal for a Third Postal Directive, art 1(10). These conditions may, however, be imposed in the context of USPs designated by the Member State. The Explanatory Memorandum justifies this distinction on the basis that designated USPs 'may be subject to a different type of a regulation as they may have to meet different objectives or operate under a distinct legal basis, such as public ownership' (Explanatory Memorandum, para 3.3.1).

168 *Altmark Trans* Case C–280/00 [2003] ECR 1 7747; See also Commission's Communication on Services of General Interest COM(2007) 724 final SEC(2007) 1514 SEC(2007) 1515 SEC(2007) 1516 – 20 November 2007. Services of general economic interest (SGEIs) are activities economic in nature, such as postal services, telecommunications, transport services and also the supply of electricity and gas. These services are also subject to the internal market and competition rules of the EC Treaty. However, if application of these rules obstructs the performance of tasks of general interest, these services may be exempted from the provisions of the Treaty.

basis of an analysis of the costs which a typical undertaking, well run and adequately provided with means of transport so as to be able to meet the necessary public service requirements, would have incurred in discharging those obligations, taking into account the relevant receipts and a reasonable profit for discharging the obligations.

(c) Access to the postal network

6.132 Access to the downstream elements of the postal network (ie sorting and delivery facilities) is not currently expressly dealt with under the Postal Directive. A new art 11a provides that transparent and non-discriminatory access conditions are made available to postcode systems, address databases, post office boxes, collection and delivery boxes, information on change of address, redirection services and return to sender services.

(d) Uniform tariffs

6.133 As discussed above, the Postal Directive allows an exception to the requirement that tariffs are geared to costs in the context of uniform tariffs for services forming part of the universal service. The European Commission takes the view that 'the mandatory provision of uniform tariffs in a fully competitive environment may lead to increasing costs for and risks to the viability of certain services, as the universal service provider will risk losing profitable business in those areas subject to competitive pressure.'[169] Accordingly, the European Commission proposes that tariff uniformity be limited to 'single piece' postal items (including those for national and EU destinations) subject to 'single piece tariffs'. This would prevent Member States from requiring USPs to provide uniform tariffs for services such as bulk mail and would, effectively, limit uniform tariffs to services paid over the counter through stamps. In addition to the pricing requirements of 'affordability', 'geared to cost', 'transparency' and 'non-discrimination' comes the new requirement that prices 'give incentives for an efficient universal service provision.'[170]

Competition Law

6.134 The Competition Authority and ComReg are jointly responsible for administering and enforcing the Competition Act 2002 in the electronic communications sector, further to the Communications Regulation (Amendment) Act 2007. Sections 4 and 5 of the Competition Act 2002 contain provisions which are closely modelled on arts 81 and 82 of the EC Treaty. Please see **Ch 7** on competition law regulation for more information in this regard.

---

169 Explanatory Memorandum, para 3.2.2.
170 ComReg suggests in its submission to the Department that a carefully designed *ex ante* price cap price control may be the only way of ensuring compliance with the tariff principles, while giving operators the appropriate freedom to respond to the initiatives of competitors and the incentive to improve efficiency. In the short term, it considers that this will need to be backed up by a detailed *ex post* review of prices.

6.135 While ComReg does not have competition law *vires* in respect of the postal sector, ComReg and the Competition Authority have overlapping concerns as postal liberalisation continues. In accordance with art 81(1) of the EC Treaty and the *Ahmed Saeed* case,[171] ComReg is obliged to ensure that its decisions are consistent with competition law. ComReg works closely with the Competition Authority when dealing with relevant issues in the postal area. As already noted, as currently implemented, the Postal Directive permits the reservation of certain services to the USP. However, the scope of the reserved area should not exceed what is necessary to guarantee the maintenance of the universal service. If the scope of the reserved area does in fact exceed what is necessary, the Member State will have infringed not only the Postal Directive but also art 86(1) EC in conjunction with art 82 EC. Where the reserved area does not go beyond what is provided for in the Postal Directive it is *prima facie* justified under art 86(2).[172] Once the Third Postal Directive is implemented, the reserved area will be abolished. In addition, art 22.2 of the consolidated Postal Directive, as inserted by the Third Postal Directive, states that NRAs may also be charged with ensuring compliance with competition rules in the postal sector. There is a European Commission Notice on the application of the competition rules to the postal sector and on assessment of certain State measures relating to postal services.[173]

ENFORCEMENT

6.136 Enforcement of the Communications Regulation Act 2002, as amended, of the Electronic Communications Regulations, of the Wireless Telegraphy Acts and Regulations and of the Postal Regulations can be both civil and criminal. This section will examine both the civil and criminal aspects of the enforcement of ComReg's powers in the area of electronic communications and postal services. In respect of electronic communications, ComReg has the choice to exercise its civil or criminal jurisdiction in respect of regulatory offences or to apply competition law to the same factual scenario. As noted above, ComReg does not have competition law jurisdiction in respect of the postal sector. Criminal enforcement is also relatively limited in the postal sector, with only summary offences provided for. In general, enforcement can happen by way of a complaint being made to a Regulator or by way of ComReg investigating a matter on its own initiative. There is also a process for dispute resolution where a dispute arises.

Complaints to ComReg and Requests for Dispute Resolutions

Complaints

6.137 There is no set format for submitting a complaint to ComReg. Complaints may be a few lines by way of an email or more sophisticated submissions drafted by lawyers

---

171 *Ahmed Saeed Luftreisen & Silver Line Reisebuero v Zentrala zur Bekaempfung Unlauterer Wettbebwerbs* Case 66/86 [1989] ECR 803.
172 The Postal Notice, para 5.4.
173 98/C 39/02.

on behalf of their clients. ComReg Document 03/20 sets out ComReg's approach to consumer complaints, as does ComReg Document 03/86 – Decision Notice D16/03.[174]

ComReg is not bound to accept a complaint; however, it does seek to consider all complaints and to respond to the complainant informing the complainant whether the matter will be investigated further and again when the matter is ultimately resolved. There is also no time limit within which ComReg has to deal with a complaint or make a decision.

There is no fee for submitting a complaint to ComReg and, given that ComReg will, if it is a valid complaint, utilise its investigate powers to examine the complaint in detail, this is often a time- and cost-effective way of dealing with a matter for a party, as opposed to private litigation.

6.138 ComReg has obligations to deal with matters confidentially. Submissions are frequently made to ComReg by parties containing commercially sensitive information. ComReg is obliged to maintain as confidential any information provided to it expressed to be confidential, except where ComReg has good reason to consider otherwise. Section 24 of the Communications Regulation Act 2002 makes it an offence, subject to a fine of €3,000, to disclose confidential information unless duly authorised by the Commissioners to do so. In respect of electronic communications, confidentiality obligations are set out in the Framework Regulations and also in the Access Regulations. ComReg's obligation to maintain as confidential any information which is provided to it on a confidential basis is set out in regs 21, 17(11) and 18(2) of the Framework Regulations. Regulation 3 of the Access Regulations also provides for the treatment by ComReg of confidential information.

6.139 ComReg has published guidelines on its website regarding the treatment of confidential information (Document No 05/24). In line with European Commission best practice,[175] complainants do not have a right of access to business secrets or other confidential information that ComReg has obtained in the course of an investigation. Notwithstanding the above, parties are of course entitled to pursue their rights as set out in the Freedom of Information Acts 1997 and 2003, which provisions, however, it must be noted also contain exceptions in relation to confidential information. Please see para **1.052** of **Ch 1** Introduction for further information on the Freedom of Information Acts 1997 and 2003.

Dispute resolution

6.140 Dispute resolution processes may be availed of under reg 31 of the Framework Regulations, reg 28 of the USO Regulations, s 57 of the Communications Regulation Act 2002, as amended, and reg 15 of the Postal Regulations.

---

174 See http://www.comreg.ie.

175 This is similar to the European Commission Notice on the Rules for Access to the Commission File in Competition Cases, 2005/C 325/07. Indeed the Court of First Instance has ruled in *Matra-Hachette SA v Commission* Case T–17/93 [1994] ECR II–595 that complainants do not have the same rights and guarantees as the parties under investigation.

Dispute resolution under the Framework Regulations

6.141 Under reg 31 of the Framework Regulations, in the event of a dispute between wholesale undertakings, subject to certain exceptions, ComReg must, at the request of either party, initiate an investigation of the dispute and make a determination to resolve the dispute as soon as possible and, except in circumstances which ComReg considers exceptional, within four months of the request being made. The dispute resolution procedure set down in reg 31 of Framework Regulations is detailed in ComReg Decision Notice D18/03 (Document 03/89). Regulation 31 also applies to disputes arising between undertakings in connection with obligations laid down in the Mobile Phone Roaming Regulation, further to reg 4 of Communications (Mobile Telephone Roaming) Regulations 2007.[176]

6.142 The main obligations arising from the legislation are:

   (i)   ComReg is obliged to issue a binding decision to resolve a dispute within four months, unless there are exceptional circumstances.

   (ii)   ComReg may decline to resolve a dispute where other mechanisms (for example mediation) may be used more effectively. However, if alternative mechanisms do not lead to resolution within four months, and if the matter has not been brought before the courts, then ComReg can issue a binding decision to resolve the dispute as quickly as possible, and in any event within four months.

   (iii) The decisions of ComReg shall be publicly available, subject to commercial confidentiality. The parties involved in the dispute shall be given a full statement of the reasons for the decision.

   (iv) The dispute resolution procedures do not preclude either party from bringing an action before the courts.

It is important to note that the issue(s) at dispute must involve a breach of specific regulations or regulatory obligations imposed by ComReg. Prior to accepting the dispute, ComReg determines whether there is a breach of obligations and that ComReg has the legal basis upon which to make a determination on the matter. Undertakings engaged or intending to engage in the provision of electronic communications networks or services or associated facilities can lodge disputes under reg 31 of the Framework Regulations.

Dispute resolution under the Universal Service Regulations

6.143 Article 34 of the Universal Service Directive requires Member States to ensure that there are out-of-court procedures in place to deal with unresolved disputes involving consumers, which concern issues covered by the Universal Service Directive. Member States may choose to extend these procedures to disputes that involve other end-users. The procedure must be transparent, simple and inexpensive and must enable disputes to be settled fairly and promptly. Under art 34(2), Member

---

176 SI 792/2007.

States are required to ensure that the legislation they adopt to implement the requirement for out-of-court dispute resolution procedures does not hamper the establishment of complaints offices. It must not hamper the provision of online services to facilitate access to dispute resolution by consumers and end-users. A system of reimbursement and/or compensation may also be adopted by a Member State where this is warranted. These procedures are without prejudice to national courts procedures, which may be invoked for resolving disputes.

Regulation 28 of the Universal Service Regulations transposes art 34 of the Universal Service Directive in Ireland. Regulation 28 also applies to disputes involving a consumer or end-user in connection with obligations laid down in the Mobile Phone Roaming Regulation, further to reg 5 of Communications (Mobile Telephone Roaming) Regulations 2007.[177]

Dispute resolution under the Communications Regulation Act 2002

6.144 Section 57 of the Communications Regulation Act 2002 provides that a network operator has the right to negotiate an agreement to share physical infrastructure with other infrastructure providers and may, upon the commencement of any negotiations, serve notice on ComReg of such negotiations. ComReg may, on its own initiative, or shall, if requested by either party, specify the period within which negotiations on physical infrastructure sharing shall be completed. Where agreement is not reached within the period specified by ComReg, it shall take such steps as are necessary to resolve the dispute in accordance with dispute resolution procedures. ComReg may:

(a) having carried out a preliminary examination of the matter, decide not to intervene in those negotiations; or

(b) discontinue the intervention in those negotiations where ComReg considers that:

(i) the request for intervention is trivial or vexatious, or

(ii) the person making the request has not taken reasonable steps to reach an agreement on physical infrastructure sharing.

6.145 ComReg shall resolve a dispute referred to it further to s 57 of the Communications Regulation Act 2002 in accordance with procedures established and maintained by it. The procedures shall be made available, on request, to interested parties free of charge. In making a decision in relation to a dispute, ComReg may impose conditions for physical infrastructure sharing and such conditions may include:

(a) conditions in respect of conformity with the relevant standards relating to establishment, operation, maintenance and repair of electronic communications infrastructure and physical infrastructure;

(b) compliance with essential requirements or the maintenance of the quality of electronic communications services; or

(c) rules for the apportionment of the costs of physical infrastructure sharing.

177 SI 792/2007.

ComReg shall notify, in writing, the network operator and physical infrastructure provider, as appropriate, of the reasons for such conditions.

6.146 The dispute resolution procedures under s 57 of the Communications Regulation Act 2002 shall include provisions for public consultation during which all interested parties shall be given an opportunity to express their views. ComReg, in reaching a decision pursuant to the dispute resolution procedures, shall take into account the:

(a)   the interests of consumers of electronic communications services;

(b)   any requirements imposed by an enactment or instrument;

(c)   the public interest, including traffic control and the protection of the environment and of amenities;

(d)   the desirability of encouraging the sharing of electronic communications infrastructure;

(e)   the provision of electronic communications services that are not available at the time of the making of the conditions;

(f)   the availability of alternatives to the physical infrastructure sharing requested;

(g)   the need to provide access to the market for electronic communications services to network operators;

(h)   the need to maintain the security of electronic communications networks and the ability of providers of electronic communications services to use different types of electronic communications infrastructure and physical infrastructure;

(i)   the nature of the request in relation to the resources available to the network operator or physical infrastructure provider concerned to meet that request;

(j)   the promotion of competition between electronic communications services providers; and

(k)   the need to maintain a universal service.

In this section, universal service is meant in the sense of electronic communications universal service.

Dispute resolution in the postal sector

6.147 Regulation 15(1) of the Postal Regulations provides that An Post and any other postal service provider with 'an annual turnover of €500,000, exclusive of VAT' must draw up:

> transparent, simple and inexpensive procedures for dealing with users' complaints, particularly in cases involving loss, theft, damage or non-compliance with service quality standards (including procedures for determining where responsibility lies in cases where more than one operator is involved). These procedures shall enable disputes to be settled fairly and promptly with provision, where warranted, for a system of reimbursement or compensation or both.

These procedures should be drawn up in accordance with guidelines laid down by ComReg in consultation with the postal service provider.

6.148 ComReg has issued legally enforceable guidelines to An Post and all operators who have indicated that they are providing services within the scope of the universal service (ComReg Doc 07/105). The main objective of these legally enforceable guidelines is to assist postal service providers who provide postal services, within the scope of the universal service, to draw up transparent, simple and inexpensive procedures for dealing with user complaints and to ensure an appropriate form of redress is available to the user in the event of loss and substantial delay,[178] theft, damage or non-compliance with service quality standards. Postal consumers in this way have an appropriate form of redress, regardless of service provider, and have the further guarantee of an appropriate compensation mechanism. The scheme for compensation in these cases can be in the form of a number of stamps and/or a cash amount, provided that the claim is in proportion to the actual cost of the mailing. These guidelines were to be fully implemented by all relevant service providers no later than 18 March 2008.

Whistleblowers

Section 24 of the Communications Regulation Act 2002 – protection of whistleblowers

6.149 Section 24A(1) of the Communications Regulation Act 2002 provides that a person who makes an appropriate disclosure of information to ComReg about the conduct of an undertaking, an associate of an undertaking or an association of undertakings incurs no civil or criminal liability for having done so. Section 24A(2) provides that a person makes an appropriate disclosure of information about the conduct of an undertaking, or an associate of an undertaking or an association of undertakings, only if:

(a) the conduct relates to the provision of an electronic communications network or service or an associated facility; and

(b) the person—

(i) believes on reasonable grounds that the information is true, or

(ii) not being able to form a belief on reasonable grounds about the truth of the information, believes on reasonable grounds that the information may be true and to be of sufficient significance to justify its disclosure.

In particular, s 24A(3) provides that ComReg may not divulge the identity of the person who has made an appropriate disclosure to it without first obtaining the person's consent, except in so far as it may be necessary to ensure proper investigation of the matters to which the disclosure relates. Section 24B provides for the tortious liability of an undertaking for victimising a whistleblower. Section 24C makes it an indictable criminal offence for whistleblowers to deliberately provide false information.

---

178 Substantial delay for domestic mail is defined as any item that has not been received within 7 calendar days and for cross-border mail within 10 calendar days.

Investigations by ComReg

6.150 ComReg has specific information-gathering powers and may require attendance before it to give evidence on oath.

Information gathering

6.151 Section 10 of the Communications Regulation Act 2002 is amended to include sub-s 10(da) the purpose of which is to confer very wide information-gathering powers on ComReg. Under this amendment, in carrying out investigations into matters relating to the supply of, and access to, electronic communications services and networks, ComReg will be able:

> [F]or the purpose of contributing to an open and competitive market and also for statistical purposes, to collect, compile, extract, disseminate and publish information from undertakings relating to the provision of electronic communications services, electronic communications networks and associated facilities and the transmission of such services on those networks …

6.152 Section 13 of the Communications Regulation Act 2002, as amended, gives the Minister and ComReg enhanced information-requesting powers. Section 13D provides ComReg with extensive information-gathering powers and may require an undertaking to provide ComReg with such written information as it considers necessary to enable it to carry out its functions. Failure to disclose information pursuant to s 13 to the Minister or ComReg is an offence and an undertaking could be liable on summary conviction to a fine of €5,000, and daily fines of €1,000 up to a maximum of €5,000. Unlike s 10(da), s 13D applies to postal services as well as electronic communications.

Information gathering through examination under oath

6.153 Section 38A enables ComReg to request that a person appear before it for the purpose of giving evidence on oath or in order to provide requested documentation. Failing to appear represents a summary offence and could entail a fine of up to €5,000. This section also applies to both electronic communications and postal services.

Information gathering under the various statutory instruments

6.154 Regulation 17 of the Framework Regulations also provides ComReg with information-gathering powers in respect of the electronic communications sector for the purpose of ensuring compliance with decisions or determinations made in accordance with the Framework Regulations, the Access Regulations, the Universal Service Regulations or the Authorisation Regulations.

Regulation 17(3) of the Postal Regulations provides that a USP in the postal sector shall furnish ComReg with any such information as ComReg may reasonably require for the purposes of his or her functions under those regulations or the Postal Directive.

Authorised officers/dawn raids

6.155 In order to investigate possible civil breaches or potential criminal offences, ComReg's may appoint authorised officers under s 39 of the Communications Regulation Act 2002 who may visit companies for the purposes of gathering information. This section applies to both the electronic communications sector and the postal sector. It provides that for the purposes of the exercise by ComReg of its functions under the Communications Regulation 2002 Act, as amended, a transferred function or any regulations made under the Act of 1972, an authorised officer may:

(a) enter, at any reasonable time, any premises or place or any vehicle or vessel where any activity connected with the provision of electronic communications services, networks or associated facilities or postal services takes place or, in the opinion of the officer takes place, and search and inspect the premises, place, vehicle or vessel and any books, documents or records found therein,

(b) require any such person to produce to him or her any books, documents or records relating to the provision of electronic communications services, networks or associated facilities or postal services which are in the person's power or control and, in the case of information in a non-legible form to reproduce it in a legible form, and to give to the officer such information as he or she may reasonably require in relation to any entries in such books, documents or records,

(c) secure for later inspection any such premises, place, vehicle or vessel or part thereof in which books, documents or records relating to the provision of electronic communications services, networks or associated facilities or postal services are kept or there are reasonable grounds for believing that such books, documents or records are kept,

(d) inspect and take extracts from or make copies of any such books, documents or records (including, in the case of information in a non-legible form, a copy of or extract from such information in a permanent legible form),

(e) remove and retain such books, documents or records for such period as may be reasonable for further examination,

(f) require the person to maintain such books, documents or records for such period of time, as may be reasonable, as the authorised officer directs,

(g) require the person to give to the officer any information which he or she may reasonably require with regard to the provision of electronic communications services, networks or associated facilities or postal services,

(h) make such inspections, tests and measurements of machinery, apparatus, appliances and other equipment on the premises or vessel or at the place or in the vehicle as he or she considers appropriate,

(i) require any person on the premises or vessel or at the place or in the vehicle having charge of, or otherwise concerned with the operation of, any machinery, apparatus, appliance or other equipment (including data equipment) or any associated apparatus or material, to afford the officer all reasonable assistance in relation thereto,

(j) take photographs or make any record or visual recording of any activity on such premises or vessel, at such place or in such vehicle.

6.156 Section 39 provides that ComReg may appoint persons to be authorised officers for the purposes of the Communications Regulation Act 2002. A person appointed shall be furnished by ComReg with a certificate of his or her appointment. The authorised officer must show his or her certificate (if requested), and inform the investigated party of the power being invoked, explaining the consequences of failing or refusing to comply, including outlining the penalties and, where appropriate, administering a caution. Most significantly, the section permits authorised officers to do certain things including entering premises where any activity connected with the provision of electronic communication services takes place and searching and inspecting books, documents or records found therein.

6.157 Section 39(6) provides that a person who obstructs, impedes or assaults an authorised officer in the exercise of a power under that section, or fails or refuses to comply with a requirement under that section, or alters, suppresses or destroys any books, documents or records which the person concerned has been required to produce, or may reasonably expect to be required to produce, or gives information which is false or misleading in a material respect, or falsely represents himself or herself, is guilty of an offence and is liable on summary conviction to a fine not exceeding €3,000.

Search warrants

6.158 Where an authorised officer in exercise of his or her powers is prevented from entering a premises, an application may be made under s 40 for a warrant to authorise such entry. In addition, an authorised officer shall not, other than with the consent of the occupier, enter a private dwelling unless he or she has obtained a warrant under s 40 authorising such entry.

6.159 Section 40 provides for search warrants and sets out that if a judge of the District Court is satisfied on the sworn information of an authorised officer that there are reasonable grounds for suspecting that information required by an authorised officer for the purpose of ComReg exercising its functions, may be found in a particular premises, the judge may issue a warrant to search those premises. The warrant authorises the authorised officer, accompanied if considered necessary by other authorised officers or members of the Garda Síochána, to enter, if need be by reasonable force, the premises, place, vessel or vehicle, at any time or times, within one month from the date of issue of the warrant, on production of the warrant (if required), and exercise all or any of the powers conferred on an authorised officer under s 39.

Indemnification of staff

6.160 Section 41 provides that where ComReg is satisfied that any member of the staff or an authorised officer has discharged his or her duties in pursuance of the functions of ComReg in a *bona fide* manner, ComReg shall indemnify such member of staff or authorised officer against all actions or claims howsoever arising in respect of the discharge by him or her of his or her duties.

Evidence and presumptions

6.161 Sections 46B, 46C, 46D and 46E of the Communications Act 2002, as amended, contain provisions to provide for admissibility of expert evidence, the provision of documents to the jury and new evidentiary presumptions. These provisions are similar to those found in the Competition Act 2002.

6.162 Section 46B provides for expert witnesses in civil or criminal proceedings and states that their opinion is admissible in evidence of matters that call for expertise or special knowledge relevant to the proceedings.

6.163 Section 46C provides that in a trial on indictment of an offence, the trial judge may order copies of any of the following documents to be given to the jury in such form as the judge considers appropriate:

(a) any document admitted in evidence at the trial;

(b) the transcript of the opening speeches of counsel;

(c) any charts, diagrams, graphics, schedules or agreed summaries of evidence produced at the trial;

(d) the transcript of the whole or any part of the evidence given at the trial;

(e) the transcript of the closing speeches of counsel; and

(f) the transcript of the trial judge's charge to the jury.

6.164 Section 46D sets out the presumptions that are to apply in civil and criminal proceedings under this Act and under the related enactments. Section 46D(2) provides that a document purporting to have been created by a person is presumed, unless the contrary is shown, to have been created by that person. A statement contained in that document is, unless the document expressly attributes the statement to some other person, presumed to have been made by that person. Section 46D(3) provides that a document purporting to have been created by a person and addressed and sent to a second person is presumed, unless the contrary is show, to have been created and sent by the person and received by the second person. Section 46D(4) covers the situation where a document is recovered from an electronic database. Again, it is presumed that the author is, unless the contrary is shown, the person who ordinarily uses the database in that person's course of business. Section 46D(5) provides that if an authorised officer who has removed one or more documents from a place gives evidence in proceedings that, to the best of the officer's knowledge and belief, the material is the property of a specified person, the material is, unless the contrary is shown, presumed to be that person's property. If an authorised officer gives evidence that material is the property of a specified person and also gives evidence that, to the best of the officer's knowledge and belief, the material relates to a particular trade, profession or other activity carried on by that person, the material is, unless the contrary is shown, presumed to be material that relates to such a trade, profession or activity.

6.165 Section 46E deals with the admissibility of evidence. It provides for the admissibility of statements contained in certain documents. If a document contains a statement from a competent person (ie a person who might reasonably be expected to have knowledge of the act or omission) that an act was done or omitted to be done, that statement is admissible in evidence in relation to proceedings for an offence, provided that certain conditions are satisfied. This section does not affect the admissibility in proceedings for an offence of a document as evidence, if the document would be admissible in the proceedings because of the operation of any other enactment or a rule of common law.[179]

Privilege

6.166 Privilege is the right of a party to refuse to disclose a document or to answer questions on the grounds of a special interest recognised by law. It covers a range of areas and examples include legal professional privilege,[180] the privilege against self-incrimination[181] and communications 'without prejudice' in the course of negotiations to obtain a settlement of litigation. There are two types of legal professional privilege

---

179 Criminal Evidence Act 1992, Pt II created a new broad exception to the hearsay rule in respect of documents compiled in the ordinary course of business. Section 5(1) of the Criminal Evidence Act 1992 provides that information contained in a document shall be admissible in any criminal proceedings as evidence of any fact stated therein of which direct oral evidence would be admissible provided that the information: (i) was compiled in the ordinary course of a business; (ii) was supplied by a person (whether or not he so compiled it and is identifiable) who had or may reasonably be supposed to have had personal knowledge of the matters dealt with; and (iii) in the case of information in a non-legible form that has been reproduced in permanent legible form, was reproduced in the course of normal operation of the reproduction system concerned. Where information is admissible under s 5 but is expressed in terms that are not intelligible to the average person without explanation, an explanation of the information is also admissible if either: (i) it is given orally by a person who is competent to do so; or (ii) it is contained in a document and the document purports to be signed by such a person. Section 6 of the Criminal Evidence Act 1992 makes provision for the proof of compliance with the conditions of admissibility by means of a certificate rather than oral evidence. Oral evidence may still be required in some instances.

180 Communication passing between a client and his lawyer, and *vice versa*, involving the giving of legal advice is privileged provided it occurred in the course of professional legal relationships between them. The privilege is that of the client and not of the lawyer, accordingly only the client can waive privilege.

181 *Heaney v Ireland* [1996] 1 IR 580; *Re National Irish Bank Ltd* [1999] 1 IR 145 where the respondents argued that there was a right under Art 38.1 of the Constitution not to have compelled testimony used against an accused during a criminal trial; *Dunnes Stores (Ireland) Co v Ryan* [2002] 2 IR 60; *Curtain v Dáil Éireann* [2006] IESC 14. A defendant will not be entitled to rely on the privilege against self-incrimination if he provides information on a voluntary basis. The privilege only comes into play were the information is compelled. While information which persons are compelled to give to ComReg (for example as a result of the exercise by ComReg of its s 39 powers) may not be used in evidence in a criminal prosecution against those persons, this does not apply to documents, as opposed to information. A caution may be issued to those providing the information voluntarily. A caution may include wording setting out that the person being investigated is not obliged to say anything unless he or she wishes to do so but that anything which the person says will be taken down in writing and may be used in evidence. (contd .../)

in Ireland – litigation privilege[182] and legal advice privilege.[183] The courts in Ireland do not distinguish between an in-house lawyer and one based in a law firm. Accordingly, any legal advice from an in-house lawyer sent to his or her client will be privileged under Irish law.

6.167 In practice, if a dawn raid is conducted by the European Commission using EC law procedures, in-house legal advice is not protected.[184] If, however, an authorised officer visit is conducted by the Irish Regulators, such as ComReg or the Competition Authority, under Irish procedures, advice provided by in-house lawyers will still be bound by the Irish legal position, which considers such documents may be privileged.

Electronic Communications – Civil enforcement

6.168 Where ComReg makes a finding of non-compliance, it can issue a direction pursuant to reg 23 of the Authorisation Regulations, reg 17 of the Access Regulations, reg 31 of the Universal Service Regulations or reg 34 of the Framework Regulations.

Obligations contained in the various regulations, in the general authorisation, spectrum license or rights of use for numbers, as well as any directions issued by ComReg under those obligations, may be enforced by means of civil procedure or by means of criminal procedure. ComReg does not have the power to impose civil fines or financial penalties; fines may only be imposed by the courts.

Civil enforcement under the Communications Regulation Act 2002 Act

Compliance notices

6.169 Section 44 of the Communications Regulation Act 2002 details a compliance procedure entailing notification of intention to prosecute and provides undertakings with an opportunity to remedy any perceived non-compliance. Under s 44, the undertaking is required to make a payment to ComReg where it remedies any non-

---

181 (contd) The person may also be reminded that he or she is there voluntarily and is free to leave at any time. In England it is recognised that a corporate entity can invoke this right; however, this has not been decided upon in this jurisdiction.

182 Litigation privilege protects from disclosure confidential communications between lawyer and client made for the dominant purpose of being used in connection with existing or contemplated litigation. The rationale behind it is to allow a litigant prepare for litigation without the danger of any documents produced for that purpose being disclosable to another party. Litigation privilege includes communications between a client or his lawyer and a third party. An example would be the report of an expert witness prepared for use in the litigation. The dominant purpose of the document's creation is to prepare for litigation, either pending or threatened.

183 Legal advice privilege can arise in circumstances where litigation is not in contemplation. Legal advice privilege protects from disclosure, confidential communications between lawyer and client, made for the dominant purpose of seeking or giving legal advice.

184 The European courts do, however, adopt a different approach: *AM&S v The Commission* [1982] ECR 1575 and *Akzo Chemicals Ltd and Akcros Chemicals Ltd v Commission of the European Communities* (CFI judgement on appeal) and do not recognise privilege for in-house lawyers in the context of a European Commission competition law investigation.

compliance. This section has been amended to increase the payment that must be made by an undertaking under this section from €1,000 to €1,500. This provision in effect commutes a criminal offence into a civil breach.

Infrastructure sharing

6.170 Section 57A gives ComReg additional power in respect of electronic communications infrastructure-sharing arrangements and allows ComReg to impose conditions on both operators and physical infrastructure providers, eg owners of ducts. ComReg can apply to the High Court for a compliance order and payment of a financial penalty in respect of matters falling under this section.

Overbilling

6.171 Section 46 provides for the civil enforcement in instances of overbilling in respect of electronic communications. If an undertaking has overbilled, or has overbilled in the past and may again, ComReg may apply to the High Court for a restraining order requiring the undertaking to cease contravening s 45 and not to repeat the contravention. Such an application is to be by motion. The High Court may make such interim or interlocutory order as it considers appropriate pending determination of an application. An application for a restraining order may be accompanied by a further application for an order directing the respondent to pay to ComReg a financial penalty of such amount as is proposed by ComReg having regard to the circumstances of the contravention, ie overbilling committed by the respondent. Factors considered by the court are:

(a)   the duration of the contravention;

(b)   the effect of the contravention on other parties to the relevant decision and on consumers;

(c)   the submission of ComReg with respect to what it considers to be the appropriate amount; and

(d)   any excuse or explanation for the contravention provided by the respondent.

If the High Court makes an order under this section, it may make such ancillary orders as it considers appropriate.

Civil enforcement under the Framework Regulations and specific regulations

6.172 Regulation 16 of the Authorisation Regulations, reg 18 of the Access Regulations, reg 32 of the Universal Services Regulations and reg 35 of the Framework Regulations make provisions for enforcement of conditions or directions by means of civil procedure. They are based on the enforcement provisions of art 10 of the Authorisation Directive.

6.173 Regulation 34[185] of the Framework Regulations sets out that ComReg may, for the purpose of further specifying requirements to be complied with relating to an obligation imposed by or under the Framework Regulations, issue directions to an undertaking to do or refrain from doing anything which ComReg specifies in the direction.

6.174 Regulation 35[186] of the Framework Regulations provides for the enforcement proceedings and provides that where ComReg finds that a person has not complied with an obligation under the Framework Regulations or under a direction, it can notify the person of those findings and give the person an opportunity to state his or her views or remedy any non-compliance not later than:

(a)   one month after issue of the notification;

(b)   such shorter period as is agreed; or

(c)   such longer period as may be specified by ComReg.

ComReg may publish any such notification subject to the protection of confidentiality. ComReg may amend or revoke any notification under this regulation.

6.175 Where, at the end of the period referred to in the notification, ComReg is of the opinion that the person concerned has not complied with the condition or the direction, then ComReg may, except where criminal proceedings have been instigated, apply to the High Court for such order as may be appropriate seeking compliance with the condition or the direction. The High Court may only make an order of compliance. The court may make an order compelling compliance with the conditions or direction, or it may refuse ComReg's application in this regard. If the court does order compliance, it must stipulate a reasonable period for the person to comply with the condition or direction.

6.176 An application for an order shall be by motion and the court, when dealing with the matter, may make such interim or interlocutory order as it considers appropriate. The court shall not deny any interim or interlocutory relief solely on the basis that the Regulator may not suffer any damage if such relief were not granted pending conclusion of the action. An application for an order may include an application for an order to pay to the Regulator such amount, by way of financial penalty, as ComReg may propose as appropriate in the light of the non-compliance. In deciding on such an application, the court shall decide the amount (if any) of the financial penalty which should be payable and shall not be bound by the amount proposed by ComReg. Any financial penalty ordered by the court to be paid by a person shall be paid to and retained by ComReg as income.

---

185 The power to issue directions is also contained in Access Regulations, reg 17; Authorisation Regulations, reg 23 and USO Regulations, reg 31.

186 Similar provisions are contained in Authorisation Regulations, reg 16; Access Regulations, reg 18 and Universal Services Regulations, reg 32.

6.177 In deciding what amount (if any) should be payable, the court shall consider the circumstances of the non-compliance, including:

    (i)   its duration;

   (ii)   the effect on consumers, users and other operators;

  (iii)   the submissions of the Regulator on the appropriate amount; and

  (iv)   any excuse or explanation for the non-compliance.

6.178 In cases where there is evidence of a breach which represents an immediate and serious threat to public safety, security or health, ComReg may issue urgent directions pursuant to reg 16(9) of the Authorisation Regulations, reg 18(8) of the Access Regulations or reg 32(4) of the USO Regulations.[187] Where ComReg has evidence of non-compliance that will, in its opinion, create serious economic or operational problems for undertakings or users of an ECN or an ECS, it may issue a direction requiring immediate compliance pursuant to reg 16(11) of the Authorisation Regulations, reg 18(10) of the Access Regulations or reg 32(11) of the USO Regulations.[188] A person may make representations to ComReg concerning a requirement made of that person under these urgent measures and ComReg must consider those representations and may confirm, amend or withdraw the requirement further to reg 16(12) of the Authorisation Regulations, reg 18(11) of the Access Regulations or reg 32(12) of the USO Regulations.[189]

6.179 Where criminal proceedings have been instituted or a notice given under s 44 of the Communications Regulation Act 2002, ComReg shall not make an application for an order further to reg 35(8) of the Framework Regulations.[190] Also, where ComReg has made an application for civil enforcement, it is precluded from bringing criminal proceedings further to reg 33(1) of the Framework Regulations in respect of the same matter.[191]

6.180 Regulation 36[192] of the Framework Regulations deals with the service of determinations, directions and notifications and provides that where the Regulator issues a determination, direction or notification, it shall be in writing, state the reasons on which it is based and be addressed to the person concerned, and, as soon as practicable, be sent or given in any of the following ways:

    (a)   by delivering it to the person;

    (b)   by leaving it at the address at which the person carries on business;

---

187 There is no such corresponding provision in the Framework Regulations.

188 There is no such corresponding provision in the Framework Regulations.

189 There is no such corresponding provision in the Framework Regulations.

190 Authorisation Regulations, reg 16(15); Access Regulations, reg 18(13); USO Regulations, reg 32(14).

191 Authorisation Regulations, reg 25(2); Access Regulations, reg 20(1); USO Regulations, reg 36(3).

192 Access Regulations, reg 19; USO Regulations, reg 34 and Authorisation Regulations, reg 24.

(c) by sending it by pre-paid registered post to the address at which the person carries on business; or

(d) in any case where the Regulator considers that the immediate giving of the determination, direction or notification is required, by sending it by means of a facsimile machine or by email.

6.181 Regulation 33 of the Universal Service Regulations provides for enforcement by the Director of Consumer Affairs, now the National Consumer Agency. The National Consumer Agency, in a case of non-compliance with reg 20(3) or (5), may issue a direction to the undertaking concerned to comply with the regulation and any stipulations contained in the direction. The Director of Consumer Affairs may appoint a person to be an authorised officer for the purposes of para (3) or (5) of reg 20. Section 39(2), (3), (4) and (5) and ss 40 and 41 of the 2002 Act apply in respect of an authorised officer appointed under para (4) and, for the purposes of those regulations accordingly, references to ComReg in those provisions should be read as including references to the National Consumer Agency.

Civil enforcement under the Roaming Regulations

6.182 The civil enforcement under reg 7 of Communications (Mobile Telephone Roaming) Regulations 2007[193] is very similar to the civil enforcement set out in the Framework and Specific Regulations. Regulation 7 of the Roaming Regulations provides for civil enforcement and compliance orders. It provides that where ComReg finds that an undertaking:

(a) being the operator of a visited network, has failed to comply with its obligations under art 3 of the Roaming Regulation[194] in relation to wholesale charges for the making of regulated roaming calls originating on that network; or

(b) being a home provider, has failed to comply with its obligations under art 4 or 6 of the Roaming Regulation[195] to roaming customers; or

(c) has failed to comply with a requirement of ComReg under art 7(4) or (6), of the Roaming Regulation;[196]

it shall notify the undertaking of those findings and give it an opportunity to state its views or remedy any non-compliance not later than:

(a) one month after issue of the notification;

(b) such shorter period; or

(c) such longer period as may be specified by ComReg.

---

193 SI 792/2007.

194 Regulation (EC) No 717/2007 of the European Parliament and the Council of 27 June 2007 OJ No L171, 29.06.2007, p 32.

195 Regulation (EC) No 717/2007 of the European Parliament and the Council of 27 June 2007 OJ No L171, 29.06.2007, p 32.

196 Regulation (EC) No 717/2007 of the European Parliament and the Council of 27 June 2007 OJ No L171, 29.06.2007, p 32.

ComReg may publish, in such manner as it thinks fit, any notification given by it under this Regulation, subject to the protection of the confidentiality. Where ComReg is of the opinion that the undertaking concerned has not complied with the obligation or the requirement, it may apply to the High Court for such order as may be appropriate to compel compliance with the obligation or requirement. The Court may, as it thinks fit, make an order compelling compliance with the obligation or requirement, or refuse the application. An order compelling compliance shall stipulate a reasonable period for the person to comply with the obligation or requirement. An application for a compliance order may include an application for an order to pay to ComReg up to €500,000, by way of financial penalty, as ComReg may propose as appropriate in the light of the non-compliance. In deciding what amount (if any) should be payable (and the Court is not bound by the amount proposed by ComReg), the Court shall consider the circumstances of the non-compliance, including:

(i)   its duration;

(ii)   the effect on roaming customers and other undertakings;

(iii) the submissions of ComReg on the appropriate amount; and

(iv) any excuse or explanation for the non-compliance.

Where criminal proceedings have been instituted or a notice given under s 44 of the Communications Regulation Act 2002, ComReg shall not make an application for a compliance order further to reg 7(7) of the Roaming Regulations.

Electronic Communications – Criminal Enforcement

6.183 ComReg also has criminal powers of enforcement. The criminal offences created in respect of communications laws are divided into two types: indictable offences and summary offences. Indictable offences, the more serious cases, are heard by a judge and jury in the Circuit Criminal Court or the Central Criminal Court, carry the most serious penalties if the court convicts the accused and are subject to appeal to the Court of Criminal Appeal. Summary offences, the less serious offences, are heard by a judge without a jury in the District Court and, on appeal, in the Circuit Court. As mentioned above, ComReg, under the 2002 Act, has been given discretion for prosecuting various summary offences as set out in the Act.

6.184 The various communications directives were transposed by statutory instruments adopted under the umbrella of the European Communities Act 1972. The Minister introduced a series of amending regulations in 2007, adopted under s 46A of the Communications Regulation Act 2002, amending the Framework Regulations, the Authorisation Regulations, the Access regulations and the Universal Service Regulations to allow for the creation of indictable offences. Indictable offences are also set out in the Communications Regulation (Amendment) Act 2007. Section 46A provides that further offences may be created by the Minister by way of statutory instrument. The Minister may make amending regulations to provide that a contravention of a prohibited act, or a failure or refusal to perform a required act, is an offence, and to provide for the offence to be triable summarily, or on indictment, if the

Minister considers it necessary for the purpose of giving effect to EC law. This section applies to:

(a) the provision of an electronic communications service, an electronic communications network or an associated facility;

(b) the radio frequency spectrum or national numbering resource; or

(c) a postal service.

The investigation and prosecution of offences are generally separate and distinct functions within the criminal justice system.[197] Like many other investigative agencies, ComReg has the power to prosecute summarily without reference to the Director of Public Prosecutions. However, the sole power to prosecute on indictment rests with the DPP.[198] ComReg is also the specialised investigating authority[199] in relation to certain offences under the Communications Regulation Act 2002, as amended, and under the various statutory instruments which provide for regulatory offences.

Criminal powers under the Communications Regulation Act 2002

6.185 Sections 13C and 13D of the Communications Regulation Act 2002, as amended, provide that it is a summary offence to fail to comply with ComReg's request for information for the purpose of enabling ComReg to perform its functions. Section 24C provides that it is an offence to disclose information about the conduct of an undertaking, knowing the information to be false or misleading. On indictment, a fine of up to €50,000 may be imposed. Section 38D provides that it is a summary offence to fail to appear before ComReg if ComReg requires attendance in pursuance of fulfilling its objectives and functions. Section 45 makes it a summary offence to overbill and gives ComReg the authority to prosecute. If a prosecution is taken, an undertaking may be liable to a fine not exceeding €5,000.

6.186 Section 42 of the 2002 Act[200] provides that where an offence is committed by a body corporate and is proved to have been committed with the consent or connivance of or to be attributable to any neglect on the part of a person being a director, manager, secretary or other officer of the body corporate or a person who was purporting to act in any such capacity, that person, as well as the body corporate, is guilty of an offence

---

197 The DPP as a general rule has no investigative function and no power to direct the investigation. The investigation of criminal offences is generally the function of An Garda Síochána.

198 The Prosecution of Offences Act 1974 conferred on the DPP the function of prosecuting both on indictment and summarily. All crimes and offences other than those prosecuted in courts of summary jurisdiction are brought in the name of the People and at the suit of the DPP (except for a limited category of offences still prosecuted at the suit of the Attorney General).

199 Although the DPP has no investigative function, the DPP may advise investigators in relation to the sufficiency of evidence to support nominated charges and the appropriateness of charges, or in relation to legal issues arising in the course of investigation. Furthermore, although the DPP is not responsible for the conduct of investigations, he is free to indicate what evidence would be required to sustain a prosecution.

200 This provision is mirrored in Framework Regulations, reg 33A; Access Regulations, reg 20A; Authorisation Regulations, reg 25A and USO Regulations, reg 27.

and is liable to be proceeded against and punished as if he or she were guilty of the first-mentioned offence.

6.187 Section 43 provides that a summary offence under this Act or a related enactment may be prosecuted only by ComReg or by some other person authorised by law to prosecute offences.

Criminal enforcement under the regulations

6.188 As can be seen from above, under s 46A, the Minister may amend a regulation, implementing EC law, and create a summary offence, and can provide that the matter is to be also triable on indictment. The Minister has exercised this power in several instances in 2007 in the Framework Amendment Regulations 2007, the Authorisation Amendment Regulations 2007, the Access Amendment Regulations 2007 and the Universal Service Amendment Regulations 2007. ComReg may take summary proceedings.

Penalties

6.189 In relation to offences which are triable summarily, a fine not exceeding €5,000 can be imposed. On indictment, fines of up to €5m or 10 per cent of turnover can be imposed. Where the defendant is not a body corporate, the maximum fine will be €500,000. Daily fines of €5,000 for a continuing offence, once tried and convicted on indictment, will be applied, and a daily fine of €500 up to a maximum of €5,000 will apply where a summary offence is involved.

Standard defences

6.190 In proceedings for most offences under the various regulations, it is a defence to establish that:

    (a)   reasonable steps were taken to comply with the relevant requirement, or

    (b)   it was not possible for that requirement to be complied with.

The Framework Regulations

6.191 Examples of offences under the Framework Regulations include:

    Provision of information

    An undertaking that fails to comply with an information request under reg 17, which provides that ComReg may require any undertaking to provide any information that ComReg considers necessary for the purpose of ensuring compliance with decisions, commits an offence which is triable either summarily or on indictment.

    Assignment of Numbers

    Regulation 22 of the Framework Regulation sets out that a person commits an offence if the person assigns to locations, terminals, persons or functions on public communications networks, numbers from the national numbering scheme that ComReg has not specifically allocated to the person. This offence is triable either summarily or on indictment. If tried summarily, it is one of strict liability, but if the offence is tried on indictment, it is a defence to establish that the person reasonably believed that the network numbers had been specifically allocated to the person by ComReg.

Accounting Separation and Financial Reports

An undertaking that fails to comply with a requirement under reg 24 commits an offence which is triable either summarily or on indictment. Regulation 24 provides that an undertaking providing a public communications network or a publicly available electronic communications service that is also engaged in another activity shall: (a) keep separate audited accounts, or (b) have structural separation for the activities associated with the provision of electronic communications networks or services. If tried summarily, an offence is one of strict liability, but if the offence is tried on indictment, the standard defences set out above apply.

Failure to comply with an SMP obligation

An undertaking that fails to comply with an SMP obligation imposed on it further to reg 27 commits an offence. The offence is triable either summarily or on indictment.

Failure to comply with a Direction

Regulation 34 provides that an undertaking that fails to comply with a direction commits an offence. An undertaking found guilty of an offence is liable on conviction to a fine not exceeding €5,000.

Failure to appear for enforcement proceedings

Regulation 35 states that failing to appear at enforcement proceedings represents a summary offence and could attach a fine of up to €5,000.

The Access Regulations

6.192 Examples of offences under the Access Regulations include:

Failure to meet obligations for interconnection and access

Regulation 5(6) provides that an undertaking that acquires information from another undertaking shall not use that information for a purpose other than that for which it was supplied. An operator that fails to comply with these obligations commits an offence. The offence is one of strict liability. An operator found guilty of an offence is liable on conviction to a fine not exceeding €5,000.

Conditional access systems and other facilities

An operator that fails to comply with reg 7 commits an offence. Regulation 7 provides that an operator of a system for conditional access to digital television and radio services broadcast to viewers and listeners by any means of transmission shall ensure that the system has the necessary technical capability for cost-effective transcontrol at redistribution system head-ends allowing the possibility for full control by operators of redistribution systems at local or regional level of the services using any such conditional access system. An offence under this regulation is one of strict liability and is triable summarily. A person found guilty of an offence under this regulation is liable on conviction to a fine not exceeding €5,000.

Transparency Obligation

An operator of conditional access services that fails to comply with a reg 10 transparency obligation in relation to interconnection or access or both interconnection and access commits an offence. An offence is triable either summarily or on indictment.

Non-discrimination

An operator that fails to comply with a reg 11 obligation of non-discrimination in relation to interconnection, access, or both, commits an offence. An offence is triable either summarily or on indictment.

Accounting separation

An operator that fails to comply with a reg 12 obligation for accounting separation in relation to specified activities related to interconnection, access, or both, commits an offence which is triable either summarily or on indictment.

Obligations of access to and use of specific network

An operator that fails to comply with a reg 13 access obligation commits an offence triable either summarily or on indictment.

Price control and cost accounting obligations

An operator that fails to comply with a reg 14 obligation relating to cost recovery and price controls, including obligations for cost orientation of prices, commits an offence which is triable either summarily or on indictment.

Directions

Regulation 17 provides that an undertaking that fails to comply with a direction issued to it pursuant to this regulation commits an offence which is triable summarily. The standard defences apply. An undertaking found guilty of an offence is liable on conviction to a fine not exceeding €5,000.

Universal Service Regulations

6.193 Regulation 36 of the Universal Service Regulations concerns the prosecution of offences under those Regulations and provides that, in respect of proceedings for an offence under reg 35, or s 39(6) of the Act of 2002 relating to an authorised officer appointed under reg 33(3), these may be brought and prosecuted by the National Consumer Agency or by any other person authorised by law to prosecute offences. In respect of all other offences under the Universal Service Regulations, proceedings may be brought and prosecuted by ComReg or by any other person authorised by law to prosecute offences.

6.194 Examples of offences under the Universal Service Regulations are as follows.

Provision of access at a fixed location

A designated USP that fails to comply with reg 3 commits an offence. Regulation 3 requires the USP to satisfy any reasonable request to provide at a fixed location: (a) connections to the public telephone network, and (b) access to publicly available telephone services. This offence is one of strict liability and is triable summarily. An undertaking found guilty of an offence is liable on conviction to a fine not exceeding €5,000.

Directory inquiry services and directories

A USP that fails to comply with reg 4 commits an offence. Regulation 4 provides that the USP shall ensure that the directory, or the directory inquiry service, comprises all subscribers of publicly available telephone services in the State who have not refused to have their personal particulars included in those directories. This offence is one of strict liability and is triable summarily. An undertaking found guilty of an offence is liable on conviction to a fine not exceeding €5,000.

Public pay telephones

A USP that fails to comply with reg 5 commits an offence that is triable summarily. Regulation 5 provides that the USP shall ensure that public pay telephones are provided to meet the reasonable needs of end-users in terms of the geographical coverage, the number of telephones, the accessibility of such telephones to disabled users and the quality of service. An undertaking found guilty of this offence is liable on conviction to a fine not exceeding €5,000.

Specific measures for disabled users

A USP that fails to comply with reg 6 commits an offence that is triable summarily. Regulation 6 provides that ComReg may, with the consent of the Minister, specify obligations applicable to USPs of ensuring that disabled end-users can enjoy access to and affordability of publicly available telephone services, including access to emergency services, directory inquiry services and directories, equivalent to that enjoyed by other end-users. An undertaking found guilty of this offence is liable on conviction to a fine not exceeding €5,000.

Affordability of tariffs

A USP that fails to comply with a requirement under reg 8 in respect of the level of retail tariffs provided by the USP, in particular in relation to national consumer prices and income, commits an offence that is triable summarily. An undertaking found guilty of this offence is liable on conviction to a fine not exceeding €5,000.

Control of expenditure

Regulation 9 sets out that the USP shall, where it provides facilities and services additional to those that form part of the universal service obligation establish terms and conditions for such additional facilities and services in such a way that the subscriber is not obliged to pay for facilities or services which are not necessary or not required by him or her. Failure to do so is a summary offence. An undertaking found guilty of this offence is liable on conviction to a fine not exceeding €5,000.

Quality of service of designated undertakings

Regulation 10 provides that a USP shall publish adequate and up-to-date information concerning its performance in relation to the provision of the universal service obligation, based on quality of service parameters, and shall supply such published information to ComReg. Failure to do so is a summary offence. An undertaking found guilty of this offence is liable on conviction to a fine not exceeding €5,000.

Financing of the Universal Service Obligation

Regulation 12 provides that where ComReg finds that the net cost of meeting the universal service obligation represents an unfair burden, it shall apportion the net cost of the universal service obligation among providers of electronic communications network and services. An undertaking which has been notified of its obligation to contribute an amount specified by ComReg shall pay that amount in the time and manner specified by ComReg. An undertaking that fails to comply with the requirement commits an offence which is one of strict liability and is triable summarily. An undertaking found guilty of this offence is liable on conviction to a fine not exceeding €5,000.

Regulatory controls on retail markets

Regulation 14 provides that, where a given retail market is not effectively competitive, ComReg may impose such obligations as it considers appropriate on undertakings with SMP on that retail market. This regulation provides for two summary offences. In relation to the first offence, relating to failure to comply with SMP obligations on a retail market and failure to comply with measures to control tariffs or measures to orient tariffs towards cost, the standard defences apply. The second offence in respect of a failure to comply with paras (5)[201] or (8)[202] of reg 14 is a strict liability offence. An undertaking found guilty of either offence is liable on conviction to a fine not exceeding €5,000.

Regulatory controls on the minimum set of leased lines

A designated undertaking that fails to comply with SMP obligations relating to a minimum set of leased lines commits an offence further to reg 15. The offence is triable summarily. An undertaking found guilty of this offence is liable on conviction to a fine not exceeding €5,000.

Carrier selection and carrier pre-selection

Regulation 16 provides that, where ComReg imposes obligations to be complied with relating to carrier selection or pre-selection by an SMP

---

201 Requirement to maintain a cost accounting system.
202 Requirement to publish in annual accounts a statement regarding compliance with the cost accounting system outlined in para 5.

undertaking, the undertaking shall ensure that pricing for access and interconnection are cost-oriented and that any direct charges to subscribers do not act as a disincentive. An undertaking that fails to comply with this commits an offence that is triable summarily. An undertaking found guilty of this offence is liable on conviction to a fine not exceeding €5,000.

Contracts

Regulation 17 provides that an undertaking that provides to end-users connection or access, or both connection and access, to the public telephone network shall do so in accordance with a contract which contains certain minimum information. An undertaking shall notify its subscribers one month in advance: (a) of a proposed modification in the conditions of the contract for that service; and (b) of their right to withdraw without penalty from such contract, if they do not accept the modification. An undertaking that fails to comply with this commits an offence that is triable summarily and is liable on conviction to a fine not exceeding €5,000.

Transparency and publication of information and quality of service

Regulation 18 provides that ComReg may specify obligations to ensure that transparent and up-to-date information on applicable prices and tariffs, and on standard terms and conditions in respect of access to and use of publicly available telephone services, is available to end-users and consumers. An undertaking that fails to comply with this commits an offence which is triable summarily. An undertaking found guilty of an offence is liable on conviction to a fine not exceeding €5,000.

Interoperability of consumer digital television equipment

Regulation 20(1) provides that a person who places on the market for sale or rent or otherwise makes available consumer equipment intended for the reception of digital television signals that is capable of descrambling digital television signals, shall ensure that such equipment possesses the capability to:

(a)   allow the descrambling according to a recognised European standards organisation, and

(b)   display signals that have been transmitted clearly.

Regulation 20(3) provides that a person who places on the market for sale or rent or otherwise an analogue television set with an integral viewing screen of visible diagonal greater than 42 centimetres shall ensure that the set is fitted with at least one open interface socket permitting simple connection of peripherals, especially additional decoders and digital receivers. Regulation 20(5) provides that a person who places on the market for sale or rent a digital television set with an integral screen of visible diagonal greater than 30 centimetres shall ensure that the set is fitted with at least one open interface socket permitting simple connection of peripherals, and able to pass all the elements of a digital television signal, including information relating to interactive and conditionally accessed services. It shall be a function of the National Consumer Agency to monitor compliance with paras (3) and (5).

A person who fails to comply with any of the above requirements commits an offence that is triable summarily and is liable on conviction to a fine not exceeding €5,000.

Operator assistance and directory inquiry services

Regulation 21 provides that an undertaking providing a publicly available telephone service shall ensure that its subscribers have the right, without charge, to have an entry in a directory and a directory inquiry service. In addition, it provides that an undertaking providing a connection to the public telephone network to end-users shall ensure that all such end-users can access operator assistance services and a directory inquiry service. An undertaking that fails to comply with these requirements commits an offence that is triable summarily and is liable on conviction to a fine not exceeding €5,000.

Single European emergency call number

Regulation 22 provides that an undertaking providing a publicly available telephone service to end-users shall ensure that they are able to call the emergency services free of charge, by using the single European emergency call number 112, or any national emergency call number (such as 999). An undertaking operating public telephone networks shall, as soon as practicable, make caller location information available to authorities handling emergencies, to the extent technically feasible, for all calls to 112 or 999. An undertaking that fails to comply with these provisions commits an offence that is triable summarily and is liable on conviction to a fine not exceeding €5,000.

European telephone access codes

Regulation 23 provides that ComReg shall ensure that the 00 code is the standard international access code. In addition, ComReg may specify requirements for compliance by undertakings for the purpose of ensuring that special arrangements for making calls between the State and Northern Ireland may be established or continued and that the end-users of publicly available telephone services in the State are fully informed of such arrangements. An undertaking operating a public telephone network shall convey all calls originating on or transiting through its network to the European telephony numbering space, without prejudice to the need for an undertaking that operates a public telephone network to recover the cost of the conveyance of calls on its network. An undertaking that fails to comply with these requirements commits an offence that is triable summarily and is liable on conviction to a fine not exceeding €5,000.

Provision of additional facilities

Regulation 25 provides that an undertaking operating a public telephone network shall make available to end-users additional facilities subject to technical feasibility and economic viability. An undertaking that fails to comply with this commits an offence that is triable summarily and is liable on conviction to a fine not exceeding €5,000.

Number portability

Regulation 26 provides that an undertaking providing a publicly available telephone service, including a mobile service, shall ensure that a subscriber to such service can, upon request, retain his or her number independently of the undertaking providing the service:

(a)   in the case of geographic numbers, at a specific location, and

(b)   in the case of non-geographic numbers, at any location.

An undertaking that fails to comply with this commits an offence. This offence is triable either summarily or on indictment.

Dispute resolution

Regulation 28 provides that an undertaking shall implement a code of practice for handling complaints from end-users in respect of alleged contravention of these regulations. ComReg may resolve disputes which remain unresolved after due completion of all the procedures of a code of practice and ComReg may issue directions to an undertaking requiring it to comply with such for the resolution of the dispute, including reimbursement of payments and payments in settlement of losses incurred. An undertaking that fails to comply with this provision commits an offence that is triable summarily and is liable on conviction to a fine not exceeding €5,000.

Directions

Regulation 31 provides that ComReg may issue directions to a person to do or refrain from doing anything which ComReg specifies in the direction. An undertaking that fails to comply with a direction commits an offence that is triable summarily and is liable on conviction to a fine not exceeding €5,000.

Offence not to comply with requirement of Director of Consumer Affairs

Regulation 35 makes it an offence for a person to fail to comply with a requirement of the Director of Consumer Affairs under reg 33. An undertaking that fails to comply commits an offence that is triable summarily and is liable on conviction to a fine not exceeding €5,000.

Authorisation Regulations

6.195 Examples of offences under the Authorisation Regulations are:

Failure to be authorised

Regulation 4 provides that any person who intends to provide an ECN or ECS shall, before doing so, notify ComReg. An undertaking shall notify ComReg of any changes to the information previously supplied to ComReg within 14 days of such change. Failure to notify accordingly constitutes an offence. The offence is triable either summarily or on indictment. If tried summarily, the offence is one of strict liability, but if the offence is tried on indictment, it is a defence to establish that reasonable steps were taken to comply with the paragraph concerned.

Conditions attached to general authorisation

Regulation 8 provides that ComReg shall specify conditions to be attached to a general authorisation as are listed in Pt A of the Sch to the Authorisation Regulations. An undertaking that fails to comply with a condition attached to its general authorisation commits an offence. An offence under this regulation is triable either summarily or on indictment.

Conditions attached to rights of use for numbers

Regulation 14 provides that ComReg shall specify conditions that shall attach to a right of use for numbers. An undertaking commits an offence if it fails to comply with a condition that ComReg has attached to an undertaking's right of use for numbers. An offence under this regulation is triable either summarily or on indictment.

Directions

Regulation 23 provides that ComReg may, for the purpose of further specifying requirements to be complied with relating to a condition of a general authorisation, a licence or a right of use for numbers, issue directions to an undertaking to do or refrain from doing anything which ComReg specifies in the direction. An undertaking that fails to comply with a direction issued to it commits an offence that is triable summarily. An undertaking found guilty of this offence is liable on conviction to a fine not exceeding €5,000.

Roaming Regulations

6.196 It is an offence under reg 6 of Communications (Mobile Telephone Roaming) Regulations 2007 for an undertaking being the operator of a visited network, fails to comply with its obligations under art 3 of the Roaming Regulation[203] in relation to wholesale charges for the making of regulated roaming calls originating on that network. It is also an offence for an undertaking being a home provider, to fail to comply with its obligations under art 4 or 6 of the Roaming Regulation[204] to roaming customers. Separately, it is an offence for an undertaking to fail to comply with a requirement of ComReg under art 7(4) or (6) of the Roaming Regulation.[205] All of the offences created are summary offences which may be prosecuted by ComReg. In proceedings for an offence in relation to compliance with art 6 of the Roaming Regulation, it is a defence to show that reasonable steps were taken to comply with the relevant obligation, or that it was not possible to comply with the relevant obligation. Section 44 of the 2002 Act applies to offences under the Roaming Regulations.

---

203 Regulation (EC) No 717/2007 of the European Parliament and the Council of 27 June 2007 OJ No L171, 29.06.2007, p 32.

204 Regulation (EC) No 717/2007 of the European Parliament and the Council of 27 June 2007 OJ No L171, 29.06.2007, p 32.

205 Regulation (EC) No 717/2007 of the European Parliament and the Council of 27 June 2007 OJ No L171, 29.06.2007, p 32.

Criminal enforcement under the Wireless Telegraphy Acts

6.197 Section 3 of the Wireless Telegraphy Act 1926, as amended, contains various offences including that it is an offence to keep, possess, work, or use any apparatus for wireless telegraphy in contravention of s 3, that is without the requisite wireless telegraphy licence. A contravention of s 3 is an either-way offence. Section 13 of the Wireless Telegraphy Act 1926 as amended, provides that the prosecution for summary offences under the 1926 Act may be brought only by the appropriate authority, by a person to whom the functions of that authority have been delegated or by some other person authorised by law to prosecute offences. The appropriate authority in relation to the use of a television set, means the Minister for Communications. In relation to wireless telegraphy apparatus associated with ships and vessels, it means the Minister for Transport, and in relation to any other matter, it means ComReg. It is an offence to breach ss 3, 4, 5, 8 or 9 of the Broadcasting and Wireless Telegraphy Act 1988. Further to s 9 of the Broadcasting and Wireless Telegraphy Act 1988, it is an offence for any person to sell, let or hire or otherwise supply apparatus for wireless telegraphy unless there has been produced on behalf of the purchaser a valid licence granted under the 1926 Act. These offences are either-way offences which may be prosecuted summarily or by the DPP on indictment.

The Postal Sector – Civil Enforcement

6.198 In respect of civil enforcement in the postal sector, ComReg can issue directions to An Post as the USP and seek compliance orders before the High Court to enforce these directions.

Directions

6.199 ComReg can issue An Post with directions in respect of the universal service. Regulation 4 of the Postal Regulations provides that users at all points in the State shall enjoy the right to a universal service involving the permanent provision of a postal service of a specified quality and, subject to reg 9(1), at affordable prices for all users. It also provides that the Regulator, after consultation with interested parties, shall issue directions to a USP: (i) in respect of the quality of the postal service to be provided, and (ii) to ensure that the density of the points of contact and of access points takes account of the needs of users. The Regulator shall publish details of any directions in *Iris Oifigiúil*. ComReg issued An Post with directions further to this regulation in May 2003 in the ComReg document entitled 'Postal Services – Universal Service Obligation, Tariff Principles and Miscellaneous Issues'.[206] ComReg also issued directions to An Post in relation to bulk mail in January 2007 in a document entitled 'Regulation of Postal Services – Universal Service Obligation – Bulk Mail Access'.[207]

---

206 Directions to An Post under European Communities (Postal Services) Regulations 2002 (SI 616/2002) Decision No D11/03, Document No 03/50, dated 13 May 2003.

207 Document No. 07/06, dated 31 January 2007.

6.200 ComReg can issue An Post with directions in respect of the tariff principles. Regulation 9 provides that the tariffs for each of the services provided by a USP which form part of its universal service shall comply with certain principles known as the tariff principles. It also provides that where the Regulator is of the opinion that a USP is not complying with the principles laid down in this regulation, the Regulator may, after consultation with the Minister, and in the case of the uniform tariff, with the consent of the Minister, issue directions to the provider for the purposes of satisfying the requirements specified in this regulation.

6.201 Regulation 10 provides that ComReg can issue An Post with directions in respect of the principles which govern cross-border terminal dues.

6.202 ComReg has issued An Post with an accounting direction.[208] Regulation 11 provides that, in accordance with directions laid down by ComReg, a USP shall keep separate accounts within its accounting systems for each of the services within the reserved sector on the one hand and the non-reserved sector on the other. The accounts for the non-reserved sector shall clearly distinguish between services which are part of the universal service and services which are not. Such internal accounting systems shall operate on the basis of consistently applied and objectively justifiable cost-accounting principles.

6.203 ComReg can issue An Post with directions in respect of quality of service of mail delivery. Regulation 13 provides that ComReg shall lay down quality standards for domestic mail. Regulation 13(4) provides that where ComReg is of the opinion that a USP's performance level does not meet these requirements, ComReg shall ensure that the USP takes corrective action where necessary. Regulation 13(5) of the Postal Regulations[209] states that, for the purpose of ensuring that the USP takes corrective action under para (4), the Regulator my give a direction to the USP to take such an action.

6.204 Regulation 14 provides that the Regulator may give directions to a USP to take corrective action where necessary when quality standards for intra-Community cross-border services which form part of the universal service are not being met.

Enforcement and Compliance Orders

6.205 Regulation 18 of the Postal Regulations[210] provides that a direction issued by ComReg shall be in writing, shall state the reasons on which it is based and be addressed to the USP, and, as soon as practicable, be delivered by hand or by registered or certified post to the registered address of the provider and shall be deemed to have been delivered as of the date so delivered. Where ComReg finds that a USP has not

---

208 'Regulation of Universal Postal Services – Accounting Separation & Costing Methodology Accounting Direction to An Post', Document No. 06/63, dated 8 December 2006.

209 As inserted by European Communities (Postal Services) (Amendment) Regulations 2008 (SI 135/2008).

210 New wording for reg 18, as inserted by European Communities (Postal Services) (Amendment) Regulations 2008 (SI 135/2008).

complied with a direction, ComReg shall notify the USP of such findings, giving the USP an opportunity to state its views or remedy any non-compliance not later than:

(i)   one month after issue of notification;

(ii)   such shorter period as may be agreed; or

(iii)   such longer period as may be specified by ComReg.

ComReg may amend or revoke a notification. ComReg may publish in such manner as it sees fit any notification given by it in this regard subject to the protection of confidentiality.

6.206 Regulation 18(3) provides that, where at the end of the period referred to above, ComReg is of the opinion that the USP has not complied with a direction, ComReg may apply to the High Court for an order to direct the USP to comply. Regulation 18(4) provides that an application for an order may include an application for a financial penalty. In deciding the amount, the court shall consider the circumstances of non-compliance, including its duration, the effect on consumers and other operators, the submissions of ComReg on the appropriate amount and any excuse or explanation offered for the non-compliance.[211]

Refusal to grant or withdrawal of authorisation

6.207 Regulation 7(4) provides that ComReg may withdraw a postal service authorisation if an operator has not complied with the authorisation or has breached the reserved area of An Post. The Regulator may withdraw an authorisation where it considers the holder has failed to comply with reg 7 of the Postal Regulations or the written declaration that it will not infringe the reserved area.

Regulation 7(5) provides that where ComReg is minded to refuse to grant an authorisation or to withdraw an authorisation, it must write to the holder advising them in writing of its reasoning and the holder has 28 days to respond. On consideration of the response, ComReg may refuse to grant or withdraw the authorisation by notifying the holder in writing (reg 7(6)). The holder then has a right of appeal to the High Court, which must be exercised within 28 days. In the event of an appeal, the decision to withdraw is suspended further to reg 7(7).

On the hearing of an appeal in relation to the decision of the Regulator to refuse to grant or withdraw a postal service authorisation, the court may either confirm the decision, allow the appeal or make any other order it considers appropriate further to reg 7(8). If the appeal is allowed in the case of a refusal to grant a postal service authorisation, the Regulator shall grant the authorisation. The decision of the High

---

211 SI 135/2008 provides that the legal basis for this provision is Communications Regulation Act 2002, s 46A(3) and (4), as amended in 2007, which provide: '(3) The Minister may make regulations for the purpose of giving effect to a provision of the treaties governing the European Communities, or an act, or provision of an act, adopted by an institution of those Communities, relating to— ... (c) a postal service. (4) Regulations under subsection (3) may contain such incidental, supplementary and consequential provisions as appear to the Minister to be necessary for the purposes of those regulations (including provisions repealing, amending or applying, with or without modification, a related enactment).'

Court on an appeal shall be final save that, by leave of that court, an appeal on a specified question of law shall lie to the Supreme Court.

Enforcement of the reserved area – right of action by An Post

6.208 Regulation 8(3) of the Postal Regulations provides An Post with a right of action to apply to the High Court for an order in respect of any breach of the reserved area and the court may make an order prohibiting the provision by any person of a service reserved to An Post and may give such other direction or make such other order as the court considers appropriate.

The Postal Sector – Criminal Enforcement

Communications Regulation Act 2002

6.209 As set out above under the electronic communications and criminal enforcement, para **6.185**, pursuant to ss 13C and 13D, it is a summary offence to fail to comply with ComReg's request for information for the purpose of enabling ComReg to perform its functions. Section 24C makes it is a summary offence to impede the role and duties of an authorised officer. Pursuant to s 38D, it is an offence to fail to appear before ComReg if ComReg requires attendance in pursuance of fulfilling objectives and functions. As set out above, s 46A provides that further offences may be created by the Minister by way of statutory instrument. The Minister may make amending regulations to provide that a contravention of a prohibited act, or a failure or refusal to perform a required act, is an offence, and to provide for the offence to be triable summarily, or on indictment, if the Minister considers it necessary for the purpose of giving effect to EC law. These sections also applies to a postal service.

Postal Services Regulations[212]

6.210 Regulation 7(10) provides that a postal service provider with an annual turnover of more than €500,000, exclusive of VAT, who operates without an authorisation is guilty of a summary offence and liable to a €3,000 fine on summary conviction. ComReg may prosecute such an offence in the District Court further to reg 7(11) of the Postal Regulations.

APPEALS AND JUDICIAL REVIEW

6.211 ComReg's decisions in relation to electronic communications may be appealed to the High Court further to regs 3 and 4 of the Framework Regulations which implement art 4 of the Framework Directive. Decisions in the postal sector may not be appealed currently, however, the Third Postal Directive does provide for an appeal mechanism once implemented in Ireland. Please see **Ch 10** on Appeals for more information in this regard. Decisions of ComReg in respect of electronic communications and post may be judicially reviewed. Please see **Ch 11** on Judicial

---

212 The Postal Regulations, as amended by SI 135/2008.

Review. The following cases concern appeals and judicial review in the communications sector.

Orange v Director of Telecommunications Regulation[213]

6.212 In 1997, ComReg's predecessor, the Director of Telecommunications Regulation, announced the holding of a competition for the award of a licence to operate a third mobile telephone service in Ireland. There were already two such services at the time, the first operated by Eircell, who had succeeded to the monopoly previously enjoyed by Telecom Éireann and the Minister for Posts and Telegraphs, and the second by Esat Digiphone, who had been granted a licence by the Director's predecessor, the Minister for Transport, Energy and Communications. The Director decided that the successful applicant would be selected by way of an open tender procedure, using what is known as the 'the best application' method, as opposed to an auction procedure under which the licence is simply awarded to the highest bidder. In the 'best application' method, a number of criteria are adopted in order to determine to whom the licence should be awarded. Bids for the licence were invited from interested parties. The tender document had stated that the bids would be subjected to a comparative evaluation on the basis of specified criteria. While a number of parties originally expressed interest in bidding for the licence, ultimately only two bids were received: from the plaintiff (Orange) and the second-named defendant (Meteor). Their bids were then subjected to an evaluation process, as a result of which Meteor was ranked first and Orange second. The Director announced the award of the licence to Meteor. Under the relevant statutory provisions at the time, Orange was entitled to appeal to the High Court from that decision. There being no rules of court in existence prescribing the procedure to be adopted in such appeals, the proceedings were instituted by way of plenary summons in the High Court, appealing from the decision of the Director. The action came on for hearing before Macken J who, in a preliminary reserved judgment delivered on 18 March 1999, made rulings as to the scope of the appeal. In her preliminary judgment, the trial judge ruled that the nature of the appeal before her was what she described as a 'review type appeal' under which the reasonableness of the Director's decision was to be ascertained by reference only to the materials which she had before her, and none other, so as to enable the court to decide whether her decision should be confirmed.

6.213 The ruling of the High Court judge ended up in the Supreme Court. The Supreme Court allowed the appeal in this case and substituted for the order of the High Court an order dismissing the appeal of Orange and disallowed Orange's cross appeal. In this case, the Supreme Court considered that the simple statement that the appellant was not the winner of the competition was the most substantive reason one could expect to get. In addition, Orange had received a summary report. The court held that the reasons given were adequate in all the circumstances. The court was also of the view that there was no justification for a finding of bias of any kind. The court considered as part of Orange's cross-appeal whether the ruling of the learned High

---

213 *Orange v Director of Telecommunications Regulation* [2000] 4 IR 136.

Court judge, excluding evidence on the reasonableness issue, was correct or not. It referred to the *O'Keeffe v An Bord Pleanála*[214] and *M & J Gleeson*[215] cases. It considered that since any issues of alleged unreasonableness which arise in the case are issues relating to the evaluators' decisions, and it was difficult to see how there could be any fresh evidence adduced which could show that any of those decisions were unreasonable in either of the senses contended for, in those circumstances, a new trial on reasonableness would be utterly pointless. It therefore allowed the appeal and dismissed the cross-appeal.

Eircom v ComReg[216]

6.214 Please see Appeals chapter (**Ch 10**) for details on this judicial review case, which dealt with the right of appeal.

Hutchison 3G v ComReg[217]

6.215 Please see **Ch 10** on Appeals for details of this case.

Vodafone, O2 and Meteor v ComReg[218]

6.216 In this case, ComReg's decision that Vodafone and O_2 had joint dominance in the market for mobile access and call origination was appealed to the Electronic Communications Appeal Panel (ECAP). An interesting issue arose in this case in respect of the disclosure of confidential information and evidence of pent-up demand. In this particular case, ComReg argued that it should not be required to produce a particular document that summarised evidence it had obtained from other operators which allegedly demonstrated a demand for wholesale access to mobile services. It was clear from the challenged decision that the document played a key role in ComReg's decision. The appellants argued that it would be unfair for them not to see a document which played such a significant part in the decision they were challenging. The panel therefore ordered its disclosure. ComReg's decision was annulled by ECAP with the consent of the parties.

Smart Mobile Ltd v ComReg[219]

6.217 This judicial review case dealt with the claim by Smart Telecom, a fixed alternative operator, against ComReg's failure to award it the fourth 3G license. Interestingly, the case was argued on the grounds of a breach of contract on ComReg's

---

214 *O'Keeffe v An Bord Pleanála* [1993] I IR 39.

215 *M & J Gleeson v Competition Authority* [1999] 2 ILRM 401.

216 *Eircom v ComReg* Case 2005 No 152 JR, judgment of McKechnie J, 29 July 2005.

217 *Hutchison 3G v ComReg* ECAP/2004/01 decision, 26 September 2005.

218 *Vodafone, O_2 and Meteor v ComReg* ECAP6/2005/03, 04 AND 05.

219 *Smart Mobile Ltd v Commission for Communication Regulation* [2006] IEHC 338, Kelly J.

part for failure to award the license. In essence, Kelly J outlined that the court has very little power to 'trespass into an area in which the court has neither competence nor expertise', therefore setting a very high standard for any party contesting the decision of a Regulator. During the hearing, ComReg pointed out the high threshold that had to be surmounted by Smart in asking the court to interfere with the decision of ComReg.[220]

6.218 Mr Justice Kelly was satisfied that, as a statutory body, ComReg must conduct its business in accordance with its statutory mandate. It must not purport to exercise powers which it does not have. In the exercise of such powers as it does have, it must act fairly, proportionately and in a manner which conforms to its statutory purposes. Kelly J continued by saying that he accepted that having been chosen as the winner of the competition, Smart was the beneficiary 'of some kind of legal right which no other person or body could claim'. For this reason, ComReg's behaviour towards Smart had to be examined with a view to ensuring that it had complied with its obligations in these regards.

6.219 Mr Justice Kelly went on to observe that, in asking the court to intervene, Smart relied only on public law entitlements; that being so, the standards which must be achieved by a successful applicant in judicial review proceedings had to be attained by Smart. Accordingly, Kelly J continued by saying that, 'the court must be astute to ensure that it does not exceed its function by acting as an appeal court from the Regulator's decision and still less to seek to sit in the Regulator's chair and so trespass into an area in which the court has neither competence nor expertise.'

It is interesting to note that Mr Justice Kelly cited the *SIAC Construction Ltd v Mayo County Council*[221] case and its citation of the *Walloon Buses*[222] case with approval. It was pointed out that a public body conducting a tender process cannot negotiate and accept criteria different from those which were contained in the tender documents. To do otherwise, would be a violation of ComReg's duties. It could not, therefore, accept conditional performance bonds having allocated marks in the comparative evaluation on the basis of unconditional performance bonds. This case may be another example of the High Court being mindful of the respective positions, roles and expertise of Regulators versus the courts.

---

220 *O'Keeffe v An Bord Pleanála* [1993] I IR 39; *SIPTU v Ashford Castle* [2004] 15 ELR 214; *SIAC Construction Ltd v Mayo County Council* [2002] 1 ILRM 401; *Walloon Buses* Case (*Commission v Belgium*) [1996] ECR 1.

221 *SIAC Construction Ltd v Mayo County Council* [2002] 1 ILRM 401.

222 *Walloon Buses* Case (*Commission v Belgium*) [1996] ECR 1.

Chapter 7

COMPETITION

PRELIMINARY AND GENERAL INTRODUCTION

7.001 Competition law in Ireland is set out in the Competition Act 2002, as amended (the 2002 Act). The Competition Act replaced earlier competition legislation, including the Competition Act 1991 (the 1991 Act), the Competition (Amendment) Act 1996 (the 1996 Act) and the Mergers, Take-overs and Monopolies (Control) Act 1978, as amended.[1] Competition law at its essence is simply stated and the consequences for businesses which have acted in breach are instantly recognisable. Pursuant to s 4(1) of the Competition Act 2002, all agreements between undertakings, decisions by associations of undertakings and concerted practices which have as their object or effect the prevention, restriction or distortion of competition in trade in any goods or services within the State, or in any part of the State, are prohibited and void. Section 5 of the Competition Act 2002 states that an abuse by one or more undertakings of a dominant position in trade for any goods or services in any part of the state is prohibited.

Undertakings in Ireland are subject to two sets of competition laws:

(i)   Irish domestic law; and

(ii)   EC law where there is an effect on trade between Member States of the EU.[2]

This chapter treats both.

7.002 Part 2 of the Competition Act sets out this *ex post* regulation of the behaviour of undertakings. It also sets out a regime for judicial supervision of such behaviour by means of private or public enforcement action through the courts. Sections 4 and 5 of the Competition Act are modelled on arts 81 and 82 of the EC Treaty, and European law jurisprudence and guidance is persuasive, although not binding, in the

---

1   Former Minister Des O'Malley who introduced the Mergers, Take-overs and Monopolies (Control) Act 1978, and the Competition Act 1991 made some interesting opening remarks on the debate on the Bill: 'I am glad to have the opportunity of saying a few words about this Bill, which I regard as enormously important for the economic future of this country. It receives little or no coverage because its significance is not understood and public interest in it is negligible. This is in contrast with attitudes in the EU and in other Member States, particularly with the interest taken in these matters in the USA where they see that the proper regulation of competition is vital to the economic well-being of the country.' Dáil Éireann – Vol 550 – 08 March 2002, Competition Bill 2001 [Seanad]: Second stage resumed.

2   For the purposes of competition law, agreements that also affect the European Free Trade Association (EFTA) member states are similarly illegal.

interpretation and enforcement of those sections. In relation to their predecessor sections in the 1991 Act,[3] the High Court has put the matter in the following terms:

> Section 4 is in identical terms to Article [81] of the Treaty, around which has grown up in the past thirty years a very considerable volume of case law from decisions of the Commission and the Court of Justice. These decisions are not binding on our Courts but in view of (a) the provisions of the Act's preamble which declares that its object is to prohibit by analogy with Article [81] the prevention, restriction and distortion of competition and (b) the fact that Article [81] of the Treaty is part of Irish domestic law and the Irish Courts are required to follow decisions of the Court of Justice in relation to it on inter-state trade, it seems to me that the decisions of both the Commission and the Court of Justice on the construction of Article [81] should have very strong persuasive force.[4]

Part 2 of the Competition Act 2002 makes a number of important technical changes relating to criminal procedure for competition offences. These relate to presumptions, defences, fines, evidence and providing information. These changes, in conjunction with the new approach to penalties, are primarily designed to facilitate the prosecution of serious competition offences while taking due account of the rights of accused persons.

7.003 Part 2 also provides for the abolition of the previous notification system under the 1991 Act. The number of notifications provided for by the earlier legislation had declined considerably, suggesting that the level of understanding of the substantive rules regarding anti-competitive agreements, decisions and concerted practices among the business community and its advisers was high.[5] A second reason for abolishing the notification system was the abolition of the comparable European notification system for an exemption under art 81(3) pursuant to Regulation 17/62.[6] This was effectively abolished by Regulation 1/2003 (the Modernisation Regulation).[7] The system of notification has been replaced by the direct application of art 81(3). The European Commission previously had exclusive competence to decide whether or not art 81(3) applied to an agreement, since the provisions of art 81(3) did not then have direct effect. As a result of this, most competition authorities allowed the European Commission to concentrate on agreements that affected inter-state trade in the Common Market. This has now changed with Regulation 1/2003. This regulation

---

3   The 1991 Act (later amended by the 1996 Act) was the first Irish competition legislation to be expressly modelled on the EC Treaty competition rules.

4   *Donovan v ESB* [1994] 2 IR 305.

5   While the availability of private civil remedies for breaches of the competition rules may not have had the widespread impact envisaged in 1991, they have nevertheless produced a useful, if small, body of Irish jurisprudence in competition law. The notification system introduced in 1991 led to the establishment of a substantial body of Competition Authority decisions, which has produced much certainty and given much guidance to business enterprises. These decision may be viewed on http://www.tca.ie.

6   EEC Council: Regulation No 17: First Regulation implementing arts 85 and 86 of the Treaty, OJ 13, 21.2.1962, p 204–211.

7   Council Regulation (EC) No 1/2003 of 16 December 2002 on the implementation of the rules on competition laid down in arts 81 and 82 of the Treaty – 4.1.2003. OJ L1/1.

provides for a consistent approach in the application of EC competition rules and national competition rules.[8] Section 4(5) of the 2002 Act provides that an agreement which may otherwise infringe s 4(1) may be permissible where it meets certain efficiency criteria and where the positive benefits outweigh the negative effects of the agreement.

7.004 The 2002 Act transferred from the Minister for Enterprise, Trade and Employment to the Competition Authority the responsibility for examining and deciding upon mergers based on competition criteria.[9] Part 3 of the 2002 Act provides the Competition Authority with merger control jurisdiction. Mergers caught by Pt 3 by virtue of being above certain turnover thresholds must be notified to the Competition Authority for prior approval.[10]

In this regard, Irish competition law mirrors the general distinction contained in EC competition law between the *ex post* application of arts 81 and 82 of the EC Treaty and the *ex ante* operation of the EC Merger Regulation.[11]

7.005 The Commission for Communications Regulation (ComReg) has concurrent competition powers together with the Competition Authority in the area of electronic communications in respect of ss 4 and 5 and arts 81 and 82. The Competition Authority, ComReg and the Courts apply arts 81 and 82 where there may be an effect on trade between member states. European law jurisprudence and guidance is binding in this respect. Articles 81 and 82 as well as the EC Merger Regulation can also be applied by the European Commission.

ECONOMIC AND POLICY CONTEXT

7.006 The purpose of the 2002 Act, from an economic and general policy, as well as political, perspective, can be best gleaned from the Dáil debates relating to it. The reason for having competition law has been summarised as follows:

> Competition between businesses protects consumers. In markets that lack effective competition, firms realise that consumers have little or no choice but to buy from them, so customers can be treated in an unfair manner. With strong competition, firms are forced to work hard to win and keep their clients. As a result, it drives down prices and drives up choice and quality. Strong competition regimes encourage open dynamic markets and, through them, innovation and value for consumers.[12]

---

8   Regulation 1/2003 does, however, allow for stricter domestic rules in respect of abuses of dominance.

9   There are, however, special additional criteria in the case of media mergers or mergers between credit institutions.

10 There are special rules for media mergers and mergers involving financial institutions.

11 Council Regulation No (EC) No 139/2004 on the control of concentrations between undertakings 2004 OJ L 24/1.

12 Charles Flanagan TD, Dáil Éireann, 28 February 2002. Dáil Éireann – Vol 550 – 28 February 2002, Competition Bill 2001 [Seanad]: Second stage.

The purpose of the 2002 Act was to reform and modernise Irish legislation relating to competition and mergers.[13] The 2002 Act introduced a more focused approach towards the penalisation of anti-competitive activities, new arrangements for handling mergers and acquisitions, and a strengthened Competition Authority geared towards making a greater impact in its core task of enforcing competition law.

7.007 The 2002 Act introduced a new distinction between two categories of infringement, namely hard-core offences such as price fixing and lesser offences such as abuse of dominance, increasing the imprisonment penalty from two to five years in the case of the more serious category, and abolishing it for the less serious category. The five-year maximum penalty also makes the offence an arrestable offence which sends the clearest possible signal that blatantly anti-consumer activities such as price fixing will not be tolerated.

7.008 It has been said that 'most economists and competition lawyers would make a clear distinction between two broad classes of anti-competitive behaviour. The first category is blatant cartels, which involve price fixing (including agreements on margins, price increases or maximum discounts), bid rigging and market sharing. The assessment of such practices is clear and unambiguous. There is no evidence that they have any beneficial effects, in fact, quite the opposite – they reduce efficiency and clearly harm consumers because, effectively, they rip-off the customer. The second category involves everything else. This includes what are called vertical agreements (exclusive distribution, franchises etc and alleged abuse of dominance). The distinction between abuse of dominance and aggressive competition can be very fine. While vertical agreements may be anti-competitive in a particular set of circumstances, they are often beneficial in the sense of promoting efficiency etc. Logically, such behaviour should be treated less severely, even when it is actually anti-competitive. It may not be possible for firms to know in advance whether they have crossed the line. If the penalties are too severe, it might actually discourage people from competing strongly for fear of prosecution'.[14]

7.009 It is important to note that the 2002 Act recognised that, in addition to vertical agreements, certain horizontal agreements may also be pro-competitive where the positive efficiencies outweigh the negative restrictions. This is particularly the case with research and development agreements and specialisation agreements. It provides

---

13   Introduced by Tánaiste and Minister for Enterprise, Trade and Employment, Mary Harney TD, Dáil Éireann – Vol 550 – 28 February 2002, Competition Bill 2001 [Seanad]: Second stage.

14   Pat Rabbitte TD, Dáil Éireann – Vol 550 – 28 February 2002, Competition Bill 2001 [Seanad]: Second stage. Deputy Rabbitte in his intervention in that debate pointed out that it is also worth noting the comments of the then Attorney General, Mr Michael McDowell, SC, at a seminar in TCD in June 1995: 'Price-fixing, bid rigging and market sharing offences would have to be specifically created. One cannot simply criminalise all anti-competitive agreements or practices as such. Still less could one imagine criminalising all behaviour which amounted to abuse of dominant position. In short, the offence has to be one which any Joe or Josephine Soap sitting in a jury box can easily see falls on the wrong side of a clearly established line. (contd .../)

for such a balancing act to be carried out using the criteria of s 4(5) of the Act which are based on the criteria set out under art 81(3).

7.010 In respect of abuse of dominance, a position of dominance may be abused by a single firm or jointly together with another firm. Dominant firms have a special responsibility under competition law not to abuse that dominance. If left unchecked, there may be a temptation for a dominant entity to behave independently of its competitors, customers and ultimately consumers.

Fennelly J in the Supreme Court decision of *Competition Authority v O'Regan*[15] explained the purpose of competition law from the courts' perspective:

> The entire aim and object of competition law is consumer welfare. Competitive markets must serve the consumer. That is their sole purpose. Competition law, as is often said, is about protecting competition, not competitors, even if it is competitors who most frequently invoke it.

7.011 Merger control is required to ensure that a particular market structure, post-merger, will not in essence be so concentrated as a result of that merger that there would be an undertaking in a position of power who might then be tempted to abuse that position. Merger control therefore operates *ex ante*, or before any market harm could actually take place, to ensure that the market structure post-merger is sufficiently competitive. In the examination of ordinary mergers and acquisitions, the test introduced by the 2002 Act is whether the result of the merger or acquisition would be to substantially lessen competition in markets for goods or services in the State. In the case of media mergers, the Minister for Enterprise, Trade and Employment retains a right to intervene where the protection of certain stated public interests requires such intervention.[16] The approach taken was to seek to identify specific public interests that should be considered in the case of media mergers and to have those interests enshrined in legislation. This is done in s 23(10) of the 2002 Act in the definition of 'relevant criteria'. This sets out five considerations that address concerns that are

---

14 (contd) We can't have the situation in which companies are in perpetual conclave with their legal advisors as to what aspect of their behaviour does or does not fall within the ambit of any proposed offence. Any new offences must be simple, obvious, and generally understood. .... It seems to me that if modern procedures, rules of evidence and evidential presumptions are introduced, it should be possible to simplify serious offences of price fixing, bid rigging or market sharing into a form that can be easily prosecuted, easily understood by the jury and the public, and in which the court is not weighed down with a mass of documentation and technical evidence which makes the trial unduly long or cumbersome.' It is to be noted that there are horizontal agreements such as research and development agreements and specialisation agreements which produce pro-competitive effects and which are not hard-core offences.

15 *Competition Authority v O'Regan* [2007] 2 ILRM 161. This case was the first appeal to the Supreme Court involving the application of substantive competition law. The case is known as '*ILCU*' as it concerned the activities of the Irish League of Credit Unions.

16 Neither the Commission on the Newspaper Industry nor the Competition and Mergers Review Group recommended a purely economic criterion of this kind for the media sector. The Dáil debate on this Act involved lengthy contributions on the media merger role of the Minister and the special role of the media. (contd .../)

specific to the media sector. The 2002 Act was amended in 2008 in relation to mergers involving credit institutions. The Government adopted the Credit Institutions (Financial Support) Act 2008 in October 2008. Section 7 of the 2008 Act provides that in the case of a merger involving credit institutions, the Minister for Finance may approve a merger, notwithstanding that the merger would substantially lessen competition, where he considers it necessary to maintain the stability of the financial system in the State and that there would be a serious threat to that stability if the merger did not proceed.

7.012 One point that is not referred to in the Act in its original form in 2002 was the matter of whether other sector Regulators should be given powers to pursue their own regulated bodies for abuses of dominant positions. This was amended in respect of electronic communications in the case of ComReg by the Communications Regulation (Amendment) Act 2007. It remains to be seen whether a similar amendment will be sought by other Regulators such as the Energy Regulator or the Aviation Regulator.

THE REGULATORS

7.013 In Ireland, the primary Regulator of competition law issues is the Competition Authority. In the case of media mergers, the Minister for Enterprise, Trade and Employment also plays a role, and in the case of mergers between credit institutions, the Minister for Finance has a statutory role. In the area of electronic communications, ComReg has concurrent competition law powers in respect of restrictive agreements and abuse of dominance. The courts are also designated Competition Authorities for the purposes of the Modernisation Regulation.[17] The European Commission is the relevant Regulator where there is an effect on trade between Member States in the case of restrictive agreements and abuse of dominance and in the case of very large mergers that trigger the threshold of the EC Merger Regulation (Regulation 139/2004).

---

16   (contd) For example, former Labour Party Minister Michael D O'Higgins made the following comments: 'It appears there are a number of assumptions at [the Competition Act 2002's] base, some of which we will leave aside for an occasion when we have much more time. To put it mildly, it is based on the assumption that perfect competition is attainable and that we have true markets, as it were. It also assumes the benefit of consumers is met almost exclusively by the elimination of inefficiencies in competition and, therefore, everybody will be better off if we proceed along this exceedingly narrow furrow. The right to have editorial diversity in society is a right of communication as a citizen, and a citizen is not simply a consumer. A citizen is in part a consumer, and competition can deal with some things that deal with one's life as a consumer, but one is entitled to read diverse opinions. One is entitled to watch films and not know that 97 per cent of them are made in a tiny place on the planet called Santa Monica. One is entitled to have a variety of radio and television production, yet there is not a single line in the Bill as to how the Government proposes to deal with those features of monopoly that are sourced in satellite technology. Does the Minister of State realise that there is a great deal more to being in Ireland than being an Irish consumer?'

17   Council Regulation (EC) No 1/2003 on the implementation of the rules on competition laid down in arts 81 and 82 of the Treaty, 2003 O.J. L 1/1.

The Competition Authority

7.014 The Competition Act 2002 provides the Competition Authority with a 'right of action' in respect of breaches of arts 81 and 82 EC as well as the national equivalents of those provisions set out in ss 4 and 5, respectively.[18] It has an *ex ante* role in respect of merger control. The Authority comprises up to five members, including one who acts as chairperson. It has staff of approximately 60 people including economists and lawyers.

ComReg

7.015 The Communications Regulation (Amendment) Act 2007 provides for the Commission for Communications Regulation (ComReg) to enforce both EC and Irish Competition law in respect of restive agreements and abuse of dominance in the electronic communications sector. ComReg is designated as a 'national competition authority'[19] for the purposes of the Modernisation Regulation (as is the Competition Authority and as are the courts). Further to the provisions of the Modernisation Regulation, ComReg is also bound to notify the European Commission under art 11 of the Modernisation Regulation when it is conducting an investigation under arts 81 or 82. Please see **Ch 6** for details on ComReg's overall remit.

The Courts as Competition Authorities

7.016 As regards the designation of the authorities responsible for the application of arts 81 and 82 of the EC Treaty, Ireland has adopted a strict separation model of competition law enforcement.[20] The Competition Authority[21] is responsible for investigating complaints and compiling evidence, while the decision and imposition of

---

18 Competition Act, s 6(1) makes it an offence to enter into an arrangement 'prohibited by section 4(1) or by Article 81(1) of the treaty.' Section 7(1) makes it an offence for an undertaking to act in a manner prohibited by s 5(1) or by art 82 of the Treaty.

19 European Communities (Implementation of the Rules on Competition laid down in arts 81 and 82 of the Treaty) (Amendment) Regulations 2007 (SI 525/2007).

20 In his general report on the Competition Topic (Topic 2) in FIDE 2004, Mr Justice John Cooke identified three broad categories of enforcement models across the various member states: (i) the 'Community Model', where a single administrative authority will investigate suspected infringements and complaints, decide cases after hearing the parties, impose remedies and fines, and where its decisions are subject to judicial review or appeal before a specialised competition tribunal or court; (ii) the 'strict separation' model, where the National Competition Authority is mainly or only responsible for investigating complaints and compiling evidence and the decision and imposition of fines and remedies is vested in a distinct judicial or quasi-judicial tribunal; and (iii) the 'hybrid model', involving systems not fitting clearly into the first two categories and where functions are dispersed among several authorities. See 'The General Report', in Cahill (ed) *Modernisation of EC Competition Law Enforcement in the EU*, (Cambridge University Press, 2004) at p 632.

21 As is ComReg in the electronic communications sector.

fines and remedies is vested in the courts.[22] This allocation of the investigation, prosecution and decision-making functions has necessitated the designation of numerous different 'national competition authorities' in Ireland. The District Court, the Circuit Court, the High Court, the Court of Criminal Appeal and the Supreme Court are designated as competition authorities for the purpose of art 5 of the Modernisation Regulation. In addition, as discussed above in para **7.015**, the Competition Authority, the Director of Public Prosecutions, ComReg were designated as competition authorities for the purposes of performing the functions assigned to national competition authorities under the Modernisation Regulation, and in particular in respect of arts 11, 27(2) and 28(2) of the Modernisation Regulation.[23]

The European Commission

7.017 The Directorate General for Competition of the European Commission polices and enforces the EC Competition rules. The procedure by which this is done is not set out in the treaty but rather in the Modernisation Regulation, which replaced Regulation 17/62.[24] In addition, the provisions of the EC Merger Regulation are directly applicable in Ireland.

THE RELEVANT LEGISLATIVE FRAMEWORK

The Competition Act

7.018 The long title of the 2002 Act expressly describes the Competition Act's provisions 'by analogy with arts 81 and 82 of the Treaty Establishing the European Community'. Sections 4 and 5 of the Act mirror the prohibitions in arts 81 and 82 of the EC Treaty on anti-competitive agreements between undertakings and abuse of a dominant position, respectively. In addition, ss 4 and 5 deal with cases that affect trade within the state, as opposed to the EC Treaty rules, which cover arrangements that affect trade between EU member states.

7.019 The 2002 Act abolished the prior notification regime for agreements, which was provided for by the 1991 Act. This means that it is no longer possible for undertakings to notify agreements to the Competition Authority for approval or exemption from the application of the provision prohibiting a restrictive agreement. Instead, undertakings now 'self-assess' to ensure that agreements comply with competition law.[25] The

---

22   Article 34.1 of the Irish Constitution states that, '[j]ustice shall be administered in Courts established by law', which has generally been interpreted to prohibit the imposition of meaningful sanctions by agencies other than Irish courts.

23   European Communities (Implementation of the Rules on Competition laid down in Art 81 and 82 of the Treaty) Regulations 2004 (SI 195/2004), as amended by SI 525/2007.

24   Council Regulation (EEC) 17/62, English Special Edition : OJ Series 1 Ch 1959 – 1962, p 0087.

25   In line with the core reform to EC competition law enforcement brought about by the Modernisation Regulation – Regulation 1/2003. (contd .../)

change pre-dated the move towards self-assessment at European level, which took effect when the Modernisation Regulation became directly applicable, on 1 May 2004. Although adopted a number of months before the Modernisation Regulation, the 2002 Act was drafted to take account of key reforms of the EC modernisation package.[26] The Competition Authority, however, retains the power to issue declarations[27] under s 4(3) of the Competition Act in respect of specified categories of agreements that in its opinion comply with the efficiency criteria set out in s 4(5) of the 2002 Act. This is similar to the power of the European Commission to issue block exemptions, and the efficiency criteria in s 4(5) are similar to the criteria contained in art 81(3) of the EC Treaty (see para **7.042** below for details of the criteria in question). The 2002 Act also has abolished licences – as of 1 July 2002, all licences and certificates were revoked by para 3(1) of the Second Schedule to the 2002 Act. The Competition Authority also issues general guidance on the application of the 2002 Act in the form of notices under s 30(1)(d). In addition, the Competition Authority in some instances publishes reasoned 'enforcement decisions' in cases where it has closed its file after an investigation of alleged anti-competitive behaviour and where it is of the view that its decision raises complex or novel issues or is of public interest.

7.020 The 2002 Act increased penalties for hard-core anti-competitive offences, ie price fixing, market sharing/customer allocation and output restrictions. Company directors or other individuals convicted of hard-core offences could face prison sentences of up to five years (increased from two years which had been inserted by the 1996 Act). Financial penalties may amount to up €4 million or 10 percent of annual turnover, whichever is the greater. There is no longer an imprisonment term for breach of s 5 (abuse of dominance) or for other lesser s 4 infringements. Part 4 of the 2002 Act also extended the investigative powers of the Competition Authority in searches popularly known as 'dawn raids'.

7.021 Part 2 of the 2002 Act made changes to the rules of evidence in relation to competition offences. It contains a number of presumptions which make the task of prosecuting competition offences easier for the Director of Public Prosecutions (DPP) and the Competition Authority, and establishes certain defences.

---

25 (contd) The Competition Act also replaced the centralised notification and authorisation system for agreements falling within the scope of s 4 with a directly applicable self-assessment system – Koeck and Karollus (eds), *The Modernisation of European Competition Law – Initial Experiences with Regulation 1/2003* (Nomos Publishers, 2008). 'Ireland' chapter contributed by Andrews, Mackey and Curran.

26 The Competition Act, which repealed and replaced the Competition Act 1991 and the Competition (Amendment) Act 1996, was adopted on 10 April 2002. Pursuant to Competition Act 2002 (commencement Order) 2002 (SI 199/2002), the majority of the provisions the Competition Act 2002, other than those parts concerning mergers, came into force on 1 July 2002. Those parts establishing the new merger control regime set out in Pt 3 of the Competition Act entered into force on 1 January 2003.

27 Similar to the category licences under the 1991 Act.

7.022 Part 3 of the 2002 Act brought about significant changes in the areas of merger control and gives the Competition Authority responsibility for decisions on merger review, although the Minister for Enterprise, Trade and Employment maintains a role in respect of media mergers, and the Minister for Finance now plays a role in respect of mergers between credit institutions.

7.023 The Competition Authority has a general function to conduct studies (either on its own initiative or at the request of the Minister for Enterprise, Trade and Employment) into practices affecting the level of competition in particular markets. The Competition Authority is also empowered to advise the government on the competition implications of new legislation, advise public authorities on competition issues arising in the exercise of their functions and comment on restraints on competition inherent in existing legislation or administrative practice.

7.024 Under s 34 of the 2002 Act, the Competition Authority has concluded co-operation agreements with certain statutory sectoral Regulators. The relevant Regulators are the Health Insurance Authority, the Broadcasting Commission of Ireland, the Commission for Energy Regulation, the Commission for Aviation Regulation, the Commission for Communications Regulation and the National Consumer Agency.[28] The purpose of these agreements is to facilitate co-operation between the Competition Authority and the statutory Regulators, to avoid duplication, and to ensure consistency of activities and decisions. These agreements also allow for the exchange of confidential information between the various agencies.

The Competition (Amendment) Act 2006

7.025 The 2006 Act[29] provides for specific rules on unilateral conduct of non-dominant firms in the grocery trade.[30] The Groceries Order[31] was the only remaining ministerial order under the former Restrictive Practices Acts 1956-1987 that had not been repealed by subsequent competition legislation until March 2006. The Order set

---

28 It has since been proposed in the Budget 2009 in Annex D Rationalisation of State Agencies that the Authority is to merge with the National Consumer Agency – www.budget.gov.ie.

29 The Competition (Amendment) Act 2006 entered into force on 20 March 2006 pursuant to the Competition (Amendment) Act 2006 (Commencement) Order 2006 (SI 127/2006).

30 According to the Minister for Trade, Enterprise and Employment when introducing the amendment Bill, '[t]he purpose of the amendments contained in the Competition (Amendment) Bill 2005 is to strengthen the existing provisions of the 2002 Act by prohibiting certain unilateral conduct on the part of non dominant undertakings in the grocery trade. These are practices which it is feared might emerge following revocation of the Groceries Order and which might not be captured by either s 4 of the 2002 Act or by s 5 because they are not the conduct of a dominant undertaking', second stage speech, 26 January 2006.

31 The Restrictive Practices (Groceries) Order 1987 (SI 142/1987), given that the order was a child of the Restrictive Practices Act 1972, practitioners may wish to familiarise themselves with that Act to understand the original legal context.

out specific obligations and prohibitions on suppliers and retailers in the grocery trade. The most important provisions were:

(1) a prohibition on price collusion, resale price maintenance, boycotts, and 'hello money';[32]

(2) a prohibition on below-cost selling by reference to the net invoice price of goods; and

(3) an obligation on suppliers to maintain and make available written terms and conditions of supply.

The 2006 Act repealed the Groceries Order in its entirety and introduced three new sections (ss 15A, 15B and 15C) into the 2002 Act prohibiting certain conduct on the part of 'grocery goods undertakings'. Pursuant to the 2006 Act, there is now no sector-specific prohibition on the sale of groceries at less than their net invoice price. Below-cost selling is now dealt with by reference to s 5 of the Competition Act.

7.026 Specifically, the 2006 Act is stated to prohibit 'grocery goods' undertakings from engaging in certain unilateral behaviour, whether or not those firms enjoy market power.[33] The prohibited behaviour is: (i) resale price maintenance,[34] (ii) unfair discrimination,[35] (iii) compelling or coercing the payment of advertising allowances,[36] and (iv) compelling or coercing the payment of 'hello money'.[37] Importantly, however, each of the foregoing prohibitions only applies to the extent that it can be demonstrated

---

32 'Hello money' is any payment, allowance, or special discount given by a supplier to a retailer on the opening or extension of a new retail outlet or after the change of ownership of an outlet.

33 'Grocery goods undertaking' is defined as an undertaking that is engaged for gain in the production, supply or distribution of grocery goods. 'Grocery goods' are defined as 'any food or drink for human consumption that is intended to be sold as groceries, and includes: any substance or thing sold or represented for use as food or drink for human consumption; any substance or thing sold or represented for use as an additive, ingredient or processing aid in the preparation or production of food or drink for human consumption; and intoxicating liquors.'

34 Pursuant to s 15(b)(1), '... a grocery goods undertaking shall not directly or indirectly attempt to compel or coerce another grocery goods undertaking, whether by threat, promise or any like means, to resell or advertise for resale any grocery goods at a price fixed directly by the first mentioned grocery goods undertaking, or a price above a minimum price fixed directly or indirectly by the first mentioned grocery goods undertaking.'

35 Pursuant to s 15B(2), '... a grocery goods undertaking shall not apply dissimilar conditions to equivalent transactions with any other grocery goods undertaking.'

36 Pursuant to s 15(b)(3), '... a grocery goods undertaking shall not directly or indirectly compel or coerce, whether by threat, promise or any like means, another grocery goods undertaking to make any payment or grant any allowance for the advertising or display of grocery goods.

37 Pursuant to s 15(b)(4), '... a retailer shall not directly or indirectly compel or coerce, whether by threat, promise or any like means, another grocery goods undertaking to make any payment or grant any allowance to the retailer in consideration of any of the following matters: (contd .../)

that the impugned conduct,'… has as its object or effect the prevention, restriction or distortion of competition in trade in any grocery goods in the State or in any part of the State.'[38] The 'relevant question' when evaluating prohibited conduct under the 2006 Act is 'does it cause consumer harm?'[39]

The Communications Regulation (Amendment) Act 2007

7.027 This Act amended the Competition Act 2002 and provided ComReg with concurrent competition law powers in the area of electronic communications. Section 47G requires the Authority and ComReg to enter into a co-operation agreement to clarify the exercise of those powers to avoid duplication of efforts. The Competition Authority and ComReg have entered into a Co-operation Agreement for the purposes of s 47G of the Competition Act covering their co-operation in respect of their concurrent competition law powers. This is in addition to the Co-operation Agreement between the parties under s 34 of the Competition Act, which covers co-operation where ComReg is exercising its *ex ante* sector-specific regulatory powers. Section 47C requires ComReg to notify the Competition Authority when it is exercising its competition law powers. Section 47D sets out the responsibilities of the Authority to notify the alleged existence of certain agreements or abuses to ComReg where these occur in the electronic communications sector. Section 47E sets out that the Authority and ComReg must make every effort to settle by agreement any question arising as to which of them should exercise their competition law functions relating to a matter. If agreement cannot be reached, the matter can be referred for resolution by the Minister for Enterprise, Trade and Employment. In making a determination under this section, the Minster for Enterprise, Trade and Employment is to consult with the Minister for Communications, Marine and Natural Resources. An undertaking is not liable to be prosecuted by both the Authority and ComReg in respect of the same offence, as provided for by s 47F.

European Competition Law

7.028 Articles 81 and 82 of the EC Treaty also apply in Ireland, as does the EC Merger Regulation. The Modernisation Regulation is also directly applicable. Article 3(1) of the Modernisation Regulation provides that national competition authorities (NCAs) and national courts, where they apply domestic competition law to agreements or unilateral practices are also obliged to apply arts 81 and 82 where these Treaty

---

37 (contd) providing space for grocery goods within a new retail outlet on or within the first 60 days after its opening to the public; providing space for grocery goods within a newly expanded or extended retail outlet on or within the first 60 days after the opening to the public of the expanded or extended part of the outlet; providing space for grocery goods within a retail outlet on or within the first 60 days after its opening to the public under new ownership.'

38 Section 15B(5).

39 See presentation by Paul Gorecki, Member of the Competition Authority, http://www.tca.ie. Gorecki, 'The Abolition of Groceries Order: Enforcement by the Competition Authority', 1 March 2006.

provisions are applicable because of an effect on inter-state trade. Article 3(2) provides that the application of national competition law may not lead to the prohibition of agreements which may affect trade between Member States but which do not infringe article 81(1) or which fulfil the criteria of art 81(3) or a block exemption. Article 3(2) does, however, allow for stricter national laws on unilateral behaviour or abuses of dominance.[40] There are various block exemptions at EC level that are directly applicable in Ireland and which include:

(i)   Vertical Restraints Block Exemption (Regulation 2790/99);[41]

(ii)   Motor Vehicle Block Exemption (Regulation 1400/02);[42]

(iii)   Research and Development Block Exemption (Regulation 2658/00);[43]

(iv)   Specialisation Block Exemption (Regulation 22658/00);[44]

(v)   Technology Transfer Block Exemption (Regulation 772/2004);[45]

(vi)   Air Transport Block Exemption (Regulation 411/2004);

(vii)   Insurance Block Exemption (Regulation 358/2003);[46] and

(viii) Consortia Between Liner Shipping Companies (Regulation 823/2000).[47]

Also relevant are the provisions of art 86 of the EC Treaty, which deals with special and exclusive rights and the provision of a service of general economic interest. The provisions of art 87 of the EC Treaty on state aid are also relevant; however, the application of the state aid rules is outside the scope of this book.

THE REGULATED ACTIVITIES

Restrictive Agreements or Cartels

Section 4 of the Competition Act

7.029 Pursuant to s 4(1) of the Competition Act 2002, all agreements between undertakings, decisions by associations of undertakings[48] and concerted practices which have as their object or effect the prevention, restriction or distortion of

---

40 This provision was requested by Germany to allow it to apply its Law Against Restrictions of Competition 1958 and in particular art 20(2) of the Law Against Restrictions of Competition which in German is known as the Gesetz gegen Wettbewerbsbeschrankungen.

41 Expires 31 May 2010.

42 Expires 31 May 2010.

43 Expires 31 December 2010.

44 Expires 31 December 2010.

45 Expires 30 April 2014.

46 Expires 31 March 2010.

47 Expires 25 April 2010.

48 The position of representative associations – which are often an association of undertakings for competition law purposes – was raised by Mr John Perry TD in the debate on the Competition Bill 2001, when he stated that, 'there are many instances where the authority has gone after representative and trade associations that have responded to actions taken by larger or more dominant players in the marketplace. (contd .../)

competition in trade in any goods or services within the state, or in any part of the state, are prohibited and void. The Act sets out a number of examples of restrictive agreements. Such agreements include those which:

(a) directly or indirectly fix purchase or selling prices or any other trading conditions;

(b) limit or control production, markets, technical development or investment;

(c) share markets or sources of supply;

(d) apply dissimilar conditions to equivalent transactions with other trading parties thereby placing them at a competitive disadvantage; or

(e) make the conclusion of contracts subject to acceptance by the other parties of supplementary obligations which by their nature according to commercial usage have no connection with the subject of such contracts.

In relation to the sanctions attaching to these examples, the Competition Act distinguishes between what have been described as mortal competition law sins and lesser venial sins against competition law.[49] Those listed at (a) to (c) above are regarded as 'hard-core' competition law offences and attract more punitive sanctions than those listed at (d) and (e).

7.030 By virtue of s 6 of the Competition Act, an undertaking which:

(a) enters into, or implements, an agreement;

(b) makes or implements a decision; or

(c) engages in a concerted practice;

that is prohibited by s 4(1) and does not meet the criteria of s 4(5) of the Competition Act is guilty of a criminal offence.[50]

In relation to the types of offences listed at s 4(1)(a)–(c), above, it is presumed by s 6(2) of the Competition Act, that such agreements, with certain qualifications, have as their object the prevention, restriction or distortion of competition in trade in any

---

48 (contd) The IFA, the licensed vintners, the veterinary profession and travel agents have all come under the focus of the authority in circumstances where they have tried to represent their members' interests in disputes with larger companies. There is an important balance to be struck in such cases. Representative and trade associations should not act to restrict competition, but it is equally important that they are allowed to represent their members in issues that affect their livelihoods.' Dáil Éireann – Vol 550 – 28 February 2002, Competition Bill 2001 [Seanad]: Second stage. Adam Smith had a different view of trade associations, as he said in his famous work *An Inquiry Into the Nature and Causes of the Wealth of Nations* (1776), 'People of the same trade seldom meet together, even for merriment and diversion, but the conversation ends in a conspiracy against the public, or in some contrivance to raise prices.'

49 Goggin, *Irish and EU Competition Law*, Irish Competition Authority, 2002, available at http://www.tca.ie.

50 Former Minister Des O'Malley, during the debate introducing the Competition Bill 2001, stated that, 'the great defect of the 1991 Act – I recognised it at the time – was that it did not contain any means to impose criminal sanctions. (contd .../)

goods or services in the state or in any part of the state unless the defendant proves otherwise. This presumption reflects an economic view that certain behaviour is unequivocally harmful to consumers. This approach may be compared to the US anti-trust system which uses the expression '*per se*' offences, that is to say, where the entering into of the agreement is itself the offence and it is not necessary to prove, in every case, that the object or effect is to prevent, restrict or distort competition.[51] While there are no provisions in Irish legislation that introduce a US style *per se* competition law offence in respect of breaches considered unequivocally harmful to consumers, s 6(2) of the 2002 Act introduces a new distinction between hard-core offences and those that are less seriously restrictive of competition.[52] As regards the types of agreement described at s 4(1)(d)–(e), the presumption does not apply to these types of offences.

7.031 Section 4 also only applies to agreements between undertakings. It is a defence if it can be proven that there is no undertaking involved.[53] Section 3(1) of the 2002 Act defines an undertaking as a person regardless of whether the person is an individual, a body corporate or an unincorporated body of persons, engaged for gain in the

---

50 (contd) I was innocent, naive and hopeful enough to think that it could be enforced by civil means, but that proved incorrect. Competition law can only be adequately enforced if it is done by a public regulatory authority, such as the Competition Authority or the Minister for Enterprise, Trade and Employment. It cannot be done 99 per cent of the time by injured or damaged parties because of their nature – they are too small and they tend to be damaged by parties that are extremely big. As a result, they never take them on.' Dáil Éireann – Vol 550 – 08 March 2002, Competition Bill 2001 [Seanad]: Second Stage (Resumed).

51 In the US, large trusts became synonymous with monopolies and the threat to the free market these trusts represented led to the Sherman and Clayton Acts being adopted as 'anti-trust laws' – hence the American term for competition law. These laws, in part, codified the common law doctrine of restraints of trade. The first two sections of the Sherman Act 1890 read as follows: Section 1. 'Every contract, combination in the form of trust or otherwise, or conspiracy, in restraint of trade or commerce among the several States, or with foreign nations, is declared to be illegal. Every person who shall make any contract or engage in any combination or conspiracy hereby declared to be illegal shall be deemed guilty of a felony, and, on conviction thereof, shall be punished by fine ....' (restrictive agreement); Section 2 'Every person who shall monopolize, or attempt to monopolize, or combine or conspire with any other person or persons, to monopolize any part of the trade or commerce among the several States, or with foreign nations, shall be deemed guilty of a felony, and, on conviction thereof, shall be punished by fine.' (abuse of dominance) The Clayton Act of 1914 was passed to supplement the Sherman Act. Specific categories of abusive conduct were listed, including price discrimination, exclusive dealings and mergers which substantially lessen competition.

52 In US anti-trust law, the comparator for these hard-core offences are the *per se* offences, where the entering into the agreement is itself the offence; importantly, and by contrast with Ireland, in the US it is not necessary to prove, in every case, that the object or effect is to prevent, restrict or distort competition. Other offences are treated on a 'rule of reason' basis.

53 The Voluntary Health Insurance Board avoided the application of the Competition Act 1991 by successfully arguing that it was not an undertaking (*Deane v VHI* [1992] 2 IR 319).

production, supply or distribution of goods or the provision of a service. The term 'gain' implies that the entity is charging in connection with its activities.[54]

It is also a defence if there is no agreement between undertakings. It is important to note that 'agreement' can be interpreted very loosely in this regard and need not be in writing. A gentleman's agreement or a nod and a wink may suffice, provided there is a meeting of minds or concurrence of wills of some sort.[55] Agreements between undertakings all belonging to the same economic entity on intra-group agreements will not trigger s 4.[56] Also relevant is the fact that the arrangement need only have the object or effect of preventing, restricting or distorting competition – it need not have both.[57]

7.032 Irish competition law applies whenever there is an effect on trade in Ireland, even if the transaction or practice also has an effect on trade outside of Ireland.[58] As a general principle, both EC and Irish competition law may apply to the same arrangement or practice.[59] It should be noted that Irish competition law may not permit any restrictive agreement that is prohibited by EC law.[60]

7.033 Competition law often divides arrangements or agreements into 'horizontal' and 'vertical' arrangements. Horizontal agreements are agreements between undertakings which are at the same level of the economic chain, such as an agreement between two or more manufacturers. Vertical arrangements involve arrangements between undertakings at different levels of the economic chain, such as an agreement between a distributor and a retailer. In general, vertical agreements often have less harmful effects on competition due to the efficiencies that they tend to generate, meaning that they can often benefit from s 4(5) or the Verticals Declaration or Verticals Notice[61] in Ireland, or the Vertical Restraints Block Exemption at EC level. Certain horizontal agreements may, however, also be considered capable of producing efficiencies, such

---

54   *Greally v Minister for Education* [1995] ILRM 481. This is to be distinguished from the position under art 81 of the EC Treaty where an undertaking does not have to be engaged for gain.

55   See by way of guidance *Bayer v Commission* Case T–41/96 [2000] ECR II–3383 [Bayer/ Adalat].

56   See by way of guidance *Viho/Parker Pen* Case T–T 77/92.

57   This approach follows the ECJ jurisprudence that, in respect of restrictions of competition by object, 'there is no need to take account of the concrete effects of an agreement' – *Consten & Grundig v Commission* [1966] ECR 299 at 342 – it is enough if the agreement is to restrict competition, the agreement does not have to be successful in its implementation or effect.

58   See also Cahill, Connery, Kennedy and Power, *European Law* (4th edn, OUP, 2008) p 138 and Competition Authority Decision No. 137 General Electric Capital/GPA, 20 October 1993.

59   *HB Ice Cream v Masterfoods* [1993] ILRM 145.

60   However, Irish competition law may be more restrictive than EC competition law in respect of abuse of dominance under the Modernisation Regulation.

61   See http://www.tca.ie for both the Verticals Declaration and the Verticals Notice.

as research and development agreements, production agreements (including specialisation agreements) and commercialisation agreements.[62]

Section 4(5) of the Competition Act

7.034 Section 4(5) provides that arrangements falling within s 4(1) may nevertheless be permitted. Under s 4(5), it has to be considered whether the pro-competitive benefits produced by an agreement outweigh the anti-competitive effects. The balancing of the anti-competitive and pro-competitive effects is conducted under s 4(5). On occasion, arrangements that are technically anti-competitive and contrary to s 4(1) may still be beneficial to the economy and therefore deserve to be permitted.

Certain criteria need to be satisfied for an arrangement to benefit from s 4(5). It must be proven that the agreement:

> contributes to improving the production or distribution of goods or provision of services or to promoting technical or economic progress, while allowing consumers a fair share of the resulting benefit and does not (a) impose on the undertakings concerned terms which are not indispensable to the attainment of those objectives, and (b) afford undertakings the possibility of eliminating competition in respect of a substantial part of the products or services in question.

Pursuant to s 4(2) an arrangement 'shall not be prohibited under subsection (1) if it complies with the conditions referred to in subsection (5).'

7.035 Sections 4(2) and (3) of the 2002 Act allow the Authority to issue declarations. Declarations are blanket exemptions from the prohibition contained in s 4(1) for those agreements which meet the criteria and provisions of the declaration. They are similar to block exemptions at an EC level. The Competition Authority has adopted a Declaration in Respect of Vertical Agreements and Concerted Practices which is published on its website. The Verticals' Declaration is similar to the provisions of the Vertical Restraints Block Exemption, discussed below. Pursuant to s 30(1)(d) of the Competition Act, the Authority also adopted a Notice in Respect of Vertical Agreements and Concerted Practices, similar to the terms of the *de minimis* Notice also discussed below.

Article 81 of the EC Treaty

7.036 The prohibition on anti-competitive agreements set out in s 4 of the Competition Act adopts almost word for word art 81 EC. Article 81 states:

> the following shall be prohibited as incompatible with the common market; all agreements between undertakings, decisions by associations of undertakings and concerted practices which may affect trade between Member States and which have

---

62 See Whish, *Competition Law* (6th edn, OUP, 2008) Ch 15. See also Commission Guidelines on Horizontal Cooperation Agreements OJ 2001 C3/2 [2001] 4 CMLR 819 and Guidelines on the Application of art 81(3) OJ [2004] C101/8. See also Block Exemptions on R&D Regulation 2658/00 and on Specialisation Regulation 22658/00, both of which expire on 31 December 2010.

as their object or effect the prevention, restriction or distortion of competition within the common market ....

It then gives examples of such agreements or arrangements, which are repeated verbatim in s 4(1) of the 2002 Act (as set out above at para **7.029**).

7.037 In EC competition law, 'undertaking' is understood to refer to any entity engaged in economic activities: 'the concept of an undertaking encompasses every entity engaged in an economic activity, regardless of the legal status of the entity and the way in which it is financed.'[63]

According to the Court of First Instance (CFI), in the *Bayer Adalat* case, the concept of agreement: 'centres around the existence of a concurrence of wills between at least two parties, the form in which it is manifested being unimportant so long as it constitutes the faithful expression of the parties' intentions.'[64]

7.038 As in the case of s 4, for an agreement to trigger art 81 it must take place between undertakings. Where two or more undertakings amount to a 'single economic entity', agreements between such undertakings belonging to the same corporate group will not trigger the application of art 81;[65] for example, in the case of a parent and its subsidiary. The ECJ held in *Viho/Parker Pen*[66] that a parent company and its subsidiaries 'form a single economic unit within which the subsidiaries do not enjoy real autonomy in determining their course of action in the market, but carry out the instructions issued to them by the parent company controlling them'.[67] Agreements must take place between undertakings.

It is important to stress that the term 'object or effect' is disjunctive and not conjunctive.[68] This means that if the parties have the object of distorting competition, then that is sufficient to found a breach of art 81. There is no need for the arrangement to have the effect of distorting competition – it is sufficient that the cartel was set up with the intention to fix prices; there is no need to prove that the cartel was competent and succeeded in its objective.

---

63 *Hofner and Elser v Macrotron* Case C–41/90 [1991] ECR I–1979 (para 21).

64 *Bayer v Commission* Case T–41/96 [2000] ECR II–3383, para 69, upheld on appeal to the ECJ by a judgment of 6 January 2004 (*BAI v Bayer and Commission* Joined Cases C–2/01 P and C–03/01 P).

65 *Viho v Commission* Case T–102/92 [1995] ECR II 17 and *Viho Europe v Commission* C–73/95 [1996] ECR I 5457 and *Bayer Adalat* Case T–41/96 [2000] ECR II–3383, para 69, upheld on appeal to the ECJ by a judgment of 6 January 2004 (*BAI v Bayer and Commission* Joined Cases C–2/01 P and C–03/01 P).

66 *Viho v Commission* Case T–102/92 [1995] ECR II 17 and *Viho Europe v Commission* C–73/95 [1996] ECR I 5457 and *Bayer Adalat* Case T-41/96 [2000] ECR II–3383, para 69, upheld on appeal to the ECJ by a judgment of 6 January 2004 (*BAI v Bayer and Commission* Joined Cases C–2/01 P and C–03/01 P).

67 Such unilateral behaviour may fall within the scope of art 82.

68 *Consten and Grundig v Commission* [1966] ECR 299.

7.039 In the *BIDS* Case[69] McKechnie J in the High Court held that each member of the Beef Industry Development Society Ltd (BIDS) was an undertaking. In addition, the court found that the BIDS was an association of undertakings for the purpose of art 81 of the EC Treaty. The court held that the arrangements put in place by the BIDS constituted a decision by an association of undertakings. The High Court did not find a breach of art 81(1). However, it did proceed in *obiter* to consider in any event the criteria of art 81(3) and concluded that they were not all met. This case is on appeal to the Supreme Court and an art 234 reference was made by the Supreme Court seeking an interpretation of art 81(1) of the EC Treaty.[70] The Supreme Court's reference to the European Court of Justice (ECJ) concerned whether a particular arrangement could have as its object, as distinct from its effect, the prevention, restriction or distortion of competition.[71] The ECJ agreed with the Advocate General's opinion,[72] on 20 November 2008 and considered that the capacity cartel was in breach of art 81(1) and reiterated that the object or effect test was disjunctive. The Supreme Court now has to apply this ruling to the *BIDS* case and may have to reverse McKechnie J's judgment in High Court. There is also a cross-appeal, on the grounds that the art 81(3) criteria are in fact all met.

7.040 There must be an appreciable effect on competition for art 81 to be triggered – the effect must not be simply *de minimis*, or minimal.[73] The European Commission has issued a notice on agreements of minor importance which do not appreciably restrict competition under art 81(1) (the *de minimis* Notice[74]). The Commission has set out in this notice that, in general, arrangements between competitors where the aggregate market share is less than 10 per cent do not have an appreciable effect on competition, while arrangements between non-competitors may involve undertakings with a

---

69 The *Competition Authority v Beef Industry Development Society Ltd and Barry Brothers (Carrigmore) Meats Ltd* [2006] IEHC 294, McKechnie J.

70 In particular, the Supreme Court asked whether the general prohibition of art 81(1) and the specific prohibition in art 81(1)(b) of measures which limit or control production should be interpreted as referring to or encompassing agreements to effect a once-off reduction in the capacity of an industry where there is no agreement to limit or control capacity or output. C–209/07 Reference from the Supreme Court to the ECJ under art 234, dated 8 March 2007, judgment on 20 November 2008.

71 Equally, even if the parties do not have the object of distorting competition, it is sufficient that the arrangement has the effect of distorting competition.

72 Advocate General Verica Trstenjak delivered her opinion on 4 September 2008. The Advocate General opined at para 109 of her opinion: 'On the basis of the above considerations, I propose that the Court reply as follows to the question referred by the Supreme Court: "An agreement with the content and under the circumstances described in the question referred has as its object the restriction of competition and is not therefore compatible with art 81(1) EC in so far as the other conditions laid down in that provision are satisfied."'

73 *Delimitis v Henninger Brau* Case C–234/90 [1991] ECR I–935; *European Night Services v Commission* Case T–374/94 [1998] ECR II–3141; *Javico v Yves Saint Laurent Parfums* C–306/96 [1998] ECR I–1983.

74 (2001) OJ C368/13.

combined market share of less than 15 per cent and not have an appreciable effect on competition. Agreements which involve certain hard-core restrictions such as price-fixing and market sharing cannot benefit from this Notice.

7.041 Article 81 of the EC Treaty applies where there is an effect on trade between member states.[75] It is important to note that there must be an appreciable effect on trade in the Common Market or any part of the Common Market.[76] The Commission and the court give quite a generous interpretation of effect on trade between member states and this is usually satisfied where something is capable of having an effect on trade. In the *Magill* case,[77] the ECJ stated:

> In order to satisfy the condition that trade between Member States must be affected, it is not necessary that the conduct in question should in fact have substantially affected that trade. It is sufficient to establish that the conduct is capable of having such an effect.

However, the effect on trade has to be appreciable.[78] Any agreements or decisions prohibited by art 81(1) and not permitted by art 81(3) shall automatically be void pursuant to art 81(2). It is to be noted that, unlike the position under s 4(1) of the 2002 Act, concerted practices, are not void under art 81(2).[79] The consequences of the voidness of an agreement is that it may not be enforced. In addition, third parties and indeed the parties to the decision itself[80] may take private damages action in respect of the decision.

Article 81(3) of the EC Treaty

7.042 Article 81(3) states that the application of art 81(1) may be declared inapplicable in the case of:

    (i)   any agreement or category of agreements between undertakings;

    (ii)   any decision or category of decisions by associations of undertakings; and

    (iii) any concerted practice or category of concerted practices;

which contribute to improving the production or distribution of goods or to promoting technical or economic progress, while allowing consumers a fair share of the resulting benefit, and which does not:

    (a)   impose on the undertaking concerned restrictions which are not indispensable to the attainment of these objectives; or

---

75   In *Wood Pulp* (Cases 114/85 etc. *A Ahlstrom Oy v Commission* [1988] ECR 5193).

76   *Volk v Vervaeke* Case 5/69 [1969] ECR 295.

77   *Radio Telefís Éireann & Independent Television Publications v Commission* Cases C–241 & 242/91 [1995] ECR I–743.

78   *Volk v Vervaecke* Case 5/69 [1969] ECR 295.

79   Order of the President of the CFI, 14 November 2008, *Artisjus Magyar, Szerzoi Jogvedo, Iroda Egyesulet v Commission* T 411/08 R.

80   *Courage v Crehan* C–452/99 [2001] ECR I 6297.

(b) afford such undertakings the possibility of eliminating competition in respect of a substantial part of the products in question.

7.043 Under art 81(3) it has to be considered whether the pro-competitive benefits produced by an agreement outweigh the anti-competitive effects. The four criteria used to do this balancing test can be summarised as two positive conditions and two negative conditions.[81] Given that these four conditions are cumulative, it is unnecessary to examine any remaining conditions once it is found that one of the conditions of art 81(3) is not fulfilled. When these four conditions are fulfilled, the agreement enhances competition within the relevant market, because it leads the undertakings concerned to offer cheaper or better products to consumers, compensating the latter for the adverse effects of the restrictions of competition. McKechnie J in the High Court considered the four-pronged art 81(3) test in the *BIDS* case, referred to above, and concluded that *BIDS* had only discharged the onus of proof in respect of three of the four criteria (although given his first conclusion that the arrangement did not infringe art 81(1), he did not need to rule on the applicability of art 81(3) so the judge's finding in this regard can only be regarded as *obiter*). The judge found that *BIDS* had not discharged the burden of proving that the arrangements allowed a fair share of resulting benefits to consumers.

The wording in art 81(3) is echoed in the wording in s 4(5) of the Irish legislation.

7.044 When an agreement is covered by a block exemption, the parties to the agreement are relieved of their burden under the Modernisation Regulation of showing that their individual agreement satisfies each of the conditions of art 81(3). The parties only have to prove that the restrictive agreement benefits from a block exemption. An agreement must satisfy all the requirements of the relevant regulation in order to benefit from the block exemption. Agreements within the terms of a block exemption are valid and this provides legal certainty. Block exemptions are blanket exemptions from the prohibition of art 81(1). The block exemptions currently in force are set out at para **7.028** above.

7.045 The most common block exemption is the Vertical Restraints Block Exemption (Commission Regulation 2790/1999). Vertical agreements generally pose a low risk of anti-competitive effect unless one of the undertakings has a high degree of market power. The Vertical Restraints Block Exemption together with the Vertical Restraints Guidelines allow companies to make their own assessment of vertical agreements under EC Competition law. The Vertical Restraints Block Exemption exempts vertical agreements from the prohibition of art 81, provided that the agreements comply with certain conditions. In order to fall within the terms of the Block Exemption, the relevant market share must be less than 30 per cent.[82] The agreement cannot contain any hard-core restrictions such as price-fixing or a restriction on passive sales. The agreement must also not contain restrictions which, although not hard-core, go beyond what is necessary to obtain the commercial objectives of the agreement. An example of such a restriction would be a non-compete in excess of five years or a post-termination

81 Cahill, Connery, Kennedy and Power, *European Law* (4th edn, OUP, 2008), p 167.

82 In the case of an exclusive distribution agreement the relevant market share is the supplier.

non-compete. The Block Exemption creates a safe harbour for vertical agreements. There is no presumption of illegality where an agreement falls outside the scope of the Vertical Restraints Block Exemption; however, businesses must then make their own assessment under the criteria of art 81(3). The Block Exemption does not apply to agreements that are the subject of another block exemption.

Abuse of Dominance

Section 5 of the Competition Act

7.046 Section 5 of the 2002 Act states that an abuse by one or more undertakings of a dominant position in trade for any goods or services in any part of the state is prohibited.[83] The section gives some examples of abuses of dominance (which are also set out in art 82 EC). They are:

(a)   directly or indirectly imposing unfair purchase or selling prices or other unfair trading conditions;

(b)   limiting production, markets or technical development to the prejudice of consumers;

(c)   applying dissimilar conditions to equivalent transactions; and

(d)   making the conclusion of contracts subject to the acceptance by other parties of supplementary obligations which by their nature or commercial usage have no connection with the subject of such contracts.

Having a dominant position alone does not raise competition law concerns; it is only when this position of economic strength is abused that concerns arise.

> Competition law does not outlaw economic power, only its abuse. Economic power may, indeed should, be the reward of effective satisfaction of consumer needs. It would be inconsistent with the objectives of free competition that successful competitors should be punished. It is not the existence but the abuse of a dominant position which offends principles of free and open competition.[84]

---

83   Former Minister Des O'Malley made some interesting comments on the competition law culture in the debate on the Competition Bill 2001: 'Activities have gone on [in Ireland] over several decades which were wrong and for which in other countries the perpetrators would have been imprisoned. However, here most people cannot see that anything is wrong. Some of these concerted practices and abuses of dominant position were so blatant, and at the same time so accepted, that they were carried out by semi-State bodies. When one or two lone voices, such as mine, raised queries about them we were looked at askance, as though we were cranks seeing crimes where no crime existed. It was assumed that a semi-State body had every entitlement to abuse its dominant position. I remember drawing attention to some of the activities of Aer Lingus for which the company was fined a substantial sum by the [European] Commission and saying that those who ran Aer Lingus would not only have received a fine if this had taken place in the USA, but would also have been sent to prison for quite a lengthy period. The reaction to that statement was one of laughter.' Dáil Éireann – Vol 550 – 08 March 2002, Competition Bill 2001 [Seanad]: Second Stage (Resumed).

84   Fennelly J in the decision in *Competition Authority v O'Regan* [2007] 2 ILRM 161.

Abuses of dominant positions can easily distort competition. For example, dominant undertakings abuse their dominance when they engage in such practices as predatory pricing, unreasonable refusals to supply and unfairly discriminating between customers in a similar situation.[85]

Article 82 of the EC Treaty

7.047 Article 82 of the EC Treaty states that:

> any abuse by one or more undertakings of a dominant position within the common market or in a substantial part of it shall be prohibited as incompatible with the common market in so far as it may affect trade between member states.

Such abuse may, in particular, consist in:

(a) directly or indirectly imposing unfair purchase or selling prices or other unfair trading conditions;

(b) limiting production, markets or technical development to the prejudice of consumers;

(c) applying dissimilar trading conditions to equivalent transactions with other trading parties, thereby placing them at a competitive disadvantage; and

(d) making the conclusion of contracts subject to acceptance by the other parties of supplementary obligations which by their nature or according to commercial usage, have no connection with the subject such contracts.

7.048 In relation to art 82, it must be shown that the undertaking is dominant and that it has abused its dominance. The ECJ in *United Brands* defined a dominant position under art 82 as:

> [A] position of economic strength enjoyed by an undertaking which enables it to prevent effective competition being maintained on the relevant market by giving it the power to behave to an appreciable extent independently of its competitors, customers and ultimately of its consumers. In general a dominant position derives from a combination of several factors which, taken separately, are not necessarily determinative.[86]

In relation to the question of whether an undertaking is dominant, a central issue will be the definition of the market in which it operates. The term 'substantial' in art 82

---

85 See also McCarthy and Power, *Irish Competition Law: The Competition Act 2002* (Tottel Publishing, 2003).

86 It may be fitting that 'dominance' is defined in a case about bananas – *United Brands Company and United Brands Continentaal BV v Commission of the European Communities*, Case 27/76, [1978] ECR 207, [1978] 1 CMLR 429. See also *Michelin v Commission* Case 322/81 [1983] ECR 3461, [1985] 1 CMLR 282 in which the court stated: 'A finding that an undertaking has a dominant position is not in itself a recrimination but simply means that, irrespective of the reasons for which it has such a dominant position, the undertaking concerned has a special responsibility not to allow its conduct to impair genuine undistorted competition on the common market', Roth (ed), *Bellamy & Child: European Community Law of Competition* (5th edn, Sweet and Maxwell, 2001), Ch 9.

refers not just to the geographical size of the market, but also to the volume of trade. In *Suiker Unie v The Commission*,[87] the ECJ said that for this purpose, 'the pattern and volume of the production and consumption of the products as well as the habits and economic opportunities of the vendors and purchasers must be considered.' In an abuse of dominance case, a defendant would be attempting to define the market as broadly as possible so that it would be more difficult to show dominance. The converse is true of plaintiffs and prosecutors.[88] A market is defined by way of its relevant product market and its relevant geographic market.[89]

Relevant product market

7.049 EC case law and EC notices are the main guides in determining how to define the relevant product market. The Competition Authority has regard to the Commission Notice on Relevant Market Definition[90] when defining markets and, in particular, uses the Small but Significant Non-transitory Increase in Price (SSNIP) test to establish substitutability. Both demand-side and supply-side substitutability is considered. In *Chanelle Veterinary Ltd v Pfizer (Ireland) Ltd*,[91] the High Court reminded the parties that in pleadings based on alleged abuse of a dominant position, the onus rests on the plaintiff to establish, on the balance of probabilities, that a distinct product market exists. In that case, the High Court ruled that the plaintiff had failed to show that Pfizer enjoyed a dominant position on any of the alternative product market definitions advanced. The Competition Authority has in a number of cases tended to define product markets narrowly. For example, in *Drogheda Independent*,[92] the Competition Authority defined a market for advertising in local newspapers in the greater Drogheda Town area. The Authority did not consider advertising on local radio, in national newspapers, local newspapers in adjacent areas, or freesheets or other media to be a sufficient substitute for local newspaper advertising. In *Competition Authority v O'Regan*,[93] the High Court accepted the Authority's contention that there was a market for credit union representation services (ie representation or advocacy services and regulatory services as provided by the Irish League of Credit Unions (ILCU) to its individual member credit unions) and a separate market for savings protection schemes (essentially deposit protection insurance offered by ILCU to credit unions and which

---

87   *Suiker Unie and Ors v The Commission* Joined cases 40 to 48, 50, 54 to 56, 111, 113 and 114-73/73 [1975] ECR 1663, [1976] 1 CMLR 295.

88   In the case of mergers, markets are often argued by the notifying parties to be quite narrow in order to minimise any risk of areas of overlap despite the risk of increased market shares with very narrow markets.

89   Market definition is also important for merger control and to avail of block exemptions or to show that an agreement does not appreciably affect competition.

90   OJ [1997] C 372/5.

91   *Chanelle Veterinary Ltd v Pfizer (Ireland) Ltd* [1999] 2 IR 365.

92   *Drogheda Independent* Competition Authority Decision No E/05/001 (Case COM/05/03), the alleged predation by Drogheda Independent Company Ltd in the market for advertising in local newspapers in the greater Drogheda area, 7 December 2004.

93   *Competition Authority v O'Regan* [2004] IEHC 330, Kearns J.

credit unions are *de facto* obliged to obtain). This case was appealed to the Supreme Court, and became the first case in which the Supreme Court had to adjudicate upon substantive competition law issues.[94] The Supreme Court overruled the High Court's decision, finding that savings protection schemes were not in fact a commercially saleable product and that the Competition Authority had failed to provide an economic analysis to substantiate its claim that representation services and savings protection schemes were distinct products in distinct product markets. At EC level, very narrow product markets have been drawn and consequently small firms have been found to have dominance on these markets.[95]

Relevant geographic market

7.050 EC case law on relevant geographic market is again persuasive in applying and interpreting the Competition Act. Where there are inherently local characteristics to a product or service market, or where there are natural or regulatory barriers to trading outside a given locality within the state, then the relevant geographic market will be that locality rather than the state, on the basis that customers cannot realistically be expected to seek alternative sources of supply outside the locality. In *Jim Blemings v David Patton Ltd*,[96] the High Court considered a dispute between a group of broiler-chicken growers and a poultry processor. In assessing the relevant geographic market for the purpose of s 5 of the Competition Act (abuse of dominance), the court considered conflicting arguments from economist expert witnesses that the market was a fifteen-mile radius around the defendant's plant or, alternatively, the entire state. The court ruled that the market was the fifteen-mile radius.[97] In general, a relevant geographic market is one where the conditions of competition are homogeneous within that geographic area.

Proof of dominance

7.051 In addition to drawing on EC precedents and guidelines, the Competition Authority has employed some more quantitatively verifiable measures of dominance tests familiar in US anti-trust law, such as the Herfindahl-Hirschman Index.[98] Evidence of the existence of barriers to market entry is also an important element in proving dominance in the Irish market.

7.052 In *Meridian v Eircell*, the High Court considered various tests of dominance in the context of an allegation by Meridian that Eircell held a dominant position in the market for mobile telephony services in the state.[99] In its analysis, the court considered

---

94 [2007] 2 ILRM 161.
95 See, for example, *Hugin v Commission* Case 22/78 [1978] ECR 1869.
96 *Jim Blemings v David Patton Ltd* [2001] 1 IR 385.
97 Narrow geographic markets include *Frankfort Airport* [1998] 4 CMLR 779 and *Holyhead Port* [1992] 5 CMLR 255.
98 US Dept of Justice & Federal Trade Commissionn, Horizontal Merger Guidelines (2 April 1992, revised 8 April 1997). CR4 is also used to measure levels of concentration on a market.
99 *Meridian Communications Ltd and Cellular Three Ltd v Eircell Ltd* [2002] 1 IR 17.

both structural aspects of the market (including market shares, number of competitors, barriers to entry and expansion, ease of switching, market growth and churn (number of subscribers who switched providers)) and behavioural issues (principally, pricing), before concluding that the plaintiffs had failed to prove that Eircell was dominant. The court found that the significance of Eircell's market share was diminished in light of its decline over a relatively short period. Esat Digifone was a strong competitor and well placed to exploit any laxity on the part of Eircell. The court was also influenced by the fact that barriers to expansion were low and by market data which suggested that Eircell's pricing behaviour was strongly constrained by Esat Digifone.[100]

7.053 In *Competition Authority v O'Regan*,[101] (see para **7.049** above) the High Court referred to EC case law in considering the issue of dominance – it noted the high market share (80 per cent and 100 per cent on the respective product markets), which had existed for some time, and the high barriers to entry. The High Court found that ILCU was in a position of 'super dominance'. On appeal to the Supreme Court, the court found that if there were truly distinct markets for the supply of representation services and savings protection schemes, then ILCU would enjoy an exceptionally large market share in each of them. Although a very high market share may, in certain circumstances, exist without the seller having that market power which is the essential characteristic of a dominant position, the court accepted that a large market share is always regarded as strongly indicative of dominance. In light, however, of the court's conclusion that the Competition Authority had not established that savings protection schemes constituted a distinct product, still less a separate product market, the court did not need to consider the issue of dominant position or its abuse.[102]

In *Ticketmaster Ireland*[103] the Competition Authority found that, although Ticketmaster held 100 per cent of the Irish market for outsourced ticketing services for events of national or international appeal, no dominant position existed due to the constraint placed on Ticketmaster by large event promoters which amounted to significant countervailing buyer power.

7.054 What is important to note from these cases is that market share alone is not enough to determine dominance. There are many indicators of dominance. Market structure has to be considered together with the market share of the dominant entity. The strength of competitors and customers also have to be analysed to consider whether there may be countervailing buyer power in the case of customers or competitive constraints exercised by competitors. With a market share of 90 per cent or more, the responsibility of a dominant firm becomes greater where the firm enjoys a position of dominance approaching monopoly, which can be known as super-dominance.[104] Under EC law, with a market share of 50 per cent or more on its own, it

---

100 In an earlier hearing in October 2000, the court had found that there was no case in respect of allegations of joint dominance for Eircell.

101 *Competition Authority v O'Regan* [2004] IEHC 330, Kearns J.

102 [2007] 2 ILRM 161.

103 *Ticketmaster Ireland* Case COM/107/02, 26 September 2005.

104 *Compagnie Maritime Belge Transports SA v Commission* Cases C-385 and 396/96P [2000] ECR II–1201.

will normally be presumed that the accused undertaking is dominant unless the undertaking can point to other factors which (when cumulatively assessed) de-accentuate, rather than amplify, the significance of its large market share.[105] A market share in the 40–50 per cent range will generally be insufficient by itself to warrant a finding of dominance. Market share of below 40 per cent is unlikely to be found to occupy a dominant position unless market structure is so otherwise fragmented that it could suggest dominance.[106] Other relevant market structure factors that are considered include vertical integration, fragmented competitors, ability to preserve market share over time, and despite competition, homogenous or innovative product market, whether the undertaking has strength to absorb losses competitors cannot sustain, the impact of any relevant intellectual property rights, oligopolistic markets for findings of collective dominance, and whether any entity owns an essential facility.

Prohibited conduct

7.055 Section 5 and art 82[107] set out a non-exhaustive list of abuses,[108] Some of the most common abuses are discussed further below.[109] It is important to note that the dominance, the abuse and the effects of the abuse need not all be in the same market.[110]

Refusal to deal

7.056 There is no absolute obligation, even on a dominant entity, to deal. Freedom to deal is a key element of commercial and contract law. There is a presumption of contractual freedom in the principle that the owner of an asset has the right to choose if, with whom and under what terms he will enter an agreement.

---

105 *AKZO Chemie v Commission* Case C-62/82 [1991] ECR I–3359.

106 The Commission found BA to be dominant with a market share of 39.7 per cent in *Virgin/BA* [2000] 4 CMLR 999, upheld by the *BA v Commission* CFI T–219/99 [2003] ECR II 5917, upheld on appeal to the *BA v Commission* [2007] ECR I 2331 ECJ C–95/04 P.

107 DG Comp issued a discussion paper in 2005 on exclusionary abuses under art 82 and expressed that it is prioritising these types of abuses. Exclusionary abuses are where a dominant firm is trying to prevent the development of competition (thereby excluding competitors and competition). Exploitative abuses are abuses designed to reduce output and increase prices above the competitive level thereby exploiting customers: http://www.ec.europea.eu/comm/competition/antitrust/art82/index.html.

108 DG Comp issued a discussion paper in 2005 on exclusionary abuses under art 82 and expressed that it is prioritising these types of abuses. Exclusionary abuses are where a dominant firm is trying to prevent the development of competition (thereby excluding competitors and competition). Exploitative abuses are abuses designed to reduce output and increase prices above the competitive level thereby exploiting customers: http://www.ec.europea.eu/comm/competition/antitrust/art82/index.html.

109 Please see Communication from the Commission of 3 December 2008 COM(2008) Guidance on the Commission's Enforcement Priorities in Applying Article 82 EC Treaty to Abusive Exclusionary Conduct by Dominant Undertakings.

110 *Michelin v Commission* C-322/81 [1983] ECR 3461; *Tetra Pak* II C–333/94 P [1996] ECR I 5951.

Refusal to deal will be considered to infringe competition law only if it is carried out by a firm enjoying a dominant position and without objective justification. *In Chanelle Veterinary Products Ltd v Pfizer (Ireland) Ltd*,[111] the plaintiff alleged, among other things, that Chanelle's decision to reduce from five to four the number of exclusive wholesalers for its veterinary products in the state amounted to abuse of a dominant position. Pfizer had refused to continue to supply the plaintiff as a wholesaler. The High Court rejected this argument. The Supreme Court affirmed the High Court's judgment.[112]

7.057 In *Meridian v Eircell*,[113] Meridian alleged that the refusal by Eircell to renew a volume discount agreement, under which Meridian received discounts of up to 40 percent on subscriptions for mobile phone air time, amounted to an abuse by Eircell of a dominant position in the mobile telephony market. The court found that Meridian had failed to prove dominance on the part of Eircell and therefore that any claims based on abuse of dominance must fail.

7.058 In *Competition Authority v O'Regan*,[114] the Competition Authority suggested that the court could consider the practices in question under two possible headings: refusal to supply and tying. It argued that Irish League of Credit Union's behaviour could be seen as a refusal to supply because it denied access to savings protection to credit unions which were not members of ILCU. The High Court, however, decided the case primarily on the tying question. In the Supreme Court, Fennelly J stated that given his finding that savings protection schemes were not a commercially saleable product, there could be no questions of an abusive refusal to supply.

7.059 The Competition Authority receives a very large number of complaints based on refusal to supply and, in December 2005, it published a Guidance Note on Refusal to Supply.[115] The Guidance Note is designed to provide guidance to complainants so that they may improve the quality of their complaints, to assist businesses in complying with the relevant competition law and to ensure maximum transparency as to how the Competition Authority deals with such complaints. A refusal to deal that is made on the basis of a commercial objective justification, such as real concerns about the risk of bad debt, would not amount to an abusive refusal to supply.

Refusal of access to essential facilities

7.060 A subset of refusal to deal or refusal to deal or refusal to supply is the doctrine of refusal to grant access to an essential facility.

The doctrine of essential facilities came from the US and has more recently been limited in its application in that jurisdiction. In the *Trinko* case, the US Supreme

---

111 *In Chanelle Veterinary Products Ltd v Pfizer (Ireland) Ltd* [1999] 2 IR 365.
112 *In Chanelle Veterinary Products Ltd v Pfizer (Ireland) Ltd* [1999] 2 IR 365.
113 *Meridian v Eircell* [2002] 1 IR 17.
114 *Competition Authority v O'Regan* [2004] IEHC 330, Kearns J.
115 Competition Authority Guidance Note: Refusal to Supply, December 2005.

Court[116] limited the applicability of the essential facility doctrine and gave the essential facilities argument short shrift. Although a US doctrine, essential facilities had never been adjudicated on by the US Supreme Court before except as part of a general refusal to deal. The court initially noted that, '[w]e have never recognized such a doctrine, and we find no need either to recognize it or to repudiate it here.'[117] The court explained that '[i]t suffices for present purposes to note that the indispensable requirement for invoking the doctrine is the unavailability of access to the "essential facilities"; where access exists, the doctrine serves no purpose.'

7.061 In the EU, in light of the *IMS Health*,[118] *Magill*,[119] *Oscar Bronner*[120] and *Microsoft*[121] cases, it would appear that the following tests have to be satisfied before there is a refusal to grant access to an essential facility:

(i) the owner of an indispensable asset refuses access and thus competition will be eliminated; and

(ii) the owner of the facility cannot show that his refusal is objectively justified.

In addition, where intellectual property rights are involved, it must be shown that the holder of an indispensable intellectual property right refuses access and thus competition will be eliminated, and that had access not been refused, new product(s) would have been introduced.

The addition of the 'new product requirement' by the ECJ in cases where the intellectual property right itself is the essential facility, such as *Magill* and *IMS Health*, shows that EC courts are more cautious with intellectual property rights than with physical property. The *Microsoft case*[122] also dealt with refusal to grant access.

7.062 In Ireland, in 1998, the Competition Authority carried out an investigation at the request of the Minister for Enterprise, Trade and Employment on the question of access by mobile phone operators to the mast sites of the national police force, An Garda Síochána, for locating mobile phone antennae. The investigation arose from a request by one of the two then existing licensed mobile operators, Eircell, for access to

---

116 *Law Offices of Curtis V Trinko v Verizon*, 540 US 398 (2004) – specifically, *Trinko* held that where a government agency has powers to enforce access to a facility, the essential facilities doctrine will not apply. The Court shared a healthy skepticism of generalist courts' ability to manage sharing: 'Enforced sharing also requires antitrust courts to act as central planners, identifying the proper price, quantity, and other terms of dealing – a role for which they are ill-suited.' – para 408. The Court explained that '[i]t suffices for present purposes to note that the indispensable requirement for invoking the doctrine is the unavailability of access to the 'essential facilities'; where access exists, the doctrine serves no purpose – at p 411.

117 540 US at para 411.

118 *IMS Health GmbH & Co OHG v NDC Health GmbH & Co KG* Case C–418/01, [2004] ECR I–3401.

119 *RTÉ and ITP v Commission* Joint Cases C–241 & 242/91, [1995] ECR I–743.

120 *Oscar Bronner v Mediaprint* Case C–7/97, [1998] ECR I–7791, para 41.

121 Commission Decision of 24 March 2004, upheld on appeal to the CFI T–201/04, dated 17 September 2007; separate appeal on T–167/08 9 May 2008.

122 Commission Decision of 24 March 2004, upheld on appeal to the CFI T–201/04, dated 17 September 2007; separate appeal on T–167/08 9 May 2008.

the Garda masts against a background where the other operator, Esat Digifone, already had an access agreement with the Garda Síochána. The Competition Authority concluded that access to Garda masts was not essential to enter the mobile telephony market and that the EC essential facilities doctrine therefore should not be applied in this case.[123]

7.063 The leading Irish case on essential facilities is *Meridian Communications v Eircell*.[124] As part of its case, Meridian (a mobile virtual network operator) claimed that the mobile network owned by licensed operator Eircell constituted an essential facility and that refusal by Eircell to give access to its network was therefore an abuse of Eircell's dominant position. In the High Court, O'Higgins J reviewed the previous US and EC case law on the doctrine of essential facilities and held that Eircell's infrastructure was not an essential facility. This was because there was an alternative to it (ie the facility of a competing licensed provider, Esat Digifone). Not only was Eircell's network susceptible to being replicated, but it had in fact been replicated by Esat Digifone and was in the course of being replicated by a third competitor, Meteor. It could not be validly asserted that the refusal of access made it difficult for Meridian or any other undertaking to compete. The cost of duplicating the facility had not been a barrier to entry for either Esat Digifone or for Meteor. The fact that there were a limited number of licensees did not, in the court's view, transform something into an essential facility that would not otherwise be such. Therefore, in the court's view, Eircell had no facility which could not be replicated.

Discrimination and discriminatory pricing

7.064 There is no Irish case law to date on abuse of a dominant position by way of discriminatory pricing.[125] The decision of the Commission in *Irish Sugar* that there had been discrimination was upheld by the CFI as infringing art 82(2)(c).[126] Section 5 of the Competition Act prohibits a dominant supplier from 'applying dissimilar conditions to equivalent transactions with other trading parties, thereby placing them at a competitive disadvantage.'

Discrimination that is based on reasonably objective criteria and which has a legitimate economic or commercial justification would likely not be prohibited; for example, differentiating between high- and low-volume customers. If, however, it can be shown that the price discrimination reflects exploitation of the dominant undertaking's strength at the expense of its customers, or that it has the object or effect

---

123 Competition Authority Annual Report 1998, at pp 31–32.

124 *Meridian Communications v Eircell* [2002] 1 IR 17.

125 In EU law discriminatory treatment and discriminatory pricing has been dealt with in such judgments as *Deutsche Post AG* [2002] 4 CMLR 598 concerning the Interception of cross border mail, it was found that it was treating different types of cross border mail in different ways and there was a concern that this amounted to discrimination and the disadvantages to consumers. See also *Akzo Chemie* case op cit.

126 *Irish Sugar Plc v Commission* T–228/97 [1999] ECR II 296.

of excluding particular players in a market, the discrimination would mostly likely amount to abuse of a dominant position.

7.065 Another area where a dominant undertaking has a special responsibility not to discriminate in terms of supply between customers is when that undertaking supplies to customers who compete with the supplier's own downstream retail arm. Examples of sectors where this issue has arisen are telecommunications, electricity and gas. In the gas sector, the Competition Authority has intervened in response to complaints against the then *de facto* monopoly supplier, Bord Gáis Éireann (BGE), to emphasise BGE's duties in this regard.[127] Specifically, the Competition Authority emphasised that BGE cannot charge different prices to firms buying similar quantities of gas to its own retail arm or offer more favourable terms to a customer in which it has an interest. It should also be noted that the telecommunications and electricity sectors are subject to specific *ex ante* control regimes by sectoral Regulators. A prohibition on unfair discriminatory treatment in particular in relation to pricing by dominant players is a feature of these regimes.

7.066 In 2004, the Competition Authority considered a case (under both art 82 and s 5) in which the Irish Simmental Cattle Society (ISCS) had increased its registration charges on the transfer of pedigree Simmental Stock from foreign herds by more than it had for transfers from Irish herds. The ISCS undertook to the Competition Authority not to discriminate between cattle on the basis of country of origin and the Competition Authority therefore took no further action.[128]

Predatory pricing

7.067 Predatory pricing, or selling below cost, can amount to an infringement of s 5 or art 82 in certain circumstances. The Competition Authority has investigated a number of complaints relating to alleged predation. It issued an enforcement decision relating to *Drogheda Independent*[129] (although it concluded that *Drogheda Independent* was not dominant in the market concerned) in order to set out its methodology for analysing such allegations. The Competition Authority follows a 'structured rule of reason approach' in analysing predation. This involves assessing: (i) the plausibility of the alleged predation on an *ex ante* and *ex post* basis – ie whether the predation makes economic sense and whether the victim went out of business and prices rose subsequently; (ii) a business justification – is there a valid business reason for dropping prices; (iii) the feasibility of recoupment – ie can the short-term losses be recovered through charging higher prices in the medium-to-longer term; and (iv) whether there has been pricing below cost. The Competition Authority's approach thus

---

127 Competition Authority Annual Report 1998, at p 16.
128 Competition Authority Annual Report 2004, at p 13.
129 *Drogheda Independent* Competition Authority Decision No E/05/001, (Case COM/05/03) The alleged predation by Drogheda Independent Company Limited in the market for advertising in local newspapers in the greater Drogheda area, 7 December 2004.

departs from the traditional EC formulaic test[130] of when pricing is predatory; only one element involves an analysis of costs, rather than the US style approach in respect of the requirement of recoupment.

Margin squeezing

7.068 A vertical margin squeeze can occur where a firm is dominant in an upstream market and supplies an input to an undertaking that competes with it on a downstream market.[131] The dominant firm, having control over the price it charges for the input, can control the ability of the firm to compete with it on the downstream market. In *Deutsche Telekom*,[132] the Commission fined Deutsche Telekom, which had a dominant position on the local loop and margin squeezed in relation to access. Deutsche Telekom's retail prices were so low when compared with its wholesale prices that it left new entrants no margin to compete for subscribers.

Fidelity rebates and discounts

7.069 To date, there has been no Irish case law on abuse of a dominant position by way of fidelity rebates and discounts. A fidelity or loyalty rebate results in the customer buying all or most of its requirements from the dominant supplier and will constitute an abuse of a dominant position under s 5 of the Competition Act if the effect of the rebate is to give rise to market foreclosure. Irish competition law is likely to follow Community precedent in relation to fidelity rebates[133] or target discounts which are designed to have loyalty inducing effect.[134]

---

130 In *Akzo v Commission* C62/86 [1991] ECR I 3359 the ECJ held that where prices are below average variable cost (AVC), predation had to be presumed since every sale would generate a loss for the dominant firm. See Case COMP/38.233 *Wanadoo Interactive,* Commission Decision of 16 July 2003. See also the CFI judgement in *France Telecom v Commission* T–340/03 [2007] ECR II 107, where the court agreed that the Commission was correct in its decision in *Wanadoo* in light of *Akzo* and *Tetra Pak* that the Commission did not have to prove recoupment of losses as a precondition to making a finding of predatory pricing on appeal to the ECJ *France Telecom v Commission* C–202/07 P – not yet decided. AVC is not always the correct standard and in certain industries other costs such as, for example, incremental cost may be the appropriate standard where fixed costs are high and variable costs are low, eg post.

131 See *Industrie des Poudres Spheriques v Commission* Case T-5/97 [2000] ECR II-3755; and see also Commission Decision in *Telefonica* Case T- 336/07 4 July 2007 under appeal and *Telefonica Espana v Commission* not yet decided.

132 *Deutsche Telekom v Commission* T–271/03, 10 April 2008.

133 *Hoffmann-La Roche v Commission* Case 85/76 [1979] ECR 461.

134 *Virgin/British Airways* Case T-219/99 *British Airways plc v Commission* [2003] ECR II 5917 on appeal to ECJ C-95/04 P *British Airways v Commission* [2007] ECR I 2331; See also *Michelin I NV Nederlandse Banden-Industrie Michelin v Commission* Case 322/81 [1983] ECR 3461 and *Michelin II Michelin v Commission* Case T-203/01 [2003] ECR II 4071.

Tying

7.070 Tying can involve a dominant firm leveraging its position in relation to the tying product to increase its position in the tied product market. The *Microsoft* case[135] dealt with tying and the Commission found (upheld by the court on appeal) that Microsoft had abused art 82(2)(d) by making the conclusion of a contract subject to the acceptance of supplementary obligations which have no connection with the contract.

7.071 In a decision involving a tour operator, *Falcon Holidays*, the Competition Authority objected to an arrangement whereby the operator made it mandatory for persons buying holiday packages from Falcon to purchase travel insurance from a particular insurance broker. Falcon had a significant share of the holiday market. The Competition Authority found that the arrangement restricted the freedom of customers to choose their own insurer and also prevented other brokers from selling their services to Falcon customers. Falcon agreed to modify its agreement and to allow customers the express option of taking the pre-arranged insurance policy or of making alternative arrangements for insurance.[136]

7.072 In a decision involving the ILCU in June 2002,[137] the Competition Authority revoked a certificate (negative clearance) previously awarded to ILCU under the 1991 Act, because ILCU had disaffiliated member credit unions which purchased insurance cover from any provider other than ILCU's own insurance subsidiary. In the subsequent litigation, *Competition Authority v O'Regan*,[138] the High Court found that there was a 'double tie' at work, namely the obligation on credit unions who sought access to ILCU's savings protection scheme to avail of ILCU's credit union representation services and also its mandatory insurance arrangements, known as a savings protection schemes. As discussed above (at paras **7.049** and **7.053**), the Supreme Court found that in order to sustain an allegation of illegal tying, it is first necessary to establish the existence, from the viewpoint of consumer demand, of an independent product market for each of the products in question, and that there is widespread sales of the tying item in unbundled form. Citing, with approval, texts on tying and bundling and a number of EC decisions, including *Tetra Pak*,[139] *Hilti*,[140] *British Airways*,[141] and the Commission's

---

135 *Microsoft Corp v Commission* Case T 201/04 [2007] ECR II 000.

136 Competition Authority Decision No 274: *Falcon Holidays/Ben McArdle Ltd*, 4 February 1994.

137 Notice under s 2(7) of the 1991 Act, 25 June 2002, Revocation of Decision No 440, Irish League of Credit Unions.

138 *Competition Authority v O'Regan* [2004] IEHC 330, Kearns J. Supreme Court appeal reported at Supreme Court [2007] 2 ILRM 161.

139 *Tetra Pak Rausing v Commission* C–333/94 [1996] ECR 1–5951, also T–51/89 [1990] ECR 11–309.

140 *Hilti AG v Commission* C–53/92 [1994] ECR 1–667, also T–30/89 [1991] ECR 11–1439.

141 *British Airways v Commission* T–219/99 [2003] ECR 11–5917.

decision in *Microsoft*,[142] the Supreme Court reached the conclusion that a savings protection scheme was not a distinct product but rather had always existed as an integral part of the bundle of services that ILCU provided to its own members.

Excessive pricing

7.073 In August 2005, the Competition Authority published a decision regarding an allegation of excessive pricing against Greenstar Recycling Holdings Ltd (Greenstar).[143] The Authority found that, although Greenstar held a dominant position in the market for the provision of household waste collection services in North East Wicklow (a suburban area adjacent to Dublin City), the prices charged by Greenstar were unlikely to be in breach of s 5 of the Competition Act for a number of reasons. It could not be shown that Greenstar's prices were excessive when compared with the social or economic value of the relevant service, or when compared with the prices charged by private operators in other markets. Even if it could be demonstrated that Greenstar's prices were excessive, the Competition Authority noted that there was an absence of an obvious effective remedy for such a breach. The Authority took the view that neither itself nor the courts was equipped to be price Regulators. It concluded that a better alternative to a price Regulator would be for contracts for household waste collection to be awarded via competitive tendering, so that competition for the market could replace the existing model of competition within the market. Excessive pricing was considered in *United Brands*.[144]

Other conduct

7.074 The introduction by the Electricity Supply Board (ESB) of an 'English clause' into supply contracts with large customers in 1998, in anticipation of liberalisation of the market for electricity, was considered by the Authority to be contrary to the 1991 Act. The clause essentially provided that a customer of ESB, which at the time had a statutory monopoly on supply, was required to notify ESB it if received an offer of supply on more favourable terms from a new market entrant when liberalisation came into effect in 2000. The customer agreed it would not take up a new offer without reverting to ESB and allowing it an opportunity to match or offer more favourable terms. The Competition Authority intervened pursuant to a complaint and insisted the clause be removed.[145] Other forms of abuse can include the taking of vexatious

---

142 Commission Decision of 24.03.04 relating to a proceeding under Art 82 of the EC Treaty. Case COMP/C–3/37.792.

143 Competition Authority Decision No E/05/002 (30 August 2005).

144 *United Brands Company v Commission* Case 27/76 [1978] ECR 207.

145 *Donovan v ESB* [1994] 2 IR 305.

litigation,[146] bundling,[147] failure to invest in a network,[148] extension of dominance[149] and leveraging.[150]

Merger Control

7.075 Irish merger control law is contained in Pt 3 of the 2002 Act. The authority responsible for the enforcement of merger control in Ireland is the Competition Authority. There is a special regime in place for media mergers and banking mergers. In respect of media mergers, the Competition Authority must refer these to the Minister for Enterprise, Trade and Employment ('the Minister'). In respect of mergers between credit institutions, the Minister for Finance has a relevant role. For large mergers that meet the turnover thresholds set out in the EC Merger Regulation, the European Commission is the relevant Regulator.[151]

The Competition Authority's Guidelines for Merger Analysis[152] explain the Authority's position on substantive issues in merger control and provide guidance on market definition. In its amended Notice (12 December 2006), guidance is provided on

---

146 *Promedia v Commission* Case T-111/96 [1998] ECR II 2937.

147 A firm may sell two or more products together as a bundle and charge more attractive prices for the bundle than for the constituent parts of it. Bundling may have the same effect as a tie-in agreement. In *De Post/La Post* the Commission imposed a fine on the Belgian Post Office for offering lower prices to customers in the case of a bundle: OJ [2002] L61/32.

148 Further to an investigation by the European Commission into E.ON, RWE and Wattenfall in respect of collective dominance, which included the abuse of discouraging investment and inefficient investment in networks, EON offered commitments to the European Commission to divest certain aspects of its business. The Commission published an art 27(4) Notice asking for interested parties' observations on the proposed commitments in June 2008 – OJ C146/34, 12 June 2008. RWE also offered commitments in May 2008 – MEMO/08/355, 31 May 2008.

149 *Greek Lignite* Case OJ C93/3 15 April 2008 – the abuse involved reinforcing dominance on the downstream market in respect of a vertically integrated company. It was held that it did not matter if the entity was not active outside of self-supply on a particular market. The Commission based its decision on the ECJ judgment in *IMS Health GmbH & Co OHG v NDC Health GmbH & Co KG* Case C–418/01, [2004] ECR I–3401.

150 Although there is arguably no independent abuse of leveraging (see O'Donoghue and Padilla, *The Law and Economics of Article 82 EC* (Hart Publishing, 2006)), leveraging may occur where an undertaking uses its dominant position in one market to be abusive in a neighbouring market for example in the Microsoft case the Commission found that Microsoft sought to leverage its dominance in computer operating systems in the related markets for operating systems software and media player – Commission Decision of 24 March 2004, upheld on appeal to the CFI T–201/04, dated 17 September 2007. Leveraging may also occur where a dominant entity extends its legitimate State monopoly into unreserved neighbouring markets.

151 Unless the so called 'two-thirds rule' is met.

152 Competition Authority Decision No N/02/004, Notice in respect of Guidelines for Merger Analysis (16 December 2002).

matters relating to calculation of turnover and the concept of undertakings involved in the merger in respect of certain terms used in Pt 3 of the 2002 Act.[153] The Competition Authority has indicated that notifying parties and their advisers can look to the European Commission Notices and Guidelines for guidance on matters not specifically covered by the Competition Authority.

7.076 On 10 July 2007, the European Commission adopted a Consolidated Jurisdictional Notice under Council Regulation (EC) No 139/2004[154] on the control of concentrations between undertakings. It provides up-to-date guidance on the Commission's jurisdiction to review transactions under the current Merger Regulation. The new consolidated Jurisdictional Notice replaces the previous four Notices, all adopted by the Commission in 1998 under the previous Merger Regulation, Council Regulation No 4064/89.[155]

7.077 The European Commission's Consolidated Jurisdictional Notice under Council Regulation (EC) No 139/2004 on the control of concentrations between undertakings also provides relevant guidance in the case of Irish merger control and where a merger is being notified to the European Commission.

Relevant mergers in Ireland

7.078 The circumstances under which a merger or acquisition is deemed to occur are set out in s 16 of the Competition Act. A merger or acquisition occurs if:

(a)   two or more undertakings, previously independent of one another, merge, or

(b)   one or more individuals or other undertakings who or which control one or more undertakings acquire direct or indirect control of one or more other undertakings, or

(c)   the result of an acquisition by one undertaking of the assets, including goodwill (or a substantial part of the assets), of another undertaking is to place the first undertaking in a position to replace (or substantially to replace) the second undertaking in the business or, as appropriate, the part concerned of the business in which that undertaking was engaged immediately before the acquisition.

---

153 On 12 December 2006, the Competition Authority amended Notice N/02/003. Two amendments have been made to Notice N/02/003, now entitled 'Notice in respect of certain terms used in Pt 3 of the Competition Act 2002'. First, art 3 has been amended to clarify the Authority's understanding of the phrase 'carries on business in any part of the island of Ireland'. Second, a new art 5 has been inserted, to give the Authority's understanding of the phrase 'within 1 month after', as used in ss 18(1) and 21(2) of the Act.

154 Available at http://www.ec.europa.eu/comm/competition.

155 Notice on the concept of concentration (OJ C 66, 02.03.1998); Notice on the concept of full-function joint ventures (OJ C 66, 02.03.1998); Notice on the concept of undertakings concerned (OJ C 66, 02.03.1998); and (iv)Notice on calculation of turnover (OJ C 66, 02.03.1998.

A merger occurs if a joint venture is created to perform, on a lasting basis, all the functions of an autonomous economic entity.

Section 16(2) of the Competition Act sets out that control shall be regarded as existing if decisive influence is capable of being exercised with regard to the activities of the undertaking.

Thresholds

7.079 Pursuant to the Competition Act, it is mandatory to notify mergers and acquisitions that reach the financial thresholds set out in s 18, which are as follows:

(i) the worldwide turnover of each of two or more of the undertakings is at least €40 million;

(ii) each of two or more of the undertakings involved carries on business in any part of the island of Ireland (ie Ireland and Northern Ireland); and

(iii) the turnover in the state (ie Ireland) of any one of the undertakings involved in the merger or acquisition is not less than €40 million.

7.080 A company is deemed to carry on business in any part of the island of Ireland where it has sales into the island of Ireland, even where it does not have a physical presence in Ireland. The Competition Authority has clarified that it understands 'turnover in the State' to comprise services supplied to customers within the State, ie the Republic (Competition Authority Decision No N/02/003).[156] Following criticism that the merger test was capturing mergers which did not have sufficient nexus to Ireland to merit falling under the merger regime, in that any merger which meets the thresholds must be notified to the Competition Authority if each of the two companies carries on business in the island of Ireland, even in the absence of a substantive overlap, the Authority adopted a *de minimis* concept. On 12 December 2006, the Competition Authority amended Notice N/02/003, 'Notice in respect of certain terms used in Pt 3 of the Competition Act 2002.' Article 3 has been amended to clarify the Authority's understanding of the term 'carries on business'. The Authority now understands that term as including undertakings that either:

(a) have a physical presence in the island of Ireland and makes sales or supply services to customers in the island of Ireland; or

(b) without having a physical presence in the island of Ireland, have made sales into the island of Ireland of at least €2 million in the most recent financial year.

7.081 Since 1 January 2003, media mergers must be notified to the Competition Authority, irrespective of whether they meet the financial thresholds set out above. As of 1 May 2007,[157] a 'media merger' means a merger or acquisition in which two or more of the undertakings involved carry on a media business in the State or,

---

156 Notice in Respect of Certain Terms Used in s 18(1) of the Competition Act 2002, as amended (18 February 2003).

157 SI 122/2007.

alternatively, one or more of the undertakings involved carries on a media business in the State, and one or more of the undertakings involved carries on a media business elsewhere. A 'media business' means:

(i)   a business of the publication of newspapers or periodicals consisting substantially of news and comment on current affairs;

(ii)   a business of providing a broadcasting service; or

(iii)   a business of providing a broadcasting services platform.

Notifying mergers to the Competition Authority

7.082 Mandatory merger notifications, fulfilling the financial thresholds as set out above (at **para 7.080**), should be made to the Competition Authority within one month of the conclusion of an agreement or the making of a public bid. All parties are obliged to make a notification, although in practice the parties usually file a joint notification. A notification will not be accepted prior to the conclusion of a binding agreement or the making of a public bid; therefore, a notification will not be accepted on the basis of a memorandum of understanding, a letter of intent or heads of agreement.[158] A filing fee of €8,000 must accompany the filing. It is an offence not to notify a merger which is required to be notified. A merger which is put into effect in advance of clearance, where clearance is required, is void.

Voluntary notifications

7.083 The Competition Authority also has a system for voluntary merger notifications which seeks to take account of a merger that does not meet the financial thresholds set out above and is thus referred to as a non-notifiable merger. A decision as to whether or not a merger should be notified, if it does not reach the thresholds set out in s 18, should be made based on a consideration of the markets that will be affected by the prospective merger and the approach that the Competition Authority has previously adopted in decisions relating to this market. The Competition Authority's Guidelines for Merger Analysis (N/02/004), explains the Competition Authority's position on substantive issues in merger control and suggest that parties should consider the following situations which highlight a particular concern: (a) where a dominant firm acquires a smaller rival or new entrant whose turnover was below €40 million; (b) the acquisition of a new entrant by another player in an otherwise oligopolistic market; or (c) the acquisition of a dominant Irish player by a strong player in a neighbouring market that had otherwise intended to enter the Irish market. If a merger does not raise competition concerns, failure to notify will not have any consequences for the parties.

---

158 On 1 January 2003, Competition Act 2002 (Notification Fee) Regulations 2002 (SI 623/ 2002), prescribing the fees payable for filing merger notifications with the Competition Authority, came into effect. A fee of €8,000 is prescribed for the purposes of a notification under s 18(8) of the Competition Act, further to SI 623/2002. Where the parties file a joint notification, only one payment of €8,000 is required. Where two separate notifications are filed, €8,000 each is required. All merger notifications must be notified to the Competition Authority on the standard form for notifications (available at http://www.tca.ie).

Assessment process

7.084 Regardless of whether a merger qualifies for a mandatory or voluntary notification, the parties may request pre-notification discussions with the Mergers Division of the Competition Authority. Pre-notification discussions are welcomed by the Competition Authority as they help the parties in the preparation of a notification and assist the Mergers Division to understand the nature of competition in the relevant market.

7.085 There is a two-phase examination process by which the Competition Authority examines mergers. The test the Competition Authority uses when assessing a merger is that of a 'substantial lessening of competition', ie if the merger does not substantially lessen competition in the market for goods or services, it will be cleared. Once the Competition Authority has determined that the merger or acquisition may be put into effect after either Phase I or Phase II, the notifying parties must complete the merger or acquisition in question within twelve months of the date of the determination.

On 1 March 2006, two documents published by the Competition Authority setting out revised procedural rules in relation to merger notifications, 'Revised Procedures for the Review of Mergers and Acquisitions' and 'Procedures for Access to the file in Merger Cases', came into effect.

7.086 Section 20(1)(a) of the Competition Act gives third parties who wish to comment on a merger the opportunity to do so. It provides that, within seven days following the receipt of the merger, the Competition Authority is obliged to publish a notice of receipt inviting third parties to comment. The Revised Merger Procedures stipulate that a third party wishing to make a submission about a merger must do so within ten days of the publication of the notice on the Competition Authority's website. The Competition Authority has a discretion to change this time limit in respect of individual cases should it wish to do so, depending on the specific circumstances.

Phase 1

7.087 Once a merger has been notified to the Competition Authority, it enters into Phase I proceedings. Phase I is an initial period of one month during which the Competition Authority must assess the proposed merger and decide to either authorise it, on the grounds that it would not substantially lessen competition, or, alternatively, carry out a more detailed investigation. This one-month period may be extended to forty-five days if competition concerns are raised and the parties and the Competition Authority negotiate undertakings or commitments to address the potential competition issues identified in the Phase I investigation. During the Phase I investigation, the Competition Authority may exercise its right under the Competition Act to 'stop the clock' and make a formal request for further information. The one-month investigation will recommence as soon as the requested information has been gathered. If at this stage the Competition Authority still has concerns that the proposed merger will substantially lessen competition in the market, it may clear the merger at the end of a Phase I investigation but make it subject to certain commitments satisfying competition concerns, or, alternatively, it may refer the merger to a Phase II. While commitments may be volunteered in Phase I, the Competition Authority may impose conditions on its determination after a Phase II investigation.

Phase II

7.088 Once a Phase II investigation has commenced, it can run for up to four months from notification or from receipt of the response to an information request, if applicable (ie normally an additional three months). During this time, the Competition Authority has to investigate the merger and decide whether it should be cleared, cleared subject to conditions or blocked. Once the Phase II investigation has commenced, notifying parties are given an initial period of 21 days to make additional submissions to the Competition Authority. A Phase II investigation involves a more detailed investigation of the relevant market(s) and may also involve an oral hearing at the request of the parties. During a Phase II investigation, the Competition Authority may negotiate undertakings or commitments with the parties to address any concerns it may have about the effects of the proposed merger on competition in the market.

7.089 The Competition Authority may issue a clearance decision or a clearance subject to conditions after eight weeks from the opening of the Phase II investigation. Within the eight-week period, or shortly thereafter, the Competition Authority will furnish a written assessment to the notifying parties addressing the competition concerns that have arisen in the course of investigations. Notifying parties in a Phase II investigation are provided with access to the Competition Authority's file during the three-week period between receipt of the written assessment and their response. Notifying parties are granted access to all documents on file, with the exception of internal working documents of the Competition Authority and confidential documents. The Access Procedures set out the Competition Authority's practice on access to non-confidential documents and its procedures for ensuring protection of confidentiality.

7.090 Pursuant to s 22(3) of the Competition Act, on completion of a full investigation, the Competition Authority makes a determination that the merger or acquisition: (a) may be put into effect, (b) may not be put into effect, or (c) may be put into effect subject to conditions specified by it being complied with, on the ground that the result of the merger or acquisition will or will not, as the case may be, substantially lessen competition in markets for goods or services in the state or, as appropriate, will not substantially lessen such competition if the specified conditions are complied with.

Media mergers

7.091 Media mergers, regardless of the financial thresholds involved, must be notified to the Competition Authority. Once the initial notification is made to the Competition Authority, a copy is sent to the Minister for Enterprise, Trade and Employment by the Competition Authority. Once the Competition Authority has made its assessment, it is obliged to refer the merger to the Minister. If after the Phase I investigation the Competition Authority is satisfied the merger will not result in a substantial lessening of competition, it must refer the merger to the Minister, who then has a period of ten days in which he or she may decide, on the basis of specified 'public interest' criteria, to direct the Competition Authority to open a Phase II investigation. The relevant criteria by which the Minister assesses a media merger include the following matters:

(a) the strength and competitiveness of media businesses indigenous to the State,

(b) the extent to which ownership or control of media businesses in the State is spread amongst individuals and other undertakings,

(c) the extent to which ownership and control of particular types of media business in the State is spread amongst individuals and other undertakings,

(d) the extent to which the diversity of views prevalent in Irish society is reflected through the activities of the various media businesses in the State, and

(e) the share in the market in the State of one or more of the types of business activity falling within the definition of 'media business' in s 23(10) that is held by any of the undertakings involved in the media merger concerned, or by any individual or other undertaking who or which has an interest in such an undertaking.

If at the end of a Phase II investigation, the Competition Authority wishes to clear a merger or, alternatively, clear the merger subject to conditions, the Minister may then, within 30 days, prohibit the merger or impose new or stricter conditions on the parties. The Minister does not have the power to implement a media merger if the Competition Authority has prohibited it on competition grounds.

Credit institution mergers

7.092 The government adopted the Credit Institutions (Financial Support) Act 2008 in October 2008, which amended the Competition Act 2002. Section 7 of that Act provides that in the case of a merger involving credit institutions, the Minister for Finance may approve a merger, notwithstanding that the merger would substantially lessen competition, where he considers it necessary to maintain the stability of the financial system in the State and that there would be a serious threat to that stability if the merger did not proceed.

Merger control under the EC Merger Regulation

7.093 The EC Merger Regulation[159] sets out the turnover thresholds for notifying mergers to DG Competition of the European Commission. The Merger Regulation applies to 'concentrations'. A concentration exists where one or more undertakings acquire direct or indirect control of the whole or parts of one or more other undertakings. In practical terms, this means that a concentration arises when there is an acquisition of sole control or of joint control. There must be a 'change of control on a lasting basis'. A merger or an acquisition would constitute a concentration. As under Irish law, a concentration can also arise in the case of joint ventures where there is joint control exercised by two or more undertakings over the joint venture which is a full-function joint-venture that is an entity which has sufficient resources to carry out the functions of an autonomous economic entity on a lasting basis. 'Control' is defined as involving 'the possibility of exercising decisive influence'. Moreover, there must be a change of control on a lasting basis for there to be a concentration for the purposes of

---

159 Council Regulation (EC) No 139/2004 of 20 January 2004.

the Merger Regulation. In order to fall within the scope of the Merger Regulation, a concentration must also be of a particular scale, ie it must have a Community dimension.

7.094 A concentration has a Community dimension when either of two tests are satisfied. The first test deals with very large mergers and involves satisfying the following criteria:

> The combined aggregate worldwide turnover, in the preceding financial year, of all the undertakings concerned in the transaction exceeds €5 billion; and the aggregate Community-wide turnover of each of at least two of the undertakings concerned exceeds €250 million.

This applies unless each of the undertakings concerned achieves more than two-thirds of its Community-wide turnover in one and the same Member State. In that case, the merger does not have a Community dimension and is subject to domestic merger rules.

7.095 If the first test is not satisfied, then there is also an alternative test. This involves satisfying the following criteria:

(i) the combined aggregate worldwide turnover of all the undertakings concerned exceeds €2.5 billion; and

(ii) in each of at least three member states, the combined aggregate turnover of all the undertakings concerned exceeds €100 million; and

(iii) in each of those three member states, the turnover of each of at least two of the undertakings concerned exceeds €25 million; and

(iv) the aggregate Community-wide turnover of each of at least two of the undertakings concerned exceeds €100 million.

This applies unless each of the undertakings concerned achieves more than two-thirds of its aggregate Community-wide turnover within one and the same member state. In that case the merger does not have a Community dimension and is subject to domestic merger rules rather than the one-stop shop under the Merger Regulation.

7.096 If a concentration falls within the Merger Regulation, it is regulated exclusively by the European Commission, unless:

(1) There is a distinct market within the meaning of art 9 of the Merger Regulation. A concentration that will significantly affect competition within a member state and which presents all the characteristics of a distinct market, or presents all the characteristics of a distinct market and which does not constitute a substantial part of the Common Market, may be referred to the member states and the Commission may forsake its jurisdiction;[160] or

(2) A prior notification request has been made by the parties to the transaction further to art 4(4) that the concentration will significantly affect competition in a market within a Member State which presents all the characteristics of a

---

160 Member States may, post-notification, request that a concentration having a Community dimension should be referred to them.

distinct market and therefore should be examined in whole or in part by that member state; or

(3)   Article 21(4) of the Merger Regulation applies where Member States may take appropriate measures to protect legitimate interests other than those taken into consideration by the Merger Regulation and which are compatible with the general principles and other provisions of Community law. The Regulation provides that public security, plurality of the media and prudential rules[161] are regarded as legitimate interests within the meaning of art 21(4);

7.097 Pursuant to art 4(5) (pre-notification) and art 22 (post-notification) of the Merger Regulation, concentrations not having a Community dimension can also be referred by Member States to the European Commission to reduce the amount of multiple filings.

Proposed concentrations with a Community dimension must be notified to the Commission 'prior to their implementation and following the conclusion of the agreement, the announcement of the public bid, or the acquisition of a controlling interest.'[162]

7.098 Notification may also be:

[M]ade where the undertakings concerned demonstrate to the Commission a good faith intention to conclude an agreement or, in the case of a public bid, where they have publicly announced an intention to make such a bid, provided that the intended agreement or bid would result in a concentration with a Community dimension.[163]

The notification must be made by the bidder in the case of a public bid, by the buyer in the case of an acquisition of sole control, or jointly on behalf of all parties to a joint venture.

7.099 Parties usually engage with the Commission before notification at pre-notification meetings. These meetings involve discussion of the jurisdiction, the contents of the notification form and any information which does not need to be filed. Notification is made to the Commission by way of Form CO,[164] which is set out in Regulation 802/2004. No filing fee is paid to the Commission. The original, 5 paper copies and 32 copies in CD or DVD must be filed. If a transaction has been notified to the Commission, then it may not be implemented unless and until it has cleared the transaction. Article 11 of the Merger Regulation enables the Commission to issue requests for information, which must be answered. Article 12 allows Member State authorities to conduct inspections on behalf of the Commission and the Commission also has the power to conduct inspections by virtue of art 13.

---

161 That is, rules designed to ensure the stability and financial adequacy of banks and credit institutions are regarded as legitimate interests.

162 Article 4(1) of the Merger Regulation.

163 Article 4(1) of the Merger Regulation.

164 There is also a short form and provision for a form RS (reasoned submission) in Regulation 802/2004.

7.100 The substantive test in the Merger Regulation is whether or not the proposed concentration would 'significantly impede effective competition in the Common Market or a substantial part of it, in particular as a result of the creation or the strengthening of a dominant position' (art 2(3)). This test is somewhat different to the 'substantial lessening of competition' test used in Ireland and to the test used under the previous Merger Regulation, which was whether or not the proposed transaction would create or strengthen a dominant position as a result of which effective competition would be significantly impeded.

7.101 The Commission's horizontal merger guidelines should be consulted in the event of a horizontal concentration. On 10 July 2007 the Commission adopted a new Commission Consolidated Jurisdictional Notice under Council Regulation (EC) No 139/2004 on the control of concentrations between undertakings. The Consolidated Jurisdictional Notice replaces the previous four Notices[165] adopted by the Commission in 1998 under the previous Merger Regulation (Regulation No 4064/89). The new consolidated Notice therefore covers a wide range of issues of jurisdiction relevant for establishing the Commission's competence under the new Merger Regulation.

7.102 The transaction must be suspended pending clearance, and gun-jumping attracts significant fines as well as the risk that the transaction is void, if it closes the transaction prior to clearance.

Phase I

7.103 The Commission deals with the vast majority of cases in Phase I but occasionally goes into a second phase. The first phase lasts for 25 working days, starting on the day which follows the receipt of the notification, but this can be extended to 35 working days if undertakings or commitments are offered, or a referral request is received pursuant to art 10(1) of the Merger Regulation. In Phase I, the Commission must decide if the proposed transaction is a concentration with a Community dimension and, if it is, then whether the Commission has serious doubts about its compatibility with the Common Market. During Phase I, if the Commission believes that the proposed transaction may be approved subject to conditions, then the Commission must issue a reasoned decision to that effect. If the Commission finds during Phase I that the transaction is not a concentration, or it is not a concentration with a Community dimension, then the Commission must make a reasoned decision to that effect. In such circumstances, Member State competition law applies unless the matter is referred back to the Commission under a procedure provided for under art 22 of the Merger Regulation. Any decision declaring a proposed concentration to be compatible is deemed to cover restrictions which are directly related and necessary to the implementation of the concentration, known as ancillary restraints.

---

165 Notice on the concept of concentration (OJ C 66, 02.03.1998); Notice on the concept of full-function joint ventures (OJ C 66, 02.03.1998); Notice on the concept of undertakings concerned (OJ C 66, 02.03.1998) and Notice on calculation of turnover (OJ C 66, 02.03.1998).

Phase II

7.104 The second phase lasts for 90 working days from the day that follows the decision to carry out the in-depth inquiry (art 10(3)). Twenty working days are added, if requested, by the notifying parties or by the Commission with the agreement of the parties. A further 15 days are added, if undertakings offer remedies after 55 working days following the initiation of the in-depth inquiry (Phase II). If the Commission believes that the proposed transaction presents 'serious doubts' that there is risk that the proposed transaction would be incompatible with the Common Market,[166] then the Commission must issues a statement of objections and initiate the Phase II process. The Commission is faced with three choices at the end of Phase II: (a) approve the merger unconditionally; (b) approve it subject to conditions; or (c) block it. The Commission issues a statement of objections to the parties during Phase II. This sets out the Commission's views as to why the proposed transaction would be incompatible with the Common Market. The parties will have a right to make a written reply to this statement of objections and present their case orally at a formal hearing. It is possible, in certain circumstances, for notifying parties to avoid a prohibition decision by making commitments or undertakings to the Commission. These may be made either during the first or second phase. The Commission prefers structural remedies (eg offers to divest) rather than behavioural remedies, which require ongoing supervision.

ENFORCEMENT

7.105 In general, enforcement can happen by way of a complaint being made to a Regulator or by way of the Authority, ComReg, or the European Commission investigating a matter on their own initiative. Enforcement by the European Commission is a civil law only matter. In both criminal and civil cases in Ireland, the Competition Authority is the main agency charged with enforcement of Irish competition law (together with the courts and, in the case of Electronic Communications, ComReg).[167] In order to enable them to discharge their functions, the Authority, ComReg and the European Commission have a number of powers to assist in the investigation of competition offences. Private enforcement of competition law is

---

166 It will be interesting to see if, in light of the recent consolidation in the banking sector, the failing firm defence will be raised in relation to some of these mergers in order to get them through.

167 Although the enforcement in this chapter focuses on the Authority, ComReg also has competition law enforcement powers in respect of electronic communications and is a member of the European Competition Network. The Communications Regulation (Amendment) Act 2007 (the 2007 Act) confers on the Irish telecommunications Regulator, ComReg, competition law powers similar to those of the Competition Authority. Part 4 of the 2007 Act amends the Competition Act 2002 to provide for co-competition powers for ComReg in relation to the communications sector. Under this part, where a matter arises under ss 4 or 5 of the Competition Act 2002 in the communications sector, ComReg and the Competition Authority are required to agree jurisdiction in respect of the matter, and if they cannot agree, the question of jurisdiction will be determined by the Minister for Enterprise, Trade and Employment, whose decision is final.

also open to parties before the court. This section will examine both the civil and criminal aspects of enforcement.

Complaints – Ireland

7.106 Complainants may bring complaints to the Competition Authority who may then investigate those complaints. The Authority screens complaints[168] to enable it to focus on the most substantive complaints and to dispose quickly of cases which do not raise competition law concerns. In relation to the rights of the complainant (and other third parties), the Competition Authority has indicated[169] that it will not comment either on the progress of a complaint or indeed on whether or not any complaint has been made. The Competition Authority will notify a complainant to acknowledge receipt of a complaint and may occasionally contact the complainant in order to seek additional information. The Competition Authority will also notify the complainant when the case is being closed. Competition Authority investigations which do not proceed to court action are usually closed in one of two ways. First, the Competition Authority may issue a letter to indicate that it is closing its file on the matter, but reserving its right to re-open the file at its discretion. Alternatively, the Competition Authority may seek undertakings from the party subject to investigation for a breach of s 4 or 5, for example, to cease the behaviour complained of and to comply in future in all respects with the Competition Act in return for the Authority not proceeding with the case to court. These undertakings may be published by the Competition Authority, either in its annual report or by way of published enforcement decision. Enforcement decisions are published by the Competition Authority in selected cases which demonstrate the Authority's approach to a particular competition issue, are of public interest, or raise issues of interest or complexity.[170]

Investigations by the Competition Authority

7.107 The primary investigative tool is the power to search the premises of suspected undertakings and the homes of individuals involved in their management. The Competition Authority has extensive investigative powers under the Competition Act. 'Dawn raids' are investigations carried out by the Competition Authority by way of unannounced visits to business premises, pursuant to a search warrant from a District Court Judge, where the Competition Authority's officers may inspect the premises, seize relevant files and interview staff. Competition Authority officers have powers to seize original documents and records, as well as to take copies of relevant material. A person engaged in an activity under investigation may be required to give any information the authorised officer may deem reasonable regarding the activity in question.

---

168 Competition Authority Annual Report 2003, at p 8.

169 Competition Authority Guidance Note: Refusal to Supply, December 2005.

170 Section 30(1)(g) of the Competition Act 2002 gives the Authority the function of 'carrying on such activities as it considers appropriate' to inform the public about competition issues.

7.108 A search is grounded on a search warrant issued to an authorised officer of the Competition Authority, by a District Court Judge pursuant to s 45(4) of the Competition Act 2002. There are no prescribed criteria for deciding whether an investigation at a business premises is justified; it is a matter of discretion for the Competition Authority, subject to the procurement of a warrant from a District Court Judge. The Authority may obtain a warrant to enter the private dwellings of directors, managers or staff of companies subject to investigation. The power to enter private dwellings may only be exercised where there are reasonable grounds to believe that records relating to the business are being kept there. As a matter of practice, sworn information to ground the application for a search warrant for either a premises or a dwelling should meet the 'reasonable grounds' standard. Searches of premises or private dwellings must be exercised within one month of the date of issue of the warrant, or within such other time period as is specified in the warrant. This search warrant allows entry by force and seizure from the premises, or connected vehicles, of any books, records and documents relating to the activity of the undertaking. This means that physical equipment, such as computers, may be removed for examination. Furthermore, persons on the premises may be required, on pain of prosecution, to answer certain questions relating to the activity engaged in by the undertaking. Similarly, any person who obstructs or impedes an investigation will be guilty of an offence attracting a fine of €3,000 and/or six months' imprisonment.

7.109 Section 45(6) was amended by the Investment Funds Companies and Miscellaneous Provisions Act 2005 to ease logistical difficulties with retaining evidence under the original wording. The original wording provided that the Authority could retain documents, computers etc for a period of six months, but in order to retain them after that time, the Authority had to apply to the District Court within the six months. The Authority now has a right to retain the evidence indefinitely without any obligation to account to the District Court which issued the initial warrant or to the owners of the property as to why it retains them. This is not unusual in criminal investigations;[171] physical objects used to commit crime are seized by the police on a daily basis as evidence and retained until trial and often forfeited and destroyed thereafter.

7.110 It is now the practice of the Competition Authority to enter premises in conjunction with members of An Garda Síochána, who are also authorised officers of the Competition Authority. To this end, there are now members of the National Bureau of Fraud Investigation assigned to the Competition Authority. When the premises of an undertaking or individual is searched, the search will not be suspended to allow legal representatives of the undertaking to arrive.[172] An undertaking's legal adviser is entitled to attend at the premises being searched. A search team should include one

---

171 *Competition Authority v District Judge O'Donnell* [2007] IEHC 390, O'Neill J. In that case, the procedure for retention was discussed together with the right of the subject of a search to give evidence as to the effect on them of having their property removed.

172 This is unlike the practice of ComReg and the European Commission who, when they are carrying out a 'dawn raid', allow a period of reasonable time for the lawyers to arrive before commencing their investigation.

officer who acts as liaison between the undertaking and the team; any requests for a list of what is being seized and other queries should be addressed to that person, for example, a request for a copy of the search warrant or sight of warrants of appointment and identification of the search team. Clearly, if the warrant is defective, any evidence garnered during the search may be excluded at a later stage. Issues concerning legally privileged documents would also be raised with the investigating officers.

7.111 Section 45(3) of the Act provides for the questioning of persons on the premises. It should be noted that these persons, be they employees or directors, are not technically in custody and therefore have no right to legal representation. In addition, certain answers may be sought on pain of penalty. However, this of course would be subject to the right to invoke the privilege against self-incrimination, if applicable. In addition, compelled statements could not be relied upon to secure a prosecution.[173]

7.112 However, it should also be noted that certain cartel offences attract a sentence of five years' imprisonment. This means that pursuant to the Criminal Law Act 1997, they are 'arrestable' offences, ie a person may be arrested without warrant on suspicion of committing such an offence.[174] Due to the length of the sentence, a person may also be detained and questioned at a nearby Garda station pursuant to s 4 of the Criminal Justice Act 1984. A person may be detained for up to twelve hours and released without charge. The power to arrest arises not only in the context of a search but also at a later stage. The situation in respect of right of access to a lawyer changes if a person is arrested and detained for questioning. A person in Garda (or presumably other) custody has a constitutional right of reasonable access to a lawyer and a refusal to permit such access will render the detention illegal.[175] However, the Court of Criminal Appeal has held that the Gardaí are not obliged to inform the person in question about that right or to proffer the assistance of a lawyer without request.[176] There is no Irish equivalent of that element of the 'Miranda warnings'[177] whereby a person in custody must be told prior to questioning that he or she has the right to legal advice. Nor, under Irish law, has a person in custody the right to the presence of a lawyer while being questioned.[178] These aspects of Irish criminal procedure have been cogently criticised in the past for failing to recognise the importance of the pre-trial stage of criminal proceedings.[179]

---

173 *In the matter of National Irish Bank Ltd (under investigation) and in the matter of the Companies Act 1990 (No 1)* [1999] 1 ILRM 321.

174 This marks a sea change in the attitude of the Oireachtas to competition offences. Offences that were previously dealt with in a somewhat gentlemanly fashion are now squarely positioned in the realm of serious criminal offences.

175 *People (DPP) v Healy* [1990] 2 IR 73.

176 *People (DPP) v Madden* [1977] IR 336.

177 So named after the US Supreme Court's celebrated decision in *Miranda v Arizona* (1966) 384 US 436.

178 *People (DPP) v Pringle* (1981) 2 Frewen 57.

179 Casey, *Constitutional Law in Ireland* (2nd edn, Sweet and Maxwell, 1992).

7.113 However, persons who are being questioned in the course of an investigation are covered by the Judges' Rules, a series of guidelines on questioning for the police drawn up by judges in the UK in response to a request from the Home Secretary in 1912. Originally four rules, they are now nine in number.[180] In essence, a person may be questioned about the circumstances of a suspected crime; once, however, that person says something that makes the questioning officer believe that the person may be a suspect, they must be cautioned to the extent that they are no longer at that stage obliged to say anything, but anything that they do say may be taken down and used in evidence. Thus, if the subject of an investigation begins to implicate himself while being questioned at the premises, the subject should be cautioned.

7.114 The Competition Authority also has the power, pursuant to s 31 of the Act, to summons persons to appear before it to answer certain questions and to produce certain documentation. The summons is a formal document, which will set out the venue, date and time of the appearance and list what the person should bring. It is very much in the form of a *subpoena duces tecum*. Once a person is before the Competition Authority, they have the same rights and privileges as a witness before the High Court. The person will be examined on oath. Accordingly, they should be legally represented and advised of the privilege against self-incrimination.[181] Failure to appear is an offence. Failure to produce any document in the person's power or control that is legally required by the Authority, or to answer questions to which the Authority may legally require an answer is also an offence. On summary conviction, one may face a fine of €3,000 and/or a term of imprisonment of up to six months. Section 31 of the Competition Act allows the Authority to summon witnesses to appear before it to give evidence under oath. In December 2005, the District Court heard a case brought by the DPP against Pat Morgan, the Managing Director of TruGas Ltd, for failure to appear before the Competition Authority following a witness summons under s 31.[182] The Competition Authority had issued the summons following a written request for information during the consultation process leading to the making of its declaration in relation to exclusive purchasing agreements in the cylinder liquid petroleum gas sector. All of the elements of the offence were found to be met and, after giving Mr Morgan time to comply with the Competition Authority's earlier request for information, the judge applied the Probation Act.[183]

---

180 Woods, *District Court Practice and Procedure in Criminal Cases* (Woods, 1994) at p 62. For an analysis of the application of the rules in this jurisdiction and their text, see *AG v Cummins* (1972) IR 312.

181 Arguably, the privilege against self-incrimination only applies to senior employees such as directors or managers, since junior employees could not be prosecuted for breaches of ss 4 or 5 given that they would not have the power to bind an undertaking. In addition, it is important to note that a statement which is compelled may not be relied upon to secure a prosecution.

182 *DPP v Morgan (Tru Gas)* (22 December 2005, unreported), District Court, Judge Ryan.

183 *DPP v Morgan (Tru Gas)* (6 February 2006, unreported), District Court, Judge Ryan.

7.115 Despite all the weapons in the Authority's investigation armoury, there are difficulties obtaining evidence. If the Authority were to summon a witness before it to give evidence under s 31 of the Competition Act, such a compelled statement could not be used to convict a person – confession evidence to secure a conviction must be given voluntarily.[184] If the Authority were to meet the suspect and voluntarily request information, the suspect could refuse to meet or could refuse to answer questions which might be self-incriminating. Even if the Authority arranged for the arrest of the suspect, in the case of an arrestable offence, even while arrested the suspect would not have to answer any questions and certainly not any questions which might be self-incriminating. In the case of economic crimes, witness evidence is vitally important given that there is no smoking gun and cartels, are by their nature secret.[185] It is for this reason that the Competition Authority and the European Commission have specific programmes for members of a cartel to provide evidence and seek either exemption from prosecution or leniency in relation to fines, as the case may be please see paras **7.176** *et seq* on leniency below.

Confidentiality

7.116 Members of the Competition Authority, members of staff of the Competition Authority and authorised officers of the Competition Authority are prohibited by s 32 of the Competition Act from disclosing information which came into their possession by virtue of the exercise by the Competition Authority of its powers to obtain information, or in a private meeting with the Competition Authority. Business secrets and other confidential information of parties which are subject to investigation by the Competition Authority should be protected from disclosure. Breach of s 32 is a criminal offence. A person who suffers loss or harm as a result of a breach of s 32 may also bring civil proceedings for relief in the form of an injunction or court declaration or damages. (In any such proceedings, the Authority is entitled to the same privilege as a minister of government.) The prohibition in s 32 does not apply to communications necessary for the performance of the Competition Authority's functions, to disclosures for the purposes of legal proceedings, or to members of An Garda Síochána, where the issue may relate to the commission of a criminal offence. In addition, under s 34 of the Competition Act, the Authority has entered into various co-operation agreements with other regulatory agencies and may exchange confidential information with those agencies. Further to the Modernisation Regulation and the Competition Authority's membership of the European Competition Network (ECN), the Authority may also share confidential information with the Commission and other members of the ECN.

---

184 *In the matter of National Irish Bank Ltd (under investigation) and in the matter of the Companies Act 1990 (No 1)* [1999] 1 ILRM 321. See also the provisions of art 38 of the Irish Constitution, Bunreacht na hÉireann, 1937 regarding trial in the due course of law.

185 In the case of non-cartel cases, what is often in dispute is the effect that the behaviour has had on the market place where it is not possible to prove the object. In this case, expert witness evidence is usually required for trial.

Aspects of European Commission Investigations and Proceedings

7.117 In relation to proceedings involving art 81 and 82, the European Commission is responsible for administering the enforcement procedure as now set out in the Modernisation Regulation.[186] By virtue of arts 5 and 6 of the Modernisation Regulation, the Competition Authority together with the courts have the powers to apply arts 81 and 82 of the Treaty in full. This has the important practical effect of meaning cases dealing with breaches of these provisions that affect trade between member states may now be heard at local level in their entirety at first instance. It is envisaged by recital 15 of the Modernisation Regulation that this extra power given to national authorities and courts will lead to the emergence of a network of public authorities applying Community competition rules in close co-operation, known as the ECN. Chapter IV of the Regulation sets out the articles governing how this network will operate. In a case involving undertakings active in a market covering three countries, rather than have the initial intervention of three national authorities and the Commission, it was considered that, due to the information exchange in the ECN, in such a case the Commission would be best placed to act, otherwise the best-placed national authority would act.[187] When investigating a matter under arts 81 or 82, the Authority must notify the Commission and the ECN further to art 11 of the Modernisation Regulation.

7.118 If the Irish Competition Authority acts, it will carry out its investigation under the Competition Act and Irish procedures will apply. If the officials of DG Competition carry out the investigation, they will use their own 'dawn raiding' powers and European Community procedures will apply. There is no criminal law element to a European Commission investigation. However, the European Commission, using European law procedures, does not recognise in-house lawyer privilege.[188] By virtue of the powers set out in arts 17–22, Ch V of the Modernisation Regulation, the Commission may enter any premises, land or means of transport belonging to an undertaking, take copies or extracts from books and records and ask for oral explanations on the spot. It is the Commission practice to give undertakings a brief period of time to allow their legal representatives attend at the premises.[189] The Commission may request assistance from the local Competition Authority officials in the carrying out of their duties. Pursuant to art 23 of the Modernisation Regulation, an undertaking may face sanctions of fines not exceeding 1 per cent of total turnover if there is obstruction. The European Commission has the power to impose fines using

---

186 Regulation 1/2003.

187 See Commission Notice on co-operation within the network of Competition Authorities, OJ C 101/43, 27.4.2004, and Commission notice on the co-operation between the Commission and the courts of the EU Member States in the application of arts 81 and 82 EC, OJ C 101/ 54, 27.4.2004.

188 *Akzo Nobel Chemicals and Akcros Chemicals Ltd v Commission* T–125/03 and T–253/03 judgment of CFI, 17 September 2007.

189 This is also the practice of ComReg, however, it is not the general practice of the Competition Authority.

civil law, unlike the Competition Authority which must apply to the court to have fines imposed utilising criminal law procedures. The European Commission recently imposed a fine on E.ON Energie AG of €38 million because a seal was broken during an on-site investigation in this regard.[190]

7.119 If the Commission believes that there is an infringement of either arts 81 or 82, it will begin proceedings by way of a statement of objections. This is an administrative system applied by the Commission, not a court proceeding. The rules regarding the way the Commission acts as investigator are set out in Regulation No 773/2004.[191] A statement of objections is a document that follows a standard format. It will set out the parties to the agreement or abuse. It will describe the infringement according to the Commission. The evidence relied on will be set out. There will then be a section stating the legal assessment. This will be a legal analysis of the infringement, its effect on trade between member states, its duration and gravity etc. The party to which the statement of objections is addressed occasionally at this stage may respond in writing to the Commission's objections, in so far as it knows them before a statement of objection issues. This may occur as a result of the party knowing what documents the Commission has seized, who has been interviewed, what has been inspected. If a submission is made to the Commission in this way, it will be answered in the statement of objections. Finally, there will be the conclusions. In response to this statement of objections, the parties to which it is addressed have an opportunity to formally respond in writing.

7.120 The next step in the procedure is an oral hearing before the Hearing Officer. Prior to an oral hearing, the parties involved have a right to access the Commission's file. This will most likely be made available in the form of a CD or DVD with all the information contained thereon. The Hearing Officer is an official of DG Competition but independent from the enforcement units. He reports directly to the Commissioner. The procedure to be followed at an oral hearing is set out in Regulation 2842/98.[192] The oral hearing is relatively informal. It is not a judicial hearing, nor is it a forum to argue the case. It is a forum in which the parties have an opportunity to put their version of events to the Commission in response to what has been stated in the statement of objections. Arising out of representation made by the parties, the Commission may

---

190 See IP/08/108 30 January 2008 and Commission Decision OJ L 240/6 19 September 2008. In this case, blue plastic adhesive (with the yellow circle of the stars of the EU) was taped to seal the door of a room which the Commission was investigating at the end of a day to preserve the room pending resuming the investigation the following day. The seal was not intact when the Commission returned. E.ON denied breaking the seal or opening the door and provided affidavits in this regard. The Commission noted that art 23 of the Modernisation Regulation did not require proof that the door had been actually opened, it was enough that the seal was tampered with.

191 Commission Regulation (EC) No 773/2004 of 7 April 2004 relating to the conduct of proceedings by the Commission pursuant to arts 81 and 82 of the EC Treaty. OJ L 123/18, 27.4.2004.

192 Commission Regulation (EC) No 2842/98 of 22 December 1998 on the hearing of parties in certain proceedings under Articles 85 and 86 of the EC Treaty.

then alter its view of events. The oral hearing will take place in Brussels and is essentially a private meeting involving the Commission, the parties to which the statement of objections is addressed and delegates from the national Competition Authorities. Generally, oral hearings do not last more than a day.

7.121 Once an oral hearing has taken place, the Commission may then proceed to make a decision. Before it does so, it must place a draft version of its decision before the Advisory Committee on Restrictive Practices and Dominant Positions. This comprises officials from the National Competition Authorities within the European Union and, if appropriate, due to the geographic scale of the infringement, the EFTA member states. The Commission is obliged to consult with the Advisory Committee before making any decision in relation to establishing an infringement of arts 81 or 82, or any decision concerning the renewal, amendment or revocation of a decision pursuant to art 81(3). This consultation is a scrutiny of the Commission's reasoning in the case. The meeting with the Advisory Committee is not a public meeting, nor is the outcome of the meeting made public.

7.122 Once this procedure has been followed through, then the Commission may make its decision, including imposing fines (see para **7.144** *et seq* below). The decision must not contain any new allegation which was not contained in the statement of objections or subsequently properly notified to the parties, nor must it contain any new evidence.[193]

CIVIL ENFORCEMENT

Antitrust Enforcement by the Competition Authority[194]

7.123 Once the Authority has gathered all the information it requires, it will issue a letter of initiation. This letter indicates that the Authority is about to commence proceedings. Undertakings can respond to this letter setting out their position. However, given that the Competition Authority can only enforce competition law before the courts, it must bring all the relevant evidence to the court for it to do so. On occasion, the undertakings may offer commitments or undertakings to discontinue the investigated practice in return for the Authority not proceeding to the court.

7.124 Under the Competition Act, an action for a breach of ss 4 or 5 may be brought in either the Circuit or the High Court, whereas previously an action for a breach of s 4 of the 1991 Act could only be brought in the High Court. The Competition Authority has a legal right to take civil proceedings. The Competition Authority may seek relief by way of injunction or court declaration, but not damages. In addition, any person (including third parties) who is aggrieved as a result of a breach of ss 4 or 5 may take a civil action in either the Circuit Court or the High Court for relief by way of injunction,

---

193 *Petrofina v Commission* Case T–2/89 [1991] ECR II – 1087 39; *Ahlstrom v Commission* Cases C –89, 104, 116, 117 and 125 – 129/85, [1993] ECR I–1037, [1993] 4 CMLR 407.

194 The same procedures would also apply to ComReg in respect of the enforcement of ss 4 and 5.

court declaration or damages (including exemplary damages). In both Competition Authority and private civil cases where the action is in respect of a breach of s 5, the court may, on its own initiative or on the application of the Competition Authority, require the adjustment of the dominant position (for example, by way of disposals) or require that the dominant position be discontinued unless specified conditions (such as behavioural undertakings) are complied with.

7.125 Where enforcement occurs through the civil route, then a civil bill, plenary summons will be served on the parties involved in the normal way. An exception to this will be an application for an injunction. This procedure will usually involve the initiation, one after the other, of three sets of proceedings. The first will be an *ex parte* application to the court for an interim injunction. This will be supported by a grounding affidavit. Secondly, an application by way of notice of motion, again supported by affidavit, served on the other side, for an interlocutory injunction will be made. Finally, a plenary summons stating the grounds to seek a permanent injunction will be served on the other side. The notice of motion, plenary summons and Order of the Court should be served immediately after securing an interim injunction.

Presumptions and admissibility of evidence

7.126 Once in court, there are a number of presumptions, set out in s 12 of the Competition Act 2002, which operate in favour of the prosecution or plaintiff in either civil or criminal proceedings. For example, where it appears that a certain person created a document, it shall be presumed they did, and any statement made therein was made by that person. Also, if the document purports to have been sent to another, it shall be presumed that it was sent and received. Where a document is retrieved from a computer file, it shall be presumed that the person who ordinarily used that computer created the document. Section 13 goes on to discuss the admissibility of certain statements in documents. These provisions are a new departure from the normal rules of evidence, which contain no such presumptions in favour of the plaintiff or prosecution. Section 12 provides for certain rebuttable presumptions to arise where documents are admitted as evidence in an action, whether civil or criminal.[195] The term 'documents' is defined as including electronic and other forms of text. Section 13 contains provisions on the admissibility of statements in documents, which are submitted in evidence. These provide that statements made by a person who has committed an offence to the effect that another person has also committed an offence may be admitted, and incorporate protections for the other person who is the subject of the statements, eg testing the witness' credibility. The document in which the statements are contained cannot be written after proceedings have started or in response to an investigation. The court may also appoint independent assessors to

---

195 This section gives effect to certain recommendations of the Competition and Mergers Review Group, providing for presumptions on the authorship, ownership, receipt and other matters relating to documents.

competition law cases in the special rules of the Superior Court for competition cases.[196]

Defences to enforcement by the Competition Authority

7.127 It may be argued as a defence to a competition law case that an agreement benefits from the efficiency criteria set out in s 4(5) of the Competition Act or art 81(3) of the EC Treaty. It may also be argued that an agreement benefits from the provisions of a declaration or block exemption or does not appreciably affect competition. In proceedings for an offence contrary to s 6(1), ie hard-core cartel offence, it is a good defence, pursuant to s 6(3), to show that the agreement, decision or concerted practice complained of, benefited from a declaration from the Competition Authority, ie that it falls within a category of agreements, decisions or concerted practices which, having regard to all the relevant market conditions, contributes to improving the production or distribution of goods or provision of services, or to promoting technical or economic progress, while allowing consumers affair share of the resulting benefit and does not—

(a) impose on undertakings concerned terms which are not indispensable to the attainment of those objectives;

(b) afford undertakings the possibility of eliminating competition in respect of a substantial part of the products or services in question.

If no declaration exists, it may be pleaded that s 4(5) or art 81(3) applies, together with a justification for its application. Furthermore, it may be pleaded in defence that the act or acts concerned was or were done pursuant to a determination made or direction given by a statutory body. The declaration replaces the former defence whereby under the previous Competition Acts, one could plead that the agreement, decision or concerted practice either benefited from a licence or a category certificate saying it did not contravene s 4. Section 13(9) provides immunity from damages where the undertaking is acting in a manner consistent with a ruling of a sectoral Regulator.

7.128 If the case is in respect of art 82, objective justification may be used as a defence to certain allegations of abuse. In addition, entities that carry out a service of general economic interest, such as a public service or universal service obligation, may argue that art 82 of the EC Treaty only applies in so far as its application would not prevent the entity from being able to carry out its service of general economic interest – art 86(2). In this way, art 86(2) may be used as a defence to actions based on art 82 for public service or universal service providers.

Right of action

7.129 The Competition Authority is entitled to bring civil actions for breaches of ss 4 and 5 in the same way as any other private party, with the restriction that it will not be

---

196 Order 63B Competition Proceedings; Rules of the Superior Courts (Competition Proceedings) 2005 (SI 130/2005).

able to recover damages. Declaratory relief is also available to the Competition Authority[197] as well as to private parties.

7.130 Injunctive relief is available to both the Competition Authority and private parties filing civil actions under the Competition Act. The grounds for securing an injunction are a matter of general Irish law and are not unique to competition law. The plaintiff must satisfy the High Court that:

(1)   there is a stateable case on the substantive issue in dispute;

(2)   damages would not be an adequate remedy; and

(3)   the 'balance of convenience' is in favour of granting the injunction.

7.131 In *Competition Authority v Avonmore Waterford Group plc*[198] the Competition Authority sought an interlocutory injunction to prevent one defendant from acquiring the second. The court was satisfied that there was a fair issue for trial. However, on the question of the adequacy of damages as a remedy, the court considered that damages would not be an adequate remedy for the defendants if an interlocutory injunction were granted. It concluded, therefore, that the balance of justice favoured refusing to grant the injunction sought.

7.132 In both Competition Authority and private civil cases where the action is in respect of a breach of s 5, the court may on its own initiative or on the application of the Competition Authority require the adjustment of a dominant position (for example, by way of disposals)[199] or require that the dominant position be discontinued unless specified conditions are complied with, further to s 14 of the 2002 Act.

---

197 As in the case of the enforcement section of this Chapter, ComReg has the same right of action as the Authority in respect of electronic communications.

198 *Competition Authority v Avonmore Waterford Group plc* [1998] IEHC 164.

199 Although this has never been used in Ireland, requiring disposals to remedy dominance has precedents in the US and in the EU. In the US, the Regional Bell Operating Companies (RBOC) are the result of the US Department of Justice anti-trust suit against the former American Telephone & Telegraph Company (later known as AT&T Corp). On 8 January 1982, AT&T Corp settled the suit and agreed to divest (spin off) its local exchange service operating companies. AT&T Corp's local operations were split into seven independent Regional Bell Operating Companies known as 'Baby Bells', which include Bell Atlantic, which was acquired by GTE in 2000 and became Verizon. In the EU, further to an investigation by the European Commission into E.ON, RWE and Wattenfall in respect of collective dominance, E.ON offered commitments to the European Commission to divest certain aspects of its business. The Commission published an art 27(4) Notice asking for interested parties' observations on the proposed commitments in June 2008 – OJ C146/34, 12 June 2008. RWE also offered commitments in May 2008 – MEMO/08/355, 31 May 2008. Also in the EU, in *Deustche Post* I Case Comp/35.151 DP 2001, which involved an abuse of dominance by cross-subsidising profits from the reserved into the non-reserved area and predatory pricing in the non-reserved area. Deutsche Post AG offered commitments to the European Commission to transfer its business parcel services to a separate company.

The 2002 Act removes from the Minister the right to take an action for a breach of the Act. Section 14 of the Act enables the court, either at its own instance or on the application of the Authority, to order the adjustment of a dominant position, or allow its continuance only on specified conditions.

Antitrust Enforcement by Private Parties

Irish law

7.133 It is open for parties to initiate private enforcement of competition law, pursuant to s 14 of the Competition Act. Any person who is aggrieved in consequence of any agreement, decision or concerted practice or abuse that is prohibited under ss 4 or 5 has a right of action. These actions may be brought in either the High Court or the Circuit Court, as appropriate. Such action is initiated in the normal civil litigation manner, ie by civil bill or plenary summons, as appropriate. The relief available includes relief by way of damages, injunction or declaration. In addition, s 14 provides structural relief and behavioural undertakings in respect of an abuse of dominance, which is not a penalty for an abuse of dominance under s 5 as criminalised by s 7. Section 14(7) gives the court discretion, when an abuse of dominance has been found under s 5 in a civil case, to require the dominant position to be discontinued unless conditions specific to the order are complied with, or require the adjustment of the dominant position, in a manner and within a period specified in the order, by sale of assets or otherwise as the court may specify. This power allows a court to break up an undertaking if needs be. This subsection has not yet been used and it will be interesting to see what test the court would set down before using this provision in light of the likely constitutional law property arguments that could be made by the dominant entity.

7.134 Damages, including exemplary damages, are available for breaches of the Competition Act. In the case of cartels, a defendant to a damages action may be able to argue that any inflated price was 'passed through' down the food chain, as it were. In this way, the amount of losses suffered by, for example, a distributor as a result of a manufacturing cartel yielding inflated prices will likely be passed on to the retailer and ultimately the consumer. It is this 'passing on' defence that makes private enforcement of competition law by consumers remote without the possibility of class actions.[200] A difficulty private parties may face is the expense of cases and the difficulty of securing a remedy in the face of opposition from a dominant undertaking or cartel. To date, it does not appear that the Authority has ever joined a notice party on its side of an argument in a civil case.[201]

---

200 In some countries, such as Germany, there are companies who fund such class actions; however, in Ireland the rule against champerty would have to be considered in this regard.

201 Order 15, r 1(1) of the Rules of the Superior Courts (SI 15/1986) states that: 'All persons may be joined in one action as plaintiffs in whom any right to relief in respect of or arising out of the same transaction or series of transactions is alleged to exist, whether jointly, severally, or in the alternative, where, if such persons brought separate actions, any common question of law or fact would arise; provided that if, upon the application of any defendant, (contd .../)

7.135 The Competition Authority can also intervene in private litigation as an *amicus curiae* (friend of the court). In October 2003, the Competition Authority made its first application to intervene in private litigation in the High Court as *amicus curiae*.[202]

7.136 Representative actions are possible under Irish law.[203] Order 15, r 9 of the Rules of the Superior Court states that:

> Where there are numerous persons having the same interest in one case or matter, one or more such persons may sue or be sued, or may be authorised by the Court to defend, in such cause or matter, on behalf or for the benefit of all persons so interested.

The main elements are that the persons on whose behalf the action is taken have a common interest and common grievance and the relief sought is of benefit to them[204] It must also be clear that the parties on whose behalf the action is being taken have authorised the applicant to represent them.[205]

European law

7.137 The European Commission published a *White Paper on Damages Actions* for breach of EC anti-trust rules.[206] The purpose of this paper was to identify the main obstacles to a more efficient system for damages claims to ensure an increased number of damages claims and to set out different options to promote private damages actions. The Commission considers that collective action should be possible through representative actions by consumer associations, State bodies, trade associations and opt-in collective actions in which victims expressly decide to combine their individual claims into a single action. It is not that the Commission wishes to encourage a litigious culture, but rather the Commission considers increased damages actions would summarily increase deterrence. In this way, also, the victims of competition law (often consumers) would be compensated for the loss they suffered. Certain cases between two parties, for example, are more suitable for resolution between private parties than by way of public enforcement. In this way, it is thought that private

---

201 (contd) it shall appear that such joinder may embarrass or delay the trial of the proceeding, the Court may order separate trials or make such order as may be expedient.' It would appear at first glance that this rule provides the vehicle by which the Competition Authority and a complainant might join forces to argue a case arising from the same set of facts seeking separate reliefs (declarations and injunctions versus damages) against the person alleged to have breached the competition act; for example, by abusing a dominant decision or perhaps leading a cartel.

202 *Calor Teoranta v Tervas Ltd* (October 2005, unreported), HC in this case, the Authority sought to intervene on the side of the court. However, this case did not go to hearing.

203 *Moore v AG (No 3)* [1930] IR 471.

204 Collins and O'Reilly, *Civil Proceedings and the State* (2nd edn, Thomson Round Hall, 2003), pp 188–189.

205 *Madigan v AG* [1986] ILRM 136.

206 COM(2008) 154 final, 2 April 2008.

damages actions would develop a competition culture similar to what happened in the US where there are class actions and triple damages.

7.138 *Courage v Crehan*[207] is a significant case in the private enforcement of competition law. Crehan was a tied pub, a party to a vertical agreement with Courage, a brewer, who was supplying beer to Crehan. Crehan sought to sue Courage on the basis of art 81 and to reclaim damages. Under art 81(2), an agreement that infringes art 81(1) and does not benefit from art 81(3) is void and unenforceable. In addition, an agreement that infringes art 81(1) without benefiting from an exemption under art 81(3) is illegal.[208] The ECJ decided that there could not be a bar to Crehan from bringing an action for damages on the basis of an illegal agreement under English law. *Courage v Crehan* clarified that even parties to an agreement which infringes art 81(1) may take damages actions against the other party. However, by way of caution, it should be noted that despite being a landmark ruling which sets a useful precedent, Crehan, after 13 years of litigation,[209] did not ultimately recover any damages, as the House of Lords found that the agreement did not breach art 81(1) after all.[210]

Irish and European law

7.139 The landmark private enforcement action in Ireland is a case which involved HB[211] and arrangements it had with retailers, whereby retailers would be offered a freezer cabinet but only on the condition that it would only be used to store HB ice cream products. Mars complained that this in effect excluded Mars from the impulse ice cream retail market as, in reality, retailers tended not to have space in corner stores for more than one freezer cabinet. The case originated before the High Court, which found that HB was entitled to refuse to share their freezers with competitors.[212] A complaint was made to the European Commission,[213] which found that the exclusivity arrangements were contrary to art 85 (now 81) on the grounds that they led to market foreclosure. It also found that the arrangements violated art 86 (now 82), as HB was determined to have dominance on the impulse ice cream market in Ireland, and its freezer exclusivity practices were considered to reinforce that dominance and contribute to market foreclosure. The European Commission decision was appealed by

---

207 *Courage v Crehan* C–453/99 [2001] ECR I 6297.

208 Under English law, a party to an agreement may not recover damages as a result of losses caused by an unlawful agreement for which he is also responsible for the illegality.

209 Whish, *Competition Law* (6th edn, OUP, 2008), pp 293–294.

210 *Courage v Crehan* [2006] UKHL 38.

211 HB subsequently became known as Van den Bergh Foods and then Unilever. Mars subsequently became Masterfoods. Article 85 subsequently became art 81, and art 86 subsequently became art 82. All these evolutions happened during the course of this lengthy litigation.

212 *Mars v HB* [1993] ILRM 145, delivered on 28 May 1992 by Keane J.

213 Commission Decision of 11 March 1998 relating to a proceeding under arts 85 and 86 of the EC Treaty (*Van den Bergh Foods Ltd* Case Nos IV/34.073, IV/ 34.395 and IV/35.496).

HB to the CFI. Subsequent to the European Commission's decision, Mars appealed the Irish High Court judgment to the Supreme Court. In the course of this appeal, the Supreme Court stayed the appeal as it deemed it necessary to make an art 234 reference to the ECJ,[214] seeking guidance from the ECJ as to what a national court should do when faced with a legal dispute which is already the subject of a Commission decision, which was in parallel being challenged to the CFI.

7.140 In response to the art 234 reference, the ECJ responded that:

1. National courts should not make rulings that conflict with existing Commission decisions.

2. National courts should avoid making rulings on matters that are likely to be at variance with an eventual decision that the Commission may make in relation to the same matter. Where it is apparent to a national court that a matter before it is likely to be the subject of a Commission decision, then the national court is obliged not to make a ruling that might be counter to the eventual Commission decision.

3. Where the national court is hearing an appeal, it should stay the outcome of the hearing of the appeal pending the CFI's judgment in order to ensure that it does not make a ruling that will ultimately be at variance with the CFI judgment. However, the court did note that the national court could make an art 234 reference to the ECJ on the validity of the Commission's decision, if it considered this was necessary.

7.141 The CFI[215] dismissed the application made by HB as unfounded and ordered HB to bear its own costs and to pay those of the Commission, and also ordered Mars to bear its costs. HB appealed the CFI decision to the ECJ. The ECJ dismissed HB's appeal and ordered HB pay the costs.[216] In April 2007, almost 15 years after the original High Court judgment, the Supreme Court instructed that the case be returned to the presiding competition judge in the High Court, McKechnie J,[217] to assess damages that could be due to Mars. It is understood that the matter then went to arbitration.[218]

7.142 As can be seen from the above case in point, private enforcement can be an arduous route and it is only generally parties with deep pockets who can indulge what can be lengthy, complex, time-consuming and expensive litigation.

---

214 *Masterfoods Ltd v HB Ice Cream Ltd* [2002] ECR I–11369.

215 *Van den Bergh Foods Ltd (formerly HB Ice Cream Ltd) v Commission* Case T–65/98 23 October 2003.

216 *Unilever Bestfoods (Ireland) Ltd v The Commission of the European Communities* (Case C–552/03 P) 28 September 2006.

217 *Masterfoods Ltd v HB Ice Cream Ltd* 1990 3359 P.

218 Last listed on competition list on 27 May 2008.

Antitrust Enforcement by the European Commission

7.143 An undertaking or association of undertakings found to have breached either arts 81 or 82 is liable to a fine pursuant to art 23(2) of the Modernisation Regulation, not exceeding ten per cent of the turnover in the preceding business year of each of the undertakings participating in the infringement. These penalties also apply to situations where an undertaking has contravened a decision ordering an interim measure in such infringement case pursuant to art 8. (This is analogous to disobeying an interim injunction granted by the court.) Similarly, undertakings failing to comply with a commitment made binding by a decision under art 9 of the regulation are liable to the same penalties. (This is analogous to breaching an undertaking to the court.)

7.144 In fixing the amount of the fine, the Commission shall have regard to both the gravity and the duration of the infringement. It is stated in the regulation that these fines are not of a criminal law nature. When considering from a practical point of view the level of fines that may be imposed on an undertaking, one should consider the guidelines issued by DG Competition[219] designed to clarify the method used in calculating fines imposed under arts 81 and 82. These state that a 'basic amount' be determined by reference to 10 per cent of the turnover, the duration and gravity of the infringement. The amount will then be raised (or lowered) if aggravating (or mitigating) circumstances exist.

7.145 In relation to the imposition of fines, the Commission is now subject to the limitation periods set out in art 25 of the Modernisation Regulation. The period after which the Commission can no longer impose fines is as follows:

(a) three years in the case of infringements of provisions concerning requests for information or the carrying out of investigations; and

(b) five years in the case of all other infringements (ie substantive infringements of either arts 81 or 82).[220]

The calculation of fines by the Commission is of interest in Ireland as it provides a template for the Irish courts when calculating fines in Irish cases which are also subject to the same fine upper limits.[221] When setting fines, the Commission takes into account the gravity of the infringement, its duration, any aggravating or mitigating circumstances, as well as the co-operation of a company. It also takes account of a company's market share in the product market concerned and its overall size. The upper limit of any fine, as in Ireland, is established at 10 per cent of a company's total annual turnover. Companies have three months in which to pay any fine imposed. The Commission considers that each cartel involving infringements of long duration, ie more than five years in this case, represent a very serious infringement of EU competition law. The Commission will consider whether the defendant was the (joint) leader and instigator of the collusive arrangements, which is an aggravating factor. The

---

219 Guidelines on the method of setting fines pursuant to art 23(2)(a) of Modernisation Regulation, 1.9.2006 OJ C210, pp 2–5.

220 Modernisation Regulation, art 25.

221 Although in Irish cases, fines may only be imposed using criminal enforcement rather than civil enforcement for breaches of the competition rules.

Commission will consider the market power of the participants as this is related to the defendant's overall ability to implement and maintain the anti-competitive agreements.

Defences to enforcement by the European Commission

7.146 An undertaking may rely on the Commission Notice on agreements of minor importance which do not appreciably restrict Competition under art 81(1) of the Treaty establishing the European Community (*de minimis*).[222] This defence is that the undertakings and agreements involved are too small to matter in the context of the wider Common Market. The basic thresholds set out are:

    (a)   if the aggregate market share held by the parties to the agreement does not exceed ten per cent on any of the relevant markets affected by the agreement, where the agreement is made between undertakings which are actual or potential competitors on any of these markets; or

    (b)   if the market share held by each of the parties to the agreement does not exceed fifteen percent on any of the relevant markets affected by the agreement, where the agreement is made between undertakings which are not actual or potential competitors on any of these markets;

in these circumstances the agreements, in the view of the Commission, do not appreciably restrict competition within the meaning of art 81(1), provided there are no hard-core restrictions such as market- sharing and price fixing. Even where the De Minimis Notice may not be availed of, it may be argued that the agreement does not appreciably effect competition[223] or appreciably effect trade between Member States[224] relying on the jurisprudence of the European Court of Justice.

In addition, it may also plead that the behaviour complained of is covered by a Commission block exemption. It should be noted that, pursuant to art 29 of the Modernisation Regulation, the Commission, where it has made a block exemption, may withdraw the benefit of an exemption in a particular case when it finds the exemption has certain effects which are incompatible with article 81(3) of the Treaty. Otherwise the action could be defended by pleading the direct applicability of art 81(3), if available.

7.147 As regards defending an allegation of an abuse of dominance contrary to art 82, the comfort of block exemptions does not apply. The market definition could be used as the starting point to build a defence to try to disprove dominance. In the alternative, it would have to be considered whether an objective justification could be found for the behaviour to disprove that it was abusive. In addition, as discussed above in **para 7.129**, in the case of entities which carry out a service of general economic interest, such entities could argue relying on art 86(2) against the application of art 82, if its application would frustrate the entity's ability to be able to carry out its service of general economic interest.

---

222 OJ C 368/13, 22.12.2001.

223 *Javico v Yves Saint Laurent Parfums* C–306/96 [1998] ECR I–1983.

224 *Volk v Vervaecke* Case 5/69 [1969] ECR 295.

EC fines

7.148 To put into context the fines in recent Irish cases, discussed below in the criminal enforcement section in para **7.169** *et seq*, it is helpful to consider some of the European Commission cases.[225] Set out below is a brief summary of some the major cartels that have been fined in Europe.

Car glass producers

7.149 The European Commission imposed fines, totalling €1,383,896,000, on Asahi, Pilkington, Saint-Gobain and Soliver for illegal market sharing and exchange of commercially sensitive information regarding deliveries of car glass in the EEA, in violation of art 81 of the EC Treaty.[226] Between early 1998 and early 2003, these companies discussed target prices, market sharing and customer allocation in a series of meetings and other illicit contacts. These four companies controlled about 90 per cent of the glass used in new cars. The Commission started the cartel investigation on its own initiative following a tip-off from an anonymous source. The Commission increased the fines on St Gobain by 60 per cent because it was a repeat offender. Asahi provided additional information to help expose the infringement and its fine was reduced by 50 per cent under the Leniency Notice. These are the highest cartel fines the Commission has ever imposed, both for an individual company (€896 million on Saint Gobain) and for a cartel as a whole.

Gas insulated switchgear cartel

7.150 The European Commission fined eleven groups of companies a total of €750.7 million for participating in a cartel for gas insulated switchgear projects.[227] Between 1988 and 2004, the companies rigged bids for procurement contracts, fixed prices, allocated projects to each other, shared markets and exchanged commercially important and confidential information. One of the companies, ABB, received full immunity from fines under the Commission's leniency programme, as it was the first company to come forward with information about the cartel. Siemens received a significant fine of €396.5 million for its use of secret codes and encrypted emails to cover up its involvement with the cartel.

Lifts cartel

7.151 On 21 February 2007, the European Commission fined members of lifts and escalators cartels over €990 million.[228]

---

225 http://ec.europa.eu/comm/competition/consumers/antitrust_en.html.
226 12 November 2008, IP/08/1685.
227 12 November 2008, IP/08/1685.
228 Case COMP.38823 21.02.07; OJ C75, 26.3.2008.

Microsoft

7.152 On 27 February 2008, the European Commission imposed a penalty payment of €899 million on Microsoft for non-compliance with its obligations under the Commission's March 2004 Decision in which it had fined Microsoft €497 million for abusing its dominant position in the market for operating systems for personal computers (PCs) between 1998 and 2004.[229] The Commission decision, adopted under art 24(2) of the Modernisation Regulation, found that, prior to 22 October 2007, Microsoft had charged unreasonable prices for access to interface documentation for work group servers. The 2004 Decision, which was upheld by the CFI in September 2007, found that Microsoft had abused its dominant position under art 82 of the EC Treaty, and required Microsoft to disclose interface documentation which would allow non-Microsoft work group servers to achieve full interoperability with Windows PCs and servers at a reasonable price. The CFI, in September 2007, also ruled that the amount of the original fine remain unchanged at €497 million.

Vitamins cartel

7.153 In 2001, the European Commission fined eight companies (including Hoffman-La Roche) for their participation in cartels designed to eliminate competition in the vitamin sector.[230] Vitamins are used in a wide variety of products, such as cereals, biscuits, drinks, animal feed, pharmaceuticals and cosmetics. This was reflected in the fine of €855.52 million.[231]

Merger Control Civil Sanctions

The Authority

7.154 In the case of *Radio 2000 Ltd/Newstalk 106*[232] the parties failed to notify the transaction to the Competition Authority within the time period set out in the Competition Act. The Competition Authority took the view that, in a further breach of the law, the acquisition by Radio 2000 of NewsTalk 106 had been put into effect before clearance had been received from the Authority. In its determination, the Competition

---

229 Commission Decision of 24 March 2004, upheld on appeal to the CFI T–201/04, dated 17 September 2007; separate appeal on T–167/08, 9 May 2008.

230 Commission Decision 2003/2/EC OJ 2003 L 6, p 1, 21 November 2001. See also judgments of the CFI in the appeals against fines by *BASF AG v Commission* (Case T 15/02) and *Daiichi Pharmaceutical v Commission*, Case T 26/02, OJ C 108/16, 6.5.2006.

231 Competition Commissioner Mario Monti said at the time: 'This is the most damaging series of cartels the Commission has ever investigated due to the sheer range of vitamins covered which are found in a multitude of products from cereals, biscuits and drinks to animal feed, pharmaceuticals and cosmetics ... The companies' collusive behaviour enabled them to charge higher prices than if the full forces of competition had been at play, damaging consumers and allowing the companies to pocket illicit profits. It is particularly unacceptable that this illegal behaviour concerned substances which are vital elements for nutrition and essential for normal growth and maintenance of life'.

232 Competition Authority Merger Notification No M/04/003.

Authority said that any merger or acquisition that has been implemented prior to Competition Authority clearance remains void until such time as the Authority issues a clearance determination. Given that the transaction is void until the determination, there is no retrospective validity given to the period between when the merger closes and when the clearance is received. For this reason, if a merged entity has engaged in gun-jumping or has put the merger into effect, it may be that contracts negotiated during this period, for example, would require renegotiation post clearance.

7.155 In addition to the Competition Authority's power to bring summary proceedings, it may also bring applications to the courts for an interim injunction or injunctive relief in the case of gun jumping. The Competition Authority may apply for an injunction if it believes that a merger has or will be put into effect without the appropriate Competition Authority approval. The Competition Authority may bring civil or criminal proceedings for the enforcement of compliance with the terms of a commitment, a determination or an order. The courts have the power to grant an injunction on the motion of the Competition Authority, or of any other person, to enforce compliance with the terms of a commitment, a determination or an order.

7.156 The Competition Authority published a news release on 'gun-jumping' on 13 May 2003. If parties are found to have breached the pre-merger waiting period, ie engaged in gun-jumping, then the transaction will be deemed void. In this press release, the Competition Authority sought to clarify its views on this issue and ensure that industry and its legal counsel were aware of the rules. The Competition Authority indicated that it would give priority to investigating any allegations that merging parties had put a merger into effect in advance of Competition Authority clearance.

7.157 Section 19 of the Competition Act sets out the limitations on a merger or acquisition being put into effect. Section 19(1) provides that a merger may be put into effect if the period within which the Competition Authority should have made its determination lapses without the Competition Authority having informed the undertaking involved of its determination in relation to the proposed merger or acquisition. The proposed acquisition by Topaz Energy Group Ltd of Statoil Ireland Ltd was notified to the Competition Authority on 12 July 2006. The Competition Authority conducted a very extensive Phase I investigation and, as a result of this investigation, the Competition Authority identified three areas in which preliminary views were expressed that the proposed acquisition would lead to competition concerns. Pursuant to the Competition Act, the Competition Authority was due to make its determination by 9 October 2006. Having identified the competition concerns prior to this date, the Competition Authority had been in discussions with Topaz, wherein Topaz had offered certain commitments. Owing to an administrative error, the Competition Authority did not make its determination by 9 October 2006. On 10 October 2006, the Competition Authority issued a statement saying that the date on which the Phase I determination in this matter could have been made had passed without any determination having been made, and that, as a result, the parties were free to put the merger into effect. Despite being allowed to put the merger into effect without conditions addressing the competition concerns, Topaz subsequently entered into further discussions with the Competition Authority and offered commitments to the Competition Authority. It remains to be seen whether a change in the law will take place to prevent mergers being put into effect by default.

A decision to terminate or suspend a contract by the Authority under this section, any other provision of this Act or a provision of the contract may be appealed by the holder of the contract to the High Court.

Merger control sanctions by the European Commission

7.158 Fines can be imposed for incomplete or misleading information in a notification. Equally, the Commission may impose a fine of up to 10 per cent of the aggregate turnover of the undertakings concerned where they intentionally put into effect a concentration before notification or before it has been declared compatible with the Common Market by the Commission. A merger is void until such time as it is cleared.

CRIMINAL ENFORCEMENT – PENALTIES AND PUNISHMENTS

7.159 Breaches of ss 4 or 5, or of arts 81 or 82 of the EC Treaty, are criminal offences that may be treated as either indictable or summary offences. Indictable offences, the more serious cases, are heard by a judge and jury in the Circuit Criminal Court or the Central Criminal Court; they carry the most serious penalties if the court convicts the accused and are subject to appeal to the Court of Criminal Appeal. Summary offences, the less serious offences, are heard by a judge without a jury in the District Court and, on appeal, in the Circuit Court. The Competition Authority has discretion for prosecuting various summary offences as set out in the Act. When determining whether or not to prosecute, the Authority follows the Director of Public Prosecution's Guidelines for Prosecutors. These consider the public interest, the strength of the evidence, and whether there has been any delay. The Prosecution of Offences Act 1974 conferred on the DPP the function of prosecuting both on indictment and summarily. The investigation and prosecution of offences are generally separate functions within the criminal justice system and the DPP, in general, has no role in the investigation of offences. The Competition Authority is both the investigator and the prosecutor in the case of summary offences.

Penalties Applicable to Offences under ss 6 and 7

7.160 Under the Competition Act, violations of ss 4 or 5 of the Competition Act, or of arts 81 or 82 of the EC Treaty, constitute criminal offences, punishable by fines and/or imprisonment. The penalties applicable to breaches of ss 4 and 5, as criminalised by s 6 and 7, are broadly the same. However, the distinction between hard-core cartel and other competition law offences is clear in that terms of imprisonment attach to individuals involved in the former but not the latter. The penalties applicable reflect this distinction.

7.161 Section 8(1) sets out the penalties applicable to undertakings and individuals found guilty of the 'hard-core' offences under s 6 to which the presumption in s 6(2) applies, ie those undertakings or individuals found guilty of breaches of s 4(1)(a)–(c). On summary conviction, undertakings are liable to a fine not exceeding €3,000.

Individuals are liable to such a fine and/or up to six months imprisonment. On conviction on indictment, undertakings are liable to a fine not exceeding whichever of the following amounts is the greater, namely, €4 million or ten per cent of the turnover of the undertaking in the financial year ending in the 12 months prior to the conviction. Individuals are subject to the same fine and/or a term of imprisonment not exceeding five years. An undertaking found guilty of a cartel offence under s 6 not covered by the above, or to an abuse of dominance offence under s 7, whether the undertaking is an individual or otherwise, is liable: (a) on summary conviction, to a fine not exceeding €3,000; or (b) on conviction on indictment, to a fine not exceeding, whichever of the following amounts is the greater, namely, €4 million or ten per cent of turnover of the undertaking in the financial year ending in the twelve months prior to the conviction. Furthermore, the Act allows for an additional fine in respect of each successive day the offence took place. By virtue of s 8(3) of the Act, if the contravention concerned continues one or more days after the date of its first occurrence, then the undertaking is guilty of a separate offence and may be fined for each successive day, €300 per day on summary conviction and €40,000 per day on conviction on indictment.

7.162 By comparison with most other member states of the European Union, one of the more unusual aspects of Irish competition law is that individuals, who are not themselves the undertakings, are liable to fines and imprisonment. The persons at risk are described in s 8(6) of the Act. They are the directors of the undertaking, its management or anyone who acts in a similar capacity. In essence, those who can be shown to be part of the guiding will and mind of the company are liable under the Act. In fact, pursuant to s 8(7), such a person is presumed to have consented to the doing of the acts by the undertaking, which constituted the commission by it of the offence concerned under ss 6 or 7. In addition, aiders and abettors are liable to prosecution under the Criminal Law Act 1997.

Defences to Prosecution

7.163 The Competition Act also lists a number of specific defences in prosecution. The main defences in relation to s 4 or art 81 are:

(1)   in proceedings for breach of s 4, it is a defence to prove that the agreement or behaviour satisfied the 'efficiency criteria' in s 4(5), or complied with a determination made or a direction given by one of the statutory sectoral Regulators; and

(2)   in proceedings for breach of art 81, it is a defence to prove that the agreement or behaviour satisfied the criteria in art 81(3), or complied with the terms of an individual or block exemption granted by the Commission, or with a determination made or a direction given by one of the statutory sectoral Regulators.

7.164 Alleged abusive conduct must always be analysed in light of whether it is objectively justified in the circumstances. In criminal proceedings for breach of s 5 or of art 82, it is also a defence to show that the act or acts concerned complied with a determination made or a direction given by one of the statutory sectoral Regulators. This is intended to cover situations where the activities of dominant undertakings are subject to directions by a sectoral Regulator, for example, in relation to pricing.

As mentioned above, evidence that is compelled, for example by way of a summons, cannot be relied upon to prosecute an individual.[233]

Parties to Proceedings

7.165 When it comes to issuing proceedings, undertakings or individuals will be summonsed in the case of criminal offences to appear in the relevant District Court to answer the charge as set out in the summons. Clearly an undertaking cannot be arrested, it being intangible. Therefore, a summons or many summonses will be served in person at the registered office of the accused undertaking to appear in the local District Court. From that point on, the matter would proceed as a normal criminal proceeding. It remains to be seen whether natural persons who are accused of competition offences under the Competition Act, 2002, will be arrested and brought to court.

7.166 The Competition Authority is competent to bring summary criminal proceedings in its own name by virtue of s 8(9). Summary proceeding may be instituted within two years of the date on which the offence was committed. This is an exception to the normal six months allowed by s 10(4) of the Petty Sessions (Ireland) Act 1851. ComReg may also institute summary proceedings for breaches of competition law, in respect of the electronic communications sector. The Director of Public Prosecution will direct trial on indictment in accordance with the general criminal law. Section 11 of the 2002 Act provides that trial on indictment of competition offences shall occur in the Central Criminal Court. This is a departure from the former regime whereby such offences were heard, along with the vast majority of jury trials, in the Circuit Criminal Court. Section 10 of the 2002 Act provides that the judge in a criminal trial may direct that certain documents be given to the jury.

Criminal Cases

7.167 There have been a number of prosecutions of note in Ireland for cartel activity. The fines imposed by the courts in Ireland further to prosecution are diminutive when compared with the quantum imposed by the European Commission by way of administrative sanction.

The Galway Heating Oil Case

7.168 In 2004, following the Competition Authority investigation into allegations of price-fixing of home heating oil products in the west of Ireland under the 1991 Act, 24 named defendants were indicted by the DPP.[234] In February and March 2006, a number

---

233 *In the matter of National Irish Bank Ltd (under investigation) and in the matter of the Companies Act 1990 (No. 1)* [1999] 1 ILRM 321.

234 *DPP v Michael Flanagan, Con Muldoon, Muldoon Oil, James Kearney, All Star Oil, Kevin Hester, Corrib Oil, Mor Oil, Alan Kearney, Sweeney Oil, Gort Oil, Pat Hegarty, Cloonan Oil, Ruby Oil, Matt Geraghty Oil, Declan Geraghty, Fenmac Oil & Transport, Michael McMahon, Tom Connolly, Eugene Dalton Snr, JP Lambe, Sean Hester, Hi-Way Oil, Kevin Cunniffe* (2 March 2006, unreported) Circuit Court.

of the defendants were found guilty of price-fixing. One defendant was fined and received a six-month custodial sentence, suspended, for aiding and abetting price-fixing. To date, 14 other participants in the cartel have been convicted of various charges relating to price-fixing. The largest fines imposed were €12,500 on a company and €15,000 on an individual. After a three-day trial, the jury returned unanimous guilty verdicts on 2 March 2006 on both counts against Mr Michael Flanagan trading as Flanagan Oil for his part in the price-fixing conspiracy. Judge Groarke imposed a fine of €3,500 in total. This was the first fine imposed in Ireland for a criminal breach of the Competition Act 1991 after a trial by jury.

7.169 Arising from the same cartel, Mr JP Lambe pleaded guilty in Dublin Circuit Criminal Court on 27 October 2005 to both counts of aiding and abetting Corrib Oil Company Ltd in price fixing. He was sentenced on 6 March 2006 by Judge Delahunt to a period of six months' imprisonment, suspended for a period of 12 months, and fined €15,000. This was the first time a custodial sentence was handed down in Ireland or Europe for a criminal breach of competition law.

The Competition Authority v Ruaidhrí Deasy, Paddy Harrington, Fintan Conway, Raymond O'Malley, Colm McDonnell and George O'Brien

7.170 In March 2003 the Competition Authority secured its first successful conviction on summary indictment under the Competition Act 2002 when the District Court fined six farmers who attempted to block the unloading of a ship of its cargo of grain in Drogheda Port for breaches of s 4 of the Competition Act 2002 arising from a blockade and a meeting, which had as its object the prevention of unloading a cargo of grain from the UK. The convictions were appealed by the defendants. On appeal, three of the convictions were upheld and the Probation Act applied by the Circuit Court in Dundalk in October 2004. This case was the first criminal case involving a breach of the Competition Act 2002.

Motor vehicles

7.171 The DPP initiated proceedings against Mr Denis Manning,[235] who was summonsed in relation to two charges alleging that he had aided and abetted the Irish Ford Dealers Association and its members in the implementation of agreements to fix the selling of Ford Motor Vehicles within the state between July 2002 and June 2003. The first of the two charges related to an offence under the 1991 Act, and the second of the two charges related to an alleged offence under the 2002 Act. The DPP agreed to drop the first of these two charges. On 9 February 2007, Mr Manning was sentenced under the 2002 Act and was given a one-year prison sentence, which was suspended for five years, and he also received a fine of €30,000, which was payable within 21 days. Judge McKechnie, in sentencing Mr Manning, noted that Mr Manning would have gone to prison only for the declining state of his health.

---

235 Under s 7 of the Criminal Law Act 1997, individuals who are found guilty of aiding and abetting the commission of an offence prohibited by s 4 of the Competition Act are guilty in the same manner as if they committed the actual competition offence.

7.172 Separately, in June 2007, the DPP initiated proceedings before the Central Criminal Court against an individual who was summonsed in relation to the charge of aiding and abetting members of the Citroën Dealers Association in distorting competition in the car market by fixing the selling prices of cars. In January and February 2008, further proceedings were issued in relation to allegations of the existence of a price-fixing agreement for the sale of Citroën motor vehicles. In May 2008, Mr James Durrigan pleaded guilty on his own behalf and as a director of his company to two counts of entering into an agreement to distort or, directly or indirectly, fix the price of Citroën cars between 1997 and 2002. He received a suspended three-month sentence and the company was fined €12,000. There are a number of similar cases due before the Central Criminal Court against other motor dealers in relation to this cartel. The Competition Authority discovered minutes of meetings showing how dealers met in hotels around the country and discussed price fixing. The delivery charges for new cars were set by the association and were the same around the country. Extras such as metallic paint were allegedly fixed at a certain rate. Maximum discounts which salesmen were allowed to give cash customers were devised. Prices were also fixed from time to time on second-hand cars. Each member of the cartel paid in €1,000 that would be forfeited in the event that a member broke any of the price-fixing rules. 'Mystery shoppers' periodically would ensure the agreement was policed.

Merger Control Criminal Sanctions in Ireland

7.173 If an undertaking or group of undertakings implements a merger, having failed to notify it to the Competition Authority, the person in control of the undertaking is guilty of a criminal offence punishable by fines. Undertakings may also be guilty of an offence if they have failed to notify the merger within the specified period or if they have failed to supply information required by the Authority within a specified period. This sanction is applied to parties to a merger since the obligation is on all the undertakings involved to make the notification. Undertakings could be liable, on summary conviction, to a fine not exceeding €3,000 or, on conviction on indictment, to a fine not exceeding €250,000. Section 11 of the Competition Act specifies a person in control of an undertaking as: (i) any officer of the body corporate who knowingly or wilfully authorises or permits the contravention, or (ii) in the case of a partnership, each partner who knowingly and wilfully authorises or permits the contravention, or (iii) in the case of any other form of undertaking, a person who knowingly and wilfully authorises or permits the contravention.

7.174 In 2004, the Competition Authority was faced with a media merger that had contravened the rules specified above. In Radio 2000 Ltd/Newstalk 106 (Competition Authority Merger Notification No M/04/003) the parties failed to notify the transaction to the Competition Authority within the time period set out in the Competition Act. The Competition Authority took the view that, in a further breach of the law, the acquisition by Radio 2000 of NewsTalk 106 had been put into effect before clearance had been received from the Authority. However, the Competition Authority, after having fully considered the matter, found insufficient evidence to seek a criminal penalty, as it was not apparent that any officer of NewsTalk 106, Radio 2000 or Communicorp knowingly and wilfully authorised or permitted the breach of the law.

LENIENCY

Leniency Programme in Ireland

7.175 As stated by the Organisation for Economic Co-operation and Development:

> the challenge in attacking hard-core cartels is to penetrate their cloak of secrecy. To encourage a member of a cartel to confess and implicate its co-conspirators with first-hand, direct "insider" evidence about their clandestine meetings and communications, an enforcement agency may promise a smaller fine, shorter sentence, less restrictive order, or complete amnesty.[236]

One area of competition law enforcement that deserves separate consideration is the presence of an immunity programme in relation to cartel offences. Many jurisdictions, including Ireland, have introduced a system whereby a party to a cartel, if it reports the cartel before the authorities are in possession of enough evidence to proceed against it, may receive total immunity from prosecuting in return for turning 'state's evidence'. The mechanisms of the programmes differ slightly but the common core principles are that the applicant must be first in, not the ringleader, cease involvement, stay quiet and be able to give the type of evidence that will crack the cartel open. The Competition Authority has also, in conjunction with the DPP, put in place a cartel immunity program under which full immunity from criminal prosecution under the Competition Act can be obtained by the first member of a cartel to come forward with sufficient evidence to warrant a referral of a completed investigation file to the DPP.

7.176 The Irish Leniency programme was published in December 2001 and may be viewed on the website of the Competition Authority[237] and on the DPP's website.[238] In order to benefit, the applicant must take effective steps, to be agreed with the Authority, to terminate its participation in the illegal activity. The applicant must do nothing to alert its former associates that it has applied for immunity. The applicant, including all relevant past and present employees, must not have coerced another party to participate in the illegal activity and must not have acted as the instigator or have been a ring leader. Throughout the course of the Authority's investigation and any subsequent prosecution, the applicant must provide complete and timely co-operation. In particular, the applicant must:

    (a)   reveal all offences under the Act in which it may have been involved;

    (b)   provide full and frank disclosure of all evidence and information; and

    (c)   co-operate fully at their own expense.

---

236 *Fighting Hard-Core Cartels – Harm, Effective Sanctions and Leniency Programmes* (OECD, 2002) at p 7.

237 http://www.tca.ie.

238 http://www.dppireland.ie.

In a case of a corporate undertaking, the application must be a corporate act. Although applications from individual directors or employees will be considered, they will not be regarded as being made on behalf of the undertaking in the absence of a corporate act. If the first applicant to request immunity fails to meet these requirements, a subsequent applicant that does meet these requirements can be considered for immunity. If a corporate undertaking qualifies for a recommendation for full immunity, all directors and employees who admit their involvement will also qualify. Applicants for immunity for an individual employed by an undertaking involved in a cartel will be considered even where the employer undertaking does not apply or otherwise co-operate under the programme.

7.177 The Authority has designated a particular officer for the purpose of the immunity programme and has provided a mobile number to be contacted on its programme document. An applicant will be allowed to place a marker with the Authority in order to bag its place as first in line in the queue in order to be able to gather sufficient information and complete the application for immunity. Joint applications from two or more accomplices will be invalid.

7.178 Although applications for immunity are made to the Authority, it is vital to note that the decision is that of the DPP's office, not the Competition Authority. The Authority would, of course, make a recommendation to the DPP to grant immunity. Any decision to grant an indemnity lies with the Director. In determining that issue, account will be taken of the following matters:

   (i)   the significance, credibility and reliability of the accomplice's testimony;

  (ii)   the degree of apparent involvement of the accomplice compared with that of the accused against whom the accomplice is testifying;

 (iii)   the strength of the prosecution evidence against the defendant without the accomplice's evidence;

 (iv)   the strength, significance and reliability of the accomplice's testimony and whether or not the evidence is reasonably necessary to secure the conviction;

  (v)   whether it is in the public interest to prosecute the accomplice;

 (vi)   whether, if the accomplice were to be prosecuted and then testify, there was a real basis for believing that his safety would be at risk;

 (vii)   whether the person agrees to testify; and

(viii)   the character, credit and criminal record of the accomplice.[239]

It is not clear whether this programme is likely to be successful in Ireland given the culture arising from the small size of the business community. A decision whether to call an accomplice or a whistleblower to give evidence presents difficulties.[240] An indemnity can be granted in respect of completed criminal conduct but cannot be

---

239 McCormick, *Prosecution of Criminal Offences under the Competition Act 2002 in Ireland: An Overview* (Office of the DPP).

240 McCormick, *Prosecution of Criminal Offences under the Competition Act 2002 in Ireland: An Overview* (Office of the DPP).

granted for future conduct. In addition, the judge would have to give the jury a direction to be cautious in respect of relying on uncorroborated accomplice evidence, which would surely undermine the usefulness of the evidence to secure a conviction. It could be argued that such evidence is being given in return for the inducement of a lighter penalty, which can lead to evidence being queried.[241]

Immunity Programme with the European Commission

7.179 The European Commission's leniency programme is called the 'Commission notice on immunity from fines and reduction of fines in cartel cases'.[242] Aventis (formerly Rhône-Poulenc) was granted full immunity in regard to its participation in the cartels in vitamins A and E because it was the first company to co-operate with the Commission and provided decisive evidence in the case of these two products. This is the first time that the Commission granted a 100 per cent reduction of a fine under the terms of the Leniency Notice. A fine was, however, imposed on Aventis for its passive participation in the vitamin D3 infringement, on which it provided no information to the Commission. At the time, former EC Competition Commissioner Mr Mario Monti said, 'the fact that the Commission has granted, for the first time, a total exemption of fines to a company illustrates its willingness to grant companies that actively co-operate at the earliest stage a unique opportunity to get off the hook. Those companies that do not seize this chance must be aware of the responsibilities they will face.' A recent ruling of the CFI in the Hoechst[243] appeal of the Sorbates cartel case concerned the Commission's immunity programme. From this ruling, it can be gleaned that it is important to be first in line with substantive documentation. Hoechst had been fined €99 million, however, there was an argument as to whether it had been the first to seek immunity. Hoechst did not demonstrate that it was in fact first into the Commission with decisive evidence.[244] The Commission did not give Hoechst immunity from fines which decision was upheld by the CFI. The CFI, however, did reduce Hoechst's fines on other grounds (down to a fine of €74.25 million.)

---

241 *DPP v Meehan* [2006] 3 IR 468 and *DPP v Gilligan* [2005] IESC 78.

242 OJ C 45/3, 19.2.2002.

243 *Hoechst GmbH v Commission of the European Communities* Case T-410/03 Judgment of 18 July 2008.

244 In this case, Hoechst's lawyers contacted the Commission indicating that Hoechst wanted to cooperate with the Commission in respect of the cartel. Another entity's lawyers had also contacted the Commission in this regard and provided detailed documentary evidence. Hoechst then provided the Commission with some information, however, it wrote to say that it would not be able to provide further evidence because of parallel pending US criminal and civil proceedings. The Commission considered this to amount to a refusal to cooperate and informed Hoechst of as much who subsequently turned up at the Commission with substantive documentary evidence in relation to the cartel.

APPEALS

Appeals in Ireland

7.180 The Competition Act provides for an appeal to the High Court against a determination of the Authority to block a merger. The Competition Act provides no right of appeal against a decision to clear a merger; however, the remedy of judicial review could be availed of. An appeal must be made within one month after the date on which the undertaking is informed by the Competition Authority of the determination concerned. Any issue of fact or law concerning the determination may form the subject of an appeal. The procedure for appeals is somewhat accelerated, in that the High Court should, by virtue of s 24(6) of the Competition Act 2002, in so far as it is practicable, hear and determine an appeal within two months after the date on which the appeal is made to it. An appeal to the Supreme Court against a decision of the High Court under any of the provisions of s 24 shall only lie on a point of law. Appeals from civil and criminal actions taken by the Competition Authority (or by the DPP on the advice of the Competition Authority) may be made under the normal rules of civil and criminal procedure. In addition, s 15 of the Competition Act makes specific provision for appeal to the High Court of a decision by the Competition Authority to grant a declaration (block exemption) under s 4(3) of the Competition Act. Such an appeal must be made to the High Court within 28 days of publication of the declaration or such greater period as the High Court may specify. On the hearing of such an appeal, the High Court may confirm, amend or annul the declaration concerned.[245]

Appeals to the European Court of First Instance

7.181 An appeal from a decision of the Commission imposing a fine only for breach of arts 81 or 82 may be made in the first instance to the CFI pursuant to art 229 of the EC treaty. The court may cancel, reduce or increase the fine imposed. An appeal on the decision at large may be made pursuant to art 230 of the Treaty, which empowers the court to review the legality of acts of the Commission on one or more of the following grounds:

(i)   lack of competence;

(ii)   infringement of an essential procedural requirement;

(iii)   infringement of the EC Treaty or of any rule of law relating to its application; and

(iv)   misuse of powers.

A right of appeal lies from the CFI judgment to the ECJ. An appeal from a European Commission decision blocking a merger would also be made to the CFI. The Commission suffered several setbacks when a number of its prohibition decisions were overturned by the CFI. In particular, the CFI has overturned merger decisions in

---

245 The first such appeal is before the courts at the time of writing: 2008 145 *MCA RYE Investments Ltd v Competition Authority* – case subsequent to the Competition Authority's decision to block a proposed acquisition by Kerry Group plc of Breeo Foods Ltd and Breeo Brands Ltd, dated 28 August 2008, M/08/009.

Airtours v Commission,[246] *Schneider Electrics v Commission*[247] and *Tetra Laval v Commission*.[248] CFI judgments may, in turn, be appealed to the ECJ on points of law, lack of jurisdiction of the CFI, breach of procedure or infringement of Community law.

OTHER FUNCTIONS OF THE AUTHORITY

Advocacy

7.182 Although this chapter focuses on its purely regulatory functions, s 30(1)(c) of the Act gives the Authority the function of studying and analysing competition matters, including developments abroad. The same section adds other powers which strengthen the advocacy role of the Authority. This role is central to changing the culture and attitude in Ireland to competition law. From a policy perspective, it is important that the Competition Authority is expressly given such a role so that there is no doubt as to the value of work done in this area. That the Competition Authority is best placed to do so is recognised by the fact that it has the power to advise the Government and Ministers concerning the implications for competition in markets for goods and services of proposals for legislation, including statutory instruments; the power to advise public authorities generally on issues concerning competition which may arise in the performance of their functions; the power to identify and comment on constraints imposed by any enactment or administrative practice on the operation of competition in the economy; and the power to carry on such activities as it considers appropriate so as to inform the public about issues concerning competition.

7.183 In this regard, the Authority submitted a number of proposed reforms regarding the Competition Act to the Department of Enterprise, Trade and Employment, in particular in relation to the reform of the merger control regime. The Authority has requested provisions to include:

(i)   permitting notifications on foot of a letter of intent;

(ii) allowing the Authority to stop the clock during Phase II; and

(iii) allowing civil fines to be imposed for criminal penalties for failure to notify a merger or failure to respond to an information request and for gun-jumping.

The Authority also proposes amending the 2002 Act to include a list of factors for judges to consider in respect of sentencing for competition offences. The Authority suggests using the European Commission's guidelines for setting fines as a basis for compiling this list of factors. The Department consulted on amending the Competition Act and this consultation closed in December 2007. No heads have yet issued in this regard at the time of writing.[249]

---

246 *Airtours v Commission* Case T– 342/99 [2002] ECR II– 2585.

247 *Schneider Electrics v Commission* Case T– 310/01 [2002] ECR II– 4071.

248 *Tetra Laval v Commission* Case T– 5/02 [2002] ECR II– 4381.

249 It has since been proposed that the Authority is to merge with the National Consumer Agency and so it remains to be seen if the legislation setting out the provisions for that amalgamation will also contain substantive amendments to the Competition Act 2002, or indeed to the Consumer Protection Act 2007.

Co-operation Agreements with Statutory Bodies

7.184 Section 34 of the Act obliges the Authority to enter into co-operation agreements with the Broadcasting Commission of Ireland, the Commission for Electricity Regulation, the Commission for Aviation Regulation and the Director of Telecommunications Regulation. The purposes of these agreements are to facilitate co-operation, to avoid duplication of activities involving determinations on competition issues and to ensure consistency in decision-making. The agreements include provisions on exchange of information, on forbearance of performance of functions by one party where the other is already performing similar functions in relation to a matter ,and provisions regarding consultation. Section 47G of the Competition Act provided for the Authority and ComReg to enter into a separate co-operation agreement regarding the exercise of ComReg's co-competition powers in the electronic communications sector, which has taken place. Copies of the various co-operation agreements are available on the Authority's website.

Arrangements with Foreign Competition Bodies

7.185 Section 46 permits the Authority to enter into arrangements with competition authorities in other countries for the exchange of information and the mutual provision of assistance. This is required as part of the Authority's role in the ECN.[250]

---

250 http://www.tca.ie/EnforcingCompetionLaw/CompetitionLaw/TheNewCompetitionAct/
TheNewCompetitionAct.aspx.

Chapter 8

ENERGY REGULATION

APPROACH OF THIS CHAPTER

8.001 This chapter examines the regulation of energy, in particular gas and electricity. The Department of Communications, Energy and Natural Resources is the responsible Government department for leading developments in this area. The relevant Regulator is the Commission for Energy Regulation (CER). The Minister for Communications, Energy and Natural Resources (the Minister) is advised by CER on the development of the energy market and also by Sustainable Energy Ireland.

HISTORY OF ENERGY REGULATION IN IRELAND

8.002 The Electricity (Supply) Act 1927 (the 1927 Act), as amended, governed the electricity market. The Electricity Supply Board (ESB) had regulatory powers, including the power to licence other operators to generate, distribute and supply electricity. The establishment of the ESB as a publicly controlled monopoly in 1927 was seen at the time as the most pragmatic approach in the prevailing circumstances. It acted both as generator, transmitter, distributor and Regulator of electricity in Ireland – all such powers given to it by statute.

The Electricity Regulation Act 1999 (1999 Act) was the first step in the process of liberalisation of the electricity sector and it came into effect on February 2000.[1] From that date, it was foreseen that the Irish market would be open to competition. From a policy perspective, the Minister[2], when introducing the legislation noted that because electricity forms such a vital component of overall energy needs,[3] the way the sector was managed by Government would have a bearing on future prosperity and development. The 1999 Act provides for a regulatory framework for the introduction of competition in the generation and supply of electricity in Ireland. It also established the Commission for Electricity Regulation, the forerunner of the CER.

8.003 The principal legislative instrument governing gas was the Gas Act 1976 (the 1976 Act), as amended, which established Bord Gáis Eireann. The Gas (Interim) (Regulation) Act 2002 (the 2002 Act) brought the gas sector within the scope of regulation. The 2002 Act also changed the name of the Commission for Electricity Regulation to the Commission for Energy Regulation (CER), and the CER has since then also been the independent Regulator for the gas sector.

---

1   Introduced by Mary O'Rourke, Minister for Public Enterprise, Dáil Éireann – Vol 499 – 3 February 1999, Electricity Regulation Bill 1998: Second Stage.

2   Mary O'Rourke, Minister for Public Enterprise.

3   Because energy is so vital, the ESB, as the Minister noted in the course of that debate, was constantly at the forefront of economic development in Ireland.

8.004 Energy policy is set out by the Department of Communications, Energy and Natural Resources (DCENR), which has overall policy responsibility for the sector. According to its website, its policy is:

(i)   To develop a competitive energy supply industry.

(ii) To ensure security and reliability of energy supply.

(iii) To develop energy conservation and end-use efficiency.[4]

Government policy in the Irish electricity sector is driven principally by the relevant EC Directives and is one of liberalisation or opening the electricity market up to competition. In March 2007, the Government published a white paper, 'Delivering a Sustainable Energy Future for Ireland', which proposed future developments of the energy sector for 2007–2020 based on increasing security, sustainability and competitiveness of energy supply.

8.005 The electricity and gas markets have been fully open since July 2007. The retail electricity market opened fully to competition on 19 February 2005 and independent companies now supply almost half of electricity consumed (by volume) in Ireland.

8.006 The Irish electricity market was fundamentally changed by the establishment of a single electricity market on 1 November 2007 under the ambit of the Electricity Regulation (Amendment) (Single Electricity Market) 2007 Act (the 2007 Act).

More recently, in 2008, there have been further developments in respect of unbundling in the electricity market. EirGrid was established in 2006 as a structurally separated entity. EirGrid is the independent State-owned body licensed by the CER to act as transmission system operator and is responsible for the operation, development and maintenance of the system. It was established on 1 July 2006. It is separate and independent from the ESB, which actually owns the transmission system. The Electricity Regulation (Amendment) (Eirgrid) Act 2008 (the 2008 Act) was adopted to enable[5] the construction by EirGrid of an interconnector to enable the transportation of electricity across and the maintenance of such an interconnector by EirGrid to enable EirGrid to own and operate such an interconnector. It also provides that EirGrid may not without the approval of the Minister for Communications, Energy and Natural Resources, given with the consent of the Minister for Finance, acquire, establish or dispose of subsidiaries or invest in other undertakings.

Also in 2008, there was functional separation with respect to the distribution system in the form of the European Communities (Internal Market in Electricity) (ESB) Regulations 2008 (SI 280/2008), which require the ESB to form a subsidiary company. The regulations provide that, with effect from the transfer date, responsibility for the operation of the electricity distribution system in accordance with these regulations shall be vested in the subsidiary company.

---

4   http://www.dcenr.gov.ie.

5   Subject to a grant of authorisation pursuant to s 16(1)(b) of the 1999 Act, and the grant of a licence under s 14(1)(i) of the 1999 Act.

8.007 The Government gas policy is driven by EC directives as well as the requirement for greater fuel security and promotion of indigenous fuel sources. The gas policy concerns security of gas supply and phased introduction of competition in gas supply, promotion of investment in infrastructure and north-south gas market developments in the context of promoting an all-island energy market. Liberalisation of the gas sector provides CER with a number of powers in the downstream developments of the gas sector; however, regulatory responsibility for the upstream elements of the sector remain the responsibility of the petroleum affairs division of the DCENR. The Energy (Miscellaneous Provisions) Act 2006 (the 2006 Act) allows for cross-border developments in respect of gas to include the participation in the development of all island energy markets.

EUROPEAN FRAMEWORK

8.008 Irish policy in the energy sector, in respect of liberalisation, is driven primarily by EC law. Directive 96/92/EC[6] (the First electricity Directive) sets out common rules for the internal market in electricity. This Directive was repealed by Directive 2003/54/EC,[7] (the Second Electricity Directive) which also establishes common rules for the internal market in electricity.

Directive 2003/55/EC[8] (the Second Gas Directive) establishes common rules for the internal market in natural gas and repeals Directive 98/30/EC[9] (the First Gas Directive). It operates together with several other directives[10] and Regulation 1775/2005[11] (the Gas Regulation) on conditions for access to the natural gas transmission networks.

8.009 The above legislation is likely to be updated with the European Commission's proposals for a Third Energy Package. The European Commission completed a sector

---

6 Directive 96/92/EC of the European Parliament and of the Council of 19 December 1996 concerning common rules for the internal market in electricity.

7 Directive 2003/54/EC of the European Parliament and of the Council of 26 June 2003 concerning common rules for the internal market in electricity and repealing Directive 96/92/EC.

8 Directive 2003/55/EC of the European Parliament and of the Council of 26 June 2003 concerning common rules for the internal market in natural gas and repealing Directive 98/30/EC.

9 Directive 98/30/EC of the European Parliament and of the Council of 22 June 1998 concerning common rules for the internal market in natural gas.

10 Directive 90/337/EEC concerning a Community procedure to improve the transparency of gas and electricity prices charged to industrial end users; Directive 94/22/EC on the conditions for granting and using authorizations for the prospecting, exploration and production of hydrocarbon (Hydrocarbons' licensing directive); and Directive 2004/67/EC concerning measures to safeguard security of natural gas supply (Security of Supply Directive).

11 Regulation (EC) No 1775/2005 of the European Parliament and of the Council of 28 September 2005 on conditions for access to the natural gas transmission networks.

inquiry into the gas and electricity markets and produced a final report in January 2007. Following the report's conclusions that competition was distorted, in September 2007 the Commission published its Third Energy Package, which included proposals for a new directive and a new regulation amending the Second Gas Directive and the Gas Regulation. It will also amend the Second Electricity Directive.[12] The Third Energy Package is expected to be adopted during the course of 2009.

8.010 The package proposes effective separation of supply and production activities from network operations as the European Commission considers that vertically integrated undertakings have an incentive to underinvest in new networks and to prefer their own sales companies. Full ownership unbundling[13] is proposed as the primary means of achieving this separation. It is argued that this may also reduce the prices of services. The alternative to ownership unbundling is the independent system operator whereby vertically integrated companies retain ownership of the network but the network assets are managed by an independent entity subject to regulatory oversight. It is also proposed to enhance the powers of national regulatory authorities in respect of monitoring and investigations. A regulation is proposed which will establish the Agency for the Cooperation of Energy Regulators (ACER) as a mechanism for national regulatory authorities to co-operate and take decisions, in particular in relation to the regulatory oversight of transmission system operators. ACER is to have decision-making powers on cross-border issues, fulfil an advisory role to the European Commission and replace the European Regulators Group for Energy and Gas and the Florence and Madrid fora.[14] There is to be increased efficient co-operation between transmission system operators, and a set of market and technical codes are proposed, as well as joint R&D planning. There is to be clearer guidelines on exemptions from the third-party access regime for new infrastructure development. There is also to be a requirement for gas undertakings to publish information used to determine wholesale price movements, eg gas stocks and forecasts, and the establishment of a true European

---

12   Documents relating to the third package proposals may be viewed at http://ec.europa.eu/ energy/gas_electricity/third_legislative_package_en.htm.

13   Further to an investigation by the European Commission into EON, RWE and Vattenfall in respect of collective dominance which included the abuse of discouraging investment, EON offered commitments to the European Commission to divest certain aspects of its business. The Commission published an article 27(4) Notice asking for interested parties' observations on the proposed commitments in June 2008 – OJ C146/34, 12 June 2008. RWE also offered commitments in May 2008 – MEMO/08/355, 31 May 2008.

14   In relation to the proposed third package consultations and contacts occurs in two forums set up to discuss issues regarding the creation of an internal electricity and gas markets between the Commission services and established stakeholder groups – the Florence (for electricity) and Madrid (for gas) forums. The participants are national regulatory authorities, Member States, the European Commission, transmission system operators, traders, consumers, network users and exchanges. The first meetings were held in 1998 for Electricity in Florence and 1999 for Gas in Madrid. The Commission's objective is to ensure that most stakeholders are fully informed throughout the preparatory process. See further, *Commission Staff working Document accompanying the legislative package on the internal market for electricity and gas Impact Assessment*, SEC, 2007 available at http:// ec.europa.eu/energy/gas_electricity/third_legislative_package_en.htm.

retail market for gas. The package will also increase co-operation to reinforce security of supply by more frequent monitoring of supply requirements, publication by storage operators of daily information on stocks of working gas and further co-operation of member states to deal with emergencies.[15]

THE RELEVANT LEGISLATIVE FRAMEWORK

8.011 The legislative framework for energy regulation includes the following Acts:

   (i)   Electricity (Supply) Act 1927;

  (ii)   Petroleum and Other Minerals Development Act 1960, as amended;

 (iii)   Gas Act 1976;

 (iv)   Electricity Regulation Act 1999;

  (v)   Gas (Amendment) Act 2000;

 (vi)   Gas (Interim) (Regulation) Act 2002;

 (vii)   Energy (Miscellaneous Provisions) Act 2006;

(viii)   Electricity Regulation (Amendment)(Single Electricity Market) Act 2007; and

 (ix)   Electricity Regulation (Amendment) (Eirgrid) Act 2008.

It includes the following statutory instruments:

   (i)   Electricity Regulation Act 1999 (Eligible Customer) Order 2002 (SI 3/2002);

  (ii)   Electricity Regulation Act 1999 and Gas (Interim) (Regulation) Act 2002 (Gas) Levy Order 2005 (SI 818/2005);

 (iii)   Electricity Regulation Act 1999 (Electricity) Levy Order 2005 (SI 819/2005);

 (iv)   Electricity Regulation Act 1999 (Criteria for Determination of Authorisations) Order 1999 (SI 309/1999);

  (v)   European Communities (Internal Market in Electricity) Regulations 2000 (SI 445/2000);

 (vi)   Public Service Obligations Order 2002 (SI 217/2002);

 (vii)   Electricity Regulation Act 1999 (Eligible Customer) (Consumption of Electricity) Order 2003 (SI 632/2003);

(viii)   European Communities (Internal Market in Natural Gas) Regulations 2004 (SI 426/2004);

 (ix)   European Communities (Internal Market in Natural Gas) (No 2) Regulations 2004 (SI 452/2004);

  (x)   European Communities (Internal Market in Electricity) Regulations 2005 (SI 60/2005);

 (xi)   European Communities (Internal Market in Natural Gas) Regulations 2005 (SI 320/2005);

---

15   Presentation by Marc van der Woude to IBC Advanced EC Competition law conference in Brussels on 13 November 2003.

(xii)   Electricity Regulation Act 1999 (Public Service Obligations) (Amendment) Order 2007 (SI 582/2007);

(xiii)   European Communities (Internal Market in Electricity) (Electricity Supply Board) Regulations 2008 (SI 280/2008); and

(xiv   European Communities (Internal Market in Natural Gas) (BGÉ) (Amendment) Regulations 2008 (SI 239/2008).

It also includes the following Directives and Regulations:

(i)   Directive 90/337/EEC concerning a Community procedure to improve the transparency of gas and electricity prices charged to industrial end users;

(ii)   Directive 94/22/EC on the conditions for granting and using authorizations for the prospecting, exploration and production of hydrocarbon (Hydrocarbons' licensing directive);

(iii)   Directive 96/92/EC of the European Parliament and of the Council of 19 December 1996 concerning common rules for the internal market (now repealed);

(iv)   Directive 2003/54/EC of the European Parliament and of the Council of 26 June 2003 concerning common rules for the internal market in electricity and repealing Directive 96/92/EC.

(v)   Directive 2003/55/EC of the European Parliament and of the Council of 26 June 2003 concerning common rules for the internal market in natural gas and repealing Directive 98/30/EC.

(vi)   Directive 2004/67/EC concerning measures to safeguard security of natural gas supply (Security of Supply Directive);

(vii)   Regulation (EC) No 1228/2003 on conditions for access to the network for cross-border exchanges in electricity Regulation Transport of Electricity; and

(viii)   Regulation (EC) No 1775/2005 of the European Parliament and of the Council of 28 September 2005 on conditions for access to the natural gas transmission networks (the Gas Regulation).

COMMISSION FOR ENERGY REGULATION

8.012 The Electricity Regulation Act 1999 established the Commission for Electricity Regulation. The policy impetus of the Act came from Directive 96/92/EC, under which Ireland was scheduled to introduce competition in the electricity industry by February 2000. The 1999 Act legislates for a radical transition in the regulation of electricity supply in Ireland. The effect of the 1999 Act is to give the power of granting licences to generate and supply, and the power to authorise the construction of plant,[16] to an independent regulatory body.

---

16   Electricity Regulation Act 1999, s 2, states that "'electric plant'" means any plant, apparatus or appliance used for, or for purposes connected with, the generation, transmission, distribution or supply of electricity, other than (a) an electric line, (b) a meter used for ascertaining the quantity of electricity supplied to any premises, or (c) an electrical appliance under the control of a consumer'.

The 1999 Act is the point of departure for a new regime.[17] Section 14 of the 1999 Act provides for the Commission for Electricity Regulation to grant licences to the ESB or to other electricity undertakings to generate and supply electricity to eligible customers. From that point on, the ESB required regulatory approval by way of licence to discharge the functions it once took for granted under statute. This important change provides the basis for competition. In this manner, the Act transferred the regulatory role of the ESB to the Commission.

8.013 The Commission for Electricity Regulation was established by s 8(2) of the 1999 Act. It is a body corporate with perpetual succession and a common seal, and power to sue and be sued in its corporate name. It has the power to acquire, hold and dispose of land, or an interest in land, and to acquire, hold and dispose of any other property.[18] Its name was changed by s 5(2) of the 2002 Act to the Commission for Energy Regulation (CER). The 2002 Act also expanded the function of CER to include natural gas regulation.[19]

The composition of CER is set out in the Schedule to the Electricity Regulation Act 1999, as amended.[20] It shall consist of at least one, but not more than three, members, each of whom shall be appointed by the Minister to hold office in a full-time capacity for a period of not less than three, and not more than seven, years. Where there is more than one member of CER, the Minister shall appoint one of them to be chairperson of CER to hold office in a full-time capacity for a period of not less than three, and not more than five, years.[21] CER is to be independent in the performance of its functions. However, CER is obliged to comply with ministerial directions and also with the fact that the Minister for Communications, Energy and Natural Resources is the ultimate owner of ESB and Bord Gáis Eireann (BGE).

---

17 A primary motivation for this liberalisation of the market was, and is, to encourage the entry of competition and new investment. The retail electricity market opened fully to competition on 19 February 2005 and independent companies now supply almost half of electricity consumed (by volume) in Ireland. Furthermore, 2007 saw the beginning of the new Single Electricity Market (SEM) for the island of Ireland.

18 The section states that judicial notice shall be taken of the seal of the Commission and every document purporting to be an instrument made by and to be sealed with the seal of the Commission (purporting to be authenticated in accordance with this section) shall be received in evidence and be deemed to be such instrument without proof unless the contrary is shown.

19 Two of the most significant pieces of legislation adding to the Commission's functions are SIs 425/2004 and SI 60/2005.

20 As amended by the Gas (Interim) (Regulation) Act 2002.

21 A member of the Commission, including the chairperson, whose term of office expires, shall be eligible for re-appointment to serve a second term, subject to a limit of serving no more than ten years on the Commission. A member of the Commission shall not be entitled to serve more than two terms of office. The Commission is obliged to designate a member of its staff as deputy member of the Commission who shall assume and carry out with the authority of the Commission all of the functions of the Commission in the absence of the members or when the membership of the Commission is vacant.

8.014 Although CER is established as a national regulatory authority, independent of the energy companies such as the ESB and BGE, as well as the Minister, using provisions similar to s 13 of the Communications Regulation Act 2002, governing the activities of the Commission for Communications Regulation, the Minister may, in the interests of the proper and effective regulation of both the electricity and natural gas markets, give general policy directions to CER relating to the exercise of its statutory functions.[22] They include directions in respect of the criteria in accordance with which an application for an authorisation may be determined by CER, public service obligations which CER is required to impose on license and authorisation holders, as well as the definitions of combined heat and power and renewable, sustainable or alternative sources of energy. Policy directions in this way cover security of supply, sustainability and competitiveness. CER must comply with such policy directions and report to the Minister on their implementation.

8.015 CER may appoint such persons to be members of its staff as it considers necessary to assist it in the performance of its functions on such terms and conditions as may be agreed. The alternative to this approach is to second members of the Minister's Department to assist CER. The secondment of civil servants of the Minister is also provided for by the establishing legislation.

FUNDING

8.016 For the purpose of meeting its expenses in the discharge of its functions, CER may make an order (referred to as a 'levy order') imposing a levy[23] to be paid each year on such classes of energy undertakings[24] as may be specified by CER in the order. Separate orders may be made in respect of electricity undertakings and natural gas undertakings. A levy order when made or amended can only take effect in the next calendar year. This provision is similar to the levy order that may be made by the Commission for Aviation Regulation or the Commission for Communications Regulation to cover their expenses. See **Chs 3** and **6** in this regard.[25]

---

22   Minister of State Brown made an interesting comment when introducing that feature of the legislation (s 6) in April 2006: 'It is important to note that such powers would be used sparingly and always in the public interest. Any policy direction which the Minister may wish to put forward will be subject to a public consultation process. Such a process can serve to improve upon the *modus operandi* of the CER by increasing its awareness of public concerns and issues.' This is imposed further to s 6 of the 2006 Act.

23   Electricity Regulation Act 1999, Sch, para 16 as amended by Gas (Interim) Regulation Act 2002, s 22. Examples of such orders are: the Electricity Regulation Act 1999 and Gas (Interim) (Regulation) Act 2002 (Gas) Levy Order 2005 (SI 818/2005) and the Electricity Regulation Act 1999 (Electricity) Levy Order 2005 (SI 819/2005).

24   '"Energy undertaking" means an electricity undertaking or a natural gas undertaking,' as defined by the Electricity Regulation Act 1999, s 2, as inserted by Gas (Interim) Regulation Act 2002, s 22.

25   Aviation Regulation Act 2001, s 23.

The Commission for Energy Regulation is obliged to separate its accounts so as to identify separately in regard to the gas and electricity sectors all elements of cost and revenue, with the basis of their calculation and the detailed attribution methods used, related to the discharge of CER's functions.[26]

FUNCTIONS OF COMMISSION

8.017 CER has the following functions:[27]

(a) to publish, pursuant to a policy direction or directions of the Minister, which shall be made publicly available when given to the CER, proposals for a system of contracts and other arrangements, including appropriate rights and obligations, for trading in electricity;

(b) to engage in a public consultation process on the procedures to be adopted by the CER to implement the proposals drawn up under paragraph (a);

(c) to advise the Minister on the impact of electricity generation in relation to sustainability, and international agreements on the environment to which the State is or becomes a party;

(d) following the public consultation process referred to in paragraph (b) and taking account of matters raised in the public consultation process, to make regulations, subject to the consent of the Minister, establishing a system of trading in electricity, including the supervision and review of such a system by the CER;

(e) to advise the Minister on the development of the electricity and gas industries, as appropriate, and on the exercise of the functions of the Minister under this Act;[28]

(ea) to regulate the activities of natural gas undertakings and natural gas installers with respect to safety;[29]

(eb) to promote the safety of natural gas customers and the public generally as respects the supply, storage, transmission, distribution, and use of natural gas (excluding such activities carried out at upstream pipelines or facilities except where such pipeline or facility is engaged in the storage of natural gas;[30]

(ec) to consult with the National Standards Authority of Ireland regarding standards and specifications relating to gas safety.[31]

---

26 Electricity Regulation Act 1999, Sch, para 25(a) and (aa), as substituted by Gas (Interim) Regulation Act 2002, s 22(e).

27 Electricity Regulation Act 1999, s 9, as amended by the Gas (Interim) Regulation Act 2002, s 6 and Energy (Miscellaneous Provisions) Act 2006, ss 3 and 4.

28 Section 9(1)(e), as substituted by Gas (Interim) Regulation Act 2002, s 6(a).

29 Section 9(1)(ea), as inserted by Energy (Miscellaneous Provisions) Act 2006, s 12(a).

30 Section 9(1)(eb), as inserted by Energy (Miscellaneous Provisions) Act 2006, s 12(a).

31 Section 9(1)(ec), as inserted by Energy (Miscellaneous Provisions) Act 2006, s 12(a).

8.018 By virtue of s 9(3) the Minister and CER are obliged to carry out their functions and exercise the powers conferred on them under the Act in a manner which:

(a) in relation to electricity, does not discriminate unfairly between holders of licences, authorisations and the Board[32] or between applicants for authorisations or licences;

(b) in relation to gas, does not discriminate unfairly between holders of licences, consents and Bord Gáis Éireann or between applicants for consents or licences; and

(c) the Minister or the CER, as the case may be, considers protects the interests of final customers of electricity or gas or both, as the case may be.[33]

8.019 Pursuant to s 9(4), in carrying out the duty imposed by subsection (3), the Minister and CER shall have regard to the need:

(a) to promote competition in the generation and supply of electricity and in the supply of natural gas in accordance with this Act;[34]

(b) to secure that all reasonable demands by final customers of electricity for electricity are satisfied;

(c) to secure that licence holders are capable of financing the undertaking of the activities which they are licensed to undertake;

(d) to promote safety and efficiency on the part of electricity and natural gas undertakings;[35]

(e) to promote the continuity, security and quality of supplies of electricity;[36]

(f) to promote the use of renewable, sustainable or alternative forms of energy;[37]

(g) to secure that there is sufficient capacity in the natural gas system to enable reasonable expectations of demand to be met;[38]

(h) to secure the continuity, security and quality of supplies of natural gas.[39]

---

32 The 'Board' is defined in the Electricity Regulation Act 1999, s 2 as the Electricity Supply Board; in the Gas (Interim) Regulation Act 2002, s 2 as meaning 'Board Gáis Eireann'. Section 6 of the 2002 Act lists the functions of the CER relative to 'the Board' in terms of electricity and of 'Bord Gáis Eireann' in relation to gas. This approach is used generally – ie the context dictates which Board/Bord is being referred to.

33 Section 9(3), as substituted by Gas (Interim) Regulation Act 2002, s 6(b).

34 Section 9(4)(a) of the 1999 Act, as substituted by Gas (Interim) Regulation Act 2002, s 6(c)(i).

35 Section 9(4)(d) of the 1999 Act, as substituted by Gas (Interim) Regulation Act 2002, s 6(c)(ii).

36 Section 9(4)(e) of the 1999 Act, as substituted by Gas (Interim) Regulation Act 2002, s 6(c)(ii).

37 Section 9(4)(f) of the 1999 Act, as substituted by Gas (Interim) Regulation Act 2002, s 6(c)(ii).

38 Section 9(4)(g) of the 1999 Act, as substituted by Gas (Interim) Regulation Act 2002, s 6 (c)(ii).

39 Section 9(4)(h) of the 1999 Act, as substituted by Gas (Interim) Regulation Act 2002, s 6(c)(ii).

By virtue of s 9(5), and without prejudice to sub-ss (3) and (4), it is the duty of CER:

    (a) to take account of the protection of the environment;

    (b) to encourage the efficient use and production of electricity;

    (c) to take account of the needs of rural customers, the disadvantaged and the elderly;

    (d) to encourage research and development into:

        (i) methods of generating electricity using renewable, sustainable and alternative forms of energy and combined heat and power, and

        (ii) methods of increasing efficiency in the use and production of electricity;

    (e) to require that the system operator gives priority to generating stations using renewable, sustainable or alternative energy sources when selecting generating stations.

8.020 Pursuant to s 9B[40] of the 1999 Act, it is a function of CER to participate in the development of an all-island energy market, including the preparation of proposals and the provision of advice to the Minister in regard to any part or aspect of the establishment, management and operation of such a market. Pursuant to s 9(5A), where the Single Electricity Market (SEM) is in operation, sub-ss (3), (4) and (5) shall not apply in relation to a matter which is a SEM matter.[41] CER also has the function set out in s 9BA of the 1999 Act[42] of taking all necessary steps to establish and facilitate the operation of the SEM, including a trading and settlement code in relation to that market. This function is to be exercised in consultation with the Northern Irish authorities. In this regard, pursuant to s 9BA(2)(b)(i), CER may require every person holding a licence under s 14(1)(a) to (d) and (h) to make available for trading under the SEM such electricity as is generated by that person or available to that person for supply above a certain threshold.

By virtue of s 9C,[43] it is a function of CER to regulate the activities of electrical contractors with respect to safety.

8.021 The European Communities (Internal Market in Electricity) (Electricity Supply Board) Regulations 2008[44] (the 2008 Regulations) set out further functions of CER. Regulation 16 of the 2008 Regulations provides that CER shall take all reasonably practicable steps to ensure that the ESB complies with the 2008 Regulations, which includes forming a subsidiary company that will take over the functions of Distribution System Operator (DSO). Regulation 17 of the 2008 Regulations obliges CER to carry out periodic reviews of the operations of the subsidiary company.

---

40   Section 9B of the Electricity Regulation Act 1999, as inserted by Energy (Miscellaneous Provisions) Act 2006, s 3.

41   Section 9(5A) of the 1999 Act, as inserted by Electricity Regulation (Amendment) (Single Electricity Market) Act 2007, s 6.

42   Section 9BA the Act of 1999, as inserted by Electricity regulation (Amendment) (Single Electricity Market) Act 2007, s 7.

43   Electricity Regulation Act 1999, s 9C, as inserted by Energy (Miscellaneous Provisions) Act 2006, s 4.

44   SI 280/2008.

THE REGULATED ACTIVITY AND THE REGULATED ENTITIES – ELECTRICITY
Authorisation

8.022 The 1999 Act provided that any person granted a permit after 1 September 1998 by the ESB to generate, distribute and supply electricity must apply to the Commission for Electricity Regulation within three months of its enactment.[45] Any existing permits granted by the ESB after 1 September 1998 expired 12 months after enactment. In accordance with s 15 of the 1999 Act, a person who has been granted a permit under s 37 of the Electricity (Supply) Act 1927 on or after 1 September 1998, must apply for a licence or an authorisation within three months of the coming into operation of this section or such other period as may be agreed by CER.[46] A permit granted under s 37 of the 1927 Act before 1 September 1998, subject to the provisions of the 1999 Act, continues in full force and effect.

8.023 CER was given the power to licence undertakings to generate, transmit, distribute and supply electricity in Ireland. Pursuant to s 14, CER may grant or may refuse to grant to any person (including the ESB) a licence to do the following activities:[47]

(a)   to generate electricity;

(b)   to supply electricity to eligible customers;

(c)   to supply electricity to final customers which is generated by that supplier or purchased by that supplier and which electricity is generated, in whole or in part, using renewable, sustainable or alternative forms of energy, in accordance with any trading arrangements provided for in regulations made under s 9(1)(d);[48] and

(d)   to supply electricity to final customers which is generated by that supplier or purchased by that supplier and which electricity is generated, in whole or in part, using combined heat and power,[49] in accordance with any trading arrangements provided for in regulations made under s 9(1)(d).[50]

---

45   Electricity Regulation Act 1999, s 15.

46   Section 15(3) states: 'A permit granted under s 37 of the Principal Act on or after 1 September 1998, shall expire 12 months after the commencement of this section or on the granting on an earlier date of a licence or authorisation by the Commission.'

47   On such terms and conditions as may be specified in the licence. Any licence granted under this section shall be deemed to contain a condition that it shall be subject to modification for the purposes of compliance with any enactment implementing, whether in whole or in part, Council Directive No 96/92/EC of the European Parliament and of the Council of 19 December 1996 concerning common rules for the internal market in electricity.

48   Section 14(1)(c) of the 1999 Act, as substituted by Energy (Miscellaneous Provisions)Act 2006, s 5.

49   '"[C]ombined heat and power" means the simultaneous generation in one process of (i) thermal energy and electrical energy, (ii) thermal energy and mechanical energy, or (iii) thermal, electrical and mechanical energy': s 2(1) of the 1999 Act, as substituted by Energy (Miscellaneous Provisions) Act 2006, s 6(a).

50   Section 14(1)(d) of the 1999 Act, as substituted by Energy (Miscellaneous Provisions)Act 2006, s 5.

8.024 The criteria which CER has regard to in determining to grant an authorisation are set out under the Electricity Regulation Act 1999 (Criteria for Determination of Authorisation) Order 1999 (SI 309/1999) and the European Communities (Internal Market in Electricity) Regulations 2005 (SI 60/2005) (the 2005 Regulations).

There are simplified authorisation procedures for generators with capacities less than 1 MW and less than 10MW.

8.025 The authorisation to operate a transmission network is a licence to discharge the functions of the transmission system operator (TSO) in accordance with the 2000 Regulations issued by CER pursuant to s 14(1)(e) of the 1999 Act. Pursuant to s 14(2A) of the 1999 Act, only EirGrid may be granted a licence as the TSO.

The authorisation to construct a transmission network is a licence to discharge the functions of the transmission asset owner in accordance with the 2000 Regulations issued by CER pursuant to s 14(1)(f) of the 1999 Act. Pursuant to s 14(2B) of the 1999 Act, only the ESB may be granted a licence as transmission asset owner.

The authorisation to construct or operate a distribution network is a licence to discharge the functions of the DSO issued by CER pursuant to s 14(1)(g) of the 1999 Act. Pursuant to s 14(2C) of the 1999 Act, only the ESB may be granted a licence as distribution system operator.

There are three different types of authorisation to supply electricity customers:

(i)   licence to supply eligible customers under s 14(1)(b);

(ii)   licence to supply all final customers with electricity from green sources under s 14(1)(c); or

(iii) license to supply all final customers with electricity produced using combined heat and power under s 14(1)(d).

8.026 Where CER refuses to grant a licence to a person, this must be done in writing setting out the reasons. The European Commission must also be notified within 28 days of the refusal. The person may appeal the refusal in accordance with s 29 of the 1999 Act. See para **8.116** below of this chapter and **Ch 10** on Appeals for further details in this regard.

8.027 Authorisations to construct or reconstruct a generating station must be granted by CER under s 16 of the 1999 Act. Importantly, and notwithstanding the Electricity (Supply) Acts 1927 to 1995, the ESB may not construct or reconstruct a generating station unless authorised to do so by the Commission.[51] In this way, anyone wishing to construct a new generating station or reconstruct an existing generating station must obtain an authorisation from CER prior to commencing work. Pursuant to s 14 of the 1999 Act, all generators must obtain a generation licence from CER, which can consider a number of factors in evaluating a licence application. These may include, for example, the availability of sufficient appropriate financial, managerial or technical resources to ensure that the generator is able to comply with the terms and conditions that govern the electricity generation licence.

---

51   Section 16(3).

Modification of Licences

8.028 Section 19 of the 1999 Act provides for licences or authorisations to be modified in a number of ways. Firstly, the holder of a licence or an authorisation may request CER to modify the conditions or requirements of the licence or authorisation. Secondly, where CER is of the opinion that a licence or an authorisation should be amended, it may do so with or without the consent of the holder of the licence or the authorisation, as the case may be. Thirdly, where CER is of the opinion that a modification of a condition or requirement of a licence or an authorisation is a modification of a class required by an order of the Minister made under ss 39 or 40,[52] CER may modify the conditions or requirements of the licence or authorisation concerned without the consent of the holder of that licence or authorisation, as the case may be. The 1999 Act envisages that such modifications are formally made in a transparent manner. A lengthy procedure is set out at s 20. In brief, before modifying a licence or an authorisation, CER must issue a public notice in the national papers; allow for representations to be made and, where it is satisfied that sufficient grounds exist to warrant a public hearing, CER may hold such a public hearing.[53] Then it must consider the representations made before giving notice of its reasoned decision. Where such modifications are not agreed, they can be imposed subject to minimum notice and certain conditions.

8.029 Section 13 of the 2007 Act states that the 1999 Act is amended by the insertion after s 14 of a new s 14A, which states that CER may modify the conditions of a particular licence where CER considers it necessary or expedient to do for the purpose of implementing, or facilitating the operation of, the SEM.[54]

Generation

8.030 A number of regulatory steps have been taken to facilitate competition in generation. Full competition has been introduced in the generation sector in Ireland although ESB still owns or controls a significant majority of the installed generating capacity. Undertakings are barred from building a generating station without the granting of plant authorisations by CER.[55] It will be recalled that the Regulator may modify any licences or plant authorisations it has granted.[56]

---

52   Electricity Regulation Act 1999, ss 39 and 40 concern public service obligations and transitional arrangements, respectively.

53   Sections 21 and 22 deal with public hearings and determinations of the Commission following a public meeting. The hearing is intended to be formal. CER may administer oaths and compel attendance of witnesses.

54   Section 14A of the 1999 Act, as inserted by Electricity Regulation (Amendment)(Single Electricity Market) Act 2007, s 13.

55   Section 15. Section 17 gives the Minister the power to specify the criteria for the granting of authorisations. These criteria may relate to the safety and security of the electricity system, protection of the environment, public service obligations, energy efficiency and other matters.

56   Sections 18 and 19.

8.031 Power generation in Ireland is carried out by ESB Power Generation (ESB PG) as well as by a number of independently owned power stations.[57] These stations generate electricity from fuels such as oil, coal and gas, as well as indigenous fuels including hydro, wind, peat and biomass.

Revenue regulation

8.032 CER regulates the revenue that ESB PG can earn. Each year it carries out an assessment of ESB PG's costs, seeking to ensure that only the efficient costs of the generation business are passed on to customers in wholesale electricity prices.[58]

Transmission

8.033 The electricity transmission system, commonly known as the national grid, is a high voltage network for the transmission of 'bulk' electricity supplies around Ireland. High voltage lines deliver electricity from Ireland's generation sources to the transformer stations, where the electricity voltage is reduced and distributed down the lines to individual customers' premises. In addition, about 18 very large commercial customers are connected directly to the transmission system.[59]

8.034 CER issues two licences in relation to the transmission system in Ireland: the Transmission System Operator (TSO) Licence and the Transmission Asset Owner (TAO) Licence. EirGrid is the independent State-owned body licensed by CER to act as TSO. ESB Networks is licensed by CER as the owner of the transmission system. The ESB owns the assets that make up the transmission network. The activity of owning the transmission system assets is a separately licensed activity and the TAO licence was granted by CER to the ESB in 2001.[60] The TAO is required to maintain the transmission system and carry out construction work for its development in accordance with the TSO's Transmission Development Plan.

8.035 An infrastructure agreement was drawn up between the TSO and the TAO to govern the ongoing relationship between the two organisations. The agreement was approved by CER and came into effect on 1 July 2006 – the same date as the legal establishment of EirGrid as the TSO.[61] EirGrid is a State-owned company that was set

---

57   The criteria for assessment for a generation licence are set out in the Electricity Regulation Act 1999 (Criteria for Determination of Authorisations) Order 1999 (SI 309/1999).

58   See, for example, Commission for Energy Regulation Direction to ESB Power Generation on Allowable Costs for 2006 and 2007, 19 October 2007, CER/07/167, http://www.cer.ie. SIs 60/2005 and 445/2000, which are cited together as European Communities (Internal Market in Electricity) Regulations 2000 and 2005 and shall be construed together as one, govern this area.

59   For example, the Aughinish Alumina factory in County Limerick.

60   The same regulations deal with the granting of a TAO licence.

61   European Communities (Internal Market in Electricity) Regulations 2000 and 2005 regulate the granting of a TSO licence.

up specifically to carry out the TSO function, and it is separate and independent from the ESB, which, as stated above, actually owns the transmission system. EirGrid's responsibilities include the operation, maintenance and development of Ireland's transmission system in a safe, secure, reliable, economical and efficient manner. It also offers terms and levies charges for the connection to and use of the system by market participants and these tariffs are regulated by CER.

8.036 The Electricity Regulation (Amendment) (Eirgrid) Act 2008 (the 2008 Act) was adopted to enable,[62] pursuant to s 2 of the 2008 Act, the construction by EirGrid of an interconnector to enable the transportation of electricity across and the maintenance of such an interconnector by EirGrid, and to enable EirGrid to own and operate such an interconnector. It also provides that EirGrid shall not lease, sell or otherwise dispose of, in whole or in part, an interconnector it has an interest in, including a proposed interconnector, to another person without the consent of the Minister, given with the approval of the Minister for Finance. EirGrid is to exercise its functions under s 2 of the 2008 Act in a manner consistent with its functions as the transmission system operator under SI 60/2005. It provides in s 3 of the 2008 Act that s 2A of the 1999 Act is to be amended so that an interconnector owned by a person other than the ESB may be construed pursuant to s 16A as being in the public interest and, where it is, it should be considered to be part of the transmission system for the purposes of calculating charges and imposing charges for use of the transmission system. In that instance, an interconnector owned by the TSO shall be regarded as part of the transmission system for the purposes of the functions of the TSO.

The 2008 Act also provides that EirGrid may not without the approval of the Minister, given with the consent of the Minister for Finance, acquire, establish or dispose of subsidiaries or invest in other undertakings. It also provides for borrowings by EirGrid and capital expenditure that may be incurred by EirGrid.

Revenue regulation

8.037 The Commission for Energy Regulation regulates the revenue both the TSO and the TAO may generate from charges for the use of their infrastructure.[63] Revenue determinations are carried out every five years, and are then reviewed annually. The latest five-year determination covers the period from 2006 to 2010 and sets out the total allowed revenues over that period.[64] As with other Regulators, in coming to its

---

62 Subject to a grant of authorisation pursuant to s 16(1)(b) of the 1999 Act and the grant of a licence under s 14(1)(i) of the 1999 Act.

63 Electricity Regulation Act 1999, s 35.

64 See the CER, *2006-2010 Transmission Price Control Review Transmission Asset Owner (TAO) and Transmission System Operator (TSO) Decision Paper*, CER/05/143, 9 September 2005, available at http://www.cer.ie. This was varied by the CER, *Determination of Transmission Allowed Revenue and Use of System Tariffs*, CER/08/178, 26 September 2008. This decision 'refines' the TSO and TAO allowed revenue for 2009 and sets out the Transmission Use of System tariffs for 2009.

decision, CER considers the operating and capital expenditure forecast of the regulated entity over the period and its cost of capital (a proxy for a reasonable rate of return on the regulatory asset base).

Distribution

8.038 The distribution network is the medium and low voltage electricity network used to deliver electricity to houses, offices, shops and street lights. The distribution system is owned and operated by ESB Networks. ESB Networks is a separate business division of ESB, licensed by CER as the DSO.[65] The licence requires that this division is completely separate from the other businesses of the ESB. ESB Networks is responsible for maintaining all the sub-transmission medium and low voltage electricity network infrastructure – this includes all overhead electricity lines, poles and underground cables in Ireland. The 2008 Regulations oblige ESB to functionally separate and form a subsidiary company that will take over the functions of DSO. Regulation 17 of the 2008 Regulations obliges the CER to carry out periodic reviews of the operations of the subsidiary company. The first periodic review shall be carried out within one year after the transfer date. Each subsequent periodic review shall be carried out within a five-year period of the previous review. As part of these reviews, CER is to ascertain:

(a) the extent to which the subsidiary company is conducting its operations in a manner consistent with the 2008 Regulations;

(b) whether the subsidiary company engages in discriminatory behaviour, in particular as regards other entities that are part of, or are related to, the ESB; and

(c) whether the subsidiary company is sufficiently resourced to discharge its functions as the DSO.

Revenue regulation

8.039 ESB Networks charges 'distribution tariffs' for using the distribution system. The tariffs are paid by the suppliers who use the system. The CER regulates the tariffs to be applied for use of the network of the DSO.[66] This is done every five years with the objective that only efficient levels of costs are permitted to be recovered from customers. The latest five-year review covers the period 2005 to 2010 and sets out the total allowed revenues over that period. However, as with generation and transmission, the revenue the licence holder (here, the DSO) is allowed to collect from customers is

---

65   Electricity Regulation Act 1999, s 14. See also SI 445/2000.

66   See, for example, CER, *2006-2010 ESB Price Control Review CER Decision Paper on Distribution System Operator Revenues*, CER 05/138, 9 September 2005, available at http://www.cer.ie.

reviewed each year and these 'allowed revenues' are used to calculate the tariffs, which are approved by CER.[67]

Grid Code and Distribution Network Code

8.040 A further innovation for the Irish market is that the ESB shall prepare a grid code or a distribution code for the operation of the electricity transmission and distribution systems, for the approval of the Regulator.[68] These codes will set out the technical aspects relating to connection to and operation of the transmission and distribution systems, for use by licence or authorisation holders. In this regard, the ESB is required to offer to enter into agreement with any licence or authorisation holder or eligible customer.[69] In addition, the ESB is obliged to prepare a statement setting out the basis for the level of system charges for connection to and use of the transmission or distribution systems.[70] That statement is to be available to licence and authorisation holders so that they may estimate and plan for their charges. Importantly, from a regulatory perspective, this statement of charges requires approval by the Regulator.[71]

An important power transferred to the Regulator is the ability to grant permission for the construction of direct lines for the transmission or distribution of electricity from licence or authorisation holders to eligible customers, where access is refused on the basis of a lack of capacity in the existing transmission or distribution system.[72]

8.041 The Distribution Network Code defines the technical aspects of the working relationship between ESB Networks, as the DSO, and all users of the distribution system. It was prepared by the ESB under the terms of the 1999 Act and was approved by CER in March 2000.

Supply

8.042 A major innovation of the Electricity Regulation Act 1999 is the definition of those customers eligible to choose their supplier of electricity.[73] Those customers were

---

67 See CER, *Decision on 2009 Distribution System Operator Allowed Revenue, Distribution Use of System Tariffs and Distribution Loss Adjustment Factors*, CER/08/173, 26 September 2008, available at http://www.cer.ie. Arguably, such an annual revenue review approach is at odds with the notion of a periodic pricing efficiency determination wherein regulated entities are expected to bear the cost of inefficiency year on year within that period, or reap the benefits from efficiencies relative to a revenue or price yield fixed at the beginning of the period that remains the same for that period.

68 Electricity Regulation Act 1999, s 33.

69 Section 34.

70 Section 35.

71 Section 36.

72 Section 37. Pursuant to s 37, the ESB must prepare a statement for the approval of the Regulator setting out estimates of future generation and transmission requirements. In simple terms, transmission lines are those massive pylon-supported lines occasionally seen in the countryside. Distribution lines are the more extensive local lines connecting to homes and factories.

73 Electricity Regulation Act 1999, s 27. This came in to force in February 2000.

initially defined by their level of electricity usage. By virtue of art 21 of Council Directive 2003/54/EC, all customers are now eligible customers.[74] Eligible customers were defined in s 27(2) of the 1999 Act as those consumers of electricity whose consumption of electricity at any single premises in any 12-month period is estimated and calculated to be, or likely to be, greater than a certain threshold, initially 4 gigawatt hours. The level was set to introduce competition to 28 per cent of the market, increasing to 32 per cent.[75] It decreased over time to 1 gigawatt hour, then 0.1 gigawatt hour then 0.1 kilowatt hours.[76] Full retail contestability was introduced in 2005. Customers do not have to change from the ESB Public Electricity Supplier, but certain large customers have done so with other operators becoming active in this market. No independent suppliers offer electricity to residential customers.

Public Service Obligation

8.043 Undertakings in the electricity sector may be subject to public service obligations (PSOs).[77] The Minister, following consultation with the Minister for the Environment and Local Government, may make an order directing the CER to impose PSOs on the ESB or other licence or authorisation holders, in the general economic interest. These obligations may relate to security of supply, regularity, quality and price of supplies, environmental protection (including energy efficiency and climate protection) and use of indigenous energy sources.[78] These PSOs may be imposed on the ESB or on holders of licences to generate or supply electricity. The cost of these

---

74 Article 21(1)(c) states that Member States shall ensure that the eligible customers are all customers from 1 July 2007.

75 In this regard, there was a Government decision in April 1996 that all electricity customers should be entitled to purchase electricity that is produced using a renewable or alternative form of energy as its primary source.

76 Section 27 empowers the Minister to vary this level of consumption by order. The Minister did so by virtue of Electricity Regulation Act 1999 (Eligible Customer) Order 2002 (SI 3/2002), wherein the reference in the Act to 4 gigawatt hours was reduced to 1 gigawatt hour. Such an order must be publicised in the national press and laid before the Houses of the Oireachtas for approval. The threshold was later reduced by Electricity Regulation Act 1999 (Eligible Customer) (Consumption of Electricity) Order 2003 (SI 632/2003). 50 watts x 20 hours = 1,000 watt hours = 1 kilowatt hour. One gigawatt hour = one billion watt hours.

77 Electricity Regulation Act 1999, s 39.

78 It is foreseen in the legislation that 'an order made by the Minister under this section [s 39] may require the Commission to impose on the Board a requirement to make such arrangements as are necessary to ensure that, in any calendar year, there shall be available to the Board a specific quantity of electricity from: (a) generating stations which use as their primary energy fuel source peat harvested within the State provided that the amount of peat used in any calendar year to generate that quantity of electricity may not exceed 15 per cent. of the overall primary energy necessary to produce the electricity consumed in the State that year, and (b) generating stations chosen as a result of a competitive process established by the Minister, the Commission or the Commission of the European Communities, as the case may be, which use as their primary fuel source such renewable, sustainable or alternative forms of energy as may be specified in the order or which operate as combined heat and power plants.'

obligations would be recovered from all electricity users. Furthermore, the Minister may by order provide for the recovery from consumers of electricity of specified costs or revenue relating to generating stations constructed before 19 February 1997.[79] To date, only the ESB has been subject to PSOs. For example, the PSO Levy is an additional charge relating to the costs to ESB of purchasing peat-generated electricity and the output of renewable, sustainable or alternative forms of energy purchased under various Government schemes. ESB is obliged by Government to make these purchases in the interests of security of supply and environmental protection. The most recent PSO order is the Electricity Regulation Act 1999 (Public Service Obligations) (Amendment) (No 2) Order 2007 (SI 583/2007), which allows for the imposition of further PSOs on the ESB, in the interest of security of supply. This order places a requirement on ESB to make payments in respect of 10-year electricity generation contracts awarded to Aughinish Alumina Ltd and Tynagh Energy Ltd on foot of the CER's Capacity 2005 Competition. It provides for the compensation of ESB for the additional costs, if any, incurred in complying with these obligations. This PSO involves CADA, which is a capacity and differences agreement between the ESB and a third-party power producer and includes alternative arrangements prepared pursuant to that agreement and in accordance with its terms.

Predicting the National Load

8.044 An important technical aspect of the legislation relates to the estimate by ESB of capacity, forecast flows and loading. Prediction of the national load is important for the avoidance of power shortages or surges. It is a key element of security of supply. Section 38 of the 1999 Act decrees that at such intervals as the Commission may direct, the transmission system operator shall prepare a forecast statement, based on the information available to it, in a form approved of by the Commission.[80] This statement shall include forecasts in respect of capacity, forecast flows and loading on each part of the transmission system of the TSO and fault levels for each electricity transmission node, together with such further information as shall be reasonably necessary to enable any person seeking use of the transmission or distribution system to identify and evaluate the opportunities available when connecting to and making use of the transmission or distribution system. This information is very important for the

---

79   Section 39. When introducing the Bill to the Dáil on 3 February 1999, the Minister said, 'I do not expect to make orders under either of those sections until the electricity directive is fully implemented. The enabling powers set out in those sections will ensure that anyone who is issued a licence by the Regulator will be aware that a public service obligation regime and a transitional levy will be part of the implementation of the electricity directive as a whole. I will use the public service obligation provision to ensure the continued use of peat-fired power stations subject to certain conditions and the promotion of renewable and alternative energy. It is also my intention that there will be a transitional regime, probably for a period of five years, which will ensure that certain ESB stations, which are effectively State investment, do not become 'stranded' or unable to operate because of the introduction of competition.'

80   Section 38 of the 1999 Act, as substituted by Electricity Regulation (Amendment)(Single Electricity Market) Act 2007, s 15.

Irish electricity market. The preparation of this forecast is to be co-ordinated with the Northern Ireland system operator.[81]

Single Electricity Market

8.045 On 23 August 2004, the CER signed a Memorandum of Understanding with the Northern Ireland Authority for Energy Regulation (NIAER), in relation to the development of an all-island electricity market. Both Regulators agreed that the establishment of an all-island wholesale electricity market, called the 'Single Electricity Market' (SEM), was the first key project of this new programme of work.

Energy (Miscellaneous Provisions) Act 2006

8.046 In April 2006, the Government[82] introduced the Energy (Miscellaneous Provisions) Act 2006[83] (the 2006 Act). The 2006 Act includes a commencement provision designed to ensure the market will be fully open to competition no later than the 1 July 2007 deadline set by the EC Directive requirements. The 2006 Act assigns the following additional functions to CER: participation in the development of an all-island energy market,[84] regulation of the activities of electricity and gas installers and the regulation and promotion of natural gas safety. Other provisions of the Act include amending the definition of combined heat and power (CHP), the conferral of power on the Minister to issue policy directions to CER, provision for the full opening of the natural gas market, and provision for the taking of emergency measures by the Minister in the event of a sudden crisis in the energy market. The primary amendment[85] to the Electricity Regulation Act 1999 was the new statutory function of CER to participate in the development of an all-island energy market.[86] In order to further an all-island energy market,[87] CER was granted the power to arrange for the establishment

---

81   Section 38(10) of the 1999 Act, as substituted.

82   Energy (Miscellaneous Provisions) Bill 2006: Second Stage, Mr John Browne, Minister of State at the Department of Communications, Marine and Natural Resources, Dáil Éireann – Vol 617 – 6 April 2006.

83   The Act implements Directive 2003/55/EC.

84   Electricity Regulation Act 1999, s 9B, as inserted by s 3 of the 2006 Act. Section 9B(6) defines 'all island energy market' as 'a market in energy for the island of Ireland resulting from the integration of the equivalent markets in Ireland with those of Northern Ireland.'

85   Energy (Miscellaneous Provisions) Act 2006, s 3.

86   Previously, policy on such a market was encapsulated in the all-island energy market development framework published in November 2004 by the Minister and his then Northern Ireland ministerial counterpart, Barry Gardiner MP. The Act of 1999 is amended by s 3 of the 2006 Act, which inserts a new section – 9B. This new section sets out the functions of the Commission regarding the all-island energy market.

87   Section 9B(6) states that a '"market in energy" includes a market in respect of (a) the generation, supply, transmission, distribution and trading, including the export or import of electricity, including electricity generated from renewable sources, (b) the storage, supply, transmission, distribution and trading, including the export and import of natural gas, (c) energy efficient services, (d) energy research and development, and (e) other sustainable activities'.

of a single market operator to operate a system of contracts and arrangements for trading in electricity on the island of Ireland.

8.047 Another important amendment to the 1999 Act provided[88] for an electricity interconnector owned by a person other than the ESB to be subject to authorisation and licence granted by CER.[89] For technical reasons relating to the definition of the electrical transmission system, the section also provides that such an interconnector shall not be part of the transmission system except where it comes to the issue of calculating and imposing charges for the transmission system's use. Under the provisions of the section, CER may also, with the consent of the Minister, secure the construction of an interconnector by specified means, including by competitive tender; by authorisation granted without a prior competitive tender, but which must be seen to be necessary and in the long-term interests of final customers; or directly, by requesting the transmission system operator to provide for its construction as part of CER's development plan.

    Provision is also made to ensure an interconnector operator shall offer access to the interconnector on the basis of published non-discriminatory terms, which will be subject to the approval or, if deemed necessary, the direction of CER.

Electricity Regulation (Amendment) (Single Electricity Market) Act 2007

8.048 To further the establishment of the SEM, in November 2006 the Government introduced the Electricity Regulation (Amendment) (Single Electricity Market) Act 2007 (the 2007 Act).[90] The SEM is defined by the 2007 Act as 'the new arrangements in the State and Northern Ireland which are (a) described in the Memorandum of Understanding,[91] and (b) designed to promote the establishment and operation of a single competitive wholesale electricity market in the State and Northern Ireland'.[92]

---

88   Sections 16 and 17 of the 1999 Act, as amended by Energy (Miscellaneous Provisions) Act 2006, s 8(4)(a) and (b).

89   East-west and north-south electricity interconnection are critical elements of the Government's energy policy. Both can provide strong physical links with Northern Ireland and mainland UK, serving to integrate Ireland into wider European markets.

90   Minister of State, Mr Browne: Electricity Regulation (Amendment) (Single Electricity Market) Bill 2006: Second Stage. Dáil Éireann – Vol 628 – 30 November 2006.

91   '[T]he "Memorandum of Understanding" means the Memorandum of Understanding relating to the establishment and operation of a single competitive wholesale electricity market in the State and in Northern Ireland entered into between the Government of Ireland and the Government of the United Kingdom of Great Britain and Northern Ireland signed on behalf of the Government of Ireland on 5 December 2006 and on behalf of the Government of the United Kingdom of Great Britain and Northern Ireland on 6 December 2006.' – Section 2 of the 1999 Act, as amended by s 3 the 2007 Act.

92   This development raises interesting constitutional law questions and questions regarding extra-territorial jurisdiction.

8.049 The 2007 Act provided for the establishment of an SEM committee to carry out SEM regulatory functions on behalf of CER.[93] A corresponding provision exists in the Northern Ireland legislation so that the same statutory framework is in place for effective decision-making for the market North and South. Up to seven members may be appointed to the SEM committee under ministerial warrants from among the members and staff of both regulatory authorities, CER in Ireland and the NIAER in the North. A member independent of both Regulators will complete the committee. CER and the NIAER will work together through the SEM committee to exercise their respective regulatory functions. The two regulatory authorities must jointly publish a statement setting out the procedures and working arrangements of the SEM committee.[94] Relevant information may be shared between the two bodies to accommodate the carrying on of all-island market business.[95]

8.050 Pursuant to the provisions of the 2007 Act, CER will make regulations for the purpose of trading in electricity on an all-island basis, including the trading and settlement code, requiring all licensees to make available for trade through the SEM all electricity generated by them above a certain threshold, according to class of licensee. These functions are mirrored by the NIAER in Northern Ireland. The day-to-day trading and settlement of the SEM will be carried out by a market operator established by licence.[96] The market operator licence is required to include appropriate terms and conditions relating to participation in, and the operation of, the SEM. The market operator must prepare a statement for the approval of CER, setting out the basis on which charges are imposed in relation to participation in the trading arrangements under the SEM. These charges may not be imposed without approval by the CER.[97] The market operator function will be carried out jointly by the two TSOs, EirGrid in the State and SONI[98] in Northern Ireland. Other licensing provisions[99] allow for modifications to licences to ensure that both existing and new licensees can participate in the SEM, together with the publication process for such modifications and breaches of licence terms and conditions.

---

93 Section 8A of the 1999 Act, as inserted by s 4 of the 2007 Act, concerns the SEM committee. Section 8B is inserted by s 5 and it discusses the Commission and working arrangements as respects the SEM.

94 Electricity Regulation (Amendment) (Single Electricity Market) Act 2007, s 5.

95 Section 8 of the 2007 Act. In this regard, s 8 inserts s 9BB into the 1999 Act; this section relates to non-disclosure of information received in the context of implementing the SEM. Arguably, these reciprocal arrangements effectively provide for the establishment of a cross-border body with executive powers.

96 Electricity Regulation (Amendment) (Single Electricity Market) Act 2007, s 11.

97 Section 36A of the 1999 Act, as inserted by s 14 of the 2007 Act. Charges relating to participation in the trading arrangements shall be calculated in accordance with directions given by the Commission under this section so as to enable the market operator to recover: (a) the costs and expenses directly or indirectly incurred in operating the trading arrangements, and (b) a reasonable rate of return on capital expenditure included in such costs.

98 System Operator for Northern Ireland (SONI) Ltd is a wholly owned subsidiary of Northern Ireland Electricity and part of the Viridian Group.

99 Sections 12 and 13 of the 2007 Act.

8.051 A primary objective[100] of the SEM is protection of the interests of consumers on an all-island basis by promoting effective competition between market players participating in the SEM. Other stated objectives include the need to ensure that all reasonable demands for electricity are met, the need to ensure co-ordinated regulation of the market, the need to have transparent pricing in the SEM, and the need to avoid unfair discrimination between consumers in Ireland and Northern Ireland.

THE REGULATED ACTIVITY AND THE REGULATED ENTITIES – GAS

8.052 The gas market has been fully open since July 2007. The Gas Act 1976 established Bord Gáis Eireann (BGE) as the owner and operator of the gas transmission and distribution systems and provided the framework for the liberalisation of gas shipping and supply.

8.053 The Gas (Interim) (Regulation) Act 2002[101] transferred certain powers and functions of the Minister for Public Enterprise to CER to provide for the independent regulation of the natural gas sector in Ireland. The legislation adapted the role of the Commission for Electricity Regulation so that it encompassed responsibility for the regulation of the natural gas sector and also changed its name to the Commission for Energy Regulation.[102] The Minister for Communications, Marine and Natural Resources retained responsibility for the licensing and regulation of offshore exploration.[103] The Act transposed Directive 98/30/EC, which set out the basic rules for initial opening of the gas sector market. It included provisions dealing with access to networks and pipeline, unbundling of integrated gas undertakings and a liberalisation timetable. Pursuant to that directive, member states were to open at least 20 per cent of national gas markets to competition from the year 2000, with further incremental increases up to 33 per cent taking effect by the year 2008.[104]

---

100 Section 9 of the 2007 Act.
101 Introduced by the Minister of State at the Department of Public Enterprise, Joe Jacob. Gas (Interim) (Regulation) Bill, 2001: Second Stage. Seanad Éireann – Volume 168 – 3 October, 2001.
102 Gas (Interim) Regulation Act 2002, s 5. The Electricity Regulation Acts 1999 and 2000 and Gas (Interim) Regulation Act 2002 may be cited together as Electricity and Gas Regulation Acts 1999 to 2002, and are to be construed together as one.
103 Because Ireland has few natural gas resources, most of the gas consumed in Ireland is bought on the international gas markets and imported to Ireland through the natural gas network or, specifically, through interconnection with the UK. As a result, Irish customers are exposed to fluctuations in international gas prices. It is unclear to what extent, if any, Irish gas suppliers hedge the future price of gas in an attempt to keep costs down to the ultimate benefit of consumers.
104 When introducing the Bill to the Senate, Minister Jacob noted that it was his 'intention to achieve full market opening by 2005, in line with the timetable proposed for the electricity sector. Full market opening will include the domestic market and the proposals fully complement the latest liberalisation proposals from the European Commission. It is my intention to adopt an orderly phased approach to full market opening in 2005 by introducing at least one intermediate step before then.'

8.054 In Ireland, this process was begun in 1995 through the Energy (Miscellaneous Provisions) Act 1995 (the 1995 Act). The 1995 Act obliged BGE to offer access to its network to customers consuming 25 million standard cubic meters of gas per annum. The term used for this arrangement is 'third-party access' and the idea is to allow consumers to source their own gas from any supplier and arrange to have it delivered through the BGE network on non-discriminatory terms and at a fair price. The 1995 Act was designed to open up the market further by reducing the annual rate of gas consumption permitting customers to acquire third-party access rights. Initially, the annual consumption threshold for eligible customers would drop from 25 million to 2 million standard cubic meters, resulting in the market opening rising from 75 per cent to over 80 per cent.[105] Third-party access involves providing regulated access to the transportation system based on published tariffs. CER approves these tariffs and the methodologies used for their calculation on an *ex-ante* basis.

8.055 The provisions of the Gas (Interim) Regulation Act 2002 (the 2002 Act) were designed to mirror, to the greatest extent possible, those set out in the Electricity Regulation Act 1999, to facilitate its implementation and so that the market would already be familiar with the principles behind the legislation. The legislation transferred various functions from the Minister to CER, as well as expanding the then current duties of CER in the light of its role regarding the natural gas sector. These duties included advising the Minister on the gas industry, promoting competition in gas supply and protecting the interest of final customers. The transferred functions also related to the construction of gas pipelines and related issues such as compulsory acquisition orders and the extinguishment of rights of way.

8.056 CER may direct pipeline operators to publish a code of operations for their pipelines in order to facilitate the interoperability of the gas transmission network and pipelines owned by different operators.[106] The CER approved a Code of Operations in 2005 for publication by BGE. The code incorporates transmission and distribution operations and facilitates an entry and exit gas transportation system. The Gas

---

105 Minister Jacob made a number of interesting comments in the course of that debate in the Seanad: 'Gas demand is growing rapidly in Ireland, mirroring trends across Europe. It is now the fuel of choice in electricity generation and its share of the domestic and industrial energy markets is also increasing. This reflects a number of factors, including competitive gas prices, the relatively high conversion efficiency of gas and the fact that gas is cleaner than other fossil fuels, such as oil and coal. Market growth is set to continue and, in a report produced last December, the ESRI estimates that over 70 per cent of Ireland's power generation will be fuelled by natural gas by 2010 and that demand for gas may grow by approximately 7 per cent per annum over this decade ... This scenario has a number of consequences. First, rising demand is driving increased investment in gas infrastructure. Second, gas has an important role to play in Ireland meeting its Kyoto targets for reducing greenhouse gas emissions. A modern gas-fired power station produces less than half as much carbon dioxide as an older coal fire station per unit of electricity generated. Gas stations also produce much lower emissions than oil stations. Hence a switch in electricity generation away from coal and oil towards gas can give rise to very large reductions in greenhouse gas emissions.'

106 Section 13 of the 2002 Act.

Regulation EC/1775/2005 on conditions of access to the natural gas transmission networks has obliged BGE since July 2006 to implement flexibility including short-term and interruptible capacity. A code modification would need to reflect this flexibility. Certain code modifications in relation to short-term services have been agreed. Capacity allocation mechanisms may also be reviewed. The balancing regime is to remain unchanged pending development of the all-island market. A code modification also allows for certain gas storage facilities. Increased market opening is facilitated by providing for the reduction of consumption thresholds above which consumers can source their own gas supplies from any supplier.[107] To provide for access to the market, BGE as a pipeline operator is also obliged to offer to deal with the following categories of undertakings on terms and conditions set down by CER:[108]

(a)   the holder of a natural gas licence under s 16 of the Gas (Interim) (Regulation) Act 2002, for the purpose of carrying out any activity for which the holder is licensed;[109]

(b)   the holder of a petroleum lease under s 13 of the Petroleum and Other Minerals Development Act 1960, for the purpose of carrying out any activity connected with the lease;

(c)   a person, including BGE, in respect of whom an order has been made under s 2(1) of the Gas (Amendment) Act 1987, for the purpose of carrying out the functions conferred on the person by the order;

(d)   a person who operates a gas-fired generating station, irrespective of its annual consumption level, for the purpose of providing energy for the generation of electricity at that station; or

(e)   a final customer (within the meaning of s 2 of the Gas (Interim) (Regulation) Act 2002), with an annual rate of consumption of not less than 2,000,000 standard cubic meters per annum (or such other rate as may stand prescribed for the time being) at a single meter installation for the purpose of delivery to that installation.

The provisions of ss 10A and 10B of the Gas Act 1976, as inserted by s 14 of the Gas (Interim) (Regulation) Act 2002, provide for the regulation by either the CER or the Minister of the charges imposed for transportation by the pipeline operator. The Minister acts in relation to 'upstream' operators.

---

107 The Act allows the Minister to reduce, by way of statutory instrument, the annual consumption threshold that defines the level of market opening. Effective from 1 January 2003, natural gas consumers who consume in excess of 500,000 standard cubic meters at a meter point are eligible to choose a natural gas licensed supplier to provide their supply.

108 Gas Act 1976, s 10A, as inserted Gas (Interim) Regulation Act 2002, s 14.

109 Dispute resolution responsibility for disagreements between a pipeline operator and licence holders seeking access to the pipelines is split between the Minister for 'upstream pipelines' and the Commission for other pipelines. See the Gas (Interim) Regulation Act 2002, s 14. That section envisages that cases involving refusal of access, dispute resolution and enforcement decisions on access are ultimately to be heard before the High Court.

8.057 A charge for connection to, or the transportation of, natural gas through a pipeline under the control of the pipeline operator must be calculated in accordance with directions given by the Minister or CER, as appropriate, so as to enable the pipeline operator to recover: (i) the appropriate proportion of the costs directly or indirectly incurred in carrying out any necessary works, and (ii) a reasonable rate of return on the capital represented by such costs as decided by the Minister or CER. Prior to applying charges, the pipeline operator must forward a statement of charges to either the Minister or CER for approval.

8.058 Following the introduction of the 2002 Act, Bord Gáis Eireann, the incumbent State monopoly, was split into Bord Gáis Networks and Bord Gáis Supply. They are separate and distinct business units within BGE and are ring-fenced according to their respective licences issued by CER. Bord Gáis Networks is the regulated system operator and is responsible for the construction, operation and maintenance of the transmission and distribution networks and developing commercial arrangements for use of the natural gas network in the Ireland. Bord Gáis Supply is a gas supplier and supplies gas to its customers.

8.059 In addition to the Energy (Miscellaneous Provisions) Act 2006, which expands the functions of CER to include its participation in the development of an all-island energy market and the regulation of natural gas safety, there have been a series of recent regulations to give effect to the Second Gas Directive. The European Communities (Internal Market in Natural Gas) (BGE) Regulations 2004 transpose parts of the Directive. Furthermore, the European Communities (Internal Market in Natural Gas) Regulations 2005 amend the Gas Act to provide common rules on third-party access to upstream and downstream facilities specifically for transportation, Liquefied Natural Gas facilitates and storage facilities. The European Commission (Internal Market for Natural Gas) (BGE) (Amendment) Regulations 2007 provide for the unbundling of transmission and distribution systems operated by BGE. An infrastructure agreement would be negotiated between BGE and its subsidiary and a transfer plan developed and implemented on a date to be fixed by the Minister. BGE is interconnected to the Transco system in the UK established under intergovernmental treaties as well as private contract and referred to in the Code of Operations as a connected system agreement.

Authorisation and Licensing

8.060 CER is now the licensing authority for undertakings that wish to engage in the supply of natural gas, the operation of distribution or transmission pipelines and the storage of natural gas.[110] CER has the power to grant to any person a licence (a 'natural gas licence') in respect of any or all of the following activities—

(a) the supply of natural gas to persons of a type mentioned in sub-s (1) of s 10A (inserted by s 14)[111] of the Gas Act 1976, or to customers of a type mentioned in art 19 of the Directive;

---

110 Gas (Interim) Regulation Act 2002, s 16.
111 Such persons are: (i) holders of a natural gas licence; (ii) the holder of a petroleum lease under Petroleum and Other Minerals Development Act 1960, s 13; (iii) Bord Gáis Eireann; (iv) a person who owns a gas fired electricity generating station; and (v) a final consumer.

(b)   the operation of a distribution or transmission pipeline; or

(c)   the storage of natural gas.

A natural gas licence is issued under s 16 of the 2002 Act for the purpose of carrying out any activity for which the holder is licensed. Pursuant to s 16 of the 2002 Act, a person may not operate a transmission pipeline or engage in the storage of natural gas without a natural gas licence issued by CER. BGE is the sole holder of a gas transportation licence which was issued by CER in 2004. Upstream pipelines were excluded from the definition of transmission pipelines and so therefore may not re-issue a licence. Licences to operate a natural gas storage facility for the purpose of a storage business are granted by CER pursuant to s 16. Section 16 also provides that CER may grant a licence for the operation of an liquefied natural gas (LNG) facility or storage facility. No such LNG licence has been issued to date. CER has the power to grant to any person a licence to operate pipelines in order to carry out the transmission of natural gas.[112]

Section 16(1) of the 2002 Act provides that CER may grant to any person a licence to carry out the distribution of natural gas to customers.[113]

8.061 A petroleum lease is required under s 13 of the Petroleum and Other Minerals Development Act 1960 (the 1960 Act) for the purpose of carrying out any activity connected with prospecting and exploring. The provisions of the Gas Act 1976 (the 1976 Act) dealing with pipeline consents were amended and a new s 39A was inserted into the 1976 Act so that BGE and all other prospective builders of pipelines will in future make their applications for consent to build pipelines under this one section.[114] There is a separate provision dealing with consent to the construction of 'upstream pipelines'. These run from gas fields to onshore terminals and require the consent of the Minister.[115] Undertakings[116] that wish to construct either type of pipeline must

---

112   Pursuant to Gas (Interim) (Regulation) Act 2002, s 16(1).

113   On 16 July 2007, the CER made a statutory order (SI 528/2007) awarding the gas distribution rights for counties Galway and Mayo to Bord Gáis Networks.

114   Gas Act 1976, s 39A(6), as inserted by Gas Interim Regulation Act 2002, s 12, states that: 'In case the holder of a consent given under ... this section constructs a pipeline the holder is obliged take all reasonable measures to protect the natural environment and to avoid injuring the amenities of the area and, in particular, the holder must take all reasonable steps while constructing the pipeline to prevent injury to any building, site, flora, fauna, feature or other thing which is of particular architectural, historic, archaeological, geological or natural interest, and when selecting the route for the pipeline the holder shall have regard to any representations made to the holder as regards the route of such pipeline by any local authority within whose functional area a proposed route, or any part of such a route would, if the pipeline were constructed, be situate, or any of the following on, in or over whose land such route or part would in such circumstances be situate ...'.

115   Gas Act 1976, s 40, as inserted by s 12(1)(b) of the 2002 Act.

116   By virtue of the provisions of Gas (Interim) Regulation Act 2002, s 17, gas undertakings will have to keep separate accounts for their different gas activities such as supply or transmission and, where appropriate, consolidated accounts for other non-gas activities. This is an attempt to avoid discrimination, cross-subsidisation and distortion of competition.

furnish to the appropriate licensing body an environmental impact assessment concerning the proposed project.[117] A refusal by CER to consent to the construction of a downstream pipeline may be appealed to the appeal panel established by the Minister (see para **8.116** below).

Production

8.062 Indigenous gas production in Ireland has been limited. BGE owns the transportation and distribution system of natural gas. BGE also owns the gas interconnectors connecting the Irish transportation system to the UK Transco system at Moffat in Scotland. Since 1999 a third-party access regime has been implemented allowing third parties to ship gas from Moffat and in the Irish system.

8.063 Private companies can participate in exploration for and production of natural gas pursuant to a licensing regime established by the 1960 Act, as amended. Natural gas exploration and production activities are subject to a regulatory and licensing regime overseen by the DCENR. Also relevant are the provisions of the Licensing Terms for Offshore Oil and Gas Exploration, Development and Production 2007. No person may explore or prospect for petroleum unless he holds an appropriate prospecting or exploration licence or is a lessee under a petroleum lease. All licences and petroleum leases incorporate licensing terms and conditions including environmental provisions set out by the DCENR. If a commercial discovery is established under an exploration licence, the license holder must notify the Minster and apply for a petroleum lease with a view to its development. Under the petroleum lease, the developer is required to obtain the Minster's approval of a plan of development prior to the commencement of commercial production operations and must comply with the plan of development for the duration of the lease which must contain a production profile of the relevant field. There are requirements for a foreshore licence under the Foreshore Act 1933 and the Planning Acts 2000 to 2006, which contain provisions in respect of infrastructure deemed to be of strategic importance to Ireland. The provisions of the Continental Shelf Act 1968, as amended, are also relevant, as is environmental legislation including the Environmental Impact Assessment Directive 85/337/EEC.[118]

Transmission Network

8.064 BGE is a vertically integrated monopoly established under the 1976 Act to own and operate the gas transmission and distribution system and undertake natural gas

---

117 Gas Act 1976, s 40A, as inserted by s 12 of the 2002 Act, states: 'A statement of the likely effects on the environment (hereafter in this section referred to as an "environmental impact statement") of a proposed pipeline of a class for the time being specified under art 24 of the European Communities (Environmental Impact Assessment) Regulations, 1989 (SI No. 349 of 1989), or under any provision amending or replacing the said art 24 shall be submitted ... [to either the Commission or the Minister as appropriate]'.

118 Council Directive 85/337/EEC of 27 June 1985 on the assessment of the effects of certain public and private projects on the environment.

supply. The transmission pipeline network is the 'national grid' of the Irish natural gas system. Transmission pipes operate at high pressures and are used to move large volumes of natural gas. When gas has reached the onshore Ireland network, it is transmitted through pipes buried in the ground and delivered to the main consumption centres (where it is distributed through the distribution pipelines). Bord Gáis Eireann was the original TSO. However, in July 2008, Gaslink Independent System Operator Limited was licensed as the TSO. BGE was licensed to own the network on the same day. The onshore network forms a ring extending through counties Dublin, Cork, and Galway. In addition, there are connections to, among other places, Louth, Cavan, and Waterford.

8.065 The purchase, sale and transport of natural gas across the Irish natural gas network are governed by a set of market rules and codes. Gaslink Independent System Operator Limited, assisted by BGE, manages these codes, which deal with issues such as capacity, balancing, allocations, nominations, measurement and maintenance. CER regulates the terms and conditions of the codes.[119] The intention of the code is to outline the rights and responsibilities of each party involved in the transportation of natural gas through the transportation system, which includes both the transmission and distribution systems. It sets out the working principles that govern the activities of the natural gas transporters and shippers, including capacity, balancing, allocations, nominations, measurement and maintenance.

8.066 CER regulates charges for connecting to and using the transmission network. The objective is to ensure that only efficient costs of operating the network are passed on to customers and also that there is fair and non-discriminatory access to the network for competitors. Charges are regulated by periodic multi-annual determinations designed to ascertain the appropriate revenue levels Bord Gáis Networks can earn over that period from this licensed activity.[120] However, each year, the revenue that Bord Gáis Networks is allowed to collect from customers is reviewed.[121] These 'allowed revenues' are used to calculate the transmission use of system (TUoS) tariffs, which are approved by CER. TUoS tariffs are charged to shippers on the basis of the amount of network capacity and energy used by their customers. There are different TUoS tariffs for the different parts of the transmission system. Pursuant to s 10A(17)(a), each pipeline operator must submit a statement setting out the basis for its charges for the transportation of natural gas and for connection to its pipeline to the CER for approval. CER may issue directions in respect of the basis for these charges with which the operator must comply. Pursuant to s 10A(4), CER may direct certain terms and

---

119 In July 2003 it directed BGE to implement an entry/exit regime to replace the then point-to-point regime in Ireland. An entry/exit regime requires the separation of entry and exit capacity in terms of definition, booking, allocation and charging.

120 Pursuant to Gas Act 1976, s 10A, as inserted by Gas (Interim) (Regulation) Act 2002, s 14. See CER, *Bord Gáis Networks Revenue Review 2007/8–2011/12 Transmission Decision Paper*, CER/07/110, 2 August 2007, available at http://www.cer.ie.

121 See CER, *Decision on BGN Revenues and Gas Transmission tariffs for 2008/9*, CER/08/151, 15 August 2008, available at http://www.cer.ie.

conditions be specified in a third-party access agreement, including price. These terms are reflected in the code of operations.

Distribution Network

8.067 Distribution pipes operate at low or medium pressure and are used for delivering natural gas to low consumption customers, typically including small businesses and residential customers. Each distribution system is connected to the higher pressure transmission system at a pressure reduction station.[122] Ireland's distribution system is completely owned and operated by Bord Gáis Éireann. Pursuant to s 16 of the 2002 Act, CER granted BGE a licence in 2004. Until 2004, a ministerial order conferred on BGE exclusive rights in relation to transmission, distribution and supply of gas. In 2004, certain supply rights were also conferred on Flogas. In 2007, the Gas (Amendment) Act 1987 (section 2) (Distribution) (Amendment) Order awarded the rights to develop the gas distribution network to certain towns to BGE. CER sets the tariffs for access to and use of distribution systems. These tariffs are paid by users of the system such as gas suppliers.

8.068 As with transmission, in the distribution side of the market, the purchase, sale and transport of natural gas across the Irish natural gas network is governed by a set of market rules and codes. CER regulates the terms and conditions of the codes.

8.069 CER regulates the charges for connecting to and using the distribution network. The objective is to ensure that only efficient costs of operating the network are passed on to customers and also that there is fair and non-discriminatory access to the network for competitors. Charges are regulated by periodic multi-annual price determinations designed to ascertain the appropriate revenue levels Bord Gáis Networks can earn over that period from this licensed activity.[123] However, each year, the revenue that Bord Gáis Networks is allowed to collect from customers is reviewed.[124] These 'allowed revenues' are used to calculate the distribution use of system (DUoS) tariffs, which are approved by CER. DUoS tariffs are charged to shippers on the basis of the amount of network capacity and energy used by their customers. There are different DUoS tariffs for different types of customers.

Gas storage

8.070 Most gas consumed in Ireland is imported through pipeline interconnection with the UK. However, gas, unlike electricity, can be stored reliably and safely without a

---

122 This is analogous to an electricity transformer station.

123 See CER, *Bord Gáis Networks Revenue Review 2007/8–2011/12 Distribution Decision Paper CER/07/111,* 2 August 2007; CER, *Decision on BGN Allowed Revenues and Gas Distribution Tariffs for 2008/9,* CER/08/152, 15 August 2008, available at http://www.cer.ie.

124 See CER, *Decision on BGN Allowed Revenues and Gas Distribution Tariffs for 2008/9,* CER/08/152, 15 August 2008, available at http://www.cer.ie.

loss of efficiency. The development of storage facilities in Ireland contributes to the security of natural gas supplies and promotes competition in supply. Marathon Oil Ireland Ltd redeveloped the Southwest Kinsale reservoir as a storage facility.[125] The Commission licensed the facility and it was made available to third parties from 1 June 2006.

Retail Market

8.071 CER also regulates the retail gas market in Ireland. A key function of CER in the retail gas market is to regulate Bord Gáis Energy Supply's tariffs, with the objective of promoting the development of competition in the market. This involves developing retail market rules and processes and ensuring that customers have adequate levels of service and protection provided to them by their suppliers. Competition in the gas market for industrial and commercial customers has been in place since 2004 and three suppliers are active in this segment. Full market opening in the Irish natural gas market took place on 1 July 2007. All gas customers are now eligible to switch supplier.

8.072 In the gas retail sector, there are two distinct activities – that of a shipper and that of a supplier. An individual or organisation can be licensed to supply or ship gas or both. A gas shipper is responsible for liaising with Bord Gáis Networks to ensure that gas is delivered to individual homes and premises. The supplier processes the sale of gas to individual customers.

Gas meter roll-out programme completion

8.073 CER was responsible for overseeing the liberalisation of the Irish natural gas market, on a phased basis, with a view to full market opening by 2007. To allow new eligible natural gas customers to change shipper or supplier, Bord Gáis Distribution, with approval from CER, undertook a programme to install daily meters to these customer sites.

Regulated revenues and tariffs

8.074 Bord Gáis Supply is licensed to supply gas, while at the same time acting as transporter and shipper of natural gas. CER regulates the prices charged, with the objective of protecting the interests of customers by ensuring that they are charged only the efficient costs of supplying natural gas.[126]

---

125 The total capacity of the Inch storage field is 7 billion cubic feet. Gas will be injected into the storage facility on an interruptible basis during the summer months when demand for gas is at its lowest. The maximum injection into the storage facility is 2.1 gigawatt hours per day. Customers may then extract gas from the storage facility and deliver it onto the onshore system during the winter months when demand is at its peak. The maximum level of extraction from the facility is 4.3 gigawatt hours per day.

126 Gas (Amendment) Act 1987, s 2(6)(A), as inserted by Gas (Interim)(Regulation) Act 2002, s 23.

8.075 Bord Gáis Supply charges are regulated by periodic multi-annual price determinations designed to ascertain the appropriate revenue levels Bord Gáis Networks can earn over that period from this licensed activity. In the revenue review, CER determines an efficient level of revenues (made up of allowed operating costs, capital expenditure, depreciation charges and an allowable margin) that can be recovered by the business from its customers over the period.[127] However, each year the allowed revenue is reviewed to calculate Bord Gáis Supply regulated tariffs. Based on this level of allowed revenue, CER sets tariffs for some specific categories of customers.[128]

Gas capacity statement

8.076 In accordance with the European Communities (Internal Market in Natural Gas) (No 2) Regulations 2004, a Gas Capacity Statement is prepared by CER each year. The statement provides a forecast of capacity, flows and customer demand on Ireland's natural gas system over the following eight years, and gives an estimate of the adequacy of Irish transmission capacity for a range of possible scenarios including a tight supply situation. The current statement covers the period 2006/07–2013/14.

Public Service Obligations

8.077 As with electricity, the Minister may introduce PSOs[129] on natural gas undertakings; for instance, with regard to security of supply, technical safety, or environmental protection.[130] Pursuant to s 21 of the 2002 Act, the Minister may direct CER to impose on such classes of natural gas undertakings as may be specified in the order in the general economic interest, PSOs that may include security of supply and technical or public safety, regularity, quality and price of supplies and environment protection. Pursuant to s 21A of the 2002 Act, BGE Supply was appointed by CER as a supplier of last resort from February 2008 to continue until such time as CER decides otherwise.

Levy

8.078 A levy may be imposed on customers in relation to the costs of delivery of natural gas. The features of the levy are set out in s 21 of the 2002 Act. A PSO order

---

127 For example, see CER, *Final Decision on Bord Gáis Energy Supply non daily metered five year Regulatory Review 2007/8–2011/12*, CER/07/158, 1 October 2007, available at http://www.cer.ie.

128 For example, see CER, *Proposed Decision Paper Interim Gas Price Increase – 1 September 2008*, CER/08/135, 25 July 2008, available at http://www.cer.ie.

129 Gas (Interim)(Regulation) Act 2002, s 21.

130 Section 21(7) specifically excludes using PSOs for non-commercial extensions of the natural gas network.

may provide for the charging of a levy by natural gas undertakings to customers in relation to:

(a)   the costs of delivery of natural gas; and

(b)   any other costs as may be deemed appropriate from time to time by the Minister, including a reasonable rate of return on the capital represented by such costs, incurred by natural gas undertakings in complying with a PSO order including costs incurred after the variation or revocation of such an order.

Single Energy Market – Gas

Energy (Miscellaneous Provisions) Act 2006

8.079 The 2006 Act also amends the 1976 Act to provide for the full opening of the natural gas market.[131] Any person shall be entitled to switch his or her natural gas supplier if he or she so wishes. Furthermore, a natural gas supplier acting on behalf of any person may be granted third-party access to gas pipelines or facilities. These provisions are designed to extend the benefits of liberalisation previously enjoyed by industrial and commercial consumers to all natural gas customers, allowing them to shop around for their supplier and to obtain the best value for their money. The policy objective is that the market is in this way fully contestable.[132]

8.080 CER is also given powers by the 2006 Act to regulate electrical contractors and gas installers.[133] It may establish standards of training for both electrical contractors and gas installers in regard to safety in their areas of work. Under the provisions of the 2006 Act, CER is entitled to designate persons to be electrical or gas safety supervisory bodies that will be required to operate in accordance with criteria and procedures published by CER. Under CER oversight, these bodies are responsible for the registration of electrical contractors and gas installers, as appropriate. They may inspect work carried out by their various members, monitor and review the training of their various members and suspend or revoke the membership of one of their members for certain specified reasons, including where work carried out by that member is unsafe or of an unsatisfactory standard. Any fees or charges imposed by any such body are subject to CER approval. Furthermore, any decision by such a body to suspend or revoke the membership of one or more of its members is subject to appeal to CER.

8.081 Section 11 of the 2006 Act provides for a natural gas TSO and a DSO to appoint a gas emergency officer, with powers to enter land and take emergency measures, where there is a danger to a person or property arising from natural gas. CER may

---

131 Gas Act 1976, ss 10A and 10B, as amended by ss 17 and 19, respectively, of the Energy (Miscellaneous Provisions) Act 2006.

132 'Contestable Market' theory is associated with the economist William Baumol. In brief, it is predicated on the absence of barriers to entry and posits that threat of entry will incentivise incumbents to behave in an economically efficient manner.

133 Electricity Regulation Act 1999, s 9C as inserted by Energy (Miscellaneous Provisions) Act 2006, s 4.

appoint a gas safety officer to assist in the carrying out of its new gas safety functions. The Minister is also granted various powers, including the power to direct CER or certain electricity or natural gas market players to take whatever safeguard measures the Minister considers necessary as emergency measures in sudden crises.[134] These provisions are in line with EU requirements on security of energy supply.

8.082 CER's functions now include the regulation and promotion of natural gas safety.[135] In this context, CER is required to consult the National Standards Authority of Ireland regarding standards and specifications relating to gas safety. CER, having consulted with the Minister, is required to establish and implement a natural gas safety framework. This framework must include, but is not limited to, inspection and testing regimes for downstream transmission and distribution pipelines, and for storage and liquefied natural gas facilities. Any such framework must also focus on the regulation and certification of natural gas installers and provide for procedures for the investigation of complaints against them.

ENFORCEMENT

Authorised Officers

8.083 Section 11 of the 1999 Act, as amended by s 18 of the 2002 Act, permits the appointment by CER of authorised officers to enforce the legislation. Authorised officers are given a wide range of powers in relation to licensed energy undertakings. Authorised officers must be furnished with a certificate of appointment by CER and when exercising a power conferred by statute shall, if requested by any person thereby affected, produce such certificate to that person for inspection. For the purposes of the exercise by CER of its functions, an authorised officer may:

(a) enter at any reasonable time any premises owned or occupied by a person to whom this section applies[136] for the purpose of exercising any powers conferred on him or her by this subsection;

(b) require a person to whom this section applies or any member, officer or employee of the person to whom this section applies to produce to the authorised officer any books, documents or records (and in the case of such information in a non-legible form to reproduce it in permanent legible form) which are in his or her power or control or to give him or her such information,

---

134 Electricity Regulation Act 1999, s 40A, as inserted by Energy (Miscellaneous Provisions) Act 2006, s 9.

135 Section 9 of the 1999, as amended by insertion of new functions by Energy (Miscellaneous Provisions) Act 2006, s 12.

136 A 'person to whom this section applies' means the ESB or a holder of an electricity licence or an authorisation or a natural gas licence granted under Gas (Interim) (Regulation) Act 2002, s 16, or a consent given under Gas Act 1976 – Electricity Regulation Act 1999, s 11, as amended by Gas (Interim)(Regulation) Act 2002, s 18.

whether oral or written, as the officer may reasonably require in relation to any entries in such records;

(bb) require any such person to give to the officer any other information, whether oral or written, which the officer may reasonably require to determine whether [the 1999 Act or the 2002 Act], are being complied with;

(c) inspect and take extracts from or make copies of any books, documents and records (including in the case of information in a non-legible form a copy of or extract from such information in a permanent legible form); and

(d) require a person to whom this section applies to maintain such books, documents and records for such period or periods of time as the authorised officer may direct.

8.084 Where an authorised officer in exercise of his or her powers is prevented from entering any premises, an application may be made under s 12 of the 1999 Act, as amended, for a warrant to authorise such entry. By virtue of s 12, if a judge of the District Court is satisfied on the sworn information of an authorised officer that there are reasonable grounds for suspecting that there has been a contravention of a condition or requirement of an electricity or gas licence or an authorisation, the judge may issue a warrant authorising the authorised officer, accompanied by other authorised officers or members of the Garda Síochána, at any time or times within one month from the date of issue of the warrant, on production if so required of the warrant, to enter such premises as are specified in the warrant, if need be by reasonable force, and exercise all or any of the powers conferred on an authorised officer under s 11.

Civil Enforcement

Dispute resolution

8.085 Various dispute resolution procedures are provided for in the energy sector. These include those detailed in this section.

8.086 In relation to electricity, the 2006 Act provides for a dispute resolution mechanism to provide for fair play between interconnector operators and applicants for access to the interconnector; a dispute appeals mechanism is also provided for with CER as final arbiter.[137]

8.087 In respect of the ESB, as provided for in the 2008 Regulations, after the formation of the subsidiary company, the ESB and the subsidiary company shall enter into negotiations in good faith with a view to entering into one or more agreements providing for the terms on which each of them will fulfil its functions with respect to the distribution system and the terms on which the ESB will provide the subsidiary

---

137 This is provided for by the 2006 Act, which amends the 1999 Act by inserting 34A(5) into the 1999 Act.

company with the resources (including financial resources) and services necessary to enable that company to fulfil its responsibility with respect to the operation of the distribution system. This agreement is made subject to approval by CER. The ESB and the subsidiary company may, from time to time, and subject to the approval of CER, vary an agreement entered into.

8.088 Regulation 18 of the 2008 Regulations provides that if, after a reasonable time, the ESB and the subsidiary company fail to enter into an agreement or, after entering into such an agreement, are in dispute over, for example, the transfer to the subsidiary company of any assets, rights or liabilities, either the ESB or the subsidiary company may request CER to make a determination with respect to the matters in dispute. This request shall be in writing. On receiving the request, CER shall in the first instance attempt to resolve the dispute by conciliation. However, if the attempt is unsuccessful, CER shall, after giving each party an opportunity to State its case, make a determination in respect of the dispute and notify the parties in writing of its determination. CER may include in such a determination such directions as it considers appropriate for resolving the dispute. A determination made is binding on the ESB and the subsidiary company and the ESB and the subsidiary company shall comply with the directions (if any) contained in the determination.

8.089 The Commission for Energy Regulation also deals with disputes about access to and use of the network in the gas sector.[138] For the purposes of art 25 of Directive 2003/55/EC,[139] CER shall be the competent authority in the State to settle expeditiously disputes concerning refusal to offer to enter into an agreement under this section within the scope of the directive.

8.090 Any dispute between an operator and any person who is, or claims to be, a person to whom the operator is obliged to make an offer for third-party access or, where appropriate, connection to a facility of the operator (and whether as to the making of an offer, the terms offered, the proposed charges or otherwise) where the operator makes an offer or refuses to make an offer, may, upon the application of that person, be determined by CER and the operator shall comply with and be bound by any such determination. Where an application is made to CER in relation to a dispute concerning a downstream pipeline, part of which is situated in the territory of another State, on the seabed under the territorial seas of another State or on the continental shelf belonging to another State, CER shall consult the relevant authorities in that other

---

138 SI 452/2004, which inserts s 21B into the 2002 Act, deals with the procedures for handling disputes, and SI 320/2005, which amends s 10B of the 2002 Act, deals with disputes under art 25 of Directive 2003/55/EC.

139 Article 25.5: 'Any party having a complaint against a transmission, LNG or distribution system operator with respect to the issues mentioned in paras 1, 2 and 4 and in art 19 may refer the complaint to the regulatory authority which, acting as dispute settlement authority, shall issue a decision within two months after receipt of the complaint. This period may be extended by two months where additional information is sought by the regulatory authorities. This period may be extended with the agreement of the complainant. Such a decision shall have binding effect unless and until overruled on appeal.'

State with respect to the application. In the event of a cross-border dispute, the deciding regulatory authority shall be the regulatory authority which has jurisdiction in respect of the system operator, which refuses use of, or access to, the system. The parties to a dispute shall provide all documents, records, accounts, estimates and other information, whether oral or written, requested from time to time, by CER, for the purpose of making a determination. In order to ensure compliance with a determination made under this section, CER may apply in a summary manner on notice to the High Court for an order requiring an operator to comply with the determination.

Electricity

Prohibition on disclosure of unauthorised information

8.091 Section 13 of the 1999 Act sets out a standard prohibition on disclosure of unauthorised information, now found in most regulatory statutes. It states that, save as otherwise provided by law, a person shall not disclose confidential information obtained by him or her while performing duties as a member of, or as a member of the staff of, or an adviser or consultant to, or as an authorised officer of, CER, unless he or she is duly authorised by CER to do so. In s 13 'confidential information' is defined as that which is expressed by CER to be confidential either as regards particular information or as regards information of a particular class or description. In expressing information to be confidential, CER shall have regard to the requirement to protect information of a confidential commercial nature.

8.092 This discretion on CER begs the question, when does it have to so express its view in order to bind those persons? In addition, this could also raise concerns about the adequate protection of the confidential nature of information relating to undertakings that operate in the energy sector.

Directions

8.093 CER has power to issue directions that may be enforced by way of a court order. CER may enforce the conditions of licences or authorisations by direction. In addition, it may apply to the High Court for an order to ensure compliance with any direction.[140] Sections 28 to 31 of the 1999 Act provide for an appeal panel to be established to hear and determine appeals regarding applications and modifications.

8.094 Where CER is of the opinion that the holder of an electricity licence or an authorisation may be contravening or may be likely to contravene a condition or requirement, it may issue a notice to the holder of the licence or authorisation specifying: (i) the condition or requirement which CER considers that the holder of the licence or authorisation may be contravening or may be likely to contravene, or (ii) the acts or omissions which in the opinion of CER may constitute or would be likely to constitute contravention of the condition or requirement concerned.[141] The licence

---

140 Sections 22 to 25.
141 Section 24 of the 1999 Act.

holder is given 28 days to make representations. On consideration of any representations or objections, CER may give a direction to the holder of a licence or an authorisation to take such measures as are necessary to cease the contravention or to prevent a future contravention. Where CER decides not to give such a direction, it may make a determination that the holder of a licence or an authorisation has committed a specified breach of a condition or requirement.[142] It appears that, in either case, where an undertaking is found in breach or directed to cease a breach, CER may seek a High Court Order to compel compliance with the licence.[143]

8.095 Pursuant to regulation 17 of the 2008 Regulations, if, in consequence of carrying out a review, CER forms the opinion that the subsidiary company:

(a)   is not conducting its operations in a manner consistent with the regulations; or

(b)   is engaging in discriminatory behaviour,

CER shall, by notice in writing given to the subsidiary company, require it to take such measures to rectify the situation as CER specifies in the notice.

8.096 A notice may include a requirement directing the subsidiary company to modify its compliance programme to such extent, and in such respects, as are specified in the relevant notice and the subsidiary company is obliged to comply with a requirement imposed on it. If, in consequence of carrying out a periodic review, CER forms the opinion that the subsidiary company is not sufficiently resourced to discharge its functions as DSO, the CER shall, by notice in writing given to the subsidiary company, request it to propose measures to address the concerns identified in the review. The subsidiary company shall respond to a notice within three months and shall propose measures to address the concerns identified in the review to CER. If CER is satisfied with the measures proposed, it shall direct the subsidiary company to implement those measures. A direction may include a requirement directing the subsidiary company to modify its compliance programme. If CER is not satisfied with the measures proposed, it shall request the subsidiary company to propose revised measures taking account of such matters as CER shall identify as requiring attention. Where CER forms the opinion that the subsidiary company's lack of sufficient resources is impacting negatively on its ability to act independently and in a non-discriminatory manner, CER may issue a notice. Where a requirement imposed by CER, or the measures proposed by the subsidiary company and agreed by CER, requires action on the part of the ESB, CER may, by notice in writing given to CER, require the ESB to adopt appropriate measures to rectify the situation.

---

142 Section 25 of the 1999 Act. This determination must be published in the national press and served on the licence or authorisation holder.

143 Section 26 of the 1999 Act, whose margin heading is 'Compliance with Direction or Determination', states that in order to ensure compliance with a direction given under s 24, CER may apply in a summary manner *ex parte* or on notice to the High Court for an order requiring the holder of a licence or an authorisation who, in the opinion of CER, is contravening or who is likely to contravene a condition or requirement to discontinue or to refrain from specified practices. The High Court may make such order as it thinks fit and may confirm, revoke or vary a direction given by CER.

8.097 Regulation 20 provides that if CER is of the opinion that a person has contravened, is contravening or is about to contravene, or has failed, is failing or is about to fail to comply with a requirement or direction, it may apply to the High Court for a compliance order against the person. An application shall be in writing and shall specify:

'(a)   the provision, requirement or direction that has been, is being or is about to be contravened or has not been, is not being or is about not to be complied with, and

(b)   the acts or omissions that, in the Commission's opinion, constitute or would constitute the contravention or failure to comply.'

An application may not be heard unless the High Court is satisfied that the person concerned has been served with a copy of the application. On being served with a copy of the application, that person becomes the respondent to the application and is entitled to appear and be heard at the hearing of the application.

8.098 Regulation 21 provides that if, on hearing an application made under regulation 20, the High Court is satisfied that the application is substantiated, it may make a compliance order directing the respondent to take such measures as are necessary to:

(a)   prevent a repetition of the contravention or failure to comply;

(b)   cease the contravention or failure to comply; or

(c)   prevent the contravention or failure to comply from occurring.

If the High Court decides to make an order, it may make such ancillary or consequential orders as it considers appropriate. The High Court may vary or revoke an order made.

Gas

8.099 Section 16(13) of the 2002 Act states that a holder of a natural gas licence shall:

(a)   operate, maintain and develop under economic conditions such facilities or systems as required for the purpose of carrying out the activity for which it is licensed with due regard to the environment and public safety;

(b)   not discriminate between system users or classes of system users particularly in favour of related undertakings;

(c)   provide any natural gas undertaking with sufficient information to ensure that transport or storage of natural gas may take place in a manner compatible with the safe, secure and efficient operation of the natural gas system;

(d)   without prejudice to any legal obligation to disclose information, preserve the confidentiality of commercially sensitive information obtained in the course of carrying out its business; and

(e)   provide all documents, records, accounts, estimates and other information, whether oral or written, requested from time to time by CER, in the form and at the times specified by CER, for the purpose of verifying that the holder of the licence is complying with the conditions of the licence, or as may be required by CER in the performance of its duties or functions imposed under this Act.

8.100 CER may also direct the holder of a licence or authorisation to discontinue or refrain from specified practices. In brief, CER may issue a direction: (i) to protect public health or safety or the environment; (ii) to protect the continuity of supplies of natural gas; (iii) to protect the interests of other licence holder; and (v) to prevent contravention of licence terms.

8.101 Court compliance orders may be obtained under s 10A.

SI 320/2005 provides also for enforcement proceedings relating to common rules for the internal market in natural gas. It provides that CER may issue directions which provide for:

(a) the matters to be specified in an agreement for third party access, including terms and conditions relating to price;

(b) the matters to be specified in an agreement for connection to or enhancement of the facility of the operator;

(c) the terms and conditions, including terms and conditions relating to price of the connection or enhancement, upon which an offer for connection to or enhancement of the facility of the operator is made;

(d) the methods for determining the proportion of the costs to be borne by the person making the application for connection to or enhancement of the facility of the operator and to be borne by the operator being costs which are directly or indirectly incurred in carrying out works under an agreement or making an enhancement or connection or modifying an existing connection;

(e) the terms and conditions upon which applications for an agreement are to be made and the period of time within which an offer or refusal pursuant to an application is to be made by the operator; and

(f) any other matters which CER considers necessary or expedient for the purpose of making an offer for third party access, or connection to a facility.

An operator shall comply with any direction made by CER within such time period as may be specified by CER in the direction.

8.102 Where an operator refuses to offer to enter into an agreement under s 10A of the 1976 Gas Act,[144] the operator shall serve notice on the applicant of the reasons for such a refusal. Where providing for third-party access or where offering terms for the carrying out of works for the purpose of connection to a facility of an operator, the operator shall not discriminate unfairly as between any persons or classes of persons.

8.103 An operator shall not, in the context of sales or purchases of natural gas by that operator or related undertakings, abuse commercially sensitive information obtained from third parties in the context of providing or negotiating third-party access to a facility under the control of the operator. CER may give directions to an operator from

144 As substituted by Gas (Interim)(Regulation) Act 2002, s 14.

time to time in respect of the basis for charges for third-party access to, or connection to, a facility under the control of the operator. Directions given by CER may provide for:

    (i)   the methods of charging to be included in the statement to be prepared by an operator;

    (ii)   the form and the extent of the information to be provided by an operator to applicants;

    (iii) the form of charges and information about those charges to be included in the statement to be prepared by an operator;

    (iv) the procedure to be adopted in the submission by an operator of a statement of charges and the approval by CER of such statement; and

    (v)   the nature of information to be provided to applicants seeking third party access to, or connection to a facility under the control of the operator and its presentation and transparency.

8.104 A charge for third-party access to, or connection to, a facility under the control of the operator shall be calculated in accordance with directions given by CER under s 10B of the Gas Act 1976,[145] so as to enable the operator to recover:

    (i)   the appropriate proportion of the costs directly or indirectly incurred in carrying out any necessary works; and

    (ii)   a reasonable rate of return on the capital represented by such costs.

8.105 Under SI 320/2005, CER shall consult with an operator and have regard to any submission made by the operator to CER prior to making a decision as to whether to approve of or not, as the case may be, a statement submitted by the operator to CER for approval. A statement and, in particular, charges referred to such statement, shall not take effect until such time as it is approved of by CER, subject to such modifications, if any, as CER considers appropriate, and published, including publication in electronic form. Any charges imposed by an operator on or before the coming into operation of this section shall, subject to the approval of the CER, continue in force until a statement has been approved of by CER under s 10B of the 1976 Act, and thereafter all charges shall be in accordance with a statement approved of by CER.

8.106 Notwithstanding this, CER may, on a case-by-case basis, following an application in writing by an operator of a storage facility, grant an exemption, on such terms and conditions as CER considers appropriate, to an operator from the provisions of those subsections in relation to the terms, conditions and charges for access to the storage facilities under the control of that operator. When granting an exemption, CER shall ensure that the granting of such an exemption would not lead to distortion of competition or to discrimination in the access to storage. CER shall, by direction, provide for the procedures and conditions under which access to the storage facility under the control of the operator shall be negotiated. A holder of an exemption shall negotiate the terms, conditions and charges for access to the storage facilities under the control of that operator in good faith and in accordance with the procedural conditions.

---

145 As substituted by Gas (Interim)(Regulation) Act 2002, s 14.

CER shall direct the holder of an exemption to publish his or her main commercial conditions for the use of the facilities under his or her control within six months of the grant of that exemption and on an annual basis thereafter.

Criminal Enforcement

Offences by bodies corporate

8.107 By virtue of s 5 of the Electricity Regulation Act 1999, where an offence has been committed by a body corporate and is proved to have been committed with the consent or connivance of, or to be attributable to any neglect on the part of a person being a director, manager, secretary or other officer of the body corporate, or a person who was purporting to act in any such capacity, that person, as well as the body corporate, shall be guilty of an offence and be liable to be proceeded against and punished as if he or she were guilty of the first-mentioned offence. Section 5 goes on to extend such liability by stating that where the affairs of a body corporate are managed by its members, sub-s (1) shall apply in relation to the acts and defaults of a member in connection with his or her functions of management as if he or she were a director or manager of the body corporate. This is an unusual departure from the normal division of corporate criminal responsibility between the company and the directors. It may be directed towards joint ventures.

8.108 Section 6 permits summary proceedings for offences under this Act to be brought and prosecuted by CER. Notwithstanding s 10(4) of the Petty Sessions (Ireland) Act 1851, summary proceedings for an offence under this Act may be instituted within 12 months from the date of the offence.

Examples of offences

8.109 Pursuant to s 11(6) of the Electricity Regulation Act 1999, a person who:

(a) obstructs or impedes an authorised officer in the exercise of a power under this section;

(b) fails or refuses to comply with a requirement under this section;

(c) knowingly alters, suppresses or destroys any books, documents or records which the person concerned has been required to produce, or may reasonably expect to be required to produce; or

(d) knowingly gives to the Commission or to an authorised officer information which is false or misleading, in a material respect;

shall be guilty of an offence and shall be liable on summary conviction to a fine not exceeding IR£1,500 or imprisonment for a period not exceeding 12 months or, at the discretion of the District Court, to both such fine and imprisonment.

8.110 A person who contravenes s 13(1) of the 1999 Act regarding the prohibition on unauthorised disclosure of information, shall be guilty of an offence and liable on summary conviction to a fine not exceeding IR£1,500 or imprisonment for a period not exceeding 12 months or, at the discretion of the District Court, to both such fine and imprisonment.

8.111 Authorisations to construct or reconstruct a generating station must be granted by CER. Importantly, and notwithstanding the Electricity (Supply) Acts 1927 to 1995, the ESB may not construct or reconstruct a generating station unless authorised by CER.[146] It is a criminal offence to engage in unauthorised construction, with those responsible being liable on conviction on indictment to a fine not exceeding IR£100,000.[147]

8.112 CER has the power to grant to any person a natural gas licence (see para **8.061** above). It is a criminal offence for any person to undertake any of the activities mentioned in s 16 of the 2002 Act without a natural gas licence. Persons found guilty of such an offence are liable on summary conviction to a fine not exceeding €3,000 or to imprisonment for a term not exceeding three months, or to both. Summary proceedings for an offence under this section may be brought and prosecuted by the CER.

8.113 Various either-way[148] offences are listed in the 2006 Act. These include offences relating to the safety of electrical and gas contractors. CER may appoint authorised officers for the purposes of carrying out work inspections in relation to electricity and a Gas Safety Officer for the purposes of carrying out work inspections in relation to gas. A person who obstructs or impedes an inspection or knowingly gives false or misleading information or turns on or reconnects the supply of natural gas or electricity, which supply has been turned off or disconnected by the inspection officer, is guilty of an offence. The punishment on summary conviction is a fine not exceeding €5,000 or a term of imprisonment not exceeding six months or both, or on conviction on indictment, a fine not exceeding €15,000 or a term of imprisonment not exceeding three years or both.

8.114 Section 34A (inserted by s 8 of the Energy (Miscellaneous Provisions) Act 2006) of the 1999 Act is amended by the 2008 Act so that a person who transports electricity across an interconnector without being duly licensed to do so under s 14(1) commits an offence and is liable:

(a) on summary conviction to a fine not exceeding €5,000 or a term of imprisonment not exceeding 12 months or to both; or

(b) on conviction on indictment to a fine not exceeding €50,000 or a term of imprisonment not exceeding three years or to both.

Summary proceedings for an offence under this section may be brought and prosecuted by CER.

---

146 Section 16(3).

147 Section 16(4).

148 An either-way or hybrid offence is an offence which may be tried summarily or on indictment.

APPEALS

8.115 Two categories of person may appeal against a CER decision to an appeal panel:[149]

(a) a person whose application for a licence or an authorisation is refused, and

(b) a person who is a holder of a licence or an authorisation and who wishes to appeal against a decision of CER:

  (i) to modify the licence or authorisation concerned, other than a modification of a class required by an order made under ss 39 or 40; or

  (ii) to refuse to modify the licence or authorisation concerned at the request of the holder of that licence or authorisation.

See **Ch 10** on Appeals for further details.

JUDICIAL REVIEW OF DETERMINATION OF COMMISSION

8.116 Section 32 of the Electricity Regulation Act 1999[150] creates a bar against a person questioning in court: (a) the validity of a decision of CER on an application made to it for the grant of a licence or an authorisation or for the modification of a licence or an authorisation; or (b) a modification by CER of a licence or an authorisation; or (c) a decision of an appeal panel under s 30; or (d) any decision made by CER under the Gas (Amendment) Act 2000, or under regulations made under that Act, otherwise than by way of an application for judicial review under Order 84 of the Rules of the Superior Court.

8.117 Such an application for leave to bring judicial review proceedings shall:

(a) be made within the period of two months commencing on the date on which the decision is given; and

(b) be made by motion on notice to:

  (i) the Commission,

  (ii) where the applicant for leave is not the applicant for or holder of the licence or authorisation concerned, the applicant or holder of that licence or authorisation, and

  (iii) any other person specified for that purpose by order of the High Court,

and such leave shall not be granted unless the High Court is satisfied that there are substantial grounds for contending that the decision is invalid or ought to be quashed. The High Court may only extend the time to bring such proceedings if it is satisfied that:[151]

(a) the applicant—

---

149 See Electricity Regulation Act 1999, s 29.

150 Section 32 of the 1999 Act, as substituted by Gas (Amendment) Act 2000, s 15.

151 Electricity Regulation Act 1999, s 32(2A), as substituted by Gas (Amendment) Act 2000, s 15.

      (i) did not become aware until after the expiration of [two months] of the material facts on which the grounds for the said application for leave are based, or

      (ii) did, before the two month's expiration, become aware of those facts but only after such number of days of that period had elapsed as would not have made it reasonably practicable for the applicant to have made the said application for leave before that period's expiration;

   (b) the applicant could not with reasonable diligence have become aware of those facts until after the expiration of that period, or, as the case may be, those number of days had elapsed, or

   (c) the said application for leave has been made as soon as is reasonably practicable after the applicant has become aware of those facts.

The determination of the High Court of such an application for leave to apply for judicial review or of an application for such judicial review shall be final and no appeal shall lie from the decision of the High Court to the Supreme Court in either case, save with the leave of the High Court, which leave shall only be granted where the High Court certifies that its decision involves a point of law of exceptional public importance and that it is desirable in the public interest that an appeal should be taken to the Supreme Court. However, this bar does not apply to a determination of the High Court in so far as it involves a question as to the validity of any law having regard to the provisions of the Constitution.

Chapter 9

REGULATORY CRIMINAL LAW ENFORCEMENT

INTRODUCTION

9.001 It is a feature of regulatory law in Ireland that many breaches are criminal offences. One of the reasons for this is that Irish regulatory law is largely based on the implementation of EC Directives. Many of these EC Directives require the imposition of financial penalties on an undertaking for breach of the provisions of the Directive. For constitutional reasons, financial penalties in Ireland are usually imposed by a court rather than directly by a Regulator.[1] In addition, for constitutional reasons, where the amount of the financial penalty is required to be substantive, the provision is usually transposed to create either-way offences, that is, offences that may be tried summarily or on indictment.[2]

This is unlike the system in many civil law jurisdictions in the EU, where civil administrative fines may be imposed directly by the Regulator. In Ireland, firms must be prosecuted in court before fines may be imposed by that court in respect of conduct which infringes the various underlying Directives. It is usually necessary for the national regulatory authority to bring summary proceedings to the court itself or to hand a file over to the DPP for prosecution on indictment. Arguably, if the underlying Directive provides that national regulatory authorities 'shall' impose financial sanctions, then the EC provision in this way overrides[3] the constitutional bar against civil administrative sanctions by virtue of the effect of Art 29.4.10°. Article 29.4.10°[4] provides that:

> [n]o provision of this Constitution invalidates laws enacted, acts done or measures adopted by the State which are necessitated by the obligations of membership of the

---

1 Article 34.1 states that 'Justice shall be administered in courts established by law by judges appointed in the manner provided by this Constitution, and, save in such special and limited cases as may be prescribed by law, shall be administered in public'.

2 See *Melling v O Mathghamhna* [1962] IR 1 which held that where a penalty is high, it is viewed as punitive and indicative of a criminal matter. See also Art 38 which provides:

1. No person shall be tried on any criminal charge save in due course of law.

2. Minor offences may be tried by courts of summary jurisdiction ....

5. Save in the case of the trial of offences under section 2, section 3 or section 4 of this article no person shall be tried on any criminal charge without a jury.

3 For reference to the new legal order created by EC law: *Van Gend en Loos* 26/62 [1963] ECR 1; *Costa v Enel* 6/64 [1964] ECR 585; See also Cahill, Connery, Kennedy & Power, *European Law* (4th edn, Oxford University Press, 2008) Ch 4.

4 *Meagher v Minister for Agriculture* [1994] 1 IR 329; *Maher v Minister for Agriculture* [2001] 2 IR 139.

European Union or of the Communities, or prevents laws enacted, acts done or measures adopted by the European Union or by the Communities or by institutions thereof, or by bodies competent under the Treaties establishing the Communities, from having the force of law in the State.

9.002 Where there is no such EC law-based requirement, where, for example, the construct 'may' as opposed to 'shall' is used, Art 29.4.10° may not be used to justify the imposition of a civil administrative sanction in this regard and the usual practice is the provision of regulatory criminal offences. An alternative construct sometimes used is that 'Member States' shall ensure that financial sanctions be imposed. This allows the Member State to exercise its discretion as to how to implement this provision in terms of whether the Regulator could apply to the court for a civil enforcement 'penalty' or whether regulatory offences should be created. Any such move must be mindful of the constitutional provisions on the administration of justice and trial of offences. Article 34.1 of the Constitution provides that 'Justice shall be administered in courts established by law by judges appointed in the manner provided by this Constitution and save in such special and limited cases as may be prescribed by law shall be administered in public.' Article 38.1 provides that: 'No person shall be tried on any criminal charge save in due course of law.' The question to be considered is whether Regulators are administering justice if they impose a financial penalty. Is this penalty so high as to be punitive and thereby in light of *Melling v O Mathghamhna*[5] indicative of a criminal matter? Is this financial penalty therefore punishment for an offence and, if so, has the firm been deprived of its right to trial in due course of law?

9.003 It is often considered under Irish law that the imposition of a significant financial penalty is punitive and thereby more appropriately dealt with under criminal law. The Financial Regulator is unique currently in Ireland in that it may impose administrative sanctions under civil law unlike other Regulators where constitutional grounds are often cited as a reason why Regulators may not impose administrative or civil financial sanctions.

It is important to note that EC law does not have criminal effect and nor does it seek to have. Regulatory offences in Ireland are often the result of implementing the requirement to impose fines.

Prior to the adoption of the European Communities Act 2007, Charleton J remarked on the corresponding increase in regulatory offences in the District Court:

> Since most of the legislation that brings into force European Directives makes the breach of them a criminal offence, these are tried in the District Court. Expressly, s 3(3) of the European Communities Act 1972, does not allow for the creation of an indictable offence by regulation, hence, absent a statutory provision, the ordinary manner of bringing European Regulations and Directives into force is by regulation which almost invariably create the remedy of a criminal prosecution for a breach. The jurisdiction of the District Court, therefore, grows ever wider, year by year.[6]

---

5   *Melling v O Mathghamhna* [1962] IR 1.
6   *Reade v Judge Reilly* [2007] 1 ILRM 504, [2007] IEHC 44.

The European Communities Act 2007 changed the policy of the legislature as regards the creation of indictable offences by way of statutory instrument. Section 2 of the 2007 Act amends s 3 of the European 1972 Act by allowing regulations under the 1972 Act to provide for indictable offences.[7] The maximum fine upon conviction of such an offence is €500,000 and the maximum term of imprisonment is three years. Section 3 of the 2007 Act provides that every regulation to which the new sub-s 3 applies shall be laid before the Houses of the Oireachtas and that either House may pass a resolution within 21 days annulling the regulation.

9.004 Most economic activity in Ireland that requires a licence or authorisation is a crime in the breach. Economic crime is described throughout this book, yet is not defined. This is because regulatory law breaches or economic crimes are simply regular crime by another name.[8] This chapter explores some practical issues that arise in enforcing that type of regulatory regime. The obvious point of departure for a chapter on criminal law enforcement is the District Court where crime commences the trial process.[9]

In criminal matters, all persons natural or legal when arrested or summonsed are brought before the District Court in the first instance. It is for the District Court Judge to ensure that the appropriate persons are processed and tried before the appropriate court.

9.005 Competition cases are dealt with centrally at the High Court sitting as the Central Criminal Court for the simple reason that a nationwide cartel arrangement may involve a number of defendants operating in different districts and circuits around the country simultaneously. Legally, these are separate local jurisdictions. In order to ensure that suspects can be tried together and the full picture given to one national court, such cases are tried before the Central Criminal Court operating on a national jurisdictional basis.

7　Section 3 of the 1972 Act specifically stated that regulations made under that Act could not create an indictable offence. In *Meagher v Minister for Agriculture* [1994] 1 IR 329 it was held by the Supreme Court that s 3 of the 1972 Act was not invalid having regard to the provisions of the Constitution.

8　For example, price fixing is a criminal offence for which a suspect may be arrested and taken into custody, much as any burglar. The potential sentence upon indictment for price fixing under the Competition Act 2002 is five years. This means it is an 'arrestable offence' as defined by the Criminal Justice Act 1997, s 2; ie a suspect may be arrested without warrant. Pursuant to the Criminal Justice Act 1984, a person arrested for an 'arrestable offence' may be detained in custody by the Garda Síochána at a Garda station for questioning. Culturally, Ireland still regards certain offences as not truly criminal. Licensing offences are an obvious example. There is talk of 'white collar crime'. This would suggest that if you're robbed by a man in a suit, it's not as bad as being robbed by a man in a track suit. Clearly, that notion is ludicrous.

9　There are some exceptions which commence in the Special Criminal Court, a 'Special Court' that combines elements of the District, Circuit and High Court criminal jurisdictions.

AUTHORISED OFFICERS

9.006 Ireland's national police force, the Garda Síochána, is not tasked at first instance with policing the economic crimes created by the regulation of economic activity. That task is primarily devolved to 'authorised officers' of the Regulators by a variety of sector-specific pieces of legislation.[10] Authorised officers are not a homogenous, specially trained body of investigators; they are usually staff of the Regulator who perform a criminal law enforcement role in addition to their normal administrative professional duties. In this regard, the same persons are both administering schemes under the Acts and then investigating and prosecuting breaches thereof. Authorised officers are 'authorised' to act only in relation to the specific activity foreseen by the legislation for which their Regulator has responsibility. These powers vary across sectors. The Competition Authority, the Commission for Communications Regulation and the Financial Services Regulator have far-reaching investigation powers. The Broadcasting Authority of Ireland, by contrast, has very few.

9.007 Most Regulators themselves can appoint undefined 'persons' as authorised officers. In the financial sector, a 'responsible authority' may appoint a 'qualified person' to act as an authorised officer.[11] Authorised officers in the sectors discussed in this book are appointed under the following legislation:

 (i)   s 11 of the Electricity Regulation Act 1999, as amended by s 18 of the Gas (Interim)(Regulation) Act 2002;

 (ii)   s 42 of the Aviation Regulation Act 2001;

 (iii) s 45 of the Competition Act 2002;

 (iv)   s 39 of the Communications Regulation Act 2002;

 (v)   s 17 of the Central Bank Act 1971;

 (vi)   s 41 of the Building Societies Act 1989;

 (vii) s 24A of the Trustee Savings Bank Act 1989;

 (viii) s 36 of the Stock Exchange Act 1995;

 (ix)   s 64 of the Investment Intermediaries Act 1995;

---

10 As stated by Keane CJ in *Dunnes Stores (Ireland) Company v Ryan* [2002] 2 IR 60 when speaking about the appointment of authorised officers under s 19 of the Companies Act 1990: 'The Oireachtas ... has assigned to the Minister, as the appropriate officer of State, significant powers to ensure that companies incorporated under the Act do not abuse the privileges which incorporation confers on them to the detriment of their members, their creditors or indeed the public in general. That has been a recognised function of the Minister and her statutory predecessor since the first decade of the twentieth century.' That logic can be extended to the appointment of authorised officers by Regulators to monitor compliance with other regulatory legislation.

11 A 'responsible authority' means the Governor of the Central Bank, the Chief Executive of the Regulatory Authority or the Registrar of Credit Unions. 'Qualified persons are either officers or employees of the Central Bank or IFSRA or some other person who in the opinion of the relevant responsible authority has the qualifications and experience necessary to exercise the powers conferred.

(x)   reg 6 of the European Communities (Undertakings for Collective Investment in Transferable Securities) Regulations 1989;[12]

(xi) s 90 of the Credit Unions Act 1997 as amended by s 31 of the Central Bank and Financial Services Authority Act of 2003; and

(xii) s 53 of the Broadcasting Authority of Ireland Bill 2008, which provides for limited rights of entry and inspection for 'investigating officers' of that Regulator.

9.008 Set out below in broad terms are the common investigative powers shared by the authorised officers of the Commission for Aviation Regulation, Commission for Communications Regulation, Commission for Energy Regulation, Competition Authority, and the Central Bank, IFSRA and the Registrar of Credit Unions.[13] Before exercising these powers, officers are obliged to produce evidence of their authorisation, eg produce a copy of their warrant or certificate of appointment.

Authorised officers commonly share the powers to:

(i)   enter, if necessary by force, and search premises at which the activity in question is carried on;[14]

(ii)   require the person who carries on an activity to provide to the officer any books, documents or records relating to that activity which are in that person's power or control, and to give to the officer such information as he or she may reasonably require in regard to any entries in such books, documents or records;

(iii) inspect and copy or take extracts from any such books, documents and records;

(iv)   require a person to give to the authorised officer any other information which the officer may reasonably require in regard to the activity in question;[15]

(v)   apply by way of information on oath for the issue of a search warrant before a judge of the District Court;[16]

(vi)   seize and retain any books, documents and records relating to the activity in question; and

(vii) require the person to maintain such books, documents or records for such period of time, as may be reasonable, as the authorised officer directs.

---

12 SI 78/1989.

13 This list is not exhaustive and readers are referred to the Acts listed above for further details of specific powers; in particular in relation to entry of 'dwellings'.

14 Such entry is generally without a warrant, except in relation to dwellings and competition cases.

15 For the Central Bank and IFSRA, see the Authorised Officers section of **Ch 4**.

16 See Electricity Regulation Act 1999, s 12; Aviation Regulation Act 2001, s 43; Communications Regulation Act 2002, s 40 and Competition Act 2002, s 45(4). On 29 October 2004, the Supreme Court gave its judgment in the case of *Creaven v The Criminal Assets Bureau* [2004] 4 IR 434 in which it was held that search warrants must be issued by a judge sitting within the district where the relevant premises are situated.

The requirements to give information may in certain circumstances represent an invasion upon the privilege against self-incrimination which is discussed further below (see paras **9.012** *et seq*).

Search warrants issued to the authorised officers mentioned above must be exercised within one month after the date of issue of the warrant. In general, a person who obstructs or impedes an authorised officer in the exercise of a power conferred is guilty of an offence.

9.009 The Competition Act 2002 helpfully defines 'records' in the sense mentioned above at s 45(11):

> 'records' includes, in addition to records in writing —
>
> (a) discs, tapes, sound-tracks or other devices in which information, sounds or signals are embodied so as to be capable (with or without the aid of some other instrument) of being reproduced in legible or audible form;
>
> (b) films, tapes or other devices in which visual images are embodied so as to be capable (with or without the aid of some other instrument) of being reproduced in visual form; and
>
> (c) photographs,
>
> and a reference to a copy of records includes, in the case of records falling within para (a) only, a transcript of the sounds or signals embodied therein, in the case of records falling within para (b), a still reproduction of the images embodied therein and, in the case of records falling within both of those paragraphs, such a transcript and such a still reproduction.

9.010 The right to retain evidence for longer than the six months provided for in the initial warrant was considered in *Competition Authority v District Judge O'Donnell*,[17] a case relating to the former provision of s 45(6) of the Competition Act (since amended). The High Court was of the opinion that the jurisdiction conferred on the District Court under s 45(6) was to provide a safeguard in respect of the rights of owners of property that has been seized on foot of warrants issued under s 45(4). In the view of the High Court, the range of consideration and thus the range of evidence that could be required by the District Court in such cases was limited essentially to two topics; firstly the progress of the investigation in respect of which the warrant was issued; and secondly, the effects on the owner of the property of the ongoing deprivation of it. A District Court Judge has discretion to refuse retention. That discretion is limited to having regard to ascertaining that the investigation is progressing in a reasonably expeditious manner and any hardship experienced by the owner of the property in question by reason of being deprived of it. Clearly, the discretion thus given to a District Court Judge enables him to make such enquiries to satisfy himself that the investigation is still ongoing and proceeding expeditiously. Beyond that, he would not be entitled to enquire into the nature of the investigation or the fruits of it. Having ascertained the ill effects of the seizure (if any) on the owner or person entitled to the documents, the District Court Judge exercising his discretion must strike a balance between these two competing interests.

---

17   *Competition Authority v District Judge O'Donnell* [2007] IEHC 390.

9.011 Section 45(6) of the Competition Act 2002 was amended by the Investment Funds Companies and Miscellaneous Provisions Act 2005, to ease logistical difficulties with retaining evidence under the original wording. The original wording provided that the Authority could retain documents, computers etc for a period of six months, but in order to retain them after that time, the Authority had to apply to the District Court within the six months. The Authority now has a right to retain the evidence indefinitely without any obligation to account to the District Court that issued the initial warrant or to the owners of the property as to why it retains them. This is not unusual in criminal investigations:[18] physical objects used to commit crime are seized by the police on a daily basis as evidence and retained until trial and often forfeited and destroyed thereafter.

Privilege against Self-Incrimination and Proportionality

9.012 Since the case of *Heaney v Ireland*,[19] which involved a challenge to the constitutionality of s 52 of the Offences Against the State Act 1939, it has been accepted that the privilege against self-incrimination, commonly called the right to silence, is enshrined in the Constitution. It has not yet been determined in this jurisdiction whether any privilege against self-incrimination is applicable to corporate bodies.

---

18   In *Competition Authority v District Judge O'Donnell*, the procedure for retention was discussed and the right of the subject of a search to give evidence as to the effect on them of having their property removed. In so far as an order made under s 45(6) is an interference with property rights in the material seized, the owner or person entitled to that material is or may be prejudicially affected by the order. Thus, having been put on notice, the notice parties in this case were entitled to give evidence of any hardships or ill effects suffered by them as a result of the deprivation of their property.

19   *Heaney v Ireland* [1996] 1 IR 580. In that case, Costello J (as he then was) quoted with approval the remarks of Lord Mustill in *R v Director of the Serious Fraud Office ex-parte Smith* (1993) AC 1, that the right to silence does not denote any single right, but rather, it 'refers to a disparate group of immunities which differ in nature, origin, incidence and importance'. Lord Mustill in that case took time (at p 30) to consider various types of immunity embraced by the term and said: 'Amongst these may be identified: (i) a general immunity, possessed by all person and bodies, from being compelled on pain of punishment to answer questions posed by other persons and bodies; (ii) a general immunity, possessed by all persons and bodies, from being compelled on pain of punishment to answer questions the answers to which may incriminate them; (iii) a specific immunity, possessed by all persons under suspicion of criminal responsibility whilst being interviewed by police officers or others in similar positions of authority, from being compelled on pain of punishment to answer questions of any kind; (iv) a specific immunity possessed by accused persons undergoing trial, from being compelled to give evidence and from being compelled to answer questions put to them in the dock; (v) a specific immunity, possessed by persons who have been charged with a criminal offence, from having questions material to the offence addressed to them by police officers or persons in a similar position of authority and (vi) a specific immunity (at least in certain circumstances which are unnecessary to explore) possessed by accused persons undergoing trial, from having adverse comment made on any failure (a) to answer questions before trial, or (b) to give evidence at the trial'.

The test for proportionality in Ireland is set out in *Heaney*[20] where Costello J considered that to be proportionate, an act must:[21]

    (a) be rationally connected to the objective and not be arbitrary, unfair or based on irrational considerations;

    (b) impair rights as little as possible; and

    (c) be such that its effect on rights is proportional to the objective.

9.013 The right to silence and privilege against self-incrimination were considered in the context of the Companies Act 1990 in *In Re National Irish Bank Limited* [1999] 1 IR 145. Inspectors appointed to investigate the bank under Pt II of that Act sought a determination from the High Court that persons from whom information, documents or evidence were requested by the inspectors were not entitled to refuse to answer questions on the grounds that the answers or documents might incriminate him, her or it. The relevant provisions were ss 10 and 18 of the Companies Act 1990. The respondents argued that the sections, when read together, constituted a breach of the privilege against self-incrimination. In the High Court, Shanley J, following the decision of the Supreme Court in *Heaney*, held that a proportionality test ought to be applied when considering restrictions placed on the right to silence by the Oireachtas. The respondents also argued that there was a right under Art 38.1 of the Constitution not to have compelled testimony used against an accused during a criminal trial. Shanley J held that this was a matter for the trial judge in criminal proceedings. On its own, the statutory obligation to answer self-incriminating questions was not inconsistent with a trial in due course of law. The case was subsequently appealed to the Supreme Court but, interestingly, the respondents in their written submissions confined their case to the rights of natural persons. The Supreme Court upheld the decision of the High Court but held that incriminating answers would not be admissible in subsequent criminal proceedings unless the trial judge was satisfied that the statements were made voluntarily.

After the decision, the Company Law Enforcement Act 2001 made a number of amendments to Pt II of the Companies Act 1990. The most significant amendment was the substituting of the word 'individual' for the word 'person' in s 18. Thus, the section now reads that an answer given by an individual may be used in evidence against him in any proceedings except for proceedings for an offence.

9.014 The issue was also considered in *Dunnes Stores (Ireland) Co v Ryan*.[22] This litigation consisted of a series of challenges to the constitutionality of s 19 of the Companies Act 1990. The relevant provisions conferred powers on authorised officers

---

20   *Heaney v Ireland* [1994] 3 IR 593.

21   Para 607.

22   *Dunnes Stores (Ireland) Co v Ryan* [2002] IEHC 61, Kearns J. This case was the last in a series of linked cases arising out of the appointment by the Minister for Enterprise, Trade and Employment of authorised officers to enquire into activities of certain companies including Dunnes Stores, having regard, amongst other things, to the McCracken Tribunal Report: *Dunnes Stores (Ireland) Co v Ryan* [2002] 2 IR 60; *Dunnes Stores (Ireland) Co v Ryan* [2000] IEHC 141; *Dunnes Stores (Ireland) Co v Maloney* [1999] 3 IR 542, [1999] 1 ILRM 119, [1998] IEHC 165.

to require production of books etc in the course of their investigation to determine whether circumstances existed for the appointment of an inspector by the High Court. Section 19(6) provided that a statement made by a person, in compliance with a requirement, could be used in evidence against that person. The applicants, two companies and one individual, sought a declaration that the provisions were contrary to Arts 38.1 and 40.1 of the Constitution. Applying the proportionality test set out in *Heaney,* Kearns J held that the requirement to produce books etc was not contrary to the Constitution. In so doing, the court emphasised the public interest in company investigations and pointed out that there was a world of a difference between the position of a vulnerable suspect in police custody and 'a large company which may engage in all sorts of stratagems and then call upon vast financial resources to protect and defend its position to the ultimate.' Kearns J did, however, hold that s 19(6) failed the *Heaney* test for failing to exclude the answers given under the subsection from use in criminal proceedings. The section was repealed and substituted by s 29 of the Company Law Enforcement Act 2001. The new subsection provides that a statement made by 'an individual' in compliance with a requirement may be used in evidence against him in any proceedings except for proceedings for an offence (other than the offence of failing to comply with the requirement by refusal to answer or giving a false or misleading answer).

In *Dunnes Stores (Ireland) Co v Ryan*, regarding the powers of authorised officers under the Companies Acts 1990, Keane CJ observed that:

> Such powers can only be exercised for the purpose for which they have been granted and are liable to be set aside ... where their invocation is not justified. In particular the exercise...of the powers ... can be set aside when ... they are being used for a purpose not contemplated by the Oireachtas. It is also clear that they can be set aside where ... the relevant authority has sought to operate them in a patently irrational fashion.[23]

9.015 The issue was considered again by Kearns J in *Environmental Protection Agency v Swalcliffe Ltd*[24] when the court found that none of the purposes underlying the privilege against self-incrimination were really at stake in the case and noted that there was no real coercion by the State body in obtaining information as the parties were not in an adversarial position when the evidence was obtained.

9.016 Persons questioned in the course of an investigation whether or not subjected to a statutory requirement to give information are the subject of the Judges' Rules, a series of guidelines on questioning for the police drawn up the Judges in the UK in response to a request from the Home Secretary in 1912. Originally four rules, they are now nine in number.[25] In essence, one may question a person about the circumstances of a suspected crime. Once, however, that person says something that makes the questioning officer believe that the person may be a suspect, they must be cautioned to

---

23   *Dunnes Stores (Ireland) Co v Ryan* [2002] 2 IR 60 at 77.
24   *Environmental Protection Agency v Swalcliffe Ltd* (21 May 2004, unreported) HC, Kearns J.
25   Woods, 'District Court Practice and Procedure in Criminal Cases' (1994) *Irish Criminal Law Journal* at p 62. For an analysis of the application of the rules in this jurisdiction and their text, see *AG v Cummins* (1972) IR 312.

the extent that they are no longer at that stage obliged to say anything, but anything that they do say may be taken down and used in evidence. Thus, if the subject of an investigation begins to implicate himself while being questioned at the premises, he should be cautioned.

9.017 A defendant will not be entitled to rely on the privilege against self-incrimination if he provides information on a voluntary basis. The privilege only comes into play were the information is compelled. Thus, if a defendant co-operates with an investigation and makes voluntary admissions, he cannot later complain that his right to silence was infringed. Statutory bodies frequently seek co-operation from persons suspected of offences, including companies, to avoid self-incrimination becoming an issue.

9.018 Arguments have been raised in other jurisdictions as to the proportionate nature of dawn raids. In the UK case of *Office of Fair Trading v X*,[26] it was alleged that a dawn raid infringed the right to protection under art 8[27] of the European Convention on Human Rights. It was held in this case that the interference with any right under art 8 was justified and proportionate given the defendant was under suspicion of being part of a cartel and there were safeguards in place to protect the defendant.

COMMENCEMENT OF PROCEEDINGS

9.019 Usually, in a regulated industry the defendants in a prosecution will be either a company or a person who has not been arrested;[28] thus the criminal law procedure to follow will be the procedure on summons. One would expect that Regulators in such cases would initiate proceedings using the procedure as set out in The Courts (No 3) Act 1986 – application to the appropriate District Court Clerk to issue a summons alleging the crime against the accused.[29]

This begs the question: who is the appropriate District Court Clerk? A related question arises as to the location of the offence. By virtue of Ord 13(1) of the District

---

26   *Office of Fair Trading v X* [2003] EWHC 1042.
27   Article 8 relates to the right to respect for private and family life. This provision may be invoked by corporate persons such as limited companies.
28   It appears to the authors that no natural person has ever been arrested and brought before the Irish courts for a 'regulatory offence' referred to in this in the book.
29   Generally, the time for commencement of proceedings pursuant to the Courts (No 3) Act 1986 is within six months of the time when the cause of complaint shall have arisen unless otherwise indicated by statute. It is not uncommon for regulatory authorities to be given much longer periods within which to initiate proceedings by statute. A new s 1 was substituted into the Courts (No 3) Act 1986 by the Civil Liability and Courts Act 2004, s 49. This provides that issue of a summons may be also be effected by transmitting it by electronic means to the person who applied for it or a person acting on his or her behalf. In addition, a summons may be issued by an office other than the appropriate District Court Office so long as it is an office of the Courts Service designated by the Courts Service for the purpose of receiving applications.

Court Rules 1997, criminal proceedings shall be brought, heard and determined either in the court area:

   (a) wherein the offence charged is stated to have been committed;

   (b) where the accused has been arrested;

   (c) where the accused resides; or

   (d) specified by order made pursuant to the provisions of s 15 of the Courts Act 1971.

For companies, points (b) and (d) will generally not apply.

9.020 A company resides in the district within which they have their registered office. A problem may arise due to the fact that some companies operating in Ireland do not have a registered address in Ireland. Presumably, it would be in order to summons them at the address they have in Ireland for service. Non-Irish companies must either register a branch in Ireland or an address and agent who will receive service of official documentation on their behalf.[30]

A further issue arises: if the company is not Irish and does not have either a registered branch or place of business in Ireland, but is trading in Ireland, it is difficult to make then amenable to an Irish summons in any simple way. For example, customers may purchase goods or services online but it then transpires the company, lacking the adequate regulatory authorisation or licence, has no Irish address for service of process etc. A question thus arises, as a matter of policing legislation, should undertakings trading in Ireland be made aware by the Regulator of their obligations under Irish company law if that is the case?

Proving a company is foreign may cause difficulty. In a prosecution, a regulatory authority has a duty to formally prove that company exists. Thus foreign company registration documentation must be authenticated before the Irish courts.

SUMMARY AND INDICTABLE OFFENCES

9.021 Increasingly, offences are created under statute as both a summary and indictable offence (an either-way offence) and many regulatory authorities are empowered to prosecute particular offences summarily. This raises the question: does the accused have a right of election? That is to say, can the accused indicate whether he wishes to be tried summarily or before a jury? In almost all instances referenced in this book, the answer is no. It is a matter for the prosecutor to decide in either-way or hybrid offences whether to proceed summarily or otherwise. This was established in the case of *State (McKevitt) v Delap*.[31] If an offence is both a summary offence and an indictable

---

30 Section 352(1)(c) of the Companies Acts 1963–2006 and the European Communities (Branch Disclosure) Regulations 1993 (SI 395/1993). The Branch Disclosures Regulations set out provisions with which foreign companies with branch activity in Ireland must comply. Their purpose is to offer members of the public information on foreign companies operating in Ireland and giving them contact persons and, importantly, authorised persons in this country upon whom legal proceedings and other important communications may be served.

31 *State (McKevitt) v Delap* [1981] IR 125.

offence, the District Court has jurisdiction to try any such case in which the prosecutor elects to treat the offence as summary. However, the District Court, having regard to the fact that it is potentially an indictable matter, would consider two points before proceeding in such a case:

    (i)   the view of the Director of Public Prosecutions; and

    (ii) whether the matter is minor.

9.022 Pursuant to the Prosecution of Offenders Act 1974, the DPP is empowered to direct trials on behalf of the People. Section 3 of the 1974 Act transfers to the DPP the functions of the Attorney General in relation to criminal matters. 'Criminal Proceedings' include the prosecutorial powers vested in the Attorney General and set out in the Criminal Justice (Administration) Act 1924, s 9:

> (1) All criminal charges prosecuted upon indictment in any court shall be prosecuted at the suit of the Attorney General of Saorstát Éireann.
>
> (2) Save where a criminal prosecution in a court of summary jurisdiction is prosecuted by a Minister, Department of State, or person (official or unofficial) authorised in that behalf by the law for the time being in force, all prosecutions in any court of summary jurisdiction shall be prosecuted at the suit of the Attorney-General of Saorstát Éireann.[32]

As mentioned above, it is a matter for a Regulator in many instances to decide whether to pursue a summary prosecution under the relevant legislation. From a Regulator's perspective, a decision to prosecute is best taken in conjunction with the DPP. Recognising the need for general guidance, the DPP has published guidance for prosecutors.[33]

9.023 Once the prosecutor treats the case as a summary offence and elects for summary disposal, the District Court must accept the case as a summary offence, unless the court decides that the offence is not a minor one. If the court decides that the offence is not a minor offence, then it must under the Constitution refuse jurisdiction and direct that the case to proceed by way of indictable trial.[34]

9.024 As Charleton J pointed out in *Reade v Judge Reilly*,[35] Art 38.5 of the Constitution gives every accused person the right to be tried by a jury except where the charge relates to a minor offence. It is defining a minor offence that causes the problem. If a case does not fit within this category, then the District Court can have no jurisdiction to deal with it, despite having apparently been given that jurisdiction by

---

32 Woods, *District Court Practice and Procedure in Criminal Cases* (James V Woods, Limerick, 1994) at p 86.

33 Director of Public Prosecutions, Guidelines for Prosecutors, June 2006, http://www.dppireland.ie.

34 Bunreacht na hÉireann, Art 38.2.

35 *Reade v Judge Reilly* [2007] 1 ILRM 504, [2007] IEHC 44 *per* Charleton J. See *Melling v Ó Mathghamhna* [1962] IR 1 and *The State (Rollinson) v Kelly* [1984] IR 248, where Henchy J doubted that certain offences, by reason of their moral turpitude, could ever be tried summarily. He instanced genocide, murder and rape. (contd .../)

statute. The test which is applied is to look to the nature of the offence, the charge that is alleged and the facts that the prosecution propose to attempt to prove against the accused and to discover the effective penalty that is likely to be imposed. However, many modern statutes give dual jurisdiction to the District and Circuit Courts and the problem is the choice of jurisdiction.

The duty of the District Court in dealing with offences which have a dual mode of trial necessarily involves the court in assessing the facts and the potential penalty that a conviction may attract. As Charleton J pointed out in *Reade,* the only way to give effect to Art 38.5 is by the District Court assuming the jurisdiction to ensure that the accused is afforded his or her constitutional right to a trial by jury where, on a judicial assessment of the facts, the charge is not a minor one. Even when a District Court Judge has elected to try a case summarily, and has embarked on the trial, circumstances may arise which entitle him, or may even make it necessary for him, to reverse his previous decision and allow the case to go forward to the Circuit Court where a higher range of sentences may be imposed.[36]

9.025 In the case of an offence triable summarily or on indictment at the option of the prosecutor, a District Court Judge is entitled to reach an opinion as to whether the offence constitutes a minor offence fit to be tried summarily either on the facts as proved or on the facts alleged against the defendant and the High Court cannot interfere with that decision on judicial review, unless it is established that it was irrational or was unsupported by the evidence before the judge.[37]

In *State (Comerford) v Kirby,*[38] Barron J decided that where an either-way or hybrid offence proceeds summarily in the District Court, the District Court judge is not deprived of jurisdiction simply because prior to the case proceeding there was no 'election' by the prosecutor for summary disposal. As the offence is a summary offence (as well as being an indictable offence), the court is entitled to determine the case on summary conviction.

---

35   (contd) In *Conroy v AG* [1965] IR 411, Walsh J indicated that the moral quality of the act is among the tests that may be useful in determining whether an offence is a minor one. At p 436 Walsh J stated: 'The court cannot accept the submission made on behalf of the Attorney General that the only test of what is or is not a minor offence is the test of the punishment it may attract. The moral quality of the act is a relevant though secondary consideration. But between the positions of grave and minimal moral guilt there is a large field which must be left to the discretion of the Oireachtas for consideration as a factor in determining whether to make an offence a minor one or not. That consideration will be reflected in the punishments which an offence may attract either by the express will of the Oireachtas in an Act or at common law without qualification by the Oireachtas.'

36   *Reade v Judge Reilly* [2007] 1 ILRM 504, [2007] IEHC 44 *per* Charleton J. See: *The State (McDonagh) v O'hUadhaigh* (9 March 1979, unreported) HC; *The State (McKevitt) v Delap* [1981] IR 125; *The State (O'Hagan) v Delap* [1982] IR 213 and *DPP v Dougan* [1996] 1 IR 544.

37   *Cummann Lúthchleas Gael Teoranta v Windle* [1994] 1 IR 525 *per* Finlay CJ. In that case Dublin Corporation were not entitled to prosecute as a common informer and in the absence of statutory authority could not prosecute the offence up to return for trial stage.

38   *State (Comerford) v Kirby* (23 July 1986, unreported) HC.

9.026 Where a Regulator is empowered by statute to proceed by way of summary prosecution, has elected for a summary trial and the District Court Judge has accepted jurisdiction, the DPP may have no involvement at all in such prosecutions, notwithstanding the fact that the offence may also be indictable. In the same case, however, the District Court Judge may refuse jurisdiction. The matter is then treated as an indictable offence and further prosecution and carriage and control of the case is outside the remit of the Regulator.

This position is distinguishable from those cases where the legislation will empower a prosecutor to try an indictable matter summarily, subject to the express consent of the DPP to summary trial.

In a case where a Regulator feels that a summary trial may not be appropriate, or is unsure, the practice is that an investigation file is submitted to the office of the DPP for directions in advance of the prosecution commencing.

SERVICE OUTSIDE THE JURISDICTION

9.027 Service outside the jurisdiction in certain cases is allowed for in the rules of the Superior Courts and was considered in the Criminal Assets Bureau (CAB) case; *Murphy v GM PB PC Ltd and GH.*[39]

9.028 This case concerned an application by CAB for an interlocutory injunction under the Proceeds of Crime Act 1996 preventing the defendants from disposing of certain cash assets. In the course of the hearing, the court considered service outside the jurisdiction and sovereignty. Mr Justice O'Higgins, giving judgment, made the following remarks:

> Order 11, Rule 1(g) of the Rules of the Superior Courts provides that:
>
> > 'Service outside the jurisdiction of an originating summons or notice of an originating summons may be allowed by the Court whenever an injunction is sought as to anything to be done within the jurisdiction … whether damages are or are not also sought in respect thereof.
>
> In the case of *Cuadron and Others v Air Zaire* [1985] IR 716, the Supreme Court held that, in order to come within Order 11, Rule 1(g), the injunction sought in the action had to be part of the substantive relief to which the Plaintiffs' cause of action entitled them, and had to be properly and necessarily sought in the Indorsement of Claim contained in the originating Summons.

9.029 The court went on to consider the point of service abroad.

> Order 11, rule 8 of the Superior Court Rules provides that "[w]here the Defendant is not, or is not known or believed to be, a citizen of Ireland, notice of the summons, and not the summons itself, shall be served upon him."
>
> In [the CAB] case the service on the Third Named Defendant on the Isle of Man was not in compliance with the Rules in that the Plenary Summons was issued

---

39   *Murphy v GM PB PC Ltd and GH* [1999] IEHC 5, O'Higgins J.

instead of Notice of the Summons. In the case of *O'Connor v Commercial General and Marine Limited and Ors* [1996] 1 IR 68 Morris J stated at p 72:

> 'The requirement for the service of notice of the proceedings, rather than the Summons itself, to be given to a non-national in another country was put by Lord Westbury in *Cookney v Anderson* (1863) 1 De GJ & S 365 as follows:
>
> > "The right of administering justice is the attribute of sovereignty and all persons within the dominions of a sovereign are within his allegiance and under his protection. If, therefore, one sovereign causes process to be served in the territory of another, and summons a foreign subject to his court of justice, it is in fact an invasion of sovereignty, and would be unjustifiable, unless done with consent; which is assumed to be the fact, if it be done in a case where a foreign judgment would, by international law be accepted as binding."

That summons was put aside.

O'Higgins J also considered the following passage of *Brownlie's Principles of Public International Law:*[40]

> Persons may not be arrested, a summons may not be served, police or tax investigations may not be mounted, orders for production of documents may not be executed, on the territory of another State, except under the terms of a treaty or other consent given.

O'Higgins J considered some other authorities; however, his decision turned on the facts. As the third named defendant in the case appeared, the court deemed this to be acceptance of the summons and to cure any defects in it. Similarly, the court deemed there was perfectly good service on the third-named defendants' solicitors in the case. Accordingly, the court deemed foreign service good.

However, the key point here from an enforcement perspective is that CAB were acting under Irish civil law rules not criminal law procedure.

It appears that an Irish criminal offence summons may not simply be served abroad for reasons of sovereignty adverted to above.

9.030 Whether a court might consider an application for a warrant for the arrest of a person outside the jurisdiction upon their return is another matter. Such a process could only apply to natural persons. Upon arrest, a person may be produced before the court and then charged with the offence by the court. The introduction of European arrest warrants (EAWs) has simplified this procedure within the EU. In relation to obtaining evidence outside of the jurisdiction, the pending adoption of the European evidence warrant in the European Union will address such matters.

Sovereignty

9.031 Article 3 of the Irish Constitution states:

> Pending the re-integration of the national territory, and without prejudice to the right of the Parliament and Government established by this constitution to exercise jurisdiction over the whole of that territory, the laws enacted by the Parliament shall

---

40 *Brownlie's Principles of Public International Law* (5th edn, OUP, 1998).

have the like area and extent as the laws of Saorstát Éireann and the like extra-territorial effect.

The effect of this Article is that the writ of the Irish criminal courts only extends to the borders of the State in most cases. It is the nature of criminal offences that they are generally local in execution and prosecution. As mentioned above, a factor in prosecuting crimes locally within national borders is the international law concept of sovereignty. In an increasingly interlinked international regulatory context such as the common market of the EU this may cause difficulties for the effective policing of some regulations. There is little mutual recognition of criminal procedures except as provided for by the EAW, which replaces international extradition arrangements within the EU. A practical concern is that a foreign-based company or person trading without a licence in Ireland may generally evade the policing of a regulation by removing themselves from the jurisdiction. Corporations cannot be extradited. From a practical perspective, it is suspects of regular, serious crime who tend to be the subjects of extradition – in years gone by this was a labour intensive, lengthy and specialised police activity.

9.032 The EAW is valid throughout the EU and has replaced extradition procedures between member states for certain serious crimes. The EAW allows for faster and simpler surrender procedures without political involvement. Its purpose is to replace lengthy extradition procedures with a new and efficient way of bringing back suspected criminals who have absconded. The State in which the person is arrested has to return the person to the State where the EAW was issued within a maximum period of 90 days of the arrest. If the person gives their consent to the surrender, the decision shall be taken within 10 days. The dual criminality principle[41] is abolished for many serious categories of offences, however, although fraud (including fraud pertaining to the financial interest of the EU and money laundering) is included, regulatory offences are not. For all offences that are not on the list, the dual criminality principle still applies. Given that regulatory offences are peculiar to Ireland, it is unlikely that the EAW will be useful in this regard. However, given that hard-core anti-trust breaches such as cartels may meet the dual criminality principle, EAWs may be used in respect of cartels in the EU.

9.033 It was in the context of the increased mobility of persons and the civil law developments mentioned above that the EAW came into being. In *The Minister for Justice, Equality and Law Reform v Altaravicius*[42] the High Court considered s 10 of the European Arrest Warrant Act 2003, which states that where a EAW has been duly issued in respect of a person within the State, that person shall, subject to and in accordance with the provisions of the Act and the Framework Decision adopted pursuant to art 34 of the Treaty on the European Union be arrested and surrendered to

---

41   Both the country requesting extradition and the country that should arrest and return the alleged criminal, recognise and accept that what he or she is alleged to have done, is a crime.

42   *The Minister for Justice, Equality and Law Reform v Altaravicius* [2007] 2 IR 265, [2006] IEHC 270.

the issuing State. The mechanism of the EAW is based on a high level of confidence between the member states.

As Murray CJ pointed out in the Supreme Court,[43] before remitting the matter to the High Court:

> The fundamental premise of mutual recognition and respect necessitates that the underlying concepts relating to judicial decisions of a judicial authority are to be seen in the context of the Framework Decision by reference to such recognition in one State of judicial authorities in other Member States.

9.034 The principles that emerged from this case are that when an EAW has been issued:

(i) An underlying domestic arrest warrant from the requesting State is not necessary.

(ii) There is a presumption that the requesting State will act in good faith in complying with the Framework Decision unless the contrary is shown. If there is cogent evidence to the contrary then an issue may arise. A mere assertion of non-compliance or the mere raising of a possibility of non-compliance is not sufficient to dislodge the presumption of compliance.

(iii) The court may require the issuing judicial authority to provide it with additional documentation or information if that provided is insufficient to enable it to perform its function.

9.035 In Ireland, when a court is requested to arrest and surrender a person, it will also consider whether there is correspondence. That is to say, if such act or omission were committed in Ireland, would it constitute an offence under the Irish law? This is the dual criminality principle. In considering correspondence, the focus of the court is on the act or omission that constitutes the offence.

This issue was considered by the Supreme Court in the *AG v Dyer*.[44] In the course of his decision, Fennelly J identified a number of principles that apply:

> 1 In considering whether correspondence has been established the court looks to the facts alleged against the subject of their quest, as opposed to the name of the offence for which he or she is sought in the requesting State, and considers whether these facts or this conduct would amount in Ireland to a crime of the necessary minimum gravity.

> 2 In considering correspondence therefore the court is concerned not with the name of the offence in the requesting country but the criminal conduct alleged in the request or warrant.

> 3 In the absence of anything suggesting that the words used in a warrant had a different meaning in the law of the requesting State, the question of correspondence was to be examined by attributing to such words the meaning they would have in Irish Law.

---

43 *Minister for Justice, Equality and Law Reform v Altaravicius* [2006] 3 IR 148, [2006] 2 ILRM 241, [2006] IESC 23.

44 *Attorney General v Dyer* [2004] 1 IR.

If such questions are to be asked in Irish courts, it is likely that the courts of other member states will have a similar approach. Correspondence of offences is a feature of extradition. This being the case, if other member states do not have criminal sanctions regimes for regulatory offences, the EAW will not apply. The corresponding breach may well occur, but simply not be a criminal offence in other member states. However, on the other hand, member states that have similar enforcement regimes to Ireland may be requested to arrest and surrender those suspected of regulatory crime committed in Ireland.

9.036 By choosing the criminal enforcement method, the State has chosen to regulate by police methods using criminal jurisprudence, which appears somewhat inflexible to the international nature of the schemes underlying regulated economic activity associated with the 'Single European Market'.[45] The Common Market is based on free movement of capital, corporations, services and people; a culture of cross-border movement that presents challenges for the adaptation of domestic criminal law to combat the breach of these freedoms.

9.037 It is illustrative by comparison to look at civil law. The Jurisdiction, Recognition and Enforcement of Judgments in Civil and Commercial Matters ('Brussels I') Regulation[46] simplifies the enforcement of judgments within the EU. It replaced the Brussels Convention with a directly applicable regulation.

Brussels I presumes that a judgment[47] in a civil or commercial matter given by the court of another Member State is to be enforced. Only in exceptional circumstances may the enforcement of a judgment under Brussels I be challenged.[48] European Enforcement Orders further simplify the process under Regulation 805/2004,[49] which sets out the procedure for cross-border enforcement of uncontested claims in civil and commercial judgments. The regulation applies to all civil or commercial judgments where a monetary award is given. As with the Brussels Regulation, judgments relating to rights in property arising from a matrimonial relationship, probate, bankruptcy, social security and arbitration are excluded from its scope. The European Communities (European Enforcement Order) Regulations 2005[50] facilitate the operation of the regulations in Ireland. A European Enforcement Order is given the same standing as a

---

45   Arguably also unsuited to the traditional skill set of the staff of Regulators' offices – few if any of these staff have any background in either police investigations or criminal prosecutions, yet they are asked to administer schemes which at their heart are now characterised as potential criminal enterprises.

46   Council Regulation (EC) No 44/2001 of 22 December 2000 on jurisdiction and the recognition and enforcement of judgments in civil and commercial matters.

47   Article 33.

48   A person will only be able to do so if it is manifestly contrary to public policy, there is insufficient time to defend the foreign proceedings or there is a risk of the judgment being irreconcilable with a judgment of the enforcing court. Thus, a defendant must raise any jurisdictional challenges before the court which adjudicated the matter.

49   Regulation (EC) No 805/2004 of the European Parliament and of the Council of 21 April 2004 creating a European Enforcement Order for uncontested claims.

50   SI 684/2005.

judgment of the High Court. It may be enforced by the High Court and have proceedings taken on it as if it was a judgment of that court. A related development is the European Order for Payment procedure.[51] This simplifies the procedure for the recovery of uncontested claims (in civil or commercial matters) between member states. The order for payment is automatically enforceable in other member states without the need for a declaration of enforceability and without any possibility of opposing its recognition.

9.038 These developments in civil and commercial matters have come into force with the deeper integration of the Common Market. In the context of Brussels I, an Irish company might sue a UK-based company in Dublin and service would be affected according to the rules on the company in the UK. If they made no appearance in Dublin, the Irish company could seek judgment in their absence in the Irish courts. If judgment was granted the Irish company could then seek to enforce that judgment in the UK.

In the absence of a flexible system of free movement of 'judgments', the internal market could not function efficiently at the level of consumers and producers in the member states.

9.039 Article 1 of Brussels I states:

> This Regulation shall apply in civil and commercial matters whatever the nature of the court or tribunal. It shall not extend, in particular, to revenue, customs or administrative matters ....

'Administrative matters' would cover regulation of economic activity. Brussels I does not expressly define 'civil or commercial matters'. Under the previous Brussels Convention, in the *Lufttransportunternehman GmbH & Co KG v Eurocontrol*,[52] the European Court of Justice (ECJ) held that this could not be determined according to national law. In that case, the ECJ excluded an action by Eurocontrol, the organisation of European National Air Traffic Controllers (such as the IAA), to recover charges payable by Lufthansa for the use of its equipment and services. The court excluded from the application of the Convention actions brought by a public authority acting in the exercise of the regulation of its public powers.[53]

Establishment

9.040 Some regulatory regimes require that the company involved be established within the European Community. Others require that such companies be controlled by member states or their nationals. These are a form of barrier to entry. In brief, the law

---

51 Regulation (EC) No 1896/2006 of the European Parliament and of the Council of 12 December 2006 creating a European order for payment procedure.

52 *Lufttransportunternehman GmbH & Co KG v Eurocontrol* Case 29/76, [1976] ECR 1541.

53 Cahill, Kennedy and Power (eds), *Applied European Law* (Law Society of Ireland, Blackstone Press, 2000) at p 99.

on establishment is set out at art 43 of the Treaty Establishing the European Community, which states:

> Within the framework of the provisions set out below, restrictions on the freedom of establishment of nationals of Member States in the territory of another Member State shall be prohibited. Such prohibition shall also apply to restrictions on the setting up of agencies, branches or subsidiaries by nationals of any Member State in the Territory of any Member State.
>
> Freedom of establishment shall include the right to take up and pursue activities as self employed persons and to set up and manage undertakings, in particular companies or firms within the meaning of the second para of art 48, under the conditions laid down for its nationals by the law of the country where such establishment is effected, subject to the provisions of the chapter relating to capital.

Article 48 states that:

> Companies or firms formed in accordance with the law of a Member State and having their registered office, central administration or principal place of business within the Community shall, for the purposes of this Chapter, be treated in the same way as natural persons who are nationals of Member States.
>
> 'Companies or firms' means companies or firms constituted under civil or commercial law, including cooperative societies, and other legal persons governed by public or private law, save for those which are non-profit making.

These provisions equally apply to the provisions on the supply of services as set out in Arts 49 to 55 of the EC Treaty.

9.041 It should be noted that, the fact that a company has registered its details with the Registrar of Companies is merely an act of compliance with domestic law governing the establishment of branches in Ireland by companies incorporated outside Ireland, be they incorporated in another Member State of the EU or in a third country. This act does not mean the company is established within the community.

STRICT LIABILITY OFFENCES

9.042 Many regulatory crimes in Ireland are strict liability offences. The mere fact of the act alone is sufficient to convict without proof of a mental element – *mens rea*. The courts are vigilant against presuming a strict liability offence exists. The law in Ireland in relation to strict liability was recently considered in joined cases *CC, PG v Ireland*.[54] In those cases, the appellants complained that they could not raise a defence of mistake as to the age of the girl with whom they had consensual sexual relations against a charge of unlawful carnal knowledge contrary to the provisions of s 1(1) of the Criminal Law (Amendment) Act 1935. In the Supreme Court, Denham J stated:

> Counsel for the applicant referred the court to *Sweet v Parsley* [1970] AC 132. This decision, of the House of Lords, held that mens rea is an essential ingredient of every offence unless some reason can be found for holding that it is not necessary and the court ought not to hold that an offence is an absolute offence unless it appears that

---

54 *CC and PG v Ireland* [2005] IESC 48, [2006] 4 IR 1.

that must have been the intention of Parliament. In that case it was held that there is a long standing legal presumption that mens rea is required for the commission of a crime. Lord Reid stated, at p 148/149:

> '... there has for centuries been a presumption that Parliament did not intend to make criminals of persons who were in no way blameworthy in what they did. That means that whenever a section is silent as to mens rea there is a presumption that, in order to give effect to the will of Parliament, we must read in words appropriate to require mens rea ...; it is firmly established by a host of authorities that mens rea is an essential ingredient of every offence unless some reason can be found for holding that that is not necessary.'

I am satisfied that this statement reflects the common law in this jurisdiction also and I would adopt and apply this statement ... The analysis in *Sweet v Parsley* was approved by Henchy J in *The People v Murray* [1977] IR 360.

9.043 In the same case, Fennelly J expanded on that mention of *Murray* when he stated:

> The leading modern Irish case on *mens rea* is *DPP v Murray*, already cited, where several members of the Court referred in more modern language to that basic proposition and also addressed the related question, so important for the present case, of the test to be applied to ascertain whether the legislature has, nonetheless, created an offence of strict liability.

In that case, Walsh J restated the principle thus:

> 'It is well established that, unless a statute either clearly or by necessary implication rules out mens rea as a constituent part of a crime, a court cannot find a person guilty of an offence against the criminal law unless he has a guilty mind.'

Henchy J at p 399, cited from the dictum of Lord Reid from the leading English case of *Sweet v Parsley* already mentioned. To similar effect, Kenny J stated at p 421:

> 'It is a general rule of our law that the act itself is not criminal unless it is accompanied by a guilty mind. The Oireachtas may make acts crimes although the accused was not aware that he was committing an offence: these are usually called crimes of strict liability. But, to effect this, clear language must be used. In the absence of such an indication, the general rule is that the guilty mind or criminal intent must be established in relation to each ingredient of the offence.'

9.044 Later on in his judgment, Fennelly J quoted with approval Lord Nicholls in *Re B(A Minor)*,[55] who in discussing the test for a strict liability offence, ie that the presumed need for *mens rea* has been negatived by the language used by parliament, said:

> The question, therefore, is whether, although not expressly negatived, the need for a mental element is negatived by necessary implication. 'Necessary implication' connotes an implication which is compellingly clear. Such an implication may be found in the language used, the nature of the offence, the mischief sought to be prevented and any other circumstances which may assist in determining what intention is properly to be attributed to Parliament when creating the offence.

---

55   *Re B(A Minor)* [2000] 1 AC 428.

In considering the matter, Fennelly J stated that two related questions arise:

> Does section 1(1) [of the Criminal Law (Amendment) Act 1935] require proof of
> *mens rea,* specifically knowledge of the age of the girl? Alternatively, does the
> section permit a defence of mistaken belief that the girl was above the statutory age? I
> have no doubt that the historic and consistent line of authority, some of which I have
> cited, would mandate a positive answer to these questions, unless, by "necessary
> implication" (as in *DPP v Murray*) or with "compelling clarity" (per Lord Nicholls in
> *B (A minor)*) that result is excluded.

9.045 This line of argument is important to bear in mind in the regulatory context in so
far as the legislature in many statutes, purports to create what on the face of it appear to
be strict liability regulatory offences. That is to say, many regulated economic acts are
now only legally done if certain circumstances obtain. The underlying morality of the
act is often not an issue but the circumstances of its performance are.

For example, in the regulatory context, the existence of a valid licence or
authorisation is a fact, not a state of mind. That fact permits action. How that action is
done requires thought. The mischief sought to be prevented by requiring a licence is
not acting with criminal intent, but acting at all. The absence of a licence prohibits
action and thus displaces consideration of *mens rea.*

9.046 It is less obvious that an offence of obstructing an investigation should be a strict
liability offence. Many statutes state that refusing to answer questions, give documents
and otherwise co-operate in some way with an authorised officer upon request
constitute obstruction, and that obstructing is an offence. This would appear to
preclude an explanation of such conduct at trial. However, precluding such an
explanation may well be disproportionate to what is trying to be achieved – assistance
in the context of a visit or search. Employees may well be under duress not to co-
operate with a search. If they are blameless in the overall scheme of things, should they
be at risk of prosecution for obstruction? Additionally, suspects may be effectively
precluded from relying on the privilege against self-incrimination.

VICARIOUS LIABILITY

9.047 Related to strict liability is the notion of vicarious liability and this was adverted
to by Denham J in her judgment in the *CC and PG* joined cases.[56]

In her judgment, Denham J in *CC* made reference to the report of the case of *Re the
Employment Equality Bill, 1996* [1997] 2 IR 321. Paragraphs 15 and 16 of the head
note to that case summarise neatly the consideration of an issue that arose: the question
of when vicarious liability for the criminal act of another might be permissible:

> 15. That in so far as it was constitutionally permissible to impose criminal liability on
> an employer for the acts of his employee, the offences in question should be
> essentially regulatory in character, apply where a person has a particular privilege or a
> duty to ensure that public standards as regards health or safety or the environment or
> the protection of the consumer are maintained, and where it might be difficult,
> invidious or redundant to seek to make the employee liable.

---

56   *CC and PG v Ireland* [2005] IESC 48, [2006] 4 IR 1.

16. That the offences provided for in the Bill for which the employer was sought to be made precariously liable were far from being regulatory in character but likely to attract a substantial measure of opprobrium. The social policy of the Bill did not justify the introduction of such a change in the criminal law. The provisions were disproportionate to the mischief sought to be avoided. To render an employer liable to potentially severe criminal sanctions in circumstances which are so unjust, irrational and inappropriate would make any purported trial of such a person not one held in due course of law and therefore contrary to Article 38, section 1 and Article 40, section 1 of the Constitution.

Denham J noted that:

[T]he judgment of the court delivered by Hamilton CJ in that Reference also referred with approval to dicta of Lord Reid in *Sweet v Parsley* cited above. The former Chief Justice particularly referred to Lord Reid's disapproval of "the public scandal of convicting on a serious charge persons who were in no way blameworthy." Of course the factual situation with which the court was dealing with in that Reference was quite different. It was referring to vicarious criminal liability. Nevertheless a constitutional requirement of an element of *mens rea* in serious offences seems to be hinted at.

9.048 The Employment Bill under scrutiny did not pass this test set out in the quoted 15 and 16 quoted above, as it had a penalty of a fine of IR£15,000 or a prison sentence of two years, or both, and covered offences which, far from being regulatory in nature, could be expected to attract a substantial measure of opprobrium. The social policy of making the Act more effective could not justify this disproportionate change to the criminal law.

CORPORATE CRIMINAL LIABILITY

9.049 A significant amount of economic crime is committed by corporations. The most common method of imposing criminal liability on corporations is to locate liability in the conduct of the company's senior officers when acting in the course of their duties. Lord Diplock stated the legal test as follows:

[W]hat natural persons are to be treated as in law as being the company for the purposes of acts done in the course of its business, including the taking of precautions and the exercise of due diligence to avoid the commission of a criminal offence, is to be found by identifying those natural persons who by the memorandum and articles of association or as a result of action taken by the directors, or by the company in general meeting pursuant to the articles, are entrusted with the exercise of the powers of the company.[57]

9.050 The Supreme Court of Canada has explained this method of attributing criminal liability to a corporation as follows:

The identification theory was inspired in the common law in order to find some pragmatic, acceptable middle ground which would see a corporation under the

---

57 *Tesco Supermarkets v Natrass* [1972] AC 153.

umbrella of the criminal law of the community but which would not saddle the corporation with the criminal wrongs of all its employees and agents.[58]

The most obvious way to avoid corporate criminal liability is to argue that the employee whose conduct is under scrutiny cannot be identified with the company.[59] In Canada it has been held that the key factor which distinguishes directing minds from normal employees is 'the capacity to exercise decision-making authority on matters of corporate policy, rather than merely to give effect to such policy on an operational basis, whether at head office or across the sea.'[60]

Defences to corporate criminal liability

Acts done contrary to express instructions

9.051 A company may argue that actions taken by an employee contrary to express instructions cannot be attributed to the corporate employee.[61] Were the law to recognise such a defence, a corporation might absolve itself from criminal consequences by the simple device of adopting and communicating to its staff a general instruction prohibiting illegal conduct and directing conformity at all times with the law. As a result of this concern, the Canadian Supreme Court has rejected the existence of such a defence:

> [T]he presence of general or specific instructions prohibiting the conduct in question is irrelevant. The Corporation and its directing mind become one and the prohibition directed by the incorporation to others is of no effect in law on the determination of criminal liability of either the directing mind or the corporation itself by reason of the actions of the directing mind.[62]

In the case *United States v Hilton Corporation*[63] the court balanced the general instructions given to a manager to maximise profits against directions to the manager to obey the anti-trust provisions of the Sherman Act and concluded that the former would in reality prevail.

---

58   *Canadian Dredge & Dock Co v The Queen* [1985] 1 SCR 662 at 701. The Canadian courts are a fertile source of judicial pronouncement on the issue of corporate criminal liability.

59   McDermott PA, 'Corporate Liability', Law Society of Ireland lecture, Dublin, June 2007.

60   *R v Church of Scientology of Toronto* (1997) 166 CCC (3d) 1.

61   McDermott PA, 'Corporate Liability', Law Society of Ireland lecture, Dublin, June 2007.

62   *Canadian Dredge & Dock Co v The Queen* [1985] 1 SCR 662 at 699.

63   *United States v Hilton Corporation* 467 F 2d 1000 (1972)(9th CCA). In that case the purchasing agent at Hilton Hotel in Portland, Oregon, threatened a supplier of goods with the loss of the hotel's business if the supplier did not contribute to a cartel arrangement. Evidence was given that this was contrary to company policy. The US court convicted Hilton Hotel Corporation of anti-trust violations because, to outsiders, the purchasing agent appeared to be acting on behalf of the corporation. This approach in the US is part inspired by the latin maxim '*Repondeat Superior*' meaning 'let the principal answer.' It expresses itself in vicarious liability as the principle that the employer is liable for the acts his employee committed in the course of his employment.

Acts done in fraud of the company

9.052 The Supreme Court of Canada has recognised that when the directing mind ceases completely to act in fact or in substance, in the interests of the corporation the identification theory begins to break down:

> Where the directing mind conceives and designs a plan and then executes it whereby the corporation is intentionally defrauded, and when this is the substantial part of the regular activities of the directing mind in his office, then it is unrealistic in the extreme to consider that the manager is the directing mind of the corporation. His entire energies are, in such a case, directed to the destruction of the undertakings of the corporation. When he crosses that line he ceases to be the directing mind and the doctrine of identification ceases to operate.[64]

Thus, in order for the identification doctrine to operate, the prosecution must demonstrate that the action taken by the directing mind:

(i)   was within the field of operation assigned to him;

(ii)   was not totally in fraud of the corporation; and

(iii) was by design or result partly for the benefit of the corporation.

9.053 In *Canadian Dredge*,[65] four companies were convicted of offences relating to public procurement after they were alleged to have made bids on a collusive basis. Each company had a manager who conducted the business of the company relating to the submission of bids for tender. The companies denied corporate criminal liability on the basis that these managers were acting in fraud of their respective employers. The Supreme Court of Canada rejected this defence and affirmed the convictions. It noted that as a result of the illegal machinations of the respective directing minds who derived personal benefits from their activities, all four companies had received contracts, sub-contracts and other benefits. Another example of an unsuccessful attempt to raise this defence is the decision of the Quebec Court of Appeal in *R V Forges du Lac Inc.*[66]

Failure to convict the directing mind

9.054 The basis of corporate liability is that a person who can be identified as the controlling mind of the company has committed an offence. Is it necessary that the employee be convicted of the offence before the company can be so convicted? Such an argument has found little favour in the courts. In *R v Ontario Chrysler*[67] a car dealership was convicted on several counts of fraud. The evidence established that 13 of its salesmen had made misrepresentations to members of the public in relation to the purchase of cars. The two individuals who represented the controlling mind of the dealership, namely the general manager and the owner, were held to have the requisite culpable state of mind. Both were aware of the practice of misrepresenting cars and

---

64   *Canadian Dredge & Dock Co v The Queen* [1985] 1 SCR 662 at 713.

65   *Canadian Dredge & Dock Co v The Queen* [1985] 1 SCR 662.

66   *R V Forges du Lac Inc* (1997) 117 CCC (3d) 71.

67   *R v Ontario Chrysler* (7 March 1994, unreported), Ontario Court of Appeal.

both authorised and condoned that practice. The dealership appealed its conviction on the ground that it could not be convicted of fraud absent the conviction of at least one of its directing minds. The Ontario Court of Appeal noted that there was no authority in favour of such a defence and concluded:

> Proof of the personal culpability of a person who constitutes the directing mind of a corporation accused may be essential in order to establish the guilt of the corporation. That proposition does not however, mean that the individual who is that directing mind must be charged and convicted.

In Ireland, it is not necessary to convict the directors to convict the company. In fact, the reverse is often the case. Directors, managers and other persons who constitute the guiding will and mind are presumed to have consented to, or connived in, the conduct of the company.

Constitutional defences for corporations

9.055 When a natural person is charged with a criminal offence, he enjoys the benefit of certain constitutional rights. To what extent can a company rely on constitutional rights? It has been suggested that, logically, if undertakings are prosecuted in a criminal court, they must be permitted the same rights and protections as a natural person.[68] However, this is not necessarily the case. It has yet to be conclusively determined in the modern era of corporate criminal liability whether or not undertakings may rely on constitutional rights such as the right to due process or the right to privacy in the same way that a natural person may.

In *NIB (No 2)*[69] Kelly J rejected a plea of double jeopardy made by the bank without considering whether or not a legal person is ever entitled to rely on such a constitutional right. In considering whether a corporation subjected to a prosecution must be permitted the same rights and protections as a natural person, one should recall that the range of sanctions available against a company is restricted – it cannot suffer imprisonment and all the deprivations that go with this penalty. Equally, the characteristics of a company are different to those of a natural person, which means that its range of actions is restricted.[70]

9.056 In *Abbey Films v AG*[71] McWilliam J suggested that an office premises was not a dwelling within the meaning of the Constitution and that a company was not a citizen.

Clearly, corporations are not human persons; therefore, they cannot be citizens. The rights of the person as a 'citizen' are the key to Constitutional protection. Article 9 of the Constitution states:

> 1.1. On the coming into operation of this Constitution any person who was a citizen of Saorstát Éireann immediately before the coming into operation of this Constitution shall become and be a citizen of Ireland.

---

68 McDermott PA, 'Corporate Liability', Law Society of Ireland lecture, Dublin, June 2007.
69 *National Irish Bank, Re (No 2)* [1993] 3 IR 190, [1999] 2 ILRM 443.
70 In an old quote attributed to Edward, Baron Thurlow, Lord Chancellor (1778-92) a corporation has '… no soul to be damned and no body to be kicked.'
71 *Abbey Films v AG* [1981] IR 158.

1.2. The future acquisition and loss of Irish nationality and citizenship shall be determined in accordance with law.

1.3. No person may be excluded from Irish nationality and citizenship by reason of the sex of such person.

2. Fidelity to the nation and loyalty to the State are fundamental political duties of all citizens.

It is clear from this Article that under the Constitution 'citizens' means physical natural persons. Corporations as abstractions are intangible, gender-neutral entities. For example, they cannot be tried for treason for the simple reason that treason attracts the death penalty, now commuted to life imprisonment. Both sentences are inapplicable to corporations.

9.057 Article 16.1 of the Constitution goes on to state that:

1. Every citizen without distinction of sex ... shall be eligible for membership of Dáil Éireann.

2.(i) All citizens, and

(ii) such other persons in the State as may be determined by law, without distinction of sex ... shall have the right to vote at an election for members of Dáil Éireann.

It is clear that by 'citizens', the Constitution means the natural people who constitute the electorate and elected of this state and whose duty is allegiance to the State. A close reading of Art 40 of the Constitution supports this view. That Article commences by stating, in Art 40.1:

[A]ll citizens shall, as human persons, be held equal before the law.

This shall not be held to mean that the State shall not in its enactments have due regard to differences of capacity, physical and moral, and of social function.

Article 40.2, which refers to titles of nobility, is clearly inapplicable to corporations.[72]

Article 40.3 details the personal rights of the citizen – such as the right to life and protection of the person from unjust attack. Corporations cannot die within the meaning of this section as they have no body to kill or attack.

Article 40.4 guarantees that no person shall be deprived of his personal liberty save in accordance with law. Again, only a physical person can benefit from this right and demand to be produced before the High Court for an inquiry into his detention at some place.

Article 40.5 set out the constitutional guarantee that the 'dwelling of every citizen is inviolable and shall not be forcibly entered save in accordance with law.'

Article 40.6 guarantees:

(i) liberty of the citizens subject to public order and morality to freely express their convictions and opinions;

(ii) peaceful assemble without arms, again subject to public order; and

(iii) freedom to form associations and trade unions.

---

72 Could one imagine a local friendly monarch bidding a memorandum and articles of association, tongue in cheek, to 'Arise, Limited Sir?!'

All of these rights attach to natural persons or flow from citizens expressing their rights as individuals.

9.058 Article 40 and its focus on citizens may be contrasted with Art 38 of the Constitution. This refers to trial in due course of law. Nowhere in this article are 'citizens' mentioned. The article states as an overarching constitutional principle: 'No person shall be tried on any criminal charge save in due course of law.' 'Person' as mentioned in this article is a much broader class of entity than that meant by the word 'citizen.'

If a citizen is to be tried in due course of law, a court must have regard to the personal rights that the State must seek to vindicate and guarantee under Art 40. Other persons do not attract this additional protection. This would seem to be the case based simply on a close reading of the Constitution. One must, of course, examine whether this view bears scrutiny having regard to the provisions of the European Convention on Human Rights.

9.059 In *Simple Imports Ltd v Revenue Commissioners*,[73] Keane J (as he then was) stated that '[p]rotection against unjustified searches and seizures is not, however, confined to the dwelling of the citizen: it extends to every person's private property.' This statement, however, does not mention the extension of the constitutional guarantee of inviolability of the dwelling to other private property. Such other property, be it a car or premises, benefits from the rules of judicial discretion as to the admissibility of evidence garnered from illegal searches; such searches not being necessarily automatically repugnant to Art 40.5 of the Constitution, but contrary to other law.

9.060 Some guidance is given by *R v Church of Scientology of Toronto*[74] where the Ontario Court of Appeal held that the application of the identification doctrine to a non-profit religious corporation did not infringe the Canadian Charter of Rights. In particular, the 'right to life, liberty and security of the person' under s 7 applied only to human beings.

THE CRIMINAL ASSETS BUREAU AND THE PROCEEDS OF CRIME

9.061 The Criminal Assets Bureau (CAB) is a multi-disciplinary law enforcement body entitled to seek to dispossess those it believes are in possession of proceeds of crime. It is entitled to make such an allegation to the High Court and discharge the burden of proof on the balance of probabilities. Proceeds of crime are broadly defined, as is criminal conduct. Taking the two together, it is possible that those who have garnered ill-gotten gains from regulatory crime may well be liable to such dispossession.

---

73   *Simple Imports Ltd v Revenue Commissioners* [2000] 2 IR 243 at 250. See also the dissenting judgment of Barron J who stated at p 257 that 'there should be a clear authority validly given before an involuntary search of premises can be enforced.'

74   *R v Church of Scientology of Toronto* (1997) 116 CCC (3d) 1.

9.062 Section 4 of the Criminal Assets Bureau Act 1996 sets out the objectives of the Bureau as follows:

(a) the identification of the assets, wherever situated, of persons which derive or are suspected to derive, directly or indirectly, from criminal activity,

(b) the taking of appropriate action under the law to deprive or to deny those persons of the assets or the benefit of such assets, in whole or in part, as may be appropriate, and

(c) the pursuit of any investigation or the doing of any other preparatory work in relation to any proceedings arising from the objectives mentioned in paragraphs (a) and (b).

9.063 By virtue of s 1 of the Proceeds of Crime Act 1996:[75]

'proceeds of crime' means any property obtained or received at any time (whether before or after the passing of this Act) by or as a result of or in connection with criminal conduct;

...

'criminal conduct' means any conduct:[76]

(a) which constitutes an offence or more than one offence, or

(b) which occurs outside the State and which would constitute an offence or more than one offence—

(i) if it occurred within the State,

(ii) if it constituted an offence under the law of the State or territory concerned, and

(iii) if, at the time when an application is being made for an interim order or interlocutory order, any property obtained or received at any time (whether before or after the passing of this Act) by or as a result of or in connection with the conduct is situated within the State;

...

'property', in relation to proceeds of crime, includes—

(a) money and all other property, real or personal, heritable or moveable,

(b) choses in action and other intangible or incorporeal property, and

(c) property situated outside the State where—

(i) the respondent is domiciled, resident or present in the State, and

(ii) all or any part of the criminal conduct concerned occurs therein, and references to property shall be construed as including references to any interest in property.

9.064 Under s 2 of the Proceeds of Crime Act 1996, the High Court may make an order that will prohibit dealing with or otherwise disposing of, or diminishing the value of, property which can be shown, on the civil standard of proof, to be the proceeds of crime and which has a value of not less than IR£10,000.

Orders under s 3 of the Proceeds of Crime Act 1996 are applied for within 21 days of the granting of a section 2 order. If this second order is granted, then specified property is 'frozen' for a period of seven years unless the court is satisfied that all or part of the property does not constitute the proceeds of crime.

---

75   As substituted by Proceeds of Crime (Amendment) Act 2005, s 3.

76   Section 1 of the 1996 Act as inserted by the Proceeds of Crime (Amendment) Act 2005, s 3.

The Proceeds of Crime Act 1996 also provides for a receivership order under s 7 of that Act.

Section 8(1) provides that where a member or an authorised officer states:

> (a) in proceedings under section 2, on affidavit or, if the Court so directs, in oral evidence, or
>
> (b) in proceedings under section 3, in oral evidence that he or she believes either or both of the following, that is to say:
>
> that the respondent is in possession or control of specified property and that the property constitutes, directly or indirectly, proceeds of crime; that the respondent is in possession of or control of specified property and that the property was acquired, in whole or in part, with or in connection with property that, directly or indirectly, constitutes proceeds of crime and that the value of the property or, as the case may be, the total value of the property referred to in both paras (i) and (ii) is not less than IR£10,000, then, if the Court is satisfied that there are reasonable grounds for the belief aforesaid, the statement shall be evidence of the matter referred to in paragraph (i) or in paragraph (ii) or in both, as may be appropriate, and of the value of the property.
>
> (2) The standard of proof required to determine any question arising under this Act shall be that applicable to civil proceedings.

9.065 On 19 March 2003, in the *Criminal Assets Bureau v Hunt*,[77] the Supreme Court rejected the appellant's submission that the CAB was only entitled to institute proceedings in pursuance of its statutory objectives under s 4 of the Criminal Assets Bureau Act 1996 where the assets were derived from criminal activity. In that case, the defendant was suspected of illegal importation of tobacco and fireworks. A tax assessment of €1.29m was raised against him. The defendant claimed there was no evidence that he had proceeds of crime and thus the application was *ultra vires* the CAB. The court stated that one of the functions of the Bureau was to ensure that the proceeds of 'suspected criminal activity' were subjected to tax and that such action could be taken where suspicion of such criminal activity was reasonably entertained by Bureau Officers. It would appear from the case that evidence must be given of the suspicion of the officers and that the trial judge must be satisfied that those suspicions are reasonably entertained by the Bureau Officers.

9.0066 In the case of *McK v M*,[78] Finnegan P (as he then was) held that service outside the jurisdiction of notice of a special summons under the Proceeds of Crime Act 1996 by a member of the Garda Síochána is good service and not in breach of any principle of international law as had been contended by the defendants.[79] The court also decided

---

77   *Criminal Assets Bureau v Hunt* [2003] 2 IR 168, [2003] 2 ILRM 481, [2003] IESC 20.

78   *McK v M* [2003] IEHC 155, Finnegan P.

79   In this case, the High Court found that it would be a breach of the comity of nations for a member of An Garda Síochána to act in that capacity within the territory of another State. However, that is not what occurred in this case. In serving notice of the Special Summons on the defendant in Northern Ireland, the member of the Garda Síochána was performing an act unrelated to his powers and status as a member of An Garda Síochána.

that it had power to order service out of the jurisdiction of proceedings, claiming relief under s 3 of the Act.

In the same case, the court decided that the Proceeds of Crime Act 1996 can apply where the defendant is out of the jurisdiction or where the offences relied upon were committed out of the jurisdiction or where both of these circumstances apply.

9.067 Having regard to the cases mentioned above, it appears the objective of the CAB is to ensure that criminals do not enjoy the proceeds of crime or of suspected criminal activity no matter where they are. Smuggling, fraud and trafficking contraband may be more the stuff of CAB's normal diet, but are not also profits, new plant, materials, vehicles and other new equipment the 'proceeds of crime' if they represent the ill-gotten gains of the unlicensed trader or cartel participant? That question has yet to be considered in Ireland, but it is a question that is there to be considered given the legislation that has been written in the Statute Book.

Chapter 10

APPEALS

INTRODUCTION

10.001 The emergence of Regulators has given rise to the emergence of appeal panels. An essential element of accountability is a system of challenge, appeal and redress. The appeals systems provide a mechanism for affected parties to assert their legal rights when they are the subject of a regulatory decision and consider that the Regulator has made a wrong decision or has acted outside the confines of its legal powers. When Regulators grant licences and set prices, levels of outputs or quality standards, they are altering market outcomes to the advantage of some and disadvantage of others. Affected parties should have recourse to appeal or judicial review. Appeals may be direct to the High Court or to an appeal panel or appeals tribunal. Appeal panels are not courts but are more akin to tribunals where, in many cases, regulated entities and, in some cases, consumers can attempt to settle their differences with their respective Regulators. The use of appeal panels in Ireland is in its infancy. Only time will tell if they will prevail against the traditional Irish bias towards court hearings. It is interesting to note that in the communications sector, the appeal panel established under secondary legislation in 2003 was disbanded in 2007 in favour of an appeal to the High Court. More recent legislation in respect of broadcasting also allows for an appeal to the High Court rather than to an appeal panel.

Over time, the appeal panels may be seen merely as stepping stones where issues can be teased out and identified before being conclusively addressed by the courts, especially given that the sectors where they operate all require significant capital expenditure by players in the market. To date, appeals to panels or tribunals do not appear to be any swifter or less expensive than appeals to the Commercial Court, for example.

10.002 Even when they are limited to a brief summary, there are significant differences in style and substance between the various appeal mechanisms. Some appeals may alter, amend, annul or vary decisions. Some appeal panel decisions may bind the parties with their decisions, while others may not. Importantly, some of the appeal panels' procedures are defined in statute, whereas others are not and their essence is much more nebulous as a result. In Ireland, none of the sectoral Regulators respond to a common appeal panel. In each applicable case, the membership of the panel is decided by the Minister responsible for the sector. The appeal panels foreseen for the Regulators in aviation, energy and financial services are all separately constituted and established on a case-by-case basis. There is no standing appeals tribunal as there is in the United Kingdom in the form of the Competition Appeals Tribunal. There are inconsistencies between sectors as to what type of decisions may be appealed and the nature of the appeals process. There are areas of regulation where there is no scope for appeal and undertakings have to rely solely on the remedy of judicial review.

10.003 The reasons for having appeal panels as opposed to an appeal to the Courts have not been subject to much analysis. Such as there is from an Irish perspective relates to the reasoning behind the establishment of other tribunals such as the Employment Appeals Tribunal, An Bord Pleanála,[1] and An Bord Uchtála.[2] There has been some comment from the OECD[3] and the European Commission on the topic. In addition, further to the government white paper on better regulation,[4] a consultation was held on regulatory appeals in Ireland which provoked substantive thought on the matter. Although appeal tribunals may be constituted to have certain expertise and to operate in a less intimidating manner than the courts, they do not have the finality and weight to their findings that comes with the judgments of a court. In addition, although the concept is to allow for a swift resolution of Regulator issues by a body with appropriate expertise, this is not always the case. The scope and standard of review are also often unclear. This leads to delay, which, when compared to the timelines followed by the Commercial Court, calls into question whether it is indeed a quicker or less expensive alternative. It is certainly an alternative that is open to regulatory gaming[5] whereby those wishing to evade the application of a regulatory decision may delay its effect by tactically appealing it.

10.004 The right to judicial review remains, despite a right of appeal being exercised. Judicial review is, however, a more limited remedy in that the review is limited to the process by which the decision is reached and, unlike an appeal, does not consider the merits of the decision itself. There may, however, be merit in selecting the same panel of judges to deal with applications for judicial review as well as appeals against Regulators in the regulated sectors, since similar issues will arise in both types of proceedings.

10.005 The following sections summarise the provisions in relation to appeals in the various regulated sectors in Ireland discussed in this book.

AVIATION APPEALS

10.006 The Aviation Regulation Act 2001 established the Commission for Aviation Regulation. Its two principal functions are to make determinations in relation to air

---

1   Planning Board.
2   Adoption Board.
3   Organisation for Economic Co-operation and Development.
4   White Paper on Regulating Better (January 2004) – available at http://www.betterregulation.ie.
5   'Regulatory gaming' arises when firms, customers and other interested parties treat the regulatory process like a game where they are opponents making tactical decisions in respect of the strategies and moves of the other player(s) based on the information each possess about the other. Each is seeking to 'win' by maximising their personal welfare. The Regulator is regarded as a kind of referee or arbitrator. Appeals are an extension of that role. Viewed in this way the regulatory process has been analysed by economists using game theory. See for example Spulber, Daniel F, *Regualtion and Markets* (MIT Press, 1989) at p 279. Regulator gaming involves the strategic use of the regulatory system in order to delay or frustrate the purpose of regulation.

charges (under s 32(2)) and air terminal services charges (under s 35(2)). The Minister for Transport, pursuant to s 40(2), must, upon request in writing from a person who is aggrieved by a determination under s 32(2) or s 35(2), establish a panel ('appeal panel') to consider an appeal by that person against the determination.

A request to establish an appeal panel shall be made promptly, but not later than three months after publication of notice of the determination to which it relates.[6] The Minister may, where he or she considers the request to be vexatious, frivolous or without substance, refuse to establish an appeal panel. A refusal by the Minister to establish the appeal panel must be in writing and state the reasons for the refusal.

10.007 Persons who may appeal the appellable determinations are an airport authority to which a determination under s 32(2) applies, the Irish Aviation Authority in respect of a determination under s 35(2) and a 'user' in respect of a determination under s 32(2) (airport charges) or s 35(2) (air terminal services charges).[7] 'User' in this context has the meaning given to it by s 33(5) of the Aviation Regulation Act[8] and connotes, amongst others, airlines, passengers, tour operators and ground handlers.

10.008 The Minister may establish an appeal panel to consider one or more requests thus one panel may deal with a number of appeals against a single determination simultaneously. Further to s 40(3), the panel is a panel of three to five persons appointed by the Minister, one of whom is chairman. It has three months to act.[9] The Appeal panel may make two decisions – it can either confirm the determination of the Commission for Aviation Regulation or refer it back to the Commission for review.

10.009 The Commission for Aviation Regulation, where it has received a referral from an appeal has two months[10] from receipt of the referral either to affirm or vary its original determination and notify the person who made the request for the appeal panel to be appointed of the reasons for its decision. In addition, it must publish a notice of the making of its decision in the national press.

10.010 The appeal panel stands dissolved, once it has referred a decision back to the Commission for Aviation Regulation further to s 40(7).

10.011 The panel therefore is a mechanism whereby an aggrieved party can ask for a review of the original determination. The Commission for Aviation Regulation is under no legal duty to change its determination. The three-month time limit on requesting the establishment of an appeal panel may be contrasted with the judicial review mechanism set out under the Aviation Regulation Act 2001, whereby one must apply for leave to review the determination within two months of its publication.[11]

---

6   Aviation Regulation Act 2001, s 32(2A) as inserted by State Airports Act 2004, s 24(c).
7   Aviation Regulation Act 2001, s 40 as amended by State Airports Act 2004, s 22(5).
8   As inserted by State Airports Act 2004, s 22.
9   Aviation Regulation Act 2001, s 40(5) as substituted by Aviation Act 2006, s 5(1)(d)(i).
10 Aviation Regulation Act 2001, s 40(8) as substituted by Aviation Act 2006, s 5(1)(d)(ii).
11 Aviation Regulation Act 2001, s 38(2)(a).

10.012 The process of appeal is relatively restricted in that not all determinations can be appealed. The decision is referred back to the Commission for Aviation Regulation; the appeal panel cannot substitute its decision for that of the Regulator. The Act does not set out what would constitute sufficient grounds for referring a decision back to the Commission for Aviation Regulation. Since the appeal panel is established on an *ad hoc* basis, this may lead to delay and a lack of developed procedures.

10.013 The essence of the appeal panel as described in this section was subject to judicial criticism in the case of *Aer Rianta v Commission for Aviation Regulation.*[12] In that case, Aer Rianta had been granted leave to bring judicial review proceedings against the determination of the Commission for Aviation Regulation in relation to air charges. The Commission sought an adjournment on the basis that an appeal panel relating to the same determination had been set up to facilitate some airport users. This adjournment was turned down. Mr Justice Kelly identified a number of drawbacks to this example of an appeal panel system:

> The appeal panel must determine its own procedure and there are no statutory guidelines. It is not clear whether it is an appeal on the merits, whether it is a review of the decision, whether there may be an oral hearing, whether written submissions may be made. These are all questions to which the statute gives no guidance.
>
> ....
>
> The Commission is given no guidance as to what it may do on receiving a referral. If it stands by its original decision, it is not clear what criteria it ought to use in so deciding. If it varies its determination, it is not clear how it may go about this function. For example, must it follow the recommendations of the appeal panel, if any.
>
> This is a witch's brew of questions – there is no reference to any statutory criteria.

In this case, Aer Rianta invoked its statutory rights and served a Notice of Motion seeking leave to apply for judicial review. Meanwhile, two other parties invoked the appeals procedure – Ryanair and the Association of Flying Groups. The Minister set up an appeal panel. In this respect, Mr Justice Kelly observed:

> The action of Aer Rianta provoked a reaction from the Commission whereby I was invited to adjourn further progress in the judicial review in circumstances where an appeal was extant ... but here [Aer Rianta] has no interest in getting involved in the appeal procedure. It should not be obliged to do so re an appellate body, which is uncertain as to the nature of its business or result. There is no clarity in the statute as to how the Commission ought to deal with the appeal. This is an exercise in conjecture and [Aer Rianta] with an existing statutory right should not be precluded from exercising it .... Moreover, I find that the legal questions are likely to survive. The Applicant is entitled to ask the Court for leave to commence proceedings. Their entitlement under section 38 at least is not in doubt, whereas the provisions of section 40 are shrouded in obscurity.

---

12 *Aer Rianta v Commission for Aviation Regulation* [2001 No 707 JR] (13 November 2001, unreported), HC, Mr Justice Kelly.

10.014 The Commission for Aviation Regulation is also responsible for licensing travel agents and tour operators. Pursuant to s 9(2) of the Transport (Tour Operators and Travel Agents) Act 1982, a person may appeal a refusal to grant a licence to the High Court. Order 102 of the Rules of the Superior Courts provides for an appeal to be by way of special summons.

In *Balkan Tours v Minister for Communications*,[13] the scope of an appeal under s 9(2) of the Transport (Tour Operators and Travel Agents) Act 1982 was considered by Mr Justice Lynch. In Balkan Tours, the Minister issued 1986/7 tour operator and travel agent licences to the defendant on 10 December 1986. A condition of the licenses was that they be reproduced in the same form exactly in any brochures for the year. Balkan Tours received the brochure from their printer on 17 December 1986. They were swiftly made available to the public. On 24 December 1986 the Minister complained that the tour operator licence as set out in the brochures was not accurate. The defendants failed to adequately explain to the Minister the reasons for this and he revoked the licence on 23 January 1987 for breach of condition. The High Court found the Minister was entitled so to do but then asked whether, notwithstanding this finding, it was entitled to vary or reverse the decision on the basis of information now before it. On the facts before it, the High Court answered in the affirmative. This was because it became clear during the High Court appeal that the printers of the brochures had not printed the correct copy of the licence and this was not the positive intention of Balkan Tours. The High Court was satisfied that, although Balkan Tours may have been careless in releasing the brochures to the industry without checking their accuracy, the effect of revocation of the licence would cause damage to Balkan Tours that was disproportionate in the circumstances to their culpability.

10.015 In so finding, the High Court considered s 9(3) and (4) of the Act.

Section 9(3) states that:

> On the hearing of an appeal under this section in relation to a refusal to grant a licence under this Act or in relation to a decision of the Minister to revoke, or vary the terms and conditions of, a licence granted under this Act, the High Court may either confirm the refusal or decision or may allow the appeal and, where an appeal is allowed, the Minister shall grant the licence or shall not revoke, or vary the terms and conditions of the licence as the case may be.

Section 9(4) states that:

> A decision of the High Court on an appeal under this section shall be final save that, by leave of that Court, an appeal from the decision shall he to the Supreme Court on a specified question of law.

Lynch J was of the view that, 'subsection (4) envisages that the High Court is to ascertain all the relevant facts of the case, whether they were before the Minister [now The Commission for Aviation Regulation] or not and is to give effect to them.' Thus, the High Court in this case varied the decision of the Minister based on information that could have been made available to the Minister but was not. Such a ruling may be

13   *Balkan Tours v Minister for Communications* [1988] ILRM 101.

distinguished from a ruling in a case based on information or events that were not in existence before a decision of an administrative body was made.

10.016 As can be perceived from *Balkan Tours*, an important question for a court upon a statutory appeal from an administrative body is the extent to which a court can hear further evidence in the appeal. In considering this question, a number of principles emerge from the case law:

(i)   One must construe the words used by the legislature to see whether the court has power to substitute its own opinion for that of the decision-maker if it considers that the impugned act was wrong on the merits and not merely wrong in law.[14]

(ii)　Making an analogy with judicial review is not that helpful, as the legislature must have intended that the court would have powers in addition to those already enjoyed at common law.[15]

(iii) The test for competition cases is not a guide for other codes.[16]

(iv) If in the opinion of the court on the hearing of any appeal the examination of further evidence by the court is necessary or desirable, then the court has ample jurisdiction within its appellate function to allow the appeal to be conducted on that basis.[17]

(v)   The jurisdiction to receive further evidence is most frequently exercised in favour of a party to an appeal where circumstances have changed since the original hearing, where basic assumptions common to both sides had been falsified by subsequent events, particularly if this had happened by the act of the defendant.[18]

---

14   Costello J in *Dunne v Minister for Fisheries and Forestry* [1984] IR 230. See also *Glancre Teo v Cafferkey* [2004] IEHC 34, Finnegan P (as he then was). Having regard to the statutory framework, see the judgment of Finnegan P in *Ulster Bank Investment Funds Ltd v Financial Services Ombudsman* [2006] IEHC 323. See *Murray v Trustees & Admin of the Irish Airlines [Gen Employee] Superannuation Scheme* [2007] 2 ILRM 196, [2007] IEHC 27 wherein Kelly J, having considered the case of *Ulster Bank Investment Funds Ltd*, stated: 'I am of opinion that, as a general rule, this court, in hearing an appeal under s 140 of the [Pensions Act 1990], is confined to the material which was before the Ombudsman. If that were not so, then parties would be at large as to what material they could put before the court by way of affidavit and the hearing in this court would be an appeal in name only.'

15   Costello J in *Dunne* above. In that case Costello J quoted with approval from *Wades Administrative Law* (5th edn, OUP, 2005) p 34: 'The system of judicial review is radically different from the system of appeals. When hearing an appeal the court is concerned with the merits of the decision under appeal. When subjecting some administrative act or order to judicial review the court is concerned with its legality. On an appeal the question is "right or wrong"? On review the question is "lawful or unlawful"?' See also *Glancre Teo v Cafferkey* [2004] IEHC 34.

16   Barron J in *Orange Ltd v Director of Telecoms (No 2)* [2000] 4 IR 159 at p 238. See also *Glancre Teo v Cafferkey* [2004] IEHC 34.

17   Walsh J in *B v B* [1975] IR 54 at 65. See also *Glancre Teo v Cafferkey* [2004] IEHC 34.

18   McLoughlin J in *B v B* [1975] IR 54 at 79. See also *Glancre Teo v Cafferkey* [2004] IEHC 34.

(vi) In exceptional cases, there would be an entitlement to adduce evidence which was not before the decision-maker when making his determination. Four conditions apply in this regard:

1. the evidence sought to be adduced must have been in existence at the time of the trial and must have been such that it could not have been obtained with reasonable diligence for use at the trial;

2. the evidence must be such that if given it would probably have an important influence on the result of the case, though it need not be decisive;

3. the evidence must be such as is presumably to be believed or, in other words, it must be apparently credible, though it need not be incontrovertible; and

4. regard should be had to the nature of the deciding body whose decision is being appealed: the proceedings before that body may well lack much of the formality which will attend a hearing before a court. An issue may arise on appeal which could not arise at a hearing; for example, an issue as to the extent of expertise of the deciding body. Thus a more flexible approach than that adopted by the Supreme Court at numbers 1 to 3 above on the admission of further evidence will be required.[19]

10.017 Persons who are refused approval to operate as ground handlers or third-party handlers under the 1998 Ground Handling Regulations[20] can appeal to the High Court. There is an appeal mechanism set out at reg 17 whereby the appellant has 21 days after the date of notice of a decision to refuse to grant an approval to appeal this decision to the High Court on a specific question of law only.

On the hearing of an appeal, the High Court, may either confirm the decision of the Commission for Aviation Regulation, or may allow the appeal, and if the appeal is allowed, the Commission shall thereupon reverse or vary his or her decision.

BROADCASTING APPEALS

10.018 In the broadcasting sector, the legislature, in the form of the Broadcasting Bill 2008, has provided for an appeal to the High Court, rather than an appeal to an appeal panel.

---

19 Kelly J in *Murray v Trustees & Admin of the Irish Airlines [Gen Employee] Superannuation Scheme* [2007] 2 ILRM 196, [2007] IEHC 27, referring to the judgment of the Supreme Court in *Murphy v Minister for Defence* [1991] 2 IR 161 subject to the modification identified by Finnegan P (as he then was) in *Ulster Bank Investment Funds Ltd v Financial Services Ombudsman* [2006] IEHC 23.

20 European Communities (Access to the Ground Handling Market at Community Airports) Regulations 1998 (SI 505/1998), transposing Council Directive 96/67/EC of 15 October 1996 on access to the ground handling market at Community Airports, OJ No L272/36 25/ 10/96.

A decision to terminate or suspend a contract by the Authority may be appealed by the holder of the contract to the High Court.

10.019 Section 51 of the Broadcasting Bill provides that the Compliance Committee may recommend to the Authority that the Authority terminate any contract entered into by the Authority under Part 6[21] or 8,[22] or suspend any contract for such period as the Compliance Committee considers reasonable and specifies in the recommendation:

(a)   if any false or misleading information of a material nature was given to the Contract Awards Committee by or on behalf of the holder of the contract before it was entered into, or

(b)   if the holder of the contract has, upon a finding by the Compliance Committee, subsequent to an investigation, failed on one or more occasions to comply with a term or condition of the contract and the nature of that failure is of such seriousness as, in the opinion of the Compliance Committee, warrants the termination or suspension by the Authority of the contract.

10.020 The Authority shall suspend the contract concerned, where the Compliance Committee recommends that the contract be suspended for such period as the Compliance Committee recommends or, having regard to all the circumstances, for such lesser period as the Authority considers appropriate. The Authority shall terminate the contract concerned or, having regard to all the circumstances, suspend the contract for such period as it considers appropriate, where the Compliance Committee recommends that the contract be terminated.

10.021 Section 51 provides that such a decision to terminate or suspend may be appealed by the holder of the contract to the High Court. Section 55 provides that the High Court or the Compliance Committee may make a determination in respect of a breach and may impose a civil financial sanction of up to €250,000. The section also provides that a broadcaster may appeal a decision of the Compliance Committee in respect of a financial sanction to the High Court.

10.022 Given that, at the time of writing, the Broadcasting Bill has not yet been adopted as an Act, it remains to be seen what standard and scope of review the High Court will apply in carrying out its appellate functions in this regard, particularly in light of the civil financial sanctions that may be imposed.

ELECTRONIC COMMUNICATIONS

10.023 In respect of electronic communications, a full right of appeal rests with the High Court. This is provided for in regs 3 and 4 of the Framework Regulations.[23] Until 2007, the Framework Regulations provided for the Minister establishing an Electronic

---

21   Part 6 deals with commercial broadcasting, ie not public service obligation broadcasting.
22   Part 8 deals with digital broadcasting.
23   European Communities (Electronic Communications Networks and Services) (Framework) Regulations (SI 307/2003, amended by SI 271/2007).

Communications Appeal Panel (ECAP). ECAP was, however, withdrawn by way of SI 271/2007 and an appeal to the High Court was provided for instead.

No provisions in the Communications Regulation Act 2002 relate to appeals. They are contained, rather, in art 4 of the Framework Directive,[24] as implemented by regs 3 and 4 of the Framework Regulations. The Framework Directive allows for the appeal of decisions adopted in relation to the Framework Directive and the following four Directives:

(i) Directive 2002/20 – the Authorisation Directive;

(ii) Directive 2002/19 – the Access Directive;

(iii) Directive 2002/22 – the Universal Service Directive; and

(iv) Directive 2002/58 – the Privacy Directive.

10.024 Article 4 of the Framework Directive sets out the right of appeal and provides:

1. Member states shall ensure that effective mechanisms exist at national level under which any user or undertaking providing electronic communications networks and/or services who is affected by a decision of a national regulatory authority has the right of appeal against a decision to an appeal body that is independent of the parties involved. This body, which may be a court, shall have the appropriate expertise available to enable it to carry out its functions. Member states shall ensure that the merits of the case are duly taken into account and that there is an effective appeal mechanism. Pending the outcome of any such appeal, the decision of the national regulatory authority shall stand, unless the appeal body decides otherwise.

2. Where the appeal body referred to in paragraph 1 is not judicial in character, written reasons for its decision shall always be given. Furthermore, in such a case, its decision shall be subject to review by a Court or tribunal within the meaning of Article 234 of the Treaty.

10.025 ECAP reached only one final decision in its time and this was in respect of *Hutchison 3G Ireland.*[25] Several other appeals were started before it; however, they were withdrawn before a final decision was handed down.[26]

---

24 Directive 2002/21/EC of the European Parliament and the Council of 7 March 2002 on a common regulatory framework for electronic communication networks and services (Framework Directive).

25 *Hutchison 3G v ComReg* ECAP/2004/01 Decision of ECAP 26 September 2005.

26 For example, *Vodafone, O2 and Meteor v ComReg* ECAP /2005/03, 04 and 05. In this case, ComReg considered that it should not be required to disclose confidential information received from third parties unless the third party waived that confidentiality. The appellants argued that it would be unfair for them not to see a document which played such a significant part in the decision they were challenging. ECAP therefore ordered its disclosure. In this case, ComReg's decision was annulled by ECAP with the consent of the parties.

Hutchison 3G v ComReg

10.026 This was the only case to go to full trial and judgment before ECAP. ECAP confined itself to considering documents produced on discovery and annexed to the parties' written submissions. The panel was established on 21 September 2004 and judgment was not handed down until 26 September 2005. In this case, the appeal was not a full re-hearing in the sense of a hearing *de novo* appeal. ECAP ruled on the scope of review in light of the cases *M&J Gleeson v Competition Authority*,[27] *Orange Communications Ltd v Director of Telecommunications Regulation*[28] and *Carrigdale Hotel v Comptroller of Patents*.[29] It decided that ECAP could focus on evidence and materials upon which the Regulator based its decision and look at the inferences and conclusions it drew from those materials. It was considered that, while the panel had appropriate expertise, and had expertise available to it, it was not the type of expertise which the Regulator itself had, for example, in collating data and information on the market and carrying out an investigation and analysis of that market. Rather it was the type of expertise which allowed the panel to understand the specialist or technical matters which the Regulator had regard to in carrying out its functions and making its decisions. To this extent, a degree of deference could be shown, but not the same degree which the court in *Orange* or *Gleeson* would have shown. The panel was therefore of the view that the standard envisaged by the Framework Regulations was broader than the standard set out in *Orange*. To overturn a decision on the grounds that it was erroneous would require errors which would need to be significant. The error should not be trivial; rather, the error should be an error which, when objectively assessed, had a bearing on the decision reached by the Regulator. However, the error need not go to the root of the decision either. Instead, it should be material in the sense that it was objectively relevant to and had a bearing on the conclusion that the Regulator came to. The standard of review was somewhere between a hearing *de novo* and the standard applied in the case of judicial review.

10.027 Traditionally, the judicial review standard is the high standard of a decision, flying in the face of reason or *Wednesbury* unreasonableness.[30] However, in the case of *SIAC v Mayo County Council*[31] the court when applying public procurement law, which is EC law implemented in Ireland, applied a lower threshold of 'manifest error' – the test applied by the European Court of First Instance when reviewing administrative decisions of the European Commission.[32]

---

27   *M&J Gleeson v Competition Authority* [1999] 2 ILRM 401.
28   *Orange Communications Ltd v Director of Telecommunications Regulation* [2000] 4 IR 159.
29   *Carrigdale Hotel v Comptroller of Patents* [2004] 3 IR 410.
30   *Associated Provincial Picture Houses v Wednesbury Corporation* [1941] 1 KB 223, [1947] 2 AC 680, [1948] 1 KB 223. See also *O'Keeffe v An Bord Pleanála* [1993] 1 IR 39.
31   *SIAC v Mayo County Council* [2002] 3 IR 148.
32   CFI 12 February 2008 *Bupa v Commission* T–289/03. Although, interestingly, the European Court of Justice itself does not use the manifest error test: see *Kali und Salz* Joined Cases C–68/94 and *France et al v Commission (Kali & Salz)* C–90/95 [1998] ECR I 1375 and, more particularly, *Commission v Tetra Laval (Tetra Laval II)* C–12/03P [2005] ECR I 987 for the ECJ's preferred standard of review.

10.028 Now, because ECAP has been disbanded, an aggrieved party can appeal a ComReg decision to the High Court within 28 days after the undertaking has been notified of the decision. An aggrieved party can also seek judicial review of a ComReg decision by the High Court.

Regulation 4 of the Framework Regulations provides that a user who, or an undertaking that, is affected by a decision may appeal to the High Court against a decision by ComReg. An appeal must be lodged in such manner as is prescribed by the Rules of the High Court and Supreme Court. This, in practice, means that an appeal is lodged by way of a notice of motion together with a grounding affidavit.

10.029 Regulation 3 provides that the appeal mechanism applies to a decision by ComReg under the Framework Regulations,[33] the Authorisation Regulations,[34] the Access Regulations,[35] the USO Regulations[36] or the Data Protection and Privacy Regulations.[37] However, it does not apply to an application or notice given under:

(i)   reg 35(1) of the Framework Regulations;

(ii) reg 18(1) of the Access Regulations;

(iii) reg 16(2) of the Authorisation Regulations;

(iv) reg 32(2) of the Universal Service Regulations;

(v)   reg 20(1) of the Data Protection and Privacy Regulations; or

(vi) s 44 of the Act of 2002.

10.030 Regulation 5 provides that the High Court may hear an appeal only if it is satisfied that a copy of the appeal has been served on the Regulator. On being served with a copy of the appeal, the Regulator becomes the respondent to the appeal.

10.031 Regulation 6 sets out the power of the High Court on hearing an appeal. It provides that the High Court shall hear and determine an appeal and may make such orders as it considers appropriate. The orders that may be made by the High Court on the determination of an appeal include:

(a) an order affirming or setting aside the whole or any part of the decision of the Regulator; and

(b) an order remitting the case to the Regulator to be re-determined, either with or without the hearing of further evidence, in accordance with the directions of the court.

---

33 European Communities (Electronic Communications Networks and Services) (Framework) Regulations, 2003 (SI 307/2003, as amended by SI 271/2007).

34 European Communities (Electronic Communications Networks and Services) (Authorisation) Regulations (SI 306/2003, amended by SI 372/2007).

35 European Communities (Electronic Communications Networks and Services) (Access) Regulations (SI 305/2003, amended by SI 373/2007).

36 European Communities (Electronic Communications Networks and Services) (Universal Service and Users Rights) Regulations (SI 308/2003, amended by SI 374/2007).

37 European Communities (Electronic Communications Networks and Services) (Data Protection and Privacy) Regulations 2003 (SI 535/2003).

10.032 Regulation 7 sets out the effect of appeal on the operation of the Regulator's decision. Lodging an appeal with the High Court from a decision of the Regulator does not, of itself, affect the operation of the decision or prevent action from being taken to implement the decision. If an appeal is lodged with the High Court, the court may make such order staying or otherwise affecting the operation or implementation of the decision of the Regulator, or a part of that decision, as the court considers appropriate for the purpose of securing the effectiveness of the hearing and determination of the appeal. If an order is in force staying the operation of a decision of the Regulator (including an order that has previously been varied on one or more occasions), the High Court may make a further order varying or revoking the order. An order in force staying the effect (including an order that has previously been varied on one or more occasions) is subject to such conditions as are specified in the order. It has effect if a period for the operation of the order is specified in the order – until the expiry of that period or, if the appeal is determined before the end of that period, until the making of the determination. If no period is so specified, it has effect until the giving of a decision on the appeal.

10.033 Regulation 8 provides for ComReg sending certain documents to the High Court and details that when an appeal is lodged in the High Court, ComReg shall send to the court all documents that were before it in connection with the proceeding to which the appeal relates. At the conclusion of the proceedings, the court shall arrange for the documents to be returned to ComReg.

Eircom v ComReg[38]

10.034 On 23 July 2008, Eircom issued a statutory appeal against a ComReg direction relating to the rental price for shared access to the unbundled local loop[39] pursuant to reg 4 of the Framework Regulations. The case was set down for a hearing in December 2008 on the commercial list. ComReg withdrew the direction, having considered *inter alia* the probability that judgment might not be delivered until well in to 2009, in the context that the decision under appeal was for an interim period of one-year only. The proceedings were therefore struck out on 27 August 2008.

10.035 The issue of the importance of preserving an undertaking's right of appeal was considered in *Eircom v ComReg*.[40] The case held that the decision of the Regulator should be subject to an effective appeals mechanism. The court considered in this case whether ComReg could enforce directions within the 28-day period within which an appeal could be brought. Eircom lodged its appeal before the Minister for Communications, Marine and Natural Resources, as was required by reg 3(3) of the Framework Regulation at that time. There was a delay between lodging the appeal with the Minister and the Minister establishing an appeal panel.[41] Eircom also sought to

---

38   *Eircom Limited v ComReg*, HC, Record No 2008/110MCA.
39   Decision No D03/08 and Document No 08/46 of 27 June 2008.
40   *Eircom Limited v ComReg* [2007] I IR 1, judgment of McKechnie J dated 29 July 2005.
41   This case was prior to the amendment of the legislation disbanding ECAP and granting a right of appeal straight to the High Court. In this case, the Minister declined to establish an ECAP pending the outcome of the judicial review case.

obtain an order of suspension since otherwise its right to an effective appeals mechanism would have been vitiated. Eircom therefore applied to the High Court for leave to bring judicial review and for an order suspending the operation of ComReg's directions on the ground that it had an unqualified right of appeal and that right would be rendered impossible by ComReg obliging Eircom to comply with the directions since this could not be reversed or undone. The court held that art 4 of the Framework Directive set out an unqualified right to appeal on the merits of a case where an aggrieved party is affected by a decision of a Regulator. The court found in favour of Eircom and asserted that there must be an effective right of appeal. The court held that 'the availability of a meaningless appeal ex post facto cannot satisfy the requirement of effectiveness or the need to preserve a person's position pending appeal' and cited *IMS Health Inc v Commission*.[42] Mr Justice McKechnie also made some observations on the scope of review under art 4 of the Framework Directive and noted, '[t]he scope of what may be appealed is extremely wide and includes errors of fact, inferences from such fact, errors of law and questions of jurisdiction and procedure. In practical terms, it is difficult to think of any issue which is not so covered.'[43]

POSTAL SECTOR

10.036 In respect of the postal sector, the only remedy available currently to operators is judicial review, although this will change once the Third Postal Directive[44] is adopted. The Third Postal Directive, however, provides at art 22.3 that member states shall ensure that effective mechanisms exist at national level under which any user or postal service provider affected by a decision of a national regulatory authority has the right to appeal against the decision to an appeal body which is independent of the parties involved. Pending the outcome of any such appeal, the decision of the national regulatory authority shall stand, unless the appeal body decides otherwise. This Directive has yet to be implemented. As part of the implementation of the Third Postal Directive, the Minister for Communications will have to consider whether a full right of appeal should rest to the High Court or whether an appeal panel should be established in respect of the postal sector in order to discharge Ireland's obligations under the new Directive.

ELECTRICITY

10.037 The Electricity Regulation Act 1999 (the 1999 Act) created the Commission for Electricity Regulation. Amongst other things, under s 14 the Commission may grant or may refuse to grant any person a licence to generate electricity, or to supply electricity to eligible customers.

10.038 Under s 13(7)(c), a person may appeal such a refusal in accordance with ss 29 and 30 of the 1999 Act. These provisions deal with the appeal panel. This panel may

---

42 *IMS Health Inc v Commission* Case T 184/01 [2001] ECR 11/2349.

43 At para 25.

44 Directive 2008/6/EC.

hear appeals from those whose application for a licence or an authorisation is refused or from a person holding a licence appealing against a modification (or refusal of a modification) of that licence. When requested to establish an appeal panel, the Minister must consult with the Competition Authority as to the composition of the appeal panel, and then within one month establish it to consider the appeal. A panel must consist of at least three persons, one of whom shall be appointed by the Minister to be the chairperson. The appeal panel is deemed to have all the powers and duties that are necessary to carry out the functions of the appeal panel under this Act. Thus it has the powers of the High Court to summon witnesses, administer oaths and compel the production of documents. No such appeal panel has yet been constituted in the energy sector at the time of writing.

The Appeal panel may confirm, annul or vary the decision of the Commission in relation to a licence. It may also direct the Commission to grant a licence or modify a licence or authorisation. It is obliged to finish its work within six months. Its procedure is set out in s 30 of the 1999 Act.

10.039 A determination of the Commission may not, however, be challenged other than by judicial review as set out in s 32 of the Electricity Regulation Act 1999. A determination in relation to a network access dispute is not appealable.

There is limited scope to appeal decisions of the Commission for Energy Regulation. Pricing decisions of the Commission are not open to appeal. It may be argued that this dilutes accountability in the decision-making process. However, these decisions are, of course, subject to judicial review.

GAS

10.040 Section 5 of the Gas (Interim)(Regulation) Act 2002 renamed the Commission for Electricity Regulation as the Commission for Energy Regulation. This body is also responsible for natural gas licensing matters. By virtue of s 16 of the Act, a person who is refused a natural gas licence may appeal under the same procedure as set out in the Electricity Regulation Act 1999. As mentioned above, no such appeal panel has yet been constituted in the energy sector at the time of writing.

FINANCIAL SERVICES

10.041 The test or standard of review in the context of statutory appeals in the financial sector was considered in the case of *Ulster Bank v Financial Ombudsman & McCarren*.[45] In that case, Finnegan P set out the following test for an appeal pursuant to the provisions of s 57CL and s 57CM of the Central Bank Act 1942 (as amended).

> To succeed on this appeal the Plaintiff must establish as a matter of probability that, taking the adjudicative process as a whole, the decision reached was vitiated by a serious and significant error or a series of such errors. In applying the test the Court will have regard to the degree of expertise and specialist knowledge of the Defendant. The deferential standard is that applied by Keane CJ in *Orange v The Director of*

---

45 *Ulster Bank v Financial Ombudsman & McCarren* [2006] IEHC 323.

Telecommunications Regulation & Anor and not that in the *State (Keegan) v Stardust Compensation Tribunal.*

The logic of the High Court in the *Ulster Bank* case was that there should be a common standard of appeal across the board in statutory appeals. This case is, however, under appeal to the Supreme Court at the time of writing.

10.042 Section 57A of the Central Bank Act 1942 (as inserted by s 28 of the Central Bank and Financial Services Authority of Ireland Act 2003) provides for the establishment of the Irish Financial Services Appeals Tribunal and Sch 5 deals with appeals. Any decision in relation to administrative sanction may be appealed to the Financial Services Appeals Tribunal and the High Court. The decision of the inquiry will not come into force when the appeal is outstanding. An 'affected person' means a person whose interests are directly or indirectly affected by an appealable decision. An 'appealable decision' means a decision of the Regulatory Authority made under a designated enactment or designated statutory instrument that has the effect of imposing a sanction or liability of a kind specified in an order made under sub-s (2) of s 57A.

10.043 Sections 57B and 57C established the Irish Financial Services Appeals Tribunal as an independent tribunal:

    (i) to hear and determine appeals under this Part;

    (ii) to exercise such other jurisdiction as is conferred on it by this Part or by any other enactment or law;

    (b) to ensure that the Appeals Tribunal is accessible, its proceedings are efficient and effective and its decisions are fair; and

    (c) to enable proceedings before the Appeals Tribunal to be determined in an informal and expeditious manner.

10.044 Membership of the Appeals Tribunal is set out under s 57D. The members are appointed by the President on the nomination of the government. Alone of all the appeal panels mentioned, its composition has guidelines. An appeal is heard by at least three members[46] A person is eligible to be appointed as the Chairperson or deputy member, but may be Chairperson only if they are either:

    (i)   a former judge of the Supreme Court or the High Court; or

    (ii) a barrister or solicitor of not less than seven years' standing.

A person is eligible to be appointed as a lay member only if the President is satisfied that the person has special knowledge or skill in relation to the provision of financial services. The members of the Appeals Tribunal are appointed for a period of five years and are eligible for reappointment at the end of that period.

---

46 Section 57E. By virtue of s 57D, the Appeals Tribunal shall consist of the following members: '(a) a Chairperson; (b) a Deputy Chairperson; (c) no fewer than 1 and no more than 5 lay members.'

10.045 Appeals must be made within 28 days of the impugned decision being notified to the appellant. The Appeals Tribunal has jurisdiction to hear and determine:[47]

    (i)   appeals made by affected persons against appealable decisions of the Regulatory Authority; and

    (ii)   such other matters, or class of matters, as may be prescribed by any other Act or law.

The Appeals Tribunal has power to do whatever is necessary for or in connection with, or reasonably incidental to, the exercise of its jurisdiction.

The Financial Services Regulatory Authority is the respondent to every appeal.

10.046 The right of appeal is set out in s 57L, which provides that an affected person may appeal against an appealable decision of the Regulatory Authority. The appeal must:

    (a) be in writing and state the grounds of appeal;

    (b) be lodged with the Registrar within 28 days after the Regulatory Authority notified the affected person of the decision concerned, or within such extended period as the Registrar may allow, after consulting the Chairperson of the Appeals Tribunal; and

    (c) be accompanied by the fee (if any) prescribed by the rules.

As soon as practicable after an appeal is lodged with the Registrar, the Registrar is required to give a copy of the appeal to the Regulatory Authority.

Section 57N provides that if the Regulatory Authority has made an appealable decision, an affected person may make a written request to that Authority for a statement setting out the reasons for the decision.

10.047 Section 57R provides that, on the application of the appellant, the Appeals Tribunal may make such orders staying or otherwise affecting the operation of the decision appealed against as it considers will secure the effectiveness of the determination of the application. The Appeals Tribunal may make an order under this section only if it considers that it is desirable to do so after taking into account:

    (i)   the interests of any persons who may be affected by the determination of the application;

    (ii)   any submission made by or on behalf of the Regulatory Authority; and

    (iii) the public interest.

The Appeals Tribunal may not make an order under this section unless the Regulatory Authority has been given a reasonable opportunity to make submissions in relation to the matter. A party to the relevant proceedings may appeal to the High Court against an order made under this section or against a refusal to make such an order.

Section 57S deals with the conditions of the stay and provides that an order in force under s 57R is subject to such conditions as are specified in the order. The stay order has effect pending the outcome of the appeal.

---

47   Section 57G.

10.048 Section 57T provides that the Appeals Tribunal shall ensure parties are given a reasonable opportunity:

(i)   to present their case (whether at a hearing or otherwise); and

(ii)   to make submissions in relation to the issues arising in the proceedings.

Section 57U deals with representation and provides that a party to proceedings before the Appeals Tribunal may appear with or without representation, or an interpreter, if necessary.

10.049 By virtue of s 57V, the Appeals Tribunal may generally determine its own procedure. It is expressly not bound by the rules of evidence and may inquire into and inform itself on any matter in such manner as it thinks fit, subject to the rules of natural justice. However, s 57V does set out detailed procedures. When hearing an appeal, the Appeals Tribunal is not limited to:

(i)   considering the evidence or grounds on which the Regulatory Authority based the decision that is the subject of the appeal, or

(ii)   applying any sanction that was imposed as a part of that decision.

The Appeals Tribunal is required to act with as little formality as the circumstances of the case permit and according to equity, good conscience and the substantial merits of the case without regard to technicalities or legal forms. This would mean that the appeal has a standard of review which is more than merely a judicial review type standard; rather it is closer to a hearing *de novo*. The scope of the review will no doubt be determined on a case-by-case basis. In proceedings before it, the Appeals Tribunal is required to act as expeditiously as is practicable and to ensure that all relevant material is disclosed to that Tribunal so as to enable it to determine all of the relevant facts in issue in the proceedings. In particular, the Appeals Tribunal may at any stage dismiss proceedings that it considers to be frivolous or vexatious or otherwise misconceived or lacking in substance. Even if the parties do not agree that the hearing should be conducted in private, the Appeals Tribunal may do so.

10.050 Section 57X deals with the power to remit and provides that at any stage of proceedings, the Appeals Tribunal may remit a decision to the Regulatory Authority for its consideration. The Regulatory Authority shall reconsider a decision remitted and on the reconsideration may:

(i)   affirm the decision;

(ii)   vary the decision; or

(iii) substitute for the decision a new decision.

If the Regulatory Authority varies the remitted decision:

(i)   the appeal is taken to be an appeal against the decision as varied; and

(ii)   the appellant may either:

    (a)   proceed with the appeal as varied, or

    (b)   withdraw the appeal.

If the Regulatory Authority substitutes for the remitted decision a new decision to replace the decision set aside:

  (i)   the appeal is taken to be an appeal against the new decision; and

  (ii) the appellant may either:

      (a)   proceed with the appeal in relation to the new decision, or

      (b)   withdraw the appeal.

10.051 Section 57Z provides that in determining an appeal, the Appeals Tribunal shall decide what the correct and preferable decision is having regard to the material then before it, including:

  (i)   any relevant factual material; and

  (ii) any applicable enactment or other law.

As soon as possible after finishing the hearing of an appeal against an appealable decision, the Appeals Tribunal shall:

  (i)   affirm the decision;

  (ii) vary the decision;

  (iii) substitute for the decision any appropriate decision that the Regulatory Authority could have lawfully made in relation to the matter concerned; or

  (iv) set aside the decision and remit the matter concerned for reconsideration by the Regulatory Authority in accordance with any directions or recommendations of the Appeals Tribunal.

10.052 The Appeals Tribunal may dismiss an appeal against an appealable decision on the ground that the appellant has failed to attend a hearing of that Tribunal, but only if it is satisfied that the appellant was notified of the date, time and place fixed for the hearing. The Appeals Tribunal may allow an appeal against an appealable decision on the ground that the Regulatory Authority has failed to attend a hearing of that Tribunal, but only if it is satisfied that that Authority was notified of the date, time and place fixed for the hearing. In that case, the Appeals Tribunal may substitute for the decision appealed against any appropriate decision that the Regulatory Authority could have lawfully made in relation to the matter concerned.

10.053 Section 57AA provides that if the members are not in unanimous agreement on a matter, the decision of the majority on the matter is the decision of that Tribunal. The Appeals Tribunal is required to give reasons for its decision in writing within 28 days after the date on which it gave its decision, unless the rules specify some other period. Those reasons must set out the findings on material questions of fact, the Appeals Tribunal's understanding of the applicable law, and the reasoning processes that led that Tribunal to the conclusions that it made. A failure to comply with this, however, does not affect the validity of a decision of the Appeals Tribunal. The Appeals Tribunal shall ensure that a copy of its decision determining an appeal is served on each party to the proceedings. Section 57AB provides that the Appeals Tribunal may reserve its decision.

10.054 Section 57AE deals with costs and facilitating payment and recovery of amounts ordered to be paid. Section 57AH also deals with costs and provides that the Appeals Tribunal may award costs in relation to proceedings before it under certain circumstances, and may determine by whom and to what extent costs are to be paid.

10.055 Section 57AF allows the Appeals Tribunal to call witnesses on its own initiative, and examine and cross-examine witnesses on oath, or by use of a statutory declaration. It may, if necessary, direct the Registrar to issue a summons to compel the attendance of the person before it. A party to proceedings before the Appeals Tribunal may apply to the Registrar for the issue of a summons compelling the attendance of a witness before it. A person who, without reasonable excuse, fails to comply with the requirements of a summons, commits an offence and is liable on summary conviction to a fine not exceeding €2,000 or to imprisonment for a term not exceeding three months, or both. A summons may be served within or outside the State. A person who attends proceedings of the Appeals Tribunal to give evidence, or attend and produce documents or other things, is entitled to the same protection and immunity as a person appearing as a witness in civil proceedings before a court.

10.056 If a person does anything that, if the Appeals Tribunal were a court of law having power to commit for contempt, would be contempt, the Appeals Tribunal may report the matter to the High Court. If the court is satisfied that there was no reasonable excuse for the act or omission concerned, then the court may make an order requiring the person concerned to comply, and if the person fails to comply with such order, may deal with the matter as if it were a contempt of that court.

Section 57AO provides that an act or omission may be punished as an offence even though it could be punished as a contempt of the Appeals Tribunal. If an act or omission constitutes both an offence and a contempt of the Appeals Tribunal, the offender is not liable to be punished twice.

10.057 Section 57AJ deals with references to the High Court and provides that when hearing an appeal, the Appeals Tribunal may, on its own initiative or at the request of a party, refer a question of law arising in the appeal to the High Court for the opinion of the court. The High Court has jurisdiction to hear and determine any question of law referred to it under this section. If a question of law arising in an appeal has been referred to the High Court under this section, the Appeals Tribunal may not:

(a)   give a decision in the appeal to which the question is relevant while the reference is pending; or

(b)   proceed in a manner, or make a decision, that is inconsistent with the opinion of the High Court on the question.

10.058 It is also possible, given the EC basis of financial services regulation, that an art 2 reference could be made to the European Court of Justice if a question of Community law arose in any particular case, and if the Appeals Tribunal was thought to fulfil the criteria of *Foto Frost*[48], *Brockmoelen*[49], *Dorsch Consult*[50] and *In Re Doris Salzman*.[51] The relevant criteria for whether a tribunal may make a reference to the Court of Justice under art 234 include whether it is permanent in nature, whether it is established under law, whether it applies the rule of law, whether its proceedings are *inter partes*, whether it is independent and whether its jurisdiction is compulsory. The tests are to be looked at cumulatively and on balance to be considered whether it is a tribunal for the purposes of art 234 of the EC Treaty. Given the Appeals Tribunal is not a tribunal in respect of which there is no judicial remedy, it would not be obliged to make the art 234 reference when requested.

10.059 A right of appeal to the High Court is provided for under s 57AK. It is not clear if it is a judicial review type standard of review that would be exercised by the High Court in the circumstances. Neither the Appeals Tribunal nor any of its members can be made a party to an appeal under this section. An appeal under this section must be made within such period and in such manner as is prescribed by rules of court of the High Court, or within such further period as that court may allow.

10.060 Section 57AL provides that the High Court is to hear and determine an appeal made under s 57AK and may make such orders as it thinks appropriate. The orders that may be made by the High Court on the hearing of such an appeal include (but are not limited to) an order affirming or setting aside the decision of the Appeals Tribunal, or an order remitting the case to be heard and decided again by that Tribunal (either with or without the hearing of further evidence) in accordance with directions. The determination of the High Court on the hearing of such an appeal is final, except that a party to the appeal may apply to the Supreme Court to review the determination on a question of law (but only with the leave of either of those courts).

10.061 Section 57AM provides that, where there is an appeal under s 57AK, this does not affect the operation of the decision appealed against, or prevent the taking of action to implement the decision, unless the High Court otherwise orders.

Westraven Finance Ltd

10.062 The Appeals Tribunal has heard one case to date: *In the matter of Part VIIA of the Central Bank Act 1942 Westraven Finance Ltd t/a Brinkspeed – and the Irish Financial Services Regulatory Authority.*[52] Westraven Finance Ltd (Westraven) applied to the Irish Financial Services Regulatory Authority under s 30 of the Central Bank Act 1997 (as inserted by s 27 of the Central Bank and Financial Services Authority of Ireland Act 2004) for an authorisation to carry on a money transmission business. The

---

48   *Firma Foto-Frost v Hauptzollamt Lübeck Ost* Case C-314/85, ECR 4199, ECJ 1987.

49   *Broekmeulen v Huisarts Registratie Commissie* Case C-246/80 [1981] ECR 2311.

50   *Dorsch Consult v Bundesbaugesellschaft Berlin* Case C-54/96 [1997] ECR I–4961.

51   *Doris Salzmann* Case C–178/99 [2001] ECR I 4421.

52   *In the matter of Part VIIA of the Central Bank Act 1942 Westraven Finance Ltd t/a Brinkspeed – and the Irish Financial Services Regulatory Authority*, Irish Financial Services Appeal Tribunal, 24/25 July 2007. Decision delivered 31 August 2007.

application was refused under s 31 of the 1997 Act. Westraven appealed the decision to the Irish Financial Services Appeals Tribunal (the Appeals Tribunal). The Appeals Tribunal, having considered the arguments advanced and the evidence adduced, decided to affirm the decision of the Financial Regulator. At the conclusion of the hearing, the Appeals Tribunal reserved its decision.

It decided that under Pt VIIA, s 57Z of the Central Bank Act 1942 (as inserted by s 28 of the 2003 Act, as amended in turn by s 14 of the 2004 Act), the power of the Appeals Tribunal on the then present appeal was either:

(i)   to affirm the decision of the Financial Regulator; or

(ii) to remit the matter concerned for reconsideration by the Regulatory Authority, together with any recommendation or direction of the Appeals Tribunal as to what aspect of the matter should be reconsidered.

10.063 The assessment and investigation of the application for authorisation made by Westraven gave rise to a multiplicity of issues. Westraven's grounds of appeal under three headings, were:

(i)   alleged want of fairness including bias on the part of the Financial Regulator or his officers and unfair procedures adopted by the Financial Regulator;

(ii) alleged errors made by the Financial Regulator in his findings or assessment in relation to the business of the Appellant and the documents maintained in relation to it; and

(iii) the failure of the Financial Regulator to recognise that the errors which did occur related to past events which had been or could be rectified.

10.064 The Tribunal considered the applicant had omitted important material from the application for an authorisation. That material consisted of the following:

(i)   The omission in the application of any reference to the formation (and subsequent striking off) of Westraven Finance (UK) Ltd.

(ii) The trade (including a money transmission business) carried on by Westraven in Germany. The carrying on of the money transmission business in Germany without authorisation in that jurisdiction was illegal and Westraven had no authorisation. The illegal activities of Westraven resulted in the police in Germany searching the premises from which Westraven carried on business in Aachen.

(iii) The suspension of the commercial relationship between Westraven and Travelex (because Westraven had underpaid Travelex a sum of €72,000).

The Tribunal was satisfied that the failure of Westraven to disclose activities in which it engaged in Germany was misleading. In the opinion of the Appeals Tribunal, the application was properly rejected by the Financial Regulator and the Appeals Tribunal affirmed that decision.

The Appeals Tribunal ordered the applicant to make a contribution of €20,000 in respect of the respondent's costs. The Appeals Tribunal directed that the order was not to be enforced unless the applicant instituted proceedings to review the decision whether by way of appeal or otherwise. No review proceedings were instituted.

COMPETITION

10.065 There is no appeal from a decision of the Competition Authority to an appeal panel.

The Competition Act 2002 provides for an appeal to the High Court against a determination of the Authority to block a merger. In addition, s 15 of the Competition Act makes specific provision for appeal to the High Court of a decision by the Competition Authority to grant a declaration (similar to a block exemption under European law) under s 4(3) of the Competition Act.

By virtue of s 4(3), the Authority may declare in writing that in its opinion a specified category of agreements, decisions or concerted practices complies with the conditions referred to in s 4(5). Such a declaration may be revoked by the Authority if it is of the opinion that the category no longer complies with the conditions set out in s 4(5). These conditions are that the agreement, decision or concerted practice, or category of agreement, decision or concerted practice, having regard to all relevant market conditions, contributes to improving the production or distribution of goods or provision of services or to promoting technical or economic progress, while allowing consumers a fair share of the resulting benefit and does not:

    (i)   impose on the undertakings concerned terms which are not indispensable to the attainment of those objectives, or

    (ii)   afford undertakings the possibility of eliminating competition in respect of a substantial part of the products or services in question.

10.066 Any undertaking or association of undertakings concerned or any other person aggrieved by the making of the particular declaration may appeal to the High Court pursuant to s 15 against the making of a declaration under s 4(3). Such an appeal must be made to the High Court within 28 days of the publication of the declaration or such longer period as the High Court may specify. On the hearing of an appeal, the High Court may confirm, amend or annul the declaration concerned. Importantly, the High Court may by order provide that, pending the hearing and determination of an appeal in relation to a declaration, the declaration shall not have effect for the purposes of s 4(2) of the Act; that is to say, the agreement may not benefit from the protection of the declaration by the Authority that it does not offend the Act.

10.067 An appeal may be made to the High Court against a determination of the Authority under paras (b) or (c) of s 22(3). These are, respectively, decisions to oppose a merger or to allow it subject to conditions. The Competition Act provides no right of appeal against a decision to clear a merger, however, the remedy of judicial review could be availed of. It is only the parties to the merger who can avail of the right of the appeal. An appeal must be made within one month after the date on which the undertaking is informed by the Competition Authority of the determination concerned.

Section 24 provides for a full appeal in that any issue of fact or law concerning the determination may be the subject of an appeal under this section. However, with respect to an issue of fact, the High Court, on the hearing of the appeal, may not receive evidence by way of testimony of any witness and shall presume, unless it considers it unreasonable to do so, that any matters accepted or found to be fact by the

Authority in exercising its powers in assessing the merger application were correctly accepted or found.

That said, the High Court, on the hearing of an appeal under s 24, may receive evidence by way of the testimony of one or more witnesses, if it considers it was unreasonable for the Authority to have accepted or found as a fact any matter concerned. The procedure for appeals is accelerated, in that the High Court should, by virtue of s 24(6) of the Competition Act 2002, in so far as it is practicable, hear and determine an appeal within two months after the date on which the appeal is made to it.

10.068 On the hearing of an appeal under s 24, the High Court may, as it thinks fit:

(i)   annul the determination concerned;

(ii) confirm the determination concerned; or

(iii) confirm the determination concerned subject to such modifications as the court determines and specifies in its decision.

10.069 There is a further appeal to the Supreme Court against a decision of the High Court, however, only on a point of law. There is currently an appeal in place against a decision of the Authority to block a merger. Issues such as the appropriate standard of review will no doubt fall to be considered in the context of this appeal.[53]

10.070 Appeals from civil and criminal actions taken by the Competition Authority (or by the DPP or by ComReg) may be made under the normal rules of civil and criminal procedure. These are not, of course, appeals from decisions of the Authority itself, but from decisions of the relevant court.

APPEAL PANELS, SPECIALIST STANDING APPEAL PANEL OR THE COURT?

10.071 From an Irish perspective, it is clear there is no particular set of principles or doctrine that has been uniformly applied in the design of various appeal panels. This much is clear from a perusal of the legislation applicable to some of the major utility Regulators together with the Competition Authority. The appeal panels that are envisaged are transitory groups with various powers, some limited, some not. The procedures by which they operate are not uniform. This flexibility is perceived as a benefit by some but not by others. The lack of clarity over the scope of review and standard of review further complicates proceedings and can lead to further delay until these issues are resolved. There is a strong criticism of such bodies for lending themselves to strategic appeals to delay the application of regulation. Certainly, with respect to the gas and electricity markets, the loss, variation or grant of the appropriate licence is of such significance to the undertaking and its competitors as to make recourse to the courts almost inevitable in order to finalise a dispute. In addition, the speed of resolution of the matters and the cost involved varies little with full appeals to

---

53   2008 145 MCA *RYE Investments Ltd v Competition Authority* – case subsequent to the Competition Authority's decision to block a proposed acquisition by Kerry Group plc of Breeo Foods Ltd and Breeo Brands Ltd, dated 28 August 2008 M/08/009.

the High Court and, in light of the speed of resolution of matters before the Commercial Court, an appeal panel may indeed prove to be slower than the High Court.

10.072 There has been little analysis of sectoral appeal panels in Ireland due to their novelty. However, there has been comment on the use of tribunals, which are related bodies, in that both are substitutes for the courts. As Hogan and Morgan have stated,[54] since most Irish tribunals are of the court-substitute type, could their functions not simply have been vested in a court of the appropriate level? They posit that the short answer is that the growth of tribunals is largely due to the failure of the legal system to respond in a flexible manner to new challenges. According to them, it is usually agreed that, by comparison with courts, tribunals carry certain practical advantages. But if an appeal panel is the High Court in disguise, why pretend it is anything else? If, in the quest for finality and authority, what is required is a court, should it not be possible to just go to court in the first place?

10.073 This state of affairs may have led the legislature in more recent times to disband the appeal panels in respect of electronic communications, where there is now a right of appeal to the High Court. In the Broadcasting Bill 2008, the right of appeal rests to the High Court rather than to an appeal panel. This may reflect the fact that appeal panels are no longer in vogue and that there is a trend towards appeals to the High Court. It may be that an appeal panel would be justified if it did in fact allow for 'faster, more cost effective and more knowledgeable resolution of disputes than current court procedures'.[55]

In the interests of expediency, appeals could go to the Commercial Court or a specialist division of the High Court such as the competition division. In the alternative, a specialist appeal panel could be established and utilised across all regulated sectors similar to the UK Competition Appeal Tribunal.

UK Competition Appeal Tribunal

10.074 There is a fundamental difference between the enforcement of competition law in Ireland and in the United Kingdom. The UK has a Competition Appeal Tribunal (CAT), a standing organisation that is very much like a court. It takes appeals from all the major utility Regulators in a uniform manner. It may strike the observer as being like a divisional sitting of the High Court, with the chairman sitting with two specialists in the particular area as appropriate. Its decision-making powers are very broad and final. It may award damages or impose penalties. The members of the panel of chairmen are judges of the Chancery Division of the High Court and other senior

---

54   Hogan and Morgan, *Administrative Law in Ireland* (3rd edn, Thomson Round Hall, 1998), p 259.

55   Commission for Communication Regulation paper, 'Future Regulation of Electronic Communications Networks and Services – ComReg submission on draft Legislation' 31 January 2003.

lawyers.[56] Its president is a judge of the Chancery Division of the High Court; in this way, it has implicitly as much authority as any appeal panel could hope to have.

There is a major difference between Ireland and the UK. In Ireland only courts may award damages against, or fine, a company for breach of competition law. In the UK an administrative body such as the Office of Fair Trade (OFT) or the CAT may do so. The CAT may also do so in its guise as the UK 'super appeal panel' for regulatory decisions. For comparative purposes, it is useful, briefly, to discuss some aspects of the UK CAT.

10.075 The CAT may hear appeals from decisions of the OFT and other Regulators made under the Competition Act 1998[57] and the Enterprise Act 2002. By contrast (generally)[58] with Ireland, most UK Regulators have competition powers in their own sector. In brief, the competition authorities whose decisions may be appealed to the CAT are: the OFT, the Civil Aviation Authority (CAA), the Competition Commission, the Office of Communications (Ofcom), the Office for the Regulation of Electricity and Gas (OFREG – NI), the Office of Gas and Electricity Markets (Ofgem), the Office of Water Services (Ofwat) and the Office of the Rail Regulator (ORR).

10.076 The CAT may also hear applications for review of decisions of the Competition Commission, OFT or Secretary of State on merger cases falling under Pt 3 of the Enterprise Act 2002 and market investigations falling under Pt 4. It may hear appeals from decisions of the Competition Commission imposing penalties under s 110 of the Enterprise Act 2002. In addition, it hears appeals under the Communications Act 2003 against decisions by Ofcom or the Secretary of State under Pt 2 of the Act (networks, services and the radio spectrum) or under the Wireless Telegraphy Acts 1949 or 1998, or against decisions by Ofcom exercising its functions in respect of broadcasting under the Broadcasting Acts 1990 and 1996 and the Communications Act 2003. It also hears appeals of decisions by Ofcom in respect of its exercise of its competition law powers. Furthermore, it hears appeals against decisions of the OFT in application of the provisions of arts 81 and 82 of the EC Treaty.

10.077 The CAT has wide powers in determining appeals and may:

(i)   confirm or set aside all or part of the decision;

(ii) remit the matter to the OFT (or the relevant Regulator);

(iii) impose, revoke or vary the amount of the penalty;

(iv) grant or cancel an individual exemption or vary any condition or obligation which relates to an exemption;

(v)   give such directions, or take such other steps, as the OFT (or sectoral Regulator) could have given or taken; or

---

56   Although the Enterprise Act 2002, Sch 2 sets out that the panel of chairmen has to comprise solicitors or barristers with at least seven years' standing, in practice, all are judges with one exception – see http://www.catribunal.org.uk.

57   See UK Competition Act, s 46(3).

58   It should be noted that ComReg has competition powers in respect of electronic communications.

(vi) make any other decision which the OFT (or sectoral Regulator) could have made.

10.078 In addition, under s 47A of the Competition Act 1998 (inserted by s 18 of the Enterprise Act 2002), any person who has suffered loss or damage as a result of an infringement of either UK or European Community competition law may bring a claim for damages or for a sum of money before the CAT in respect of that loss or damage. Under s 49 of the Competition Act (as amended by para 4, Sch 5 of the Enterprise Act) a further appeal lies from decisions of the CAT either on a point of law or as to the amount of penalty. Any such appeal lies to the Court of Appeal in the UK and Northern Ireland and to the Court of Session in Scotland.

10.079 Consequently, the CAT has effectively the same power within its jurisdiction as the High Court has generally. An obvious question to ask is, why not use the High Court? The answer is that the CAT is a specialist body which has built up the requisite expertise by dealing with appeals from the national regulatory authorities as well as from the OFT and the Competition Commission and cases are heard before a panel consisting of three members: either the President or a member of the panel of chairmen and two ordinary members. The members of the panel of chairmen are judges of the Chancery Division of the High Court and other senior lawyers. The ordinary members have expertise in law and/or related fields. The CAT is thus a specialist judicial body with cross-disciplinary expertise in law, economics, business and accountancy. There is no similar body in Ireland – whether one is desirable is another issue. Access rather than expertise may be the real issue. There is sufficient expertise on the Irish bench for the High Court sitting in division to perform the same role in appropriate cases – if necessary, appointing an expert technical assessor or adviser in appropriate cases.

Advantages of Appeal Panel System

10.080 Hogan and Morgan identify a number of advantages and disadvantages of tribunals such as appeal panels by contrast with the courts.[59]

One advantage of an appeal panel may be that the procedure before an appeal panel is simpler and more flexible than that of a court. Although an appeal panel should not adopt procedures which are unfair or which imperil a just result, many appeal panels are given wide discretion as to their procedures, and particularly whether to depart from the strict rules of evidence. These features, together with the fact that proceedings may in some circumstances be held in private and in a less formal atmosphere than that of a court, arguably may make an appearance before an appeal panel a more attractive proposition.

Furthermore, many appeal panels possess particular expertise. As they are established by Ministers, generally on an *ad hoc* basis, their composition can be tailored to suit the circumstances. For example, a three-person panel may comprise a lawyer, economist and engineer, with a background in the regulated sector, who are able to draw on their expertise.

---

59 Hogan and Morgan, *Administrative Law in Ireland* (3rd edn, Thomson Round Hall, 1998), pp 259–263.

In addition, tribunals are supposedly quicker and cheaper for all the parties concerned. It has been argued in their favour that it is usually unnecessary for lawyers to appear on behalf of interested parties. However, the experience of appeal panels to date is that this is not the case and, in fact, expert evidence is also often proffered to a panel, particularly in the form of economists' expert reports.

10.081 Appeal panels may take a less rigid attitude to questions of statutory interpretation and to precedent.[60] This can be a blessing as well as a curse. However, where points of law are concerned, tribunals must apply the law, employing the standard principles of statutory interpretation and following the decisions of the High Court and Supreme Court.

Disadvantages of Appeal Panel System

10.082 Against these advantages, the question of allocating certain judicial functions to bodies such as appeal panels rather than courts has been questioned by Mr Justice Walsh. Writing extra-judicially in the context of the work of An Bord Uchtála (The Adoption Board), the judge commented that:

> [C]ertain aspects of family law are of such fundamental importance, such as those cases which can alter the legal status of a person, that they should be decided in the High Court ... This prompts one to question the wisdom or desirability of permitting legal adoptions to take effect without judicial intervention or confirmation ... [the powers of An Bord Uchtála] are limited. It cannot decide – questions concerning the validity of the marriage of couples who seek to adopt. Yet if adoption is approved for a couple whose marriage is not a valid subsisting marriage in the eyes of the State the resulting invalidity of the adoption may not be discovered until it is too late to avoid ... the inevitable legal consequences.[61]

What Mr Justice Walsh is warning against here is misjudgement on profound Constitutional rights of the citizen by non-judicial bodies, given that the courts are the guardians of the Constitution. In answer to that concern, one may suggest that it is unlikely that an appeal panel will be weighed down in such a manner, mainly due to the fact that in reality the more likely appellants are corporations who do not enjoy the personal rights of the citizen. That said, they do enjoy the right to fair procedures and property rights. Thus appeal panels are duty bound to act fairly and respect due process and constitutional justice.

10.083 Webster J indicated another range of difficulties in considering prison disciplinary tribunals in *R v Home Secretary ex p Tarrant*.[62] In brief, it appears his argument was that the more a body such as an appeal panel had to deal with questions of law and fair procedures, the less suited that body was to the task which was more in

---

60 Hogan and Morgan, *Administrative Law in Ireland* (3rd edn, Thomson Round Hall, 1998), pp 260–262.

61 In the forward to Binchy, *A casebook on Irish Family Law* (1984, Butterworths), p vii.

62 *R v Home Secretary ex p Tarrant* [1995] QB 251.

the realm of the courts.[63] This view is eminently sensible. The policy reason for an appeal panel is to have technical questions of fact – such as methodology, complex calculations and expert theoretical approaches – questioned and tested before a panel personally qualified by its own professional expertise to understand and assess them. Such an assessment may well be unforthcoming from a judge, who by contrast is eminently more suited to deciding questions of law and procedure. Therein lies the desired division of labour between the courts and appeal panels.

10.084 In respect of the wisdom of establishing a panel to deal with electronic communications appeals, ComReg considered the OECD view and the European Commission's view.[64]

The OECD has analysed the use of an appeal panel in Denmark and noted:

> [I]n practice, the existence of the Telecommunications Complaints Board in Denmark has served to weaken the regulatory authority and independence of the NTA, and has led to significant delays in the implementation of regulatory decisions. This has had a negative consequence for the development of competition in the Danish telecommunications market.

The OECD also noted the existence of what lawyers would refer to as tactical appeals and what economists would refer to as regulatory gaming: 'The existence of the Board has provided a relatively easy and cheap way to delay implementation of key decisions aimed at fostering competition.'

Having a third body, in addition to the Regulator applying and the courts interpreting relevant legislation, leads to delay. In this regard, the OECD stated:

> the Telecommunications Complaints Board has caused delays in all the regulatory issues that were filed to the Board ... such a delay is a large burden for a rapidly evolving market such as the telecommunications sector, and has resulted in imposing a market disadvantage to new entrants in many cases.

10.085 The European Commission's *7th Report on the Implementation of the Telecommunications Regulatory Package* (2001) in para 4.2.1 identified the tendency of operators in Ireland to use appeal procedures strategically: 'It appears that incumbents have, as a matter of strategy, continued the practice of appealing systematically against NRA decisions.'

10.086 The former Department of Public Enterprise's review[65] of appeal mechanisms underlined the risk of second-guessing the Regulator. The Department review noted at para 4.1.2 of the report:

> There is the danger that provision for the appeal of a regulatory decision on its merits can give rise to a situation where so many decisions of the Regulator are referred

---

63   See Hogan and Morgan, *Administrative Law in Ireland* (3rd edn, Thomson Round Hall, 1998), p 263.

64   The following points are made in the Commission for Communication Regulation's paper of 31 January 2003 in Appendix I – extracts of views from official reports of potential drawbacks of appeal panels – Commission for Communication Regulation Document No 3/12, 31 January 2003, 'The future Regulation of Electronic Communication Networks and Services.'

65   *Governance and Accountability in the Regulatory Process: Policy Proposals March 2000.*

onward to the appeal body for second consideration that the appeal body becomes, in effect, the real Regulator for the sector in question. Appeals on merit could also be used as a delaying tactic to postpone the effective implementation of Regulators' decisions.

10.087 Appeals panels may not always have the necessary expertise, particularly where they are not a standing appeals panel but rather are constituted on an *ad hoc* basis.

10.088 Since an appeals panel is not a court, it does not have the same certainty of procedures which courts apply and follow. In addition, the difference between the various appeals bodies mean that different procedures are followed and different standards of review and scopes of review are applied.

10.089 Appeals panel systems are often unable to grant urgent stays, injunctive relief or interim measures. This can lead to a duplication of actions whereby the appellants also need to invoke the jurisdiction of the court for urgent relief via judicial review as well as appealing the decision to the appeal panel. Where appeals panels do have the power to grant suspension, pending the hearing of an appeal, this may be used tactically by appellants to frustrate the impact of regulation.

10.090 The fact that judicial review and an appeal mechanism are not mutually exclusive may give rise to an intricate web of related proceedings. Since the appeals panel is not a court, there is a lack of finality with its decision-making, given the right to judicially review both the underlying decision of the Regulator as well as that of the appeals panel. This can lead to further delay in the process.

Direct Recourse to the Courts

10.091 It has been considered whether it would be best to have a right of appeal straight to a general court or to a specialist court or, indeed, to a general court supplemented by expert assessors.[66] Regulatory appeals could be (and have been) dealt with by the Commercial Court, which, due to its efficient use of case management and accelerated court procedures, is often a swifter route than an appeals panel. Having a direct route of appeal to the Commercial Court could remove the additional layer of regulation that is the appeal body and could ensure the swift resolution of an appeal.

10.092 Under ord 63A of the Rules of the Superior Courts, the Commercial List means the list in which proceedings have been entered into. 'Commercial proceedings' mean under r 1(a):

[P]roceedings in respect of any claim or counterclaim, not being a claim or counterclaim for damages for personal injuries, arising from or relating to any one or more of the following:

(i) A business document, business contract or business dispute where the value of the claim or counterclaim is not less than €1 million.

66　See paras **10.98** *et seq* on Better Regulation.

(ii) The determination of any question of construction arising in respect of a business document or business contract where the value of the transaction the subject matter thereof is not less than €1 million;

Rule 1(b) provides that even if a case does not fall within the definition, it is still possible to be admitted onto the list. The test is subjective and will depend on whether the judge considers the case to involve:

proceedings in respect of any other claim or counterclaim, not being a claim or counterclaim for damages for personal injuries, which the Judge of the Commercial List, having regard to the commercial and any other aspect thereof, considers appropriate for entry in the Commercial List.

Order 63A, r 1(g) of the Rules of the Superior Courts provides that the term 'commercial proceedings' includes:

any appeal from, or application for judicial review of, a decision or a determination made or a direction given by a person or body authorised by statute to make such decisions or determinations or given such direction, where the Judge of the Commercial List considers that the appeal or application is, having regard to the commercial or any other aspect thereof, appropriate for entry in the Commercial List.

10.093 Order 84C deals with statutory appeals[67] and does make reference to r 4(2) of ord 63A to allow for an application to the judge of the Commercial List for an order entering the appeal as proceedings in the commercial list. *Eircom v ComReg*,[68] which was a regulatory appeal, was admitted to the Commercial List of the High Court. It is arguable that matters which are mainly administrative law or constitutional in nature, but to which a commercial issue is tagged on, may not be appropriate for the Commercial List. No doubt each case will be considered on its own facts. Cases may also be transferred out of the Commercial List, where it is just or equitable to do so.

10.094 It should be noted that even where litigation falls within the definition of commercial proceedings, there is no automatic entry onto the Commercial List. Cases are admitted onto the Commercial List on application to the judge in charge of the list. Alternatively, ords 63A, 84 and 84C could be amended to explicitly provide that all

---

67 Order 84B, which is contained in the same statutory instrument as ord 84C (namely SI 14/2007), provides for rules of procedure relating to compliance actions relating to enactments by relevant authorities such as sector Regulators. Order 84B provides at r 1(2): 'Where any enactment provides for an appeal to be made to the High Court or to a judge of the High Court from a decision or determination made or direction given by a person or body, other than a court, which person or body is authorised by any enactment to make such decision or determination or give such direction (in this Order referred to as "the deciding body"), and provision for the procedure applicable is not made either by the enactment concerned or by another Order of these Rules, the procedure set out in the following rules of this Order shall apply, subject to any requirement of the relevant enactment. Rule 10 provides 'Where the Court considers it appropriate having regard to the nature of the proceedings, it may adjourn the proceedings to enable one or more of the parties to make an application pursuant to rule 4(2) of Order 63A to the Judge of the Commercial List for an order entering the appeal as proceedings in the Commercial List.'

68 *Eircom v ComReg* HC, Record No 2008/110MCA.

administrative proceedings relating to the regulated sectors could be processed through the Commercial Court.

10.095 In the alternative, the competition division of the High Court hears competition appeals and has competition law expertise. Rule 24(5) and ord 63B contain the Competition List Rules. In order for litigation to get onto the Competition List, it must fall within the definition of 'competition proceedings'. This involves:

   (i)   private party civil actions under s 14(1) of the Competition Act 2002;

   (ii)   proceedings in exercise of a right of action conferred on the Authority under s 14(2) of the Act;

   (iii)   an appeal against a declaration of the Authority under s 4(3);

   (iv)   an appeal against a determination of the Authority in respect of its merger control decisions;

   (v)   proceedings for judicial review of a decision of the authority;

   (vi)   proceedings seeking to apply arts 81, 82, 86, 87 or 88 of the EC Treaty;

   (v)   proceedings related to restraint of trade; or

   (vi)   proceedings which concern the application of a provision of the Competition Act.

The Competition List Rules allow the court to appoint its own expert, an assessor to assist it in proceedings. This process is to be recommended to any court hearing regulatory appeals. Although, of course, both sides will no doubt each present evidence of independent expert witnesses, it could be beneficial for the court to have its own independent assessor.[69] The High Court did this in *Competition Authority v O'Regan*,[70] in which Kearns J explained the remit of the assessor as follows:

> It was agreed that the expert thus appointed should attend so much of the hearing and submissions as might be necessary to assist the court, both then and afterwards, in properly understanding and clarifying, where necessary, the economic evidence given so as to enable the court to discharge its obligation to carry out a proper economic analysis in the case. As part of this remit, the court confirmed that if the assessor, in relation to any significant point of economic evidence, expressed or offered an opinion which was contrary to any initial assessment or preliminary view taken by the court, or put forward a view which had not been addressed in the submissions of the parties, then the court would in such circumstances reconvene to hear further submissions from the parties on any such view or opinion. Any decision or judgment

69 Communications Regulation Act 2002, s 46B allows for opinions of expert witnesses and provides: '(1) In civil or criminal proceedings under this Act or a related enactment, the opinion of any witness who appears to the court to possess the appropriate qualifications or experience about the matter to which the witness's evidence relates is admissible in evidence of matters that call for expertise or special knowledge relevant to the proceedings. (2) A court that admits evidence under subsection (1) may, if it is of the opinion that it is in the interests of justice to do so, direct that the use of the evidence is to be limited to specified purposes only.'

70 *Competition Authority v O'Regan* [2007] 2 ILRM 161.

on any portion of the economic evidence would at all times remain the decision of the court and not the assessor.

The Competition Rules allow for observations to be submitted by the Competition Authority as *amicus curiae.*

Order 63B, which deals with competition cases, could be amended to include regulatory appeals, which frequently involve similar concepts as competition law cases, such as rights of access or discriminatory treatment by undertakings in a dominant position.

10.096 There may be a reluctance on the part of judges to be involved in the implementation of politically made decisions about economic matters, absent the existence of a manifest error or an error which goes to the root of the decision.

Due to the doctrine of the separation of powers and the independence of the judiciary, however, the court may not wish to become involved in regulatory decision-making or substituting its decision for that of the Regulator except in cases of *ultra vires, mal fides* or irrationality. However, in this manner a full right of appeal on the merits of a case would be limited to a scope similar to that of judicial review.

10.097 The Bar Council, in its submission to the consultation paper on regulatory appeals published by the Better Regulation Appeals sub-group,[71] considered the jurisprudence of the Irish courts in relation to regulatory appeals. Historically, it transpires that the Irish courts engaged in a full merits-based review in respect of appeals from administrative bodies.[72] A change in attitude occurred in *MJ Gleeson v Competition Authority*[73] where the High Court refused to entertain a right of appeal as a *de novo* appeal. The court relied on the concept of curial deference and concluded that it was obliged to defer to the Regulator and would only second guess its findings where it could be said to have committed a serious or significant error that went to the root of the decision made. This approach was upheld by the Supreme Court in *Orange v Director of Telecommunications (No 2)*,[74] and in the High Court in *Carrigdale v Comptroller of Patents*[75] and *Henry Denny & Sons (Ireland) Ltd v Minister for Social Welfare,* in which case CJ Hamilton commented:

> [T]he courts should be slow to interfere with the decisions of expert administrative tribunals. Where conclusions are based upon an identifiable error of law or an unsustainable finding of fact by a tribunal such conclusions must be corrected. Otherwise it should be recognised that tribunals which have been given statutory tasks to perform and exercise their functions, as is now usually the case, with a high degree of expertise and provide coherent and balanced judgments on the evidence and

---

71　Bar Council of Ireland Submission on Regulatory Appeals, dated 31 October 2006.

72　*Philadelphia Storage Batteries v Controller of Industrial and Commercial Property and NV Philips' Gloeilampenfabrieken* [1935] IR 575; *Dunne v Minister for Fisheries* [1984] IR 230, Costello J; *Balkan Tours v Minister for Communications* [1988] ILRM 1010, Lynch J.

73　*MJ Gleeson v Competition Authority* [1999] 2 ILRM 401.

74　*Orange v Director of Telecommunications (No 2)* [2000] 4 IR 159 Keane J.

75　*Carrigdale v Comptroller of Patents* [2004] 2 ILRM 401.

arguments heard by them it should not be necessary for the courts to review their decisions by way of appeal or judicial review.[76]

Although the Bar Council is of the view that the Irish courts do not wish to review decisions of regulatory bodies because it 'invites the Court to run too close to its constitutional boundaries', it may be, in fact, that were the courts to hear both appeals and judicial review, there would be little difference in practice between the standards of review. This may be particularly so in the case of an appeal utilising the *Gleeson*[77] standard (serious or significant error that went to the root of the decision made) or the *Ulster Bank*[78] test of 'vitiated by a serious and significant error or a series of such errors' and the standard of judicial review outlined in *SIAC*[79] ('manifest error').

BETTER REGULATION

10.098 The Department of the Taoiseach published a white paper on Better Regulation in January 2004. As part of this white paper,[80] the development of an improved approach to regulatory appeals was proposed. Also considered was whether the same appeal panel and the same approach could be used for each sector, and whether appeals should be on merit and the options that should be available to the appeal panel. For example, should the appeal panel be able to substitute its decision for the decision reached by the Regulator or should it merely have the power to remit the matter back to the Regulator? It was also suggested that, given the availability of an appeal body, consideration should be given to recourse to the courts being limited to points of law. The issue of the use of the appeals structure in a vexatious or delaying manner was highlighted, together with what disincentives could be introduced in this regard, such as regarding costs. It was proposed that the issue of whether the decision of the Regulator could stand during the appeal process should be considered and consulted upon. It was also proposed that the courts service was to continue to improve and streamline case management practices in cases relating to sectoral regulation in order to expedite the process. Expert panels of judges were to be established within the court system to deal with specified cases of competition and sectoral regulation.[81]

10.099 A sub-group of the Better Regulation Group was established to provide recommendations to the Better Regulation Group for an improved approach to the appeal of Regulators' decisions. It engaged in a public consultation on regulatory appeals and focused on six sectoral regulatory authorities: ComReg, CAR, CER, the Competition Authority, the Financial Regulator and the Commission for Taxi Regulation. The consultation closed at the end of October 2006. The sub-group produced a report on the matter to the government. The Report of Submissions on

---

76   *Henry Denny & Sons (Ireland) Ltd v Minister for Social Welfare* [1998] 1 IR 34 at 37.

77   *MJ Gleeson v Competition Authority* [1999] 2 ILRM 401.

78   *Ulster Bank v Financial Ombudsman & McCarren* [2006] IEHC 323.

79   *SIAC v Mayo County Council* [2002] 3 IR 148.

80   White Paper on Regulating Better (January 2004), p 44 – available at http:// www.betterregulation.ie.

81   White Paper on Regulating Better (January 2004), p 46.

Regulatory Appeals[82] contains an overview of the various responses received. Submissions received were critical of the appeals panels in terms of the delay and the lack of clarity surrounding the standard of review and the scope of review.

10.100 The Report of Submissions addressed whether the appeals body or the court, in the case of an appeal, should be able to replace the decision of a Regulator with one of its own, or whether it should simply have the power to remit the decision back to the Regulator for reconsideration. The current practice in this regard is not uniform throughout the various sectors and so it is no surprise that the respondents' views were divergent in this regard. Many considered that the appeals body should not have the power to replace a decision of the Regulator and that the power to remit the decision back to the Regulator should be sufficient because of concerns that the appeal body (or court) would otherwise become the *de facto* Regulator. Some respondents did, however, suggest that the High Court should retain the power to substitute its decision for a decision which it quashes on an error of law, if the court is satisfied that there would only have been one decision that could be reached in that instance.

10.101 Suspension was also considered as part of this report and, in particular, whether decisions should be suspended pending the hearing of an appeal.[83] In general, it was considered that it should be possible to suspend or stay decisions until an appeal is heard. One respondent was of the view that the only circumstance in which suspension should not be granted is where damages would be an adequate remedy. Another view was that there should be no damages unless the overturned decision was one that no reasonable regulatory body could have reached. Another respondent was of the view that the decision should stand unless three conditions were met:

    (i)   irredeemable harm would come from letting the decision stand;

    (ii)   no other postponed remedy would adequately address the resulting harm; and

    (iii)   the balance of convenience made it necessary.

Another respondent suggested that the decision should stand unless the appellant could demonstrate that it had a *prima facie* case and that it would suffer irreparable harm if the decision was implemented.

10.102 The report highlighted the inconsistency in the various appeals processes in relation to what decisions could be appealed and the divergences in the mechanisms in place to hear appeals. Most respondents did consider that there should be a mechanism for appealing regulatory decisions, as well as the right to seek judicial review. The majority also considered that a merits-based appeal should be available for regulatory decisions. It was also considered that the appeals body should have specialist expertise at its disposal, either by way of it being a standing specialist multisectoral appeals panel (similar to the UK CAT) or a (specialist) court with access to expert assessors (similar to the Competition Division of the High Court).

---

82   http://www.betterregulation.ie.

83   Report of Submissions on Regulatory Appeals, p 32 – http://www.betterregulation.ie.

CONCLUSION

10.103 Oversight and accountability of decisions made by Regulators is essential, particularly so when those decisions can have a significant impact on their addressees. Recourse to a high-quality and expedient appellate body is therefore vital. This role may be effectively carried out by a court with, if required, access to an expert assessor, or by a specialist standing multisectoral appeal body (similar to the CAT in the UK). Where the role is carried out by various *ad hoc* appellate bodies which need to be constituted on a case-by-case basis together with, in some instances, the courts, there are divergent standards of review and scopes of review applied which leads to a lack of consistency in approach as between sectors, and sometimes even within the same sector.[84] Even where suspension is available before appeal panels, the delay in constituting *ad hoc* appeal panels may force parties to apply to the courts for urgent injunctive relief. In addition, due to the decision of the appeal body, as well as the underlying decision of the Regulator both being subject to judicial review, and the fact that judicial review and recourse to appeal are not mutually exclusive, this leads to a 'witches' brew' of legal issues and delay in the decision-making process, which reduces legal certainty for all stakeholders.

---

84 For example, the Electronic Communications Appeal Panel ECAP, when it was established, was not bound by the approach it adopted in previous decisions.

Chapter 11

JUDICIAL REVIEW

INTRODUCTION

11.001 Judicial review is the basic procedural mechanism by which the High Court scrutinises public bodies in the exercise of public law functions. Public law bodies include the Central Bank, the Financial Services Regulator, the Competition Authority, the Commissions for Aviation, Communications and Energy Regulation and the Broadcasting Authority, all of which have been discussed in this book.[1] The High Court intervenes to quash, prevent, require or declare as appropriate. Intervention takes place not because the court disagrees with a merits judgment, but rather so as to right a recognisable wrong, whether unlawfulness, unreasonableness, unfairness or a procedural issue.[2] This chapter attempts to introduce the basic principles of judicial review as one might expect to encounter in a case involving the decision of a regulatory body.

11.002 In Ireland, standard judicial review procedure is set out in Ord 84 of the Rules of the Superior Courts 1986.[3] Rule 18 identifies the main orders that may be sought:

   (i)   *certiorari* – whereby a decision of an inferior court or public body upon review may be quashed either in part or in full;

   (ii) *mandamus* – an order compelling a public person or body to perform a public duty;

---

1   The High Court reviews the determination of other lower courts, Regulators, tribunals and other public authorities, for example county councils and planning authorities.

2   See generally, Hogan and Morgan, *Administrative Law in Ireland* (3rd edn, Round Hall, 1998); de Blacam *Judicial Review* (2nd edn, Tottel Publishing, 2009); Bradley, *Judicial Review in Ireland* (Round Hall, 1999); Fordham, *Judicial Review Handbook* (3rd edn, ART publishing, 2001). As Fordham notes, in a judicial review, the High Court is not being asked to substitute a merits judgment, rather there is some recognised vitiating flaw, for example: (i) error of law; (ii) excess of jurisdiction or power; (iii) failure to ask the right questions; (iv) frustration of the legislative purpose; (v) unjustified interference with European Convention human rights; (vi) breach of EC law; (vii) unreasonableness; (viii) error as to a precedent fact; (ix) error of established and relevant fact; (xi) failure of inquiry; (xii) absence of evidence; (xiii) substantially unfair outcome; (xiv) unjustified breach of a legitimate expectation; (xv) unjustified inconsistency; (xvi) bad faith; (xvii) improper motive; (xviii) unlawful abdication; (xix) improper delegation; (xx) fettering of discretion; (xxi) failure to consider a relevancy; (xxii) considering an irrelevancy; (xxiii) manifestly disproportionate act; (xxiv) breach of express procedural duty; (xxv) basic procedural unfairness; (xxvi) real danger of bias; (xxvii) absence of adequate reasons; (xxviii) relevant external wrong.

3   SI 15/1986.

(iii)   prohibition – an order restraining a public body from exceeding its powers, acting contrary to the rules of natural justice or restraining a public authority in the exercise of their judicial or quasi-judicial powers;

(iv)   a declaration or injunction;[4] and

(v)   *quo warranto* – an order directing an enquiry into the authority by which a person purported to exercise public powers.

In relation to an application for an order of *certiorari*, the court may quash the decision of the public body concerned. Generally, in relation to judicial review concerning regulatory decisions, the court may remit the matter to the public body concerned with a direction to reconsider the decision and make a new decision in accordance with the findings of the court. As stated by Charleton J in *Davy v Financial Services Ombudsman*,[5] '[i]t is not the function of the High Court, however, on judicial review of a decision to substitute its own view as to the merits of any case.'

11.003 The claimant must be a person with sufficient interest,[6] who lacks any suitable alternative remedy for example an appeal. The claimant must obtain the leave of the High Court and must commence proceedings promptly. In judicial review proceedings, all parties must make full and fair disclosure.

Persons seeking to bring judicial review proceedings must act promptly in seeking the High Court's leave to commence such proceedings.[7] Generally leave is sought on an *ex parte* basis, that is to say, the body who took the decision is not on notice of the application to obtain leave of the court to review the decision. The leave stage is a filtering device. Applicants must show that they have a *prima facie* case. If the High Court so directs, the grant of leave to bring judicial review proceedings may act as a stay on the proceedings or decision challenged.

11.004 A feature of certain legislation establishing Regulators is that these Acts may set out specific procedural rules for judicial review that apply to the particular Regulator. For example, an application for leave to bring judicial review proceedings regarding a determination of the Commission for Aviation Regulation may not be

---

4   See *CRA v Minister for Justice Equality and Law Reform* [2007] 2 ILRM 209 (High Court MacMenamin J) for injunctions in judicial review.

5   *Davy v Financial Services Ombudsman* [2008] IEHC 256, *per* Charleton J. In that case the applicants sought to impugn the decision of the Financial Services Ombudsman on the basis that he had misconstrued his powers under the statute and had fallen into unconstitutional procedures.

6   See *Harding v Cork County Council & Anor* (2 May 2008, unreported), SC, Murray CJ, Kearns J and Finnegan J dated 2 May 2008 for a restatement of the law relating to sufficient interest in respect of judicial review

7   Order 84, r 21. 'Promptly' is undefined. However, the application must be brought within six months from the date when grounds for the application arose if one seeks an order of *certiorari* or three months for the other orders mentioned above. As a rule of thumb, it is prudent to take the view that promptly means as quickly as possibly and well within the respective time limits see *Dekra Eireann Teo v Minister for Environment* [2003] 2 IR 27 in this regard.

made *ex parte* but rather on notice and within two months of the date on which notice of the determination was first published.[8]

In that instance, no appeal shall lie from the decision of the High Court to the Supreme Court save with the leave of the High Court, which leave shall only be granted where the High Court or the Supreme Court certifies that the decision involves a point of law of exceptional public importance and that it is desirable in the public interest that an appeal should be taken to the Supreme Court.

11.005 Similarly, s 32 of the Electricity Regulation Act 1999[9] creates a bar against a person questioning in court:

(i) the validity of a decision of the Commission on an application made to it for the grant of a licence or an authorisation or for the modification of a licence or an authorisation;

(ii) a modification by the Commission of a licence or an authorisation;

(iii) a decision of an Appeal Panel under s 30; or

(iv) any decision made by the Commission under the Gas (Amendment) Act 2000, or under regulations made under that Act otherwise than by way of an application for judicial review under Order 84 of the Rules of the Superior Court.

The application must be brought within two months of the date on which the decision was given.

In addition, no appeal shall lie from the decision of the High Court to the Supreme Court save with the leave of the High Court which leave shall only be granted where the High Court certifies that its decision involves a point of law of exceptional public importance and that it is desirable in the public interest that an appeal should be taken to the Supreme Court.

By contrast there are no statutory provisions setting out a particular judicial review procedure for the Broadcasting Authority, the Competition Authority, the Central Bank and Financial Services Authority or the Commission for Communications Regulation.

APPLYING FOR JUDICIAL REVIEW

11.006 An applicant must comply with various rules and go through a filtering process before a court will hear the substantive argument. Accordingly, before considering some of the more salient substantive points that tend to arise in judicial review, it is appropriate to first look at some procedural points touching upon the application for leave to bring judicial review proceedings.

---

8   Aviation Regulation Act 2001, s 38; Electricity Regulation Act 1999, s 32, which also extends to gas by virtue of Gas (Interim) (Regulation) Act 2002, s 5.

9   Section 32 of the 1999 Act, as substituted by s 15 of the Gas (Amendment) Act 2000.

Application for Leave

11.007 Order 84, r 20(1)[10] requires that no application for judicial review shall be made unless the prior leave of the court has been obtained. An application for leave must be made by motion *ex parte* by a notice containing details of the relief sought and the grounds upon which it is sought, together with a grounding affidavit verifying the facts relied upon.[11] Leave will not be granted unless the applicant has a sufficient interest in the matter to which the application relates.[12] If the court grants leave, it may impose such terms as to costs as it thinks fit, and may require an undertaking as to damages.[13]

11.008 The requirement as to leave is a distinctive feature of judicial review procedure. It serves as a filtering device[14] designed to discourage unmeritorious claims that a particular decision is invalid.[15] The standard to be applied when considering whether to grant leave was comprehensively set out by Finlay CJ in *G v Director of Public Prosecutions*:[16]

> An applicant must satisfy the Court in a *prima facie* manner by the facts set out in the affidavit and submissions made in support of his application of the following matters:
>
> (a) That he has sufficient interest in the matter to which the application relates to comply with rule 20(4);
>
> (b) That the facts averred in the affidavit would be sufficient, if proved, to support a sustainable ground for the form of relief sought by judicial review;

---

10   Rules of the Superior Courts 1986 (SI 15/1986).

11   Where material facts are not disclosed the court is entitled to refuse the relief on discretionary grounds: *State (Nicolaou) v An Bord Uchtála* [1966] IR 567; *Cork Corporation v O'Connell* [1982] ILRM 505; *G v DPP* [1994] 1 IR 374 at 378 *per* Finlay CJ. See also *Gordon v DPP* [2002] 2 IR 369, [2003] 1 ILRM 81, and *Akujobi & Anor v Minister for Justice* [2007] 3 IR 603, [2007] 2 ILRM 209.

12   Order 84, r 20(4).

13   In practice, these orders are unlikely to be made – costs are usually reserved and an undertaking as to damages usually only arises in the case of a party seeking a stay or an interim injunction. In addition, it may not be the case that a Regulator would usually be obliged to give such an undertaking, given that this is not the general practice in other jurisdictions such as the UK and Australia.

14   This is one of the reasons given by the House of Lords in *O'Reilly v Mackman* [1983] 2 AC 237 as to why challenges to administrative action brought by plenary summon (in the case of a declaration or injunction) and which thus circumvent the leave requirement should be struck out as an abuse of process.

15   *G v DPP* [1994] 1 IR 374; *O'Reilly v Cassidy (No 1)* [1995] 1 ILRM 306. In *Keane v An Bord Pleanála* (20 June 1995, unreported), HC, Murphy J observed that the burden which the applicant must discharge at this stage is 'modest' and in *TH v DPP* [2006] 3 IR 520 at 533 Fennelly J observed that it was a 'low standard'.

16   *G v DPP* [1994] 1 IR 374.

(c) That on those facts an arguable case in law can be made that the applicant is entitled to the relief which he seeks;

(d) That the application has been made promptly and in any event within the three months or six months time limits provided for in Order 84., r.21(1), or that the court is satisfied that there is a good reason for extending this time limit...;

(e) That the only effective remedy, on the facts established by the applicant, which the applicant would obtain would be an order by way of judicial review or, if there be an alternative remedy, that the application by way of judicial review is on all the facts of the case, a more appropriate method of procedure.[17]

As mentioned above, applications for leave to bring judicial review proceedings against certain Regulators' decisions are on notice. The applicant must also meet the standard required set out above, at a minimum. In addition, it has been said that in such a contested leave application, the applicant must disclose an argument that is 'reasonable', 'arguable' and 'weighty', not 'frivolous' or 'vexatious'.[18]

11.009 In a similar vein, in the case of *Potts v Minister for Defence*,[19] the applicant's case involved a challenge to the statutory framework currently in existence for the summary disposition of charges to be laid against members of the Defence Forces such as the applicant.

In the course of that case, Mr Justice Clarke compared and contrasted the different thresholds for granting leave, depending on whether the application for leave is *ex parte* or on notice to the other side:

> In the ordinary way in an *ex parte* application seeking leave to commence judicial review proceedings the principles applicable to the granting of leave are those set out in the case of *G v DPP* [1994] 1 IR. In such a case an applicant is required to show an arguable case based on stateable grounds in order to obtain such leave from this court.

That said, considering the provisions of both s 50 of the Planning and Development Act 2000 and s 5 of the Illegal Immigrants (Trafficking) Act 2000, Clarke J noted that the statutory cases require that the court, prior to granting leave, must be satisfied that there are substantial grounds for contending that the matter intended to be challenged is invalid or ought to be quashed. He then went on to state that:

> In the jurisprudence of the courts in relation to both the above sections it has been accepted that a higher threshold for the grant of leave is required in such cases. That threshold has been variously described as being equivalent to 'reasonable', 'arguable' and 'weighty' but not 'frivolous' or 'tenuous'. See for example *VZ v Minister for Justice, Equality and Law Reform* [2002] 2 IR 135. It seems to me that the existence of such an established statutory regime in respect of matters where the Oireachtas has determined that leave should only be granted where a more onerous threshold is passed is a matter that needs to be considered in a case such as this.

---

17 Reaffirmed in *DC v DPP* [2005] IESC 77.

18 *VZ v Minister for Justice, Equality and Law Reform* [2002] 2 IR 135.

19 *Potts v Minister for Defence* [2005] 2 ILRM 517, Clarke J.

DISCOVERY

11.010 Discovery is available to parties to a judicial review proceeding. However, this is limited by various factors. Firstly, the facts are generally not the subject of controversy in judicial review proceedings. Secondly, as judicial review is normally concerned with procedure rather than substance, this inevitably will narrow the range of documents which are relevant.[20] Public bodies are under a duty to disclose information to the court upon which they relied. Discovery will not normally be regarded as necessary if the judicial review application is based on procedural impropriety, as ordinarily that can be established without the benefit of discovery.[21] Thirdly, discovery will generally be refused where the applicant has made out no positive case on a particular ground, but where discovery is simply sought 'in the hope of turning up something out of which he could fashion a possible challenge'.[22] If the challenge is based on irrationality or unreasonableness grounds, discovery will not normally be necessary 'because if the decision is clearly wrong it is not necessary to ascertain how it was arrived at.'[23] Discovery in judicial review application is thus generally confined to cases where information is improperly withheld or where there is a relevant and material conflict of fact on the affidavits.[24]

---

20 As Geoghegan J said for the Supreme Court in *Carlow Kilkenny Radio Ltd v Broadcasting Commission of Ireland* [2003] 3 IR 528 at 531: 'It is trite law that judicial review is not concerned with the correctness of a decision, but rather with the way the decision is reached. It follows that the categories of document which a court would consider were necessary to be discovered will be much more confined than if the litigation related to the merits of a case.'

21 *Carlow Kilkenny Radio Ltd v Broadcasting Commission of Ireland* [2003] 3 IR 528 *per* Geoghegan J at p 537.

22 *Re Rooney's Application* [1995] NI 398 at 414–415 *per* Carswell LJ. This point was also expressed by Bingham MR in the Court of Appeal in *R v Health ex parte Hackney LBC* [1994] COD 432, when in dealing with the issue of necessity as regards discovery and production, he said: 'It is not open to a plaintiff in a civil action or to an applicant for judicial review, to make a series of bare unsubstantiated assertions and then call for discovery of documents by the other side in the hope that there may exist documents which will give colour to the assertion that the applicant, or the plaintiff, is otherwise unable to begin to substantiate.' A similar point was expressed by Murray J in *Acquatechnologie Ltd v National Standards Authority of Ireland et al* [2000] IESC 64 when he said that 'an application for discovery must show it is reasonable for the Court to suppose that the documents contain information which may enable the applicant to advance his own case or to damage the case of his adversary. An applicant is not entitled to discovery based on mere speculation or on the basis of what has been traditionally characterised as a fishing expedition' Murray J *nem diss*.

23 *Carlow Kilkenny Radio Ltd v Broadcasting Commission of Ireland* [2003] 3 IR 528 *per* Geoghegan J at p 537.

24 *Carlow Kilkenny Radio Ltd v Broadcasting Commission of Ireland* [2003] 3 IR 528 *per* Geoghegan J at p 538; see also O'Caoimh J's judgment in *Shortt v Dublin City Council* [2003] 2 IR 69.

BARS TO RELIEF

Lack of Good Faith

11.011 A failure to put all relevant material before the court upon making an application for leave may justify the leave order being set aside.[25] In the words of Mr Justice Kelly:

> On any application made *ex parte* the utmost good faith must be observed, and the applicant is under a duty to make a full and fair disclosure of all the relevant facts of which he knows, and where the supporting evidence contains material misstatements of fact or the applicant has failed to make sufficient or candid disclosure, the *ex parte* order may be set aside on that very ground.[26]

The issue of lack of candour on the part of public authorities also may arise which may involve a lower standard then set aside.[27] This obligation extends to counsel and there is a particular obligation to draw the court's attention to materials that would suggest an order of the type sought ought not to be made. It follows that absence of good faith or suppression of material facts in the evidence presented before the court may ground a refusal of relief at the hearing of the application.[28]

11.012 In *Smart Mobile Ltd v Commission for Communication Regulation (ComReg)*,[29] Kelly J again considered the notion of good faith and how it applies to judicial review:

> The relief which is sought by Smart is declaratory. The grant of declaratory relief is a matter for the discretion of the court. I have already refused it. Lest however I am wrong in so doing, I propose to express my views as to whether, even if Smart had made out a case, the court ought as a matter of discretion to grant the declaratory relief sought.
>
> If I had found in favour of Smart on the substantive claim I would have been disinclined to grant the declaration sought. This is because of the behaviour of Smart, both in its dealings with ComReg and with this court. I do not find its methods of trying to solve its problems in the least bit attractive. Part of the tactics set out in the email of Mr Casey, of 29th January 2006, were, in my view, carried into effect. The deliberate attempt to try and "engineer" a situation where ComReg would feel pressured to grant a further extension of time was not an honourable way to behave towards it. Assertions were made in support of this approach which were not correct. That in particular arose in the material which I have already identified from Smart's solicitors of 30th January, 2006.
>
> Whatever about the approach adopted by Smart towards its Regulator, it is an entirely different matter when it comes to dealing with the court. From the outset Smart

---

25 *Gordon v DPP* [2002] 2 IR 369, 375 *per* Fennelly J.

26 *Adams v DPP* [2001] 2 ILRM 401 at 416.

27 *Gordon v DPP* [2002] 2 IR 369.

28 *de Róiste v Minister for Defence* [2001] 1 IR 190, at p 200 *per* Fennelly J, referring to *State (Vozza) v Ó'Floinn* [1957] IR 227; see also *Akujobi & Anor v Minister for Justice* [2007] 3 IR 603, [2007] 2 ILRM 209, at pp 214–18 *per* McMenamin J.

29 *Smart Mobile Ltd v Commission for Communication Regulation* [2006] IEHC 338, Kelly J.

asserted its entitlement to a decree of specific performance. It was never in a position to provide bonds fit for purpose and had not obtained, either from its banks or its partners, the necessary approval in respect of them. It could never have obtained a decree of specific performance and such should not have been claimed.

I deprecate the obtaining of an *ex parte* interim injunction on the basis of sworn material which, in one important respect, was simply untrue. I have already identified that averment earlier in this judgment. I cannot see how such an averment could have come to be made by the deponent. There might be some explanation if the affidavit had to be sworn in great haste. Such was not the case. The application to Laffoy J came at the end of a moratorium of in excess of ten days which gave ample time to ensure that all of the facts deposed to were correct. Whilst an apology was tendered for this during the trial that does not remedy the position.

Apart from the specific performance claim other claims were maintained right up to the trial. Many of them were abandoned or not pursued amidst a number of shifts in position which occurred during the course of the hearing. I do not believe that Smart dealt with ComReg in an appropriate fashion. Neither did it do so with the court.

In such circumstances, even if I had found that there had been some breach of Smart's entitlements I would have required a lot of persuasion before I would have been prepared to grant declaratory relief.

Futile or Moot

11.013 Judicial review is unavailable where it would serve no useful purpose.[30] Circumstances rendering the granting of relief futile may exist at the commencement of the proceedings or come into being later, in which case the application may be refused for being moot.[31] The refusal of relief on this ground is an expression of the overarching principal that people should not go to court for no useful purpose, ie waste the court's time.

Delay

11.014 Some regulatory legislation imposes comparatively short time limits for the challenge of administrative decisions.[32] In delivering the judgment of the court in the case of the *Illegal Immigrants (Trafficking) Act 2000*, Keane CJ drew attention to the public policy in this field:

There is a well established public policy objective that administrative decisions, particularly those taken pursuant to detailed procedures laid down by law, should be capable of being applied or implemented with certainty at as early a date as possible

---

30 *Barry v Fitzpatrick* [1996] 1 ILRM 512 at 515, *per* Hamilton CJ; *Ahern v Minister for Industry and Commerce* (No. 2) [1991] 1 IR 462 at 470 *per* Blayney J; *Minister for Labour v Grace* [1993] 2 IR 53 at 56 *per* O'Hanlon J; *Ryan v Compensation Tribunal* [1997] 1 ILRM 194 at 203 *per* Costello P.

31 See *G v Collins* [2005] 1 ILRM 1 at 13, *per* Hardiman J.

32 For example, the Aviation Regulation Act 2001 and the Electricity Regulation Act 1999.

and that any issue as to their validity should accordingly be determined as soon as possible.[33]

Applicants for judicial review must apply for relief promptly. Order 84, r 21(1) of the Rules of the Superior Courts 1986 provides that, in general, all applications for judicial review, 'shall be made promptly and in any event within three months from the date when the grounds for the application first arose, or six months when the relief sought is *certiorari*.' The court has discretion to extend the time limits where there is a good reason for so doing. It is possible for an applicant who has not moved promptly for judicial review to be defeated on delay grounds;[34] however, this usually would require the respondent to show special factors such as prejudice. That said, 'matters have not reached a stage where an application made within time can be defeated in the absence of some special factor',[35] although litigants who for whatever reason wait until the end of the relevant time period 'are running a serious risk by deferring proceedings for such periods of time.'[36]

11.015 In *Dekra Éireann Teo v Minister for Environment*,[37] the losing party in a public procurement tender commenced proceedings a few weeks after the three-month time period prescribed by the public procurement review rules in Ord 84A.[38] An opposing motion was brought to strike out those review proceedings for non-compliance with the time limits in Ord 84A by SGS Ireland Ltd, who had been awarded the contract. Mr Justice O'Neill, in the High Court, when hearing that motion to strike out, was not satisfied that the applicant had either justified or excused this delay; however, he was also not satisfied that either the Minister or the successful third-party tenderer (SGS Ireland Ltd) had suffered the degree of prejudice as would warrant the striking out of the proceedings. Thus he declined to strike out the Dekra Éireann application for leave and made an order extending the time to make that application in exercise of his discretion. These findings and order were appealed by both Dekra Éireann and the Minister. The Supreme Court allowed the appeal. Denham J in her judgment stated:

> Dekra did not comply with the time limit in Order 84A, rule 4 of the Rules of the Superior Courts. Dekra neither explained nor gave excuses which justified the delay. There were no good reasons given for extending the time limit. I would allow the appeal. I would set aside the order of the High Court granting the extension of time and I would refuse the application by Dekra for judicial review of the public contract in issue.

---

33 Keane CJ in *The matter of Article 26 of the Constitution and the Illegal Immigrants (Trafficking) Bill, 1999* [2000] 2 IR 360 at 394.

34 See, for example, *Twomey v DPP* [2004] 3 IR 232 *per* Quirke J.

35 *O'Brien v Moriarty* [2005] 2 ILRM 321 at 336.

36 *Sandyford Environmental Planning and Road Safety Group Ltd v Dun Laoghaire Rathdown County Council* [2004] IEHC 133, McKechnie J.

37 *Dekra Eireann Teo v Minister for Environment* [2003] 2 IR 27.

38 See Rules of the Superior Courts (No 4), Review of the Award of Public Contracts (SI 374/1998).

In the other judgment in the case, Fennelly J made the following observations, which have resonance for Regulators whose statutes contain special provision regarding judicial review time limits:

> The three-month period from the date when the decision was made, or when the grounds first arose, if later, is available in every case. The obligation to move at the earliest opportunity reinforces the obligation to act quickly. I do not find it possible to attach any great importance to the choice of this expression rather than the word, *'promptly'*.

11.016 Fennelly J found that O'Neill J had been influenced by the following passage from the judgment of McCarthy J in *O'Flynn v Mid-Western Health Board*:[39]

> There is ample ground for saying that both in principle and in precedent an application for judicial review should not fail merely because it is out of time: *The State (Furey) v Minister for Defence* [1988] ILRM 89. In principle it is right to relieve against delay in challenging an administrative decision where the delay has not prejudiced third parties.

As stated by Fennelly J, the proposition there enunciated could no longer be regarded as good law. The precedent upon which it was based, *State (Furey) v Minister for Defence,* was disapproved by the Supreme Court in *de Róiste v Minister for Defence* [2001] 1 IR 190. Having found that the statement above in *O'Flynn* does not now correctly represent the law, the court went on to state:

> [T]hat the legislative tendency towards the imposition of stricter time limits is matched by corresponding judicial development. An applicant, who is unable to furnish good reason for his own failure to issue proceedings for Judicial Review 'at the earliest opportunity and in any event within three months from the date when grounds for the application first arose' will not normally be able to show good reason for an extension of time. In particular, he cannot, without more, invoke the absence of any prejudice to the opposing party as the sole basis for the suggested good reason. The strictness with which the courts approach the question of an extension of time will vary with the circumstances. However, public procurement decisions are peculiarly appropriate subject matter for a comparatively strict approach to time limits. They relate to decisions in a commercial field, where there should be very little excuse for delay.

11.017 Here Dekra showed no good reasons for their delay. What are good reasons? Fennelly J considered this briefly:

> The wording of Order 84, rule 21 of the Rules of the Superior Courts, which is very similar to that of the rule now under consideration, was considered by Costello J (as he then was) in *O'Donnell v Dun Laoghaire Corporation* [1991] ILRM 301. He said, at p 315:
>
> 'The phrase "good reasons" is one of wide import which it would be futile to attempt to define precisely. However, in considering whether or not there are good reasons for extending the time I think it is clear that the test must be an objective one and the court should not extend the time merely because an aggrieved plaintiff believed that he or she was justified in delaying the institution of proceedings. What the plaintiff

---

39   *O'Flynn v Mid-Western Health Board* [1991] 2 IR 223.

has to show (and I think the onus under O 84, r 21 is on the plaintiff) is that there are reasons which both explain the delay and afford a justifiable excuse for the delay.'

11.018 It must be remembered that the obligation to apply for judicial review 'promptly' is independent of any stipulated time limit. This point was made by Herbert J in *O'Connell v Environmental Protection Agency*[40] where, although the applicant had brought the judicial review proceedings within the two months stipulated by s 85(8) of the Environmental Protection Agency Act 1992, it was contended, but not accepted by the court, that the applicant had not move promptly as required by Ord 84, r 21(1):

> This requirement of promptness in seeking the comprehensive new remedy of judicial review has always been an incident of the former prerogative remedies of *certiorari*, mandamus and prohibition. In my judgment, s 85(8) while imposing a non-expandable upper time limit within which an application for leave to apply for judicial review must be brought does not in any way suspend or lessen the requirement that every application for leave to apply for judicial review must be made promptly within that stipulated period.

11.019 There may be instances where it will be incumbent on the applicant to move with great speed, especially where the challenge is to the award of licences to third parties[41] or where the impugned decision affects 'major infrastructural projects where huge expense and inconvenience inevitably may be expected to arise where delay occurs.'[42] The context of an application will thus often be material to the issue of delay; for example, in a commercial or procedural case.[43] In such a context, the case of *Veolia v Fingal County Council*[44] concerned the award of a contract for the survey, design and installation of a water metering system for non-domestic water for the four Dublin local authority areas. Fingal acted as the lead authority in relation to the award process. Veolia was an unsuccessful tenderer and sought to challenge the award on a number of grounds. In its defence, Fingal contended that Veolia were out of time for bringing the challenge. It was held in this case that time runs from the date the grounds first arose and this may be a further burden on applicants in such proceedings as they may not be able to wait until the conclusion of the public procurement award process before moving to the High Court.

11.020 In considering when time begins to run, Clarke J was satisfied that:

> [O]n its ordinary reading Order 84A requires that time begin to run in relation to the making of an application for judicial review when the events giving rise to the

---

40   *O'Connell v Environmental Protection Agency* [220] 1 ILRM 1.

41   *Dekra Eireann Teo v Minister for the Environment and Local Government* [2003] 2 IR 270.

42   *Noonan Services Ltd v Labour Court* [2004] IEHC 42, *per* Kearns J. In *Mulcreevy v Minister for Environment*, Keane CJ observed that in such cases where 'substantial expense may result to the public as a result of unnecessary delay, the time fact requires special attention', [2004] 1 IR 72 at 80, [2004] 1 ILRM 419, [2004] IESC 5.

43   *SIAC Construction Ltd v National Roads Authority* [2004] IEHC 128, Kelly J; *Veolia Water UK plc v Fingal County Council* [2007] 1 ILRM 216; *CityJet v Irish Aviation Authority* [2005] IEHC 206, Kelly J.

44   *Veolia Water UK plc v Fingal County Council* [2007] 1 ILRM 216, [2006] IEHC 137.

grounds upon which the challenge is intended to be brought occur. Those events may be said to have occurred when any formal adverse consequence has crystallised to the extent of a formal step in the process being taken adverse to the interests of the applicant concerned.

Clarke J went on to observe that:

> the Supreme Court had occasion to consider the question of an extension of time in public procurement matters in *Dekra*. The principle behind the strict time limits in public procurement was stated in the following terms by Fennelly J:
>
> > 'Public procurement decisions are a peculiarly appropriate subject matter for a comparatively strict approach to time limits. They relate to decisions in a commercial field, where there should be very little excuse for delay.'

Existence of an Alternative Remedy

11.021 The existence of an alternative remedy is of itself a ground for refusing relief by way of judicial review.[45] This is separate to not being granted leave due to having already commenced proceedings seeking an alternative remedy. In *Buckley v Kirby*[46] the Supreme Court *per* Geoghegan J considered, amongst other things, circumstances where an applicant appeals and brings judicial review proceedings and the:

(a)   appeal has been fully or partly heard by the time the judicial review proceedings come on for hearing;

(b)   does so in circumstances where both remedies are equally appropriate and the appeal is pending at the time the judicial review proceedings come on for hearing;

(c)   the applicant has both appealed and brought judicial review proceedings in circumstances where at the time of the judicial review hearing the appeal is still pending but where in all the circumstances, appeal, rather than judicial review, is clearly the more appropriate remedy; or

(d)   the applicant has not brought an appeal at all but has gone the route of judicial review in circumstances where an appeal is much the more appropriate remedy though it would be open to a court to grant leave for judicial review.

11.022 Geoghegan J ruled that the first of these situations is governed by *State (Roche) v Delap*, where Henchy J, after finding there was an error of law on the face of the impugned order, held that:

> it does not follow from this conclusion that *certiorari* should have issued. The prosecutor elected to appeal to the Circuit Court. There he allowed the appeal to be opened and did not contend that his conviction (as distinct from the sentence) was other than correct. While that appeal was pending, it was not open to him to apply for *certiorari*; see *R (Miller) v Monaghan JJ*[47] which shows that he should have elected either for an appeal or for *certiorari*. It was not within the competence of the high

---

45   *Buckley v Kirby* [2000] 3 IR 431 *per* Geoghegan J.

46   *Buckley v Kirby* [2000] 3 IR 431.

47   *R (Miller) v Monaghan JJ* (1906) 40 ILTR 51.

court to intervene by *certiorari* to quash a conviction and sentence when an appeal had not alone been taken to the Circuit Court but that appeal was actually in the process or being heard in that Court.[48]

11.023 With regard to the second situation, Geoghegan J approved the following passage form the judgment of Barron J in *McGoldrick v An Bord Pleanála*:

> The real question to be determined where an appeal lies is the relative merits of an appeal against granting relief by way of judicial review. It is not just a question whether an alternative remedy exists or whether the applicant has taken steps to pursue such a remedy. The true question is which is the more appropriate remedy considered in the context of common sense; the ability to deal with the questions raised and principles of fairness; provided, of course, that the applicant has not gone too far down one road to be estopped from changing his or her mind.[49]

11.024 On points (c) and (d), the court observed that:

> [T]his is not a case where either remedy would have been equally appropriate. Judicial review in this case would appear to be singularly inappropriate as compared with an appeal and it is extremely doubtful whether in the event of leave being granted, it would ultimately be held that judicial review lay at all. It has long been established that *certiorari* will not be granted merely on the grounds of an absence of evidence to support a finding. In the well known case of *R (Martin) v Mahoney* [1910] 2 IR 695 Lord O'Brien CJ said the following:

> 'To grant *certiorari* merely on the ground of want of jurisdiction, because there was no evidence to warrant a conviction, confounds, as I have said, want of jurisdiction with error in the exercise of it. The contention that mere want of evidence to authorise a conviction creates a cesser of jurisdiction, involves, in my opinion, the unsustainable proposition that a magistrate has, in the case I put, jurisdiction only to go right; and that, though he had jurisdiction to enter upon an inquiry, mere miscarriage in drawing an unwarrantable conclusion from the evidence, such as it was, makes the magistrate act without and in excess of jurisdiction.'

> 9. That passage is cited in Mr Conleth Bradley's new book on judicial review at p 719 as still being the authority for the proposition set out. It has recently been cited with approval in two judgments of this Court one delivered by Keane J (as he then was) in *Killeen v DPP* [1998] 1 ILRM 1 and the other by the same judge as Chief Justice in *DPP v Judge Kelleher* unreported judgment 24th May, 2000. It is therefore wrong to grant leave for judicial review merely on the grounds that there was a lack of evidence to support the judge's decision. The proper remedy is appeal. This was clearly the view of O Caoimh J and I agree with it.

The court went on to observe that in a case where an appeal would clearly be the more appropriate remedy, an applicant ought not necessarily be granted leave to bring judicial review proceedings merely because he has not in fact appealed. In those circumstances, if he ought to have appealed, the court in its discretion may refuse leave.

---

48 *State (Roche) v Delap* [1980] IR 170, 173.

49 *McGoldrick v An Bord Pleanála* [1997] 1 IR 497, 509, also approved in *Tomlinson v Criminal Injuries Compensation Tribunal* [2006] 4 IR 321, 325 *per* Denham J.

11.025 The court went on to emphasise the final condition which had to be complied with to justify judicial review as set out in *G v DPP*, where Finlay CJ stated:

> [T]he only effective remedy, on the facts established by the Applicant, which the Applicant could obtain would be an order by way of judicial review or, if there be an alternative remedy, that the application by way of judicial review is, on all the facts of the case, a more appropriate method of procedure. These conditions or proofs are not intended to be exclusive and the court has a general discretion, since judicial review in many instances is an entirely discretionary remedy which may well include, amongst other things, consideration of whether the matter concerned is one of importance or of triviality and also as to whether the applicant has shown good faith in the making of an *ex parte* application.

As Geoghegan J went on to note, it would seem to follow from that last passage that it is within the discretion of the court granting leave to refuse leave where the point raised is a trivial one and the alleged defect in procedure, if un-remedied, results in no substantial injustice or where perhaps it should more appropriately be dealt with by a private law rather than a public law remedy.

Having made that observation Geoghegan J, ruled that:

> It cannot be said that the point raised in this case is trivial but equally it cannot be said that "the application by way of judicial review is, on all the facts of the case, a more appropriate method of procedure." Since this is a case of an alleged incorrect assessment of the evidence or lack of it, an appeal is quite obviously the appropriate remedy. That is why this appeal had to be dismissed.

11.026 Judicial review may be the only remedy available to an applicant on the facts of the situation. For example, in *Ryanair Ltd v Commission for Aviation Regulation*[50] the proceedings were initially a purported appeal by way of special summons related to a decision made by the Commission on 10 March 2008, in relation to charging certain fees in respect of check-in desks at Dublin Airport. The Commission successfully applied to have the action struck out on the ground that it had been improperly brought. It contended that the only remedy available to Ryanair was through the medium of judicial review. The court found that the entitlement to make the decision was conferred by the European Communities (Access to the Ground Handling Market at Community Airports) Regulations.[51] The actual relief sought in these was 'an order overturning the decision of the defendant dated the 10th March, 2008'. Kelly J went on to state that:

> The relief which is sought is in effect an order quashing that decision. That ought to be done by judicial review unless there is a clear statutory remit to make an order to quash of the type sought. There is no such remit in the present case.

Discretionary Bars

11.027 When seeking judicial review, the applicant must recall that the grant of the order sought is a matter of discretion for the court. Delay, alternative remedy, futility

---

50   *Ryanair Ltd v Commission for Aviation Regulation* [2008] IEHC 278.
51   SI 505/1998.

and other headings adverted to above are all discretionary bars to relief. Otherwise, the applicant is entitled to relief if he has a direct interest in the subject matter of the application and shows grounds. The common law has restricted the exercise of judicial discretion to acting according to 'the rules of reason and justice, not according to private opinion ... according to law, and not humour ... Not arbitrary, vague, and fanciful, but legal and regular.'[52] As Denham J has observed:

> *Certiorari* may be granted where the decision maker acted in breach of fair procedures. Once it is determined that an order of *certiorari* may be granted, the Court retains a discretion in all the circumstances of the case as to whether an order of *certiorari* should issue. In considering all the circumstances, matters including the existence of an alternative remedy, the conduct of the applicant, the merits of the application, the consequences to the applicant if an order of *certiorari* was not granted and the degree of fairness of the procedures, should be weighed by the Court in determining whether *certiorari* is the appropriate remedy to attain a just result.[53]

It has been suggested that one could have no argument with this passage if 'the merits of the application' refers to the merits of the judicial review application as opposed to the underlying facts of the matter.[54]

11.028 Other cases have seen judges describe a somewhat less defined discretion. For example, in *Connors v Delap*,[55] Lynch J stated the following:

> It has been emphasised on a number of occasions by the Supreme Court that the primary function of the Courts established by and pursuant to the Constitution is to do justice between the parties before the Court. See for example the *State (Healy) v O'Donoghue*.[56] In this case the parties before this Court are the applicant on the one hand and people of Ireland through the Director of Public Prosecutions on the other hand. If I were to make an order of *certiorari* in favour of the applicant based on the technical points on which he relies it would clearly deprive the people of Ireland of the just retribution to which they are entitled in respect of the crime committed by the applicant.

Later Mr Justice Barr approved and followed this approach in *White v Hussey*,[57] stating:

> The relief which the applicant seeks is a discretionary remedy. It seems to me that in declining whether or not discretion should be exercised in his favour, it is proper that

---

52 *per* Lord Chancellor Halsbury in *Sharp v Wakefield* [1891] AC 173, 179 [1886–90] All ER 651.

53 *Stefan v Minister for Justice, Equality & Law Reform* [2001] 4 IR 203, 217 *per* Denham J.

54 Anthony M Collins SC, 'Judicial Discretion in Judicial Review' Judicial Review Conference 2007, Royal College of Physicians, Kildare Street, Dublin 2, 1 December 2007. In that regard, see the analysis of Henchy J in *State (Abenglen Properties Ltd) v Dublin Corporation* [1984] IR 381, 400–401 where the relief sought was refused, amongst other reasons, in relation to the exercise of the court's discretion of the ground that it would have been futile to do so.

55 *Connors v Delap* [1989] ILRM 93, 97.

56 *State (Healy) v O'Donoghue* [1976] IR 325.

57 *White v Hussey* [1989] ILRM 109, 111 & 113.

I should take all of the relevant considerations into account and then decide whether justice requires that the convictions complained of should be set aside. Similar considerations apply regarding the exercise of discretion to extend time for making the application ... in determining whether to quash a conviction regard must be had also to the interests of the people of Ireland who are entitled to redress where the facts establish, or clearly imply, that the applicant was in fact guilty of the offence the subject matter of the conviction which he challenges on a technical ground that has no relevance to the merits of the case.

GROUNDS FOR REVIEW

The Threefold Division – Unreasonableness, Unlawfulness, Unfairness

11.029 Judicial review is primarily concerned only with the legality of the decision-making process, not with the merits of a decision.

In *O'Keeffe v An Bord Pleanála*,[58] Mr Justice Henchy made the following observations:

Judicial Review is concerned, not with the decision, but with the decision making process. Unless that restriction on power of the Court is observed, the Court will in my view, under the guise of preventing the abuse of power, be itself guilty of usurping power ... Judicial Review, as the words imply, is not an appeal from a decision, but a review of the manner in which a decision was made.

11.030 The concept of unreasonableness is an exception to the rule that a court will generally not review the merits of a decision. Mr Justice Henchy's explanation of the concept is worth quoting:

I conceive of the present state of evolution of administrative law in the Courts on this topic to be that when a statute confers on a non judicial person or body a decision-making power affecting personal rights, conditional on that person or body reaching a prescribed opinion or conclusion based on subjective assessment, a person who shows that a personal right of his has been breached or is liable to be breached by a decision purporting to be made in exercise of that power has standing to seek, and the High Court has jurisdiction to give, a ruling as to whether the pre-condition for the valid exercise of the power has been complied with in a way that brings the decision within the express, or necessarily implied, range of the power conferred by the statute. It is to be presumed that, when it conferred the power, Parliament intended the power to be exercised only in a manner that would be in conformity with the Constitution and within the limitations of the power as they are to be gathered from the statutory scheme or design. This means, amongst other things, not only that the power must be exercised in good faith but that the opinion or other subjective conclusion set as a precondition for the valid exercise of the power must be reached by a route that does not make the exercise unlawful – such as by misinterpreting the law, or by misapplying it through taking into consideration irrelevant matter of fact, or through ignoring relevant matters. Otherwise, the exercise of the power will be held to be invalid for being *ultra vires*.[59]

---

58   *O'Keeffe v An Bord Pleanála* [1993] 1 IR 39.
59   *State (Lynch) v Cooney* [1982] IR 337 at 380.

That said, the discretion afforded under stature is subject to '[the] necessarily implied constitutional limitation of jurisdiction in all decision-making which affects rights or duties, requires, *inter alia*, that the decision-maker must not flagrantly reject or disregard fundamental reason or common sense in reaching his decision.'[60]

11.031 The judgment in *O'Keeffe* sets a high threshold for the applicant. Arguably, in *Aer Rianta v Commissioner for Aviation Regulation*[61] the High Court went further in stating that:

> The type of grievous error so reviewable is of a completely different order. It is not reached by the extension of the line on which are to be found mere errors, serious errors, multiple errors and fundamental errors because that is a line of rational attempt no matter how misguided the outcome. But the kind of error that produces invalidity in one which no rational or sane decision maker, no matter how misguided, could essay. To be reviewably irrational it is not sufficient that a decision maker goes wrong or even hopelessly and fundamentally wrong: he must have gone completely and inexplicably mad; taken leave of his senses and come to an absurd conclusion. It is only when the last situation arises or something akin to it that a court will review the decision for irrationality.

The final sentence of that quote is very important. The court may intervene on other grounds. One should also recall that it may also be that the applicant has other avenues open to him to challenge a decision – such as a normal appeal or an appeal to an appeal panel.

11.032 Unreasonableness and unlawfulness were also considered by the Supreme Court in the case of *DPP v Kelliher*.[62] A District Judge in preliminary examination refused to send an accused forward for trial on a rape charge having regard to the evidence presented for examination. The DPP sought *certiorari* in the High Court against that order to remit the matter to the District Court with such directions as the

---

60   *State (Keegan) v Stardust Victims Compensation Tribunal* [1986] IR 642 at page 658.

61   *Aer Rianta v Commissioner for Aviation Regulation* [2003] IEHC 12, O'Sullivan J [2001 No 707 JR] at p 48, cited with approval in *Kildare County Council v An Board Pleanála* [2006] IEHC 173, MacMenamin J, at p 78. There are two main judgments in *Aer Rianta v Commission for Aviation Regulation*. The second was given by Mr Justice O'Sullivan [2003] IEHC 168. When giving his January judgment, Mr Justice O'Sullivan went on to state at p 49 that, 'in no way could it be said that in making these errors [the Commissioner for Aviation Regulation] was guilty of an abandonment of plain reason and common sense …In my opinion the train of errors, miscalculations and misapplication of theory and practice so eloquently rehearsed by counsel for [Aer Rianta – and taking his characterisation of these alleged mistakes as correct] in no way approaches the height of absurdity and whimsicality necessary before a Court will review the decision for irrationality.' The court went on to state that, 'it cannot have been the intention of the law makers who inserted s 38 into the Act of 2001 [JR procedure section], that errors which have only come to light as a result of painstaking discovery and long after the two month limitation period has elapsed should nevertheless be subject to irrationality review. The plain purpose of the Act of 2001 in my opinion is that errors of this kind shall be referred for correction to an appeal panel'

62   *DPP v Kelliher* [2000] IESC 60, *per* Keane CJ.

High Court deemed appropriate. Keane CJ succinctly set out the argument before the President of the High Court:

> The learned President, having referred to the arguments advanced on behalf of the applicant and having cited a passage from the judgments of this Court in *Killeen v The Director of Public Prosecutions* [1998] ILRM 1, a well known passage from the judgment of Lord Justice O'Brien, Lord Chief Justice in *R (Martin) v Mahony* 1910 2 IR 695 and having also referred to an argument that had been advanced on behalf of the applicant based on the dicta of Lord Greene in *Associated Provincial Picture Houses Limited v Wednesbury Corporation* [1947] 2 AC 680 and the statement of the law by Mr Justice Henchy in the *State (Keegan) v Stardust Compensation Tribunal* and the statements of the law of this Court in *O'Keeffe v An Bord Pleanála* [1993] IR 39 said that the argument essentially advanced in reliance on those decisions was that, since the decision of the District Judge lacked reason and was fundamentally at variance with commonsense, the Court should set it aside.

11.033 He said that, however, in his view, that argument was not open to the applicant in the present proceedings because the grounds upon which leave was granted were, in summary, that the respondent had acted in excess of jurisdiction, that he carried out the preliminary examination otherwise than in accordance with s 7 of the Criminal Procedure Act 1967, that he acted without jurisdiction in failing to consider the statement of the complainant and that he acted in excess of jurisdiction in discharging the notice party.

He said that, in his view, none of those grounds, all of which amounted to an allegation of a failure on the part of the District Judge to carry out his functions in accordance with the Criminal Procedure Act 1967, permit an argument to be made seeking to set aside the order on the grounds that it is at variance with reasonable common sense and he accordingly refused the relief sought.

This order of the High Court for those reasons was affirmed by the Supreme Court in that case.

11.034 In the UK, a commonly used classification of judicial review is Lord Diplocks's threefold division from the *GCHQ*[63] case, into illegality (unlawfulness), irrationality (unreasonableness) and procedural impropriety (unfairness). As Fordham notes,[64] it has aged well, resting as it does on two important distinctions: the first, between substance (legality and irrationality) and procedure (procedural impropriety); the second, between hard-edged questions (legality and procedural impropriety) and soft questions (irrationality). It is also a very helpful summary of the concept. In that case, Lord Diplock stated:

> Judicial Review has I think developed to a stage today when ... one can conveniently classify under three heads the grounds upon which administrative action is subject to

---

63 *Council of Civil Service Unions v Minister for the Civil Service* [1985] AC 374. This case is known in the UK as the '*GCHQ*' case, as it involved a ban on union membership by employees at Government Communications Headquarters (GCHQ). The UK government pleaded risk to national security as a defence to procedural unfairness in the way the ban was imposed.

64 Fordham, *Judicial Review Handbook* (3rd edn, ART publishing, 2001), p 686.

control by judicial review. The first ground I would call 'illegality', the second 'irrationality' and the third 'procedural impropriety'. That is not to say that further development on a case-by-case basis may not in the course of time add further grounds ... but to dispose of the instant case the three already well established heads that I have mentioned will suffice. By 'illegality' as a ground for judicial review I mean that the decision maker must understand correctly the law that regulates his decision making power and must give effect to it. Whether he has or not is par excellence a justiciable question to be decided, in the event of a dispute, by those persons, the judges, by whom the judicial power of the state is exercisable. By 'irrationality' I mean what can now be succinctly referred to as *Wednesbury* unreasonableness ... It applies to a decision which is so outrageous in its defiance of logic or of accepted moral standards that no sensible person who had applied his mind to the question to be decided could have arrived at it. Whether a decision falls within this category is a question that judges by their training and experience should be well equipped to answer or else there would be something badly wrong with out judicial system ... I have described the third head as 'procedural impropriety' rather than failure to serve basic rules of natural justice or failure to act with procedural fairness towards the person who will be affected by the decision. This is because susceptibility to judicial review under this head covers also failure by an administrative tribunal to observe procedural rules that are expressly laid down in the legislative instrument by which jurisdiction is conferred, even where such failure does not involve any denial of natural justice.

Where the Court is considering the legal propriety of an exercise of discretionary power, the traditional approach involves identifying the "bundle" of familiar grounds referred to in the *Wednesbury*[65] case, namely, misdirection in law and (1) disregard of relevancies; (2) consideration of irrelevancies; and (3) patent unreasonableness.

If when exercising his statutory functions, the Regulator reaches a decision unsupported by the facts, this error as to fact may be challenged as unreasonable.

Error of Law or Misdirection in Law

11.035 Generally, in Ireland, an error of law made by a statutory or administrative tribunal, or by a court of limited jurisdiction, if made within jurisdiction, would not be reviewed unless the error appears on the face of the record.[66] In Ireland, the consideration of the impact of error in a decision is treated differently than in the UK. In essence, in Ireland, if the error by the tribunal is such as not to go to the jurisdiction of the Regulator, then the courts will not review the decision; instead, it should be appealed. In the UK a tribunal has no power to decide any question of law incorrectly; any error of law would render its decision liable to be quashed as *ultra vires*.[67] The UK position arises from the judgment in *Anisminic v Foreign*

---

65   *Associated Provincial Picture Houses Ltd v Wednesbury Corporation* [1948] 1 KB 223.

66   *R (Martin) v Mahony* [1910] 2 IR 695. See also *State (Keegan) v Stardust Victims Compensation Tribunal* [1986] IR 642 and *The State (Abenglen Properties Ltd) v Corporation of Dublin* [1984] IR 381.

67   Wade and Forsyth, *Administrative Law* (9th edn, OUP, 2004), p 264.

Compensation Commission.[68] By contrast, in Ireland, the case law maintains a division and Ireland has a jurisprudence developed on notions of fair procedures and constitutional justice.[69] What this means is that if an error, here meaning an error of law, is made by a Regulator when coming to a decision, unless that error is set out in his decision and goes to the root of the manner in which he has made that decision, then the decision will not be subject to judicial review. For example, where the Regulator has misinterpreted law and consequently gone outside its jurisdiction in taking certain things into account or, in the alternative, failed to take into account that which he should have done, then this error may be reviewed.

11.036 It is important to bear in mind that the decision may nevertheless be subject to an appeal. In many ways, the above statements delineate the subject matters of appeal versus review. One reviews the process by which a decision was made but one appeals the actual substance of the decision.[70]

Strategically, regulated entities may prefer to use the threat of review, as the order usually sought in such a review – *certiorari* – is a blunt instrument. *Certiorari* quashes the decision. The Regulator has to start again. By contrast, an appeal is a different process whereby the appeal panel (or court) may confirm, condemn or vary the Regulator's decision. It may, in fact, be unattractive for a litigant to have a varied decision if they oppose a positive decision in any guise. Thus review, if available, may be a better option for the litigant looking for a knock-out blow. This assumes the court will so exercise its discretion. In an appeal, if one sets out the grounds why the appeal should be allowed, the appeal panel is obliged to act. In a review there is residual discretion in the High Court not to grant the order sought.

11.037 The development of Irish jurisprudence would seem to support an assertion that if a decision by a Regulator is legally within jurisdiction, but arguably based on insufficient evidence to support that decision, it may not be quashed on review.[71] The proper challenge is an appeal. The reason is that even though a Regulator may have gotten it wrong, he was entitled to be wrong within his own jurisdiction having regard to the evidence before him.

---

68 *Anisminic v Foreign Compensation Commission* [1969] 2 AC 147. The significance of *Anisminic* in the UK is further enforced by judgments such as *In Re Rascal Communications Ltd* [1981] AC 374; *O'Reilly v Mackman* [1983] 2 AC 237 and *R v Hull University Visitor ex parte Page* [1993] AC 682.

69 See for example, *East Donegal Co-operative Livestock Marts Ltd v AG* [1970] IR 317 and *Glover v BLN Ltd* [1973] IR 388.

70 Put simply, review is concerned with a 'decision done right' as opposed to the 'right decision'. See **Ch 6** on communications regulation, which discusses the experience of the Electronic Communications Appeals Panel which panel considered that the standard of review in respect of appeals by regulatory bodies is not a full *de novo* hearing. The panel this has now been replaced by an appeal to the High Court.

71 *R (Martin) v Mahony* [1910] 2 IR 695.

11.038 The UK approach to the fact that the courts have a general supervisory role of correcting mistakes of law has been explained thus by Lord Justice Diplock:[72]

> [B]y 'illegality' as a ground for judicial review I mean that the decision maker must understand correctly the law that regulates his decision making power and must understand correctly the law that regulates his decision making power and must give effect to it. Whether he has or not is par excellence a justiciable question to be decided, in the event of dispute by those persons, the judges, by who the judicial power of the State is exercisable.

One would have to show that the error was material, ie an error in the actual making of the decision that affected the decision itself. Jurisprudence in the UK tends to indicate that if an error is made that does not affect the outcome, then the court should be slow to exercise its discretion.[73]

11.039 In *SIAC Construction Ltd v Mayo County Council*,[74] the applicant unsuccessfully submitted a tender to be awarded by the County Council for a major sewerage works at Ballinrobe. SIAC sought to review the award decision and appealed the finding of the High Court in favour of the County Council. Amongst other things, it argued that in a case involving EC public procurement rules, a 'Wednesbury unreasonableness' test was incorrect. SIAC argued that there should be a different test used in such a review, more suited to the Community law nature of the remedy, especially the principle of effectiveness. It was noted that the Remedies Directive applied in this case.[75]

11.040 In considering this argument, the court found that the state is required to provide a judicial remedy for the purposes of the EC public procurement rules. The courts of the state must render those provisions effective in favour of those in a position to invoke them. The two classic principles applicable to that situation are those of equivalence, ie the remedy must be at least as favourable as that available in national law for a similar complaint, and effectiveness, ie as the Remedies Directive itself

---

72 *Council of Civil Service Unions v Minister for the Civil Service* [1985] AC 374, 410F.

73 Fordham, *Judicial Review Handbook* (3rd edn, ART publishing, 2001).

74 *SIAC Construction Ltd v Mayo County Council* [2002] 3 IR 148; [2002] 2 ILRM 401; [2002] IESC 39, *per* Fennelly J *nem diss.*

75 European Communities (Review Procedures for the Award of Public Supply and Public Works Contracts) Regulations 1992 (SI 38/1992) gave effect in the state to the Remedies Directive in place at that time. These rules have been updated and replaced by (a) the European Communities (Award of Contracts by Utility Undertakings) Regulations 2007 (SI 50/2007) which give effect to Directive 2004/17/EC of the European Parliament and of the Council of 31 March 2004 on the co-ordination of procurement procedures of entities operating in the water, energy, transport and postal services sectors (as amended by Directive 2005/51/EC of 7 September 2005) and (b) the European Communities (Award of Public Authorities' Contracts) Regulations 2006 (SI 329/2006) which give effect to Directive 2004/18/EC of the European Parliament and of the Council of 31 March 2004 on the co-ordination of procedures for the award of public works contracts, public supply contracts and public service contracts (as amended by Directive 2005/51/EC dated 7 September 2005 and Directive 2005/75/EC dated 16 November 2005).

makes clear, a remedy that will offer appropriate and sufficient protection for the Community law rights in question.

11.041 The Supreme Court considered that it seems to be well established by a significant line of case law of the Court of First Instance that a Community institution, when in a comparable situation to the awarding authority of a member state, enjoys 'a wide discretion' as to the criteria by which it will judge tenders and, moreover, its decisions will be annulled only if a 'manifest error' can be demonstrated.[76]

11.042 That said, the Supreme Court ruled that it is not conceivable that the courts of the member states are required to apply a different standard of judicial review to their own awarding authorities. This emerges clearly from a reading of *Upjohn Ltd v Licensing Authority established by the Medicines Act 1968*[77]. In that case, answering a reference to it by the UK Court of Appeal, the European Court of Justice (ECJ) stated:

> 34. According to the Court's case-law, where a Community authority is called upon, in the performance of its duties, to make complex assessments, it enjoys a wide measure of discretion, the exercise of which is subject to a limited judicial review in the course of which the Community judicature may not substitute its assessment of the facts for the assessment made by the authority concerned. Thus, in such cases, the Community judicature must restrict itself to examining the accuracy of the findings of fact and law made by the authority concerned and to verifying, in particular, that the action taken by that authority is not vitiated by a manifest error or a misuse of powers and that it did not clearly exceed the bounds of its discretion (see, in particular, Joined Cases 56/64 and 58/64 *Consten and Grundig v Commission* [1996] ECR 299, Case 55/75 *Balkan-Import Export v Haputzollamt Berlin-Packhof* [1976] ECR 19, paragraph 8, Case 9/82 *Ohrgaard and Delvaux v Commission* [1983] ECR 2379, paragraph 14, Case C–225/91 *Marta v Commission* [1993] ECR I–3203, paragraphs 24 and 25, and Case C–157/96 *National Farmers' Union and Others* [1998] ECR I–2211, paragraph 39).

> 35. Consequently, Community law does not require the Member States to establish a procedure for judicial review of national decisions revoking marketing authorisations, taken pursuant to Directive 65/65 and in the exercise of complex assessments, which involves a more extensive review than that carried out by the Court in similar cases.

> 36. Nevertheless, any national procedure for judicial review of decision of national authorities revoking marketing authorisations must enable the court or tribunal seised of an application for annulment of such a decision effectively to apply the relevant principles and rules of Community law when reviewing its legality.

---

76 See, for example, the decision of the Court of First Instance in *Adia Interim SA v Commission* Case T–19/95 [1996] ECR II–321; *Alsace International Car Services v European Parliament of 2000* Case T–139/99, which refers to *Agence Européenne d'Intérims v Commission* Case 56/77 [1978] ECR 2215, para 20; *Adia Intérim v Commission* Case T–19/95 [1996] ECR II–321, para 49; and *Embassy Limousines & Services v Parliament* Case T–203/96 [1998] ECR II–4239, para 56.

77 *Upjohn Ltd v Licensing Authority established by the Medicines Act 1968* Case C–120/97, [1999] ECR I–223.

11.043 The Supreme Court noted that a decisive additional consideration in the area of public procurement is the explicit concession of a wide margin of discretion to awarding authorities.

That said, Fennelly J went on to state:

> 83. I do not think, however, that the test of manifest error is to be equated with the test adopted by the learned trial judge, namely that, in order to qualify for quashing, a decision must 'plainly and unambiguously fly in the face of fundamental reason and common sense.' It cannot be ignored that the Advocate General thought the test should be "rather less extreme." Such a formulation of the test would run the risk of not offering what the Remedies Directive clearly mandates, namely a judicial remedy which will be effective in the protection of the interests of disappointed tenderers.

> 84. The courts must be ready, in general, to render effective the general principles of the public procurement, already discussed. Where a failure to respect the principles of equality, transparency or objectivity is clearly made out, there is, of course, no question of permitting a margin of discretion ...

> 85. Therefore, I am satisfied that the courts, while recognising that awarding authorities have a wide margin of discretion, must recognise that this cannot be unlimited. The courts must exercise their function of judicial review so as to make the principles of the public procurement directives effective. In the case of clearly established error, they must exercise their powers. The application of these principles may not, in practice, lead to any real difference in result between the judicial review of purely national decisions and of those which require the application of Community law principles.'

11.044 In *Commission v Tetra Laval*[78] a different expression of 'manifest error' as a standard of review was challenged. The Court of First Instance (CFI) overturned a Commission concentrations decision, on appeal to the ECJ, the Commission complained that the CFI, whilst claiming to apply the test of manifest error of assessment, in fact applied a different test requiring the production of convincing evidence. In doing so, it claimed the CFI infringed art 230 EC by failing to take account of the discretion conferred on the Commission with regard to complex factual and economic matters.

The Commission case argued that the review by the Community judicature of the exercise by it of discretion in reaching a decision on a concentration must take account of the discretionary margin implicit in the provisions of an economic nature which form part of the rules on concentrations.[79]

---

78 *Commission v Tetra Laval* C–460/02 [2004] ECR I–11547. In this case, the Commission of the European Communities appealed to the ECJ to set aside the judgment of the CFI in *Tetra Laval v Commission* Case T–5/02 [2002] ECR II–4381 by which the CFI annulled Commission Decision 2004/124/EC of 30 October 2001 declaring a concentration to be incompatible with the common market and the EEA Agreement (Case No COMP/M.2416 – Tetra Laval Sidel) (OJ 2004 L 43, p 13).

79 See *France v Commission (Kali & Salz)* Joined Cases C–68/94 and C–30/95 [1998] ECR I–1375, paras 223 and 224; *Gencor v Commission* Case T–102/96 [1999] ECR II–753, paras 164 and 165; and *Airtours v Commission* Case T–342/99 [2002] ECR II–2585, para 64.

11.045 The ECJ found in favour of the test applied by the CFI. It stated that 'whilst the Court recognises that the Commission has a margin of discretion with regard to economic matters, that does not mean that the Community Courts must refrain from reviewing the Commission's interpretation of information of an economic nature. Not only must the Community Courts, *inter alia*, establish whether the evidence relied on is factually accurate, reliable and consistent but also whether that evidence contains all the information which must be taken into account in order to assess a complex situation and whether it is capable of substantiating the conclusions drawn from it. Such a review is all the more necessary in the case of a prospective analysis required when examining a planned merger with conglomerate effect.'

11.046 This test, in competition cases, equates more to a rationality test, ie a relevance and reasonableness test. In other words, was the information considered relevant and sufficient, and were the conclusions drawn reasonable having regard to the evidence before the Commission? As the ECJ pointed out in its judgment, the CFI explained and set out the reasons why the Commission's conclusions seemed to it to be inaccurate in that they were based on insufficient, incomplete, insignificant and inconsistent evidence. By contrast, the manifest error test often used by the CFI is an argument akin to error or misdirection in law.

Excess of Jurisdiction and Ultra Vires

11.047 Jurisdiction is a way of describing *ultra vires* in the sense that a public body has exceeded the boundaries of its received power. The word 'jurisdiction' has also been described as a synonym for 'power'.[80] Furthermore, it has been said that the word 'jurisdiction' best describes the nature of the power, duty or authority committed to the person or body which is amenable to the supervisory jurisdiction of the court.[81] The cases discussed below display the various approaches of the courts in considering whether the decision maker actually acted outside their jurisdiction, and how they got to that point. There are various aspects of acting unlawfully under this heading.

11.048 Jurisdiction may be wrongfully asserted or exercised. In other words, a Regulator might do something that is not within its power. Equally, it may wrongfully decline to do something that it is within its power.[82]

11.049 One may also act without jurisdiction if the necessary conditions precedent are not satisfied. In the words of Pearce LJ in the seminal English case, *Anisminic*,[83] 'lack

---

80   *Per* Sir George Ormrod in *R v Manchester City Magistrates Court, ex p Davies* [1989] QB 631.

81   *Per* Lord Hope in *West v Secretary of State for Scotland* 1992 SLT 636.

82   See, for example, *Ryanair Holdings plc v Irish Financial Services Regulatory Authority* [2008] IEHC 231, *per* Kelly J. In this case, Ryanair sought, unsuccessfully, to compel IFSRA to investigate a complaint made to it by Ryanair that Aer Lingus had acted in breach of the Market Abuse (Directive 2003/6/EC) Regulations 2005. Alternatively, it sought *mandamus* to compel IFSRA to decide whether it was going to investigate the matter and to give reasons for its decision.

83   *Anisminic Ltd v Foreign Compensation Commission* [1969] 2 AC 147.

of jurisdiction may arise in various ways. There may be an absence of those formalities or things which are conditions precedent to the tribunal having any jurisdiction to embark on an enquiry.' This point is directly relevant to holding a review of a price determination if substantial grounds must have arisen upon which a review may be founded, ie they are a condition precedent of a review. Therefore, the start point for a challenge to a review might well be that no such grounds in fact exist. Morris LJ captured the point in the *Anisminic* case when he stated:

> [I]t is sometimes the case that the jurisdiction of a tribunal is made dependent upon or subject to some condition. Parliament may enact that if a certain state of affairs exists then there will be jurisdiction. If in such a case it appears that the state of affairs did not exist, then it follows that there would be no jurisdiction. Sometimes, however, a tribunal might undertake the task of considering whether the state of affairs existed. If it made an error in that task such error would be in regard to a matter preliminary to the existence of jurisdiction. It would not be an error within the limited jurisdiction intended to be conferred.

Thus one may question whether the substantial ground upon which the review is based is actually a substantial ground for the purposes of the relevant statute. If a court answered this question in the negative, then the decision made after such review would be struck down.

11.050 Another aspect of unlawful jurisdiction is improper delegation. Usually this applies to a situation where some authority believing it can do so, delegates some executive act to another to perform. In the case of a Regulator charged with making a determination, it must do so and be seen to do so. To the extent that consultants are retained to do work this must be directed by the Regulator and the results if appropriate put out to the industry for comment and then the consultants work accepted or rejected by reference to any comment with reasons given.

11.051 In brief, 'where there is a want of jurisdiction as opposed to a failure to follow procedural requirements, the result is a nullity'.[84] By contrast, 'where there is jurisdiction but there has been a miscarriage of natural justice, the decision stands good until quashed.'[85] This is an important distinction, although in each case the decision would of course stand until the High Court would declare otherwise.

11.052 It does not necessarily follow that a Regulator who commences a decision-making process within jurisdiction will continue making his decision within jurisdiction. For any number of reasons, he may exceed jurisdiction and thereby make its decisions liable to being quashed on *certiorari*. In the words of Henchy J, speaking about whether a District Court judgment followed the required statutory procedures:

> For instance, [the court or tribunal] may fall into an unconstitutionality, he may breach the requirements of natural justice, or he may fail to stay within the bounds of the jurisdiction conferred on it by statute. It is an error of the latter kind that prevent

---

84 *Per* Hodson LJ in *Ridge v Baldwin* [1964] AC 40.
85 *Per* Devlin LJ in *Ridge v Baldwin* [1964] AC 40 at p 584.

the impugned order in this case from being held to have been made within jurisdiction.[86]

11.053 In the later case of *The State (Abenglen Properties Ltd) v Dublin Corporation*[87] Mr Justice Henchy again returned to this theme. In that case Dublin Corporation successfully appealed to the Supreme Court from an order of *certiorari* of the High Court, which overturned the Corporations earlier decision to grant an outline planning permission. Henchy J in delivering the majority judgment of the Supreme Court assumed that the Corporation erred in law in wrongly identifying the relevant plan and wrongly interpreting the prescribed plot ratio:

> For the purpose of this appeal I am prepared to assume (without so holding) that the respondents erred in relation to those matters to the extent found by the judge in the High Court. If they did so err, their errors do not appear on the face of their decision. The alleged errors arose in the course of identifying and construing the relevant development plan. There is no doubt but that, on a true reading of the relevant Acts and regulations, the respondents, as the appropriate planning authority, had jurisdiction to identify and construe the relevant development plan in its relation to Abenglen's application. If therefore, the respondents erred in either respect they erred within jurisdiction and any error that they may have made does not appear on the face of the record. In such circumstances the remedy of *certiorari* does not lie: see the judgments of the House of Lords *In re Rascal Communications Ltd* [1981] AC 374 and that of the Privy Council in *SE Asia Fire Bricks v Non Metallic Products* [1981] AC 363. Where an inferior court or tribunal errs within jurisdiction, without recording that error on the face of the record, *certiorari* does not lie. In such cases it is only when there is an extra flaw that the Court or tribunal acted in disregard of the requirements of natural justice that *certiorari* will issue. In the present case, there is no suggestion that the respondents, in dealing with Abenglen's application acted in disregard of any of the requirements of natural justice.[88]

11.054 Error within jurisdiction was also addressed in *State (Keegan) v Stardust Victims Compensation Tribunal*.[89] Having quoted from the *Martin* and *Abenglen* case mentioned above, Blayney J concludes: 'I consider that this statement of law applies equally to the facts of this case and accordingly I must allow the course shown and discharge the conditional order of *certiorari*.'

Mr Keegan appealed that decision. He sought *certiorari* of the decision of the tribunal based on unreasonableness grounds as set out the case of *Associated Provincial Picture Houses Ltd v Wednesbury Corporation*.[90] The Supreme Court confirmed the High Court decision:

> In short, the decision of the High court was that if the Tribunal was in error it was an error within its jurisdiction and that it had not exceeded its jurisdiction nor gone

---

86   *State (Holland) v Kennedy* [1977] IR 193. Such an error would not appear on the face of the record but leads to *certiorari*.

87   *State (Abenglen Properties Ltd) v Dublin Corporation* [1984] IR 381.

88   *State (Abenglen Properties Ltd) v Dublin Corporation* [1984] IR 381, 399–400.

89   *State (Keegan) v Stardust Victims Compensation Tribunal* [1986] IR 642 at 50.

90   *Associated Provincial Picture Houses Limited v Wednesbury Corporation* [1941] 1 KB 223.

outside it and that therefore the remedy of *certiorari* did not lie. It was further held in the High Court that the decision of the Tribunal was not arbitrary or capricious and that therefore it was unnecessary to decide , even it were, whether that would lead to the quashing of that decision on *certiorari*. In this Court Counsel on behalf of the prosecutors mainly relied on the principles enunciated in the decision of the *Associated Provincial Picture Houses Ltd v Wednesbury Corporation* [1948] 1 KB 223 a decision of the Court of Appeal in England.

11.055 The grounds on which the High Court can set aside a decision of a body such as a Commission established by the Oireachtas with specified functions and powers have been made clear in a number of decisions. As Keane J noted,[91] the *locus classicus* is the frequently cited passage from the judgment of Lord Greene, MR in *Associated Provincial Picture Houses Ltd v Wednesbury Corporation*,[92] namely:

> The court is entitled to investigate the actions of the ... authority with a view to seeing whether they have taken into account matters which they ought not to take into account, or, conversely, have refused to take into account or neglected to take into account matters which they ought to take into account. Once that question is answered in favour of the ... authority, it may be still possible to say that, although the ... authority have kept within the four corners of the matters which they ought to consider, they have nevertheless come to a conclusion so unreasonable that no reasonable authority could ever have come to it. In such a case, again, I think the court can interfere. The power of the court to interfere in each case is not as an appellate authority to override a decision of the ... authority, but as a judicial authority which is concerned, and concerned only, to see whether the authority have contravened the law by acting in excess of the powers which Parliament has confided in them.

This passage was adopted by the Supreme Court in *State (Keegan) v Stardust Victims Compensation Tribunal*[93] where Henchy J defined the test of unreasonableness as: 'Whether the impugned decision plainly and unambiguously flies in the face of fundamental reason and common sense.'

11.056 In *Ryan v Compensation Tribunal*[94] Costello P dismissed a challenge to a determination of the Compensation Tribunal established to deal with the Hepatitis C scandal. The tribunal's decision was challenged in *certiorari* proceedings on the grounds that the tribunal had failed to interpret correctly the relevant legislation. As the court held that the tribunal had correctly applied the law, the issue of error within jurisdiction did not arise. However, Mr Justice Costello made the followings observations:

> [B]efore leaving this part of the case I should observe that this submission [of the claimant] is a claim that the tribunal erred in law in failing to take into account the provision of section 2 of the 1964 Act [Civil Liability (Amendment) Act 1964]. But if

---

91 *Radio Limerick One Ltd v Independent Radio and Television Commission* [1997] 2 IR 291, *per* Keane J *nem diss.*

92 *Associated Provincial Picture Houses Ltd v Wednesbury Corporation* [1948] 1 KB 223.

93 *State (Keegan) v Stardust Victims Compensation Tribunal* [1986] IR 642.

94 *Ryan v Compensation Tribunal* [1997] 1 ILRM 194.

it has so erred it was not an error on the face of the record. Further an error of law cannot be a ground for challenging the decision on the ground of irrationality as it does not follow that a tribunal which made an error of law thereby flies in the face of fundamental reason and common sense. But the law relating to *certiorari* has been developed in England and as a result in particular of two cases decided in the House of Lords, *Anisminic Limited v Foreign Compensation Tribunal* [1969] AC 682 and *R v Hull University Visitor, ex parte Page* [1993] AC 682) the English courts will now quash the decision of a tribunal which has made any error of law and it is no longer necessary to show that the error was on the face of the record. If therefore, I had concluded that the tribunal in this case had so erred I would have re-listed the case to hear further submissions as to whether or not I should apply similar principles in this case.[95]

This meaning of the principle in *Anisminic*, although championed in certain Irish cases, has yet to be considered adopted by the Superior Courts in Ireland. It has been argued that the conclusion expressed in *Killeen's* case below is wholly consistent with the approach taken by the majority of the House of Lords in *Anisminic* but not recognised as such.[96]

11.057 A key question to be considered in this regard by the court upon review is whether the error is an error of law or of fact. In *Killeen v Director of Public Prosecutions*,[97] a District Judge had erroneously discharged two accused persons on the basis that their warrants of arrest were invalid. The appeal came before the Supreme Court after the High Court had restrained the DPP from proceeding further against Killeen. The Supreme Court first had to decide whether the error made by the District Court was an error of law or an error of fact:

> It is clearly not possible for any tribunal, including the District Court, upon which a particular jurisdiction has been conferred by statute, as here, to extend or confine the boundaries of that jurisdiction by an erroneous determination of fact: see the *State (Attorney General) v Durcan* [1964] IR 279. In this case, however, there is no question of the District Judge having made an erroneous finding of fact in relation to a matter which was a condition precedent to his assuming jurisdiction. If the District Judge was of the opinion that the defect in the warrant of itself precluded him from sending forward the applicants for trial and was wrong in so holding, that was an error of law.[98]

The key point here is not the defect in the warrant – piece of evidence – but rather the process in which the District Judge was engaged – preliminary examination. At preliminary examination stage, the job of the court is to assess, taking it at its height, whether the evidence before it (assuming it is all received by the trial court) establishes a *prima facie* case sufficient to put the accused on trial. The validity of the warrant is not an issue to be considered at this stage of the process. By entering into an inquiry as

---

95 *Ryan v Compensation Tribunal* [1997] 1 ILRM 194 at 217.

96 James O'Reilly SC, '*Anisminic* – Jurisdictional Error and Judicial Review' Paper delivered at the Judicial Review Conference 2007. organised by Thompson Round Hall, December 2007 at the Royal College of Physicians in Dublin.

97 *Killeen v DPP* [1997] 3 IR 218.

98 *Killeen v DPP* [1997] 3 IR 218 at 227.

to the legality of certain evidence, the District Judge had misdirected himself in law as this was not his task at preliminary examination.

11.058 Having determined that the error in issue was an error of law, rather than an error of fact, Keane J, as he then was, continued: 'It may be that an error of law committed by a tribunal acting within its jurisdiction is not capable of being set aside on *certiorari*: see *The State (Davidson) v Farrell*.[99] It is otherwise where the error of law has its consequence the making of an order which the tribunal had no jurisdiction to make.'[100] In his judgment, Keane J concluded that the order made was consequent to an error of law not within the jurisdiction of the District Judge to make:

> The question posed in this case can now be stated as follows. If the District Judge in the present case discharged the applicants because he considered he was precluded from sending them forward for trial by reason of the defect in the warrant, was that an error of law which was within his jurisdiction to make? I am satisfied that it was not. If the District Judge was of that view, it follows that he failed to determine the precise question assigned for decision to the District Court [on preliminary examination], ie as to whether on the materials before the Court, there was a sufficient case to put the applicants on trial. If that was his decision, it constituted an error of law which rendered his order a nullity in accordance with legal principles already set out.

11.059 As described in the cases mentioned above, the paradigm of *ultra vires* in administrative law is where a statute confers limited powers on a public body, but the body acts beyond those limits. One may extend this logic in two directions:[101] firstly, to include incompatibility with constraints inherent in the Regulator's statute; and secondly, to include constraints which are prescribed by any legal source to which the Regulator is subject. A number of scenarios then arise, ranging, for example, from judicial review of primary legislation for its incompatibility with Community law to judicial review of a decision for its incompatibility with other rules.[102]

11.060 Aer Rianta used the latter route when challenging the approach the Commission for Aviation Regulation used when making its first airport charges determination.[103] Aer Rianta were essentially making the point that the Commission's method used in this decision was *ultra vires* its powers under the Aviation Regulation Act 2001, having regard to Aer Rianta's statutory role as set out by provisions in Air Navigation and Transport (Amendment) Act 1998.

---

99 *State (Davidson) v Farrell* [1960] IR 438.

100 *Killeen v DPP* [1997] 3 IR 218 at 227.

101 Fordham, *Judicial Review Handbook* (3rd edn, ART publishing, 2001), p 703.

102 Laws LJ described *ultra vires* as being, 'perfectly respectable shorthand to identify that legal defect or vice which consists in the making of a subordinate instrument which is not authorised by the text of its supposed parent in the main legislation, given the correct construction of both measures' – *R v Secretary of State for Trade and Industry, ex p Thompson Holidays Ltd* (2000) *The Times*, 12 January.

103 *Aer Rianta v Commissioner for Aviation Regulation* [2003] IEHC 168, O'Sullivan J.

11.061 In the *Law Society of Ireland v Competition Authority*,[104] the Law Society pleaded that the Competition Authority 'Notice in Respect of Legal Representation of Persons Attending before the Competition Authority',[105] was *ultra vires* its powers. The kernel of this notice was that:

> [W]here the Authority was of the opinion that the integrity of its investigation processes may be compromised by the fact that the same lawyer represents more than one person in any particular matter it would permit that lawyer to appear before it on behalf of only one of those persons.

As the representative body for solicitors, the Law Society sought *certiorari* on the grounds that the Notice, and position of the Competition Authority set out therein, was *ultra vires* its powers and functions as set out in s 30 of the 2002 Act.

11.062 O'Neill J held that:

> the following passage from the judgment of Hamilton CJ in *Keane v An Bord Pleanála (No 2)* [1997] 1 IR 484 states the law in regard to the powers of statutory corporations. In that instance he was referring to the powers of the Commissioners of Irish Lights where he says:
>
>> 'The powers of the Commissioners, being a body created by statute, are limited by the statute which created it and extend no further than is expressly stated therein or is necessarily and properly required for carrying into effect the purposes of incorporation or may fairly be regarded as incidental to or consequential upon those things which the legislature has authorised.'

However, he went on to state that the notice was not *ultra vires* the powers of the respondent merely because the express provisions of ss 30(1)(d) or 37(5) of the Act did not expressly provide for that power, the power in question being necessarily incidental and consequential upon the functions and powers conferred in ss 30 and 31 of the Act.

Rather, the court agreed that content of the notice, ie the restriction on the choice of legal representation contained in the notice, unreasonably and disproportionately infringed the right of persons appearing before the respondents to the lawyer of their choice and thus infringed the right to fair procedures guaranteed by Art 40.3 of the Constitution.

As mentioned above, it does not necessarily follow that a Regulator who commences a decision-making process within jurisdiction will continue making his decision within jurisdiction. For any number of reasons, he may exceed jurisdiction and thereby make its decisions liable to being quashed on *certiorari*.

A summary of the position in Ireland is set out in the judgment of McGuinness J in *Hughes v Garavan*.[106] In that case, Mr Hughes argued that he should not have been sent forward for trial on all eight of the drugs charges against him, on the basis that the evidence considered by the District Judge so to do had been served by way of additional evidence after preliminary examination was technically over. In her judgment, McGuinness J stated: 'In my view, once the District Court judge had passed

---

104 *Law Society of Ireland v Competition Authority* [2005] IEHC 455, O'Neill J.
105 28 July 2004.
106 *Hughes v Garavan* [2003] IESC 65.

on to hear submissions under s 7 it was not open to him to receive the additional evidence which purported to be served under s 6(4) or to take it into account in reaching his decision to return the accused for trial on this particular charge.'

Later on she stated:

> On balance, I would allow the appeal and substitute for the order of the High Court an order of *certiorari* setting aside the order of the District Court returning the applicant for trial on charge No 8 in the statement of charges and remitting that charge to the District Court judge to proceed with it in accordance with law.

In arriving at the decision, McGuiness J, for the court, summarised the Irish jurisprudence on the topic of the limited scope of *certiorari* in cases where a determination has been made by the District Court:

> [Counsel for the DPP] submitted that the order of the District Court should be quashed only where there had been a breach of natural or constitutional justice. There is well-settled authority on this issue. In *State (Holland) v Kennedy*[107] Henchy J in this court stated (at p 201):

> The real question in this case, as it seems to me, is whether the order of the District Court is reviewable on *certiorari*. Counsel for the respondent has submitted that as the order is good on its face and as the error, if any, made by the respondent was an error made within jurisdiction, the procedure to remedy it should be held to be by appeal and not by *certiorari*.

> Having considered the authorities, I am satisfied that the error was not made within jurisdiction. The respondent District Justice undoubtedly had jurisdiction to enter on the hearing of this prosecution. But it does not necessarily follow that a court or a tribunal, vested with powers of a judicial nature, which commences a hearing within jurisdiction will be treated as continuing to act within jurisdiction. For any one of a number of reasons it may exceed jurisdiction and thereby make its decision liable to be quashed on *certiorari*. For instance, it may fall into an unconstitutionality, or it may breach the requirements of natural justice, or it may fail to stay within the bounds of the jurisdiction conferred on it by the statute. It is an error of the latter kind that prevents the impugned order in this case from being held to have been made within jurisdiction.

> [McGuiness J continued] Thus a failure to abide by the terms of the relevant statute giving jurisdiction to the District Court in that case gave grounds for judicial review. *Killeen v DPP*[108] again dealt with the scope of review of the District Court. In his judgment in that case, Keane J (as he then was) stated (at p 8):

> 'It may be that an error of law committed by a tribunal acting within its jurisdiction is not capable of being set aside on *certiorari*; see *State (Davidson) v Farrell* [1960] IR 438. It is otherwise where the error of law has as its consequence the making of an order which the tribunal had no jurisdiction to make.'

Keane J went on to refer to the passage already quoted from *State (Holland) v Kennedy* and continued:

> Further guidance as to the circumstances which may render the decision of a tribunal a nullity, although it had jurisdiction to enter upon the inquiry, can be derived from

---

107 *State (Holland) v Kennedy* [1977] IR 193.
108 *Killeen v DPP* [1998] 1 ILRM 1.

this passage in the speech of Lord Reid in *Anisminic Limited v Foreign Compensation Commission* [1969] 2 AC 147:

'... there are many cases where, although the Tribunal had jurisdiction to enter on the inquiry, it has done or failed to do something in the course of the inquiry which is of such a nature that its decision is a nullity. It may have given its decision in bad faith. It may have made a decision which it had no power to make. It may have failed in the course of the inquiry to comply with the requirements of natural justice. It may in perfect good faith have misconstrued the provisions giving it power to act so that it failed to deal with the question remitted to it and decided some question which was not remitted to it. It may have refused to take into account something which it was required to take into account. Or it may have based its decision on some matter which, under the provisions setting it up, it had no right to take into account. I do not intend this list to be exhaustive. But if it decides a question remitted to it for decision without committing any of these errors it is as much entitled to decide that question wrongly as it is to decide it rightly'.

11.063 More recently, in *O'Shea v O'Buachalla and DPP*, Denham J, speaking on behalf of the court, said: 'There is well settled Irish law that a court, even if it commences acting within jurisdiction, may fall into unconstitutionality or breach natural justice or fail to stay within its bounds of jurisdiction.'[109]

Similarly, the task set for many Regulators is to determine a price cap according to statute. If that determination is made in a manner whereby the Regulator has acted outside his jurisdiction as set out in statute – usually the Act establishing the Regulator – or has failed to abide by the rules of natural justice, then that decision may be set aside.

Incorrect Application or Interpretation of the Law

11.064 By contrast, the High Court would strike down the same decision predicated on the incorrect application or interpretation of the law by a Regulator as being either illegal or outside his powers – ie ultra vires, the simple reason being that in considering questions of law, the Regulator has moved into the realm in which the High Court is expert. This distinction was explained by Mr Justice Kinlen in *Lambert v An t'Árd*

---

109   *O'Shea v O'Buachalla and DPP* [2001] 3 IR 137, p 5. Denham J went on to refer to the previously quoted passage in *State (Holland) v Justice Kennedy* and continued:'The obligation of a district judge is to conduct a preliminary examination in accordance with the provisions of the 1967 Act. This permits the preliminary examination to be conducted and completed on the basis of the book of evidence alone or on the basis of the depositions sought.

From these authorities it is clear that where a district judge, having considered the materials for him, forms an opinion either that there is a sufficient case to put the accused on trial or there is not, his order sending the accused forward for trial or discharging him cannot be set aside on certiorari. However, if the district judge acts in a way which is not within jurisdiction, for example, by acting outside the jurisdiction conferred by statute or by breaching the requirements of natural justice, his decision is open to review and may be set aside. If, therefore, the applicant in the instant case can establish that the District Court judge either exceeded the bounds of his jurisdiction under the Act of 1967 or failed to abide by the rules of natural justice the decision of the first-named respondent may be set aside.'

Chláraitheoir, a challenge to the decision of the Registrar General to refuse to recognise the applicant's foreign divorce: [110]

> It seems to the court that the respondent's reliance on the doctrine of unreasonableness, and in particular the latitude which that doctrine affords to decision main tribunals, is misconceived. This case is not concerned with a situation where an administrative tribunal has been afforded a discretion in an administrative matter, and to this extent it can be distinguished from, for example, the Stardust case. The present case turns on the determination of a legal issue. The Registrar General is only entitled to refuse to issue a licence or certificate in a case where there is a 'lawful impediment' to a marriage. In the context of the present proceedings, this issue falls to be determined on the correct interpretation of the law relating to the recognition of divorces, *viz* whether or not one of the parties to the first marriage was domiciled in England prior to the divorce proceedings in that jurisdiction. The Supreme Court, in *T v T* [1983] IR 29 at page 33, stated that the determination of a person's domicile is a mixed question of law and fact. On the facts of a particular case, the Supreme Court held that the District Justice and the High Court Judge involved have misdirected themselves in law in holding that the husband had acquired an Irish domicile of choice. It is clear that the determination of a person's domicile involved consideration of a legal issue; the Registrar General cannot enjoy any discretion in the determination of this matter. The determination of the Registrar General of an issue of law need not be treated with same deference as the determination of a specialised tribunal on an issue of fact. Thus, the current case is clearly distinguishable from the fact of *O'Keeffe v An Bord Pleanála* [1993] 1 IR 39, a case concerning a specialised Tribunal, *viz,* An Bord Pleanála, of its discretion in a matter peculiarly within its expertise.[111]

Relevancy and Irrelevancy

11.065 A public body entrusted with discretionary powers owes several basic duties to the public, the breach of which can justify the court's intervention. For example, a Regulator has a duty of inquiry, that is to say, a duty to take reasonable steps to inform itself of such matters necessary to make a decision. To paraphrase Lord Diplock, did the Regulator ask itself the right question and take reasonable steps to acquaint itself with the relevant information to enable it to answer it correctly?[112] Public bodies generally have a duty to act in the public interest, as noted by Wade,[113] who states:

> The powers of public authorities are therefore essentially different from those of private persons. A man making his will may, subject to any rights of his dependants,

---

110 *Lambert v An t'Árd Chláraitheoir* [1995] 2 IR 372.

111 The comments of Kinlen J here add weight to the argument that the principles in *O'Keeffe* be limited in their application to planning cases.

112 *Secretary of State for Education and Science v Tameside Metropolitan Borough Council* [1977] AC 1014. See also *Secretary of State for Education ex parte London Borough of Southwark* [1995] ELR 308 *per* Laws J: 'the decision maker must call his attention to considerations relevant to his decision, a duty which in practice may require him to consult outside bodies.'

113 Wade, *Administrative Law* (5th edn, OUP, 1982) at pp 355–356.

dispose of his property just as he may wish ... This is unfettered discretion. But a public authority may do neither unless it acts reasonably and in good faith and upon lawful and relevant grounds of public interest. Unfettered discretion is wholly inappropriate to a public authority, which possess powers solely in order that it may use them for the public good.

As mentioned earlier, a key question to be considered by the court is the relevance of the materials considered.

It is a basic principle of administrative law that a public body should take into account all relevant considerations and no irrelevant ones. Failure to do so is a common ground for judicial review. As accepted by the Supreme Court, in the above-mentioned *Killeen v DPP*,[114] taking into account an irrelevancy or failing to take into account a relevancy may be the basis for having a decision quashed.[115] Another aspect of relevancy is guidance or policy as a relevant condition. For example, a Ministerial direction may be given, of which account must be taken when making a determination.[116]

11.066 Relevancy is a matter of law for the courts; however, the weight to be given to relevant considerations is for the decision-maker. It is noted that where statute provides that the decision-maker 'have regard in particular', then such factors, having mandatory consideration status, carry the most weight.[117] This is no more than common sense.

Procedural *Ultra Vires*

11.067 In the *GCHQ* case,[118] Diplock LJ distinguished procedural *ultra vires* from procedural unfairness as follows:

> I have described the third head as 'procedural impropriety' rather than failure to observe basic rules of natural justice or failure to act with procedural fairness towards the person who will be affected by the decision. This is because susceptibility to judicial review under this head covers also failure by an administrative tribunal to observe procedural rules that are expressly laid down in the legislative instrument by

---

114 *Killeen v DPP* [1998] 1 ILRM 1.

115 Another example of relevancy is given by Kerr J *R v Westminster City Council, ex p Monahan* [1990] 1 QB 87 regarding a planning application: 'Financial constraints on the economic viability of a desirable planning development are unavoidable facts of life in an imperfect world. It would be unreal and contrary to common sense to insist that they must be excluded from the range of considerations which may properly be regarded as material in determining planning applications ... [P]rovided that the ultimate determination is based on planning grounds and not on some ulterior motive, and that it is not irrational, there would be no basis for holding it to be invalid in law solely on the ground that it has taken account of, and adjusted itself to, the financial realities of the overall situation.'.

116 See, for example, s 10 of the Aviation Regulation Act 2001.

117 *R City of Westminster Housing Benefit Review Board, ex p Mehanne* [2001] UKHL 11, [2001] 1 WLR 539.

118 *Council of Civil Service Unions v Minister for the Civil Service* [1985] AC 374.

which its jurisdiction is conferred, even where such failure does not involve any denial of natural justice.

Examples of express procedural duties include express duty to consult,[119] express duty to give reasons and express notice requirements. A Regulator may be under an express duty to:

(i) ensure that its determinations are objectively justified, non-discriminatory, proportionate and transparent;

(ii) give notice of its intention to make a determination by publication in a national daily newspaper or on its website;

(iii) give interested parties and the public a period of time within which they can make representations with respect to the proposed determination;

(iv) consider those representations and either accept or reject them; and

(v) report on its determination giving an account of its reasons for making that determination and reasons for accepting or rejecting any representations made.

11.068 The issue has been considered in the UK of whether statutory provisions are mandatory or discretionary. Diplock LJ put it thus:[120]

> Where the legislation which confers upon a statutory tribunal its decision making powers also provides expressly for the procedure it shall follow in the course of reaching its decision, it is a question of construction of the relevant legislation, to be decided by the Court in which the decision is challenged, whether a particular procedural provision is mandatory, so that its non observance in the process of reaching the decision makes the discretion itself a nullity, or whether it is merely directory, so that the statutory tribunal has a discretion not to comply with it if, in its opinion, the exceptional circumstances of a particular case justify departing from it.

Lord Hailsham had previously spoken of this notion, stating:[121]

> [T]he first task is to construe the statute, and ask the question whether the duty in question is mandatory or directory. If it be mandatory, the second task is to ask what remedy is available for non compliance. If the statute specifies the remedy, well and good. If it is silent, the ordinary remedies ... proceedings for [judicial review] should be pursued as appropriate.

In another case[122] it was stated that the effect of failure to comply with a statutory duty to give summary reasons 'depends on the importance of the requirements in the context of the particular statutory scheme'. In that case, the context was important protection in the context of intrusive power, so failure would provide grounds to set aside the decision, subject to the court's discretion to refuse a remedy. One would

---

119 '*[A]udi alterem partem*, the first rule of natural justice is expressly required to be observed by the Commission at this stage' – *R v Commission for Racial Equality, ex p Hillingdon London Borough Council* [1982] AC 779.

120 *O'Reilly v Mackman* [1983] 2 AC 237.

121 *London & Clyeside Estates Ltd v Aberdeen District Council* [1980] 1 WLR 182.

122 *R v Mac Donald (Inspector of Taxes), ex p Hutchinson and Co Ltd* [1998] STC 680.

imagine such thinking would apply to any lack of reasoning in a Regulator's decision, given their intrusive nature on free enterprise.

Proportionality

11.069 The principle of proportionality in essence amounts to this:

> [A] measure which interferes with a Community or human right must not only be authorised by law but must correspond with a pressing social need and go no further than strictly necessary in a pluralistic society to achieve its permitted purpose; or more shortly, must be appropriate and necessary to its legitimate aim.[123]

An example of where this principle might apply is in the context of an express legal requirement on a Regulator to act proportionately in making a determination. For example, by s 5(4) of the Aviation Regulation Act 2001, the Commission must ensure that all such determinations are objectively justified, non-discriminatory, proportionate and transparent. Neill LJ explained this EC law concept very succinctly when stating that it is:

> [A] well established concept in Community law ... The principle required that the means used to attain a given end should be no more than what is appropriate and necessary to attain the end. In the context of an administrative decision this means that there must be a reasonable relationship between the objective which is sought to be achieved and the means used to that end.[124]

11.070 In *Montemuino v Minister for Communications*,[125] the master of the fishing boat *Ocean Enterprise* was charged with illegal fishing offences contrary to the Fisheries Acts. Upon conviction, in such cases, a person is liable to fines and forfeiture. Mr Montemuino contended that the sanction of the forfeiture of the entire catch on the facts of this case would amount to a disproportionate penalty. The mandatory statutory provision providing for forfeiture under s 224B of the Fisheries (Consolidation) Act 1959, offends against the principle of proportionality. Mr Justice Feeney considered the principle of proportionality as considered by Costello J in *Heaney v Ireland*:[126]

> In that case the constitutionality of section 52 of the Offences Against the State Act, 1939, was considered in circumstances where that Section required a person arrested to give an account of his movements. The issue before the Court was whether such a provision amounted to a legitimate restriction on the privilege against self

---

123 *Per* Sedley LJ in *B v Secretary of State for the Home Department* [2000] UKHRR 498 referring to the principle of proportionality in both the Luxembourg [CFI/ECJ] and Strasburg [CHR] courts.

124 *R v Secretary of State for the Environment ex parte National & Local Government Officers Association* (1993) 5 Admin LR 785.

125 *Montemuino v Minister for Communications* [2008] IEHC 157, *per* Feeney J.

126 *Heaney v Ireland* [1994] 3 IR 593.

incrimination and the right to remain silent. In considering the matter, Costello J applied a test which is now referred to as the rationality test (at p 607):

'The objective of the impugned provision must be of sufficient importance to warrant overriding a constitutionally protected right. It must relate to concerns pressing and substantial in a free and democratic society. The means chosen must pass a proportionality test. They must:

(a) be rationally connected to the objective and not be arbitrary, unfair or based on irrational considerations;

(b) impair the right as little as possible; and

(c) be such that their effects on rights are proportional to the objective.

11.071 The Supreme Court considered the application of a form of test in *Employment Equality Bill 1996*[127] in the following terms, when Hamilton CJ stated:

In effect a form of proportionality test must be applied to the proposed section.

Is it rationally designed to meet the objective of the legislation?

(b) Does it intrude into constitutional rights as little as reasonably possible?

(c) Is there a proportionality between the Section and the right to trial in due course of law and the objective of the legislation? ... or to put it a slightly different way, section 63, sub-s 3, when read in the context of the Bill is a failure to protect the constitutional rights of the citizen and not warranted by the objectives which it sought to secure.

The principle of proportionality has not only developed in Irish law but also is a long established principle in community law. The approach identified in community law mirrors the proportionality test identified by Hamilton CJ in the *Employment Equality Bill 1996* case.

11.072 There is jurisprudence in the UK comparing proportionality and reasonableness. Take, for example, Ackner LJ's comment[128] that, '[counsel] has contended in issuing these directives the Secretary of State has used a sledgehammer to crack a nut. Of course this is a picturesque way of describing the *Wednesbury* irrationality test.' In a later case,[129] Laws J explicitly compared the notion of a proportionality review with the review on traditional grounds. He stated:

[T]he difference between *Wednesbury* and European review is that in the former case the legal limits lie further back. I think there are two factors. First the limits of domestic review are not, as the law presently stands, constrained by the doctrine of proportionality. Secondly, at least as regards a requirement such as that of objective justification in an equal treatment case, the European rule requires the decision maker to provide a fully reasoned case.[130] It is not enough merely to set out the problem, and assert that within his jurisdiction the Minister chose this solution or that

---

127 *Employment Equality Bill 1996* [1997] 2 IR 321 at p 383.

128 *R v Secretary of State for the Home Department, ex parte Brind* [1991] 1 AC 696.

129 *R v MAFF, ex parte First City Trading* [1997] 1 CMLR 250.

130 Such a requirement for reasons is replicated in the Commission's obligation to provide reasons set out in section 32 of the Aviation Regulation Act 2001.

solution, constrained only by the requirement that his decision must have been one that a reasonable Minister might make. Rather the court will test the solution arrived at [for proportionality], and pass it only if substantial factual considerations are put forward in its justification: considerations which are relevant, reasonable and proportionate to the aim in view. But as I understand the jurisprudence the court is not concerned to agree or disagree with the decision; that would be to travel beyond the boundaries of proper judicial authority and usurp the primary decision-maker's function. Thus *Wednesbury* and European Review are different models, one looser one tighter of the same judicial concept, which is the imposition of compulsory standards on decision makers so as to secure the repudiation of arbitrary power.[131]

Procedural Unfairness

11.073 The common law imposes minimum standards of procedural fairness. They are traditionally known as the rules of natural justice, although one may also speak of procedural fairness and due process. The concept of procedural fairness connotes a fair hearing and the absence of bias.[132] Lord Denning summed it up thus:

> The rule against bias is one thing. The right to be heard is another. Those two rules are the essential characteristics of what is often called natural justice. They are the twin pillars supporting it. The Romans put them in two ways: *nemo judex in causa sua* [no one can be a judge in his own cause] and *audi alterem partem* [hear the other side]. They have recently been put into two words – impartiality and fairness. But they are separate concepts and are governed by separate considerations.

Bias

11.074 Originally, classic administrative law was expressed in just two Latin maxims: *audi alterem partem*, that both sides must be heard, and *nemo iudex in sua causa* , the rule against bias.[133] It has been repeatedly recognised in Ireland, as in other

---

131 An interesting comment on the difference is made by Weir who states that, 'although it is sometimes said that the [*Wednesbury*] test and the Community law principle are similar in their operation, the better view seems to be that Community law imposes a more exacting standard, and one that is more fully articulated. It provides for an explicit weighting of interests, and is therefore perhaps better suited to review of legislative measures for which *Wednesbury* was not of course intended. At the same time proportionality provides a flexible test; it allows for account to be taken of fundamental rights of the individual, and of fundamental public interests ... It seems to me a rational and well structured test, which provides useful guidance to Courts, and which may even reflect the way in which administrative measure are (or ought to be) arrived at.' – Weir, 'Is EC Proportionality the same as Wednesbury Reasonableness?' (1999) *JR* 263.

132 The Court of Appeal made a pithy link between the concept of natural justice and decisions affecting the rights of individuals when it said, 'the Minister was a person having legal authority to determine a question affecting the rights of individuals. This being so it is a necessary implication that he is required to observe the principles of natural justice when exercising that authority.' – *AG v Ryan* [1980] AC 718.

133 *Per* Hardiman J in *Ardagh v Maguire* [2002] 1 IR 385.

jurisdictions, that the adjudication of disputes by a tribunal that is not only impartial but seen to be impartial is an essential feature of the administration of justice.[134]

11.075 There are two fundamental principles within the wider concept of bias. Firstly, that there should be no actual bias – a subjective test. And secondly, that there should be no reasonable apprehension that there is bias – an objective test.[135] This distinction also underlies the oft quoted dictum of Lord Hewart LCJ in *R v Sussex Justices, ex parte McCarthy*, that:

> It is not merely of some importance but is of fundamental importance that justice should not only be done, but should manifestly and undoubtedly be seen to be done.[136]

11.076 In the Supreme Court hearing in *Orange Telecommunications Ltd v Director of Telecommunications Regulation*,[137] Murphy J[138] pointed out that to condemn as biased the decision of a judge or other decision-maker involves two conclusions. Firstly, that the adjudicator is affected by some factor external to the subject matter of his decision and, secondly, that in relation to the particular decision, the external factor operated so as to tilt the judgment in favour of the successful party. He explained that the distinction is crucial. The existence of the extraneous factor must be proved as a fact on the balance of probabilities: The operative effect of an impermissible factor (where it does exist) is presumed.

---

134 *Radio Limerick One Ltd v Independent Radio and Television Commission* [1997] 2 IR 291, Keane CJ *nem diss.*

135 See *Dublin Well Woman Centre Ltd v Ireland* [1995] 1 ILRM 408, Supreme Court, *per* Denham J.

136 *R v Sussex Justices, ex parte* McCarthy (1924) 1 KB 256 Lord Hewart's *obiter dictum.*

137 *Orange Telecommunications Ltd v Director of Telecommunications Regulation (No 2)* [2000] 4 IR 159. The background to that case was that the Director of Communications Regulation granted Meteor a licence to operate a third mobile telephone service in Ireland. Orange was the other unsuccessful tender candidate. It unsuccessfully appealed the decision, alleging bias amongst other things.

138 In his judgment in *Orange*, Mr Justice Murphy mentioned *Laird v Tatum* 409 US 824 (34 L Ed 2d 50) where Justice Rehnquist made the following point in a motion to disqualify himself: 'proof that a Justice's mind at the time he joined the [US Supreme] Court was a complete *tabula rasa* in the area of constitutional adjudication would be evidence of lack of qualification, not lack of bias.' He further quoted Rehnquist J as referring with approval to extracts from the often quoted judgment of Justice Franck in *In re JP Linahan* 138 F2d 650. As Mr Justice Murphy stated, a particularly attractive passage from that judgment is in the following terms: 'Democracy must, indeed, fail unless our Courts try cases fairly, and there can be no fair trial before a judge lacking in impartiality and disinterestedness. If, however, 'bias' and 'partiality' be defined to mean the total absence of preconceptions in the mind of the judge, then no one has ever had a fair trial and no one ever will. The human mind, even at infancy, is no blank piece of paper. We are born with predispositions; and the process of education, formal and informal, creates attitudes in all men which affect them in judging situations, attitudes which reasoning in particular instances and which, therefore, by definition are prejudices.'

11.077 As Denham J later stated in the same court in the case of *O'Callaghan v Judge Mahon*,[139] the law on objective bias is well established in Ireland. In *O'Neill v Beaumont Hospital Board*[140] Finlay CJ stated:

> The bias alleged in this case is a bias consisting of pre-judgment. The plaintiff's case, in very brief summary, is that a consideration of the question of the making of the decision as to the continuance or termination of his service as a consultant in the hospital cannot fairly be carried out by reason of the fact that the persons who should carry it out have pre-judged his case. There is no suggestion of personal animosity, personal gain or personal self-interest in any member of the board as a form of bias. The sole form of bias alleged is pre-judgment ...
>
> I am satisfied that the proper standard to be applied by this Court which does not appear to be wholly different, though it may be subtly different from the standard which was applied in the High Court, is the question as to whether a person in the position of the plaintiff, Mr O'Neill, in this case who was a reasonable man, should apprehend that his chance of a fair and independent hearing of the question as to whether his services should be continued or terminated does not exist by reason of the pre-judgment of the issues which are involved in that by the members of the board. That in my view is the proper test to be applied in this case, and it fulfils what I understand from the authorities to be the test which has been accepted in this country and by this Court in relation to a case of this description.

11.078 That standard was applied in *Dublin Wellwoman Centre Ltd v Ireland*,[141] where Denham J stated:

> That standard is applicable to this case. In the High Court there was no suggestion of personal favour or personal interest, ie subjective bias of the learned High Court judge. The actual state of mind of the judge was and is not in issue. What was and is in issue is the objective test: as to whether a person in the position of the appellant in this case, being a reasonable person, should apprehend that his chance of a fair and independent hearing of the question at issue does not exist by reason of the previous non-judicial position, statements and actions of the learned High Court judge on issues which are at the kernel of this case.

---

139 *O'Callaghan v Judge Alan Mahon* [2007] IESC 17.

140 *O'Neill v Beaumont Hospital Board* [1990] ILRM 419 at p 438.

141 *Dublin Wellwoman Centre Ltd v Ireland* [1995] 1 ILRM 408 at p 420. As the Supreme Court later noted in *Orange*, in most of the reported cases involving an allegation of bias against a judge, the existence of some extraneous factor relating to the circumstances of the judge is admitted or acknowledged. For example, in the leading Irish case, *Dublin Wellwoman Centre Ltd v Ireland* it was immediately recognised that Ms Justice Carroll had acted as Chairperson of the Commission on the Status of Women so that the argument in the case, and the decision on it, turned on to whether that fact might affect the impartiality of the Judge or, more correctly, give rise to a perception of bias. Similarly, in the leading English case of *ex parte Pincohet Ugarte* [1999] 2 WLR 272 the fact that Lord Hoffman had links with Amnesty International was not in dispute. The issue was whether that association might be perceived as affecting his judgment.

11.079 Bias was further considered in *Ardagh v Maguire*,[142] where McGuinness J noted that the test of objective bias was neither in a court nor in a committee to be applied in an over-strict or exaggerated way. However, in the context of that case, it was unacceptable for members of an inquisitorial committee to make public comments on the subject matter of the inquiry, both in the run up to the inquiry and during its actual currency. This view was echoed by Hardiman J in the same case when he said that:

> [A] person who sits in judgment on the actions of another must act in a *quasi* judicial fashion. He must clearly avoid bias; what is less well understood is that he must also avoid the appearance of bias. One obvious course of conduct which risks giving rise to an appearance of bias is to discuss either the issues being inquired into, or the procedures adopted for the inquiry, outside the context of the inquiry itself. It is therefore undesirable for persons sitting in a *quasi* judicial capacity to make themselves available for interview, discussion programmes, or comment of any sort on either substantive or procedural issues during the hearing.

11.080 As the court stated in *Ardagh v Maguire,* the issue of bias relates to two aspects – subjective and objective. Subjective bias means actual bias and in the court's view no committee member who has subjective bias could participate in such an inquiry. Objective bias is a matter which is also a component of fair procedures. Therefore, a committee member in such an inquiry may not sit if in all the circumstances a reasonable person would have a reasonable apprehension of bias – an apprehension that the committee member might not bring an impartial and unprejudiced mind to the hearing. This would refer to considerations relating to matters prior to the establishment of the committee and during the hearings of the committee. Thus, indications of a view being held by a committee member whilst the hearing is proceeding would be contrary to the concept of fairness.

11.081 Regulated entities may have grounds for review if a Regulator, in his dealings leading up to a decision, appears to have pre-judged the outcome of that decision.[143]

Disclosure

11.082 Lord Diplock considered disclosure in the following way:[144]

> [F]airness requires that the objectors should have an opportunity of communicating to the Minister the reasons for their objections to the scheme and the facts on which they are based. The [Act] requires that the form in which that opportunity is to be afforded to them is a local inquiry. Fairness, as it seems to me, also requires that the objectors should be given sufficient information about the reasons relied on by the department as justifying the draft scheme to enable them to challenge the accuracy of

142 *Ardagh v Maguire* [2002] 1 IR 385.
143 See for a discussion of bias the recent case of North Wall Property Holding Company Ltd and Sean Dunne v Dublin Docklands Development Authority and North Quay Investments Ltd (9 October 2008, unreported)
144 *Bushell v Secretary of State for the Environment* [1981] AC 75.

any facts and the validity of any arguments upon which the departmental reasons are based.[145]

A duty on a Regulator to put information in the public domain may encounter claims of confidentiality. This has been considered in the UK by Simon Brown LJ, asking,[146] 'does the public interest in making the limited disclosure now sought outweigh the remaining confidentiality in the report? That in turn seems to me to depend upon whether disclosure to the requesting states is required in the interests of fairness. If fairness demands disclosure, then to my mind disclosure clearly becomes the overriding public interest.'[147]

Consultation

11.083 The requirements of adequate consultation have been described in following terms by Auld LJ:[148]

> [T]he classic statement of the basic requirements of consultation is that formulated by Mr Stephen Sedley QC, as he then was, in argument, and adopted by Hodgson J in his judgment in *R v Brent London Borough Council, ex p Gunning* 919850 84 LGR 168, and approved by Webster J in R v Sutton London Borough Council, ex p Hamlet (unreported) namely ...: 'First ... consultation must be at a time when proposals are still at a formative stage. Secondly ... the proposer must give sufficient reasons for any proposal to permit of intelligent consideration and response. Thirdly ... adequate time must be given for consideration and response and finally, fourthly, the product of consultation must be conscientiously taken into account in finalising any ... proposals.'

The process described above is one providing for the give and take of information and views between the relevant parties before a final proposal is made. It is predicated on early disclosure of sufficient information facilitating an informed response to be made. Whether or not persons take the chance to be involved in a consultation is their choice.

---

145 See also Moses J, who stated that, '... generally [the duty of fairness] will require the decision maker to identify in advance areas which are causing him concern in reaching the decision in question.' – *R (on the application of Interbrew SA) v Competition Commission* [2001] EWHC Admin 367.

146 *R v Secretary of State for the Home Department, ex parte Kingdom of Belgium* (15 February 2000, unreported), Divisional Court.

147 Disclosure, in the context of the proper performance of duties, was also considered by Lord Chief Justice Bingham, who stated 'when, in the course of performing its public duties, a public body ... comes into possession of information relating to a member of the public, being information not generally available and potentially damaging to that member of the public if disclosed, the body ought not to disclose such information save for the purpose of and to the extent necessary for performance of its public duty or enabling some other public body to perform its public duty ... The principle rests on a fundamental rule of good public administration which the law must recognise and if necessary enforce.' – *R v Chief Constable of the North Wales Police, ex parte AB* [1999] QB 396.

148 *R v London Borough of Barnet, ex p B* [1994] ELR 357.

However, those affected should be given that chance in a meaningful way so that they may become involved.[149]

The requirement for adequate consultation has not yet been incorporated into Irish jurisprudence as a ground for judicial review. It may arise where there is a mandatory statutory requirement to consult and may then form part of the lack of procedural fairness ground for review, or indeed in the case of the absence of any consultation where one is statutorily required, the procedural *ultra vires* ground for review.

Representations

11.084 Affording parties an opportunity to present various sides of an issue is fundamental to fair procedures. On 30 July 2008, the High Court ruled that the Financial Services Ombudsman failed to follow fair procedures in the way in which he upheld a complaint by Enfield Credit Union against stockbrokers J & E Davy.[150] The court quashed the decision of the Financial Services Ombudsman by an order of *certiorari* and directed the Ombudsman to conduct a new investigation into the complaint against Davy according to 12 procedures outlined by the court, which included conducting an oral hearing and full exchange of complaint documentation. Charleton J stressed that when determining complaints, both complainants and respondents must be treated equally.

11.085 In respect of the right to the oral hearing, the court noted that there is no absolute right to an oral hearing – *State (Williams) v Army Pensions Board*.[151] However, for reasons of natural justice, an oral hearing may be appropriate. The court quoted Costello J in *Doupe v Limerick*,[152] where the learned judge stated, 'As to the extent of the duty to disclose in some cases, natural justice may require that disclosure of all relevant documents be made prior to an oral hearing … [natural justice] does not

---

149 In an unreported case concerning consultation, Legatt LJ made the following interesting comments: 'it is difficult to see what difference favourable to the [claimant] it could have made if the consultation document had contained other or more accurate information. Whatever its deficiencies, the consultation process had the effect of evoking opposition to the closure proposal on a large scale … Even if there was a failure to consult specifically a few named organisations which might with advantage have been consulted, it is, in my judgment, impossible that any of them was unaware within the time permitted of the existence of the consultation process and of the opportunity to make submissions, if any of them saw fit; … there can be no question of the procedure for consultation having in any or all of the respects alleged been so unfair as to vitiate the decision making process – *R v Secretary of State for Health, ex p London Borough of Hackney* (25 April 1994, unreported). Those sentiments echo Moses J in *Wiseman v Borneman* [1971] AC 297 who stated 'I feel bound to express my prima facie dislike of a situation in which the tribunal has before it a document (which might contain both facts and arguments) which is calculated to influence the tribunal but which has not been seen by a party who will be affected by the tribunals determination.'

150 *J & E Davy trading as Davy v Financial Services Ombudsman* [2008] IEHC 256, *per* Charleton J.

151 *State (Williams) v Army Pensions Board* [1983] IR 308.

152 *Doupe v Limerick* [1981] ILRM 456.

require that every administrative order which may adversely affect rights must be preceded by a judicial type hearing involving the examination and cross examination of witnesses.' In *Galvin v Chief Appeals Officer*[153] the applicant successfully reviewed the defendant on the basis that he had been deprived of an oral hearing. An oral hearing with examination and cross-examination should take place if natural justice requires it or it may in other circumstances suffice if written submissions were made and the oral hearing only related to cross examination. The judge was of the view that in this case the fact that an oral hearing was required was 'inescapable' in order for a fair determination of the dispute.

11.086 In relation to the exchange of documents, the court in that case noted at para 47 that a procedure cannot be fair if the party against whom a complaint is made is not enabled to make a response. Central to the ability to make a response is that a party should have reasonable notice of the nature of the complaint. It is unfair if the appendices to a letter of complaint are excluded. It was, according to the court, 'a mistake' for the Ombudsman not to provide the documentation appended to the letter of complaint, since this constituted as a whole the complaint:

> They are entitled to latitude as to how they order their procedures but they may not imperil a fair resolution of a conflict in consequence of adopting a procedure which infringes fundamental principles of constitutional fairness – *Gallagher v The Revenue Commissioners (No 2)* [1995] 1 IR 55. Tribunals are entitled to depart from the rules of evidence, they are entitled to receive unworn evidence, they are entitled to act on hearsay and they are entitled to ensure that procedures unlike court procedures are informal. The guiding principle is evenness of treatment towards each side. The principle of evenness of treatment would arguably seem, on the basis of the analysis of the Act that I have conducted to be absent from the intention of the legislature. However, the legislature cannot, as a matter of constitutional law, have intended unfair procedures and I must not presume that, unless no constitutional interpretation of an Act is possible. A balance has to be maintained. If for instance, submissions are allowed by one side, they have to be allowed by both. If oral evidence is heard from one side then both sides must be entitled to make submissions. If one party is allowed to call and cross-examine a witness, then the other party should have the same facility ... As to what is required in terms of the procedures will vary with the particular circumstances. In the interpretation of the act there is a clear legislative bias towards minimal formality, subject to the fairness of procedures.

Many of the comments above will have resonance for those in regulated industries where important decisions taken may have an impact for years thereafter. It is no surprise then that formal consultation in some guise is a feature of regulation in Ireland.

Duty to give reasons

11.087. Regulators, usually by statute, have a duty to report on their decisions or determinations and give reasons for accepting or rejecting representations on their draft determinations. The importance of giving reasons is well recognised in

---

153 *Galvin v Chief Appeals Officer* [1997] 3 IR 240.

administrative law. The primary purpose for disclosing reasons behind decisions is to show transparency. It explains to those affected the basis upon which a decision has been taken. Importantly, a person can then assess how and if their point of view has been taken into account. The purpose for giving reasons has also been described in the courts. Giving reasons:

> allows the [claimant] to see whether the decision is legally challengeable; facilitates review by the Courts; ... adequate reasons expose any errors of law, unsubstantial findings and extraneous considerations; ... informs third parties since they to are entitled to know of the reasons for a decision; ... public confidence in the decision making process is enhanced by the knowledge that supportable reasons must be, and are, given; and giving reasons is also a self disciplining exercise. Decisions are more likely to be correct if they are carefully considered and properly articulated. Writing brings clarity and precision to thought.[154]

11.088 In *Deerland Construction Ltd v The Aquaculture Licences Appeals Board*[155] the applicant, amongst other things, sought to quash on *certiorari* a decision of the first respondent (ALAB), of 17 of July 2007, to grant an aquaculture licence to a third party. Kelly J considered the absence of reasons given by ALAB fatal given its statutory duty to do so. It is worth quoting his judgment at length as he summarised Irish law on the nature of the requirement to give reasons:

> ALAB is under a statutory obligation to ensure that both the determination of an appeal and the notification of that determination, state the main reasons and considerations on which the determination is based. That is provided for in s 40(8) of the 1997 Act, which in turn was inserted by s 10 of the Fisheries (Amendment) Act 2001 ...
>
> I do not accept that a pro forma recitation of the matters which are contained in ALAB's decision amounts to a compliance with its statutory obligation to state its reasons for such decision. The reference to it being satisfied that it was in the public interest to make the determination is a conclusion reached by it but no clue is given as to how such a conclusion was reached.

At this stage there is an abundance of case law indicating what must be done by a body such as ALAB if it is to satisfy its obligation of setting forth the reasons for its conclusions. I mention just a few. [Kelly J continued] In *O'Donoghue v An Bord Pleanála*,[156] Murphy J said:

> It is clear that the reason furnished by the Board (or by any other tribunal) must be sufficient first to enable the courts to review it and secondly, to satisfy the person having recourse to the tribunal that it has directed its mind adequately to the issues before it. It has never been suggested that an administrative body is bound to provide a discursive judgment as a result of its deliberations.

---

154 *R v London Borough of Islington ex p Hinds* (1995) 27 HLR 65.
155 *Deerland Construction Ltd v The Aquaculture Licences Appeals Board* [2008] IEHC 289, *per* Kelly J.
156 *O'Donoghue v An Bord Pleanála* [1991] ILRM 750.

Kelly J went on to observe that the matter was again considered by the Supreme Court in *Ní Eilí v Environmental Protection Agency*[157] where Murphy J considered and followed the principles enunciated by Finlay CJ in *O'Keeffe v An Bord Pleanála*[158], and then went on to say:

Where a decision to grant a licence is made, the position is different. In that event, by definition, objections will have to be made to, and submissions received by the Agency in relation to such objections. If a licence is indeed granted, it might be inferred that those objections had been overruled or the submissions rejected. That would not be an adequate compliance with the Regulation. Those who have gone to the trouble and expense of formulating and presenting serious objections on a matter of intense public interest must be entitled to obtain an explanation as to why their submissions were rejected.

In *Mulholland v An Bord Pleanála* [2006] ILRM 287, I [Kelly J] had to deal with the statutory obligation to give reasons and state considerations which now forms part of the planning code. I said

'The obligation at (b) above to state the considerations on which a decision is based is, of course, new. I am of opinion that, in order for the statement of considerations to pass muster at law, it must satisfy a similar test to that applicable to the giving of reasons. The statement of considerations must therefore be sufficient to:

1. give to the applicant such information as may be necessary and appropriate for him to consider whether he has a reasonable chance of succeeding in appealing or judicially reviewing the decision;

2. arm himself for such hearing or review;

3. know if the decision maker has directed its mind adequately to the issues which it has considered or is obliged to consider; and

4. enable the courts to review the decision'.'

Finally, [Kelly J noted] in *R v Westminster City Council*[159], Hutchinson LJ said:

It is well established that an obligation, whether statutory or otherwise, to give reasons for a decision is imposed so that the persons affected by the decision may know why they have won or lost and, in particular, may be able to judge whether the decision is valid and therefore unchallengeable, or invalid and therefore open to challenge.

There are numerous authoritative statements to this effect …

It is possible to state two propositions which the judgments of *ex parte* Grahams support. (1) If the reasons given are insufficient to enable the court to consider the lawfulness of the decision, the decision itself will be unlawful; and (2) The court should, at the very least, be circumspect about allowing material gaps to be filled by affidavit evidence or otherwise.'

The latter part of the quotation from Hutchinson LJ is apposite because that is precisely what ALAB sought to do in the present case. It has sought to fill the

---

157 *Ní Eilí v Environmental Protection Agency* [1999] IESC 64.

158 *O'Keeffe v An Bord Pleanála* [1993] 1 IR 39.

159 *R v Westminster City Council* [1996] 2 All ER 302.

material gaps by affidavit evidence.ALAB's determination of 17th July, 2007, insofar as it relates to Bed 30A is quashed. The matter will not be remitted to ALAB.'[160]

In the regulatory context, this judgment has much resonance. The majority of Regulators are obliged by their statutes to give reasons for their major statutory decisions. Many Regulators also make use of external consultants to give expert technical advice on matters pertaining to those decisions, for example, on matters such as the appropriate cost of capital for a regulated entity to be used in price-cap decisions, and the capacity of and/or the reasonable construction costs of the utility in question. In such circumstances, it is best practice that a Regulator makes explicit reference to its reliance on such reports and the adoption of their findings for the reasons set out in those reports.

Legitimate Expectation

11.089 In *Gorman v Minister for the Environment and Local Government*[161] Mr Justice Carney restated the principle that has been recognised in case law that the principles of constitutional justice do not apply with equal force in every situation and indeed, in some circumstances where decisions are taken by public bodies, such as a decision to enact a particular piece of legislation by the Oireachtas, the *audi alteram partem* rule, or the duty to consult and hear submissions, does not arise at all. This is because the State is exercising legislative power. The citizen is not consulted in relation to increased taxation in the budget. There may, of course, be various practices in place to consult interested bodies or persons before legislative decisions are taken, but this is undertaken as a matter of *practice*, not of *law*.

11.090 In the course of his judgment, speaking about the legitimate expectations persons might have of public bodies, Carney J went on to observe that:

> 80. A public body is entitled to resile from its previous practice or representation where there actually exists in the particular case objective reasons which justify this change of position. A person or groups of persons who have benefited from a previous policy can legitimately make representations as to why the policy should not be changed. They cannot, however, legitimately expect to fetter the body's statutory discretion to adopt a new policy in the public interest, as it is the public interest and not the private rights incidentally created that the public body must ultimately seek to vindicate.
>
> Where a public interest emerges to make another policy the appropriate one to follow in the altered circumstances, the expectation that the beneficiary of the previous

---

160 See also *Aer Rianta v An Bord Pleanála* [2002] IEHC 69, in which the High Court permitted the statement of reasons to be taken from a combination of the formal decision itself and the inspector's report; also *Fairyhouse Club Ltd v An Bord Pleanála* [2001] IEHC 106, in which the High Court allowed the formal decision of An Bord Pleanála to be supplemented by reference to the inspector's report, notwithstanding the fact that the members of An Bord Pleanála had nowhere stated that they had adopted his recommendation or reason.

161 *Gorman v Minister for the Environment and Local Government* [2001] 2 IR 414; [2001] IEHC 47.

policy can legitimately expect is a procedural rather that a substantive one. As was stated by Keane J (as he then was) in *Pesca Valentia Limited v Minister for Fisheries* [1990] 2 IR 305 at 323:

> 'While the Plaintiffs were undoubtedly encouraged in their project by semi-state bodies, they were not given any assurance that that the law regulating fishing would never be altered so as adversely to affect them nor, if such an assurance had been given, could any legal right have grown from it. No such estoppel could conceivably operate so as to prevent the Oireachtas from legislating or the executive from implementing the legislation when enacted.'

Inconsistency

11.091 Consistency is a basic principle of good administration. There are several types of 'unjustified inconsistency' that may warrant the intervention of the courts on judicial review. Fordham[162] suggests it is helpful to think of three presumptive rules:

(1)   that 'like cases should be treated alike', which can be thought of as a rule of equality or equal treatment;

(2)   that distinct cases should not be grouped together indiscriminately, which can be thought of as a rule against arbitrariness; and

(3)   that a given case should be approached on a consistent and stable basis, which can be thought of as a rule of certainty.

None of these principles is absolute but a court will look to a public body to provide an adequate explanation for apparently 'inconsistent' treatment of any of these three types. There may well be a good reason, especially given that:

(1)   different case are hardly ever identical;

(2)   public bodies are allowed to have broad policies; and

(3)   they are also allowed to change their minds (and their policies).

11.092 In the context of a review of a determination, the possible outcomes are either no change or a variation. Carnwath J touched on this topic of later change when considering the reversal of a decision previously reached. Reviewing various authorities in the United Kingdom, he referred[163] to:

> a broad principle ... that where a formal decision has been made on a particular subject matter or issue affecting private right by a competent public authority that decision will be regarded as binding on other authorities directly involved, unless and until circumstances change in a way that can be reasonably found to undermine the basis of the original decision. That change may be change in the factual circumstance or sometimes in the underlying policies affecting the decision ... Underlying the various approaches to changing a decision is the common sense view that, in the public sphere, once the matter has been formally decided it should stay decided until circumstances change in some material respect.

---

162 Fordham, *Judicial Review Handbook* (3rd edn, ART publishing, 2001), p 770.

163 *R v Cardiff County Council, ex parte Sears Group Properties* [1998] 3 PLR 55.

Later in the same case he stated that, 'the question of whether there is sufficient change in the circumstances, justifying a departure from the decision is one which will normally be for the authority subject only to *Wednesbury*[164] grounds.' This would suggest that the inconsistency would have to be such as to fly in the face of reason to be considered to be grounds for judicial review.

---

164 *Associated Provincial Picture Houses Ltd v Wednesbury Corporation* [1948] 1 KB 223.

INDEX

Entry control
methods of economic regulation, and,
2.049

Error of law
judicial review, and, 11.035–11.046
electricity sector regulation, and, 8.022–
8.027

**Estimate of capacity, forecast flows and
loading**
electricity sector regulation, and, 8.044

European Central Bank (ECB)
financial services regulation, and, 4.021

European Commission
competition, and, 7.017

European Competition Network
generally, 1.024

European Monetary Union (EMU)
financial services regulation, and, 4.021

Examination
administrative sanction procedure, and,
4.171–4.172
electronic communications, and, 6.153

Excess of jurisdiction
judicial review, and, 11.047–11.063

Excessive pricing
abuse of dominant position, and, 7.073

Exit control
methods of economic regulation, and,
2.049

Externalities
economic regulation, and, 2.018

Failure to invest
abuse of dominant position, and, 7.074

Fees
financial services regulation, and,
4.042–4.048

Fidelity rebates and discounts
abuse of dominant position, and, 7.069

Financial sanctions
broadcasting regulation, and,
5.141–5.142

Financial Services Authority of Ireland
And see **Financial services regulation**
appeals against decisions, 4.194
civil enforcement
administrative sanction procedure,
4.158–4.188
authorised officers, 4.156–4.157
complaints to the Ombudsman, 4.155
consultation, 4.039
enforcement
civil, 4.155–4.188
criminal, 4.189–4.193
introduction, 4.154
establishment, 4.018
functions, 4.037
generally, 4.026–4.031
introduction, 4.018
judicial review, 4.194
objectives, 4.040
powers, 4.038
regulated activities, and
anti-money laundering, 4.131–4.138
banking supervision, 4.050–4.068
bureaux de change, 4.119–4.121
consumer protection, 4.125–4.127
credit institution supervision,
4.050–4.068
credit unions, 4.105–4.112
directors of financial services entities,
4.128–4.130
disclosure of information,
4.139–4.147
dormant accounts, 4.151
electronic money, 4.148–4.150
fit and proper standards, 4.128–4.130
funds, 4.096–4.099
home reversion firms, 4.122–4.124
insurance, 4.088–4.094
insurance intermediaries,
4.100–4.104
introduction, 4.049
investment intermediaries,
4.100–4.104
investment services, 4.095
managers of financial services
entities, 4.128–4.130
money laundering, 4.131–4.138
money transmission services,
4.119–4.121
moneylenders, 4.113–4.118